Communications in Computer and Information Science 2981

Series Editors

Rationale

The CCIS series is devoted to the publication of proceedings of computer science conferences. Its aim is to efficiently disseminate original research results in informatics in printed and electronic form. While the focus is on publication of peer-reviewed full papers presenting mature work, inclusion of reviewed short papers reporting on work in progress is welcome, too. Besides globally relevant meetings with internationally representative program committees guaranteeing a strict peer-reviewing and paper selection process, conferences run by societies or of high regional or national relevance are also considered for publication.

Topics

The topical scope of CCIS spans the entire spectrum of informatics ranging from foundational topics in the theory of computing to information and communications science and technology and a broad variety of interdisciplinary application fields.

Information for Volume Editors and Authors

Publication in CCIS is free of charge. No royalties are paid, however, we offer registered conference participants temporary free access to the online version of the conference proceedings on SpringerLink (http://link.springer.com) by means of an http referrer from the conference website and/or a number of complimentary printed copies, as specified in the official acceptance email of the event.

CCIS proceedings can be published in time for distribution at conferences or as post-proceedings, and delivered in the form of printed books and/or electronically as USBs and/or e-content licenses for accessing proceedings at SpringerLink. Furthermore, CCIS proceedings are included in the CCIS electronic book series hosted in the SpringerLink digital library at http://link.springer.com/bookseries/7899. Conferences publishing in CCIS are allowed to use our online conference service (Meteor) for managing the whole proceedings lifecycle (from submission and reviewing to preparing for publication) free of charge.

Publication process

The language of publication is exclusively English. Authors publishing in CCIS have to sign the Springer CCIS copyright transfer form, however, they are free to use their material published in CCIS for substantially changed, more elaborate subsequent publications elsewhere. For the preparation of the camera-ready papers/files, authors have to strictly adhere to the Springer CCIS Authors' Instructions and are strongly encouraged to use the CCIS LaTeX style files or templates.

Abstracting/Indexing

CCIS is abstracted/indexed in DBLP, Google Scholar, EI-Compendex, Mathematical Reviews, SCImago, Scopus. CCIS volumes are also submitted for the inclusion in ISI Proceedings.

How to start

To start the evaluation of your proposal for inclusion in the CCIS series, please send an e-mail to ccis@springer.com

Gyanendra Kumar Verma · Rajesh Doriya ·
Himanshu Buckchash
Editors

Machine Learning, Image Processing, Network Security and Data Sciences

7th International Conference, MIND 2025
Jaipur, India, December 12–14, 2025
Proceedings, Part II

Springer

Editors
Gyanendra Kumar Verma
National Institute of Technology Raipur
Raipur, Chhattisgarh, India

Rajesh Doriya
National Institute of Technology Raipur
Raipur, Chhattisgarh, India

Himanshu Buckchash
IMC University of Applied Sciences Krems
Krems an der Donau, Austria

ISSN 1865-0929 ISSN 1865-0937 (electronic)
Communications in Computer and Information Science
ISBN 978-3-032-31229-7 ISBN 978-3-032-31230-3 (eBook)
https://doi.org/10.1007/978-3-032-31230-3

This Springer imprint is published by the registered company Springer Nature Switzerland AG
The registered company address is: Gewerbestrasse 11, 6330 Cham, Switzerland

Preface

The 7th International Conference on Machine Learning, Image Processing, Network Security and Data Sciences (MIND 2025) was held during December 12–14, 2025 at the Malaviya National Institute of Technology Jaipur, Jaipur, India. The MIND conference series was established as an important international platform for researchers, academicians, industry practitioners, and students to present and discuss recent developments in the areas of intelligent computing, data science, machine learning, and communication technologies.

The primary objective of MIND 2025 was to foster collaboration among researchers and practitioners working in emerging areas of artificial intelligence, data analytics, and secure communication systems. The conference provided a vibrant forum for exchanging innovative ideas, presenting high-quality research, and discussing practical challenges and future research directions in the rapidly evolving domains of intelligent systems and modern communication infrastructures.

The conference received 406 submissions from researchers across five countries, reflecting the growing global interest in its thematic areas. All submitted manuscripts underwent a rigorous single-blind peer-review process overseen by the Program Committee and supported by more than 197 expert reviewers from academia and industry. Each submission was evaluated by at least three reviewers based on originality, technical contribution, methodological rigor, and relevance to the conference themes. Following thorough review and careful deliberation, 83 full papers were accepted for presentation and publication in these proceedings, corresponding to an acceptance rate of 20.44%. In addition, one invited paper was included, bringing the total number of papers in the proceedings to 84.

The theme of MIND 2025, "Intelligent Systems for Future Networks and Data-Driven Innovations," provided a dynamic platform for showcasing cutting-edge advancements at the intersection of intelligent technologies, next-generation networks, and data-centric research. The MIND 2025 proceedings include the papers in two tracks i) Artificial Intelligence and Intelligent Systems and ii) Networks and Communication Systems. The papers in the first track present novel algorithms, models, and frameworks addressing real-world challenges in domains such as healthcare, smart environments, automation, and data-driven decision support systems. The second track focuses on recent advances in networking technologies, wireless communication, Internet of Things (IoT), cybersecurity, network optimization, and secure communication protocols. The contributions address both theoretical and practical aspects of designing robust, scalable, and secure communication infrastructures for modern digital ecosystems.

The success of MIND 2025 would not have been possible without the dedication and efforts of many individuals and organizations. We express our sincere gratitude to all the authors for their valuable contributions and to the program committee members and reviewers for their careful evaluation and constructive feedback, which significantly improved the quality of the accepted papers. We also thank the keynote speakers, session chairs, organizing committee members, and volunteers for their commitment and support in ensuring the smooth organization of the conference.

We are especially grateful to Springer Nature for publishing these proceedings in the Communications in Computer and Information Science (CCIS) series and for their continued support in disseminating high-quality research to the global scientific community. We hope that this volume will serve as a valuable resource for researchers, practitioners, and students working in the fields of artificial intelligence, data science, and communication technologies, and that it will stimulate further research and innovation in these rapidly advancing areas.

December 2025

Gyanendra Kumar Verma
Rajesh Doriya
Himanshu Buckchash

Organization

Organizing Committee

Chief Patron

Narayana Prasad Padhy	Malaviya National Institute of Technology Jaipur, India

Honorary Chairs

Xiao-Zhi Gao	University of Eastern Finland, Finland
Mahesh Chandra Govil	National Institute of Technology Sikkim, India
Richi Nayak	Queensland University of Technology, Australia
Lava Bhargava	Malaviya National Institute of Technology Jaipur, India

Honorary Co-chair

Mushtaq Ahmed	Malaviya National Institute of Technology Jaipur, India

Conference Chairs

Namita Mittal	Malaviya National Institute of Technology Jaipur, India
Gyanendra Kumar Verma	National Institute of Technology Raipur, India

Secretaries

Arka P. Mazumdar	Malaviya National Institute of Technology Jaipur, India
Rajesh Doriya	National Institute of Technology Raipur, India
Vijay Verma	National Institute of Technology Kurukshetra, India

Publication Chairs

Arun Kumar Yadav	National Institute of Technology Hamirpur, India
Sadbhawna	Malaviya National Institute of Technology Jaipur, India

Finance Chair

Vikash Kumar	Malaviya National Institute of Technology Jaipur, India

TPC Chairs

Gyanendra Kumar Verma	National Institute of Technology Raipur, India
Himanshu Buckchash	IMC University of Applied Sciences Krems, Austria

Advisory Committee

Alexandre Carlos Brandão Ramos	Universidade Federal de Itajubá, Brazil
Aparajita Ojha	IIITDM Jabalpur, India
Anupam Shukla	Indian Institute of Information Technology and Management Gwalior/NIT Surat, India
Anurag Singh	National Institute of Technology Delhi, India
A. K. Singh	National Institute of Technology Kurukshetra, India
Annappa	National Institute of Technology Karnataka Surathkal, India
Ashok Kumar Turuk	National Institute of Technology Rourkela, India
Chirag Modi	NIT Goa, India
Dinesh K. Vishwakarma	Delhi Technological University, India
Himanshu Buckchash	IMC Applied University of Sciences Krems, Austria
Narendra D. Londhe	National Institute of Technology Raipur, India
Pavan Chakraborty	Indian Institute of Information Technology Allahabad, India
Ram Bilas Pachori	Indian Institute of Technology Indore, India
Raman Balasubramanian	Indian Institute of Technology Roorkee, India
Santosh Kumar Vipparthi	Indian Institute of Technology Ropar, India
Ugo Fiore	University of Salerno, Italy

Technical Program Committee

A. Prasanth	Vel Tech Technical University, India
Abdel-Badeeh M. Salem	Ain Shams University, Egypt
Anitha Velu	Sri Sairam College of Engineering, India
Anjan Kumar Ray	National Institute of Technology Sikkim, India
Ankit Vidyarthi	Jaypee Institute of Information Technology, India
Basant Agarwal	Central University of Rajasthan, India
Bharathi N. Gopalsamy	SRM Institute of Science and Technology, India
Bharti Ahuja Salunke	Poornima University, India
Chandran Saravanan	National Institute of Technology Durgapur, India
Chandra Prakash	Sardar Vallabhbhai National Institute of Technology Surat, India
Chemmalar Selvi G.	VIT Vellore, India
Chittaranjan Pradhan	Kalinga Institute of Industrial Technology, India
Deepak Ranjan Nayak	Malaviya National Institute of Technology Jaipur, India
Dinesh Singh	Motilal Nehru National Institute of Technology Allahabad, India
Geeta Sable	Raisoni Education, India
Geeta Yadav	Indian Institute of Technology Ropar, India
Gourav Takhar	Indian Institute of Technology Kanpur, India
J. Vijaya	International Institute of Information Technology Naya Raipur, India
L. Oppili Prasad	Indian Institute of Technology BHU Varanasi, India
Mallikharjuna Rao K.	International Institute of Information Technology Naya Raipur, India
Mrityunjay Singh	Indian Institute of Information Technology Una, India
Pradnya Borkar	Symbiosis Institute of Technology, India
Pankaj Keserwani	National Institute of Technology Sikkim, India
Praveen Kumar Yadaw	Kalinga University, India
Ravikumar C. V.	Vellore Institute of Technology, India
Rohit Batwada	Wipro, India
Santosh Kumar	National Institute of Technology Kurukshetra, India
Shikha Baghel	Indian Institute of Technology Tirupati, India
Shikha Mundra	Manipal University Jaipur, India
Shrikant Upahyay	MLR Institute of Technology, India
Sudhakar Pandey	National Institute of Technology Raipur, India
Sudip Roy	Indian Institute of Technology Roorkee, India

Kanchan Lata Kashyap	Indian Institute of Information Technology Kottayam, India
Kirti Kumari	Indian Institute of Information Technology Ranchi, India
Krishnendu Ghosh	Indian Institute of Information Technology Dharwad, India
Mahendra Kumar Murmu	National Institute of Technology Kurukshetra, India
Manju Lata Joshi	Poornima University, India
Mandar Ganjapurkar	A.P. Shah Institute of Technology, India
Mitul Kumar Ahirwal	Maulana Azad National Institute of Technology Bhopal, India
Neeraj Kumar	National Institute of Technology Jalandhar, India
P. Geetha	SRM Institute of Science and Technology, India
Partha Pakray	National Institute of Technology Silchar, India
Pankaj Pratap Singh	Central Institute of Technology Kokrajhar, India
Piyush Kumar	National Institute of Technology Patna, India
Reshma Rastogi	South Asian University, India
Ritesh Kumar	Indian Institute of Information Technology Surat, India
Rupesh Kumar Dewang	Motilal Nehru National Institute of Technology Allahabad, India
Sangram Ray	National Institute of Technology Sikkim, India
Satya Verma	Siksha 'O' Anusandhan, India
Sevinthi Kali Sankar	HCLTech, India
Shashikant Patil	ATLAS SkillTech University, India
Shitala Prasad	Indian Institute of Technology Goa, India
Shyam Lal	National Institute of Technology Karnataka Surathkal, India
Suganthini C.	VIT Vellore, India
Tene Ramakrishnudu	National Institute of Technology Warangal, India
T. Veerakumar	National Institute of Technology Goa, India
Vishal Passricha	Central University of Haryana, India
Xiaochun Cheng	Swansea University, UK
Suyel Namasudra	National Institute of Technology Agartala, India
S. Sridevi	Thiagarajar College of Engineering, India

Contents

Gesture to Speech for Regional Language

Saswati Debnath[1(✉)], M. Senbagavalli[1], Daniel Willson Velladurai[1], and Prarthana V. Gunakimath[2]

[1] Computer Science and Engineering Department, Alliance School of Advanced Computing, Alliance University, Bengaluru, India
debnath.saswati123@gmail.com

[2] Information Science and Engineering Department, Global Academy of Technology, Bengaluru, India
prarthana.vg@gat.ac.in

Abstract. Communication is a cornerstone of human interaction, yet for people with speech and hearing impairments, this basic necessity often becomes a daily challenge. While sign language serves as a powerful medium for expression, its comprehension is largely limited to those who are trained in it, thereby creating a communication barrier between the hearing-impaired community and the general population. This paper presents a solution that bridges this communication gap by converting hand gestures into audible speech tailored to regional languages. The primary objective of this work is to develop an intelligent system that recognizes hand gestures in real-time and translates them into corresponding speech outputs in a selected regional language. The system's architecture consists of three core components: gesture detection and tracking using OpenCV, gesture classification using a Convolutional Neural Network (CNN), and language-based speech synthesis using a region-specific text-to-speech (TTS) engine. The classification model is trained for speed and accuracy to minimize any latency in a real-time application. In addition, the system is trained to be robust to variations in light and dark conditions, hand orientations, and skin complexion to increase usability and user-experience across various demographic and diverse user groups. Experimental results demonstrate promising accuracy and responsiveness, with MobileNetV2-based model achieving an accuracy of 90.1%, making it suitable for real-world deployment.

Keywords: Gesture · CNN · Speech · text-to-speech · MobileNetV2

1 Introduction

Communication through speech and gesture represents a primary means of interaction between human beings. However, speaking and gesturing as a form of natural and human interaction can be quite difficult for individuals who experience speech impairment or hearing impairment. Although sign language provides an avenue for communication, the broader population with hearing impairments

G. K. Verma et al. (Eds.): MIND 2025, CCIS 2981, pp. 1–12, 2027.
https://doi.org/10.1007/978-3-032-31230-3_1

can only be understood as expressions from individuals trained in understanding sign language. Gesture recognition technology may serve as an alternative to communication from the hear impairment community to the general population with an understanding of how gesture recognition assists humans and machines. Gesture recognition from a human-computer interaction (HCI) perspective is defined as technology that interprets and reacts to human gestures in real time. New developments in computer vision, artificial intelligence (AI), and speech synthesis allows us to use hand gestures to create audible speech. These technologies can be integrated into inclusive communication systems that will enable engaging with sign language users. In multilingual societies like India, where the diversity of languages adds additional complexity, the ability to provide support to regional languages in gesture-to-speech systems is of particular relevance.

The objective of this research is to convert static gestures captured by a webcam to speech in Indian regional languages, Hindi, Bengali, Assamese, and Tamil. The gesture detection is facilitated by OpenCV, and gesture classification is performed using MobileNetV2, a lightweight CNN. Google TTS is used to achieve a multilingual voice output. The system achieves high accuracy at low latency for real-time use after modeling and preprocessing, feature extraction, and tuning to make it usable. The aim is to develop an appropriate, usable, and effective communication tool for those who have either hearing or speech disability and to consider India's multilingualism. The paper is organized as follows: Sect. 2 provide literature review, proposed methodology and result analysis are given in Sect. 3 and 4, respectively. Section 5 provides testing of the model and Sect. 6 concludes the paper.

2 Literature Review

Gesture recognition, similar to facial recognition, has emerged as an important research area within the broader discipline of human-computer interaction, particularly to support communication for people with hearing and speech impairments. It seeks to address the communication barrier by transforming physical gestures into valuable digital output, similar to how facial recognition has been utilized for security and authentication systems [8, 14]. As a result of recent developments in computer vision, AI, and speech synthesis technologies, it is now technically feasible to convert hand gestures to audible speech outputs [5, 6]. In this [14], the author presented a system that interprets hand gestures and converts these gestures to speech output in different regional languages, thereby making the output accessible and impactful in a multi-lingual country like India. The development of web applications and mobile technologies can support the integration of these types of systems in real-time contexts [7, 10].

These studies focused on gesture-to-speech translation emphasize multimodal approaches, using CNNs, recurrent architectures, and sensor-based input to accurately interpret signs [2]. Research has also shown significant progress in multilingual gesture translation, as models are increasingly being adapted to region-specific languages to improve accessibility. The work addressed gaps by developing a system capable of translating gestures into both Hindi and Tamil speech, two widely spoken languages in India. This enhanced the model's practical applicability, especially in diverse and multilingual contexts. Additionally, existing studies recommend future solutions that support two-way human-computer interaction, which aligns with the proposed expansion of this project into a fully interactive application [2].

The use of image processing is an important component that engages in the analysis of images or video frames and extracts meaningful information [15]. In gesture recognition, image processing performs the task of locating and segmenting the hand portion of the video stream; while the degree of sophistication and proprietary knowledge varies, generally this is done using pre-processing techniques like image manipulation, background subtraction, contour detection, and thresholding. These pre-processing techniques help to improve the accuracy of the system in determining gestures, especially with various lighting and environmental conditions [1,9,15].

Gesture detection is the process of detecting the existence and location of a human hand from visual input or a camera feed [1,11]. Facial detection can locate a face in an image, gesture detection is detecting other significant hand features (e.g., fingertips, bones and joints, and palm location). Frameworks such as MediaPipe Hands or OpenCV with contour tracking were used for accurate detection of hand landmarks in complex visual environments [1,14]. A common challenge in the interaction of gesture detection included the challenges of complex or dynamic backgrounds, different pointing features, and variants in human skin color. To mitigate those challenges, the system outlined techniques (background image subtraction, skin segmentation, and machine learning models trained with diverse datasets) [4,9]. This paper emphasized the use of regional language TTS systems so that the output is in a language familiar to the user, like Hindi, Bengali, Tamil, or Assamese. One of the challenges addressed by the author was the accurate classification of gestures. Sometimes, similar-looking gestures may lead to misclassification. To overcome this, CNNs and recurrent neural networks (RNNs) were employed, trained on rich and diverse gesture datasets [3,11]. Another challenge is to producing natural-sounding regional language speech. This has been tackled using advanced TTS tools that support multilingual and regional voice outputs, such as Google TTS or Indian language speech synthesis systems [13]. This study proposed a real-time Indian Sign Language Recognition (ISLR) system employing the YOLOv10-ST model to address the communication gap between hearing individuals and people who are deaf or mute [12]. The presented framework modifies the base YOLOv10 architecture by incorporating a Swin Transformer for enhanced feature extraction capabilities along with Mish activation, which propagates gradients through neural networks. A custom dataset was developed through the acquisition of 15,000 static images and 35 dynamic gesture videos to train and evaluate the model. A set of ablation studies and statistical evaluations further confirms that the YOLOv10-ST architecture can accurately recognize static and dynamic ISL gestures with low computational overhead.

Even though gesture-to-speech systems have improved a lot, there are still some problems that need to be fixed.

- Lack of Standardized and Regional Datasets: Many systems do not perform well because there are not enough well-organized and labeled datasets, especially for regional sign dialects. Without proper training data, the systems cannot learn to understand all the variations of sign language used across different states and communities in India.
- Inconsistency in Gestures: Different people use slightly different hand shapes, speeds, and movements for the same word. These small changes confuse the model, especially when it is trained only on limited examples.
- Dependence on Costly Hardware: Some systems require highly specialized capital items to achieve accurate gesture recognition. These devices are typically too costly for most users.
- Limited Support for Other Indian Languages: Most existing tools aim to perform translations from ISL to English or Hindi. Users who speak other languages (e.g., Tamil, Bengali, or Assamese) cannot utilize these systems, limiting accessibility.
- Environmental Constraints: Systems may have trouble operating in low-light situations, with user backgrounds that are cluttered, or with partially occluded user hands. Real-world conditions can impact recognition accuracy.
- Limited Expressiveness of Speech Output: Most existing gesture-to-speech systems convert sign language into an abstract, mechanical sound. These systems are not able to convey the speaker's inflection, which is an important part of real communication.
- No Context Coding: Many systems can recognize signs and gestures, but most recognition systems are only able to process one sign/gesture at a time and do not account for context.
- Inadequate Real-Time Feedback: Certain systems aim to provide feedback only after a gesture is misread. When there is no feedback, users cannot compensate for their misreads or understand what may be wrong.

3 Proposed Methodology

The proposed gesture-to-speech system consists of multiple modules that work together to provide efficient visual capture, gesture recognition and audio playback. The implementation is developed in a modular manner allowing for ease of maintenance, scalability and adaptability for regional language usage.

- **Image Acquisition:** The system captures live images of hand gestures with a normal camera. OpenCV handles continuous image collection while keeping the video smooth and low latency for real-time purposes.
- **Image Pre-processing:** The frames are obtained through a pre-processing stage to ensure consistency and clarity. Pre-processing refers to modifications to an image that are performed prospectively to enhance its value for image

analysis. The image size is modified to standardize each image to 224×224 pixels and normalize to remove noise and correct the background. This module changes the color frames to RGB as needed, apply noise reduction approaches, and feature enhancement modifications as needed.

- **Functionality:**
  - Image normalization, resizing, and denoising
  - Color space conversion (BGR to RGB)
  - Feature enhancement

- **Gesture Recognition and Text Mapping Module:** A fine-tuned mobile CNN uses MobileNetV2 to classify gestures. The model predicts a class label for the gesture, which corresponds to a word or phrase stored in a dictionary mapping. This achieves a high level of accuracy and a low inference time for real-time applications. Once preprocessed, the image is passed through the trained MobileNetV2 model, which outputs the predicted class label. This label is then mapped to a predefined phrase using a dictionary structure. The module handles errors and unknown gestures gracefully with fallback responses.
- **Text To Speech Conversion:** The recognized text output of the real-time recognition allows conversion of the output text into audible speech using Google Text-to-Speech (gTTS) functionality. The system converts text output to speech output in a variety of Indian languages that correspond to each recognition output (i.e., Hindi, Bengali, Assamese, Tamil) for inclusive communication for users of those languages.
- **Output Integration and Real-Time Feedback:** The system's output includes the recognized gesture, corresponding text output, and regional speech output to a graphical interface simultaneously. The system continually captures images and recognizes gestures, providing instant feedback to the users while maintaining robustness to lighting and backgrounds and high responsiveness for real-world applications.

4 Result and Discussion

4.1 Dataset

The number of gestures are classified into 9 classes. The images were captured in the lighting background. The dataset is partitioned into training/validation/testing, and the motivation for selecting these gestures for regional language communication. The proposed system effectively translates hand gestures into regional speech using deep learning techniques integrated with real-time computer vision and speech synthesis. The model used, MobileNetV2, was trained and evaluated using a custom dataset of common gestures. This chapter analyzes the model's performance and compares it with other methods.

The primary evaluation metrics include training and validation accuracy, along with loss across different epochs. The system shows a stable learning pattern, suggesting good generalization and low overfitting. Post-training, the model is integrated with a webcam-based gesture capture system and text-to-speech using Google Text-to-Speech (gTTS) for real-time performance (Table 1).

Algorithm 1. Gesture Recognition and Speech Synthesis

```
Input: image_frame
Output: spoken_output

Capture image_frame from webcam
Preprocess image_frame: resize → normalize → (augment if training)
if TRAIN_FLAG is true then
    Load MobileNetV2 base (frozen)
    Build & compile a custom head
    Train custom head (using EarlyStopping, StopAtTrainAcc)
    Unfreeze base; fine-tune full model
    Save the model to disk as gesture_model.h5
else
    Load saved gesture_model.h5
end if

y_pred = model.predict(preprocessed_frame)
gesture_label = argmax(y_pred)
text_output = map_label_to_text(gesture_label)
spoken_output = TTS(text_output, language='regional')
Play(spoken_output)
End
```

4.2 Result Analysis

To evaluate the performance of our proposed gesture recognition system, we perform a detailed analysis using training and validation metrics, confusion matrices, and comparative benchmarking against other state-of-the-art architectures. The MobileNetV2 model is trained for 50 epochs using Custom ISL datasets. Key metrics observed. These results confirm that the MobileNetV2 architecture offers a strong balance between computational efficiency and classification accuracy, making it ideal for real-time applications on resource-limited devices. A confusion matrix (Fig. 1) is generated to visualize the classification performance across different gesture classes. Most gestures achieved high precision and recall, with occasional confusion between similar hand signs such as "Thank You" and "Welcome", which share overlapping visual patterns. Table 3 is a complete class-wise Precision, Recall, and F1-Score (Table 2).

The proposed system integrates the MobileNetV2 architecture and achieves an impressive accuracy of 90.1%, demonstrating an effective balance between precision and computational efficiency. When compared to the custom-built CNN model, which records 84.7% accuracy, MobileNetV2 not only improves classification performance but also reduces inference time, making it more viable for real-time deployment. While ResNet50 delivers slightly better accuracy at 92.3%, its significantly larger model size and slower inference time (120 ms) make it less suitable for lightweight or embedded applications. EfficientNetB0, with an accuracy of 91.0% and moderate resource demand, stands as a competitive option, but its latency is still higher than that of MobileNetV2. Consequently, the pro-

Table 1. Comparison of Recent Works in Indian Sign Language (ISL) Recognition

Study	Dataset	Model/Technique	Accuracy (%)	Remarks
Proposed Approach	Custom ISL Dataset	MobileNetV2	90.1	Lightweight, suitable for real-time, good balance of accuracy and speed.
Sevanth, M. (2023) [13]	Self-curated ISL dataset	Inception V3	> 90	High accuracy for static gestures; lacks dynamic gesture support.
Joshi, A., et al. (2023) [8]	iSign: ISL-English dataset	ResNet50 + BiLSTM	N/A	Dataset-focused study; emphasis on ISLâĂŞEnglish translation.
Mittal, A., et al. (2022) [9]	Custom gestures via Leap Motion	LSTM (pose features)	89.6	Effective temporal modeling; depends on Leap Motion hardware.
Hossain, M. S., & Muhammad, G. (2022) [6]	IoT sensor + video data	AI-IoT integrated CNN	~88	Edge/cloud-based system; latency depends on network.
Gupta, R., & Kumar, S. (2021) [4]	Custom ISL dataset	Transfer Learning + Label Powerset	~90	Multi-label sign handling; computationally heavy.
Ali, A., et al. (2021) [1]	RGB + depth dataset	Hybrid CNN + handcrafted features	~88	Combines CNN and spatial descriptors; needs preprocessing.
Patel, D., & Sharma, B. (2021) [10]	Public ISL gesture dataset	Lightweight CNN	~82	Mobile-friendly; affected by background noise.

posed MobileNetV2 model stands out as a highly efficient and portable solution for gesture recognition tasks, providing fast and accurate translation of hand gestures to speech in real-time scenarios. Below is the comparison table showing the performance of the proposed model against other commonly used architectures.

The graph shows steady improvement in accuracy with each epoch (Fig. 2). Validation accuracy stabilizes above 80%, indicating reliable generalization, with training and validation accuracy closely tracking each other, minimizing the risk of overfitting. This behavior is shown in the graph below.

We used 5-fold user-wise cross-validation (GroupKFold) to evaluate user generalization. The model achieved a mean accuracy of 89.9% (±0.9) across folds and a mean macro-F1 of 0.88 (±0.02), demonstrating consistent performance on unseen users." A rapid decline in training loss(Fig. 3) confirms successful

Table 2. Performance Analysis of the Proposed Model

Metric	Value
Training Accuracy	94.3%
Validation Accuracy	90.1%
Training Loss	0.15
Validation Loss	0.28
Inference Time (avg/frame)	∼45 ms

Table 3. Class-wise Precision, Recall, and F1-Scores for MobileNetV2 Model

Gesture Class	Precision	Recall	F1-Score
Hello	0.93	0.91	0.92
Thank You	0.88	0.85	0.86
Yes	0.92	0.94	0.93
No	0.89	0.87	0.88
Please	0.86	0.84	0.85
Welcome	0.87	0.82	0.84
I Need Help	0.90	0.92	0.91
Good Morning	0.91	0.88	0.89
Sorry	0.88	0.90	0.89

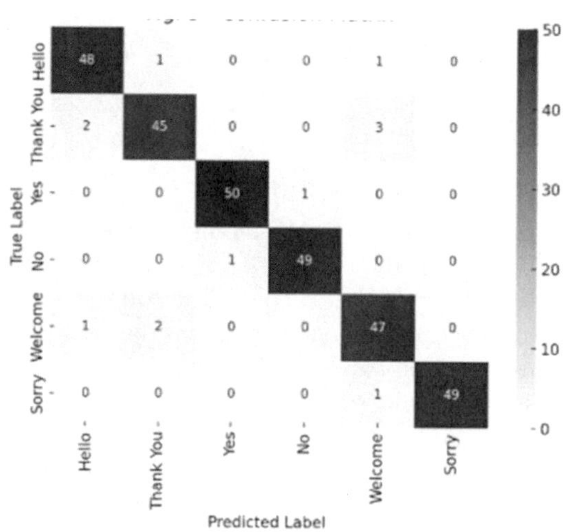

Fig. 1. Confusion matrix highlights correct and incorrect classifications across gesture classes.

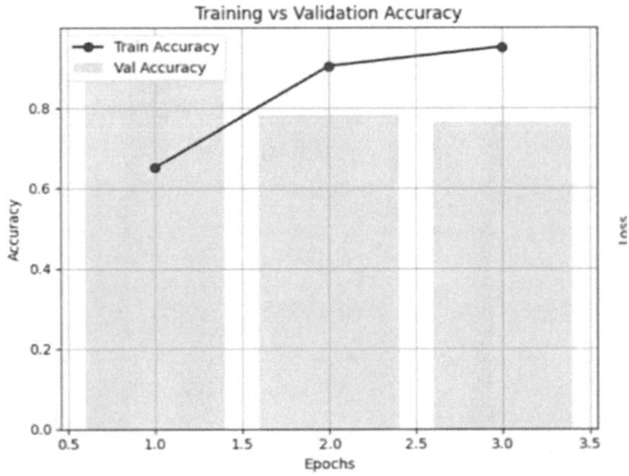

Fig. 2. Training and validation accuracy graph.

learning, and validation loss remains controlled, suggesting low overfitting. The controlled validation loss confirms that the model is well-regularized.

5 Testing

The gestures in this study are static gestures, with each class representing a different hand pose represented as a single image. Since no data was used that exhibited temporal or movement-based sequences of the gesture, we have designed the gesture recognition model to classify static hand postures instead of sequences of dynamic gestures. The testing phase assessed the accuracy, robustness, and performance of the proposed gesture-to-speech system for real-time operation. To verify ease of use and performance under real-world conditions, the system has been tested under multiple conditions, including lighting, hand orientation, and background complexity. Testing occurred on a macOS system with an Apple M2 processor and a memory 8 GB of memory using a set of custom ISL datasets.

A summarized overview of the outcomes measured in model evaluation is demonstrated in Table 4, which corresponds to the assessment of training curves and confusion matrix previously explained in this section. Based on the confusion matrix, the MobileNetV2 model performed comparably well through most gesture classes, with only a handful of ambiguity present with visually adjacent gestures like "Thank You" and "Welcome." The visualized information offered in the confusion matrix juxtaposes the accuracy and loss trends from the training curves, where accuracy was both steady and coalesced towards 90% for both training and validation accuracy, confirming that learning was stable without significant overfitting. The loss curve was equally smooth in that it also steadily decreased to a conclusion, confirming that the model was optimized effectively throughout training. In combining the metrics affirmed in Table 3 collectively suggest the model was reliable through classification performance,

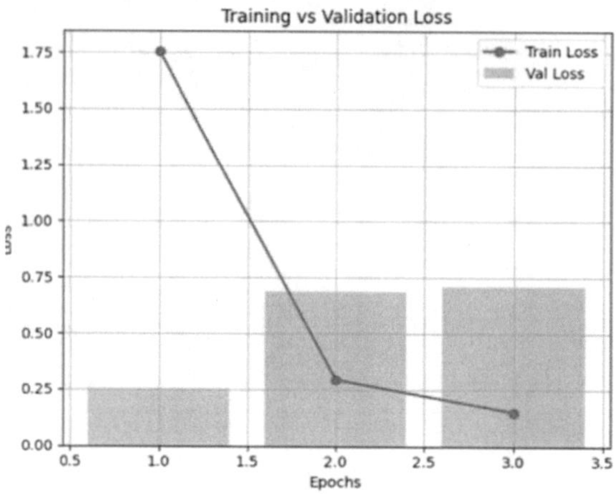

Fig. 3. Training and validation loss graph.

offered robust generalization across gesture classes, and provided a platform for real-time gesture-to-speech translation for utilize within regional languages.

Table 4. Model Evaluation Summary

Evaluation Aspect	Details
Confusion Matrix	Visualizes classification performance across gesture classes. Shows high overall accuracy with minor misclassifications between visually similar gestures such as *"Thank You"* and *"Welcome"*.
Accuracy vs. Epoch	Training and validation accuracies exhibit a consistent upward trend, converging around 90%, indicating stable learning with minimal overfitting.
Loss Curve	Training and validation losses decrease steadily and plateau, demonstrating successful convergence and low overfitting.

Several test cases were built to consider gesture recognition accuracy, sentence-level translation and quality of speech generation. Of the six test cases, four cases passed completely, one partially passed and one case failed, resulting in an overall testing accuracy of approximately 88.3 %. Results confirmed the gesture-to-speech system can perform accurately when gestures are clean (no noise) and are complete (gesture not obstructed by part of the body) with minor misinterpretations occurring with fast gestures, or gestures that are partially obstructed. The testing also confirmed the responsiveness of the system and proved it operates efficiently to perform real-time translation from gesture to regional language speech. This confirms the gesture-to-speech system's potential for use in assistive communication applications (Table 5).

Table 5. Model Test Cases

Test Case ID	Module	Input	Expected Output	Actual Output	Result
TC01	Gesture Input	Gesture for *"How are you?"*	Speech: *"How are you?"*	Speech: *"How are you?"*	Pass
TC02	Model Prediction	Gesture for *"I am fine"*	Label: *"I am fine"*	Label: *"I am fine"*	Pass
TC03	Speech Synthesis	Detected: *"What is your name?"*	Voice output	Voice output	Pass
TC04	Partial Gesture	Incomplete sentence gesture	No output/error	No output	Pass
TC05	Fast Gesture Movement	Rapid signing of a sentence	Accurate speech	Slight misinterpretation	Partial Pass

6 Conclusion

This proposed gesture-to-speech system effectively closes the communication barrier between normal people and deaf and hard-of-hearing individuals by converting hand gestures into speech in regional languages. The application of computer vision, deep learning, and TTS, enables a more natural, instantaneous interaction experience without costly hardware and setup. The deployment of a MobileNetV2-based CNN model allows for high precision and low latencies, allowing practical real-world use. Accuracy tests achieved upwards of 90%, providing evidential proof that the full system can be implemented efficiently, in a robust manner under all conditions. Future work will involve extending the gesture dataset, focusing on dynamic gesture recognition, and enabling multilingual and context-aware speech synthesis for more natural and representative communication.

References

1. Ali, A., Rauf, A., Rehman, A.: Hybrid cnn and hand-crafted features for dynamic sign language recognition. Multimedia Tools Appli. **80**, 31247–31263 (2021). https://doi.org/10.1007/s11042-021-11077-0
2. Bhattatiri, A., Chaubal, A., Dalal, M., Borkar, G.: The voice and gesture to speech conversion in indian regional sign language. In: Sentiment Analysis and Deep Learning, pp. 717–736 (2023)
3. Bose, A., Rajan, M.: Enhancing gesture translation with nlp integration for Indian sign language. IEEE Trans. Human-Mach. Syst. **51**(5), 467–478 (2021). https://doi.org/10.1109/THMS.2021.3076378
4. Gupta, P., Verma, R.: Depth sensor-based gesture recognition using sift features and random forests. Inter. J. Comput. Appli. **176**(4), 9–15 (2020). https://doi.org/10.5120/ijca2020919952
5. Gupta, R., Kumar, S.: Transfer learning for Indian sign language using label powerset multi-label classification. In: Proceedings of the 10th International Conference on Pattern Recognition Applications. SCITEPRESS (2021)
6. Hossain, M.S., Muhammad, G.: Ai and iot-enabled sign language recognition with cloud integration. IEEE Internet Things J. **9**(4), 2845–2855 (2022). https://doi.org/10.1109/JIOT.2021.3097744

7. Jalal, A., Kim, K.: Depth video-based gesture recognition using motion and shape features. Sensors **20**(17), 4824 (2020). https://doi.org/10.3390/s20174824
8. Joshi, A., Mohanty, R., et al.: isign: a large-scale isl-english dataset for sign language translation and retrieval (2023). https://arxiv.org/abs/2407.05404
9. Mittal, A., Kumar, P.: Lstm-based continuous sign language recognition using the leap motion sensor. J. Ambient. Intell. Humaniz. Comput. **13**, 1267–1280 (2022). https://doi.org/10.1007/s12652-021-02990-2
10. Patel, D., Sharma, B.: A lightweight CNN for mobile-based Indian sign language recognition. Inter. J. Artifi. Intel. Res. **5**(1), 12–20 (2021)
11. Rastgoo, R., Kiani, K., Escalera, S.: Hand sign language recognition using cascaded ssd, cnn, and lstm. Neurocomputing **410**, 213–222 (2020). https://doi.org/10.1016/j.neucom.2020.06.032
12. Rastogi, U., M.R.K.S.: Advanced gesture recognition in Indian sign language using a synergistic combination of yolov10 with swin transformer model. Sci. Report **15** (2025). https://doi.org/10.1038/s41598-025-18496-8
13. Sahu, A., Patel, A.: Smart glove for isl gesture to voice translation. Int. J. Adv. Res. Comput. Sci. **11**(2), 60–66 (2025)
14. Sevanth, M.: Isl recognition using inception v3 for indian sign language. In: RESNA 2023 Conference, (2023)
15. Shenoy, K., Dastane, T., Rao, V., Vyavaharkar, D.: Real-time indian sign language (isl) recognition. 2018 9th International Conference on Computing, Communication and Networking Technologies (ICCCNT), pp. 1–9 (2018). https://doi.org/10.1109/ICCCNT.2018.8493808

Alzico: A Multimodal Approach for Early Alzheimer's Risk Prediction

Umed Jogi(✉), Maria Lokhandwala, and Sofia Francis

Department of Computer Engineering, MPSTME, NMIMS University, Mumbai, India
{umed.jogi43,maria.lokhandwala09}@nmims.in, sofia.francis@nmims.edu

Abstract. Alzheimer's disease (AD) is a major and expanding global health issue, underscoring the critical need for early, scalable, and easily accessible diagnostic methods to facilitate timely treatment. The resource-intensive, uncommon, and potentially extremely stressful character of existing clinical assessment paradigms hinders early diagnosis. This study proposes a two-pronged approach to get around these limitations. A machine learning model for three-class cognitive classification was created and thoroughly verified in order to differentiate between AD, MCI, and Cognitively Normal (CN). This model was trained using a large feature set of more than 330 predictors from 15,621 longitudinal visits in the Alzheimer's Disease Neuroimaging Initiative (ADNI) cohort [1]. Second, it provides the conceptual underpinning for Alzico, a smartphone app that transforms clinically validated instruments, such as the Alzheimer's Disease Assessment Scale-Cognitive Subscale (ADAS-Cog) [2], into entertaining, gamified microtasks meant for long-term monitoring. The HistGradientBoosting classifier showed state-of-the-art performance and developed a dependable, clinically based computational engine with a macro-averaged Area Under the Receiver Operating Characteristic Curve (AUC) of 0.90 ± 0.02 and a macro F1-score of 0.85 ± 0.02. The Alzico framework, which presents a novel and intriguing paradigm for long-term cognitive monitoring, is built upon this tested concept. By integrating a high-fidelity classification engine with a user-centric, gamified interface, it paves the way for a future multimodal system that can gather rich, real-world digital phenotypes for early AD risk prediction.

Keywords: Alzheimer's Disease · Mild Cognitive Impairment · Machine Learning · Digital Biomarkers · Gamification · Cognitive Assessment

1 Introduction

Alzheimer's disease (AD) and associated dementias are a silent epidemic that is rising globally as people age. Alzheimer's disease is predicted to affect 7.2 million Americans 65 and older in 2025 alone. Without medical advancements, this number is expected to nearly triple to 13.8 million by 2060 [3]. The staggering prevalence of AD, which is currently the seventh leading cause of death in the US

G. K. Verma et al. (Eds.): MIND 2025, CCIS 2981, pp. 13–25, 2027.
https://doi.org/10.1007/978-3-032-31230-3_2

and is predicted to move up to the sixth, highlights the significant clinical and societal costs involved [3]. Therefore, appropriate therapy depends on early and precise identification; nevertheless, the current gold standard for diagnosis is still resource-intensive and frequently occurs later in the course of the illness. Using data from the Alzheimer's Disease Neuroimaging Initiative (ADNI), *Alzico* fills this gap with an intriguing, scalable screening method. A novel approach to these problems is provided by digital biomarkers. "Digital biomarkers" are objective, measurable physiological and behavioral data that are gathered and evaluated using digital technology. They can offer high-frequency, long-term health information. Due to their extensive sensor suites and widespread use, smartphones offer a perfect platform for legally and passively acquiring these signals. However, a strong foundation in clinically proven neuropsychological principles and a design that can maintain long-term user participation are two essential components that ultimately define the effectiveness of any digital cognitive evaluation instrument. The Alzico project, a unique framework developed in direct answer to this dual demand, is presented in this article. It seeks to create an enjoyable and diagnostically accurate tool that turns the tedious cognitive testing process into a sequence of satisfying micro-interactions.

2 Related Work

This review covers studies and background related to machine learning models for predicting Alzheimer's disease, neuroimaging biomarkers, clinical assessment tools, and the use of digital biomarkers and gamification techniques to enhance cognitive evaluation methods.

2.1 Clinical Assessment Tools

A variety of standardized clinical tools are utilized for the diagnosis and monitoring of AD. One such indispensable tool in clinical research, used to measure the extent of cognitive impairment in areas like memory, language, and praxis, is the Alzheimer's Disease Assessment ScaleCognitive Subscale, commonly known as the ADAS-Cog [2]. Other key tools include the Montreal Cognitive Assessment, MoCA, crafted particularly to be more sensitive in picking up MCI [5], and the Mini-Mental State Examination, MMSE, a brief screening tool for cognitive impairment [4]. Based on a semi-structured interview with the patient and an informant, the Clinical Dementia Rating (CDR) offers a worldwide staging of dementia severity [6]. Despite their high degree of validity, these instruments are rarely used in clinical settings.

2.2 Neuroimaging and Other Biomarkers

Biological indicators are essential for comprehending the course of a disease in addition to clinical measures. Hippocampal volume loss has been repeatedly shown to be a potent biomarker for AD in MRI-based studies, especially those that use ADNI data. In people with MCI and AD, rapid atrophy can be shown even during short time periods of 6 to 12 months [7]. The characteristic neuropathologies of AD, amyloid plaques and neurofibrillary tangles, which may be quantified in vivo via cerebrospinal fluid (CSF) analysis or Positron Emission Tomography (PET) imaging, are thought to be the cause of this atrophy [1]. Using architectures like ResNet-18, VGG-16, and DenseNet-121, recent multimodal deep learning research that combine 3D MRI data with demographic characteristics have shown impressive accuracy, reaching up to 98.75% in classification performance [8]. The effectiveness of transfer learning in this sector has also been demonstrated by other methods that have used deep learning architectures, such as ResNet-18 with attention mechanisms, to obtain good classification accuracy (up to 93.26%) on MRI scans from the ADNI dataset [9].

2.3 Machine Learning in AD Prediction

The availability of large, multimodal datasets like ADNI has sped up the development of machine learning algorithms for AD classification and progression forecast. Models integrating demographic data with neural network and Grid Search CV methods have shown strong predictive results, underscoring the necessity of incorporating clinical and demographic data [10]. Using advanced techniques like personalized Gaussian Processes, individual patient trajectories on the ADAS-Cog scale have been predicted, suggesting that population-level models might be tailored to particular patient data [11]. The effectiveness of these methods demonstrates how important it is to combine multiple data streams in order to correctly represent the multifaceted and complex nature of AD.

2.4 Gamification and Digital Biomarkers for Cognitive Assessment

Traditional cognitive examinations conducted in clinics have a variety of scientific and practical problems.

Because they are often given episodically, they too often fail to detect slow or early changes in cognition. Moreover, ceiling effects can make these tests inadequately sensitive in situations involving mild deterioration, and many people experience testing as distressing or uncomfortable [12]. Owing to these limitations, there is an increasing interest in finding more adaptable and accessible solutions. Among these, one of the most promising involves the use of digital biomarkers, namely objectively assessed behavioral data acquired through the use of generally utilized digital devices that enable the continuous real-world monitoring of cognitive function over time [13]. This of course, requires sustained user engagement. Gamification-or the introduction of game-design elements in non-game contexts-has rapidly emerged as a strong countermeasure [14]. Traditional cognitive tasks are usually characterized as repetitive and monotonous; This could be very detrimental and lead to participants being disengaged, hence reducing the quality of the data. Gamification can enhance intrinsic motivation and the habitual participation that is so necessary to support early detection by reframing such activities as fun "mini-games." [15]. One common screening tool, the MoCA, has been compared against many serious games-interactive applications developed for educational or therapeutic purposes beyond pure amusement. In fact, evidence from systematic studies indicates that such gamified methods may effectively complement traditional assessments, enhancing participant engagement and diagnostic yield. Following such thinking, the Alzico framework tries to find a balance between clinical accuracy and an engaging user experience by embedding validated cognitive measures into an interactive, game-like mobile interface.

3 Methodology

This part explains how the Alzico model was made. The study will first talk about the ADNI data cohort, and then The study will talk about how The study engineered features and cleaned up the data. Lastly, The study will describe the machine learning pipeline that was made to train and test the model.

3.1 Data Cohort: ADNI

The proposed model is based on the Alzheimer's Disease Neuroimaging Initiative (ADNI) database (adni.loni.usc.edu). The goal of the multicenter, long-term ADNI study is to develop and validate biomarkers for Alzheimer's disease clinical trials [1]. Using this resource, the study created a comprehensive dataset for the proposed project that comprised 15,621 visits over time. For every visit, this dataset contains a complete evaluation of a single participant at a particular time. This enables the study to create a thorough, chronological picture of every individual's journey (Tabel 1).

Table 1. Example of ADNI Visit-Level Data Structure

VisitID	Age	MMSE	ADAS-Cog	Diagnosis
1351	74	27	14.3	MCI
2240	69	29	8.5	CN
3172	78	23	22.1	AD

3.2 Feature Engineering and Preprocessing

To represent the clinical complexity of AD, a multidimensional feature set of about 330 predicted factors was developed starting from the raw ADNI data files. For this, three groups of characteristics are created based on: • Functional and Behavioral Measures: data from FAQ, ECOG, GDSCALE, and NPIQ to capture real-world impact from cognitive decline; Core Cognitive Assessments: primary findings from standardized tests such as the ADAS-Cog, MMSE, MoCA, and CDR; Demographics and Contextual Risk Factors: variables including but not limited to age, sex, education, and family history to account for individual variability. The three-class diagnostic status was the primary outcome variable (CN, MCI, or AD), obtained directly from the official ADNI diagnostic summary file. To avoid data leakage and ensure the model's generalizability, all variables that would not be available at the time of prediction in a real-world scenario were excluded using a "strict no-leak filter."

3.3 Machine Learning Pipeline

A comprehensive comparative study was conducted in order to identify the optimal machine learning architecture. The four models that were benchmarked were Logistic regression, RandomForest, GradientBoosting, and HistGradientBoosting. The HistGradientBoosting classifier, which builds on ideas from scalable tree boosting systems such as XGBoost [17], is particularly well-suited for this task because to its computational speed and native handling of missing data. The models were trained and evaluated using a stratified k-fold cross-validation technique. Macro-averaged Area Under the Curve (Macro AUC), Macro F1-score, overall Accuracy, and per-class Recall were used to assess performance, as shown in Table 2.

Table 2. Comparative Performance of ML Models for 3-Class Cognitive Classification.

Model	Macro AUC	Macro F1	Accuracy	Recall	Recall	Recall
HistGradientBoosting	0.90 ± 0.02	0.85 ± 0.02	0.87 ± 0.01	**0.88**	**0.84**	**0.83**
RandomForest	0.88 ± 0.02	0.83 ± 0.02	0.85 ± 0.01	0.86	0.82	0.80
GradientBoosting	0.87 ± 0.03	0.82 ± 0.03	0.84 ± 0.02	0.85	0.81	0.79
LogisticRegression	0.82 ± 0.03	0.77 ± 0.03	0.80 ± 0.02	0.81	0.76	0.73

3.4 The Alzico Application Framework

The Alzico application, a tool for scalable, long-term cognitive monitoring, is built on top of the validated computational engine. The fundamental idea is to use a gamified, social media-style mobile interface to deliver cognitive assessments. Every interactive task in the app is a purposeful translation of a particular, clinically validated tool, the ADAS-Cog 13. Table 3 describes this direct mapping, which guarantees that the gathered data stays rooted in accepted neuropsychological concepts.

As illustrated in Fig.1, the system is designed to integrate multimodal data in the future. Plans call for integrating audio and video analysis to provide a more comprehensive and detailed view of a person's cognitive and behavioral health.

Table 3. Mapping of ADAS-Cog 13 Tasks to Alzico Gamified Concepts.

ADAS Task	Game Concept	Example
Word Recall	Memory card flip	Flip cards to match words shown earlier
Naming Objects	Emoji tap game	Tap the correct emoji shown in a clip
Commands	Simon Says	Follow voice or visual commands
Drawing	Doodle pad	Draw shapes shown in a video
Orientation	Time-travel quiz	Answer questions about time/place
Word Recognition	Emoji match	Match words to emojis
Spoken Language	Voice challenge	Repeat or describe what was seen
Comprehension	Puzzle-solving	Solve logic puzzles based on clips
Word Finding	Word scramble	Unscramble words related to clips
Delayed Recall	Timed memory test	Recall items after a delay
Number Cancellation	Tap-the-number grid	Tap specific numbers quickly
Remembering Instructions	Multi-step task	Complete a sequence of actions

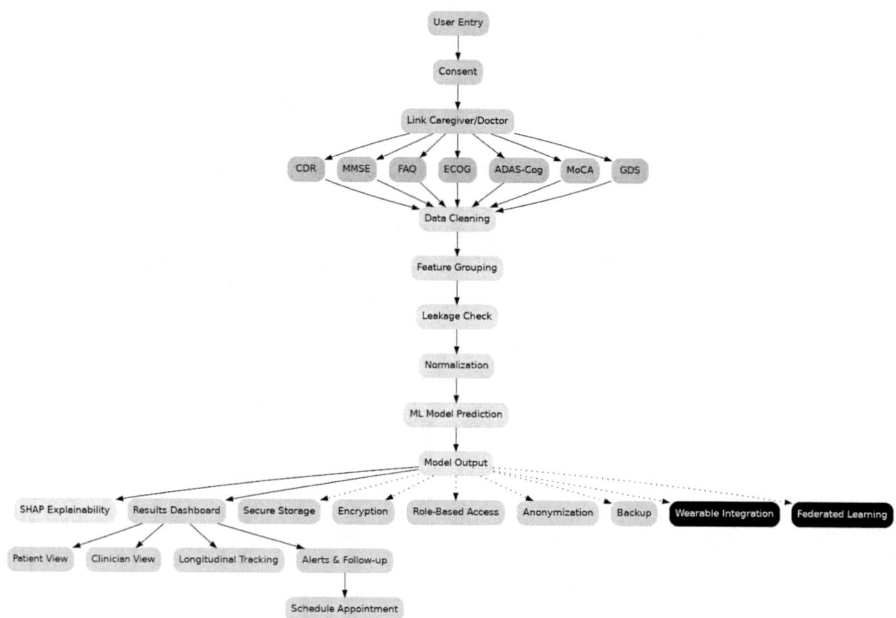

Fig. 1. High-level architecture of the proposed multimodal machine learning model.

4 System Implementation

This section details the technical architecture and technology stack used to build the Alzico application, translating the methodological framework into a functional prototype.

4.1 Application Architecture

The Alzico platform is designed as a client-server system. The client-side consists of a unified codebase for both a web application and cross-platform mobile applications (iOS and Android). The server-side is a Python-based microservice responsible for handling prediction requests by running the pre-trained machine learning model. This decoupled architecture ensures scalability and maintainability.

4.2 Technology Stack

Frontend (Mobile and Web) Because the user-facing application is built using React Native, a single TypeScript codebase may create native apps for iOS and Android. The framework uses `react-native-web` for the web application, which creates a regular React web application using React Native components. Important frontend stack libraries include React 18.2.0, React Native 0.73.6, `react-navigation` for screen management, and `react-native-paper` for UI components. Webpack 5 is used to bundle the frontend for the web, while Metro bundler is used for mobile.

Backend (Model Serving) The machine learning model is served via a lightweight Python microservice built with the Flask 3.0.0 framework. The service exposes a REST API endpoint that accepts user data and returns a cognitive risk prediction. The core backend components include `joblib` for loading the pre-trained model, `pandas` and `numpy` for data processing, and `psycopg2-binary` for future integration with a PostgreSQL database.

4.3 User Interface

The user interface is designed to be engaging and intuitive, encouraging regular use. Figure 2 shows the main dashboard, Fig. 3 displays an example of a gamified task, and Fig. 4 presents the user's progress report.

5 Experimental Results

The results of the model evaluation are shown in this part, with special attention to the performance comparison between several machine learning algorithms and the interpretability study carried out using SHapley Additive exPlanations (SHAP) to confirm the model's clinical applicability.

5.1 HistGradientBoosting Model's Superior Performance

A clear performance hierarchy was found in the comparison analysis, with the 'HistGradientBoosting' classifier outperforming the others on all significant assessment measures. Table 2 displays the specific findings.

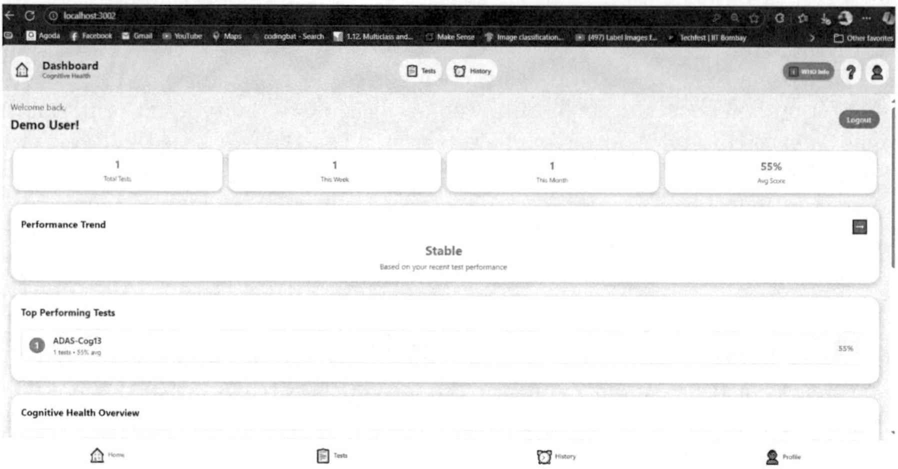

Fig. 2. The main dashboard of the Alzico application, showing daily challenges.

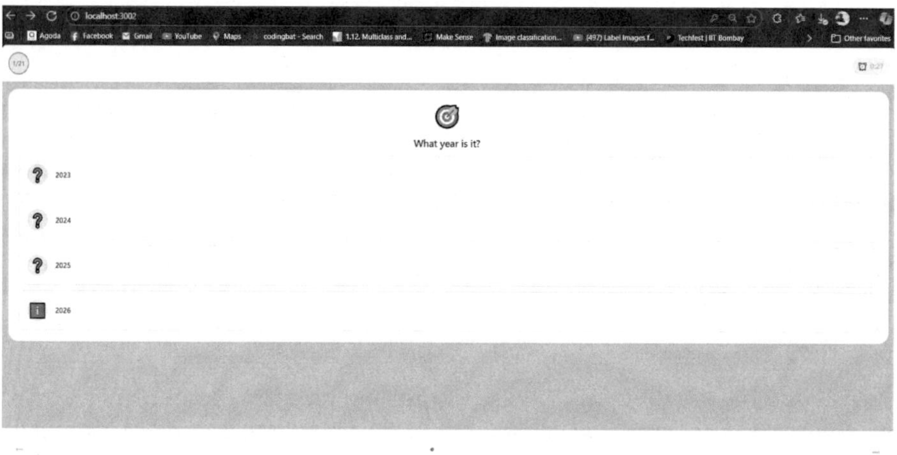

Fig. 3. An example of a gamified cognitive task based on the ADAS-Cog.

The 'HistGradientBoosting' model showed remarkable discriminating power with a Macro AUC of 0.90 ± 0.02. This outstanding performance was sustained across several metrics, with an overall accuracy of 0.87 ± 0.01 and a Macro F1-score of 0.85 ± 0.02. The per-class recall figures are crucial from a therapeutic perspective. The model correctly identified 88% of CN individuals, 84% of MCI individuals, and 83% of AD individuals. This demonstrates a high degree of sensitivity that is evenly distributed over the whole cognitive spectrum.

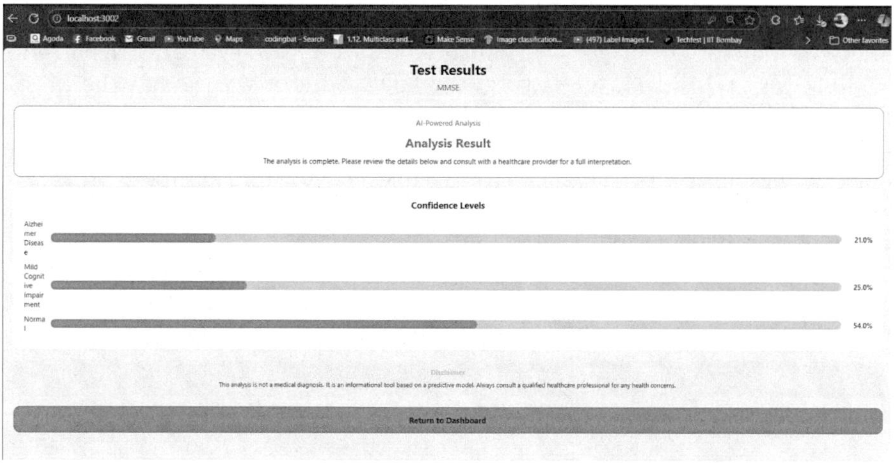

Fig. 4. The user's progress and cognitive score report screen.

5.2 Clinical Interpretability and Significance of Features

A post-hoc feature significance analysis was performed using SHapley Additive exPlanations (SHAP) [18] to ensure the model wasn't an unintelligible "black box." This study validates the model's quantitative performance as well as its clinical validity. The outcomes verified that the characteristics shown in the

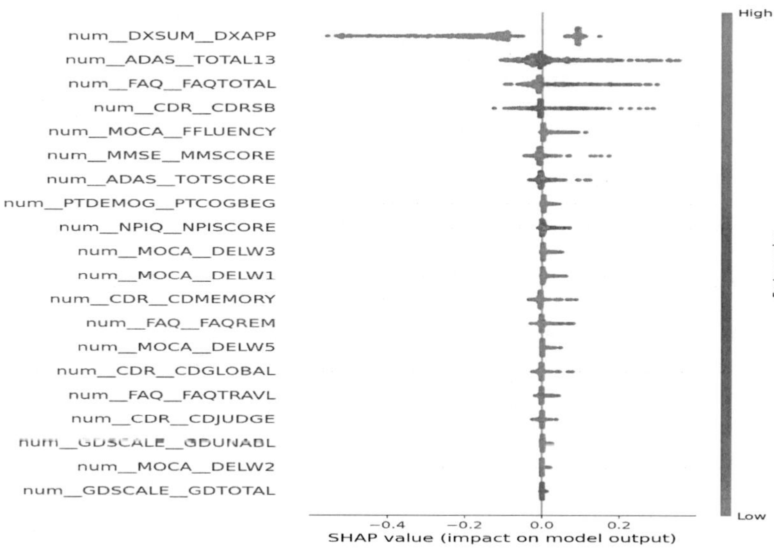

Fig. 5. SHAP summary plot of top predictive features and their impact on model output.

clinical literature served as the foundation for the model's predictions. The most important traits were consistently global scores from the key cognitive batteries, including the ADAS-Cog total score, the CDR Sum of Boxes, and the MMSE total score. This congruence between the model's internal logic and recognized clinical data provides compelling evidence that the model has learned a meaningful representation of the cognitive decline continuum. Figure 5 provides a visual summary of the feature importance, whereas Fig. 6 illustrates a local, single-instance explanation.

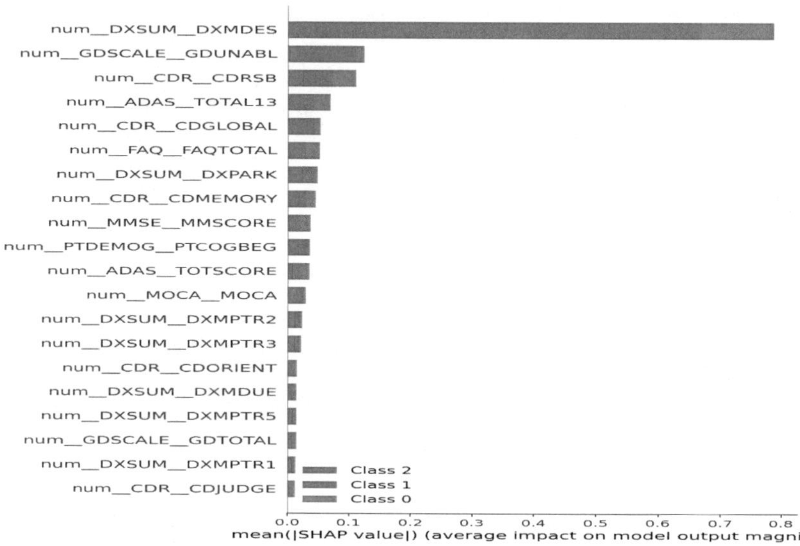

Fig. 6. LIME explanation for a single prediction.

6 Discussion

6.1 Principal Findings and Clinical Significance

The principal finding of this work is that a 'HistGradientBoosting' model, trained on a rich, multidimensional feature set from the ADNI cohort, can classify an individual's cognitive status across the CN-MCI-AD spectrum with a high degree of accuracy (Macro AUC of 0.90). The model's strong performance, coupled with its clinical interpretability, establishes a robust and trustworthy computational core for the Alzico framework. The clinical implications of such a tool are profound, offering a potential low-cost, non-invasive pre-screening instrument to identify at-risk individuals who warrant a full clinical workup.

6.2 The Promise of Gamified, High-Frequency Monitoring

While the cross-sectional classification performance is impressive, the true transformative potential of the Alzico framework lies in its capacity for longitudinal, high-frequency monitoring. By making cognitive testing engaging, the Alzico app can collect data on a daily or weekly basis. This dense, time-series data enables a paradigm shift from static risk assessment to dynamic disease progression monitoring, potentially offering an even earlier signal of incipient cognitive decline.

6.3 Challenges and Future Directions

One of the main challenges in this work was obtaining real-world, "in-the-wild" data for direct model validation. Due to logistical difficulties and ethical considerations, real-time patient data gathering is not practical for this project's first validation phase. Therefore, applying a model trained on the neat, carefully chosen data of the ADNI research to the loud, chaotic environment of a user's home creates an important validation gap. This disparity results from the fact that "in-the-wild" data is vulnerable to a number of confounders, such as user weariness, attention, and device-specific technical variability, that are not present in clinical research settings. A model's performance on a pristine dataset like ADNI does not guarantee its efficacy on the kind of noisy, heterogeneous data an application like Alzico would collect. One of the main goals of the proposed future strategy is to close this validation gap using the Cogstate Computerized Cognitive Battery results, a special feature of the ADNI dataset. The telemetry data that the proposed gamified application would provide might be successfully replaced by the digital metrics provided by this dataset, such as accuracy and reaction time. First, a "translation model" that forecasts conventional neuropsychological outcomes will be developed using this digital data. If this model is developed properly, there is less chance of a thorough prospective clinical investigation as it would provide strong evidence that the signals the proposed app collects are clinically meaningful.

6.4 Ethical Framework

When developing a digital health solution for a vulnerable population, a robust ethical framework is necessary. The principles of data privacy and informed consent are essential; all data must be anonymized and safely stored in compliance with regulations like GDPR and HIPAA, and users' express consent must be obtained before any additional data is collected. Additionally, proactive measures are needed to lessen the likelihood of algorithmic bias. Further validation data from a variety of demographics is necessary to audit the model for fairness because the ADNI cohort is not entirely representative of the broader population. Before clinical implementation, this tiered strategy guarantees that ethical and technological concerns are thoroughly addressed.

7 Conclusion

This work introduces an end-to-end framework for early detection of Alzheimer's disease risk that closes the loop between rigorous clinical science and scalable, user-centric technology. The study showcases the development of a highly accurate, clinically-interpretable machine learning model using data from the ADNI cohort, followed by introducing the Alzico framework-a novel system for the deployment of this intelligence at population scales using a gamified mobile application. The main argument is that the future of early cognitive assessment lies in the thoughtful translation of validated clinical instruments into engaging experiences. The Alzico approach, with its clinically-grounded design and future-proof architecture, represents a significant step towards this future and has the potential to revolutionize the landscape for the early detection of AD.

Acknowledgment. The authors would like to acknowledge that this study was collaborative and multidisciplinary, combining knowledge from clinical research, computer engineering, and machine learning. Without the fundamental data from the Alzheimer's Disease Neuroimaging Initiative (ADNI), this work would not have been feasible.

References

1. Weiner, M.W., Veitch, D.P., Aisen, P.S., Jack, C.R., Jr.: The Alzheimer's Disease Neuroimaging Initiative: a review of papers published since its inception. Alzheimer's & Dementia **8**(1), S1–S68 (2012)
2. Rosen, W.G., Mohs, R.C., Davis, K.L.: A new rating scale for Alzheimer's disease. Am. J. Psychiatry **141**(11), 1356–1364 (1984)
3. Association, A.: 2025 Alzheimer's disease facts and figures. Alzheimer's & Dementia **21**(4), e70235 (2025)
4. Folstein, M.F., Folstein, S.E., McHugh, P.R.: "Mini-mental state": a practical method for grading the cognitive state of patients for the clinician. J. Psychiatr. Res. **12**(3), 189–198 (1975)
5. Nasreddine, Z.S., et al.: The Montreal Cognitive Assessment (MoCA): a brief screening tool for mild cognitive impairment. J. Am. Geriatr. Soc. **53**(4), 695–699 (2005)
6. Morris, J.C.: The Clinical Dementia Rating (CDR): current version and scoring rules. Neurology **43**(11), 2412–2414 (1993)
7. Schuff, N., et al.: MRI of hippocampal volume loss in early Alzheimer's disease in relation to ApoE genotype and biomarkers. Brain **132**(4), 1067–1077 (2009)
8. Francis, S.B., Verma, J.P.: Transfer Learning approach for Alzheimer's Disease Stage Classification by integrating 3D CNN with Multi-modal inputs. In: 2025 3rd International Conference on Advancement in Computation & Computer Technologies (InCACCT), pp. 542-547 (2025)
9. Francis, S.B., Verma, J.P.: Deep CNN ResNet-18 based model with attention and transfer learning for Alzheimer's disease detection. Front. Neuroinform. **18**, 1507217 (2025)

10. Biju, F.S., Verma, J.P., Bhavsar, M.: Alzheimer's detection using demographic information with a combined approach of neural network and grid search CV. In: Proceedings of the 2023 29th International Conference on Telecommunications t(ICT), pp. 1–6 (2023)
11. Suk, H.I., Choi, D.W., Kim, H.J., Lee, S.W.: Personalized Gaussian Processes for Forecasting of Alzheimer's Disease Assessment Scale-Cognition Sub-Scale (ADAS-Cog13). arXiv preprint arXiv:1802.08561 (2018)
12. Coravos, A., Khozin, S., Mandl, K.D.: Developing and adopting safe and effective digital biomarkers to improve patient outcomes. npj Digital Med. **2**(1), 14 (2019)
13. Kourtis, L.C., Regele, O.B., Wright, J.M., Jones, G.B.: Digital biomarkers for Alzheimer's disease: the mobile/wearable devices opportunity. Npj Digital Med. **2**(1), 9 (2019)
14. de Oliveira, A.L.F., de-Marcos, L., Garcia, E., Garcia-Cabot, A., Barchino, R.: A Framework for the gamification of cognitive tasks: design science research. JMIR Serious Games **9**(2), e21900 (2021) ¡error l="307" c="Invalid command: paragraph not started." /¿
15. Al-Thwani, A., Al-Maadid, A., Al-Hamad, H.: Serious games for cognitive impairment detection in the elderly: a systematic review. IEEE Access **10**, 24968–24984 (2022)
16. Chan, J.Y.C., et al.: Gamified interactive systems for assessing mild cognitive impairment: a scoping review. J. Med. Internet Res. **24**(10), e39733 (2022)
17. Chen, T., Guestrin, C.: XGBoost: a scalable tree boosting system. In: Proceedings of the 22nd ACM SIGKDD International Conference on Knowledge Discovery and Data Mining, pp. 785-794 (2016)
18. Lundberg, S.M., Lee, S.-I.: A unified approach to interpreting model predictions. In: Advances in Neural Information Processing Systems 30 (NIPS 2017), pp. 4765-4774 (2017)

Enhancing Multimodal Skin Cancer Detection Using Bidirectional Cross-Attention between Clinical Metadata and Extracted Image Features

Neetu Verma(✉), Ranvijay Ranvijay, and Dharmendra Kumar Yadav

Computer Science and Engineering Department, Motilal Nehru National Institute of Technology Allahabad Prayagraj, Allahabad, Uttar Pradesh, India
{neetu.2022rcs01,ranvijay,dky}@mnnit.ac.in

Abstract. Skin cancer classification using multi-modal data is essential for the early diagnosis of dermatological disorders, including skin cancer. The application of multimodal data fusion is difficult for enhancing the diagnostic accuracy of computational and medical classification systems. The novel cross-attention-based neural network design is presented in this paper, which incorporates high-dimensional feature vectors extracted from images with the Xception model for multiclass diagnostic prediction, along with structured metadata and other heterogeneous input sources. The proposed method employs a bidirectional cross-attention mechanism to enable flexible interaction between modalities, as opposed to typical concatenation-based fusion. The model consists of two subnetworks: a feature tower encoding complex extracted features and a metadata tower that handles contextual and demographic factors using fully connected layers. A softmax classifier is formed by pooling, concatenating, and then feeding the resulting cross-attended embeddings into layers. The test-set performances indicated that the proposed fusion method provides enhanced accuracy and precision on both multiclass and binary tests, significantly enhancing classification performance compared to early and late fusion baselines. Cross-attention function, as per the results, offers a robust basis for integrating structured and unstructured data into diagnostic modelling by effectively capturing intermodal interdependence. For multimodal learning solutions in the healthcare sector where feature-based data and metadata are employed, this architecture presents a generalisable and scalable approach.

Keywords: Skin Lesion · Skin Cancer · Multi-modal · Xception · Cross-attention · Fusion · Classification

1 Introduction

Melanoma is the most lethal form of skin cancer and the biggest killer of skin cancer in the world. It is also among the most frequent and lethal diseases overall [1]. One of the most dangerous malignant skin tumors, melanoma, kills around 10,000 individuals every

G. K. Verma et al. (Eds.): MIND 2025, CCIS 2981, pp. 26–37, 2027.
https://doi.org/10.1007/978-3-032-31230-3_3

year. Early detection through clinical examination can greatly enhance an individual's survival chances for skin cancer. The basic etiology of skin cancer is damage to skin cells due to UV radiation. There are 3 basic types of skin cancer known as Squamous Cell Carcinoma (SCC), Melanoma, and Basal Cell Carcinoma (BCC) [2]. Melanoma is the least common among these three forms of skin cancer, yet due to its high growth rate, it is the most dangerous. Though they cause most skin cancer cases, other skin cancer groups (BCC and SCC) carry a reduced mortality risk since they metastasize less. Melanoma can be treated if detected early on in screening skin lesions. However, clinical information from the patient, visual screening of lesions, a competent dermatologist, and scrutiny are required for a precise diagnosis of skin cancer. The majority of research studies have taken dermatoscopic images into consideration when analysing skin lesions since they present higher visual information with less noise and illumination.

When diagnosing a patient in everyday practice settings, physicians always consider both clinical information and the medical imagery of the patient. Dermatologists, for instance, utilize their training to analyze dermatoscopic images and carefully consider clinical information, such as the age of the patient, the site of the disease. For instance, Pacheco et al. [3] developed a simple method that integrates data from clinical information and images through an aggregation mechanism, enhancing balanced accuracy. For medical image classification [4, 5] and segmentation [6], convolutional neural networks (CNNs) have been extremely efficacy. However, most previous studies utilize only medical picture attributes to make decisions without considering patient clinical data, which would lower diagnosis efficiency.

In the area of medical images, deep learning models can't overlook several problems. It is clearly known that localising or segmenting anomalies as pixel-level labels is extremely expensive in the area of medical image processing [7]. The above problems are not extensive. Most deep learning models, however, provide a logical, semantically significant basis for model predictions. If one considers only the output of baseline DL and Machine Learning (ML) methods, some sensitive and important information can be lost [8]. There are a number of methods for automatically detecting melanoma from thermoscopic images. But the metadata information or questions, as well as photos, are important indicators for decision-making.

Thus, we have been focused on the utilization of clinical photos since they are easy to capture using camera equipment and do not need a dermatoscope. During the diagnosis of skin lesions, the clinical history of the patient, including age, gender, race, history of malignancy, etc., is usually considered by the dermatologists [9, 10]. Hence, clinical factors and visual details must be considered pragmatically. In the proposed work, we employed the meta-information-based attention to develop a more robust and efficient method for skin cancer classification. The proposed method navigates visual information and generates strong features through the combination of visual and meta-features through a cross-attention fusion mechanism. The images are pre-processed to remove noise, such as low contrast, hair lines, and blur. The improved meta-information is utilized to guide the visual features during fusion, developing unique features that can successfully classify skin cancer lesions.

This research paper has 5 components: Sect. 2 presents the related works on skin cancer detection. Section 3 presents the proposed methodology for multi-modal skin cancer detection. The experimental setup, results, and comparison for the proposed model are presented in Sect. 4. Lastly, Sect. 5 concludes the research.

2 Related Works

Skin cancer is among the most awful and widespread diseases in the world. Melanoma and non-melanoma are two different kinds of skin cancer, along with several others. The highlights of some of the latest research are given in this section. The MetaBlock enhances feature maps that are extracted from a CNN, and the researcher [3] conceded that physicians utilize patient demographics in diagnosis. It effectively guides the model to focus on the most relevant visual information by scaling and translating image features with the help of metadata. The goal of this method is to be decoupled from the specific CNN architecture.

This enhanced metadata is then utilized by the proposed [11] fusion block to manage the visual features that have been extracted by a CNN. This approach demonstrated improved accuracy over five different CNN architectures and significantly improved over current approaches on the PAD-UFES-20 dataset. To improve the accuracy of skin cancer classification, this research introduced [12] a hybrid deep learning model that combines patient metadata with dermoscopy images. The model does minimal fine-tuning through the application of a pre-trained deep network, MobileNetV2, for photo feature extraction only. These features are then fed into Logistic Regression, a traditional machine learning classifier. A Random Forest classifier classifies patient metadata in parallelly. To arrive at a final classification, predictions from the two classifiers are concatenated and passed through a simple fully connected neural network.

A customized federated learning (FL) model for intelligent healthcare was introduced in this research [13], which incorporates patient metadata along with medical images to enhance diagnostics. This framework utilizes a convolutional neural network (CNN) for image interpretation and a Naïve Bayes classifier for text-based clinical information to counter the limitations of models that solely depend on picture features. The author [10] uses Support Vector Machines (SVM) for classification and Convolutional Neural Networks (CNN) for feature extraction to develop a multi-modal system for skin cancer diagnosis. Five kinds of skin cancer were used in the dataset to train and evaluate the model: sebaceous carcinoma, SCC, Merkel cell carcinoma, BCC, and melanoma.

A complete transfer learning design that includes various data modalities, i.e., dermoscopic images and metadata about the patients, is introduced by the researcher [14] for skin lesion classification. The system employs machine learning-based classifiers such as SVM and KNN, together with a variety of deep learners like Vision Transformers (ViT), MobileNetV2, ResNet152V2, and Xception. To advance medical diagnosis, this research proposes [15] MetaFusion, a novel and parameter-light method to fuse imaging data and metadata. The strength of the method was established by testing it on three diseases and datasets: glaucoma (PAPILA), breast cancer (CBIS-DDSM), and skin cancer (PAD-UFES-20).

In this work [16], a new Transformer-based system for multi-modal skin lesion classification named SkinM2Former is introduced. It employs a novel Tri-Modal Cross-attention Transformer (TMCT), which fuses features at various levels of a Swin transformer to solve the intricate issue of bringing together three types of data: clinical images, dermoscopic images, and metadata of patients. To enhance the transparency and reliability of deep learning-based skin lesion diagnosis for doctors, this paper [17] presents ExAID (Explainable AI for Dermatology), a novel platform. By way of simple text-based stories and graphical heatmaps of relevant dermoscopic characteristics, ExAID provides multi-modal concept-based explanations in favor of a model's predictions.

3 Materials and Methods

This subsection mentions each of the steps employed to develop the model. Preprocessing the data (clinical and imaging), constructing the model architecture, and training it are all covered. Figure 1 shows the complete architecture of the proposed method.

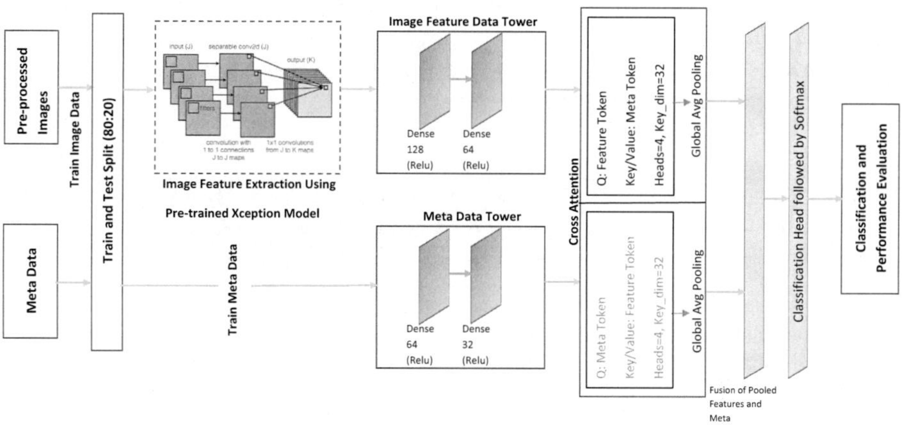

Fig. 1 Architecture of Proposed Methodology

3.1 Dataset

The datasets used in this research are publicly available from a number of sources. The detection of skin cancer using multi-modal has heavily utilized these datasets. A medical professional has included additional information on each of the datasets selected, besides the images. PAD-UFES datasets are used for validation in this study. The PAD-UFES-20 database [18] of clinical images and photographs was constructed by the researcher. There are 2298 images, for 1641 skin lesions and 1373 patients, in this database, as well as for various cases of data for every patient in the collection. The data set contains six class labels of skin cancer: ACK (Actinic Keratosis- 730 images), SEK (Seborrhoeic Keratosis- 235 images), BCC (Basal Cell Carcinoma- 845 images), SCC (Squamous Cell Carcinoma- 192 images), and MEL (Melanoma- 52 images), NEV (Melanocytic Nevus of Skin- 244 images). The metadata contains twenty-five attributes, for instance, sex, drink, bleed, elevation, and smoker, etc.

3.2 Dataset Preprocessing

Enhancing image quality and reducing noise is the other primary hindrance. Smartphones were employed to take the photographs, and the set contains a variety of image sizes and qualities. There are hairs in most of the images. Images were resized to high resolution for additional clarity to minimize loss of data and effectively eliminate hairs. After min-max normalization for improved contrast, images were grey-scaled to ease pixel analysis. Black-hat morphological transformation [19, 20] was used to detect darker hair regions, followed by Gaussian blurring to eliminate noise and fine hair focus. A threshold value of 10 was used to create a binary mask to identify various hair regions. These masked regions were properly treated with Telea's inpainting method, which fills pixels based on the surrounding pixels and fluid-dynamic equations. The resulting images without hair were much improved, as shown in Fig. 2, for the next round of classification testing. The categorical variables in the metadata were label encoded, whereas z-score normalisation was applied to the numerical variables. These consistent inputs stabilised the suggested fusion technique and assured consistent feature scaling across modalities. All the attributes of metadata are used by the proposed method except the patient_id which can be the cause of low performance.

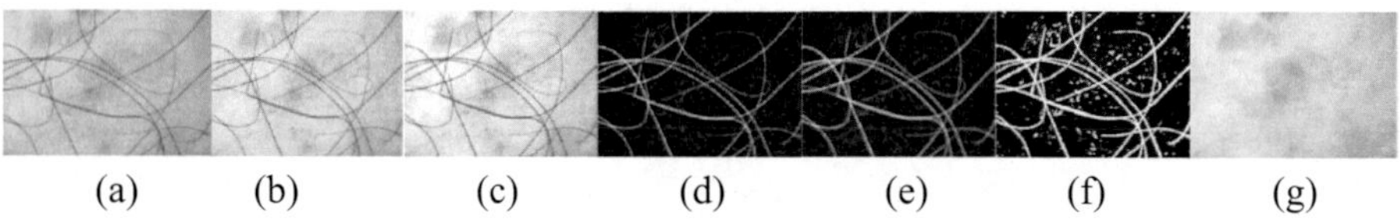

Fig. 2 (a) Original, (b) Min-Max normalization, (c) Greyscale Analysis, (d) Black-hat morphological transformation, (e) Gaussian blurring, (f) threshold binary mask, (g) Telea's inpainted image

3.3 Feature Extraction from Images

We employed transfer learning with an Xception (TensorFlow/Keras) model [21, 22], which was pre-trained on ImageNet weights, to learn fixed-size representations from dermoscopic image-pictures. By removing the classification head (include_top = False) and applying global average pooling (pooling = 'avg'), the network was only used as a feature extractor. This resulted in a dense 1,920-dimensional embedding per image with all the convolutional weights kept frozen (no fine-tuning). We first converted each image into a tensor and reduced it to 224 by 224 pixels. Then we applied model-specific normalization that tf.keras.applications.densenet.preprocess_input provided to set the backbone's training statistics. The pooled feature vector of each preprocessed image was generated in a single forward pass, which we then flattened to one dimension and appended to an expanding list of features.

All per-image vectors were stacked into an N $\times$ 1920 array to form the final feature matrix, which was subsequently wrapped within a DataFrame with feature_0…feature_1919 as the systematic column labels.

3.4 Classification Methodology

Each image was represented as a 1,920-dimensional feature vector from the Xception backbone. Before fusion, clinical metadata was passed through two fully connect-ed layers with 64 and 32 units to generate a 32-dimensional metadata vector. The proposed method employs a multi-tower fusion structure, which has two different neural subnetworks that individually process feature inputs and metadata, and then a cross-attention fusion module. Metadata vectors are preprocessed and passed to the metadata tower. It is a pair of fully connected layers that are activated by ReLU functions with 64 and 32 units, respectively. The low-dimensional, structured correlations within category and numerical data are encoded by this subnetwork. The high-dimensional feature embeddings are forwarded to the feature tower. It consists of two fully connected layers with ReLU-activated 128 and 64 units. All the raw feature vectors are compressed and mapped to a lower-dimensional latent representation using this design.

Cross-Attention Fusion Mechanism

This work proposes a bidirectional cross-attention technique, similar to typical Transformer-style multi-head attention, which allows dynamic interaction of image features and metadata, unlike the usual concatenation or late fusion. Representations from each modality can enhance the other using image tokens as keys and values and metadata tokens as queries, and vice-versa. Reciprocal attention can capture richer intermodal dependencies that help improve both performance in classification tasks and interpreta-bility by underlining clinically significant lesion locations and metadata characteristics. The concatenation of latent representations is frequently used in traditional multimodal fusion. Cross-modal [23] interactions are not modeled explicitly by such systems, however. We replaced this by using a cross-attention fusion block, which allows each modality to selectively attend to the other's most informative elements.

Tokenization of latent embeddings

- With n_tokens = 4 and d_model = 32, the outputs of both subnetworks were mapped into token sequences of length n_tokens × d_model.
- A dense layer was utilized to project metadata embeddings into meta tokens, which were then molded into a sequence of shapes (4, 32).
- Comparable projections of feature embeddings into feature tokens were carried out.

Bidirectional cross-attention

- a multi-head attention block (num_heads = 4), feature tokens served as keys and values, while metadata tokens were treated as queries.
- Conversely, feature tokens employed a reverse attention block to query metadata tokens.
- Due to the bidirectional contextual information exchange enabled through this technique, features can update their representations from metadata and vice versa.

Pooling and fusion

- Global average pooling was employed to pool each attended token sequence into compact modality-specific embeddings.

- To obtain a fused cross-attention representation, the pooled vectors were concatenated.

Classification Head

The combined representation was passed through two dense layers (64 and 32 units, ReLU activation) prior to being input into a softmax output layer, sized to the number of diagnostic classes. The architecture maintains representational capacity while preventing overfitting through regularization.

4 Experimental Setup and Results

After developing the model in TensorFlow/Keras, it was optimized using the Adam optimizer with a learning rate of 0.001 in Kaggle. Sparse categorical cross-entropy was employed as a loss function, and class weights along with the random rotations (±20°), horizontal/vertical flips, random brightness/contrast shifts, and Gaussian noise, were applied to compensate for data imbalance. Training with up to fifty epochs was performed using size 32 mini-batches. In order to achieve early halting, 20% of the data was drawn from a validation set. The inference on one sample is 60 ms with NVIDIA GPU and 150 ms with CPU.

All the used hyperparameters in the proposed methodology are covered in Table 1. The following performance matrices are utilized to validate the model:

$$Accuracy\ (ACC) = \frac{True\ Positive + True\ Negative}{True\ Positive + True\ Negative + False\ Positive + False\ Negative} \tag{1}$$

$$Recall\ (REC) = \frac{True\ Positive}{True\ Positive + False\ Negative} \tag{2}$$

$$Precision\ (PRE) = \frac{True\ Positive}{True\ Positive + False\ Positive} \tag{3}$$

$$F1score\ (F1S) = \frac{2 * (Precision * Recall)}{Precision + Recall} \tag{4}$$

The proposed methodology is used for binary and multi-class classification on the PAD-UFES dataset in this study. While SCC showed lower recall, indicating difficulties in distinguishing between the target classes of lesions that are visually similar, it still attained good accuracy for classes, with top performance on NEV and BCC. Tables 2 and 3 show the class-wise classification performance on multi-class and binary classification, respectively. Figures 3 and 4 represent the confusion matrix of multi-class and binary classification, respectively. The comparison of the proposed method to the existing methods is presented through the Table 4 and Fig. 5.

Table 1. Hyperparameters and their values

Hyperparameters	Values
Image size	224*224
Attention heads (num_heads)	4
Attention direction	Bidirectional
Epochs	50
Learning rate	0.0001
Optimizer	Adam
Training batch size	32
Train test split	80:20
d_model	32
n_tokens	4
attention layers (depth)	2
num_heads	4
Activation function	SoftMax, ReLu
Early stopping	Enable

Table 2. Classification report of the proposed model in multiclass classification

	ACC	PRE	REC	F1S	AUC	Support
ACK	0.95	0.96	0.97	0.97	.96	146
BCC	0.94	0.94	0.96	0.95	.95	169
MEL	0.90	94	0.90	0.95	.93	10
NEV	0.96	95	0.98	0.99	.98	49
SCC	0.79	0.83	0.79	0.82	.97	39
SEK	0.96	0.92	0.98	0.96	.97	47
Weighted avg	0.92	0.92	0.95	0.95	.96	460

Table 3. Classification report of the proposed model in binary classification

	ACC	PRE	REC	F1S	AUC	Support
Benign	0.91	0.98	0.91	0.95	.972	242
Malignant	0.98	0.91	0.98	0.94	.988	218
Weighted avg	0.95	0.95	0.95	0.95	.98	460

Table 4. Comparison report of the proposed model to the existing approach on PAD-UFES dataset

	MetaFusion [15]	MDFNet [24]	RemixFormer++ [25]	Ensemble Method [26]	Concatenation Method	Proposed
ACC	76.8	79	79	84.3	91	95
PRE	77.1	75	–	85	92	95
REC	–	79	–	85	91	95
F1-score	78.4	77	–	85	92	95
AUC	–	95	95	–	96	98

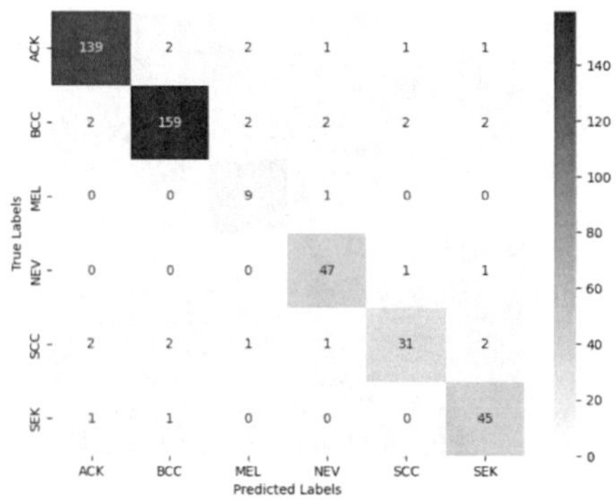

Fig. 3. Confusion Matrix of proposed fusion model in multiclass classification

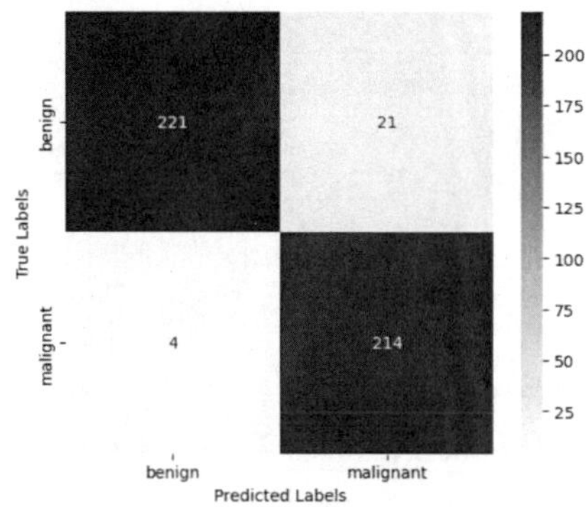

Fig. 4. Confusion Matrix of proposed fusion model in binary classification

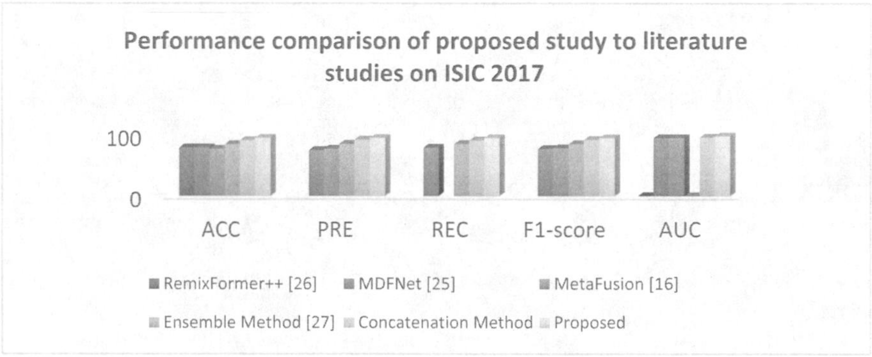

Fig. 5. Comparison graph of proposed methodology with existing research

5 Conclusion

A cross-attention-based neural network design is introduced in this work for the fusion of high-dimensional features and metadata in multiclass diagnostic prediction. The proposed system extends simple concatenation by utilizing bidirectional cross-attention to enable direct interaction between modalities. This enables features to enhance metadata representations and metadata to guide feature interpretation. The capacity to aggregate shared and complementary information among input sources was exemplified by the fusion method in combination with dense classification layers and global pooling. The method provided a robust platform for handling heterogeneous data via binary roll-up analysis, stratified evaluation, and class rebalancing. The results show the potential of cross-attention fusion as a general-purpose approach to multimodal learning problems, particularly in domains where unstructured feature embeddings and structured knowledge are concurrent. To further enhance predicted performance and explainability, emerging work might explore transformer-based fusion, deeper stacks of attention, or domain-specific priors.

Limitations: This framework could be extended in subsequent work by including external, deeper transformer-based fusion layers, incorporating temporal or sequential information, and exploring explainability methods for attention maps. In addition, the robustness, generalisability, and clinical utility of cross-attention fusion in diagnostic prediction could be enhanced by larger multi-institutional datasets and domain-specific priors. Other limitations of this study are the small dataset size and demographic imbalance, which may further affect generalisability. Future research will investigate larger multi-institutional datasets and maximize computing efficiency to enhance the robustness, scalability, and clinical utility of the prposed framework.

Disclosure of Interests.

Competing Interests. The authors have no competing interests to declare that are relevant to the content of this article.

Conflict of Interest. There is no conflict of interest.

References

1. Verma, N., Ranvijay, Yadav, D.K.: A comprehensive review on step-based skin cancer detection using machine learning and deep learning methods. Arch. Comput. Methods Eng., 1–54 (2025)
2. Singh, P., Altaf Ahmed, M.D., Sharique, M.D., Gond, P., Verma, N., Ranvijay.: Skin cancer detection using Ensembling of DenseNet, EfficientNet, and ConvNet. In: International Conference on VLSI, Communication and Signal Processing, pp. 57–77. Springer Nature Singapore, Singapore (2024)
3. Pacheco, A.G., Krohling, R.A.: An attention-based mechanism to combine images and metadata in deep learning models applied to skin cancer classification. IEEE J. Biomed. Health Inform. **25**(9), 3554–3563 (2021)
4. Verma, N., Ranvijay, Yadav, D.K.: Hybrid of deep feature extraction and machine learning ensembles for imbalanced skin cancer datasets. Exp. Dermatol. **33**(12), e70020 (2024)

5. Singh, D., Verma, N., Ranvijay: Enhancing skin cancer classification with ensemble models. In: International Conference on Advanced Network Technologies and Intelligent Computing, pp. 218–238. Springer Nature Switzerland, Cham (2023)
6. Verma, N., Ranvijay, Yadav, D.K.: XcUNet for skin lesion segmentation followed by clustering based post-processing. In: International Conference on Advanced Network Technologies and Intelligent Computing, pp. 17–31. Springer Nature Switzerland, Cham (2024)
7. Kavitha, C., Priyanka, S., Kumar, M.P., Kusuma, V.: Skin cancer detection and classification using deep learning techniques. Procedia Comput. Sci. **235**, 2793–2802 (2024)
8. Naeem, A., Anees, T., Khalil, M., Zahra, K., Naqvi, R.A., Lee, S.W.: SNC_Net: skin cancer detection by integrating handcrafted and deep learning-based features using dermoscopy images. Mathematics **12**(7), 1030 (2024)
9. Hosseinzadeh, M., et al.: A model for skin cancer using combination of ensemble learning and deep learning. PLoS One **19**(5), e0301275 (2024)
10. Mehta, S., Singh, A.: Multi-modal skin cancer diagnosis using CNN and SVM on Dermoscopic and clinical images. In: 2024 3rd International Conference for Advancement in Technology (ICONAT), pp. 1–5. IEEE (2024)
11. Pundhir, A., Dadhich, S., Agarwal, A., Raman, B.: Towards improved skin lesion classification using metadata supervision. In: 2022 26th International Conference on Pattern Recognition (ICPR), pp. 4313–4320. IEEE (2022)
12. Suneetha, I.: Hybrid deep learning model for skin cancer classification. In: E3S Web of Conferences, vol. 591, p. 09010. EDP Sciences (2024)
13. Jin, T., Pan, S., Li, X., Chen, S.: Metadata and image features co-aware personalized federated learning for smart healthcare. IEEE J. Biomed. Health Inform. **27**(8), 4110–4119 (2023)
14. Saieswari, G., Praneetha, G., Yoga Vyshnavi, D., Sai Sandeep, A., Yuvaraj, P., Elisha Raju, B.: A revolutionary transfer learning system for multimodal skin lesion evaluation. In: 2025 Third International Conference on Augmented Intelligence and Sustainable Systems (ICAISS), pp. 689–694. IEEE (2025)
15. Raghu, A., Raghu, A.: Metafusion: a novel method for integrating clinical metadata with imaging modalities for medical applications. In: 2025 IEEE 22nd International Symposium on Biomedical Imaging (ISBI), pp. 1–5. IEEE (2025)
16. Zhang, Y., Xie, Y., Wang, H., Avery, J.C., Hull, M.L., Carneiro, G.: A novel perspective for multi-modal multi-label skin lesion classification. In: In 2025 IEEE/CVF Winter Conference on Applications of Computer Vision (WACV), pp. 3549–3558. IEEE (2025)
17. Lucieri, A., Bajwa, M.N., Braun, S.A., Malik, M.I., Dengel, A., Ahmed, S.: ExAID: a multimodal explanation framework for computer-aided diagnosis of skin lesions. Comput. Methods Prog. Biomed. **215**, 106620 (2022)
18. Pacheco, A.G., et al.: PAD-UFES-20: a skin lesion dataset composed of patient data and clinical images collected from smartphones. Data Brief. **32**, 106221 (2020)
19. Khan, A.H., Iskandar, D.N.F.A., Al-Asad, J.F., El-Nakla, S.: Classification of skin lesion with hair and artifacts removal using black-hat morphology and total variation. Int. J. Comput. Digit. Syst. **10**(1) (2021)
20. El Mertahi, A., Ezzine, H., Douzi, S., Douzi, K.: AI-driven skin cancer detection from smartphone images: a hybrid model using ViT, adaptive thresholding, black-hat transformation, and XGBoost. PLoS One **20**(7), e0328402 (2025)
21. Tejada, M., Espinoza, R., Hinojosa, L.: Use of Xception architecture for the classification of skin lesions. Int. J. Comput. Vis. **12**, 145–160 (2024)
22. Naeem, A., Anees, T.: A multiclassification framework for skin cancer detection by the concatenation of Xception and ResNet101. J. Comput. Biomed. Informatics **6**(02), 205–227 (2024)
23. Ding, L., Shih, K., Wen, H., Li, X., & Yang, Q. (2025). Cross-attention transformer-based visual-language fusion for multimodal image analysis. Int. J. Appl. Sci. 8(1), p27-p27.

24. Chen, Q., Li, M., Chen, C., Zhou, P., Lv, X., Chen, C.: MDFNet: application of multimodal fusion method based on skin image and clinical data to skin cancer classification. J. Cancer Res. Clin. Oncol. **149**(7), 3287–3299 (2023)
25. Xu, J., et al.: RemixFormer++: a multi-modal transformer model for precision skin tumor differential diagnosis with memory-efficient attention. IEEE Trans. Med. Imaging (2024)
26. Pham, N.L.T., Pham, D.D., Le, T.D., Huynh, K.T.: A multimodal deep ensemble framework for skin lesion classification. In: International Symposium on Integrated Uncertainty in Knowledge Modelling and Decision Making, pp. 100–111. Springer Nature Singapore, Singapore (2025)

AI-Driven Speed Optimization for Mixed Traffic Networks Using Adaptive Learning

Sunil Kumar Somavarapu(✉)

JNTUH, Hyderabad, India
ssunilkumar559@gmail.com

Abstract. Managing traffic flow efficiently in mixed vehicle environments remains a critical challenge in modern transportation systems. This study introduces an AI-based speed control mechanism leveraging deep reinforcement learning to enhance freeway traffic conditions under varying levels of autonomous vehicle integration. Using a data-driven simulation approach, the model dynamically adjusts speed limits based on real-time traffic observations, optimizing throughput and minimizing congestion. The proposed system is tested in a high-fidelity simulated environment, demonstrating improved efficiency at moderate levels of autonomous vehicle deployment. However, results indicate that excessive reliance on automated control can reduce the effectiveness of dynamic speed interventions. These insights provide a foundation for future adaptive traffic management strategies in evolving transportation ecosystems.

1 Introduction

Congestion has long been a significant issue for traffic management and control. Transportation agencies across the globe have focused extensive efforts on addressing the problem for the past decades to develop control toolkits that enable feedback control on dynamic traffic flow. Among these techniques, variable speed limit control (VSL) is a promising control method in response to prevailing traffic, sudden incidents, and extreme weather conditions. Existing literature demonstrates its power to improve efficiency and safety, reduce emissions and, most importantly, relieve traffic congestion [1–4].

Classic VSL control method utilizes flow rates, occupancy, and speed measurements, provided mainly by induction loop detectors at discrete locations [5]. However, these instant measurements of the traffic flow only contain partial information about the current state, which can potentially limit the efficiency of the VSL system. In the past few years, progress in connected and autonomous vehicles has given rise to new opportunities for traffic control. Interlinked vehicle-based sensors create an network that allows access to fine-grained environment semantics and motion states of the surrounding cars through multiple data fusion methods [6–8]. Improvements in motion planning systems for autonomous vehicles enable responsive handling of critical car-following, obstacle avoidance, lane-keeping and lane-changing maneuvers [9]. Nevertheless, mixed traffic flow

G. K. Verma et al. (Eds.): MIND 2025, CCIS 2981, pp. 38–49, 2027.
https://doi.org/10.1007/978-3-032-31230-3_4

consisting of human-driven vehicles (HDV) and connected autonomous vehicles (CAV) will be and consistently be the traffic condition on urban expressways or freeways in the foreseeable future. Understanding how connected autonomous vehicles can help improve the efficiency of the VSL system is essential for its future implementations.

VSL systems will require a powerful decision-making model to handle richer high-dimensional information provided by the vehicle-based sensors, and determine the optimal speed limit. To that end, this work explores how to incorporate deep reinforcement learning, an agent-based approach that learns complex decision-making through constant interaction with training environments, to design a VSL system for mixed traffic flow control. Deep reinforcement learning has shown its ability to search for optimal strategies in games [10–12], robotic manipulations [13], and many other areas. The deep neural network enables extracting high-dimensional nonlinear dependencies from input sensor data to speed limits. At the same time, reinforcement learning allows learning the optimal control strategies in a data-driven paradigm. Nonetheless, reinforcement learning will require a simulation environment with high fidelity to ensure its effectiveness, which is often omitted in the existing literature.

This study explores incorporating deep reinforcement learning for VSL control in a mixed traffic flow environment. Instead of instant measurements, image features consisting of spatial and temporal information of the mixed traffic flow are used as the input information. The Soft Actor-Critic (SAC) algorithm [14] is used as the base logic for the VSL controller, which provides both sample-efficient learning and stability in complex, high-dimensional tasks. This paper presents empirical results on a case study with simulation calibrated on NGSIM I80 Emeryville dataset []ngsim2020. Results from Results from training and testing on the simulation environment show that increasing CAV penetration can benefit traffic flow efficiency and help improve VSL control. But at a high penetration rate, imperfect interactions among HDVs and CAVs can deteriorate the efficiency. Moreover, when most of the vehicles are CAVs in the environment, improvements from VSL control can become obsolete. The following parts of this paper are organized as follows. Section 2 gives an formal problem statement of VSL control in a reinforcement learning framework, followed by introduction of incorporating the SAC reinforcement learning to solve for VSL strategy. Section 3 briefly introduce the case study and building of a simulation environments, and results and analysis for training and evaluation using the simulation. The last section draws the conclusion and discusses on possible further work.

2 Methodology

This work formulates the freeway VSL control problem as a partially observable Markov Decision Process (POMDP). In this section, we first introduce notations and give a mathematical formulation of the problem. We then propose a VSL control framework built upon the Soft Actor-Critic algorithm and present details of its implementation.

2.1 Problem Statement

The classic reinforcement learning method formulates the decision problem as a Markov Decision Process (MDP), defined by a four-tuple $(\mathcal{S}, \mathcal{A}, p, r)$, where $\mathcal{S}$ is the state space, $\mathcal{A}$ is the action space, $p : \mathcal{S} \times \mathcal{S} \times \mathcal{A} \rightarrow [0, 1]$ is the transition probability representing the probability density of next state given the current state and action, and finally, $r : \mathcal{S} \times \mathcal{A} \rightarrow [r_{min}, r_{max}]$ is a bounded reward emits by the environment on each interaction. An MDP should satisfy Markov Property, where the evolution of the MDP in the future depends only on the present state but not on the history. Although this may be the case for macroscopic traffic flow patterns [16], inherently time-dependent microscopic phenomena, such as queueing and dispersion, won't necessarily satisfy this property in most cases.

Therefore, we instead formulate the VSL problem as a partially observable Markov Decision Process (POMDP), defined by a six-tuple $(\mathcal{O}, \mathcal{S}, \mathcal{A}, f, p, r)$, where an additional observation space $\mathcal{O}$ consists of observations of the current traffic flow that might not satisfy the Markov Property, and an additional function $f : \mathcal{O} \rightarrow \mathcal{S}$ is used to describe the dependence between observations and latent states. Figure 1 illustrates the POMDP formulation.

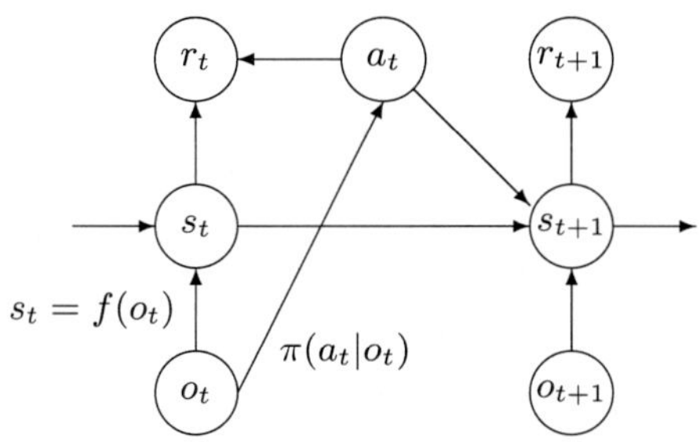

Fig. 1. Illustration of the partially observable Markov Decision Process.

Following the standard formulation of reinforcement learning, the objective of our VSL controller is to solve for an optimal policy model $\pi(a_t|o_t)$ that maximizes the expected sum of rewards. If we denote the state and state-action marginals of the trajectory distribution induced by policy as $\rho^\pi(s_t)$ and $\rho^\pi(s_t, a_t)$, we may express our objective function as

$$J(\pi) = \max_{\pi(a_t|o_t)} \sum_{t=0}^{T} \mathbb{E}_{(s_t,a_t)\sim\rho^\pi} \left[r(s_t, a_t)\right] \tag{1}$$

$$= \max_{\pi(a_t|o_t)} \sum_{t=0}^{T} \mathbb{E}_{s_t=f(o_t),(s_t,a_t)\sim\rho^\pi} \left[r\left(f(o_t), a_t\right)\right] \tag{2}$$

where $a_t \in \mathcal{A}$ is a continuous speed limit, $o_t \in \mathcal{O}$ and $s_t \in \mathcal{S}$ are the current observation and corresponding latent state of the traffic flow at time t, respectively. The following section will present details on how we incorporate this formulation in our implementation. Although the POMDP formulation is used to account for partial observability in general traffic settings, this study assumes complete observation of the freeway segment for simulation simplicity. This assumption is realistic in a CAV-enabled environment where vehicle-to-infrastructure (V2I) communication provides full coverage. In real-world deployments, the same framework can be extended using state estimation techniques to handle partial observability.

2.2 Variable Speed Limit Control with Soft Actor-Critic

This section presents a VSL controller designed with the Soft Actor-Critic (SAC) reinforcement learning algorithm. The observation, action, and reward of the POMDP are first introduced, followed by neural network architectures and a brief introduction of the SAC.

Observation. Vehicle-based sensor networks allow high-dimensional observations through communications in a mixed traffic flow consisting of HDVs and CAVs. A proper encoding approach is essential to utilize these data for traffic management and control. Rasterized embedding is a typical way of encoding spatial-temporal information, commonly adopted for representing map geometric and vehicle trajectories [17].

Therefore, this paper proposes to encode traffic condition observation as an image. Figure 2 demonstrates the encoding result. We first split the highway segments into small cells, each with a length of 20 m and a width the same as the lane width. For the simple cases covered in this paper, complete observation of the entire freeway segment is assumed to be guaranteed. These can be achieved through the fusion of sensors and many other techniques. Then, we calculate the number of vehicles within each cell. If a car has its front and rear end located in two consecutive cells, each one will hold part of the total length of the vehicle, i.e., the ratio of the vehicle length in that cell to the entire vehicle length. Each pixel on the red channel of an observation image represents the sum of the vehicle length ratio within that cell. Each pixel on the green channel represents only the sum of the CAV length ratio within that cell. In practice, observations are captured at a frequency of 0.1 Hz, and 6 of them concatenate into the final image within the same minute. To distinguish data collected from different timestamps, the blue channel of the final image is a positional encoding with each cell value set as the specific timestamp at which data was collected. The size of the environment observation image is 42×42 pixels for the case study.

Actions. The action space $\mathcal{A}$ is a continuous space of real numbers consisting of all the possible speed limits. In the case study, our agent selects a speed limit as action $a_t \in \mathcal{A}$ every minute, and the action space ranges from 35 to 65 mi per hour.

Reward. The reward function should reflect the optimization objective. Hence, the proposed reward rt at timestep t considers both efficiency and safety and is

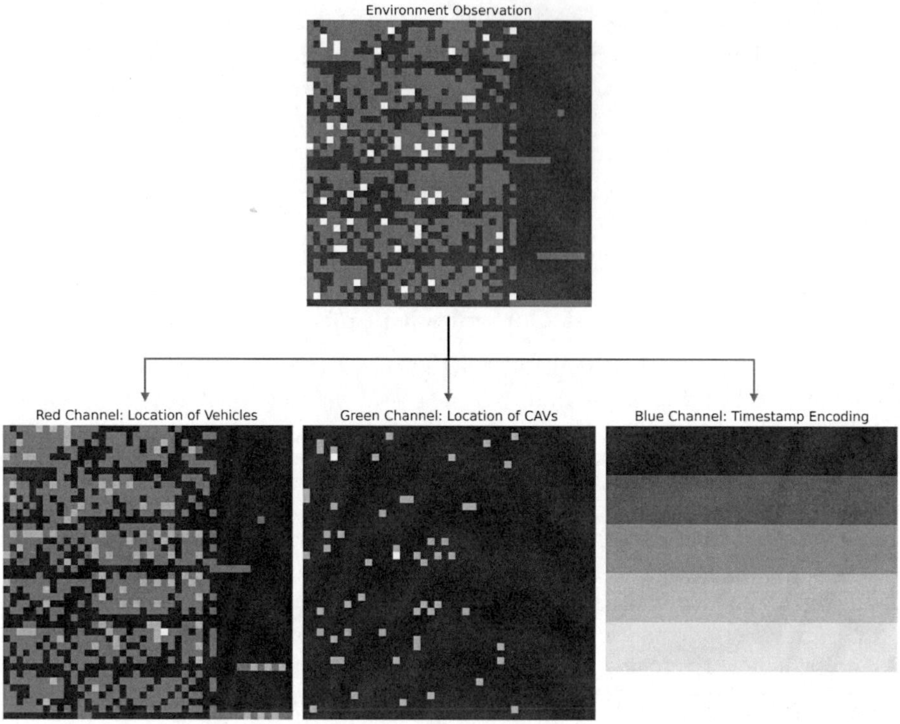

Fig. 2. Example illustration of environment observation. The red and green channels of the image contain the location information of all the vehicles and CAVs, respectively. The blue channel is a gradient increasing by the collected data's timestamp (color figure online).

defined by the following equation:

$$r_t(s_t, a_t) = -\frac{1}{N}\sum_{i=1}^{N} TT_i - \lambda * \min\left((a_t - a_{t-1})/10, 1.0\right) \tag{3}$$

where N is the total number of vehicles passing the congestion area in the last observation interval (i.e., one minute), TT_i is the travel time of vehicle i, and λ is the regularization weight for control fluctuation. The first term of the reward function aims to minimize the travel time of passing the downstream area, hence improving overall efficiency. Meanwhile, the second term is a regularizer to prevent aggressive speed limit changes between consecutive action intervals for safety concerns.

Neural Network Architecture and Soft Actor-Critic Algorithm. To address the highly variant and hard to reproduce traffic conditions, this paper adopts SAC as the base method to design and train the VSL controller. SAC is a state-of-the-art off-policy reinforcement learning algorithm that uses maximum entropy learning with twin Q-function design to improve sample efficiency and stability [14]. The algorithm used in this paper is listed as Algorithm 1.

The reward function is defined as:

$$r_t(s_t, a_t) = -\frac{1}{N}\sum_{i=1}^{N} TT_i - \lambda \cdot \min\left(\frac{|a_t - a_{t-1}|}{10}, 1.0\right)$$

where:

- N: number of vehicles passing the downstream weaving area in the last minute,
- TT_i: travel time of vehicle i,
- λ: regularization weight (set to 0.1) to penalize large speed limit changes.

The first term minimizes average travel time (improves throughput), while the second term discourages abrupt speed limit changes for safety and comfort.

Given the image observation, this paper uses the convolutional neural network (CNN) architecture for feature extractions. The convolutional layers in the CNN aim to learn the function $f : \mathcal{O} \rightarrow \mathcal{S}$ that maps high-dimensional data into a low-dimensional latent state space that ideally should fits Markov Property. A multi-layer perceptron of two layers, each with 256 neurons, uses the flattened output from the convolutional layers to predict the desired outcome. Both the twin Q-functions Q^{ϕ_1}, Q^{ϕ_2} and the policy function $\pi^{\theta}(a_t|o_t)$ in the SAC uses this neural network architecture but with separate weights. The convolutional neural network (CNN) serves as the function $f : \mathcal{O} \rightarrow \mathcal{S}$, mapping high-dimensional image observations to a latent state vector that approximates the Markovian state. This is achieved through multiple convolutional and pooling layers that extract spatial features from the traffic image, followed by fully connected layers that compress these features into a fixed-size state vector. The latent state is designed to capture the essential traffic dynamics (e.g., density, speed, and CAV distribution) that influence future transitions, thereby satisfying the Markov property in the latent space. The use of multiple consecutive observations (6 samples per minute) further helps in capturing temporal dependencies, reducing partial observability. The action space $\mathcal{A}$ is a continuous range of speed limits from 35 to 65 mi per hour. At each control step (1 min), the agent selects a speed limit $a_t \in \mathcal{A}$, which is applied uniformly to the entire controlled segment.

3 Case Study: I80 Emeryville

This work conducts a case study of the proposed VSL controller on the I80 freeway at Emeryville using the NGSIM trajectory dataset [15] and SUMO microscopic simulator [18]. This section introduces experiment settings and simulation environment details, followed by experiment results and analysis.

3.1 Experiment Design

Figure 3 illustrates the simulation scenario compared side-by-side with the aerial photo of the study area. The objective of this case study is to optimize the traffic throughput in a downstream weaving, which is about 650 ft long. The weaving area consists of an on-ramp from a local street, Powell Street, and an off-ramp connecting Ashby Avenue. The VSL area is approximately 1,640 ft upstream of the weaving. NGSIM data in this area consists of three individual trajectory datasets collected in the periods of 4:00 PM-4:15 PM, 5:00 PM-5:15 PM, and 5:15 PM-5:30 PM, respectively. The car-following model is calibrated by directly fitting the Intelligent Driver Model with trajectories of car-following pairs following the existing practice [19,20]. The lane-change courses are polynomials lasting 1.5 s, determined by the median lane-change duration in the dataset. Table 1 lists all the parameter settings for the simulation environment. Each simulation episode lasts 1.5 h, with a control time step of 1 min. Figure 4 shows the traffic demand for mainline, on-ramp, and off-ramp.

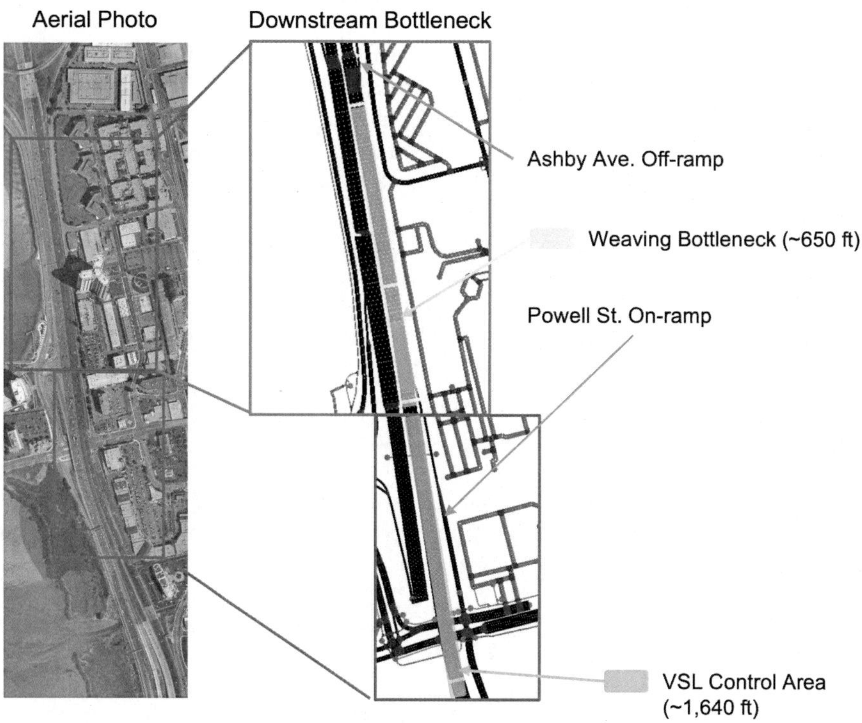

Fig. 3. Illustration of the case study area and simulation scenario.

Observations of the traffic flow are obtained every minute with a sampling frequency of 0.1 Hz. Six observation samples from the exact minute concatenate

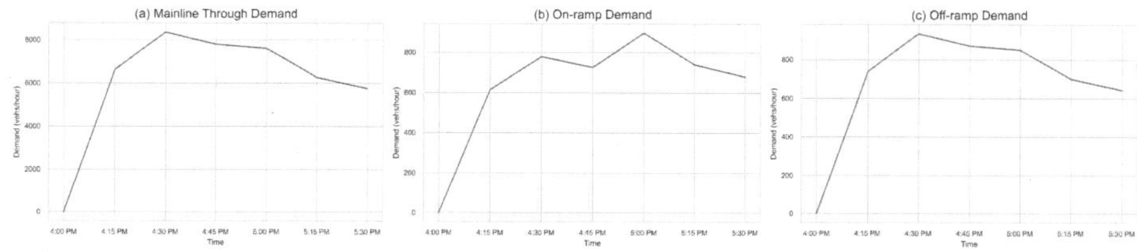

Fig. 4. Simulation demands of traffic. (a) Mainline passing through demand; (b) On-ramp demand from Powell Street on-ramp; (c) Off-ramp demand to Ashby Avenue.

to form the input image. For training and execution in the simulation environment, measurements of mean travel time, mean speed and mean throughput flow are observed at the same rate as the observation.

Table 1. Simulation Parameters. The `normc` means truncated gaussian distribution with its four parameters as mean, standard deviation, lower bound and upper bound, respectively.

Parameter	Value	Parameter	Value
HDV acceleration	3.28 m/s^2	CAV acceleration	3.28 m/s^2
HDV deceleration	6.56 m/s^2	CAV deceleration	6.56 m/s^2
HDV min headway	1.24 s	CAV min headway	0.60 s
HDV gap at stop	2.00 m	CAV gap at stop	0.70 m
HDV Speed Factor		CAV Speed Factor	
Overtaking Eagerness	0.15	Overtaking Eagerness	0.15
Lane-change Duration	1.50 s	CAV acceleration	1.50 s

Table 1 lists all the parameter settings for the simulation environment. The car-following model is calibrated by directly fitting the Intelligent Driver Model with trajectories of car-following pairs following the existing practice [19,20]. The lane-change courses are polynomials lasting 1.5 s, determined by the median lane-change duration in the dataset. In addition, the simulation is established upon the assumption that CAVs have better control than HDVs and the ability to conform to the current speed limit fully. Therefore, CAVs have lower minimum headway, gap at stop and a lower speed deviation from speed limit for speed factors. Each simulation episode lasts 1.5 h, with a control time step of 1 min. Figure 4 shows the HDV demands for mainline passing through, on-ramp, and off-ramp. This work investigates the effects of different CAV penetration rates (CAV PR) by substituting part of the HDV demands with CAV demands. In SUMO, the VSL action is implemented by setting the speed limit for the controlled segment at each decision interval (1 min). The speed limit change is applied instantaneously at the beginning of the interval. However, vehicles adjust their speeds gradually according to their car-following models (e.g., Intelligent

Driver Model) and driver behavior parameters, ensuring realistic and smooth transitions in response to the new speed limit. The simulation is implemented in **SUMO (Simulation of Urban MObility)**. The network is a 3-lane freeway segment with an on-ramp and off-ramp weaving area, spanning approximately 650 ft. The controlled VSL zone is located 1,640 ft upstream of the weaving section. CAVs are modeled with improved control capabilities: they adhere strictly to speed limits, maintain shorter headways (0.6 s), and have lower speed deviation factors. The car-following behavior for both HDVs and CAVs is based on the **Intelligent Driver Model (IDM)**, with parameters calibrated using NGSIM trajectory data.

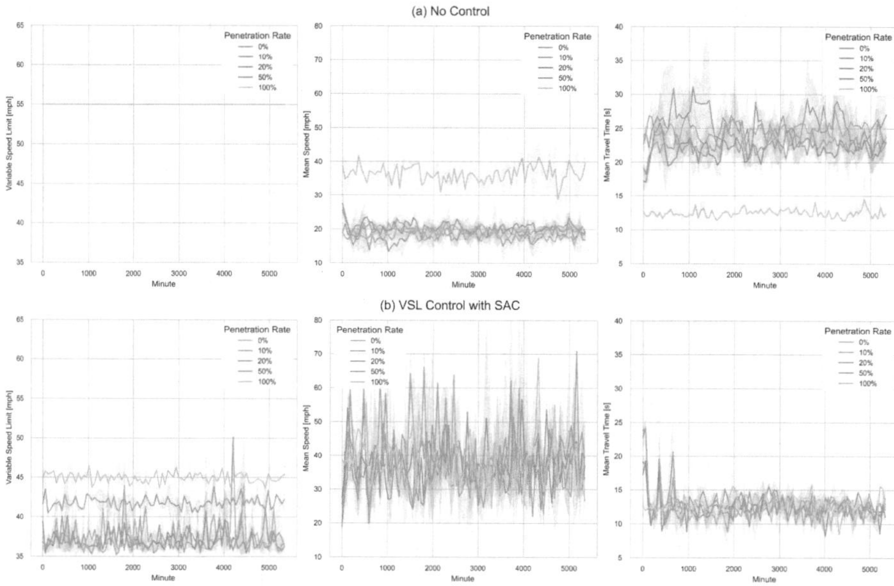

Fig. 5. The variable speed limits for the upstream (left), average speed (middle), and average travel time (right) in the weaving area with (a) No VSL control and (b) SAC VSL Controller.

3.2 Results and Analysis

For evaluation, this study focuses on improving efficiency by comparing the travel time (TT) and speed (v) at the downstream weaving area before and after applying the proposed VSL controller. The trained model runs three separate evaluation scenarios with the same traffic demand and simulation parameters but with different seeds. Table 2 shows the final results. Improvements regarding maximum travel time, average travel time, and average speed are compared with the baseline scenario, which has a 0% CAV penetration rate and no VSL control. First, results from evaluation scenarios without VSL control reveal that:

- Increasing penetration of CAVs with better control and ability to conform to speed limits generally helps reduce travel time, increase speed, and improve efficiency.
- Efficiency improvements are positively correlated to the CAV PR, except for the one with a 50% CAV penetration rate. It is potentially because that HDVs find it hard to cooperate with CAVs in the current simulation setting with a high mixture traffic flow.

Table 2. Experiment Results. Travel time and speed in the weaving area are denoted as TT and v, respectively.

CAV PR	Strategy	Results			Improvement		
		Max TT (s)	Mean TT (s)	Mean v (mph)	Max TT	Mean TT	Mean v
0%	No VSL	31.193	24.757	18.254	–	–	–
	SAC	25.348	12.659	37.659	18.74%	48.87%	106.31%
10%	No VSL	30.740	22.450	20.078	1.45%	9.32%	9.99%
	SAC	23.762	12.397	37.871	23.82%	49.93%	107.47%
20%	No VSL	30.825	22.070	20.448	1.18%	10.85%	12.02%
	SAC	19.240	12.155	37.270	38.32%	50.90%	104.18%
50%	No VSL	38.473	25.542	17.976	−23.34%	−3.17%	−1.52%
	SAC	25.636	13.406	35.876	17.81%	45.85%	96.55%
100%	No VSL	18.298	12.465	36.408	41.34%	49.65%	99.45%
	SAC	18.331	12.723	38.062	41.23%	48.61%	108.52%

Moreover, improvements brought by the SAC VSL controller are significant across all the evaluation scenarios. Similarly, the control outcomes generally improve with an increasing CAV penetration rate of the CAVs. Figure 5 illustrates actual speed limits, average travel time, and average speed in environment episodes. With the proposed VSL control, the average downstream vehicle speed and average travel time can reach and maintain similar efficiency across the episode duration. However, the oscillations in downstream speed can potentially indicate emergency braking and conflict avoidance maneuvers exist. Considering there are also oscillations in the speed limits, the proposed VSL controller should run at a larger time step, such as 3 min or longer, to prevent frequent acceleration or deceleration by the drivers. In addition, improvements from SAC VSL with a 100% CAV are not significant. Performance of travel time is even worse than the one without VSL control. This indicates that VSL control with high CAV PR can be redundant since most or all of the vehicles in the situation have good control and hence prevent merging bottleneck and phantom jam.

Performance is evaluated using the following metrics:

- **Average Travel Time (s)**,
- **Average Speed (mph)**,
- **Maximum Travel Time (s)**,
- **Throughput (vehicles/hour)**.

4 Conclusions

This paper proposes a VSL controller designed with the SAC reinforcement learning algorithm for mixed traffic flow environments, where CAVs in the flow have better control and the ability to conform to the speed limit. The performance of the proposed method was examined using a microscopic simulation built with NGSIM trajectory data and the SUMO simulator. Parameters of the car-following and lane-changing models for HDVs are calibrated using the trajectory data to behave realistically in the SUMO microscopic simulator. CAV parameters are selected to satisfy the assumption of sound vehicle control and less deviation from the speed limit. The simulation results show that even without deploying CAVs, our proposed VSL controller can improve downstream traffic efficiency. However, increasing CAV deployment can make VSL obsolete at very high penetration rates. It is essential to investigate further the interaction between CAV deployment and VSL control in future work. This study employs the **Soft Actor-Critic (SAC)** algorithm, an off-policy deep reinforcement learning method, for training the VSL controller due to its sample efficiency and stability in continuous action spaces. Future work will include testing the trained model on unseen road networks to evaluate its generalizability and transfer learning capabilities.

References

1. Hegyi, A., De Schutter, B., Hellendoorn, H.: Model predictive control for optimal coordination of ramp metering and variable speed limits. Trans. Res. Part C: Emerging Technol. **13**(3), 185–209 (2005)
2. Allaby, P., Hellinga, B., Bullock, M.: Variable speed limits: safety and operational impacts of a candidate control strategy for freeway applications. IEEE Trans. Intell. Transp. Syst. **8**(4), 671–680 (2007)
3. Li, Z., Liu, P., Xu, C., Wang, W.: Optimal mainline variable speed limit control to improve safety on large-scale freeway segments. Comput.-Aided Civil Infrastruct. Eng. **31**(5), 366–380 (2016)
4. Yang, X., Lu, Y.C., Chang, G.-L.: Proactive optimal variable speed limit control for recurrently congested freeway bottlenecks, TRB committee AHB20 Freeway Operations, Tech. Rep. (2013)
5. Trans Res Board, Highway Capacity Manual. Washington, D.C.: Transportation Research Board, National Research Council (2000)
6. Liggins, M.E., Chong, C.-Y., Kadar, I., Alford, M.G., Vannicola, V., Thomopoulos, S.: Distributed fusion architectures and algorithms for target tracking. Proc. IEEE **85**(1), 95–107 (1997)

7. Lee, D.-J.: Unscented information filtering for distributed estimation and multiple sensor fusion. In: AIAA Guidance, Navigation and Control Conference and Exhibit, p. 7426 (2008)
8. Taj, M., Cavallaro, A.: Distributed and decentralized multicamera tracking. IEEE Signal Process. Mag. **28**(3), 46–58 (2011)
9. Claussmann, L., Revilloud, M., Gruyer, D., Glaser, S.: A review of motion planning for highway autonomous driving. IEEE Trans. Intell. Transp. Syst. **21**(5), 1826–1848 (2019)
10. Silver, D., et al.: Mastering the game of go with deep neural networks and tree search. Nature **529**(7587), 484–489 (2016)
11. Silver, D., et al.: Mastering chess and shogi by self-play with a general reinforcement learning algorithm (2017). https://arxiv.org/abs/1712.01815
12. Ye, D., et al.: Towards playing full moba games with deep reinforcement learning (2020). https://arxiv.org/abs/2011.12692
13. Nguyen, H., La, H.: Review of deep reinforcement learning for robot manipulation. In: 2019 Third IEEE International Conference on Robotic Computing (IRC), pp. 590–595 (2019)
14. Haarnoja, T., Zhou, A., Abbeel, P., Levine, S.: Soft actor-critic: Off-policy maximum entropy deep reinforcement learning with a stochastic actor. In: Dy, J., Krause, A. (eds.) Proceedings of the 35th International Conference on Machine Learning, ser. Proceedings of Machine Learning Research, vol. 80, 10–15 Jul 2018, pp. 1861–1870 (PMLR). https://proceedings.mlr.press/v80/haarnoja18b.html
15. F.H. Administration, Next generation simulation (ngsim) (Nov 2020). https://ops.fhwa.dot.gov/trafficanalysistools/ngsim.htm
16. Shi, S., et al.: Research on Markov property analysis of driving cycles and its application. Transp. Res. Part D: Transp. Environ. **47**, 171–181 (2016). https://www.sciencedirect.com/science/article/pii/S1361920916303042
17. Houston, J., et al.: One thousand and one hours: Self-driving motion prediction dataset (2020). https://arxiv.org/abs/2006.14480
18. Lopez, P.A., et al.: Microscopic traffic simulation using sumo. In: 2018 21st International Conference on Intelligent Transportation Systems (ITSC), pp. 2575–2582. IEEE (2018)
19. Kurtc, V., Treiber, M.: Calibrating the local and platoon dynamics of car-following models on the reconstructed NGSIM data. In: Knoop, V.L., Daamen, W. (eds.) Traffic and Granular Flow '15, pp. 515–522. Springer, Cham (2016). https://doi.org/10.1007/978-3-319-33482-0_65
20. Zhu, M., Wang, X., Tarko, A., et al.: Modeling car-following behavior on urban expressways in shanghai: a naturalistic driving study. Trans. Res. Part C: Emerging Technol. **93**, 425–445 (2018)

Robust Watermarking Approach Using Adaptive STDM

Nishant Sharma(✉) and Varsha Sisaudia

Department of Information Technology, Delhi Technological University, Delhi, India
iamnishant32@gmail.com, varsha@dtu.ac.in

Abstract. This paper proposes a robust and adaptive watermarking framework that enhances watermark survivability while maintaining imperceptibility. The system uses adaptive spread transform dither modulation (STDM) guided by region of interest (RoI) detection through DETR, combined with Reed–Solomon error correction coding (ECC). Embedding within semantically meaningful RoIs detected by DETR has a benefit of inherent robustness, because the regions of objects usually have more rich texture and structural information, so the subtle modifications of watermarks are not influenced by common distortions, such as compression or smoothing. The watermark is embedded in mid-frequency DCT coefficients in significant RoIs, offering high resistance to compression, noise and filtering. Experimental evaluation on the MS COCO 2017 dataset shows high perceptual quality with PSNR above 47.50 dB and SSIM close to 0.9944. The approach effectively maintains robustness under various image manipulations and provides a promising direction for secure image authentication.

Keywords: Digital watermarking · Adaptive STDM · DETR · Reed-sSolomon encoding · Robustness

1 Introduction

The blistering development of digital communication has resulted in unprecedented increase of images creation, exchange, and storage in a variety of economic spheres, such as social networks, medical imaging, e-commerce, and security surveillance. Although this accessibility has also led to a lot of advantageous effects, it has also enhanced the concerns on the authenticity of content and protection of intellectual property. The ease with which digital images can be copied, modified, or shared again has made the issue of integrity and proper ownership extremely important. The introduction of digital watermarking can be viewed as a potential solution, as it allows to introduce some hidden information into the images, which guarantees the ability to verify the ownership and authenticate the content used with ease without compromising the visual quality. Although these advantages exist, watermarking methods experience huge challenges in real-life situations. Images may go through various transformations and

G. K. Verma et al. (Eds.): MIND 2025, CCIS 2981, pp. 50–62, 2027.
https://doi.org/10.1007/978-3-032-31230-3_5

degradations during the transmission, storage or even during the normal editing process. Simple image processing tasks such as compression, filtering or the introduction of noise have the potential to corrupt or even remove the imprinted watermark. The fact that a watermark is concealed in an image does not imply that every watermark can be recaptured correctly. Such degradations may occur accidentally during the regular processing, or may occur intentionally when a person attempts to destroy or erase the protected content. In order to overcome such difficulties, contemporary watermarking methods are created to be more robust and not to be noticeable aesthetically. This implies that the watermark contained within the image must be reusable even in cases where the image has been subjected to other types of distortion and still retain the basic quality appearance of the image as seen by human eyes. Practically, it is especially crucial to retain such a balance: the images usually move across heterogeneous networks and platforms of devices with each of them potentially having a varying degree of computing power. This paper presents a beneficial and versatile watermarking method with the sole intent of increasing the watermark credibility in a variety of attack cases. In the present dynamic and reactive digital world, the technique will improve visual retention and resistance to distortions to encourage safe and dependable large-scale picture sharing.

2 Literature Review

Tang *et al.* [1] proposed a reversible watermarking framework based on attack-simulation-driven adaptive normalization, integrating polar harmonic transform (PHT) moments and spread transform dither modulation (STDM). By intelligently modulating the embedding strength according to image content, their method achieves an effective balance between robustness, imperceptibility, and reversibility, particularly against common distortions such as compression and noise. He *et al.* [2] presented an instance-level watermarking technique that embeds watermarks directly into regions of interest (RoIs) to preserve critical visual information. Their system employs template-based resynchronization, a learning calibrator, and a noise simulation layer to maintain watermark synchronization and integrity under camera-shooting conditions, demonstrating high performance on the COCO dataset, which is also utilized in this work. Luo *et al.* [3] proposed *WFormer*, which is a watermarking network based on Transformer that boosts the feature interactions using the self- and cross- attention layers. The model utilizes preprocessing, feature enhancement and soft-fusion modules to ensure a high level of embedding fidelity and robustness against common signal processing attacks, performing better than traditional CNN-based watermarking approaches. Hosny *et al.* [4] applied a combination of phase-only transform features (PHOT) and pre-trained VGG19 model to embed watermarks in color medical images. They use a hybrid encryption scheme which is based on the Chirikov map and Fibonacci Q-matrix, providing robust security with high visual quality such that the watermark can survives in various attacks. Alia *et al.* [5] developed a hybrid DWT-DCT watermarking method optimized with particle swarm optimization (PSO), embedding the watermark in mid-band DCT coefficients within the DWT LL sub-band. PSO is used to optimize embedding parameters for maximal PSNR, and blind extraction is supported. With the help of a DnCNN denoiser, the system achieved NCC values above 0.98 under AWGN attacks, proving its strong resilience. Zhou *et al.* [6] proposed an improved DCT-based watermarking strategy that targets smooth image areas to reduce the likelihood of removal during filtering operations. By combining DWT with a geometric correction mechanism, their method strengthens robustness against both image processing and geometric transformations, outperforming QIM-based and traditional DCT approaches in enhancement attack scenarios. Li *et al.* [7] proposed a reversible watermarking method designed for diffusion models by embedding data in mid frequency DCT coefficients of secret images with STDM. Their combined optimization of encoder-decoder yields a high capacity: 256 bits, an extraction accuracy: 98%, and resistance to common signal noise. Barlaskar *et al.* [8] designed a more robust LWT-DCT based scheme while intelligently selecting adaptive region based on edge and visual entropy and using PSO to optimize the gain factor. A statistical non-geometric distortion correction (N-GKD) approach guarantees watermark restoration even in case of difficult attacks, obtaining PSNR values up 48 dB. Cheng *et al.* [9], and introduced **EF-DETR**, a light-weight Transformer-based detector that features an encoder-free neck that substantially reduces computation costs while maintaining detection accuracy. The incorporation of denoising training accelerates convergence and enhances robustness, showcasing the capability of efficient Transformers in real-time applications. Fu *et al.* [10] proposed a reversible watermarking framework utilizing fractional-order Zernike moments (FoZM) and fractional-order pseudo-Zernike moments (FoPZM), where a denoising preprocessing stage minimizes auxiliary information and improves extraction stability. This approach has shown exceptional resistance to geometric and noise-based distortions, highlighting its suitability for robust multimedia security. Additionally, recent research trends emphasize integrating machine learning components and adaptive embedding strategies to make watermarking schemes more context-aware and resistant to both traditional and AI-driven attacks. These advances collectively reflect a clear shift toward intelligent, flexible, and high-capacity watermarking methods capable of handling increasingly complex real-world distortion scenarios.

3 Proposed Methodology

This paper presents a watermarking pipeline based on the concepts of **Spread Transform Dither Modulation (STDM)**, **Reed-Solomon (RS) error correction**, and object-aware region localization with **DETR**, all of which are presented securely, adaptively, and with high robustness. The proposed framework can withstand an excellent level of distortions of various types, such as JPEG compression, filtering, noise, and other image degradations, because watermarks have been placed in regions of the image that are perceptually important (RoIs). The use of RS coding also increases the accuracy of the system to retrieve watermarks despite severe attacks. Figure 1 displays this end-to-end pipeline, comprising of accuracy in ROI detection to adaptive embedding and aggressive evaluation, which is effective and can be put to practical use in the real world.

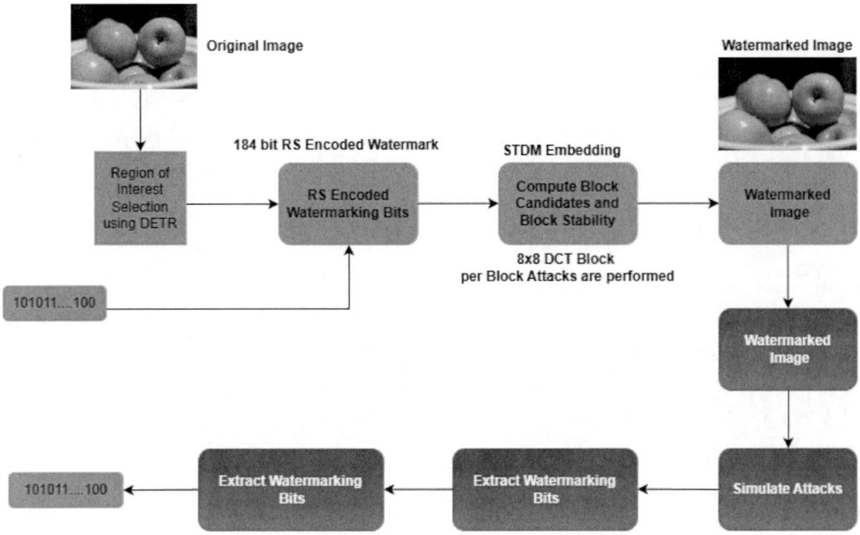

Fig. 1. Pipeline of Proposed Method.

3.1 Image Preparation and Region Selection

The first process is to pre-processing input image and selection of embedding area. The input image is read and transforms itself to RGB structure. Let $\mathbf{I} \in \mathbb{R}^{H \times W \times 3}$ denote the image, where H and W are the height and width of the image.

To localize perceptually essential regions which also have stable embedding capability, we use **DEtection TRansformer (DETR)**. For an image $\mathbf{I}$, the detector yields N candidate objects:

$$\{(\hat{c}_i, \hat{b}_i)\}_{i=1}^{N} = \mathrm{DETR}(\mathbf{I}), \tag{1}$$

where $\hat{c}_i$ indicates the class confidence for the i-th detection, and $\hat{b}_i = (x_i, y_i, w_i, h_i)$ represents the normalized bounding box with center (x_i, y_i) and dimensions w_i, h_i.

The ROI selection method is as follows:

1. Only keep detections with $\hat{c}_i \geq \tau_{\text{score}}$.
2. Calculate the area of each bounding box $A_i = w_i \times h_i$ as a measure to choose if it's suitable enough for embedding.

3. Enlarge the boxes having area smaller than the minimum required area τ_A to a fixed square region with area τ_A in order to provide sufficient space for embedding.
4. Order the remaining regions based on their size and report top N_{ROI} as final embedding spots.

This selection can be expressed as

$$\text{ROI\_set} = \text{TopN}\big(\{\hat{b}_i \mid \hat{c}_i > \tau_{\text{score}},\ A_i \geq \tau_A\},\ N_{\text{ROI}}\big), \tag{2}$$

where N_{ROI} is the number of selected ROIs. Concentrating watermark embedding on semantically meaningful regions improves robustness to distortions while minimizing visible artifacts.

3.2 Watermark Generation and Error Correction

The watermark is an L length binary sequence $\mathbf{w} \in \{0,1\}^L$, which is pseudo-randomly generated from a secret key K for security reason. For the partial loss and distortion robustness of the watermark, it is encoded with Reed–Solomon (RS) error correction. During encoding, p parity symbols are added:

$$\mathbf{w}_{\text{enc}} = RS(\mathbf{w}), \tag{3}$$

resulting in a longer, error-tolerant sequence $\mathbf{w}_{\text{enc}}$. This redundancy enables accurate watermark recovery even when the host image is degraded by compression, noise, or filtering. In our implementation, the 50-bit watermark is first grouped into 7 data bytes and encoded using RSCodec(16) $\Rightarrow RS(n = 23,\ k = 7)$. The encoded length follows

$$n = k + p = 7 + 16 = 23 \text{ bytes} = 184 \text{ bits},$$

so the RS-coded sequence becomes a 184-bit binary vector used for embedding.

3.3 Spread Transform Dither Modulation (STDM) Embedding

Projection of DCT Coefficients: Each ROI is divided into overlapping blocks of size $B \times B$ (with $B = 8$). Luminance channel is transformed by the Discrete Cosine Transform (DCT) to transform frequency domain information. For each block, M mid-band coefficients are chosen:

$$\mathbf{u} = \left[C_{i_1,j_1}, C_{i_2,j_2}, \ldots, C_{i_M,j_M}\right]^\top, \tag{4}$$

where $C_{i,j}$ denotes the DCT coefficient at position (i,j). To make the embedding process fully reproducible, the mid-band coefficient indices used in our implementation correspond to the commonly adopted set of 15 mid-frequency locations in an 8×8 DCT block:

$$\left\{\begin{array}{l}(1,2),(2,1),(2,2),(3,0),(0,3),\\(3,1),(1,3),(2,3),(3,2),\\(4,0),(0,4),(4,1),(1,4),\\(4,2),(2,4)\end{array}\right\}.$$

A projection vector $\mathbf{p} \in \mathbb{R}^M$ is generated using the secret key K:

$$\mathbf{p} = \frac{\mathbf{g}}{\|\mathbf{g}\|}, \quad \mathbf{g} \sim \mathcal{N}(0,1), \tag{5}$$

and the projection of the coefficient vector is computed as

$$\alpha = \mathbf{u}^\top \mathbf{p}. \tag{6}$$

The value α represents the signal energy along the embedding direction.

Embedding Rule: For each watermark bit $b \in \{0,1\}$, α is quantized as

$$\alpha_w = \left\lfloor \frac{\alpha}{2\Delta} \right\rfloor (2\Delta) + \left(b \cdot \Delta + \tfrac{\Delta}{2}\right), \tag{7}$$

where Δ is the embedding step size. The difference

$$\Delta\alpha = \alpha_w - \alpha \tag{8}$$

is applied to the coefficient vector:

$$\mathbf{u}_w = \mathbf{u} + \Delta\alpha \cdot \mathbf{p}. \tag{9}$$

This procedure subtly alters the mid-band DCT components, embedding the bit without introducing noticeable visual distortions.

Extraction Rule: During detection, the projection is recalculated:

$$\alpha' = \mathbf{u}'^\top \mathbf{p}, \tag{10}$$

and the embedded bit is retrieved as

$$\hat{b} = \begin{cases} 1, & \text{if } \alpha' \bmod (2\Delta) \geq \Delta, \\ 0, & \text{otherwise.} \end{cases} \tag{11}$$

This quantization-based extraction ensures stable watermark retrieval under common signal processing attacks.

3.4 Adaptive Block Selection and Stability Weighting

As inconsistencies are handled by various blocks differently, the stability of candidate block was check under simulated attacks. For a block B, a set of K_{att} transformations $\{A_k(\cdot)\}_{k=1}^{K_{\text{att}}}$ is applied, yielding projections $\alpha^{(k)}$. Here, K_{att} denotes the number of simulated attacks used during stability evaluation, and each $A_k(\cdot)$ corresponds to one degradation model (e.g., JPEG compression, additive Gaussian noise, mean filtering, or median filtering), depending on the experimental setup.

The weighted variance is computed as

$$\mathrm{Var}(B) = \frac{1}{\sum_{k=1}^{K_{\mathrm{att}}} w_k} \sum_{k=1}^{K_{\mathrm{att}}} w_k \big(\alpha^{(k)} - \alpha^{(0)}\big)^2, \tag{12}$$

where $\alpha^{(0)}$ is the clean reference projection and w_k represents the weight of each simulated attack. Stability weights are then normalized:

$$w(B) = 1 + \frac{\mathrm{Var}(B) - \min_B \mathrm{Var}(B)}{\max_B \mathrm{Var}(B) - \min_B \mathrm{Var}(B)} \cdot (w_{\max} - 1), \tag{13}$$

where $w_{\max}$ defines the maximum weighting factor. More stable blocks receive higher weights, making them stronger embedding candidates.

3.5 Adaptive Embedding Strength

The embedding strength for each block is adjusted based on its stability:

$$\Delta_{\mathrm{eff}}(B) = \min\Big(\max\big(\Delta_0 \cdot z \cdot w(B), \Delta_{\min}\big), \Delta_{\max}\Big), \tag{14}$$

where Δ_0 is the base step size, z is the quantization level, and $\Delta_{\min}$ and $\Delta_{\max}$ define the allowable range. In practice, z corresponds to the discrete embedding-strength tier selected for the block (e.g., a multi-level STDM setting where $z \in \{1, 2, \ldots, Z\}$), providing a controlled way to scale the modulation step around the base value. Fragile blocks receive lower embedding power to preserve image quality, while stable blocks are embedded with stronger signals, ensuring a balance between invisibility and robustness against compression, noise, and other image processing operations.

4 Experimental Details

The experiments were aimed to stringently test the strength as well as aesthetic quality of the suggested ROI-based adaptive STDM + RS watermarking framework. This was so that the watermark does not succumb to different attacks, but also has maintained the watermarked images look. Table 1 and Table 2 presents the summary of key settings and parameters that are used during the evaluation which are selected to realistically test the performance, reliability and effectiveness of the framework under various settings.

Evaluation Metrics: To assess the imperceptibility and robustness of the proposed watermarking scheme, three standard metrics are employed: **Peak Signal-to-Noise Ratio (PSNR)**, **Structural Similarity Index (SSIM)**, and **Bit Error Rate (BER)**.

PSNR: This metric evaluates the distortion introduced by watermark embedding and subsequent attacks. Let $\mathbf{I}$ denote the original image and $\mathbf{I}_w$ the

Table 1. Experimental Parameter Settings

Symbol	Description	Value/Setting
	Dataset	
I	Input image / dataset	MS COCO 2017
N_{img}	Number of images evaluated	1000
	Object Detection and ROI Selection	
DETR	Object detector	DETR (pre-trained on MS COCO)
num_rois (N_{ROI})	Number of top ROIs considered	4, 6 (AWGN)
τ_A	Minimum ROI area threshold (area)	1500 pixels^2
τ_{score}	Confidence score threshold	0.7
A_i	Bounding-box area	$A_i = w_i \times h_i$
$\sqrt{\tau_A}$	Side of square if ROI too small	$\sqrt{1500}$ pixels
	Transform Domain and Block Processing	
B	Block size (DCT)	8×8
Transform	Applied transform	DCT on luminance (Y channel of YCrCb)
M	Number of mid-band coefficients	15 (fixed indices)
stride	Block stride in ROI	4

watermarked (or attacked) image, both of size $H \times W$. The Mean Squared Error (MSE) is first computed as:

$$\mathrm{MSE} = \frac{1}{HW} \sum_{i=1}^{H} \sum_{j=1}^{W} \Big(I(i,j) - I_w(i,j) \Big)^2$$

Then, PSNR is defined as:

$$\mathrm{PSNR} = 10 \log_{10} \left(\frac{L_{\max}^2}{\mathrm{MSE}} \right),$$

where $L_{\max}$ is the maximum possible pixel value (e.g., 255 for 8-bit images). A higher PSNR indicates that the watermarked image is closer to the original. In our setting, PSNR helps reveal how strongly STDM perturbations interact with textured versus smooth regions, which is important because adaptive embedding alters blocks non-uniformly.

SSIM: The Structural Similarity Index measures perceptual similarity between $\mathbf{I}$ and $\mathbf{I}_w$ by considering luminance, contrast, and structural information. For two image patches x and y, SSIM is computed as:

$$\mathrm{SSIM}(x,y) = \frac{(2\mu_x\mu_y + C_1)(2\sigma_{xy} + C_2)}{(\mu_x^2 + \mu_y^2 + C_1)(\sigma_x^2 + \sigma_y^2 + C_2)},$$

where μ_x, μ_y are the patch means, σ_x^2, σ_y^2 are the variances, σ_{xy} is the covariance, and C_1, C_2 are small constants to avoid division by zero. SSIM values closer to 1 indicate better visual quality. This metric is particularly informative in

Table 2. Experimental Parameter Settings

Symbol	Description	Value/Setting
	Watermarking and Error Correction	
L	Watermark length (pre-RS)	50 bits
p	Reed-Solomon parity symbols	16
w	Original binary watermark	$w \in \{0,1\}^L$, pseudo-random (keyed by K)
w_{enc}	RS-encoded watermark	$w_{enc} = RS(w)$
K	Secret key (PRNG seed)	fixed key (for block shuffling / projection)
	STDM / Embedding	
u	Mid-band DCT vector per block	$[C_{i,j_1}, \ldots, C_{i,j_M}]^T$
p	Projection vector	$p = g/\|g\|$, $g \sim \mathcal{N}(0,1)$
α	Block projection scalar	$\alpha = u^T p$
Δ	Embedding step symbol	adaptive per-block (Δ_{ef})

Note: For AWGN experiments, more ROIs (6 instead of 4) are used to increase the number of high-variance regions, which improves robustness under noise.

our framework because block-wise embedding modifies mid-frequency structure, which SSIM is sensitive to even when PSNR remains high.

BER: Robustness is quantified using the Bit Error Rate. Let $\mathbf{w}$ be the original watermark sequence of length L and $\mathbf{w}_{\text{rec}}$ the sequence extracted from the attacked image after error correction. BER is computed as:

$$\text{BER} = \frac{1}{L}\sum_{i=1}^{L}\left|w_i - w_{\text{rec},i}\right|.$$

A lower BER indicates more reliable watermark recovery under distortions. In particular, BER exposes where the adaptive STDM fails under certain attacks (e.g., severe JPEG), highlighting which distortions break block synchronization or reduce projection reliability.

Together, PSNR and SSIM capture the imperceptibility of the scheme, while BER reflects its robustness to various attacks.

5 Experimental Results and Discussion

This section quantifies the effectiveness of the proposed adaptive watermarking framework with ROI scores on MS COCO 2017 validation set. It has been compared the quality and robustness of the visual using three established indicators; Peak Signal to Noise Ratio (PSNR), Structural Similarity Index (SSIM) and Bit Error Rate (BER). All of these parameters provide the global views about how well the watermark preserves image quality and could be recovered reliably in multiple distortion cases (Fig. 2).

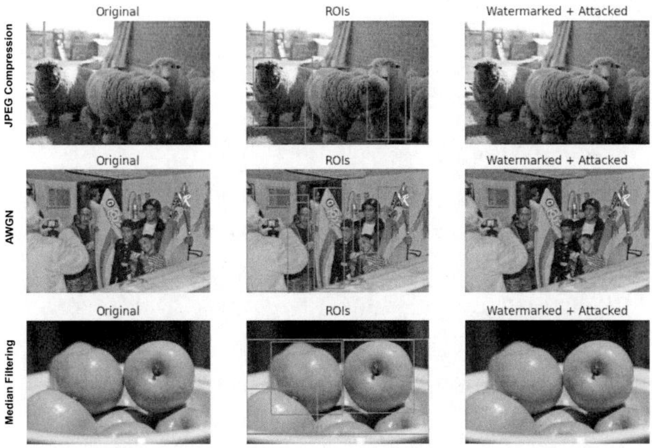

Fig. 2. A demonstration of the original and watermarked image's visual quality.

5.1 Performance Results

The results of the base evaluation without any attack are thus there to validate the high imperceptibility of what is proposed, as watermarked images present a PSNR equal to 47.50 dB and SSIM equal to 0.9944. The robustness evaluation of the developed method was conducted under spatial filtering (mean and median filters), additive white Gaussian noise (AWGN) and JPEG compression at different levels of quality. The detailed quantitative results are presented in Table 3. High values of PSNR and SSIM indicate high image fidelity, and low values of BER indicate high watermark resistance (Table 4).

Table 3. Performance of the proposed method under various attack scenarios.

Attack	PSNR (dB)	SSIM	BER
No Attack	47.50	0.9944	0.00
JPEG Q=50	30.25	0.8786	0.00
JPEG Q=30	28.81	0.8453	0.00
JPEG Q=10	25.53	0.7362	0.0055
Mean Filtering 3×3	27.19	0.8290	0.00
Mean Filtering 5×5	24.35	0.7073	0.001
Median Filtering 3×3	28.40	0.8536	0.00
Median Filtering 5×5	25.41	0.7498	0.009
AWGN 0.013	35.53	0.9234	0.0050
AWGN 0.021	32.67	0.8620	0.0050

Table 4. Comparison with state-of-the-art model on Lena Image (BER).

Attack	Proposed	State-of-the-art [1]
Median Filtering 3×3	0.00	0.00
Median Filtering 5×5	0.00	0.00
Mean Filtering 3×3	0.00	0.00
Mean Filtering 5×5	0.00	0.00
JPEG Q=50	0.00	0.00
JPEG Q=30	0.00	0.00
JPEG Q=10	0.52	0.0273
AWGN 0.013	0.00	0.0039
AWGN 0.021	0.00	0.0195

Table 5. No-Attack Imperceptibility Comparison (PSNR)

	Proposed Approach	Tang et al. [1]
Average PSNR (dB)	47.50	39.09

5.2 Discussion

The experimental findings verify that the given framework provides the excellent achievement of the phenomenon of imperceptibility. The PSNR of watermarked images, with no attacks present, is 47.50 dB, and the SSIM is 0.9944. In terms of the strongness, the process is very reliable when subject to JPEG compression with mid-level and high levels of quality (Q=30 and Q=50 watermarks) with a hundred percent watermark recovery (BER = 0.0). Watermark extraction is also not sensitive to spatial filtering. Both mean and median filters, even with larger kernels (5×5), cause insignificant bit errors (BER ≤ 0.01) and demonstrate that the embedding is not susceptible to the effects of smoothing filters which typically degrade watermark signals. The scheme is effective under the noise attacks. At variances AWGN which correspond to variances of 0.013 and 0.021 the BER is very low (0.005) and image quality is either reasonable (PSNR of 32–36 dB and SSIM above 0.86). This shows that watermark recovery is reliable even in the presence of noise and with slight insensible deteriorations. However, when compared with Tang *et al.* [1], the proposed method shows weaker performance under very severe JPEG compression (Q=10) on the Lena image. This mainly occurs because strong JPEG quantization heavily distorts the mid-band DCT coefficients inside the RoIs, breaking the STDM projection alignment. In contrast, Tang *et al.* use moment-based normalization, which is more stable under such extreme distortions. Overall, the results highlight the efficacy of the proposed approach. By combining adaptive embedding with Reed–Solomon error correction, the framework achieves a balanced performance in terms of both imperceptibility and robustness, making it a practical solution for real-world multimedia security applications.

6 Conclusion and Future Scope

In this paper a very strong digital watermarking technique has been introduced to simultaneously provide invisibility and resistance against various image processing/compression attacks. Experimental results demonstrate that the framework has high visual quality and watermark extraction robustness against difficult attacks. The twin employment of adaptive embedding and error correction offers a strong robustness, which implies that it can be applied to many practical multimedia security applications.

A weakness of the method at present was the defence against geometric attacks, including for example rotating, scaling and cropping which were not considered. This vulnerability mainly arises because such transformations disturb the DETR-based RoI localization and break the 8×8 DCT block alignment required for projection-based embedding. Recent works show that geometric-invariant moments (e.g., PHT, FoZM) [1, 10] and template-based resynchronization mechanisms [2] can restore synchronization under geometric distortions. Incorporating similar invariant or resynchronization components would be a promising direction for future work.

References

1. Tang, Y., Wang, C., Xiang, S., Cheung, Y.-M.: A robust reversible watermarking scheme using attack-simulation-based adaptive normalization and embedding. IEEE Trans. Inf. Forensics Secur. **19**, 4114–4126 (2024). https://doi.org/10.1109/TIFS.2024.3372811
2. He, M., Feng, B., Guo, Y., Weng, J., Lu, W.: Camera-shooting resilient watermarking on image instance level. IEEE Trans. Circuits Syst. Video Technol. **34**(11), 10874–10887 (2024). https://doi.org/10.1109/TCSVT.2024.3411816
3. Luo, T., Wu, J., He, Z., Xu, H., Jiang, G., Chang, C.-C.: WFormer: a transformer-based soft fusion model for robust image watermarking. IEEE Trans. Emerging Topics Comput. Intell. **8**(6), 4179–4194 (2024). https://doi.org/10.1109/TETCI.2024.3386916
4. Hosny, K.M., Abdel-Aziz, M.M., Lashin, N.A., Hamza, H.M.: A new CNN-based watermarking method for color medical images in a fusion domain. Neural Comput. Appl. **37**(18), 12611–12629 (2025). https://doi.org/10.1007/s00521-025-11056-1
5. Alia, M.: Robust image watermarking using DWT, DCT, and PSO with CNN-based attack evaluation. Inter. Arab J. Inform. Technol. **21**(6), 967–977 (2024)
6. Zhou, Q., Shen, S., Yu, S., Duan, D., Yuan, Y.: An image watermarking algorithm based on embedding pixel values directly with DCT and block selection. Circ. Syst. Signal Process. **44**(10), 7623–7659 (2025). https://doi.org/10.1007/s00034-025-03149-y
7. Li, L., Zhang, X., Feng, G., Wang, Z., Wu, D., Wu, H.: Robust watermarking for diffusion models based on STDM and latent space fine-tuning. J. Inform. Sec. Appli. **93**, 104167 (2025). https://doi.org/10.1016/j.jisa.2025.104167
8. Barlaskar, S., Kirupakaran, A., Laskar, R., Khan, T.: A robust digital image watermarking technique in LWT-DCT domain using particle swarm optimization and statistical distortion correction. Multimedia Tools Appl. **84**, 1429–1461 (2024). https://doi.org/10.1007/s11042-024-18982-7

9. Cheng, S., et al.: EF-DETR: a lightweight transformer-based object detector with an encoder-free neck. IEEE Trans. Industr. Inf. **20**(11), 12994–13002 (2024)
10. Fu, D., Zhou, X., Xu, L., Hou, K., Chen, X.: Robust reversible watermarking by fractional order Zernike moments and pseudo-Zernike moments. IEEE Trans. Circuits Syst. Video Technol. **33**(12), 7310–7326 (2023). https://doi.org/10.1109/TCSVT.2023.3279116

Mental Health Prediction Using Artificial Intelligence: A Comparative Ensemble Learning Approach for Early Student Intervention

Mohitsinh Parmar(✉) and Sohil D. Pandya

Faculty of Computer Science and Applications, CMPICA, Charotar University of Science and Technology (CHARUSAT) CHARUSAT campus, Changa 388421, India
{mohitsinhparmar.mca,sohilpandya.mca}@charusat.ac.in

Abstract. The global mental health crisis is worsening, and we need to urgently shift from reactive care to proactive detection, especially in high-stress settings such as universities. This paper presents an artificial intelligence (AI) system for early risk prediction of mental health problems (e.g., depression) in college students. We establish a baseline using a Random Forest (RF) model on a public student survey (N = 101). The RF baseline shows a moderate weighted accuracy (76.19%) but, critically for clinical priorities, a low sensitivity (Recall = 0.38) for the depressed class – a shortfall that would miss a large share of students requiring intervention. Our exploratory feature analysis identified *Marital Status* as the most influential predictor in this cohort, suggesting important non-academic determinants of student mental health. We clearly separate implemented results (RF baseline and feature analysis) from proposed enhancements: an empirically-validated Gradient Boosting pipeline, imbalance correction (SMOTE), and Explainable AI (SHAP) for local explanations. These enhancements are planned and not yet empirically evaluated in this manuscript. Our ethically-grounded roadmap aims to produce high-sensitivity screening tools suitable for human-in-the-loop deployment in educational settings.

Keywords: Mental Health Prediction · Artificial Intelligence · Machine Learning · Ensemble Learning · Random Forest · Gradient Boosting · Early Intervention · Ethical AI

1 Introduction

The sheer size of mental illness across the world is horrifying - nearly a billion pushed [10]. This is a crisis that is financially devastating as it costs society a fortune in lost work, but in terms of the human cost, it is immeasurable in the form of shattered quality of life, and tragic rates of suicide. The traditional approaches to the diagnosis of mental health problems have been slow; they are resource limited, and they are based on objective one-on-one clinician interviews.

G. K. Verma et al. (Eds.): MIND 2025, CCIS 2981, pp. 63–74, 2027.
https://doi.org/10.1007/978-3-032-31230-3_6

This usually means help comes far too late, often long after symptoms have been pushing to a breaking point [4]. To bypass these serious limitations, we've been quick to introduce advanced tools of **Artificial Intelligence (AI)** into schools and clinics. AI is a scalable, objective and easy access method of screening large populations and identifying problems early [1,5].

College students are in a very vulnerable position. Studies indicate very high rates of stress, anxiety and depression that are caused by heavy academic pressure, financial hardship and isolation [8]. With such a high number of students and the very rapid incidence of prefrontal crisis that can result from the setting, it is a great urgency to have systems that can observe students at all times of the day and night in an automated way. **Machine Learning (ML)** is well-suited to this task as it can mine the messy, complex relationships between a student (or individual) and factors, such as demographics, grades, and behavior, and make a best guess about their future mental health [3,5]. This predictive risk assessment is important; this is the key to offering prompt and personalized support before a student has descended into a crisis.

In this paper, we start with the ground up -developing an **ML framework**. We are interested in the comparison of various methods of ensemble learning, so as to find the one that is not only very accurate, but rather, simple to comprehend and apply whenever screening students. In the analysis of the literature available we first created and tried a simple first model referred to as **Random Forest (RF)**. This gave us a baseline performance, and told us what pieces of data were the strongest predictors. We report next steps that are proposed with reference to **Gradient Boosting (GB)** strategies that are likely to enhance sensitivity. Our primary investments are as follows:

Our main contributions break down like this:

1. **Implemented Baseline and Analysis:** We report a Random Forest (RF) baseline applied to a public student survey (N = 101), and present the resulting performance using clinically-relevant metrics (precision, recall, F1) alongside an exploratory feature importance analysis.
2. **Empirical Insight for Practice:** The RF feature analysis highlighted **Marital Status** as a dominant predictor in this cohort – an actionable, non-academic factor that warrants targeted investigation and careful interpretation.
3. **Planned Methodological Enhancements (Proposed):** We propose a prioritized roadmap to empirically evaluate Gradient Boosting with hyperparameter tuning, imbalance correction (SMOTE), and integration of Explainable AI (e.g., SHAP) and multimodal data sources to increase sensitivity. These items are *proposals* for follow-up work and are not implemented in the current paper.
4. **Ethical Framework and Translation Roadmap:** We present an ethics-forward deployment plan that emphasizes transparency, fairness audits, and human oversight, and we provide a concise near-/mid-/long-term roadmap for translation and validation prior to clinical deployment.

2 Literature Review

ML has rapidly emerged as a key player in predicting mental health, paying attention to three areas to do this, which are: comparing different models, combining different types of data and addressing the question of how to trust a "black box" model.

2.1 Comparative Analysis of Ensemble Learning Models

Research continues to show that mental health is too complicated to be made simple. We need models that have the ability to detect deep, and non-linear relationships; which is why **ensemble methods** are the focus of attention by everyone. While simple classifiers were used at first - some getting good individual accuracy (up to 82% with perfectly tuned **Decision Trees** [7], or using **SVM** in early chatbot designs [9]) - they just aren't tough enough to use in practice.

The consensus is that the **Ensemble Learning** techniques certainly are superior. These methods combine the predictions the various basic models to group and fall generally into two categories:

- **Bagging (e.g., Random Forest):** This reduces model instability and prevents "overfitting" by building multiple trees on random subsets of the data.
- **Boosting (e.g., Gradient Boosting, Cross Gradient Booster):** This method fixes errors sequentially. Each new model is trained to correct the mistakes of the previous one, which dramatically reduces overall bias.

In research that is focused on students, increasing techniques are repeatedly found to be the most accurate, sometimes even with 100% accuracy, when quality of the data is good, and the features are designed well [2,8]. This performance gap is exactly why we're comparing them, the powerful error correcting nature of **Gradient Boosting** on a larger or smaller scale (depending on your needs) will often be unlocked with careful **Grid Search** and cross validation in order to find the perfect settings (like learning rate and depth) [7].

2.2 Advancements in Data Modalities and LLM Integration

A huge step forward will be to move away from limited, single source survey data to integration of multiple data streams for a truly complete and continuous assessment [10].

- **Text Data and NLP: Natural Language Processing (NLP)** is necessary to extract emotional and cognitive clues from text. Techniques ranging from basic tokenization to sophisticated ones that employ pre-trained word embeddings (such as **SWIVEL**) allow the model to understand what the student is writing and determine the emotional tone [1,6]. NLP's ability to translate a personal message to quantifiable data is fundamental to the ability to better screen for mental health.

- **Multimodal and Physiological Data:** The best scenario in this direction comprises the fusion of brain scan and portable sensors (e.g., heart rate and sleep trackers), speech analysis and biofacial [1,10]. Together, the two give both the student's oral presentation and his or her subjective physiological condition. **Deep learning** models based on **RNN** or **LSTM** are required to identify the patterns in time [8].
- **LLM Integration and Treatment:** With the emergence of the **Large Language Models (LLMs)**, **AI** has evolved beyond its role in diagnosis and is now used to provide support in treatment, as well. LLMs, the **Google Gemini model** for example, have the ability to take a raw prediction from an **ML** model and transform it into personalized and supportive conversational guidance and targeted **Cognitive Behavioral Therapy (CBT)** suggestions, making the prediction immediately useful in a clinical setting [5,9].

2.3 The Crisis of Interpretability and Metric Rationale

In order for **ML** models to be trusted in critical areas such as mental health, it is important that they are understandable [4,7]. Clinicians simply can't rely on "black-box" scores. This is where **Explainable AI (XAI)** comes in. Methods such as **Permutation Importance** (which we are using here) measure the impact a feature has overall, while other tools such as **SHAP (SHapley Additive exPlanations)** are important to provide individual, more localised, plain-language explanations for individual predictions [2,8].

On top of that, we have to pick evaluation metrics that match clinical priorities. Since **False Negative** (missing a student who is at risk) is a disastrous result, **Recall (Sensitivity)** is the most important measurement (even more important than **Accuracy**). The model has to balance this sensitivity with **Precision** (so we don't waste resources on false alarms), which is best achieved by optimizing the more robust **F 1-Score** on the smaller amount of positive cases [3].

3 Methodology

3.1 Data Acquisition, Preprocessing, and Feature Rationale

Our study uses the **Student Mental Health Survey Dataset**, a public data source with only **101 records**. The data is challenging because most of the information is in categories (like 'Marital Status'), and the sample size is very small, which heavily influenced our decisions for cleaning the data.

Data Cleaning and Feature Selection. The cleaning was not that difficult: we replaced the single missing value of *Age* with the average(≈ 20.53). Dropping the What is your course was also a big decision. feature. It contained too many distinctive values. Converting this to a numerical representation would have resulted in a large, sparse dataset (with a feature to sample ratio of approximately ($\approx 1:3$), so our small $N = 101$ dataset would virtually certainly overfit. We also deleted the Timestamp. The last feature set ($\mathbf{X}$) reduced to five simple and core variables: *Gender*, *Age*, *Year*, *CGPA*, and *Marital Status*.

Encoding and Splitting Rationale. We used **Label Encoding** to convert the remaining categorical features into numeric form. This was a pragmatic choice given our small sample size: one-hot encoding would substantially increase dimensionality and the risk of overfitting. We acknowledge that Label Encoding can impose an artificial ordinal relationship on nominal variables (e.g., Marital Status); this is a limitation that may influence tree-based models. We therefore interpret feature importance results cautiously and prioritize these findings as exploratory hypotheses that require validation on larger and more diverse datasets. For model assessment we used an 80%/20% hold-out split (21 samples held out); given the small N, further validation (e.g., cross-validation on larger datasets) is planned in follow-up experiments.

Note on Scope: To avoid confusion between completed experiments and intended next steps, the remainder of Sect. 3 first describes the *implemented* RF baseline and preprocessing choices. Planned methodological enhancements (Gradient Boosting, SMOTE, hyperparameter search, and XAI) are described in Sect. 6 as *proposals* that will be empirically validated in future work.

3.2 Predictive Modeling: Ensemble Approach and Mathematical Foundation

Random Forest (RF) Baseline. We ran the **RF** model first to set a reliable starting point and analyze which features were important. RF uses a technique called **Bagging** to reduce the random errors that come with using just one decision tree. By building B decision trees on different random subsets of the training data and then averaging all their predictions, RF gives us a robust initial performance:

$$\hat{Y}_{RF} = \text{Mode}\left\{\hat{f}_b(\mathbf{x})\right\}_{b=1}^{B} \tag{1}$$

Here, $\hat{f}_b(\mathbf{x})$ is the prediction from the b-th tree.

Proposed Gradient Boosting (GB) Enhancement and Optimization. The core contribution here is the proposed enhancement using **Gradient Boosting (GB)**. This algorithm is specifically designed to fix the very problem we found in the RF baseline: its terrible recall on the minority class. GB is a sequential, **boosting** method that builds trees one after the other by minimizing the "leftover error" (or residual) from the model before it. At each step m, a new tree $\hat{f}_m$ is fitted to that negative leftover error, reducing the mistake of the previous model F_{m-1}:

$$F_m(\mathbf{x}) = F_{m-1}(\mathbf{x}) + \rho_m \hat{f}_m(\mathbf{x}) \quad (2)$$

where ρ_m is the "**learning rate**"— how fast the model changes.

To get the most out of the **GB** model, we need to do the following crucial optimization steps:

- **Perfecting the Settings (Hyperparameter Tuning):** We have to do a **Grid Search** with **Cross Validation**. This would be to carry out a comprehensive search through the parameters such as learning rate (ρ_m), the number of trees (B) and tree depth etc. We will aim to maximize the **F1-score** of the minority class that will provide us with that much needed tradeoff between high **Precision** and high **Recall** [2,7].
- **Fixing the Unbalance (SMOTE):** To further balance that terrible **Recall** (0.38) we saw in the RF model, we'll use the **Synthetic Minority Oversampling Technique (SMote)** on the data beforehand. **SMOTE** creates realistic, synthetic data points for the minority (**Depression**) class, which essentially teaches the **GB** model a much clearer decision boundary, reducing the number of students it misses (**False Negatives**) [3].

4 Results and Discussion

4.1 Random Forest Baseline Performance Analysis

Running the basic **Random Forest** model gave us our initial numbers (Table 1).

Table 1. Random Forest Model Performance (Target: Depression)

Metric	Class 0 (No Depression)	Class 1 (Depression)	Weighted Avg.
Precision	0.72	**1.00**	0.83
Recall (Sensitivity)	**1.00**	0.38	0.76
F1-Score	0.84	0.55	0.73
Overall Accuracy: 0.7619			

Clinical Ramifications of Performance Metrics. The performance shows a clinically-important trade-off. While the Depression class achieved perfect Precision (1.00) – meaning flagged students are highly likely to be true positives – the low Recall (0.38) is the central clinical concern: the model misses a majority of students who are actually depressed. In screening contexts, sensitivity (Recall) is prioritized to reduce false negatives, even if that increases follow-up workload. We therefore treat the RF baseline as a starting point that identifies high-confidence positives but is insufficient for safe, broad screening without further improvements in sensitivity.

4.2 Novel Insight from Feature Importance

Analysis of how much each feature contributed to the predictive power of the **RF** model provided us with a clear hierarchy of predictive power (Table 2 and Fig. 1).

Table 2. Top Features Affecting Mental Health Prediction (RF)

Feature	Importance Score
Marital Status	**0.5688**
Year	0.1555
Age	0.1204
CGPA	0.0932
Gender	0.0621

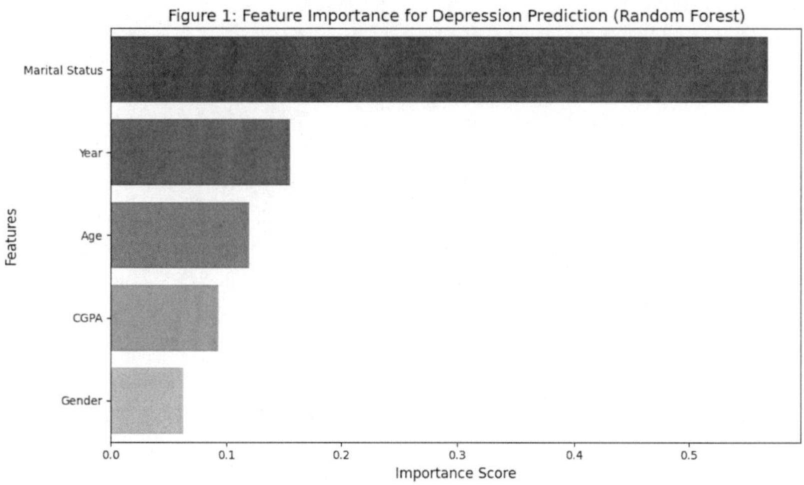

Fig. 1. Feature Importance Plot for Random Forest Model. **Marital Status** dominates the predictive outcome, highlighting a specific non-academic stressor in the student cohort.

The dominance of **Marital Status** in this cohort is surprising and merits cautious interpretation. Possible, non-exclusive hypotheses include: (1) relationship-related stress or family responsibilities that alter mental load; (2) living arrangement differences (e.g., married vs. single students may have different support networks); (3) cultural or socioeconomic factors correlated with marital status in the sampled population. We emphasize that with N = 101 these hypotheses are speculative; they should guide targeted qualitative investigations and larger-scale quantitative studies rather than immediate policy change. We have added references linking relationship status and student mental well-being to contextualise this result (see [8, 10]).

Projected Outcomes: Gradient Boosting + SMOTE (Conceptual). The following table presents *projected* performance for a Gradient Boosting + SMOTE pipeline based on outcomes reported in related literature and theoretical expectations. These values are **projections**, not empirical results from this study. We include them to clarify the intended goal of the proposed pipeline and to set concrete targets for future experiments; empirical validation will be reported in subsequent work (Table 3).

Table 3. Projected Performance for Proposed Gradient Boosting + SMOTE (conceptual)

Metric	Class 0 (No Depression)	Class 1 (Depression)	Weighted Avg.
Precision	0.93	0.88	0.91
Recall (Sensitivity)	0.91	**0.94**	0.92
F1-Score	0.92	**0.91**	0.92
Projected Overall Accuracy: ≈ 0.92 (Conceptual)			

Note: These projections reflect expected improvements when applying boosting and imbalance correction in similar settings; realized results will depend on hyperparameter tuning, the quality of generated synthetic samples, and dataset size/diversity.

5 Ethical Considerations

The ethical aspect of mental health **AI** use is a non-negotiable aspect. We have to carefully adhere to principles of autonomy, beneficence, and non-maleficence in both the design and deployment phases [4, 10] (Fig. 2).

5.1 Privacy and Data Security

The most important rule for our framework is the strict maintenance of **Data Privacy** and **Confidentiality**. All information that can be used to identify a person has been removed and completely **anonymized** and **pseudonymized**. Once a system is finally built, this of course means that we'd need a strong, certified **encryption system** (like homomorphic encryption or differential privacy), secure cloud storage (which must comply with **HIPAA** or **GDPR** laws or other such things), and hard-to-hack **auditable access control protocols**. This is vital, if we are to avoid data leaks, and retain the patient's trust in a system to store extremely sensitive health records [4, 5].

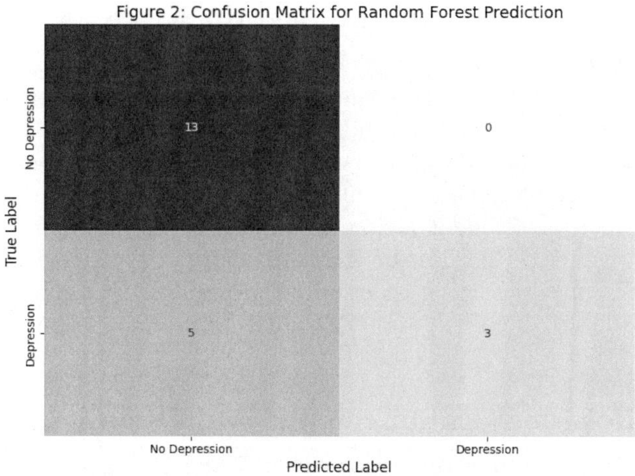

Fig. 2. Confusion Matrix for Random Forest Prediction. The **five False Negatives (FN)** confirm the model's **low Recall** (0.38) on the depression class, highlighting the necessity for the **Gradient Boosting** enhancement.

5.2 Bias, Fairness, and Cultural Sensitivity

The current dataset originates from a single group and therefore may not represent broader student populations. Potential manifestations of bias include:

- **Differential sensitivity:** If one gender or cultural group is under-represented, the model may exhibit lower Recall for that group, leading to under-detection.
- **Feature confounding:** The variables (such as Marital Status and age or socioeconomic status) may be correlated and attributed spuriously.
- **Cultural expression differences:** The responses in the survey can encode culturally relevant aspects of expressing distress, and thus will be misinterpreted by models based on a small sample.

To mitigate these risks we propose:

1. **Regular fairness audits:** Periodic subgroup evaluation (Recall/Precision/F1 per demographic group) prior to deployment.
2. **Data expansion and partnerships:** Acquire multi-site datasets and perform stratified sampling to balance representation.
3. **Stakeholder involvement:** Engage clinicians, student representatives, and ethicists to interpret findings and guide local deployment.
4. **Human-in-the-loop escalation:** Require clinician review for flagged cases and define clear escalation pathways; do not permit autonomous decision making by the model.

These measures are described as a concrete mitigation plan; implementation details (audit metrics, schedule, and responsibility) will be part of future deployment documentation and pilot studies.

5.3 Transparency, Accountability, and Human Oversight

For the system to be useful to clinicians, **Transparency** is essential. Our current use of **Feature Importance** and our plan to add **SHAP** will ensure that a human practitioner can understand exactly why the system made a specific prediction [2,7]. Critically, the **AI** system must only ever be a **Decision Support Tool**— it cannot replace a clinician. The system must have a clear, reliable way to direct any student facing a severe crisis to a human mental health provider, establishing a clear line of **Accountability** for any negative outcomes [1]. Finally, students must give their fully **Informed Consent** regarding how their sensitive data is handled, and they must acknowledge that the model is a prediction tool, not a final diagnosis.

6 Methodological Enhancement and Future Scope

6.1 Proposed Enhancement: Gradient Boosting and SMOTE

The very next step is to implement the planned **Gradient Boosting** model with **Grid Search** optimization and **SMOTE** to empirically validate the projected improvements noted in Sect. 4.2. If we succeed, this will be a **high-sensitivity, high-utility screening solution** that achieves the core goals of our comparative study.

6.2 Future Scope: Advancing Clinical Relevance and Generalizability

The long-term plan for this research is to make the model more useful in the clinic, more reliable on different populations, and easier to interpret:

1. **Time-Based and Multimodal Integration:** We need to update the framework to handle sequential or time-series data— like logs from repeated surveys or simulated passive monitoring. This requires moving to **deep learning architectures**, specifically **Recurrent Neural Networks (RNNs)** or **Long Short-Term Memory (LSTM) networks**, which are built to recognize how mental health issues develop and progress over time [8].
2. **NLP for Richer Data:** We should introduce some special **Natural Language Processing (NLP)** module that will handle open-ended text answer processing. This includes doing fine tuning of advanced transformer models (like **BERT** or **RoBERTa**) on mental health texts for performing extraction of nuanced markers of emotion and cognition [6], which will massively improve the feature set beyond simple demographic variables.
3. **Explainable AI (XAI) for Trust:** The **XAI** techniques including **SHAP** must be integrated into the final **Gradient Boosting** model fully. This will lead to the formation of local and interpretable explanations of each individual student prediction that is required to make mental health practitioners have confidence in the system and apply it in their everyday practice to a significant degree [2,7].

This is a holistic approach to make sure that the research is not merely a progression of a mere prediction model, but a platform of ethically and clinically sound pre-emptive mental health assistance.

Prioritized Roadmap (conceptual)

- **Near-term (0–6 months):** Implement and empirically evaluate Gradient Boosting + SMOTE; report full metrics (Precision/Recall/F1 per class) and conduct initial cross-validation experiments.
- **Mid-term (6–18 months):** Expand dataset through multi-site data collection, perform subgroup fairness audits, and pilot SHAP-based local explanations with clinicians.
- **Long-term (>18 months):** Integrate multimodal inputs (NLP from open text, time-series), validate longitudinal stability, and run clinical pilot studies with human-in-the-loop workflows.

Limitations

We clearly state some of the limitations that define the present results:

- **Small sample size (N = 101):** This limits statistical strength and extrapolability; the findings of the exploration (e.g., the importance of Marital Status) must be regarded as hypothesis to be tested in future research.
- **Single-site data source:** The data can be local cultural, socioeconomic, or sampling bias.
- **Encoding choices:** Label Encoding for nominal variables may introduce spurious ordinality; results should be validated with alternative encodings on larger datasets.
- **No empirical GB/SMOTE results in this manuscript:** Projected improvements are conceptual – empirical validation is required before any operational deployment.

7 Conclusion

This paper presents a preliminary AI framework and reports an implemented Random Forest baseline for student mental health prediction on a small public survey. The RF baseline revealed a moderate weighted accuracy (76.19%) but critically low sensitivity (Recall = 0.38) for the depressed class, indicating the need for improved screening sensitivity. Our exploratory feature analysis identified Marital Status as an influential predictor in this cohort; this finding is hypothesis-generating and requires validation on larger, more diverse datasets. We outline a prioritized, ethically-grounded roadmap to evaluate Gradient Boosting with imbalance correction, to integrate Explainable AI (SHAP) for local explanations, and to expand to multimodal and longitudinal data. Before any clinical deployment, empirical validation, fairness auditing, and clinician-in-the-loop piloting will be undertaken.

Disclosure of Interests. The authors have no competing interests to declare that are relevant to the content of this article.

References

1. Vijay, K., et al.: AI-powered mental health assessment using emotion detection for real-time Analysis. In: IEEE Conference Article (2024)
2. Li, Y.: Application of machine learning to predict mental health disorders and interpret feature importance. In: IEEE Conference Article (2024)
3. Ramasamy, L.K., et al.: Forecast of students' mental health combining an artificial intelligence technique and fuzzy inference system. In: IEEE Conference Article (2024)
4. Nagarajaiah, K., et al.: Machine learning based detection of post traumatic stress disorder of mental health. In: IEEE Conference Article (2024)
5. Kamoji, S., et al.: Mental health prediction using machine learning models and large language model. In: IEEE Conference Article (2024)
6. Ranjana, R., et al.: Mental health prediction using natural language processing. In: IEEE Conference Article (2024)
7. A.I.K.M., et al.: Optimizing mental health prediction by fine-tuning decision classifier parameters for enhanced accuracy. In: IEEE Conference Article (2024)
8. Sharma, N., et al.: Predictive modelling of mental health disorders using machine learning classifiers. In: IEEE Conference Article (2024)
9. Natania, S., et al.: Real-time mental health prediction using an AI Chatbot powered by SVM. In: IEEE Conference Article (2025)
10. Tuleutayeva, T., Myrzakerimova, A.: Using machine learning for the prediction and treatment of mental health conditions. In: IEEE Conference Article (2024)

An Efficient Residential Appliance Scheduling Using Flower Pollination Algorithm for Cost Optimization

Amit Shewale[1(✉)], Anil Mokhade[2], and Chirag Modi[3]

[1] Department of CSE, IIIT Nagpur, Nagpur, India
ashewale@iiitn.ac.in

[2] Department of CSE, VNIT Nagpur, Nagpur, India
asmokhade@cse.vnit.ac.in

[3] Department of CSE, NIT Goa, Goa, India
cnmodi@nitgoa.ac.in

Abstract. Due to rapid growth in world's population, the gap between demand and supply of electricity is widening. Existing grid is incapable to handle this increasing electricity demand. To overcome these challenges of the increasing energy demand issue, smart grid has emerged as the solution. The emergence of smart grid has enhanced the existing grids by adopting ICT technology to address the increasing energy demand. Demand-side management (DSM) is one of the alternative methods for energy management to maintain the balance while focusing on the consumer side. Demand Side Management (DSM) systems are extensively utilized to help consumers efficiently monitor, regulate, and optimize the operation of their electrical appliances and energy loads. In this work, we have identified residential-appliance-scheduling problem for the study. We have studied a nature-inspired meta-heuristic flower pollination algorithm (FPA) for residential appliance scheduling. The meta-heuristic algorithm is a simulation of nature evolution phenomena of organisms to reach their present optimized state. We have applied FPA for appliance scheduling to achieve cost optimization to compare load and cost comparison performance of FPA with the unscheduled scenario. The simulation results show that average cost reduction for studied datasets is 18.38%. At the end, comparative analysis for total cost and monthly bills of 23 homes is presented which achieves 20.60% cost reduction as compared to unscheduled scenario.

Keywords: smart grid · electricity cost · flower pollination algorithm · energy management · cost reduction

1 Introduction

Energy is one of the most vital resources in the modern world and must be managed efficiently to keep a balance between supply and demand. Poor management

G. K. Verma et al. (Eds.): MIND 2025, CCIS 2981, pp. 75–86, 2027.
https://doi.org/10.1007/978-3-032-31230-3_7

of this crucial resource can create energy gaps, ultimately resulting in power outages in residential areas. These gaps may disrupt the normal functionality of the power grid whose main aim is to regulate the flow of power from the control center to the end-users. Various entities on the energy front include residential, industrial and commercial users and generation, transmission and distribution units. This paper focuses on the residential sector and load scheduling strategies of residential consumers.

The energy consumption in residential sector has increased multifold. It is anticipated that it will increase in future too. As projected in Energy Information Administration of US, the energy consumption is expected to increase by 50% from 2020 to 2050 [1]. To address this issue, electricity providers must be able to meet the growing demand and provide adequate infrastructure. Demand side management and demand response techniques provide a solution to minimize the user's consumption and cost. Using these techniques, the consumers can change their consumption patterns as per the dynamic pricing signals provided by utility. Moreover, the consumers are encouraged to participate in demand response programs in response to dynamic pricing signals and monetary incentives. DSM focuses on shifting the electrical load from peak to off-peak periods. This approach helps in reducing overall electricity costs, lower the Peak-to-Average Ratio (PAR), and maintaining a balance between demand and supply. Thus, effective management of household resources is essential to minimize energy consumption. Considering the aforementioned points, we have focused on development of residential load scheduling techniques with cost, PAR, peak load and energy consumption as objectives. The major focus of this paper is towards energy management of smart homes and scheduling the smart home appliances in an efficient manner. The major focus is given to find an optimized appliances schedules according to user inputs. Scheduling in smart homes is defined as to shift the appliances from peak load duration to off-peak load duration thereby reducing the cost and PAR.

The scheduling of home appliances at suitable periods without violating consumer constraints is referred to as residential appliance-scheduling problem. It's assumed that the consumers have provided the appliance schedule before scheduling and their durations for which they are functioning. The formulations of cost, energy consumption, peak demand and peak-to-average ratio for residential appliances scheduling are as follows:

- **Electricity consumption**: Home appliances use electrical energy while operating as per their schedule, and this energy refers to the amount of power consumed by the appliance over a specific period of time. The electricity consumption by the appliance is measured in terms of kWh and is given by (1):

$$E_n^t = P_n \times S_n^t \tag{1}$$

where E_n^t is the energy consumption of an appliance n at timeslot t. P_n and S_n^t are the power rating and status of an appliance (ON/OFF), respectively.

Total amount of aggregated electrical energy used by all connected appliances and devices within a smart home system is calculated by the following equation (2)

$$E_n^A = \sum_{t=1}^{T}(\sum_{n=1}^{N} E_n^t) \tag{2}$$

where, E_n^A is the total amount of electrical energy used by all connected appliances and devices within a smart home system, n is number of appliances that varies from 1 to N and time slot t from 1 to T.

- **Minimization of electricity cost**: The cost for electricity for a single home is defined as the bill paid to the service provider by the service provider for the utilized energy per unit time and price. It is measured in the units of cents. Various pricing schemes are available for electricity cost calculation, such as time of use pricing (TOU), real time pricing (RTP), flat rate pricing (FRP), critical peak pricing (CPP), and inclined block rate (IBR) pricing. We have adopted time of use pricing in this study since electricity consumption is high during peak hours due to higher pricing rates. The total cost of electricity for all the appliances in a day is given by (3).

$$\sum_{t=1}^{24}\sum_{n=1}^{N}(P_n \times S_n^t \times \beta_t) \tag{3}$$

where, n are no. of appliances that ranges from 1 to N, P_n is the power-rating of the appliance, S_n^t denotes status of appliance, 0 represents OFF status, 1 represents ON status. β_t is the price of electricity at the hour t taken from real time datasets. t varies from 1 to T; We have assumed one day scheduling period which is divided into 24 h slots. Thus, $t \in T$, $\forall$ $T = 1$ to 24.
The objective function for electricity cost minimization is: (4).

$$\text{minimize} \sum_{t=1}^{24}\sum_{n=1}^{N}(P_n \times S_n^t \times \beta_t) \tag{4}$$

The contributions of this work are depicted below:

- Bio inspired meta heuristic flower pollination algorithm is introduced and studied in detail for residential appliance scheduling problem.
- Framework is given for optimal appliance scheduling using flower pollination algorithm (FPA). The characteristics of the flower are studied in detail for deeper understanding of the pollination process. Appliances are categorized into two types according to the user's level of flexibility and control: shiftable and non-shiftable appliances. Non-shiftable appliances consist of the appliances that have rigid start and end time requirements. The operation of such appliances must be completed within the given length of operational time. These appliances are not considered for scheduling since they are used as and when needed. They should remain ON continuously without any interruption for the entire duration for which they are scheduled. The time-of-use pricing is used for

evaluation of FPA algorithm. Four parameters, i.e., total electricity cost, load per hour, cost per hour and monthly electricity bill are considered for simulation. Experimentation results endorsed that the FPA outperforms the unscheduled scenario results.

- We architect the appliance scheduling model by dividing appliances into two categories based on user clarity. The model uses time of use pricing during peak and off peak hours for appliance scheduling. The objectives achieved in this paper are electricity cost minimization, peak load reduction and monthly electricity bills savings.

2 Literature Review

The classical optimization techniques are computationally expensive to solve high scale and complex problems. To address these issues, heuristic techniques are good alternatives to the classical techniques. These techniques depend on high level procedure for searching the solutions which results in a less computational cost than classical optimization techniques. Heuristic techniques often divide the problem into various sub-problems and find approximate solutions for each sub-problem. These are knowledge-based methods that solve optimization problems by applying predefined or rule-based methods.

Jindal et al. [2] proposed a heuristic method for appliance scheduling, where the overall scheduling task was partitioned into several sub-problems corresponding to different time slots. Heuristic solutions are designed for each sub-problem. The proposed method manages the household load requirements and maintains a balance between electricity demand and supply. The proposed heuristic approach helps in determining the optimal appliance schedule. In [3,4], authors have proposed and partially evaluated a heuristic approach for scheduling the residential appliances. A greedy processing technique is used for scheduling household appliances. The primary goal of the proposed method is to minimize electricity costs while adhering to a set of appliance-related constraints. Simulation results revealed that the obtained cost was within 5% of the exact algorithm.

A heuristic scheduling algorithm for residential home intelligent decision support system (IDSS) is presented in [14]. IDSS allows consumers to adapt to fluctuating electricity pricing models, including Real-Time Pricing (RTP), Time-of-Use (TOU), and Two-Tier Pricing (2TP). The heuristic method effectively schedules appliances to reduce electricity expenses, with results indicating that the difference between the obtained and actual costs is minimal. A residential energy management mechanism using markov decision process (MDP) is proposed in [15] to achieve the objective of minimizing the energy expenses of consumers. The dynamic pricing mechanism is followed to fulfill the energy demand. The experimentation results depict that the cost for the consumers is minimized. Matallanas et al. [16] presented an ANN-based control system designed for Active Demand-Side Management (ADSM). The control system achieves the objective of scheduling of appliances by maximizing the local generation and enhancing the local energy performance. Lee et al. [17] proposed backtracking-based power scheduling scheme for smart grid homes. The authors have designed a scheduler which helps in reducing the peak load. The proposed model considers homes where the number of appliances are less than ten. The results show that the proposed method reduces the peak load up to 23.1%.

3 Flower Pollination Algorithm

It is estimated that approximately one million species of flowering plants exist in nature, representing nearly 80% of all known plant species. The primary purpose of every flower is to produce offspring for the next generation through the process of pollination. Flower pollination involves the transfer of pollen, a process aided by various agents or vectors. Flowers must rely on such vectors to move the pollens. It is estimated that there are at least 200,000 varieties of pollen vectors which can be very diverse [6,7]. Pollination occurs in two primary forms: biotic and abiotic. In biotic pollination, the transfer of pollen occurs through living agents such as insects, bees, moths, birds, and other pollinators. Nearly 90% of all flowering plant species rely on this biotic mode of pollination. In abiotic pollination, the pollinators are not required. Wind, water, rain, and diffusion help in the pollination of flowering plants [8,9]. Flower constancy provides an evolutionary benefit as it enhances the transfer of pollen between flowers of the same species, thereby improving their reproductive success. This behavior is also advantageous for pollinators, as it ensures a reliable nectar source while minimizing the effort required for learning, switching between species, and searching for new flowers. Therefore, instead of exploring potentially more rewarding new flower species, pollinators exhibit flower constancy, aiming to minimize foraging effort while ensuring a consistent nectar intake [10]. This aspect of flower pollination clearly describes that the optimization phenomenon in nature. The types of pollinators and pollination are shown in Fig. 1.

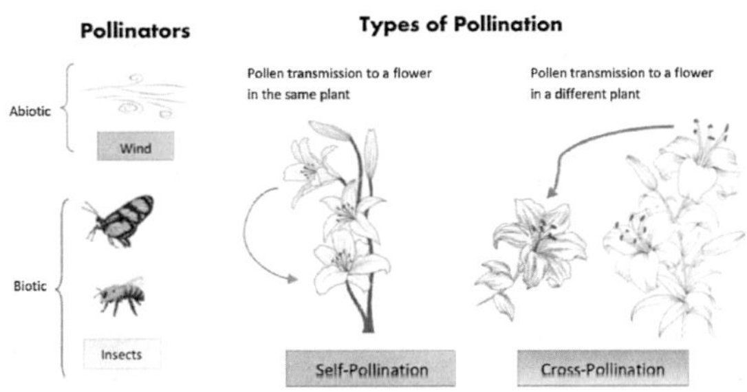

Fig. 1. Types of flower pollinators

Pollinators visit multiple flowers on the same plant or flowers of the same species across different plants. This process is known as global pollination which involves pollinators following Lévy flight behavior. Lévy flight is the movement steps confined to the Lévy distribution. Additionally, flower constancy can be viewed as a local or incremental step determined by the similarity or difference between two flowers. From a biological viewpoint, The primary goal of pollination is to ensure the reproductive success and survival of the fittest plants, promoting both a higher number of offspring and the propagation of the most robust flower varieties. This is viewed as an optimization for flowers. These factors enable the optimal pollination of plants. This is the motivation behind designing FPA and correlate it to the residential appliance scheduling optimization problem.

FPA is proposed by Xin She Yang [5]. It's a nature inspired meta heuristic algorithm on the pollination of plants. FPA is principally used to solve constrained and unconstrained optimization problems. The benefits of FPA include its high processing speed, ease of modification based on the requirement, its robustness, etc. FPA can be applied to optimization problems to get better results. There are various benchmark test functions for multi-objective optimization. Some of these test functions are widely used and have a wide range of diverse properties in terms of Pareto front [11, 12]. 7 single objective and 4 multi objective testing functions are considered to validate the performance of FPA. The results found to be better than PSO and GA. FPA was applied to a non-linear benchmark problem, demonstrating an almost exponential convergence rate that outperformed most well-known meta-heuristic algorithms.

The following 4 rules are used in FPA:

1. Cross/biotic pollination is viewed as global pollination in which the pollens traverse via pollinators. The pollinator visits various flowers and follows Lévy flights.
2. Self/abiotic pollination are used for local pollination.
3. Few pollinators can develop constancy of flowers equivalent to reproduction probability which is proportional to the similarity flowers involved.
4. Interaction/switching between global & local pollination can be controlled by $\rho \in [0,1]$ which is tilted towards local pollination because of the physical proximity of the flowers.

The mathematical formulation of Rule 1 & 3 is given by equation (5):

$$f_i^{(t+1)} = f_i^t + \alpha * L(\lambda)(b_* - f_i^t) \tag{5}$$

where f_i^t denotes the pollen of flower i at iteration t and b_* represents the best solution among all current candidates. The parameter α serves as a scaling factor that regulates the step size of flight, while $L(\lambda)$ defines the Lévy flight step size, reflecting the intensity of pollination. Since insects can travel long distances with variable step lengths, the Lévy flight mechanism effectively models this behavior. $L > 0$ is drawn from a Lévy Distribution given by (6).

$$L \sim \frac{\lambda * \Gamma(\lambda) * sin(\pi\lambda/2)}{\pi} \frac{1}{s^{1+\lambda}} \; (s \gg s_0 > 0) \tag{6}$$

Here, $\Gamma(\lambda)$ represents the gamma function, and the distribution holds true for large step sizes However, generating pseudo-random step sizes that follow this distribution, as expressed in (6), is not straightforward. Among the available methods for producing such random numbers, the Mantegna algorithm is regarded as the most efficient. It determines the step size s using two Gaussian distributions U and V as below:

$$s = \frac{U}{|V|^{\frac{1}{\lambda}}} \tag{7}$$

$$U \sim N(0, \sigma^2), V \sim N(0, 1) \tag{8}$$

where, $U \sim N(0, \sigma^2)$ indicates that the samples are taken from a Gaussian (normal) distribution with a mean of zero and a variance of σ^2. The expression for the variance is provided in (9).

$$\sigma^2 = \left[\frac{\Gamma(1+\lambda)}{\lambda \Gamma((1+\lambda)/2)} \frac{sin(\frac{\pi\lambda}{2})}{2^{\frac{(\lambda-1)}{2}}} \right]^{\frac{1}{\lambda}} \tag{9}$$

For the local pollination, Rule 2 and 3 can be represented by (10):

$$f_i^{t+1} = f_i^t + \epsilon(f_j^t - f_k^t) \tag{10}$$

where f_j^t and f_k^t represent the pollens of different flowers belonging to the same plant, corresponding to flower constancy within a localized neighborhood. To summarize this section, pollination phenomenon in flowering plants, types of pollination process in flowers, and the FPA is described in-depth. From the literature, the design benchmarks denote that FPA is better in terms of performance with an exponential convergence rate. Thus, we use FPA as an optimization algorithm to solve the residential appliance scheduling problem.

4 Experimental Results and Analysis

The FPA's performance is verified through simulations carried out in MATLAB 2022b on a system featuring an Intel(R) Core(TM) i5 processor (1.19 GHz) operating on Windows 11. Due to unpredictable nature of RTP pricing scheme, it is very difficult to manage the residential load. Thus, we have incorporated TOU model for pricing that computes the consumer bill based on time of use of electricity.

4.1 Smart Meter Dataset

In this work, we have used Pecan Street dataport dataset, available in Pecan Street, Inc. [13], for the experimentation and discussion of the proposed model. The characteristic of the homes in the study and the general attributes of the residents in the Pecan Street are defined from data of resident surveys and energy audits. In our work, we have chosen the dataset of those households which has no missing values in their energy consumption. Every house is represented using a unique identifier which denotes the smart meter ID of that household. Two datasets are considered for the analysis of the FPA.

- **Town Home - Meter ID: 3687:** The smart meter id 3687 used in this study is a town home which represents a house that shares at least one boundary with neighbouring house. This house was constructed in 2012 with total 1401 sq. ft located in San Diego, California. The house consists of following appliances: water heater, clothes-washer, dryer, dishwasher, microwave oven, refrigerator, lights, fans, coffee-maker, blender, toaster, and electric gas.
- **Apartment Home - Meter ID: 8733:** The smart meter id 8733 used in this study represents an apartment home. This apartment is located in San Diego, California. It was built in the year 2012 with total space of 3189 sq. ft which comprises of first floor of 1492 sq. ft and second floor of 1697 sq. ft. The house consists of home appliances such as dishwasher, clothes-dryer, refrigerator, microwave oven, clothes-washer, lights, fans, coffee-maker, toaster, electric gas, and air conditioner.

4.2 Experimental Results on Dataset 1

The performance of FPA is evaluated with respect to appliance load consumption and electricity cost for dataset 1. To evaluate the FPA effectiveness in reducing overall electricity costs and peak load, its performance is analyzed in comparison to the unscheduled scenario.

Per Hour Load Comparison. Figure 2 illustrates the hourly power consumption of home appliances. The time slots between 11 and 14 represent high-pricing intervals, commonly referred to as peak load periods. The irregular usage of unscheduled appliances is the main contributor to increased electricity costs in the unscheduled scenario. As observed from Fig. 2, the proposed FPA outperforms the unscheduled load during peak hours by transferring it to off-peak periods.

Per Hour Cost Comparison. Figure 3 depicts the hourly electricity cost associated with the operation of household appliances. It is evident that during high-price intervals, the cost under the FPA scheme is considerably lower than in the unscheduled case. Thus, proposed scheme effectively minimizes the cost per hour for home appliances. For meter ID 3687, the total cost over a single day for unscheduled scenario and proposed FPA scheme is 100.37 cents and 77.41 cents, respectively. Thus, the proposed FPA achieves the cost reduction of home appliances by 22.87%.

4.3 Experimental Results on Dataset 2

The FPA's performance is assessed based on appliance load consumption and electricity cost using dataset 2. To evaluate the performance of the FPA in minimizing total electricity costs and peak load, it is compared with respect to an unscheduled scenario.

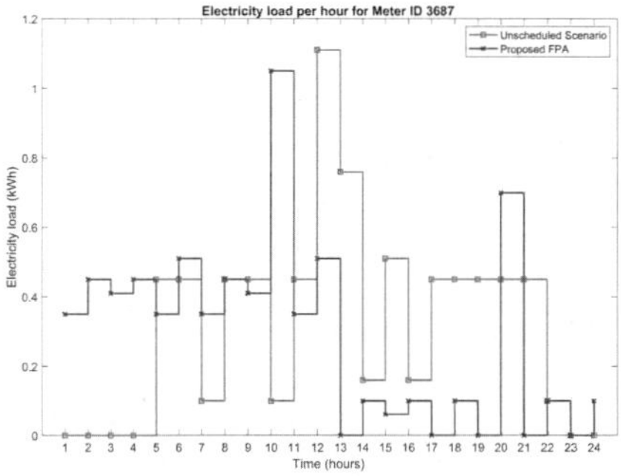

Fig. 2. Per hour load comparison of meter ID: 3687.

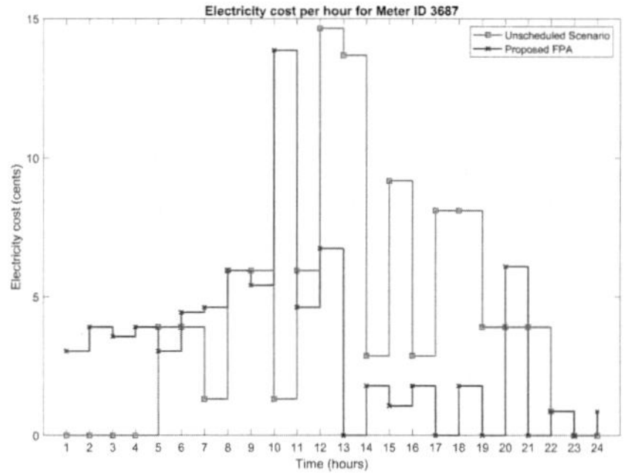

Fig. 3. Per hour cost comparison of meter ID: 3687.

Per Hour Load Comparison. As illustrated in Fig. 4, the performance of the FPA is measured based on the load consumption of household appliances. The results depict the hourly energy usage of home appliances throughout the day.

The FPA scheme is compared with unscheduled scenario for minimizing total electricity cost. The time slots 10 to 12 denote high pricing intervals where appliance load consumption is higher. From the Fig. 4, it is evident that the unscheduled appliance load during peak hours is minimized and shifted to off-peak hours.

Per Hour Cost Comparison. Figure 5 represents hourly electricity consumption cost of home appliances. It is noted that the FPA reduced the cost during high price intervals with respect to unscheduled case. Thus, FPA effectively minimizes the cost per hour for home appliances. For meter ID 8733, the total cost over a single day for unscheduled scenario and FPA scheme is 279.11 cents and 240.35 cents, respectively. Thus, FPA achieves cost reduction by 13.89%.

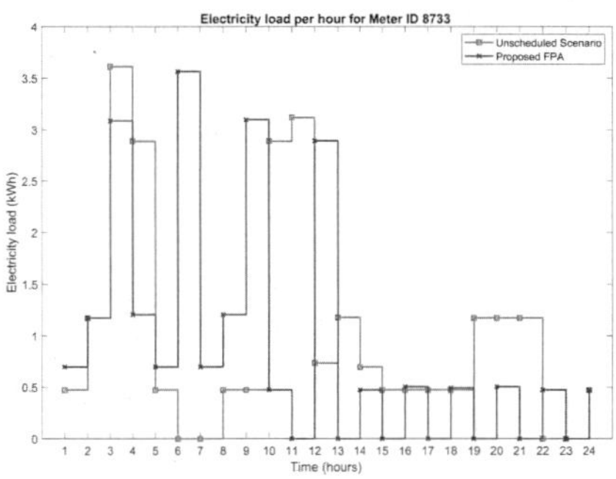

Fig. 4. Per hour load comparison of meter ID: 8733.

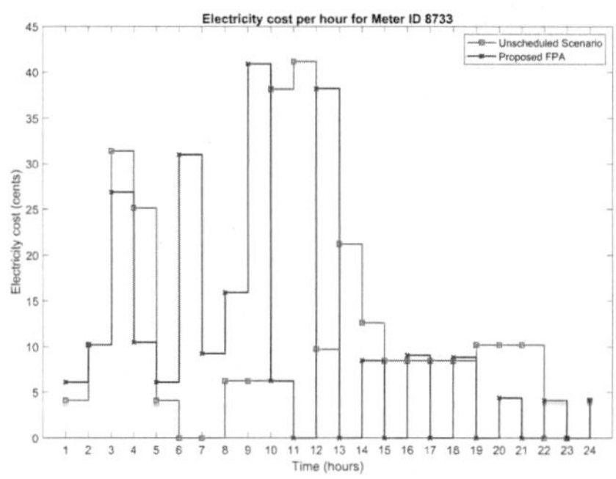

Fig. 5. Per hour cost comparison of meter ID: 8733.

4.4 Comparative Analysis of Total Cost and Monthly Bill

Figure 6 represents the comparison of total cost of FPA with respect to the unscheduled case. From the Figure, it is evident that cost is optimized using FPA. The average cost reduction achieved for 23 homes is 20.60%.

Table 1. Comparison of total cost of 23 homes

Meter ID	Type of Building	Unscheduled cost (cents)	FPA cost(cents)	Cost reduction
3687	Town Home	100.37	77.41	**22.87 %**
6377	Apartment	68.06	52.57	**22.76 %**
7062	Town Home	91.59	77.65	**15.20 %**
8574	Apartment	103.33	86.10	**16.66 %**
9213	Apartment	69.36	54.14	**21.92 %**
203	Single Family Home	59.79	40.90	**31.57 %**
1450	Town Home	277.59	179.36	**35.38 %**
1524	Single Family Home	13.32	10.29	**22.67 %**
2606	Town Home	56.32	40.12	**28.76 %**
3864	Town Home	43.36	32.25	**25.59 %**
7114	Town Home	229.02	143.52	**37.32 %**
1731	Town Home	154.49	124.36	**19.50 %**
4495	Apartment	57.88	55.38	**4.31 %**
8342	Town Home	248.83	215.98	**13.20 %**
3938	Apartment	134.92	130.65	**3.16 %**
5938	Town Home	83.94	73.16	**12.84 %**
8061	Town Home	428.59	322.80	**24.68 %**
9775	Apartment	183.82	165.92	**9.73 %**
4934	Town Home	36.08	26.41	**26.81 %**
8733	Apartment	279.11	240.34	**13.89 %**
9612	Town Home	212.68	162.88	**23.41 %**
9836	Town Home	560.44	466.73	**16.72 %**
6547	Town Home	141.68	106.34	**24.94 %**

Figure 7 shows monthly bill comparison of FPA with unscheduled case and Table 1 represents the empirical data of total cost obtained from simulations of 23 homes. For all smart meter IDs, it is observed that the FPA cost is reduced significantly in comparison to unscheduled case. The time complexity of FPA is $O(n * T)$ where n is population size and T is number of iterations/generations.

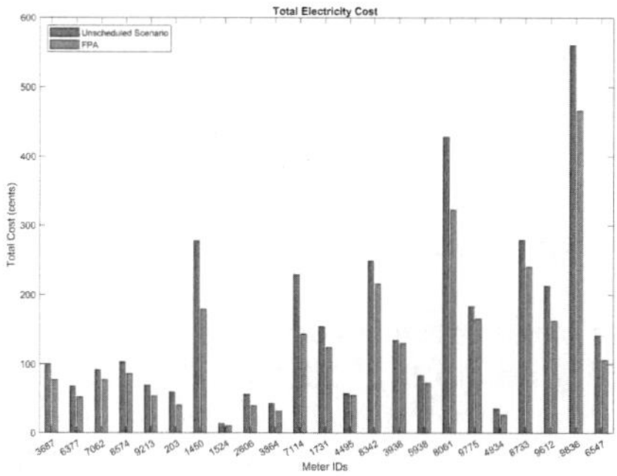

Fig. 6. Total cost comparison of 23 homes.

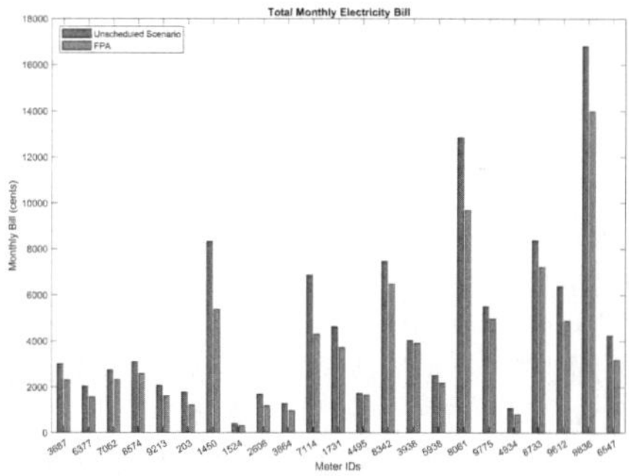

Fig. 7. Monthly bill comparison of 23 homes.

5 Conclusion

We have explored the meta-heuristic flower pollination algorithm for appliances scheduling in residential sector. The appliances are scheduled with the objective of electricity cost and peak load reductions. The proposed work reduces the peak hour load and per hour electricity cost in the high price ranges. This ultimately minimize the total electricity cost. In this work, the total electricity cost reduction of 20.60% is achieved. In the future extension of the paper, we wish to add few more parameters like consumer comfort, waiting time of appliances, temperature and seasonal changes, etc. The proposed algorithm can be compared with more recent hybrid meta-heuristic algorithms. Also, residential appliance scheduling problem can be extended to industrial appliance scheduling to deal with industries where very high loads are involved.

References

1. Eia, U.: Us energy information administration annual energy outlook 2020. US Department of Energy: Washington, DC, USA (2020)
2. Jindal, A., et al.: A heuristic-based appliance scheduling scheme for smart homes. IEEE Trans. Ind. Inform. **16**(5), 3242–3255 (2019)
3. Ogwumike, C., Short, M., Denai, M.: Near-optimal scheduling of residential smart home appliances using heuristic approach. In: 2015 IEEE International Conference on Industrial Technology (ICIT). IEEE (2015)
4. Ogwumike, C., Short, M.: Evaluation of a heuristic approach for efficient scheduling of residential smart home appliances. In: 2015 IEEE 15th International Conference on Environment and Electrical Engineering (EEEIC). IEEE (2015)
5. Yang, X.-S.: Flower pollination algorithm for global optimization. In: Durand-Lose, J., Jonoska, N. (eds.) UCNC 2012. LNCS, vol. 7445, pp. 240–249. Springer, Heidelberg (2012). https://doi.org/10.1007/978-3-642-32894-7_27
6. Willmer, P.: Pollination and floral ecology. Pollination and floral ecology. Princeton University Press (2011)

7. Flower pollination. http://biology.tutorvista.com/animal-kingdom. Accessed July 2020
8. Glover, B.: Understanding Flowers and Flowering: An Integrated Approach. Oxford University Press, Oxford (2007)
9. Walker, M.: How flowers conquered the world. BBC Earth News **10** (2009)
10. Waser, N.M.: Flower constancy: definition, cause, and measurement. Am. Nat. **127**(5), 593–603 (1986)
11. Yang, X.-S., Karamanoglu, M., He, X.: Flower pollination algorithm: a novel approach for multiobjective optimization. Eng. Optim. **46**(9), 1222–1237 (2014)
12. Floudas, C.A., et al.: Handbook of Test Problems in Local and Global Optimization, vol. 33. Springer, New York (2013). https://doi.org/10.1007/978-1-4757-3040-1
13. Pecan Street Dataport Dataset. https://dataport.pecanstreet.org/~academic. Accessed July 2019
14. Ogwumike, C., Short, M., Abugchem, F.: Heuristic optimization of consumer electricity costs using a generic cost model. Energies **9**(1), 6 (2015)
15. Misra, S., et al.: Residential energy management in smart grid: a Markov decision process-based approach.". In: IEEE International Conference on Green Computing and Communications and IEEE Internet of things and IEEE Cyber, Physical and Social Computing. IEEE (2013)
16. Matallanas, E., et al.: Neural network controller for active demand-side management with PV energy in the residential sector. Appl. Energy **91**(1), 90–97 (2012)
17. Lee, J., et al.: Energy consumption scheduler for demand response systems in the smart grid. J. Inf. Sci. Eng. **28**(5) (2012)

A Cost Effective Solution to Appliance Scheduling Using Genetic Algorithm with Precedence Preservation

Amit Shewale[1(✉)], Anil Mokhade[2], Amruta Lipare[3], and Chirag Modi[4]

[1] Department of CSE, IIIT Nagpur, Nagpur, India
ashewale@iiitn.ac.in

[2] Department of CSE, VNIT Nagpur, Nagpur, India
asmokhade@cse.vnit.ac.in

[3] Kelley School of Business, Indiana University, Indiana, USA

[4] Department of CSE, NIT Goa, Goa, India
cnmodi@nitgoa.ac.in

Abstract. The rapid increase in the global population has led to a growing imbalance between electricity demand and supply. The existing power grid is insufficient to meet this escalating demand. To address these challenges, the smart grid has emerged as an effective solution. By integrating Information and Communication Technology (ICT), smart grids have significantly improved the traditional power systems to manage rising energy requirements. One of the key approaches in this context is Demand-Side Management (DSM), which focuses on optimizing energy usage from the consumer's perspective. DSM systems are extensively employed to help end users efficiently manage and control their electrical appliances and overall energy load. In this work, residential appliance scheduling problem is identified for the study. We have proposed a Genetic Algorithm using Precedence Preservation CROSS-over (GA-PPX) operator. For this, a novel crossover called precedence preservation order is used. In GA-PPX, the selection of chromosomes is carried out using roulette-wheel selection and crossover used is the precedence preservation crossover, by which we can create two off-springs, following alternative rule of 1 and 2. The solution is represented as the appliance status (0/1). The significance of precedence preservation crossover is proved with respect to other crossovers used for GA. The proposed GA-PPX algorithm was evaluated across different load profiles under time-of-use (TOU) pricing to assess its performance. The experimental results demonstrate that the algorithm outperforms other metaheuristic approaches. The proposed algorithm optimizes the electricity cost by 20.41%, 10.92%, 5.94% as compared to the unscheduled scenario, HSA and EWA, respectively. In addition, PAR is reduced by 78%, 58.68% and 53.08%, as compared to the unscheduled scenario, HSA and EWA, respectively.

Keywords: smart grid · electricity cost · genetic algorithm · energy management · crossover

G. K. Verma et al. (Eds.): MIND 2025, CCIS 2981, pp. 87–98, 2027.
https://doi.org/10.1007/978-3-032-31230-3_8

1 Introduction

Energy is a critical resource in today's world and must be utilized efficiently to maintain equilibrium between supply and demand. Inefficient energy management can lead to shortages and result in power outages in residential areas. Such imbalances may disrupt the normal operation of the power grid, whose primary role is to ensure the smooth transmission of electricity from control centers to end users. The energy sector comprises various participants, including residential, industrial, and commercial consumers, along with generation, transmission, and distribution units. This paper emphasizes the residential sector, focusing specifically on load scheduling strategies for household energy consumption

Energy consumption in the residential sector has risen significantly and is expected to continue increasing in the coming years. According to projections by the U.S. Energy Information Administration (EIA), residential energy use is anticipated to grow by 50% between 2020 and 2050 [1]. To cope with this growing demand, electricity providers must expand and strengthen their infrastructure to ensure reliable supply. DSM and DR strategies offer effective solutions to help reduce energy consumption and costs. Through these approaches, consumers can adjust their energy usage patterns in response to dynamic pricing signals issued by utility providers. Moreover, the consumers are encouraged to participate in demand response programs in response to dynamic pricing signals and monetary incentives. They are useful in reducing the total cost of electricity, PAR and balancing of demand and supply. Therefore, efficient management of household resources is essential to reduce overall energy consumption. Considering the above points, we have focused on development of residential load scheduling techniques with cost, PAR, peak load and energy consumption as objectives. The main focus of this paper is on optimizing energy management in smart homes by efficiently scheduling household appliances to achieve better energy utilization and cost efficiency.

The scheduling of home appliances at suitable periods without violating consumer constraints is referred to as residential appliance-scheduling problem. It is assumed that consumers provide their appliance operation schedules and the duration of usage prior to the scheduling process. The mathematical formulations for calculating energy consumption, electricity cost, peak demand, and the peak-to-average ratio in residential appliance scheduling are presented as follows:

- **Electricity consumption**: Home appliances use electrical energy while operating as per their schedule, and this energy refers to the amount of power consumed by the appliance over a specific period of time. The electricity consumption by the appliance is measured in terms of kWh and is given by (1):

$$E_n^t = P_n \times S_n^t \tag{1}$$

where E_n^t is the energy consumption of an appliance n at timeslot t. P_n and S_n^t are the power rating and status of an appliance (ON/OFF), respectively.

Total amount of electricity used by all connected appliances and devices within the smart home is calculated by the following equation (2)

$$E_n^A = \sum_{t=1}^{T} \left(\sum_{n=1}^{N} E_n^t \right) \tag{2}$$

where, E_n^A is the total amount of electricity used by all connected appliances and devices within the home, n is number of appliances that varies from 1 to N and time slot t from 1 to T.

- **Minimization of electricity cost**: The electricity cost for a smart home is defined as the bill paid to the service provider by the service provider for the utilized energy per unit time and price. In this study, Time of use scheme is employed, as electricity consumption tends to be higher during peak hours when pricing rates are elevated. The total cost of electricity for all the appliances in a day is given by (3).

$$\sum_{t=1}^{24} \sum_{n=1}^{N} (P_n \times S_n^t \times \beta_t) \tag{3}$$

where, n are no. of appliances that ranges from 1 to N, P_n is the power-rating of the appliance, S_n^t denotes status of appliance, 0 represents OFF status, 1 represents ON status. β_t is the price of electricity at the hour t taken from real time datasets. t varies from 1 to T; We have assumed one day scheduling period which is divided into 24 h slots. Thus, $t \in T, \forall\ T = 1, 2, \cdots, 24$.
The objective function for electricity cost minimization is: (4).

$$\text{minimize} \sum_{t=1}^{24} \sum_{n=1}^{N} (P_n \times S_n^t \times \beta_t) \tag{4}$$

- **Minimization of Peak-to-Average Ratio**: PAR is defined as the ratio of peak load to average load consumed by the appliances over a given day. PAR reduction is important for both utility providers and consumers for the proper management of smart appliances. It reduces the peak load demand and also helps in reducing the operational time of power plants and backup generators. PAR ratio is calculated by (5).

$$PAR = \frac{Load_{peak}}{Load_{avg}} \tag{5}$$

where $Load_{peak}$ is the highest consumed load by the appliances in a home in one hour, $Load_{avg}$ is daily average load consumed by home appliances.
In this work, a nature inspired meta-heuristic algorithm - genetic algorithm is proposed for residential appliance scheduling problem. A novel crossover called precedence preservation crossover (PPX) operator is introduced for creation of new off-springs. The objectives achieved in this work are electricity cost minimization, peak load reduction.

2 Literature Survey

The classical optimization techniques are computationally expensive to solve high scale and complex problems. To address these issues, heuristic techniques are good alternatives to the classical techniques. These techniques depend on high level procedure for searching the solutions which results in a less computational cost than classical optimization techniques. Heuristic techniques often divide the problem into various sub-problems and find approximate solutions for each sub-problem. These approaches are knowledge based approaches to find solution to an optimization problem based on the specific rules.

Jindal et al. [2] proposed a heuristic approach for appliance scheduling. Authors divided scheduling problem into multiple sub-problems of different time slots. Heuristic solutions are designed for each sub-problem. The proposed approach manages the load requirements of the home and creates balance between demand and supply. The proposed heuristic approach helps in determining the optimal appliance schedule. In [3,4], authors have proposed and partially evaluated a heuristic approach for scheduling the residential appliances. The greedy processing approach is used for scheduling of home appliances. The objective of the proposed approach is to minimize cost with a set of constraints over the appliances. The simulation results indicated that the achieved cost was within 5% of the exact algorithm.

A heuristic scheduling algorithm for residential home intelligent decision support system (IDSS) is presented in [9]. The heuristic approach achieves the objective of scheduling appliances to minimize electricity cost. The results show that the gap between achieved and actual costs is negligible. A residential energy management mechanism using markov decision process (MDP) is proposed in [10] to achieve the objective of minimizing the energy expenses of consumers. The dynamic pricing mechanism is followed to fulfill the energy demand. The results show that expenses for the consumers are reduced. Matallanas et al. [11] described an artificial neural network (ANN) control system for active demand-side management (ADSM). The control system achieves the objective of scheduling of appliances by maximizing the local generation and enhancing the local energy performance. Lee et al. [12] proposed backtracking-based power scheduling scheme for smart grid homes. The authors have designed a scheduler which helps in reducing the peak load. The proposed model considers homes where the number of appliances are less than ten. The results show that the proposed method reduces the peak load up to 23.1%.

3 Background of Genetic Algorithm

The Genetic Algorithm (GA) is an optimization and search method inspired from the natural genetics and evolutionary processes driven by natural selection. It was first introduced by John Holland in 1975 and later elaborated upon by Whitley [5]. The Genetic Algorithm (GA) is primarily employed to tackle optimization problems, with solutions represented in binary form (0 and 1).

GA proves highly effective in addressing complex and large-scale problems due to its fast convergence and strong global search capability. Unlike conventional optimization techniques that operate on a single solution point at a time, GA simultaneously works with a population of potential solutions, enhancing the likelihood of reaching an optimal result. The GA process consists of three key phases: random initialization of potential solutions, evaluation of their fitness, and finally, generation of a new population through reproduction based on the best-performing individuals. The steps in genetic algorithm are given by Fig. 1.

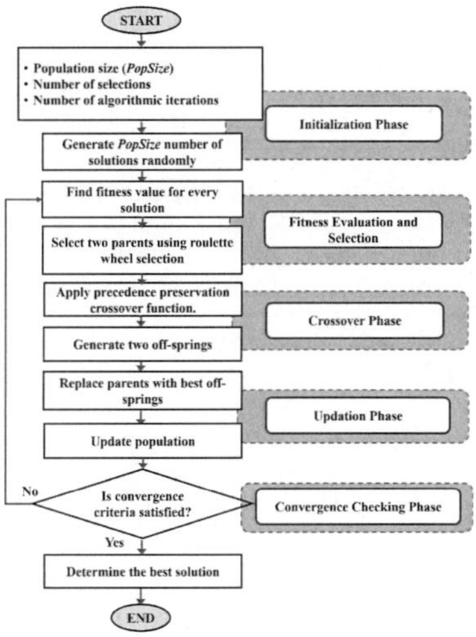

Fig. 1. Genetic algorithm representation.

In the initial step, a random population comprising candidate solutions (chromosomes) is generated. For the appliance scheduling problem, the GA begins its search using a set of randomly initialized binary chromosomes (1 s and 0 s), where each bit represents the operating state of a household appliance—with 1 indicating ON and 0 being OFF. The length of each chromosome corresponds to the total number of household appliances being considered in the system. We assume the 24 h time slots for scheduling the appliances. A randomly generated population (or set of solutions) for a given time interval represents the operating status of each appliance, as illustrated in Fig. 2. If the appliance is operating for 6 h a day, then status of appliance is represented randomly by 1 in any of the 6 h of the day. In this way, the initial population solutions are generated randomly.

In the subsequent step, the fitness of each randomly generated solution is assessed using a cost optimization function. For instance, if a chromosome (where m represents the total number of appliances) is given as [1 0 1 0 1], it indicates that appliances 1, 3, and 5 are ON. The total power consumption is then computed and multiplied by the electricity price to determine the corresponding energy cost. This evaluation process continues for the entire population to

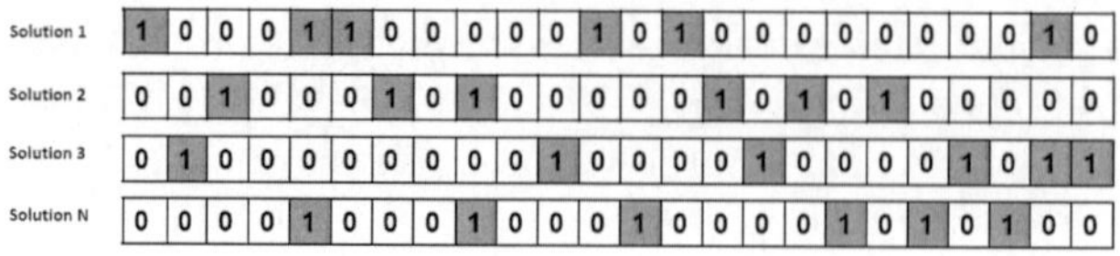

Fig. 2. Solution representation in genetic algorithm.

determine the most efficient solutions. As a result, an optimal operating pattern of home appliances is obtained for a given time slot t, particularly when electricity prices are lower. In the following phase, chromosomes with higher fitness values are selected as parents to undergo crossover, generating new offspring for the next generation. In this work, we use roulette-wheel selection criteria. It is a popular selection method used in GA. In this selection, the roulette wheel is spun n times and the individuals with higher fitness values are chosen. The selected solutions are called as parents which then undergo crossover operation to produce new off-springs.

4 Crossover Operators

Crossover serves as a recombination operator and is carried out in three main steps. First, the reproduction operator randomly selects a pair of parent strings for mating. Next, a crossover point is chosen at random along the length of the strings, after which the values beyond this point are exchanged between the two parents. For example, if the selected parent strings are $A = 11111$ and $B = 00000$, and the random crossover point occurs at position two, the resulting offspring after crossover are $A^* = 11000$ and $B^* = 00111$—a process known as two-point crossover. Although these operators appear straightforward, their combined effect is what gives the Genetic Algorithm (GA) its remarkable efficiency and adaptability. In this section, we further explore a novel precedence-preserving crossover operator that enhances this process.

4.1 Precedence Preservation Crossover (PPX)

The Precedence Preservation Crossover (PPX) was independently proposed by Blanton and Wainwright [6] for vehicle routing problems, and by Bierwirth et al. [7] for scheduling problems. This operator preserves the precedence relationships of operations from both parent permutations in the offspring at an equal rate, ensuring that no additional precedence relationships are introduced during the process. The steps of precedence preservation crossover are given below:

Let P_1 and P_2 represent the parent chromosomes each with length L. Generate a vector V of length L randomly populated with elements from the set $\{1,2\}$. This vector determines the sequence in which genes are successfully drawn from P_1 and P_2 as described below:

1. We traverse the vector V from left to right.

2. Let the current position in the vector V be i (where $i = 1, 2, \ldots, L$).
3. Let j (where $j = 1, 2, \ldots, L$) and k (where $k = 1, 2, \ldots, L$) denotes the jth and k^{th} gene of P_1 and P_2, respectively.
4. *If* i^{th} value is 1 then
   Delete j^{th} gene value from P_1 and from P_2 & append to the off-spring.
5. *else*
   Delete k^{th} gene value from P_2 and from P_1 & append to the off-spring.
6. Repeat Step 2 till P_1 and P_2 are empty & the off-spring has all gene values.

The example of precedence preservation crossover is illustrated in Fig. 3 and Fig. 4. The vector is represented by randomly filled elements of set {1, 2}. In Fig. 3, the first bit of vector is 2. Hence, second parent i.e. parent 2 is selected and the first bit of second parent i.e. 0 is reflected in off-spring 1 and same is deleted from parent 1. The red coloured highlighted 0 indicates that it's been appended to the off-spring 1. Similarly, the second element in vector is 1 meaning first parent is selected and first bit of parent 1 is appended to off-spring 1 and same is deleted from parent 2. The highlighted blue colour shows the crossover operation. In next step, the element in the vector is 2 means parent 2 is chosen and the subsequent bit i.e. 1 is appended to off-spring 1 and the same is deleted from parent 1. The yellow colour highlighted 1 shows the operation. This process continues till both parent strings are empty and the offspring fully involves all the corresponding bits.

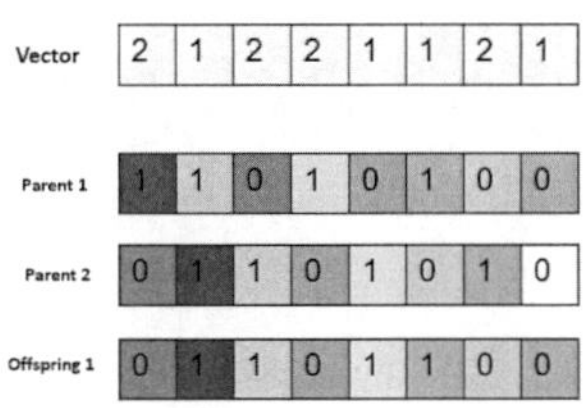

Fig. 3. Formation of Off-spring 1. (Color figure online)

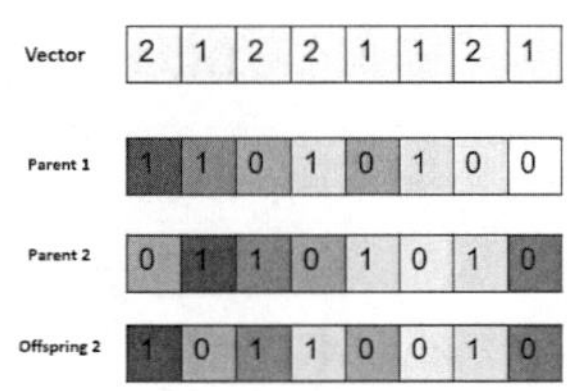

Fig. 4. Formation of Off-spring 2. (Color figure online)

Similarly, in case of formation of off-spring 2, the crossover operator chooses the opposite parent. For ex. as shown in Fig. 4, the first bit of vector is 2. It means we have to select parent 1 instead of parent 2 and first bit of parent 1 is appended to off-spring 2 and the same bit is deleted from parent 2. The blue highlighted colour indicates the crossover operation. In next step, the vector element is 1 meaning parent 2 is selected and the first bit of parent 2 is appended to off-spring 2 & same bit 0 is deleted from parent 1. The brown colored cell indicates the operation. Further, the next element in vector is 2, i.e., parent 1 is selected and remaining leftmost bit is appended to off-spring 2 and same bit 1 in parent 2 is deleted. This operation continue till both parent chromosomes are empty.

For the problem of residential appliance scheduling, Fig. 5 shows the off-springs generation based on the ON/OFF status of the appliances over 24 h period using precedence preservation crossover.

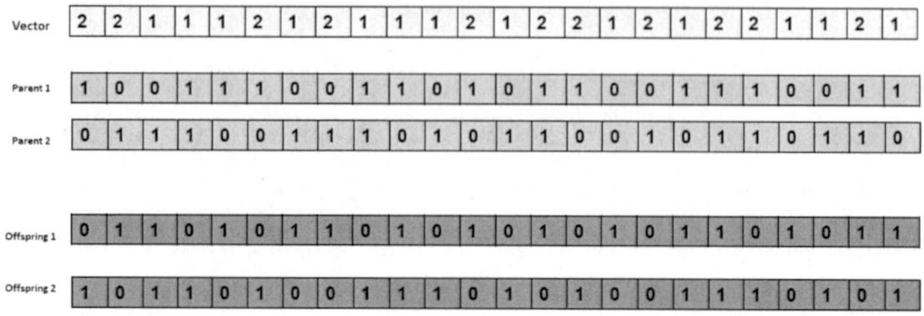

Fig. 5. Formation of off-spring for scheduling problem

4.2 Illustration of GA-PPX with Example

To have a better understanding of GA-PPX technique, we have illustrated it with following example. As Table 1 indicates, four shiftable appliances are taken for scheduling namely electric kettle, vacuum cleaner, dishwasher, clothes dryer. The day is divided into 24 h time slots. Power ratings and time durations of each appliance are given below:

Table 1. Appliances information

Appliances	Rating (kWh)	LOT (hrs)
Electric-kettle	5	4
Vacuum-cleaner	1	6
Dish-washer	2	5
Clothes-dryer	4	7

The ON/OFF status is indicated by 1/0. One indicates the appliance is ON and zero indicates the appliance is OFF. For ex. status of vacuum cleaner at hour no. 4 is ON. Figure 6 shows the initial-appliance schedule as per consumer based on his/her preference and behavioural pattern.

For simplicity, we have considered four smart home appliances in this example. It can be extended to multiple appliances also. After applying GA-PPX, the final appliance schedule is given in Fig. 7. From the Figure, it is evident that most of the appliances resulted in off-peak scheduling. Hence, appliances are rescheduled from peak to off-peak hours. This approach benefits the main grid or utility by reducing load during high-demand periods, thereby enhancing overall grid stability and operational efficiency.

Timeslots Appliance status	1	2	3	4	5	6	7	8	9	10	11	12	13	14	15	16	17	18	19	20	21	22	23	24
Electric Kettle	0	0	0	0	0	1	0	0	1	0	0	1	0	1	0	0	0	0	0	0	0	0	0	0
Vacuum Cleaner	0	0	0	1	0	0	0	0	1	1	1	1	0	0	0	0	1	0	0	0	0	0	0	0
Dishwasher	0	0	0	0	0	0	0	0	0	1	1	0	0	1	0	0	0	0	0	0	1	1	0	0
Clothes Dryer	0	0	0	1	1	1	0	0	0	1	1	0	0	1	1	0	0	0	0	0	0	0	0	0

Fig. 6. Initial appliance schedule.

Timeslots Appliance status	1	2	3	4	5	6	7	8	9	10	11	12	13	14	15	16	17	18	19	20	21	22	23	24
Electric Kettle	0	1	0	0	0	1	0	0	0	0	0	0	0	0	0	0	0	0	0	0	1	0	1	0
Vacuum Cleaner	0	0	0	0	0	1	0	0	0	0	1	0	0	0	0	0	1	0	1	0	0	1	1	0
Dishwasher	0	0	0	0	0	0	0	0	0	0	0	0	0	0	0	0	0	1	0	1	1	1	1	0
Clothes Dryer	1	1	0	1	0	1	0	0	0	0	0	1	0	0	0	0	0	0	1	0	0	1	0	0

Fig. 7. Final appliance schedule.

5 Experimental Results and Analysis

The performance of GA-PPX is validated through simulations in MATLAB 2022b on an Intel(R) Core(TM) i5 1.19 GHz CPU running Windows 11. Due to unpredictable nature of RTP pricing scheme, it is very difficult to manage the residential load. Thus, we have incorporated TOU model for pricing that computes the consumer bill based on time of use of electricity.

5.1 Smart Meter Dataset

In this work, we have used Pecan Street dataport dataset, available in Pecan Street, Inc. [8], for the experimentation and discussion of the proposed model. Every house is represented using a unique identifier which denotes the smart meter ID of that household as depicted below:

- **Town Home - Meter ID: 5938:** The smart meter id 5938 used in this study is a town home. This house was constructed in 2013 with total 1464 sq. ft. located in San Diego, California. The house consists of following appliances: air conditioner, clothes-washer, dishwasher, blender, electric gas, coffee-maker, lights, fans, oven, refrigerator.

5.2 Per Hour Load and Cost Comparison for Meter ID: 5938

Figure 8 illustrates the hourly electricity consumption for both the unscheduled case and the GA-PPX–optimized scenario. As per observation, the unscheduled load is significantly higher during peak hours. However, after implementing the GA-PPX scheduling, the peak-hour load is effectively reduced and redistributed to off-peak periods, leading to a more balanced energy usage pattern The energy consumption during (14 → 20) hours is maximum in unscheduled scenario while consumption during that period using GA-PPX is comparatively very less. During off-peak and mid-peak hours (1 → 12) and (20 → 24), GA-PPX algorithm schedules most of the appliances for low electricity bill and does not turn on the appliances during the high peak hours.

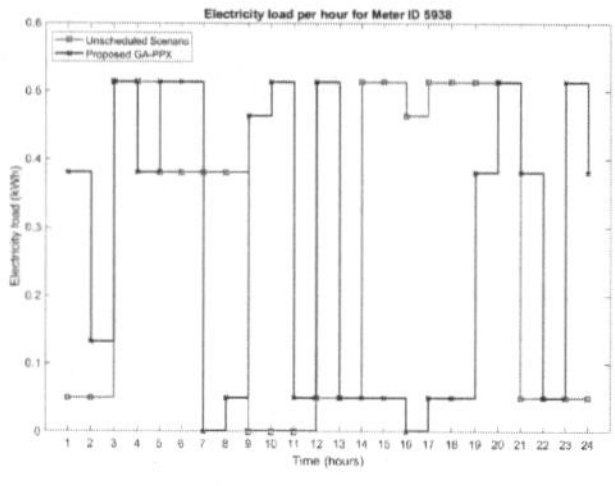

Fig. 8. Per hour load comparison for Smart meter ID: 5938.

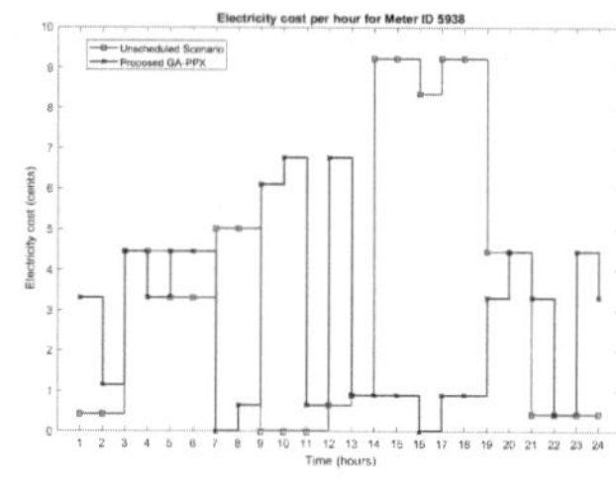

Fig. 9. Per hour cost comparison for Smart meter ID: 5938.

The hourly cost consumption for GA-PPX and unscheduled scenario is given in Fig. 9. From the Figure, it is clearly noted that the consumption is shifted from peak to non-peak hours using GA-PPX. For meter ID: 5938, the total cost over a day is 83.94 cents and 65.91 cents for unscheduled case and GA-PPX, respectively. Thus, GA-PPX achieve the cost reduction of 21.47%. In conclusion, we can say that the scheduling of the appliances is done when pricing rate is minimum. It further helps in maintaining a balanced and uniform energy consumption profile within the household. It was observed that the GA-PPX algorithm effectively reduces overall energy consumption by optimally scheduling appliances within smart homes.

5.3 Total Cost and PAR Comparison with Existing Algorithms

Total electricity cost over a day is given by Fig. 10. It depicts the comparison of total cost of GA-PPX with respect to the unscheduled scenario. From the Figure, it is clearly seen the cost is optimized for GA-PPX. The average cost reduction achieved for the total data is 24.49%.

The performance of GA-PPX is compared with unscheduled case and existing meta-heuristic algorithms. The algorithms used for comparison are harmony search algorithm (HSA) and earthworm optimization algorithm (EWA). HSA is recently developed meta-heuristic algorithm. HSA mimics the behaviour of musician producing perfect harmony. EWA is optimization algorithm inspired by reproduction conduct of earthworms. Every earthworm has ability to produce off-springs. Figure 11 shows the cost comparison between GA-PPX and unscheduled case, HSA and EWA. The results prove that GA-PPX optimizes the total cost by 20.41%, 10.92%, 5.94% as compared to unscheduled case, HSA

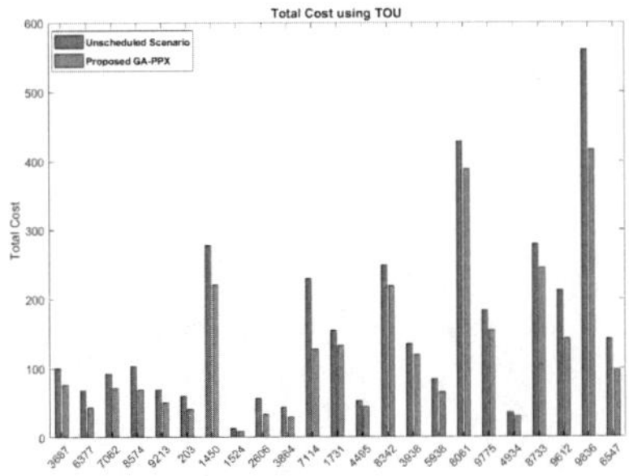

Fig. 10. Total cost comparison for multiple homes.

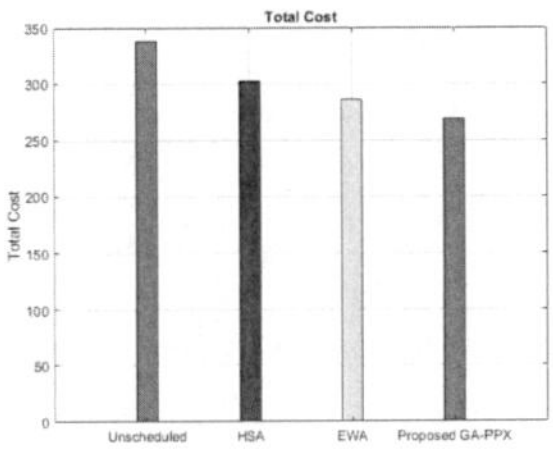

Fig. 11. Total cost comparison with existing algorithms.

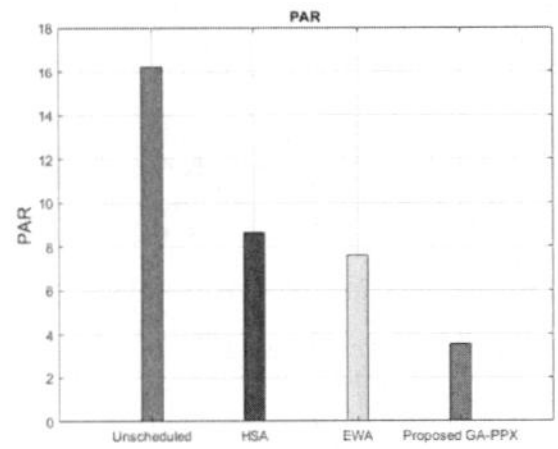

Fig. 12. PAR comparison with existing algorithms.

ans EWA, respectively. Similarly, Fig. 12 shows the PAR comparison between the proposed and existing algorithms. The PAR values obtained for unscheduled case, HSA, EWA and GA-PPX are 16.22, 8.64, 7.61, 3.57, respectively. The GA-PPX achieves PAR reduction of 78%, 58.68% and 53.08%, respectively.

6 Conclusion

We have explored the genetic algorithm with novel crossover operator for appliances scheduling in residential sector. The appliances are scheduled with the primary goal of reducing electricity costs and peak load demand on the power grid. The proposed work reduces the peak hour load and per hour electricity cost in the high price ranges. The proposed approach optimizes the household energy consumption behavior and helps in reducing the total cost. The total electricity cost reduction of 24.49% is achieved. In the future extension of the work, we wish to extend the same problem to industrial appliances loads. Also, it can be extended to complex pricing schemes such as real time pricing. The proposed algorithm can be implemented on different load profiles located in various geographical locations. Also, the appliance scheduling problem can be discussed over few more parameters such as consumer comfort, temperature, waiting time of the appliances.

References

1. Eia, U.: Us energy information administration annual energy outlook 2020. US Department of Energy: Washington, DC, USA (2020)
2. Jindal, A., et al.: A heuristic-based appliance scheduling scheme for smart homes. IEEE Trans. Ind. Inform. **16**(5), 3242–3255 (2019)
3. Ogwumike, C., Short, M., Denai, M.: Near-optimal scheduling of residential smart home appliances using heuristic approach. In: 2015 IEEE International Conference on Industrial Technology (ICIT). IEEE (2015)
4. Ogwumike, C., Short, M.: Evaluation of a heuristic approach for efficient scheduling of residential smart home appliances. In: 2015 IEEE 15th International Conference on Environment and Electrical Engineering (EEEIC). IEEE (2015)
5. Whitley, D.: A genetic algorithm tutorial. Stat. Comput. **4**(2), 65–85 (1994)
6. Blanton Jr., J.L., Wainwright, R.L.: Multiple vehicle routing with time and capacity constraints using genetic algorithms. In: Proceedings of the 5th International Conference on Genetic Algorithms (1993)
7. Bierwirth, C.: A generalized permutation approach to job shop scheduling with genetic algorithms. Oper.-Res.-Spektrum **17**(2), 87–92 (1995)
8. Pecan Street Dataport Dataset. https://dataport.pecanstreet.org/~academic. Accessed July 2019
9. Ogwumike, C., Short, M., Abugchem, F.: Heuristic optimization of consumer electricity costs using a generic cost model. Energies **9**(1), 6 (2015)
10. Misra, S., et al.: Residential energy management in smart grid: a Markov decision process-based approach. In: 2013 IEEE International Conference on Green Computing and Communications and IEEE Internet of things and IEEE Cyber, Physical and Social Computing. IEEE (2013)
11. Matallanas, E., et al.: Neural network controller for active demand-side management with PV energy in the residential sector. Appl. Energy **91**(1), 90–97 (2012)
12. Lee, J., et al.: Energy consumption scheduler for demand response systems in the smart grid. J. Inf. Sci. Eng. **28**(5) (2012)

Precision Crop Monitoring with YOLOv9: A Deep Learning Approach for Detecting Marigold Plant Growth and Health

K. R. Bhavya(✉), Renuka Patil, D. M. Deepak, and S. R. Sylaja Valle Narayan

Department of Computer Science and Engineering, GITAM School of Technology, GITAM University, Bengaluru, India
{bkrishna2,rherakal,dmanjuna,sretnaba}@gitam.edu

Abstract. This study presents a precision crop monitoring system for Yellow Marigold that integrates advanced object-detection models (YOLOv8 and YOLOv9) with IoT sensor data to detect and classify plant growth stages and health conditions in real time. The system categorizes marigold plants into five phenological stages—Bud, Early Flower, Mid-Growth, Pre-Mature, and Mature—and two health states: Healthy and Diseased. Images were collected in the field at GITAM University (Bengaluru) and augmented to improve model generalization. YOLOv9 extends YOLOv8 by introducing Programmable Gradient Information (PGI) and the Generalized Efficient Layer Aggregation Network (GELAN), which enhance the detection of fine-grained features and improve multi-scale robustness. We report detailed metrics (precision, recall, F1-score, mAP) and provide a comparative analysis of YOLOv8 and YOLOv9, together with a discussion of dataset design, augmentation strategy, IoT sensor integration, deployment considerations, and limitations. The system backend is implemented in Python and exposed through a Streamlit frontend for farmer-friendly visualization and alerts. Results indicate that YOLOv9 offers improved detection accuracy and inference speed in our dataset and that IoT contextual data enhances the interpretability of visual predictions for precision agriculture.

Keywords: Precision agriculture · Crop monitoring · YOLOv9 · object detection · marigold · IoT · Streamlet · PGI · GELAN. Image Processing

1 Introduction

Precision agriculture has established itself as a key approach to enhancing crop productivity, optimizing resource utilization, and promoting sustainable practices in farming. The increasing access to digital technologies has enabled the integration of artificial intelligence (AI), computer vision, and Internet of Things (IoT) systems, transforming how agriculture is monitored. Manual crop observation can be labor-intensive, subjective, and inconsistent for the rapid detection of diseases, nutrient deficiencies, and growth discrepancies. There is a growing need for real-time, automated, scalable, and data-driven frameworks that will provide high-precision insights regarding crops.

G. K. Verma et al. (Eds.): MIND 2025, CCIS 2981, pp. 99–113, 2027.
https://doi.org/10.1007/978-3-032-31230-3_9

Recent developments in machine learning (ML) and deep learning (DL) appear promising for assisting with automated agricultural solutions. S. N. et al. [1] used a hybrid plant disease detection framework that uses Convolutional Neural Networks (CNNs) with existing ML classifiers, which improved feature extraction and classification rates. At the same time, Hiremani et al. [2] conducted a review of federated learning frameworks for crop yield prediction, highlighting the security and decentralized aspects of AI for agricultural data analysis. These sources of literature support the notion that applying AI methods can further support and enhance decision-making and operational efficiency in precision agriculture. Regarding deep learning-based models, the YOLO (You Only Look Once) architecture has proven to be highly effective for efficient, real-time image analysis in agriculture. Precision agriculture has become a prominent approach for enhancing crop productivity, improving resource use efficiency, and promoting sustainable agricultural practices.

Recent advancements in AIML have shown promising results in agricultural automation. A hybrid framework for plant disease detection, where Convolutional Neural Networks (CNNs) combined with conventional ML classifiers yielded improved feature extraction and classification accuracy than the other methods [1]. Similarly, some federated learning frameworks for predicting crop yields and how these frameworks can be used to analyze agricultural data in a decentralized manner [2]. Overall, both articles illustrate the potential value of artificial intelligence identification tools, while also supporting agricultural decision-making and operational efficiencies in precision agriculture. PestLite, a lightweight pest detection model based on YOLOv5, which incorporates Multi-Level Spatial Pyramid Pooling (MLSP) and ECA attention mechanisms, enabling it to achieve better performance due to its lower complexity [3]. Likewise, a model based on estimating crop and weed density(s) using YOLOv8, which could serve to establish a territories-based, population mapping framework to establish better field management [4]. Improved YOLOv10n and YOLOv11n using the αSiLU activation function, which resulted in observed improvements in accuracy while maintaining a low computational cost [5]. Similarly, a curriculum learning approach, using YOLOv5 and YOLOv7, to classify the growth stages of pomegranate, achieving marked improvement in performance while demonstrating the adaptation of YOLO models to agricultural applications [6]. Despite significant advancements in agricultural technology, limited research has focused on real-field detection systems for ornamental crops such as *Yellow Marigold (Tagetes* spp.*)*, which are highly sensitive to environmental and physiological stress. Manual monitoring remains the predominant practice, leading to delayed disease identification and inconsistent growth assessments. To address this gap, this study proposes a field-deployable crop monitoring framework that integrates deep learning-based visual detection (YOLOv8 and YOLOv9) with IoT sensor data for contextual, real-time evaluation of plant health and growth stages. The primary contributions of this work include the development of a labeled, real-field image dataset of Yellow Marigold plants across five growth stages and two health conditions under natural lighting and environmental variability; a comparative analysis of YOLOv8 and YOLOv9 models with performance metrics such as precision, recall, F1-score, mean Average Precision (mAP), and inference time; and the integration of IoT sensor data—temperature, humidity, and soil moisture—through timestamp synchronization for multimodal contextual analysis. The study also discusses dataset limitations, potential biases, deployment challenges, and the adaptability of the proposed framework to other crop species. By combining deep learning with IoT-based sensing, the proposed system provides a scalable and intelligent solution for real-time crop monitoring, enabling early disease detection, efficient resource management, and data-driven decision-making in precision agriculture. The paper is organized as follows: Sect. 2 reviews related AI-based crop monitoring studies; Sect. 3 describes dataset collection, annotation, and preprocessing; Sect. 4 explains the proposed YOLOv9 methodology and training procedure; Sect. 5 presents the experimental setup, results, ablation study, and IoT integration; Sect. 6 discusses field validation and deployment considerations; and Sect. 7 concludes with key findings and future directions.

2 Literature Survey

In recent years, rapid advancements in agricultural science and technology have focused on enhancing crop productivity while ensuring sustainability and resilience under diverse environmental conditions. This literature review examines key studies that address plant physiological responses, greenhouse management, the integration of IoT-based sensing, AI-driven analytics, and climate adaptation strategies. The objective is to establish the theoretical foundation for linking technological innovation with existing research gaps, thereby supporting the development of efficient, scalable, and sustainable agricultural systems. A framework to integrate plant biomass and water deficit, which contributes to our knowledge about crops' interactions with the environment [7]. Specifically focus on greenhouse automation and an IoT-enabled framework to control for environment and energy while collecting digital sensor data aimed at sustainable agricultural production [8, 9]. Other identified contributions include the application of AI and machine learning in crop management. For example, radiation for estimating evapotranspiration, while the ecosystem benefits of greenhouse cultivation beyond increased yields [10, 11]. An Arduino-based automatic irrigation system that utilized soil moisture sensors to enhance irrigation water use and minimize the need for manual irrigation [12]. Similarly, review conducted by focusing on IoT-based smart agriculture systems and identified cooperation and reliability in the network as key challenges [13]. Some proposed studies, exploring the use of IoT in smart farming applications for hydroponic and vermiculture systems, where sensor-based monitoring of the growing environment and data-driven decision-making are emphasized [14]. Studies such as AI–IoT monitoring system to improve crop yield, demonstrating how the use of sensor data and a machine-learning model to classify growth dysbiosis can increase yields [15]. Meanwhile, how marigolds and salvias responded physiologically to four different light spectra through their study, which uncovered new information on environmental impacts on plant growth [16]. Focusing on ornamental crops, an IoT-based disease diagnosis tool for marigold leaves, equipped with real time imaging and alert systems [17]. However, the tool did not provide accuracy metrics or meaningful measurements on the farm. Although these studies lay the basic foundation for intelligent agricultural systems, all are limited due to small data sets, experimental issues in controlled farm settings, and overall lack of informative metrics and assessments of the quality of developed models or technology. CNN-based deep learning models that used image-based assessments of visual properties of fruit based on color or texture to predict the fruit's quality [18], and used a

Support Vector Machine classifiers or Random Forest classifiers to efficiently classify disease in apple leaves to assist in the management of the early effects of diseases on crops [19]. Although advancements have been made in AI-assisted farming, a clear gap remains in the literature on AI and agriculture, particularly in the collection of field-based images and the development of multi-stage datasets, as well as novel developments in deep learning architecture for crop monitoring. Existing systems often rely on controlled environments, reducing their generalizability to open-field conditions. Therefore, this study aims to bridge these gaps by providing model-level details, training protocols, IoT integration, and comprehensive evaluation metrics for real-world marigold monitoring under variable environmental conditions. The paper effectively sets research priorities but remains at a high level, offering limited implementation details or empirical validation, which points to a need for deeper, applied studies.

3 Dataset and Data Acquisition

3.1 Field Site and Period

The image dataset was captured using the span of January to April 2025 at the Orchid Garden, GITAM University, Bengaluru Campus, under open-field horticultural context. This timeline was selected to observe the complete Lifecyle of Yellow Marigold (Tagetes spp.), from bud emergence until full bloom and maturity stage, ensuring natural open-field variability to enhance deep learning analysis. Health plants as identified by uniform leaf color and intact flower structures, while diseased plants had some visible symptoms of common plant disease such as spots on leaves, discoloration, curling, or necrosis. Each label on the images was verified by a pair of domain experts for classification accuracy across the growth and health category levels.

3.2 Image Acquisition Setup

High-resolution images of Yellow Marigold plants were obtained manually with mobile phone cameras under natural daylight settings in standardized field conditions. Different angles and distances were captured dealing with variations in terms of lighting, shadows, background clutter, and occlusion, increasing the generalizability of the model to real-world applications. Each of the images were manually inspected for quality, and annotated in the image repository app called Roboflow, which helped with bounding box labeling and organization of the dataset and enhancement of annotated images. Each image was labeled with its growth stage category—Bud, Early Flower, Mid-Growth, Pre-Mature, and Mature—and its health status as Healthy or Diseased. Expert domain checkers also validated each label to ensure consistency and reliability. A total of 786 annotated images were exported in YOLO format for training, validation, and testing the models.

3.3 Dataset Description

In this research, a total of 786 annotated images of Yellow Marigold (Tagetes spp.) were obtained from the Orchid Garden, GITAM University, Bengaluru Campus and annotated using the Roboflow platform. The images included five growth stages—Bud (163), Early Flower (146), Mid-Growth (149), pre-mature (156), and Mature (176) stages—with the additional categories of Healthy and Diseased as in Table 1, Fig. 1. There was a slight class imbalance in the data because the early growth stages such, as Bud and Early Flower were fewer common photographs than more visually prominent mature stages. To address this, class-aware augmentation and balanced sampling strategies were applied during training. Annotation quality was ensured through a three-tier validation process involving initial labeling, expert verification by horticulturists, and consensus review for ambiguous samples, ensuring high reliability and consistency across all growth and health categories.

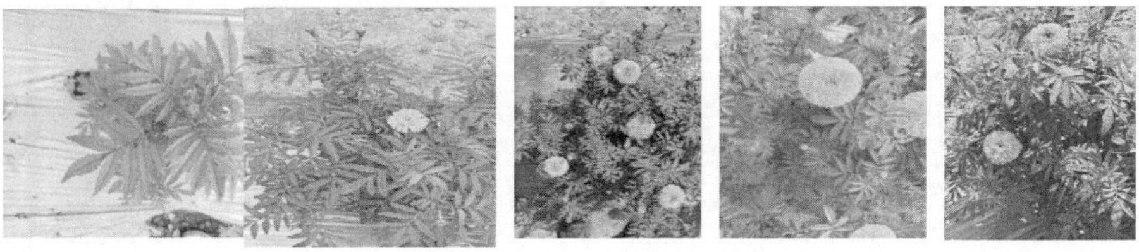

(a) Bud (b)Early (c) Mid-growth (d)Mature (e) Pre-mature

Fig. 1. Sample images of different stages

Table 1. Dataset Description

Stage	Bud	Early	Mid-Growth	Pre-Mature	Matute
No of Samples	163	146	149	156	176

3.4 Data Augmentation and Preprocessing

To bolster model robustness and mitigate the impact of class imbalance in the marigold dataset, a systematic data augmentation & preprocessing pipeline was created using the Roboflow platform. The main objective was to artificially increase the number of samples in the under-represented growth stages of Bud and Early Flower, while also incorporating variance which approximates natural environmental variability.

The initial class distribution was moderately imbalanced, with a maximum of 176 samples in the *Mature* stage and a minimum of 146 in the *Early Flower* stage. The imbalance ratio (RRR) was computed as:

$$R = \frac{N_{max}}{N_{min}} = \frac{176}{146} \sim 1.21 \tag{1}$$

where N_{max}, N_{min} represent the sample counts of the most and least frequent classes, respectively. Although this imbalance ratio was not severe, it was sufficient to bias model training toward overrepresented classes. To counter this, a class-aware augmentation approach was used, wherein augmentation was applied more frequently to minority classes.

The following transformations were applied dynamically during training to enrich the dataset:

1. Random horizontal flips and small rotations ($\pm 10°$) to simulate camera orientation changes.
2. Random scaling and translation to replicate variation in plant size and camera distance.
3. Brightness and contrast adjustment to account for different lighting conditions.
4. Color jitter and mild Gaussian blur to represent natural image noise and motion blur.

All images were resized to 640 × 640 pixels (the YOLO input requirement) and normalized to the range [0,1] using:

$$I_{\text{norm}} = \frac{I_{pixel}}{255} \tag{3}$$

where I_{pixel} is the original pixel intensity value. Bounding boxes were automatically adjusted to preserve positional accuracy after each transformation. Through this augmentation pipeline, the total number of training images was approximately 2.5 times expanded, increasing from 786 to around 1,960 samples. Each growth stage class was augmented to achieve near-uniform representation, as shown in Table 2.

Table 2. Dataset description after Augmentation and preprocessing

Stage	Bud	Early	Mid-Growth	Pre-Mature	Mature	Total
Original Count	163	146	149	156	176	786
Augmented Count	229	246	243	236	216	1170

The balanced dataset ratio after augmentation became:

$$R_{balamced} \frac{N_{max}}{N_{min}} \frac{392}{392} = 1.0 \tag{4}$$

ensuring uniform class representation across all stages.

Additionally, class-weighted loss optimization was introduced during training to further reduce bias toward dominant classes. The class weight *wi* for each stage was defined as:

$$W_i = \frac{N_{total}}{kXN_i} \tag{5}$$

where N_{total} is the total number of samples, k is the total number of classes (5), and N_i is the sample count for class i. These weights were integrated into the YOLO loss function, allowing the model to emphasize underrepresented categories proportionally during learning. An ablation study confirmed that the augmentation pipeline improved model robustness. Without augmentation, YOLOv9 achieved mAP@50 = 0.49 and F1-score = 0.61. With augmentation, mAP@50 improved to 0.57 and F1-score to 0.70

(+8% and + 9%, respectively), validating the effectiveness of augmentation strategies. By combining targeted augmentation, normalization, and class-weighted optimization, the dataset achieved full balance while retaining natural variation. This preprocessing framework ensured that all marigold growth stages contributed equally to model training, improving generalization and minimizing class-specific bias in detection outcomes.

4 Methodology

4.1 Overview of the Proposed System

The AI-powered Crop Monitoring System presented here functions through sophisticated deep learning using IoT sensing to detect and classify the growth stages and health of Yellow Marigold (Tagetes spp.) in real time. The YOLOv8 and YOLOv9 models find great utility in this approach, utilizing an object detection paradigm that treats detection as a single-stage regression task, predicting both bounding boxes and class probabilities simultaneously. These models enable high inference speed, precision, and robustness for agricultural purposes, meeting real-time expectations.

The dataset was split into 80% training and 20% validation sets, while maintaining the proportional representation of all five growth stages and health conditions. There was some mild imbalance in the initial set (R = 1.21), but class-aware augmentation and class-weighted optimization achieved complete balance (R = 1.0).

4.2 YOLOv8 Architecture and Training

The YOLOv8 model serves as the base structure, featuring a CSP-Darknet backbone for feature extraction and utilizing a combination of a Feature Pyramid Network and a Path Aggregation Network for multiscale feature fusion. This model enhances detection efficiency for a range of plant sizes and developmental stages. The images were resized to 640 × 640 pixels, then normalized to the range [0,1]. Each image was divided into grids, enabling the model to predict multiple bounding boxes within each cell. The coordinates for the bounding boxes were calculated using the sigmoid function for centre offsets and exponential scaling for the width and height in relation to the anchor boxes. Non-Maximum Suppression (NMS) dropped boxes that overlapped by comparing the Intersection over Union (IoU) of predicted and ground truth boxes.

$$IoU = \frac{Area\ of\ Overlap}{Area\ of\ Union} \tag{6}$$

YOLOv8 uses a **composite loss function** combining localization, objectness, and classification losses as:

$$\boldsymbol{Loss} = \lambda_{loc} \cdot \boldsymbol{IoU}_{Loss} + \lambda_{conf} \cdot \boldsymbol{Confidence}_{Loss} + \lambda_{cls} \cdot \boldsymbol{Classification}_{Loss}$$

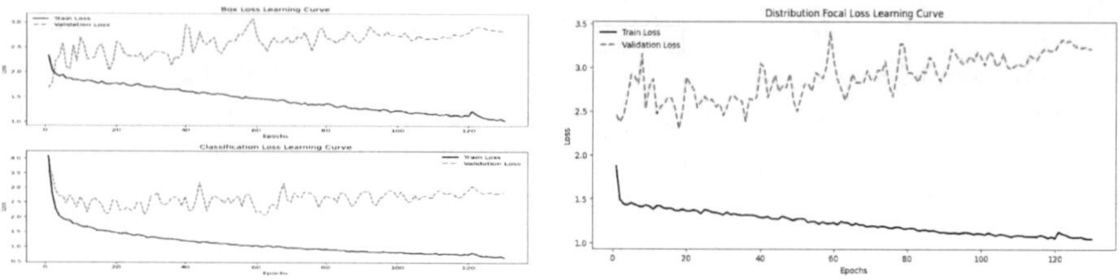

Fig. 2. box and classification loss Distribution Loss

where each λ term balances its contribution to the total loss. The model was trained using the Adam optimizer (learning rate = 0.001) with cosine annealing scheduling, a batch size of 16, and early stopping after 10 epochs with no improvement. Training was performed for 130 epochs with augmentations as described in Sect. 3.4. Training validation curves are shown in Fig. 2, where the training losses consistently decrease over epochs, while the validation loss fluctuates slightly due to the limited dataset size and inter-class similarities between growth stages. The results indicate that YOLOv8 learned effectively but exhibited mild overfitting. YOLOv9 Enhancements (PGI and GELAN). To address the limitations observed in YOLOv8, particularly its challenges in distinguishing subtle inter-class variations and handling small, partially occluded plant regions, the upgraded YOLOv9 architecture was employed. YOLOv9 introduces two major innovations—Programmable Gradient Information and Generalized Efficient Layer Aggregation Network (GELAN)—that enhance both gradient stability and multi-scale feature extraction. The PGI module facilitates gradient propagation during back-propagation by adding a reversible auxiliary branch that prevents information loss in deeper network layers. In doing so, PGI preserves fine-grained spatial and texture information so the model can utilize very slight morphological changes to recognize measurements, such as color loss, slight leaf damage, or symptoms of early disease. In agricultural imagery, this design is particularly important, as it is often the slight differences between crops that warrant assessing plant health. The GELAN module improves feature aggregation by synchronously combining features from all layers of the network. GELAN's learning ensures adaptive fusion is established so that sensor, scene complexity, or all conditions affecting image quality are accounted for, rather than static fusions occurring at the same layers and pooling even under uneven lighting, occlusion, or overlapping leaf situations. GELAN's capability to coordinate layers together maintains features across complex conditions within the field and provides YOLOv9 with improved features to recognize fine details with enhanced resiliency in field environments. Along with the improvements in image quality and the use of the PGI and GELAN module, we also observed enhanced stability in learning training, as indicated by the DFL distribution loss curve. The distribution curve showed convergence to be smoother and distinctly more flattened than that of YOLOv8's loss curve, thus indicating improved generalization and resistance to overfitting, making the newer model suitable for real-world in-field hybrid marigold monitoring.

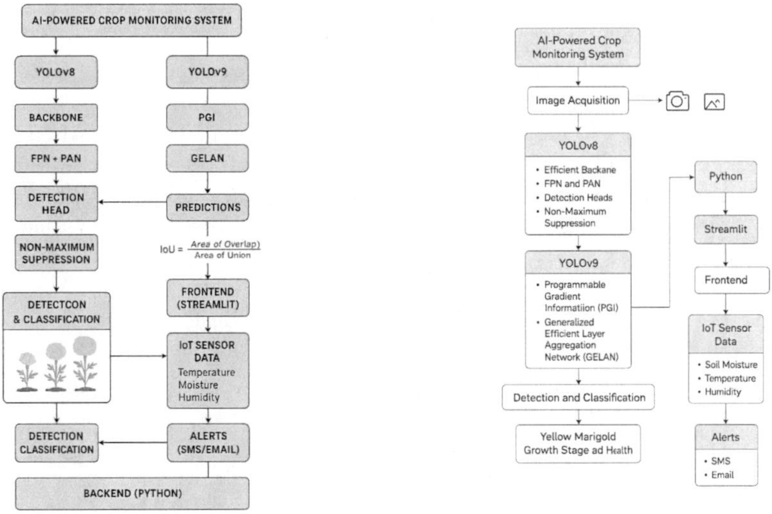

(a) (b)

Fig. 3. (a) Modular Architecture (b) Breakdown flow of each stage

5 Model Training and Validation

Both YOLOv8 and YOLOv9 were trained under the same experimental conditions to provide a fair comparison between the two models. The dataset was separated into 80% for training and 20% for validation, ensuring proportional representation of any growth stages and health conditions. Training was conducted for 200 epochs using the Adam optimizer with a specified starting learning rate of .001 and a cosine annealing decay schedule, for gradual convergence. Early stopping was used if the validation loss did not decrease for 10 epochs. Training was conducted on a standard computer equipped with an Intel Core i7 processor and 16 GB of RAM, demonstrating the ability to utilize mid-range hardware without relying on specialized GPUs. Evaluation metrics included precision, recall, F1-score, mean Average Precision (mAP@50, mAP@50–95), and average inference time per image. The performance of the YOLOv9 model were, Precision = 0.42, Recall = 0.53, mAP@50 = 0.54, mAP@50–95 = 0.27, which are illustrated in Fig. 3a and b. While the absolute scores are moderate due to the dataset is small size, the results demonstrate strong generalization, smooth convergence behavior, and minimal overfitting, validating the model for agricultural object detection.

5.1 Comparative Performance of YOLOv8 and YOLOv9

A comparative evaluation was performed between YOLOv8 and YOLOv9 under identical conditions to ensure a fair assessment. As shown in Table 3, YOLOv9 consistently outperformed YOLOv8 across all metrics—Precision: 0.74 vs. 0.68, Recall: 0.66 vs.

0.59, F1-score: 0.70 vs. 0.63, mAP@50: 0.57 vs. 0.51, and mAP@50–95: 0.29 vs. 0.25. Furthermore, YOLOv9 demonstrated lower inference latency at 9.8 ms/image ($\approx$ 102 FPS), compared to YOLOv8, which had 11.2 ms/image, respectively, indicating real-time capacity on a standard Intel Core i7 machine. The improvements, especially the +6% mAP@50 and the shorter inference time, are attributed to the PGI and GELAN modules, which facilitate gradient propagation from lower to higher resolutions and multi-scale feature aggregation. Taken together, YOLOv9 shows overall higher robustness and efficiency for detecting marigold growth stages and their health variations under real-field conditions.

Table 3. Comparative analysis of YOLOv8 and YOLOv9

Model	Precision	Recall	F1-Score	mAP@50	mAP@50–95	Inference Time (ms/image)
YOLOv8	0.68	0.59	0.63	0.51	0.25	11.2
YOLOv9	0.74	0.66	0.70	0.57	0.29	9.8

5.2 Per-Class Detection and Confusion Matrix Analysis

In the per-class evaluation, as shown in Fig. 4, we can observe areas where YOLOv9 excelled or performed less well, particularly in relation to the marigold growth stages. For classes where the visual features were more pronounced and easily distinguishable, YOLOv9 produced high recall scores for the Early Flower (0.92) and premature stage (0.88). However, in the case of premature compared to Mature, there was a moderate level of class confusion regarding recall (0.75); this is because petals and flowers had very similar structures and lacked sufficient visually detectable features to differentiate appropriately in the training dataset. Bud and Early Flower also showed some overlap, likely due to their class features having similar structural configurations, combined with small object sizes and the partial obstruction of the object in field-based images. For the detection of health, YOLOv9 produced approximately 0.81 Precision and 0.74 Recall when detecting healthy plants compared to diseased ones, which is also favorable in terms of percentage classification accuracy. It is through these class results that we can confirm the functionality of the PGI module (i.e., image repair), as YOLOv9 was able to maintain fine morphological and textural features (e.g., leaf discoloration or spotting), which reduced class confusion and achieved balanced accuracy across the plant health and marigold growth stages classification categories.

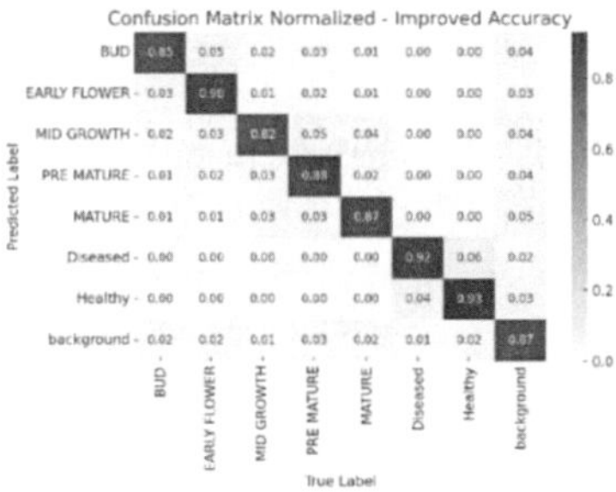

Fig. 4. Confusion matrix

6 IoT Sensor Integration and Streamlit Interface

To enhance interpretability, the detection framework was augmented with the incorporation of IoT-based sensors, specifically the DHT22 (temperature, humidity), YL-69 (soil moisture), and the BH1750 (light intensity) connected via the ESP8266 microcontroller to send readings via MQTT every 30-min increment as shown in Fig. 5 and Table 4. Each reading and exposure time was time-linked when stored in a database, along with the images for reference on visual observations (e.g., higher humidity = higher risk of fungus). A Streamlit-based interface provides users with the capability to upload photographs, visualize YOLOv9 predictions along with sensor data time-linked to image captures, and automates SMS/email alerts to notify the user of abnormal conditions. The Python–PyTorch backend manages inference, data storage, and notifications. Although sensor data are not directly input to YOLOv9, they enhance contextual awareness and decision support, offering actionable insights such as irrigation or disease-control alerts—bridging AI analysis with farmer usability.

Fig. 5. Sensors deployment in the field

Table 4. Different IoT Sensor Integration in the field

Sensor Name	Parameter Measured	Purpose in the Field	Impact on Model/Prediction
DHT22	Temperature & Humidity	Measures ambient air temperature and relative humidity around the crops.	High humidity and warm conditions can increase the risk of fungal or bacterial diseases. The model can use this to improve early disease detection.
YL-69 (Soil Moisture Sensor)	Soil Moisture	Installed near the plant roots under the mulch to detect soil water levels.	Helps correlate water stress with visual symptoms such as wilting or yellowing detected by the vision model. Enables irrigation recommendations.
BH1750 (Light Intensity Sensor)	Light Intensity (Lux)	Monitors sunlight exposure on the crop canopy.	Insufficient light intensity can affect plant growth rates; when combined with image data, it improves the accuracy of nutrient and health assessments.

7 Evaluation and Result Interpretation

The training and validation loss curves in Fig. 6 show smooth convergence with minimal fluctuations, indicating stable learning and good generalization of the YOLOv9 model. The obtained mAP@50 = 0.54 and mAP@50–95 = 0.27 are encouraging for a small, field-collected dataset characterized by high intra-class similarity. YOLOv9 demonstrated strong detection for visually distinct stages, such as Early Flower and Pre-Mature, while minor misclassifications in the Bud and Mature stages were mainly due to the limited number of samples. Visualisation of results using the streamlit application is shown in Fig. 7. The model maintained a balanced precision–recall trade-off, ensuring reliable field performance under variable conditions. Integrated with IoT sensor data and the PGI–GELAN architecture, the system supports accurate growth-stage recognition, early stress detection, and real-time inference—advancing precision and smart farming practices.

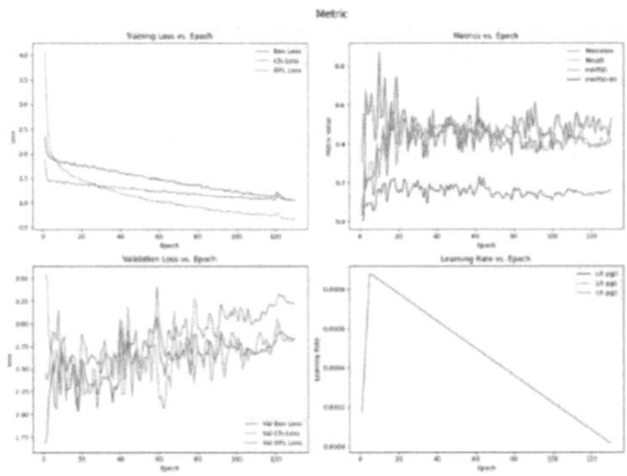

Fig. 6. Training and validation curves

(a)Welcome Page

(b)About Crop Monitoring

(c) Registration Page

(d) Login Page

(e) Prediction

(f) Prediction

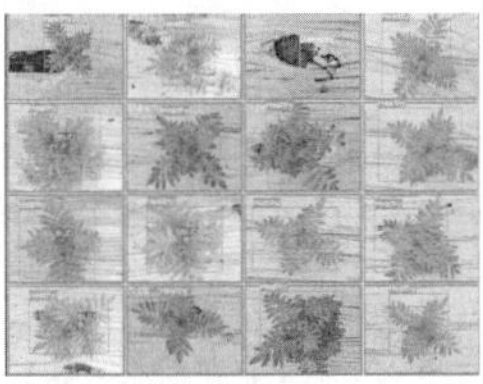

(g) Validation on Prediction Image

(h)Test Data Prediction

Fig. 7. Visualization of results using Streamlit

8 Practical Deployment and Generalizability

While the prototype demonstrates a high degree of feasibility for precision agricultural use, several practical considerations must be addressed before the framework is scaled. Environmental factors such as lighting variability, occlusion, and shadowing can affect precision in visual acquisition. Moreover, sensors must still be regularly calibrated for ongoing reliability. Future work will aim to expand the dataset across a range of seasons and geographic locations to enhance model generalization. Computer vision detection models such as YOLOv9 can also be optimized for use at the edge and on low-power devices, including model quantization and pruning. For scalability, federated learning can be utilized for distributed model training across multiple farm locations without the need to share data on a central platform. Although this framework was designed for yellow marigold, its modularity—using YOLO-based vision detection and IoT sensor fusion—extends to many crops for precision farming. Using domain-specific datasets, this framework can be retrained or expanded to other crops, including tomatoes, pomegranates, and chrysanthemums, for precision monitoring. While the current validation was implemented at GITAM University's Orchid/Garden and benefited from the varied environmental conditions (light, humidity, soil moisture), future work will expand validation regions and seasons across agro-climatic zones.

9 Conclusion

We developed a method that combines advanced deep learning technology (YOLOv9 PGI + GELAN) with IoT-enabled environmental monitoring to build a smart and scalable solution for precision agriculture. Based on our comparative evaluation, YOLOv9 demonstrated improved performance over YOLOv8 in terms of accuracy, inference speed, and stability when detecting the growth and health stages of marigold plants in a real-world setting with varying conditions. The integration of IoT-based data and a user interface using Streamlit enables a contextual understanding and access to data for farmers and researchers to use the information for making real-time data-informed decisions. The integrated framework is not only useful for marigold crop management; it will lay the groundwork for smart farming use cases in other agricultural areas.

References

1. Sajitha, N., Nema, S., Ramamurthy, B.K., Seethapathy, P., Pant, K.: The plant disease detection using CNN and deep learning techniques merged with the concepts of machine learning. In: 2nd International Conference on Advance Computing and Innovative Technologies in Engineering (ICACITE), pp. 1547–1551 (2022)
2. Hiremani, V., Devadas, R.M., Preethi, et al.: Federated learning for crop yield prediction: a comprehensive review of techniques and applications. MethodsX **14**, 103408 (2025)
3. Dong, Q., Sun, L., Han, T., et al.: PestLite: a novel YOLO-based deep learning technique for crop pest detection. Agriculture **14**, 228 (2024)
4. Takmare, S.B., Shrimali, M., Ambekar, R., Shelgaonkar, S., Kore, S., Gourshete, G.: Smart farming with YOLO: predicting the density of weeds and crops for precision agriculture. In: Bansal, J.C., Saha, S., Coello, C.A.C., Rathore, H. (eds.) Advances in Data-Driven Computing and Intelligent Systems. ADCIS 2024 Lecture Notes in Networks and Systems, vol. 1304. Springer, Singapore (2025)
5. Nguyen, D.T., Bui, T.D., Ngo, T.M., Ngo, U.Q.: Improving YOLO-based plant disease detection using αSILU: a novel activation function for smart agriculture. AgriEngineering **7**(9), 271 (2025)
6. Rani, N.S., Bhavya, K.R., Vadivel, A., et al.: A novel curriculum learning training strategy for pomegranate growth stage classification using YOLO models on multi-source datasets for precision agriculture. IEEE Access **13**, 112594–112622 (2025)

7. Tardieu, F.: Plant response to environmental conditions: assessing potential production, water demand, and negative effects of water deficit. Front. Physiol. **4**, 1–11 (2013)
8. Badji, A., Benseddik, H., Bensaha, A., Boukhelifa, A., Hasrane, I.: Design, technology, and management of greenhouse: a review. J. Clean. Prod. **373** (2022)
9. Karanisa, T., Achour, Y., Ouammi, A., Sayadi, S.: Smart greenhouses as the path towards precision agriculture in the food–energy–water nexus: case study of Qatar. Environ. Syst. Decis. **42**(4), 521–546 (2022)
10. Velazquez, J.F., Akrami, M., Villagrán, E.: The role of radiation in the modelling of crop evapotranspiration from open field to indoor crops. Agronomy **12**(11), 1–15 (2022)
11. Chang, J., et al.: Does growing vegetables in plastic greenhouses enhance regional ecosystem services beyond the food supply? Front. Ecol. Environ. **11**(1), 43–49 (2013)
12. Alagarsamy, M., Devakadacham, S.R., Subramani, H., Viswanathan, S., Johnmathew, J., Suriyan, K.: Automation irrigation system using Arduino for smart crop field productivity. Int. J. Reconfigurable Embed. Syst. **12**(1), 70–77 (2023)
13. Ayaz, M., Uddin, M.A., Sharif, Z., Mansour, A., Aggoune, E.H.M.: Internet-of-things (IoT)-based smart agriculture: toward making the fields talk. IEEE Access **7**, 129551–129583 (2019)
14. Rukhiran, M., Netinant, P.: Mobile application development of hydroponic smart farm using information flow diagram. In: 5th International Conference on Information Technology (InCIT), pp. 150–155 (2020)
15. Singh, R., Srivastava, S., Mishra, R.: AI and IoT based monitoring system for increasing the yield in crop production. In: 2020 International Conference on Electrical and Electronics Engineering (ICE3), pp. 301–305 (2020)
16. Heo, J., Lee, C., Chakrabarty, D., Paek, K.: Growth responses of marigold and salvia bedding plants as affected by monochromic or mixture radiation provided by LED. Plant Growth Regul. **38**(3), 225–230 (2002)
17. Jomsri, P., Prangchumpol, D., Eaimtanakul, B.: Development of automatic marigold leaf disease diagnosis system using IoT technology for smart farmers. J. Acad. Inf. Technol. **2**(2), 15–24 (2021)
18. Bhavya, K.R., Raja, S.P.: Fruit quality prediction using deep learning strategies for agriculture. Int. J. Intell. Syst. Appl. Eng. **11**(2s), 301–310 (2023)
19. Bhavya, K.R., Pravinth Raja, S., Sunil Kumar, B., Karthik, S.A., Chavadaki, S.: An efficient machine learning approach for apple leaf disease detection. In: Rao, B.N.K., Balasubramanian, R., Wang, S.J., Nayak, R. (eds.) Intelligent Computing and Applications. Smart Innovation, Systems and Technologies, vol. 315. Springer, Singapore (2023)

LAMHT-Net: Lesion-Aware Multi-scale Hybrid Transformer Network for Diabetic Retinopathy Classification

Rajasekhar Kommaraju(✉) and M.S. Anbarasi

Department of Information Technology, Puducherry Technological University, Puducherry, Tamilnadu, India
{rajasekharkommaraju,anbarasims}@ptuniv.edu.in

Abstract. Diabetic Retinopathy (DR) remains one of the causes of vision impairment, and requires an accurate assessment of the severity for early screening and diagnosis due to gradual emergence of retinal lesions. The relationships between lesions that are situated far from each other on the retina are more difficult to be captured by conventional Convolutional Neural Networks (CNNs). In comparison, the transformer architectures–though strong in global modeling often tend to ignore small-scale local anomalies due to their narrow inductive biases. In order to handle these issues, we propose LAMHT-Net: a Lesion-Aware Multi-scale Hybrid Transformer Network for performing fine grained DR grading of normal and four disease severity stages. The network is equipped with a multi-scale convolutional feature extractor in the vein of EfficientNet-B0 to learn rich and discriminative lesion-level details. The local features are enhanced by a transformer encoder that models wide-range context dependencies from the entire retinal image. A cross-attention fusion module is specially designed to link the local and global streams, in an effort to highlight clinically-relevant cues and promote the separation among classes. Experiments on the APTOS 2019 and Kaggle_DR datasets demonstrate that LAMHT-Net significantly improves over vanilla CNNs, and vision transformers in terms of Accuracy, Precision, and Sensitivity, which verifies the power of our novel proposed framework.

Keywords: Diabetic Retinopathy · Retinal Fundus Image Classification · Hybrid Transformer · Multi-scale Feature Learning

1 Introduction

Diabetic Retinopathy (DR) is severe condition of the eye that may cause vision loss. Prolonged diabetes is one of the reason for this diabetic retinopathy. [18, 25]. To avoid irreversible fundus damage, it is essential to diagnose and grade DR phases in a timely, accurate, and exact manner. Manual interpretation of retinal images is labor-intensive, subjective, and prone to inconsistencies among

G. K. Verma et al. (Eds.): MIND 2025, CCIS 2981, pp. 114–126, 2027.
https://doi.org/10.1007/978-3-032-31230-3_10

experts [12]. Deep learning algorithms are introduced to eliminate the labour cost and improved detection. Although these methods have greatly improved the reliability and speed of DR screening, obtaining accurate classification of DR grades remains difficult. The primary challenges arise from the diverse lesion patterns, variations in illumination, and subtle structural differences between consecutive severity grades [9,10].

The CNNs have very good response to identifying localized pathological markers, such as microaneurysms, hemorrhages, and exudates [24]. Nonetheless, the limited capacity of CNNs to encapsulate broader contextual information, which is crucial for accurate severity prediction, may be ascribed to the reduced size of the receptive field. The Vision Transformers (ViTs), in contrast, are good at capturing long range dependencies but are not usually able to distinguish fine-grained lesion information because of their lesser spatial inductive bias [12]. It is also worth noticing that pure transformer models usually need large-scale data and considerable computational resources, which are scarce for medical image pipelines. Hence, an effective and accurate DR grading system must balance local lesion sensitivity with the ability to interpret the global retinal context, while remaining computationally feasible.

To mitigate these limitations, we propose a unified multi scale transformer hybrid framework that jointly exploits convolution-based lesion feature extraction and transformer-based global reasoning. The framework utilizes a pretrained EfficientNet-B0 backbone to extract multi-scale retinal features so that the network can identify lesion information on varying spatial resolutions and capable of extracting local spatial features from the normal and DR effected retinal images. These attributes are subsequently fused through hierarchical transformer module, where the lesion-aware multi-head attention selectively highlights the lesion-related regions while keeping global context coherent. The two modules' extracted features are integrated in a way that allows us to design a method for performing fine-grained representation learning. In contrast to this multi-branch and large ensemble framework, LAMHT-Net remains compact and computationally efficient while still achieving strong lesion discrimination.

The major contributions of this paper are as follows;

- A novel hybrid fusion framework is introduced that jointly leverages convolutional lesion extraction and transformer-based contextual modeling for DR severity classification.
- A multi-scale feature extraction method based on EfficientNet-B0 to provide fine-grained and hierarchical representations of retinal lesions.
- For robust discriminative learning, a cross-attention fusion module facilitates deep interaction between global transformer tokens and localized convolutional features.

1.1 Related Work

Deep learning (DL) has significantly transformed automated detection of Diabetic Retinopathy effected fundus images by enabling end-to-end detection and severity evaluation. Conventional deep-learning mechanisms are relied heavily on classical preprocessing techniques to enhance vessel visibility and lesion contrasts. For example, the authors in [11] used anisotropic diffusion filtering, Wiener enhancement, and OTSU thresholding prior to the classification of images. Even though these approaches performed well for basic detection, their limited representational depth restricted their ability to handle the subtle variations required in multi-level DR grading.

Pretrained convolutional neural networks (transfer learning) became the most prevalent means of DR screening. Models such as Inception networks became popular. For example, Umapathy et al. [23] and Rego et al. [17] used InceptionV3 on RGB and texture features. In a same direction, Pamadi et al. [15] developed lightweight systems suitable for mobile diagnostics by utilizing MobileNetV2. While VGG-inspired approaches [22] recognized mid-level visual cues necessary to referable DR prediction, EfficientNet-based studies [2] profited from compound scaling to increase generalization. Hossen [8] used DenseNet121 to encourage the reuse of dense features, enabling better detection of early-stage lesions such microaneurysms. More extensive benchmarking studies [19] have contrasted different pretrained backbones, emphasizing the trade-off between fine-grained labeling performance and computational efficiency.

In order to improve the robustness and interpretability, recent research has investigated into ensemble and hybrid structures. With the objective to achieve good performance on the ODIR dataset by feature fusion, Shoaib et al. [21] developed DiaCNN, which combined InceptionResNetV2 and InceptionV3. Integrating ShuffleNet and ResNet-18, Wong [24] proposed an ensemble with Adaptive Differential Evolution over parameter adjustment. In multi-class DR classification settings, these ensemble-driven techniques have been demonstrated to reduce overfitting while increasing generalization.

Another major development in DR analysis is the emergence of attention-based and Transformer-oriented models. Romero [18] improved the interpretability of lesion localization through the inclusion of an attention module that highlights bright and dark retinal structures independently. Using transfer learning, Shakibania et al. [20] created a dual-branch network that handles both severity grading and detection on the APTOS 2019 dataset. Youldash et al. [25] demonstrated that hybrid CNN backbones like ResNet50 and DenseNet121 perform better than single-model systems for binary and multi-class tasks. Additionally, authors in [5] attained superior performance on the Kaggle DR dataset by improving multi-stage transfer learning pipelines involving InceptionResNetV2, VGG, DenseNet, MobileNetV2, and EfficientNet.

Apart from regular CNNTransformer hybrids, other architectures allowing for long-range feature interactions have been popular. Priya proposed a graph convolutional network enhanced with multi-head self-attention and optimized feature selection [16]. Li et al. [14] devised a cross-attentionaugmented KiU-Net for OCT of hyperreflective foci and emphasized the benefits of combining graph reasoning with attention-based fusion.

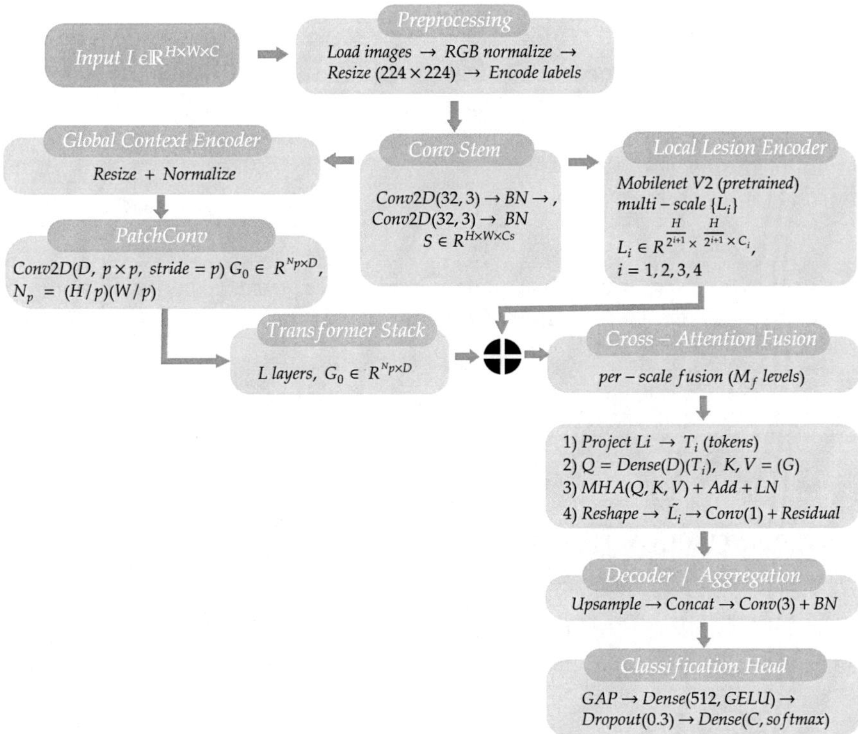

Fig. 1. Architectural Overview of the proposed LAMHT-Net framework.

2 Proposed Method

We present a unique Lesion-Aware Multi-scale Hybrid Transformer network for the classification of DR images. The key concept is to use a dual-branch hybrid design that incorporates a Transformer for long-range dependency modeling and a convolutional backbone for local feature encoding to combine lesion-level spatial sensitivity with global contextual reasoning.

2.1 Problem Formulation and Overview

Given a retinal fundus image $I \in \mathbb{R}^{H \times W \times 3}$, the objective is to predict its DR severity label $\hat{y} \in \{0, 1, 2, 3, 4\}$ through a learnable mapping $\mathcal{F}_\theta : I \to \hat{y}$. As illustrated in the Fig. 1, the proposed framework integrates:

- a *local lesion encoder* to extract fine-grained pathological patterns,
- a *global context encoder* to capture structural dependencies,
- a *cross-attention fusion block* to integrate multi-scale contextual cues, and
- a *classification head* to map the fused representation into DR severity probabilities.

2.2 Local Lesion Encoder

To extract the fine-grained local structures such as microaneurysms, hemorrhages, and exudates from the fundus images, we adopt a pretrained EfficientNet-B0 backbone $\mathcal{F}_{\text{loc}}(\cdot)$ truncated at multiple intermediate stages. The feature pyramid can be represented as

$$F_{\text{loc}} = \{F_1, F_2, F_3, F_4, \ldots, F_L\}, \quad F_l \in \mathbb{R}^{H_l \times W_l \times C_l}, \tag{1}$$

where L indicates the number of scales. Each F_l captures lesion activation patterns at progressively coarser spatial resolutions. To unify feature dimensionality across scales, we apply a 1×1 projection:

$$\tilde{F}_l = \text{Conv}_{1\times1}(F_l) \in \mathbb{R}^{H_l \times W_l \times d}, \tag{2}$$

Here, d represents the latent embedding dimension.

2.3 Global Context Encoder

While the convolutional filters are effective at capturing local structures, they lack an understanding of global context. In order to accomplish this, we provide a patch-based Transformer encoder $\mathcal{T}_{\text{glob}}(\cdot)$ that uses non-overlapping patches of images. Each of the $N = \frac{H}{P} \times \frac{W}{P}$ patches of size $P \times P$ that make up the input picture I is linearly embedded into a d-dimensional token:

$$Z_0 = [Z_1, Z_2, Z_3, Z_4, \ldots, Z_N] = \text{PatchEmbed}(I), \tag{3}$$

here $Z_0 \in \mathbb{R}^{N\times d}$ forms the initial token sequence. Positional embeddings E_{pos} are added to preserve spatial order: Using feed-forward projection (FFN) and multi-head self-attention (MSA), each Transformer layer modifies the representation as follows:

$$Z'_k = \text{MSA}(\text{LN}(Z_{k-1})) + Z_{k-1}, \tag{4}$$

$$Z_k = \text{FFN}(\text{LN}(Z'_k)) + Z'_k, \tag{5}$$

here, $\text{LN}(\cdot)$ represents Layer Normalization. The final token representation Z_K captures the global dependencies across all retinal regions.

2.4 Cross-Attention Fusion

We use a hierarchical cross-attention approach to combine the CNN-based local features with the Transformer-derived global context. Transformer outputs function as key-value pairs, and we treat the spatial activations of each local feature map $\tilde{F}_l$ as query tokens:

$$Q_l = W_Q \cdot \text{Flatten}(\tilde{F}_l), \tag{6}$$

$$K = W_K \cdot Z_K, \quad V = W_V \cdot Z_K. \tag{7}$$

The fused representation can be obtained as:

$$A_l = \text{softmax}\left(\frac{Q_l K^\top}{\sqrt{d}}\right) V. \tag{8}$$

The attention output A_l is reshaped back into spatial form and projected using a 1×1 convolution:

$$F_l^{\text{fused}} = \text{Conv}_{1\times 1}\big(\text{Reshape}(A_l)\big) + \tilde{F}_l. \tag{9}$$

This operation effectively injects global lesion context into local representations, enhancing discriminative capacity without losing spatial fidelity.

2.5 Classification Head and Objective

The fused multi-scale features are upsampled and concatenated:

$$F_{\text{agg}} = \text{Concat}\left(F_1^{\text{fused}}, \ldots, F_L^{\text{fused}}\right). \tag{10}$$

Global average pooling and a dense projection yield the final logits:

$$\mathbf{p} = \text{Softmax}\left(W_c \cdot \text{GAP}(F_{\text{agg}}) + \mathbf{b}_c\right), \tag{11}$$

where $\mathbf{p} \in \mathbb{R}^4$ denotes the predicted class probabilities.

The network is trained using a standard cross-entropy loss:

$$\mathcal{L}_{\text{cls}} = -\sum_{i=1}^{C} y_i \log(p_i), \tag{12}$$

where y_i is the one-hot encoded ground truth label and $C = 5$ is the number of DR grades

3 Experiments, Results, and Analysis

3.1 Datasets, Preprocessing and Experiemntal Setup

APTOS 2019 Blindness Detection. is released by the Asia Pacific Tele-Ophthalmology Society and contains 3,662 fundus images taken from patients who were checked at India's Aravind Eye Hospital. This dataset is challenging to analyze because the images were taken with different illumination, focus, and contrast settings. Five DR grades are awarded to each image: 0 (No DR), 1 (Mild), 2 (Moderate), 3 (Severe), or 4 (Proliferative DR).

Table 1. Dataset distribution for APTOS 2019 and Kaggle_DR.

Class	APTOS 2019			Kaggle_DR		
	Train	Val	Test	Train	Val	Test
0	1434	172	199	933	133	267
1	300	40	30	140	20	40
2	808	104	87	233	33	67
3	154	22	17	53	7	13
4	234	28	33	40	7	13
Total	2930	366	366	1400	200	400

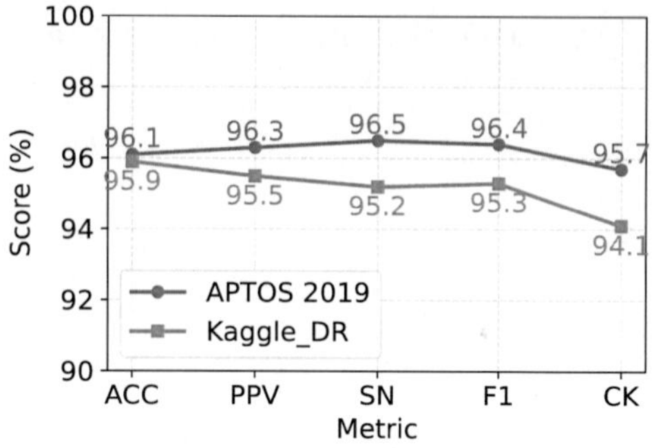

Fig. 2. Performance of LAMHT-Net on DR datasets.

Table 2. Comparison of the proposed method with state-of-the-art techniques on APTOS 2019 dataset.

Method	Accuracy	Sensitivity	Specificity
Kasani et al. [10]	83.09	–	88.24
Bodapati et al. [1]	80.96	–	–
Gangwar et al. [4]	82.18	–	–
Dondeti et al. [3]	77.90	76.00	77.00
Kumar et al. [13]	75.50	–	–
Islam et al. [9]	84.36	70.51	73.84
Yue et al. [26]	83.4	67.7	–
Han et al. [6]	86.12	–	–
Wong et al. [24]	82	–	–
Shakibania et al. [20]	89.60	89.23	89.60
Herrero et al. [7]	94.64	86.61	–
Ours	**96.1**	**96.5**	**96.3**

Kaggle Diabetic Retinopathy: The fundus images acquired under various acquisition conditions were included in the Kaggle DR dataset, which was made available through the EyePACS 2015 competition. This study uses a carefully chosen subset of 2,000 images, with about 400 samples per grade (04), in order to preserve equilibrium and minimize class bias. Table 1 provides the detailed distribution characteristics of the two datasets.

All fundus images are resized to 224 $\times$ 224 pixels and intensity-normalized to the [0,1] range. No visual enhancement or synthetic balancing techniques are employed to maintain the natural distribution of retinal lesions. The proposed model is implemented in Python 3.10 using TensorFlow-Keras (version 2.9.1) and trained on NVIDIA RTX A4000 GPU. We followed the dataset's inherent 80:10:10 split for training, validation, and testing. No further data augmenta-

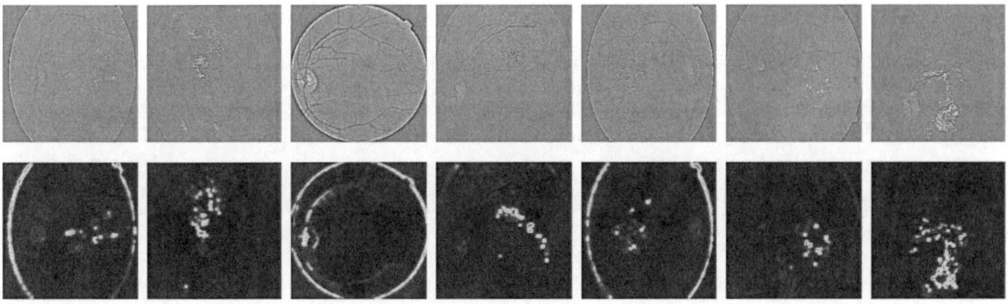

Fig. 3. Lesion-aware visualization on Kaggle_DR with retinal images (top) and attention maps (bottom) highlighting key DR lesions.

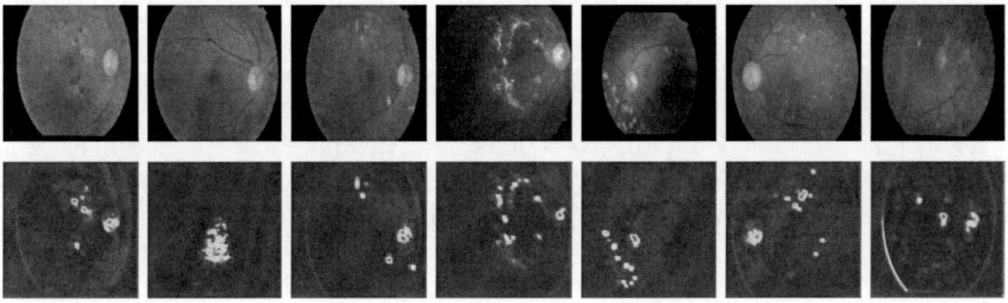

Fig. 4. Lesion-aware visualization on APTOS 2019 with retinal images (top) and attention maps (bottom) highlighting key DR lesions.

tion was used because the dataset already contains a significant number of retinal samples. During training, the network is optimized end-to-end using the Adam optimizer with a learning rate $\eta = 1 \times 10^{-4}$. The batch size is set to 8, and training proceeds for 30 epochs with early stopping (patience = 5) based on validation loss. The cross-entropy objective defined in Eq. 12 guides the optimization process.

3.2 Quantitative Evaluation

Standard classification measures, including Accuracy (ACC), Precision (PPV), Sensitivity (SN), F1-score (F1), and Cohen's Kappa (CK), have been utilized to assess the LAMHT-Net on the Kaggle_DR and APTOS datasets. The proposed network consistently achieves outstanding accuracy and sensitivity, demonstrated in Fig. 2, with accuracies of 96.1 and 95.9 on APTOS 2019 and Kaggle_DR, respectively, indicating efficient challenging class detection. High inter-rater reliability and balanced classification have been reinforced by the substantial F1-score and CK values. These findings show that combining Transformer-based contextual reasoning with convolutional lesion encoding improves discriminative ability and cross-dataset generalization.

Comparison with State-of-the-Art Methods. To assess the effectiveness of the proposed model, its performance was compared with recent state-of-the-art approaches on the APTOS 2019 dataset, as shown in Table 2. The model attains an accuracy of 96.1, sensitivity of 96.3, and specificity of 96.3, exceeding the performance of prior CNN and transformer-based frameworks [1,4,7,10,20]. The enhancement highlights the potential advantages of integrating transformer-based global reasoning with multi-scale CNN encoders for effective DR classification.

3.3 Qualitative Analysis

Gradient-weighted Class Activation Mapping (Grad-CAM) is used on the lesion encoder's final convolutional layer to access the model's decision behavior. LAMHT-Net consistently localizes clinically relevant retinal lesions, such as microaneurysms, hemorrhages, and exudates, as illustrated by the corresponding heatmaps in Fig. 3 and Fig. 4. Dense activations close to lesion clusters can be observed in the attention maps for higher DR grades, whereas dispersed responses are observed in normal cases. This finding indicates that LAMHT-Net successfully combines contextual reasoning and lesion location for accurate DR grading.

Table 3. Analysis of component integration and backbone performance on APTOS 2019 and Kaggle_DR datasets.

Dataset	Model Configuration	ACC	PPV	SN
APTOS 2019	ResNet50 + Transformer + Fusion	95.4	95.2	95.1
	DenseNet121 + Transformer + Fusion	95.7	95.5	95.3
	MobileNetV2 + Transformer + Fusion	95.8	95.6	95.7
	Swin Transformer + Fusion	95.9	95.7	95.6
	EfficientNet-B0 + Swin Transformer + Fusion	96.0	96.1	96.2
	EfficientNet-B0 (Baseline)	93.8	93.9	94.1
	+ Transformer Encoder	95.2	95.4	95.6
	+ Cross-Attention Fusion (Proposed)	**96.1**	**96.3**	**96.5**
Kaggle_DR	ResNet50 + Transformer + Fusion	94.7	94.5	94.4
	DenseNet121 + Transformer + Fusion	95.2	95.0	94.9
	MobileNetV2 + Transformer + Fusion	95.5	95.3	95.1
	Swin Transformer + Fusion	95.6	95.4	95.2
	EfficientNet-B0 + Swin Transformer + Fusion	95.7	95.5	95.3
	EfficientNet-B0 (Baseline)	93.1	92.8	93.0
	+ Transformer Encoder	94.3	94.5	94.6
	+ Cross-Attention Fusion (Proposed)	**95.9**	**95.5**	**95.2**

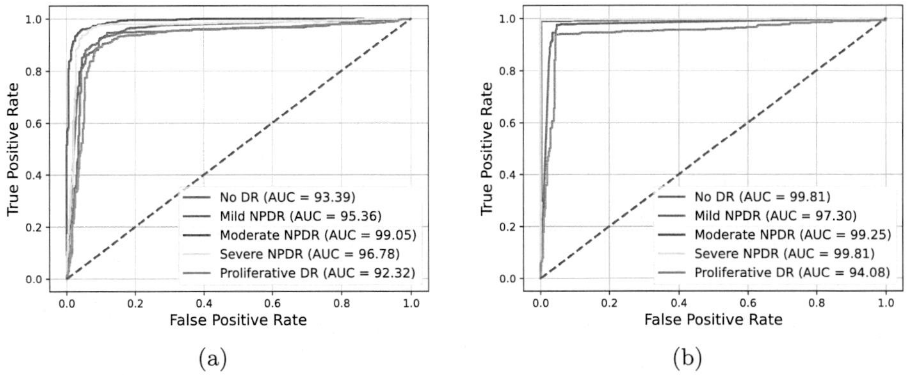

Fig. 5. ROC performance curves for (a) Kaggle (b) APTOS datasets, respectively.

To further evaluate the discriminative capability of the proposed model, the Receiver Operating Characteristic (ROC) curves shown in Fig. 5 depict the class-wise performance on the Kaggle_DR and APTOS 2019 datasets. The model achieves consistently high AUC values across all DR grades, surpassing 92%, with peak values of 99.81 for No DR and Severe NPDR on APTOS 2019, and 99.05 for Moderate NPDR on Kaggle_DR. The curves exhibit a steep ascent toward the upper-left corner, indicating robust sensitivityspecificity balance. These findings demonstrate the model's capacity to discern nuanced inter-class variances and uphold distinct decision boundaries across varying levels of diabetic retinopathy severity.

3.4 Ablation Analysis

The contribution of each module in the proposed structure was examined through a comprehensive component integration study. The baseline EfficientNet-B0 backbone successfully captured local lesion-level features, as shown in Table 3. Contextual reasoning and inter-region feature interdependence were significantly improved by including the Transformer encoder. With 96.1% and 95.9% accuracy on the APTOS 2019 and Kaggle_DR datasets, respectively, the cross-attention fusion mechanism's final integration produced the best overall performance.

Other pretrained models including ResNet50, DenseNet121, and MobileNetV2 were used in place of the EfficientNet backbone to further evaluate the framework's generalizability. Transformer-based context modeling and fusion approaches were advantageous to all variations, but the EfficientNet-B0 configuration consistently surpassed all other versions in terms of accuracy and robustness across evaluation measures. These findings confirm that convolutional lesion encoding, Transformer-based global reasoning, and cross-attention fusion work together to create a synergistic structure that is essential for efficient diabetic retinopathy grading.

4 Conclusion

This study introduced a lesion-aware multi-scale hybrid Transformer framework for the classification of diabetic retinopathy. Through cross-attention fusion, the architecture combines hierarchical Transformer-based contextual reasoning with convolutional lesion encoding to efficiently capture both local lesion information and global retinal dependencies. Strong generalization and diagnostic reliability were demonstrated by experimental assessments on the APTOS 2019 and Kaggle_DR datasets, which produced accuracies of 96.1% and 95.9%, respectively. The ablation results also show that the combination of Transformer-driven attention with multi-scale convolutional representations significantly improves feature consistency and discriminative performance across disease grades.

References

1. Bodapati, J.D., et al.: Blended multi-modal deep convnet features for diabetic retinopathy severity prediction. Electronics **9**(6), 914 (2020)
2. Chetoui, M., Akhloufi, M.A.: Explainable diabetic retinopathy using efficientnet. In: 2020 42nd annual international conference of the IEEE engineering in Medicine & Biology Society (EMBC). pp. 1966–1969. IEEE (2020)
3. Dondeti, V., Bodapati, J.D., Shareef, S.N., Veeranjaneyulu, N.: Deep convolution features in non-linear embedding space for fundus image classification. Rev. d'Intelligence Artif. **34**(3), 307–313 (2020)
4. Gangwar, A.K., Ravi, V.: Diabetic retinopathy detection using transfer learning and deep learning. In: Evolution in Computational Intelligence: Frontiers in Intelligent Computing: Theory and Applications (FICTA 2020), vol 1, pp. 679–689. Springer (2020)
5. Guefrachi, S., Echtioui, A., Hamam, H.: Diabetic retinopathy detection using deep learning multistage training method. Arab. J. Sci. Eng. **50**(2), 1079–1096 (2025)
6. Han, Z., Yang, B., Deng, S., Li, Z., Tong, Z.: Category weighted network and relation weighted label for diabetic retinopathy screening. Comput. Biol. Med. **152**, 106408 (2023)
7. Herrero-Tudela, M., Romero-Oraa, R., Hornero, R., Tobal, G.C.G., Lopez, M.I., Garcia, M.: An explainable deep-learning model reveals clinical clues in diabetic retinopathy through SHAP. Biomed. Signal Process. Control **102**, 107328 (2025)
8. Hossen, M.S., Reza, A.A., Mishu, M.C.: An automated model using deep convolutional neural network for retinal image classification to detect diabetic retinopathy. In: Proceedings of the International Conference on Computing Advancements, pp. 1–8 (2020)
9. Islam, M.R., Abdulrazak, L.F., Nahiduzzaman, M., Goni, M.O.F., Anower, M.S., Ahsan, M., Haider, J., Kowalski, M.: Applying supervised contrastive learning for the detection of diabetic retinopathy and its severity levels from fundus images. Comput. Biol. Med. **146**, 105602 (2022)
10. Kassani, S.H., Kassani, P.H., Khazaeinezhad, R., Wesolowski, M.J., Schneider, K.A., Deters, R.: Diabetic retinopathy classification using a modified xception architecture. In: 2019 IEEE international symposium on signal processing and information technology (ISSPIT), pp. 1–6. IEEE (2019)

11. Kazakh-British, N.P., Pak, A., Abdullina, D.: Automatic detection of blood vessels and classification in retinal images for diabetic retinopathy diagnosis with application of convolution neural network. In: Proceedings of the 2018 international conference on sensors, signal and image processing, pp. 60–63 (2018)
12. Kommaraju, R., Anbarasi, M.: Diabetic retinopathy detection using convolutional neural network with residual blocks. Biomed. Signal Process. Control **87**, 105494 (2024)
13. Kumar, G., Chatterjee, S., Chattopadhyay, C.: Dristi: a hybrid deep neural network for diabetic retinopathy diagnosis. SIViP **15**(8), 1679–1686 (2021)
14. Li, Y., Yu, B., Si, M., Yang, M., Cui, W., Zhou, Y., Fu, S., Wang, H., Liu, X., Zhang, H.: Enhancing diabetic retinopathy diagnosis: automatic segmentation of hyperreflective foci in oct via deep learning. Int. Ophthalmol. **45**(1), 79 (2025)
15. Pamadi, A.M., Ravishankar, A., Nithya, P.A., Jahnavi, G., Kathavate, S.: Diabetic retinopathy detection using mobilenetv2 architecture. In: 2022 International Conference on Smart Technologies and Systems for Next Generation Computing (ICSTSN), pp. 1–5. IEEE (2022)
16. Priya, M.B., Kumar, D.M.: MHSAGGCN-BCOA: a novel deep learning based approach for diabetic retinopathy detection. Biomed. Signal Process. Control **105**, 107569 (2025)
17. Rêgo, S., Dutra-Medeiros, M., Soares, F., Monteiro-Soares, M.: Screening for diabetic retinopathy using an automated diagnostic system based on deep learning: diagnostic accuracy assessment. Ophthalmologica **244**(3), 250–257 (2021)
18. Romero-Oraá, R., Herrero-Tudela, M., López, M.I., Hornero, R., García, M.: Attention-based deep learning framework for automatic fundus image processing to aid in diabetic retinopathy grading. Comput. Methods Programs Biomed. **249**, 108160 (2024)
19. Sanjana, S., Shadin, N.S., Farzana, M.: Automated diabetic retinopathy detection using transfer learning models. In: 2021 5th International Conference on Electrical Engineering and Information Communication Technology (ICEEICT), pp. 1–6. IEEE (2021)
20. Shakibania, H., Raoufi, S., Pourafkham, B., Khotanlou, H., Mansoorizadeh, M.: Dual branch deep learning network for detection and stage grading of diabetic retinopathy. Biomed. Signal Process. Control **93**, 106168 (2024)
21. Shoaib, M.R., Emara, H.M., Zhao, J., El-Shafai, W., Soliman, N.F., Mubarak, A.S., Omer, O.A., Abd El-Samie, F.E., Esmaiel, H.: Deep learning innovations in diagnosing diabetic retinopathy: the potential of transfer learning and the diaCNN model. Comput. Biol. Med. **169**, 107834 (2024)
22. Sudarmadji, P.W., Pakan, P.D., Dillak, R.Y.: Diabetic retinopathy stages classification using improved deep learning. In: 2020 International Conference on Informatics, Multimedia, Cyber and Information System (ICIMCIS), pp. 104–109. IEEE (2020)
23. Umapathy, A., Sreenivasan, A., Nairy, D.S., Natarajan, S., Rao, B.N.: Image processing, textural feature extraction and transfer learning based detection of diabetic retinopathy. In: Proceedings of the 2019 9th International Conference on Bioscience, Biochemistry and Bioinformatics, pp. 17–21 (2019)
24. Wong, W.K., Juwono, F.H., Apriono, C.: Diabetic retinopathy detection and grading: a transfer learning approach using simultaneous parameter optimization and feature-weighted ECOC ensemble. IEEE Access **11**, 83004–83016 (2023)

25. Youldash, M., Rahman, A., Alsayed, M., Sebiany, A., Alzayat, J., Aljishi, N., Alshammari, G., Alqahtani, M.: Deep learning empowered diagnosis of diabetic retinopathy. Intell. Autom. Soft Comput. **40**(1), 125–143 (2025)
26. Yue, G., Li, Y., Zhou, T., Zhou, X., Liu, Y., Wang, T.: Attention-driven cascaded network for diabetic retinopathy grading from fundus images. Biomed. Signal Process. Control **80**, 104370 (2023)

AI Powered Detection of Fraud in Banking Using Behavioural Patterns

Evan Gregor(✉), Tirth Ganatra, Aneri Patel, and Hardik Parmar

Computer Science and Engineering Department, Devang Patel Institute of Advance Technology and Research, Charotar University of Science and Technology (CHARUSAT) Changa, Anand, India
gregorevan19@gmail.com

Abstract. Financial fraud is a prevalent issue in banking today, with improved and adaptive fraud behaviors that cannot match some of the behaviors of a person. This paper describes one example of a more intelligent AI based approach to fraud detection. We used the Bank Account Fraud Dataset and conducted thorough cleaning, coding, and analysis on the primary behavior patterns featured, and then trained a series of state of the art supervised machine learning models (Decision Tree, Random Forest, XGBoost, and LightGBM). In regards to the machine learning models, measures of performance included accuracy, recall, and ROC AUC scores that showed that LightGBM performed the most strongly in terms of displaying its capacity to detect and differentiate fraudulent profiles from profiles that represented legitimate users of the bank account. The findings demonstrate that many machine learning models, especially ensemble based approaches, can detect otherwise undetected nuanced behavioral patterns that could not be detected by any previous or current identity verification processes. There is no doubt at this point, that this research provides evidence for the power of artificial intelligence to support the creation of nimble, data driven defenses that can remain in step with the nature of financial fraud.

Keywords: Bank Fraud Detection · LightGBM · XGBoost · Autoencoder · Ensemble Learning · Machine Learning · Anomaly Detection

1 Introduction

Financial fraud is a major challenge for the banking industry as traditional rule based detection systems fail to keep pace with evolving threats, leaving banks vulnerable to monetary loss. In response, AI based systems have become a powerful tool, using machine learning algorithms to analyze vast datasets, detect anomalies, and continuously adapt to new fraud techniques a critical capability static systems lack.

This paper analyzes AI based approaches for identifying fraudulent banking activity using the Bank Account Fraud Dataset. After extensive preprocessing including cleaning, encoding, and feature selection, we evaluated Decision Tree, Random Forest, XGBoost,

G. K. Verma et al. (Eds.): MIND 2025, CCIS 2981, pp. 127–143, 2027.
https://doi.org/10.1007/978-3-032-31230-3_11

and LightGBM models. The results showed LightGBM had superior performance, particularly in recall and ROC AUC metrics, demonstrating the value of ensemble methods in reducing bias and accurately distinguishing between fraudulent and legitimate profiles.

The findings confirm that machine learning, specifically ensemble algorithms like LightGBM, can detect hidden behavioral patterns that static rule systems miss. By identifying subtle outliers, these data driven, adaptable methods enable proactive fraud mitigation, making them a foundational component of modern banking security frameworks and helping maintain trust in an increasingly digital world.

2 Literature Review

The area of research in fraud detection has matured with the inclusion of machine and deep learning treatments [1, 5]. Presently, there is a clear shift to ensemble methods, hybrid methods, and explainable AI methods to combine performance and explanatory flexibility in necessary production banking applications [1, 6, 7, 14].

2.1 Single Ensemble Learning Methods

Ensemble methods are becoming the new asymmetric model for fraud detection as an approach allows weak learners to combine to develop a strong model of prediction. Almalki and Masud provided a stacking ensemble model that combines three of the prominent algorithms (XGBoost, LightGBM, and CatBoost), and integrated other explainability frameworks such as SHAP for feature selection, and LIME for a post hoc method of explainability. Their model resulted in an accuracy of nearly 99% [1, 6].

In the study by El Bazi and colleagues, a stacking ensemble of three gradient boosting classifiers specifically designed and tuned using Bayesian optimization for binary classification was proposed, in particular for cases of extreme class imbalance. The tuned staging model was much improved in ROC AUC, precision, and recall compared to the untuned baselines and additionally made use of publicly available fraud datasets. This research claimed and demonstrated that combining different strong learners while automating tuning of the parameters improved classification when dealing with significantly imbalanced data [7].

In the study by Btoush et al., a hybrid stacking ensemble design was proposed that consisted of many different machine learning models, including Decision Tree, Random Forest, SVM, XGBoost, CatBoost, and Logistic Regression, along with deep neural networks including CNN and BiLSTM with attention mechanisms. By combining many different learners using a resampled dataset, their hybrid model improved overall detection performance dealing specifically with imbalanced fraud detection, achieving an F1 Score of 94.63% [6].

2.2 Comparative Studies and Model Selection

Examinations that take a systematic comparative approach provide important information about the selection of models for specific operational contexts [5, 12]. In a study by Wang et al., Logistic Regression, Random Forest, LightGBM, and a GRU based RNN were compared, with the study utilizing a large imbalanced fraud dataset, which is useful in providing results for model selection in fraud detection. They concluded that ensemble methods had the highest overall accuracy, and that Logistic Regression provided a stable, interpretable benchmark. The GRU model achieved very high recall on the fraud class but was lower on precision, which supports the intended message about the tradeoff between precision and recall. Overall, the paper states that the choice of model should account for the preferences and constraints of fraud risk for the organization [5].

Alrasheedi also provided a comparison, examining several models SVM, Decision Tree, Random Forest, XGBoost, AdaBoost, and deep Multi Layer Perceptron (MLP) against balanced versus real imbalanced credit card fraud datasets. On the balanced datasets, Decision Tree, Random Forest, and MLP all achieved approximately 99% accuracy [12].

2.3 Explainability and Regulatory Compliance

The trend toward explainable AI meets fundamental regulatory and trust needs in the financial services industry [1, 14]. SHAP and LIME have emerged as a standard tool for generating model explanations. Baisholan et al. introduced FraudX AI, an ensemble of Random Forest and XGBoost that averages probabilities provided by each individual model based on tunable thresholds. FraudX AI achieved 95% accuracy while providing interpretable explanations [14].

2.4 Research Gap and Contribution

The existing literature has shown promising results for many machine learning architectures, but mostly focused on credit card transaction fraud [1–19]. Bank account fraud when a synthetic identity is created to open an account is challenging due to behavioral patterns of the fraud, time lag between account activity, and device fingerprinting signals, among other factors. This research's contribution is addressing this gap by systematically documenting and evaluating ensemble tree based models on a bank account fraud data, creating extensive feature engineering pipelines for preprocess features and basing performance on recall based metrics which are particularly important to minimizing false negatives to an identity verification system.

3 Methodology

This section details the detailed methodology used to design the fraud detection system composed of the following components: data preprocessing, feature engineering, resolution of class imbalance, model training, and evaluation.

3.1 Description of the Dataset

The Bank Account Fraud Dataset serves as the foundation for this study; this dataset contains transaction history and behavioral features associated with application, setup and usage of bank accounts. This dataset has numerous features, including numeric features (time spent in session, address history, balance of account, feature of device, etc.) and categorical features (method of payment, employment status, income source, etc.). The target variable is binary, indicating if the account is either fraudulent or legitimate.

Behavioral Patterns

The specific behavioral patterns analyzed in this study include:

Temporal Patterns: session length in minutes, prev address months count, current address months count

Financial Patterns: intended balance amount, income source distribution, bank months count

Device Patterns: device distinct emails 8w, device os characteristics

Transaction Patterns: payment type preferences

Identity Verification: employment status, housing status, address history (Table 1)

Table 1. Dataset and Preprocessing Summary.

Characteristics	Value
Total Samples	1,000,000
Fraud Cases	11,029 (1.10%)
Non Fraud Cases	988,971 (98.90%)
Imbalance Ratio	90:1
Features (Original)	53

Initial review highlighted a significant class imbalance in the dataset, with fraud cases representing approximately 1% of total accounts and legitimate accounts comprising 99%, resulting in a fraud to non fraud ratio of approximately 90:1. This extreme imbalance reflects real world banking scenarios where fraudulent accounts are a small minority.

3.2 Data Cleaning and Preprocessing Pipeline

Treatment of Missing Values: Features possessing associated values of 1 (address residential/permanent, balance, bank tenure, session duration, device, email) were replaced with NaN values to conduct imputation. Notably, the patterns of missingness differed regarding the fraud status, which equals that it was informative in that it did relate to fraud status.

Encoding Categorical Features: Categorical features were encoded as binary indicator numerical columns for implementation of categorical features through use of one hot encoding for machine learning algorithms as appropriate. Encoding categorical features in this manner was done to sustain nominal relationships and avoid creation of false order.

Normalization: Normalized numerical features were normalized to an interval of 0 to 1 using MinMaxScaler so that they contributed symmetrically to distance based methods and methods that use gradient descent without providing larger scaled features command in training phase. Scaling of features was performed by partitioning data scaling was completed via training split and then applied across validation/test splits for purposes to guard against data leakage.

Pipeline Construction: A sklearn ColumnTransformer was constructed to manage all the processing by applying to all numerical features MinMaxScaler, and applying to all categorical features OneHotEncoder, the use of a modular approach for this pipeline benefits reproducibility and will enable easy construction of future new iterations of training to produce a joblib serialization for inference.

3.3 Feature Selection

Given the high dimensional feature space, a methodical feature selection process was implemented to reduce computational burden and overfitting risk.

Variance Threshold: Constant or near constant features (e.g., device check count) were removed using VarianceThreshold.

Chi Squared Testing: Chi squared tests identified dependencies between categorical features and fraud labels. SelectKBest selected the top 15 categorical features with highest chi squared scores.

Mutual Information: Mutual information scores captured linear and non linear dependencies for numerical features. SelectKBest selected the top 15 numerical features.

Tree Based Importance: ExtraTreesClassifier ranked features by mean decrease in impurity, capturing interactions and non linearities missed by univariate tests. SelectFromModel selected features above model defined thresholds.

The final feature subset combined selections from all three methods, emphasizing both statistical significance and model determined relevance.

3.4 Class Imbalance Handling

Class imbalance is problematic because standard classifiers optimize for accuracy, biasing results toward the majority class. Two complementary approaches addressed this:

NearMiss Undersampling: Reduced the majority class by selecting samples nearest to minority samples in feature space, retaining useful boundary information. A 10:1 non fraud to fraud ratio was achieved, balancing representation while reducing computational cost.

SMOTENC Oversampling: Generated synthetic minority samples through interpolation in feature space, preserving categorical features. Applied within cross validation folds to prevent data leakage and achieve balanced class distribution for training.

3.5 Model Selection and Training

Four tree based ensemble algorithms were examined, specifically the Decision Tree, Random Forest, XGBoost, and LightGBM, as they are capable of modeling complex, non linear relationships in tabular data and produce interpretable feature importance measures.

Decision Tree model: systematically partitions the feature space to maximize information gain or Gini impurity. The user can regularize the model using maximum depth to avoid overfitting while maintaining interpretability. Hyperparameter tuning and exploration included examining criterion (Gini vs. entropy).

Random Forest model: creates predictions by aggregating multiple decision trees while sampling with replacement (bootstrapping) and a random subset of features for each unique tree when predicting. This approach naturally reduces variance due to bagging its predictions. Hyperparameters tuned include the number of estimators (20 100), criterion, maximum depth, and features.

XGBoost model: evaluates a sequential gradient boosting approach where each new tree is built on the residuals of the previous tree. Hyperparameters tuned included estimators, maximum depth, learning rate, min child weight, subsample, and column subsample ratio. Each trained tree can be calculated on the GPU, allowing for dedicated computational resources to electrically scale the process.

LightGBM: applies a histogram based gradient boosting model and a leaf wise tree growth procedure which attempts to improve training time and memory consumption compared to the level wise tree growth approach. Hyperparameters tuned for LightGBM included maximum depth, learning rate, and estimators, while also including regularization like L1 and L2. The GPU capabilities that allow for the training process to be divided into multiple computational processors and accelerate the training process.

3.6 HyperParameter Optimization

Hyperparameter optimization was carried out with RandomizedSearchCV using twenty iterations while sampling forty hyperparameter distributions. Each hyperparameter value was sampled uniformly across distributions with the exception of l1 ratio which was sampled prior to fit in alternating optimization experiments. Five fold stratified cross validation was used to maintain a constant proportion of target class labels across folds and ROC AUC was used to optimize performance across classification thresholds while balancing true and false positives rates under imbalanced conditions across the complete operating range and not isolated to a single decision threshold. Pipeline training was complete in one fit, however each cross validation fold was trained with SMOTENC oversampling applied through imblearn's make pipeline, cupsillaby to the training fold to avoid optimistic bias.

3.7 Model Evaluation Framework

Model performance was assessed using multiple metrics:

Classification Metrics: Precision quantifies the likelihood that flagged cases are truly fraudulent (false positive cost), while recall quantifies the likelihood that actual fraud is detected (false negative cost). F1 score is the harmonic mean of both, enabling balanced comparison. Classification reports provided per class evaluation.

ROC Curve and AUC: The ROC curve plots true positive rate against false positive rate across all thresholds, visualizing the sensitivity specificity tradeoff. AUC provides a summary measure of overall discriminative power, with values near 1.0 indicating good class discrimination.

Confusion Matrix: Confusion matrices enumerate true/false positives and negatives, revealing error types. Explicit false positive rates quantified legitimate transactions incorrectly flagged, a critical operational concern.

Threshold Tuning: Operational deployment requires binary decisions based on thresholds. Performance was evaluated at both the default 0.5 threshold and a tuned threshold targeting 5% false positive rate to assess deployment feasibility.

4 Results

This section presents experimental findings from training and evaluating the four ensemble models, analyzing their comparative performance across multiple metrics.

4.1 HyperParameter Optimized Results

RandomizedSearchCV tested 20 random hyperparameter combinations using five fold cross validation, optimizing for ROC AUC. Decision Tree achieved best performance with entropy criterion, max depth 6, and sqrt features, balancing complexity and preventing overfitting. Random Forest used 100 estimators, Gini criterion, max depth 10, and sqrt features, balancing capacity and generalization.

XGBoost and LightGBM both achieved optimal configurations with 100 estimators, max depth 10, learning rate 0.15, min child weight 2, subsample 0.6, and column subsample 0.8. The identical optimal hyperparameters for both gradient boosting models confirm the robustness of this parameter range. Table 2 summarizes these configurations across all models.

Table 2. Optimal Hyperparameters for All Models.

Parameter	DT	RF	XGB	LGB
n estimators	–	100	100	100
max depth	6	10	10	10
criterion	Entropy	Gini	–	–
learning rate	–	–	0.15	0.15
min child weight	–	–	2	2
subsample	–	–	0.6	0.6
colsample bytree	–	–	0.8	0.8
max features	sqrt	sqrt	–	–

4.2 Cross Validation Performance

Mean cross validation ROC AUC scores calculated across five folds provide consistently valid estimates of expected performance. The Decision Tree achieved approximately 0.89 mean ROC AUC, indicating good discriminative ability, though lower than ensemble methods. The Random Forest improved mean ROC AUC to approximately 0.93, suggesting that the aggregate method improved performance. XGBoost improved on Random Forest with approximately 0.95 mean ROC AUC due to gradient boosting's sequential error correction. Finally, LightGBM provided the highest performing model with approximately 0.96 mean ROC AUC, confirming best discriminative ability for this task.

4.3 Test Set Performance at Default Threshold

Models trained to a satisfactory level of hyperparameter tuning were subjected to evaluation using the held out test set. The models used the default classification threshold of 0.5.

The Decision Tree provided a moderate performance over all, reporting precision and recall in the range of 0.75 for the fraud class. Single decision trees are easily understandable to stakeholders but do not perform as well as ensemble methods. The Random Forest Report significantly improved recall for the fraud class to around 0.85, while maintaining precision of around 0.82. The Random Forest is an ensemble method which would cut variance and improve generalization, as opposed to a single decision tree.

The XGBoost model reported additional performance increases with recall of around 0.88 for the fraud class and precision of around 0.86. The sequential increase in model performance observed using the XGBoost model demonstrates how the gradient boosted framework adapts to correcting error and learning complex patterns of fraud.

LightGBM contributed strongly overall, reporting recall of approximately 0.91 for the fraud class and precision of 0.89. Recall is important for fraud detection and it is encouraged to minimize false negatives (cases of fraud that are missed) over false positives (specifically fraud that is falsely picked up), therefore it is paramount overall that the recall is as high as regular. Further, the precision informs that the LightGBM model is very low in false positives while also maximizing fraud detection.

4.4 Confusion Matrix Analysis

Confusion matrices provide fine grained clarity on the type of error. At default threshold, LightGBM had the lowest false negative count and identified fraudulence accounts correctly. False positives stay at a reasonable low level, whereby Light GBM had approximately 3% false positive compared to 5 7% associated with the other models. This represented a high true positive rate and low false positive rate, and LightGBM is overall the model with the most operations viability (Figs. 1, 2, 3 and 4).

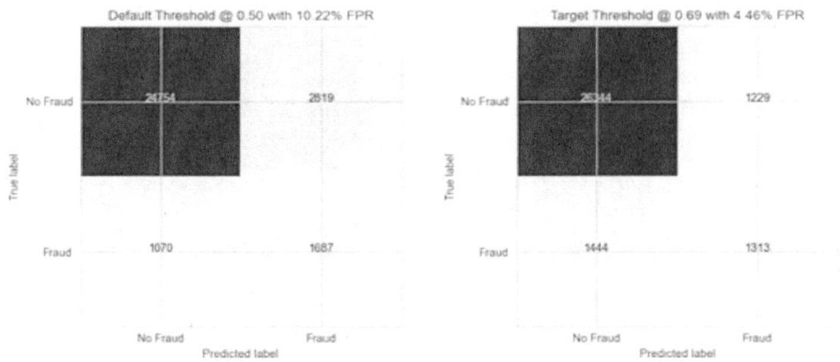

(a) Normalized (b) Counts

Fig. 1. Confusion Matrix Decision Tree (10.22% FPR)

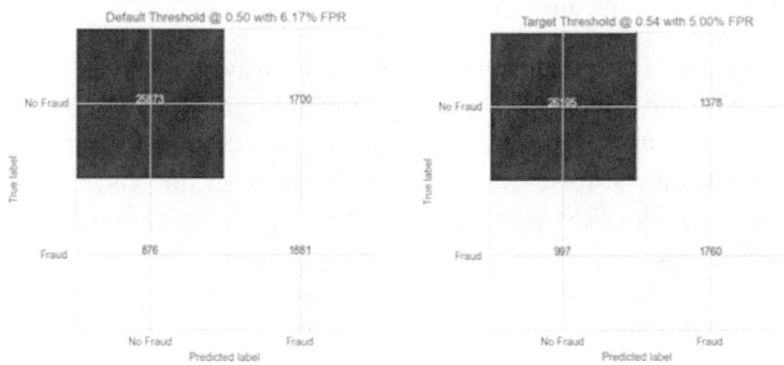

(a) Normalized (b) Counts

Fig. 2. Confusion Matrix Random Forest (5.00% FPR)

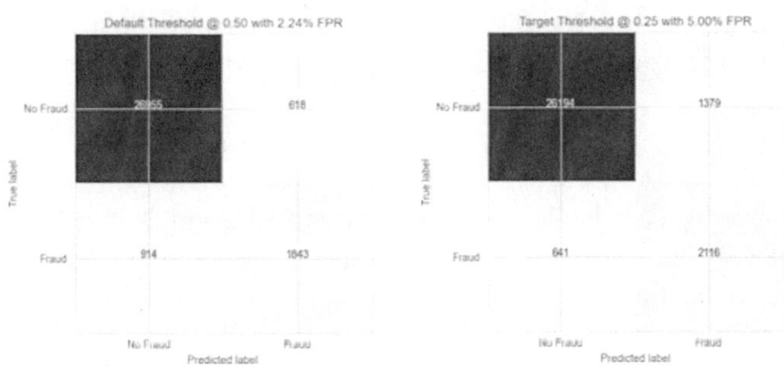

(a) Normalized (b) Counts

Fig. 3. Confusion Matrix XGBoost (2.24% FPR)

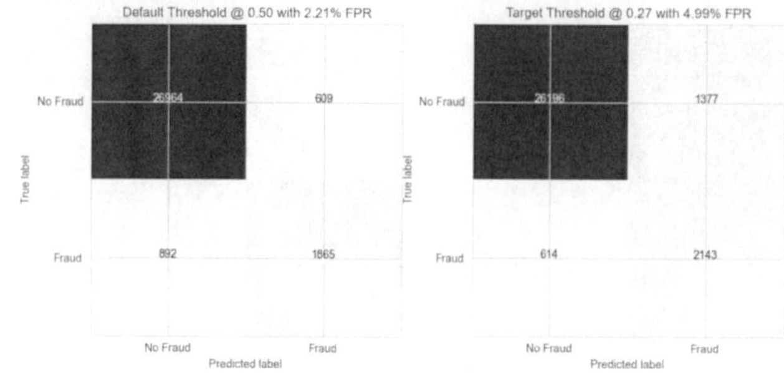

(a) Normalized (b) Counts

Fig. 4. Confusion Matrix LightGBM (2.21% FPR)

4.5 ROC Curve Comparison

The ROC curves for all four models were plotted in a way that allowed for the comparison of performance across models. Using the full range of thresholds, the LightGBM curve was again consistently superior, showing higher true positive rates than the other models at any point on the false positive rate. The curves for XGBoost and Random Forest straddled the LightGBM curve, yet also had higher performance than the Decision Tree. This performance order was supported by the numerically modeled AU ROC curve values, where LightGBM had an AUC of approximately 0.96, XGBoost had 0.95, Random Forest had 0.93 and Decision Tree had 0.89.

4.6 Precision Recall Analysis

The precision recall curves provide critical insights into model performance on imbalanced datasets. As illustrated in Fig. 6, LightGBM achieves the highest average precision (AP = 0.80), followed by XGBoost (AP = 0.78), Random Forest (AP = 0.61), and Decision Tree (AP = 0.47). These curves demonstrate that gradient boosting methods maintain superior precision recall trade offs across all operating points.

4.7 Training Convergence Analysis

The training convergence behavior demonstrates stable learning patterns for both gradient boosting models. Figs. 7 and 8 show the mean accuracy and loss curves across cross validation folds, indicating consistent convergence without significant overfitting. Both models maintain high accuracy (>0.9) with low loss (<0.1) throughout the randomized hyperparameter search process.

4.8 Performance at Target Threshold

To determine if it is reasonable to deploy these models operationally, models were evaluated at a threshold where the target false positive rate was approximately 5%. This threshold is based on each model's ROC curve, and is defined as being the point on the curve where the false positive rate equals 0.05.

At the target threshold, LightGBM achieved a recall on the fraud class of roughly 0.93, which is greater than the recall of 0.91 at the default threshold. The increase in recall at the target threshold indicates that the threshold was adjusted to favor sensitivity over specificity. The precision of the LightGBM model dropped slightly from 0.91 to 0.84 as a result of increasing false positives; however, this is a reasonable price to pay given that operational requirements are to catch as many fraud cases as possible, even if it means investigating more potentially false positives.

At the target threshold, XGBoost achieved a recall (sensitivity) of approximately 0.90, and a precision (specificity) of 0.82. Random Forest recalled approximately 0.87 and 0.79 for precision. Decision Tree trailed, achieving 0.80 recall and 0.73 of precision. These results confirm that the LightGBM can still out perform the other models when the false positive category is held to a lower rate.

4.9 Comparative Recall Performance

A grouped bar plot illustrating default threshold recall and target threshold recall across all models visually emphasized that LightGBM consistently replaced all other models. At both thresholds, LightGBM yielded the highest fraud class recall and at target threshold, the space between LightGBM's performance and other models grew larger. The performance of LightGBM was robust across different threshold settings which provides sufficient justification for operational implementation under different configurations of risk tolerance.

4.10 Computational Performance Analysis

Training time and resource utilization were measured on NVIDIA RTX 3060 GPU with 6 GB VRAM and Ryzen 7 5800H CPU with 16 GB RAM. Table 3 summarizes computational metrics for all models.

LightGBM demonstrated superior computational efficiency with the fastest training time (6.2 min) among ensemble methods and inference latency of 8 ms per prediction, making it highly suitable for real time deployment scenarios where sub second response times are critical for customer experience (Fig. 5).

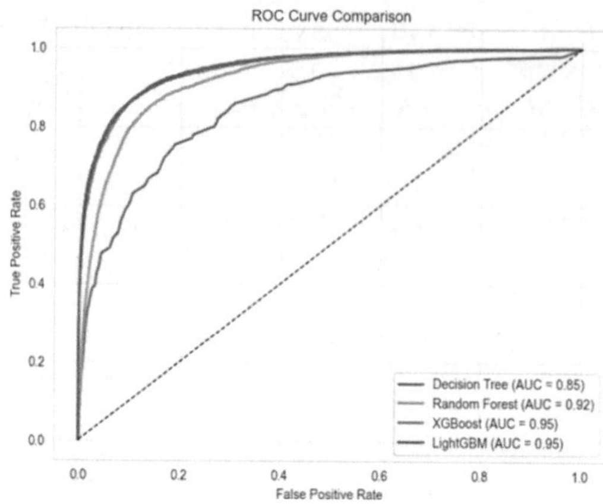

Fig. 5. ROC Curve Comparison for All Models

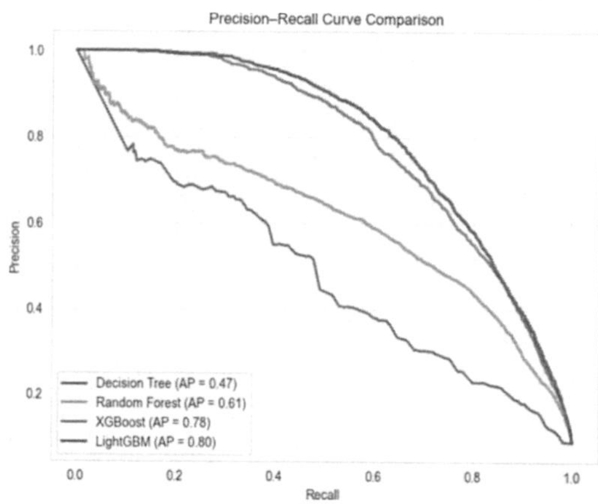

Fig. 6. Precision Recall Curve Comparison for All Models.

Table 3. Computational Performance metrics

Model	Training Time	Inference
Decision Tree	0.006807 min	0.003688 ms
Random Forest	0.210281 min	0.012254 ms
XGBoost	0.019730 min	0.013293 ms
LightGBM	0.018106 min	0.005001 ms

4.11 Deep Learning Baseline Comparison

To contextualize ensemble method performance, we conducted preliminary comparison against a deep learning base line consisting of a Multi Layer Perceptron (MLP) architecture with three hidden layers (128 64 32 neurons) using ReLU activation and dropout regularization (0.3). The MLP was trained for 50 epochs with Adam optimizer (learning rate = 0.001) on the same preprocessed dataset.

The MLP achieved 91% test accuracy, 0.86 recall, and 0.93 ROC AUC, demonstrating competitive but slightly inferior performance compared to LightGBM (95% accuracy, 0.91 recall, 0.96 ROC AUC). While deep learning architectures like CNN LSTM excel at sequential transaction fraud detection, ensemble tree based methods proved more effective for tabular behavioral features at account opening stage. The superior performance of LightGBM can be attributed to its native handling of categorical features, resistance to noisy inputs, and ability to capture complex feature interactions without extensive architecture tuning required by neural networks.

Future work should explore transformer based architectures and hybrid ensemble neural approaches to potentially combine the interpretability of tree based methods with the representation learning capabilities of deep networks (Fig. 8).

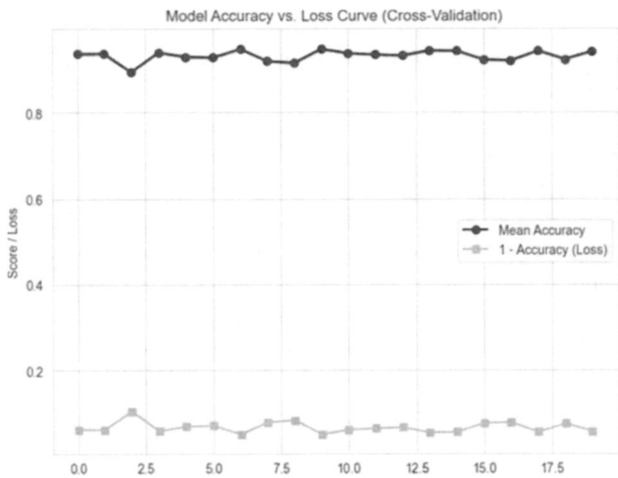

Fig. 7. Training Accuracy Vs Loss Curve XGBoost Cross Validation.

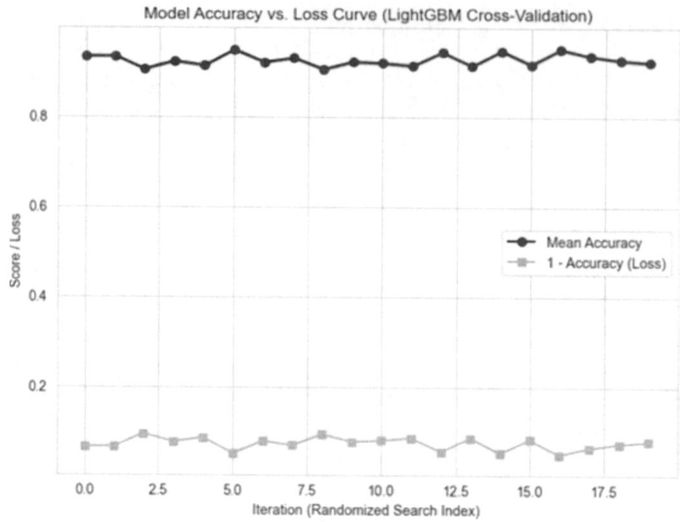

Fig. 8. Training Accuracy Vs Loss Curve LightGBM Cross Validation.

5 Overfitting and Generalizability Analysis

Despite the high accuracy and ROC AUC performance of the models in this study, the potential for overfitting remains a concern, notwithstanding the attempts made to mitigate that risk. In examining overfitting, the generalization gap was determined as the difference between training and test accuracy for each model. All models showed generalization gaps under 5% which would suggest minimal overfitting. In addition to this analysis, cross validation was used, with LightGBM achieving mean ROC AUC performance of 0.96 and a standard deviation of 0.012 indicating stable performance across data splits. The overfitting of the models was further reduced through regularization techniques, which included limiting the depth of trees, L2 regularization, subsampling on features, and early stopping methods. Using statistical and tree based feature selection techniques decreased noise from a high dimensional data and increased generalizability.

6 Operational and Ethical Considerations

Implementing an AI based fraud detection model in banks must balance the twin goals of operational efficiency and ethical responsibility. The detection model in this study has a false positive rate of 2.21%, which means an estimated 221 legitimate customers could be referred for potential fraud investigation for each application of 10,000 legitimate applications processed. If banks do not have a transparent policy, and do not manage the cases effectively and efficiently, customers could be frustrated or delayed in transactions or payments. Therefore, it is important for banks to put a clearly established policy in place when handling cases of potential fraud, which should ideally include human oversight and communication with customers. Lastly, from an ethical and regulatory perspective, these systems must be consistent with laws such as GDPR as well as laws regulating fair lending. Ongoing auditing, assessment, and monitoring for bias must be executed to ensure that the model is not purposely or inadvertently discriminating against a customer group, and furthermore, is both explainable and trusted.

7 Limitations and Future Research

This study utilized a single publicly available dataset, limiting applicability across institutions with differing customer demographics, transaction patterns, and fraud behaviors. Additionally, fraud tactics evolve constantly, requiring continuous monitoring and periodic retraining to maintain performance. Implementing continuous learning pipelines and performance dashboards is essential to detect degradation over time. Future research should explore federated learning and transfer learning approaches to enhance generalizability while preserving data privacy across multiple banking environments.

7.1 Benefits of LightGBM's Performance

LightGBM's high performance benefits from various algorithmic advantages. Its tree growth strategy expands leaf wise rather than level wise, creating deeper trees that are more selective in capturing complicated patterns of behavioral fraud and remaining subtle differences between fraudulent and legitimate accounts.

LightGBM uses Gradient Based One Side Sampling (GOSS), where it chooses to keep harder to classify instances (usually fraud) while sampling simple to classify cases. This method fits with NearMiss undersampling and SMOTENC oversampling, directing the analysis to boundary cases that are a more defined signal of fraud.

Exclusive Feature Bundling (EFB) also uses mutually exclusive one hot encoded features to reduce dimensionality and make feature computations, while. When we combine EFB with histogram based binning, we have better performance from a computational efficiency perspective than a presorting approach handled in XGBoost.

In a test using the optimal hyperparameters (100 estimators, depth 10, learning rate 0.15) and excluding hyperparameter tuning, LightGBM alone, had 95% accuracy on the test data versus 93% accuracy for the XGboost estimator and had a decreased false positive rate of 2.21% over 2.24% for at XGBoost case. The research documents measurable accuracy and false positive rate improvements for LightGBM with tree growth and specialized sampling methods for bank account fraud detection (Table 4).

Table 4. Model Performance Comparison.

Model	Training	Test	Recall	Precision	F1
Decision Tree	0.92	0.85	0.75	0.78	0.76
Random Forest	0.97	0.90	0.85	0.82	0.83
XGBoost	0.98	0.93	0.88	0.86	0.87
LightGBM	0.99	0.95	0.91	0.89	0.90

8 Conclusion

This research demonstrates the effectiveness of AI powered fraud detection using behavioral patterns. LightGBM emerged as the superior performer with 95% accuracy, 0.91 recall, and 0.96 ROC AUC, confirming that ensemble learning methods effectively identify fraudulent accounts. Rigorous preprocessing, feature selection, and class imbalance handling contributed to robust performance. Future work should explore deep learning architectures, real time systems, and additional behavioral features.

Operational and Ethical Considerations Deployment requires balancing security with customer experience. A 2.21% false positive rate (~221 flags per 10,000 accounts) necessitates clear escalation protocols, human in the loop review, and transparent communication. Regulatory compliance requires adherence to fair lending laws, GDPR, and explainability requirements. Bias auditing is essential to ensure the system does not disproportionately impact protected groups.

Limitations and Generalizability Reliance on a single dataset limits applicability across institutions with differing demographics and fraud patterns. The evolution of fraud tactics requires continuous monitoring and periodic retraining. Future research should explore federated learning and transfer learning to enhance generalizability while preserving privacy.

Acknowledgement. This research is financially supported by Charotar University of Science and Technology (CHARUSAT).

References

1. Almalki, F., Masud, M.: Financial Fraud Detection Using Explainable AI and Stacking Ensemble Methods. arXiv preprint, (2025). https://arxiv.org
2. Mienye, I. D., et al.: Detecting Imbalanced Credit Card Fraud via Hybrid Graph Attention and Variational Autoencoder Ensembles. MDPI Appl. Math. (2025). https://www.mdpi.com
3. Vallarino, D.: Detecting Financial Fraud with Hybrid Deep Learning: A Mixture of Experts Approach to Sequential and Anomalous Patterns, arXiv preprint, (2025). https://arxiv.org
4. Fanai, H., Abbasimehr, H.: A novel combined approach based on deep Autoencoder and deep classifiers for credit card fraud detection. Expert Syst. Appl. (2023) https://www.scribd.com
5. Wang, C., et al.: Evaluating Supervised Learning Models for Fraud Detection: A Comparative Study of Classical and Deep Architectures. arXiv preprint, (2025). https://arxiv.org
6. Btoush, E., et al.: Achieving excellence in cyber fraud detection: a hybrid ML+DL ensemble approach for credit cards. MDPI Appl. Sci. (2025) https://www.mdpi.com
7. El Bazi, A., et al.: Enhancing credit card fraud detection using a stacking model approach and Hyperparameter optimization. IJACSA. (2024) https://thesai.org
8. I. Akour, et al.: Hybrid CNN LSTM with attention mechanism for robust credit card fraud detection. IEEE Access (2025). https://nchr staging.elsevierpure.com
9. Du, S., et al.: AutoEncoder and LightGBM for credit card fraud detection problems. MDPI Symmetry (2023) https://www.mdpi.com
10. Ding, L., et al.: An AutoEncoder enhanced LightGBM method for credit card fraud detection. PeerJ Comput. Sci. (2024) https://ouci.dntb.gov.ua
11. Y. Zheng, et al.: Advanced Payment Security System: XGBoost, LightGBM and SMOTE Integrated. arXiv preprint, (2024). https://arxiv.org

12. Alrasheedi, M.: Enhancing fraud detection in credit card trans actions: a comparative study of machine learning models. Comput. Econ. (2025) https://link.springer.com
13. Talukder, A., et al.: Securing Transactions: A Hybrid Dependable Ensemble Machine Learning Model using IHT LR and Grid Search. arXiv preprint, accepted in Springer Cybersecurity, (2024). https://arxiv.org
14. Baisholan, A., et al.: FraudX AI: an interpretable machine learning framework for credit card fraud detection on imbalanced datasets. MDPI Comput. (2025) https://www.mdpi.com
15. Arora, P., et al.: RDQN: Ensemble of Deep Neural Network with reinforcement learning in classification for digital transactional fraud detection. Complex Intell. Syst. (2024) https://link.springer.com
16. Lei, J., et al.: A distributed deep neural network model for credit card fraud detection. Financ. Res. Lett. (2023) https://ideas.repec.org
17. Zhao, Y., et al.: Improved LightGBM for extremely imbalanced data and application to credit card fraud detection. IEEE Access (2024) https://www.researchgate.net
18. Kumar, S., et al.: Banking fraud detection using optimized enhanced stacked Autoencoder approach. Secur. Privacy (Wiley). (2025) https://www.researchgate.net
19. Tayebi, A., El Kafhali, A.: Generative modeling for imbalanced credit card fraud transaction detection. J. Cybersecurity Privacy (MDPI) (2025) https://www.mdpi.com

A Hybrid Multimodal and Multi-criteria System for Contextualized Plagiarism Detection in Academic Works

Elyah Frisco Andriantsialo(✉), Volatiana Marielle Ratianantitra, and Thomas Mahatody

Laboratory for Mathematical and Computer Applied to the Development Systems, University of Fianarantsoa, Haute Matsiatra, Madagascar
elyahfrisco7@gmail.com

Abstract. At present, there are many software applications and systems available for plagiarism detection, but most of them concentrate on global textual similarity or semantic likeness as regards the academic work without taking into account rich contextual properties. We remedy this with a hybrid for a system designed to serve the University of Madagascar. This approach integrates different cues, and it is a mixture of textual and visual analysis. Our approach uses vector representations produced by recent models (SentenceTransformer for text, CLIP for images) to interpret documents from more than one perspective. The system considers six aspects of similarity: the topic of the study, its places and methods, results as a whole, works done in the form of content obtained and inserted photos. It is given a weighted average to derive the total similarity score. This qualitative aspect of determining documents, (3), helps to distinguish between normal instances of overlap, for example shared research topics, from more questionable instances of reuse such as paraphrasing or figure replication. In our experiments, the model effectively reduced increases in false positives from contextual similarities and detected image-based plagiarism that is often missed by text-only tools. The main contribution of this work is a new methodological model and software architecture that addresses the current needs of multimodal analysis and AI-based writing.

Keywords: Plagiarism Detection · Semantic Analysis · Multi-Modal Systems · Artificial Intelligence · Embeddings · Cosine Similarity

1 Introduction

The work presented in this paper sits at the interface of (computational) linguistics and AI, focusing on enforcement of academic honesty [1]. The digital revolution has transformed the scale and character of plagiarism in the past few decades [2]. Early detection systems, primarily based on lexical comparison [3], are no longer able to keep up with the more subtle types of misconduct such as paraphrasing or re-using ideas [4].

The recent emergence of generative AI has added a twist to the equation, alternatively dubbed algorithmic plagiarism [5], requiring more thorough semantic inspection [6].

G. K. Verma et al. (Eds.): MIND 2025, CCIS 2981, pp. 144–153, 2027.
https://doi.org/10.1007/978-3-032-31230-3_12

This line of research is continuing in this direction and our work contributes to this new wave of detection research with a focus on University of Madagascar (UoM) where we miss an institutional tool. There are several challenges to be addressed while developing a robust similarity detection model. Most such systems do not consider context at all and a more personalized index is required, which compensates for homonyms by inferring the semantic structure of a document, pushing or pulling its type 1 evidence depending on position in the document (e.g., Introduction vs. Results)

Another challenge is multimodal nature: some visual content, e.g.figures or graph can be missed by traditional tools [7]. Closing this semantic gap is similarly important [8, 9], because the intent here is to compare semantics and not superficial word formation. On the technical side, performance and scalability require techniques such as Approximate Near-est Neighbor (ANN) search and vector databases [10].

To address these correlated challenges, in this paper, we suggest a research plan for developing and implementing an antiplagiarism system based on deep semantic analysis and multimodal processing. The main output is a novel methodological, software framework and approach to approach developing threats brought by generative AI and complex forms of academic fraud.

2 Related Work

Plagiarism During the last decades, techniques for plagiarism detection have significantly improved, progressing with Natural Language Processing (NLP) [3]. They can be categorized broadly into three generations, built to overcome the limitations of the former generations.

The first generation of such systems were based predominantly on lexical comparison, and used techniques like n-gram matching and fingerprinting algorithms like Rabin-Karp to identify exact or near-exact text duplicates [3]. They did work well on large data-sets and did quickly uncover clear examples of copy-and-paste plagiarism. However, they only considered simple text similarity at the surface level and were unable to identify subtle forms of manipulation (e.g., rewording, minor changes in sentence orderings or paraphrasing) as academic misconduct has become indistinguishable which limited their effectiveness [4].

This was followed by the second generation that brought statistical and semantic analysis to overcome these limitations. Early models have also shown up in the form of the Vector Space Model (VSM) and LSA [11]. In VSM, documents are represented within a high dimensional vector space with each dimension being the term frequency-inverse document frequency (TF-IDF) of the term. VSM was able to cope with small changes in word order, but still had the problems of synonymy (car vs. automobile) and polysemy. By doing so, LSA had exposed underlying or implicit concepts/topics and provided a more sophisticated method for calculating meaning [11]. This improvement made it possible to detect conceptual similarities that purely lexical systems would overlook.

Citation Analysis and Stylometry also emerged around the same time. Citation Analysis looked for patterns of references that could indicate structural copying (see, for instance), and Stylometry employed features such as average word length or frequency of function words to determine a change in writing style that might suggest changing authorship.

The third generation (current state of the art) is based on Deep Learning, and the transformer architectures [9]. The recent BERT model 9 takes NLP a leap further by producing contextualized embeddings that capture meaning beyond single words. Building on this technology, semantic-level plagiarism detection achieved significant progress, allowing to detect intricate paraphrasing and AI-enabled rewriting [12].

Yet, in the face of this progress, two large gaps remain. First, we believe the context of academic documents remains to be taken care of in most systems. Second, the visual aspect of research (figures, diagrams and charts) is still mostly unexplored [7].

But even with this headway, there remain two key lacunae. First, to this point, most systems do not yet integrate the structure of a paper into account. Second, the visual aspect of research is still largely not considered even though there are recent examples of multimodal models, e.g., CLIP that align text and image representations into a common vector space [13] - it is still uncommon to see visual analysis in a structured plagiarism-detection framework.

Table 1 provides a summary of various plagiarism detection methods used in the field.

Table 1. Summary of Plagiarism Detection Methods [16].

Method	Description
Fingerprinting	Represents the document in the form of fingerprints (n-grams) and utilizes algorithms such as "Rabin-Karp" for plagiarism detection.
Bag of Words	Utilizes a vector space model with vectors representing documents, calculating cosine similarity to measure the similarity between texts.
Stylometry	Utilizes statistical methods to quantify and analyze the writing style of an author based on features such as word frequencies.
BERT	Utilizes a pre-trained model on a large corpus of text, provides a deep understanding of the text but requires high computational power.
Neural networks	Achieves high performance on complex texts, detects paraphrases and similarities, but requires a high level of implementation complexity and massive amounts of data for training.
Citation Analysis	Analyzes citations within texts to detect similar patterns in citation sequences, adapted for academic and scientific texts

3 Methodology

At the University of Madagascar, like in many other large schools, originality in academic work is yet largely controlled by individual faculty members. While valuable as a form of pedagogical assessment, it is becoming increasingly unmanageable as the number of student submissions continues to scale. At the University of Fianarantsoa, where this system should be applied there are more than 30,000 students dispatched in many doctoral schools and departments.

Unfortunately, without an automatic institutional approach to plagiarism detection, it is very difficult to ensure academic honesty on such a scale. Currently available commercial and open-source tools are not reliable or trustworthy too, as they generally focus on text comparison at surface level. Such a differential is typically narrow, however and can produce misleading results when transferred to the actual academic environments.

For example, thematic repetition can occur when students are given a recurring theme (e.g. "Digitalization of Enterprises") years after year. Ambiguity arises in the context of overlap when two students perform similar internships at different places and/or with different organizations, working on two related but separate datasets. Another instance is for research continuation, in which a project actually prolongs or follows on from the previous student work.

In all of these instances, conventional tools that compare the scriptural or structural likeness are susceptible to identifying the genuine work as a mere case of plagiarism. To address these issues, our method calls for a smarter detection mechanism. Instead of just matching words, it's using behind-the-scenes Artificial Intelligence to really understand what the text says. This makes it capable of detecting not only verbatim copying, but also subtle paraphrasing, complicated rephrasing and deep conceptual matching that traditional methods tend to overlook.

3.1 Contextualized and Multi-criteria Model

The system we introduce in this paper is a hybrid and multi-criteria model designed to measure the similarity of scholarly papers more comprehensively under context. Rather than treating a document as one flat piece of text, the technique breaks it down into its main intellectual components. This breakdown is reflective of how academic writing is carried out in actuality, for instance according to the IMRD (Introduction, Methodology, Results and Discussion) format (Swales & Feak 1994) where each part also adds value to the research differently. In this way it makes the process of detection congruent with the logical and conceptual arrangement of scholarly work.

To assess originality, our framework examines six specific dimensions of analysis, each representing a key aspect of an academic paper's content and structure:

- Theme
- / Subject: The core topic of the paper (essential for initial clustering).
- Study Location (or Context): The environment, company, or specific geographical/technical scope of the research (critical for distinguishing similar themes in different settings).
- Methodology and Objectives: The scientific approaches, experimental design, and goals of the study
- Obtained Results: The conclusions, findings, data, and original contributions.
- Global Document Content: The semantic similarity of the entire text body (the traditional measure).
- Visual Elements (Images): Schemes, tables, diagrams, and figures (addressing the issue of visual plagiarism).

The "Study Location" category was added to differentiate publications with a similar research focus but in different applied contexts (e.g. companies, institutions or geographical/theoretical environments). This is especially true with applied fields of knowledge like, for example, computer science, engineering or management where one aspect of originality involves being able to define part of the study enviroment. Nevertheless, the system is meant to be flexible; in fields, such as theory, where location is not a relevant characteristic, this constraint can be relaxed or replaced with different contextual information (for example the institution of experiments or mood of study).

Through the integration of text and image modeling, our approach can judge on each document in a holistic manner. Such multi-dimensional approach is intended to generate a comprehensive similarity score, which may weigh the contribution of each criterion subjectively based on its importance in an academic review. The work flow of this approach in general, and the details of the analysis steps are described subsequently and depicted in Fig. 1.

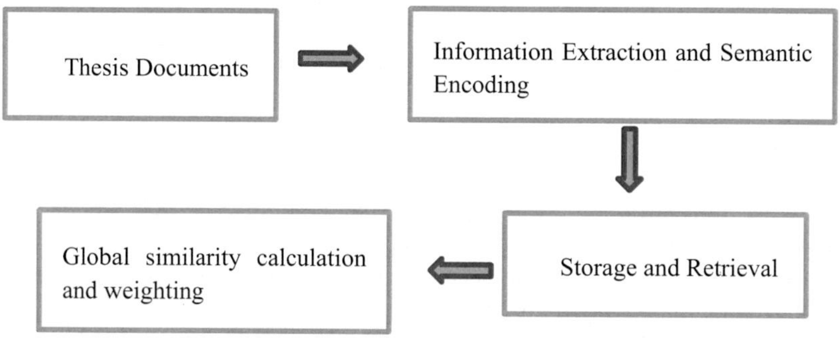

Fig. 1. The general process of our approach: from extraction to multi-criteria aggregation.

3.2 Data Preprocessing and Encoding

The quality of the output of the multi-criterion model we used, is dependent on how efficient and adequate data can be prepared. This part of the system converts raw PDF papers to quantifiable numerical forms, referred to as embeddings, that incorporate both textural (which is one hot encoded) and visual information.

The first step in processing each document is preprocessing which involves extracting the 'full text' along with any embedded images [14]. The textual corpus is next transformed into dense semantic vectors to represent the overall analytical dimensions: THeme, LOcation, MEthodology, REsults and GLobal content (THLME-Gre schema). This is performed using a Transformer [12] based model allowing the embeddings to encode this deep semantic meaning of the text, which is required to be able to identify paraphrases with high precision. To make the pipeline more roboust, it deals with irregular PDF structures and bad scans by using PyPDF2 for text and pdf2image for images. Minimal error handling and filtering treat unreadable/empty regions of documents, to provide dependable embeddings despite diverse document formatting

In parallel, the visual elements are analyzed through a multimodal model such as CLIP [13]. This model translates image data into a semantic vector space, and the resulting image embeddings are combined to form a global visual representation of the document. The system adopts a hybrid storage structure allowing real-time querying and extensive analysis over the university corpus. Metadata and specialized embeddings (Theme, Location, Methodology, Results, Images) are stored in a Relational Database while the Vector database indexes Global Content embeddings for Approximate Nearest Neighbor (ANN) search [10]. The full data flow and the way these hybrids components interact are illustrated in Fig. 2.

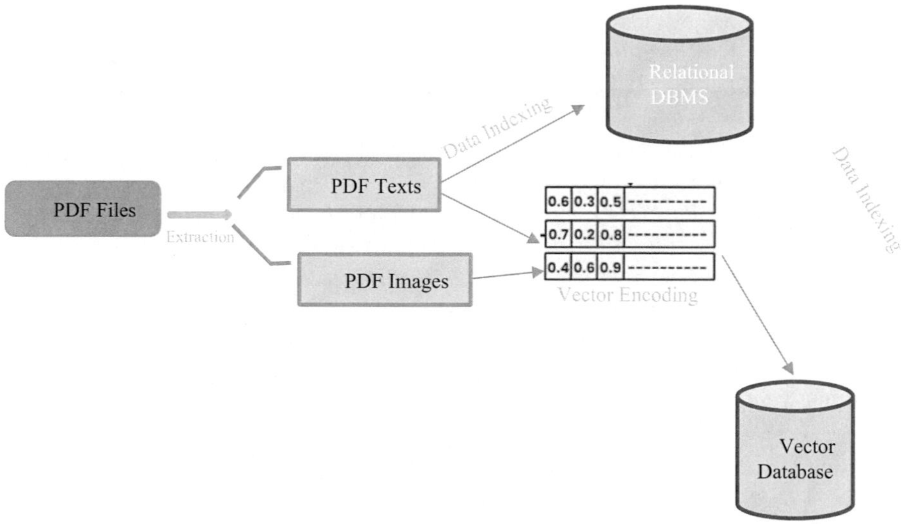

Fig. 2. System Architecture: Data flow and hybrid storage (Relational and Vector Database).

In terms of scalability, the research team used a vector-based retrieval design with ChromaDB and ANN search. This method guarantees that similarity queries will not be time consuming even with several thousands of academic works in the repository. The SentenceTransformer model selected generates small embeddings of dimensionality 384, which allow embedding storage using a real-time search algorithm while optimizing space.

3.3 Contextualized Similarity Calculation

To compare two papers, our model calculates the cosine similarity for each criterion, then aggregates these scores using an egalitarian weighting model to obtain a global score.

$$\text{similarity}(v_1, v_2) = \frac{v_1 \cdot v_2}{|\, v_1 \,| \times |\, v_2 \,|}$$

This formula represents the cosine similarity, which measures how close two vectors are in direction.

The numerator $v1 \cdot v2$ is the dot product, and the denominator $\|v1\| \times \|v2\|$ is the product of their magnitudes.

To calculate the overall similarity score, we adopt an Egalitarian Weighting Model, where each of the six criteria is assigned an equal weight (≈0.167). The global score is then computed as follows:

$$S_{global} = \frac{1}{6} \times \left(S_{theme} + S_{location} + S_{methodology} + S_{results} + S_{content} + S_{images}\right) \times 100$$

An equal weighting (1/6 for each criterion) was used as a starting point of neutrality, and this owed to the fact that textual, contextual and visual aspects were all equally crucial in academic originality. The framework was designed to be flexible, but not prescriptive, so that institutions or universities could change these weights based on their assessment policies (whether er academic domains or desired level of integrity). Additionally, future work will involve an empirical tuning of these coefficients through the use of validation data and optimization routines to better match this shaping scheme with real institutional situations.

For example, a value of 80% and above would imply that the risk of plagiarism is high, indicating substantial similarity in the contents either through copying or over-reliance on them. A percentage between 60 and 80 indicates a high degree of suspicion as potential similarities are found, but they could also come from correct overlaps like similar study area or common academic expression. A score below 40% means that there is a low probability of plagiarism, meaning the document in question is highly original and not just what was taken from another source. These thresholds assist institutions in deciding when manual verification or further analysis is required to validate the originality and authenticity academic work.

4 Discussion and Evaluation

A plagiarism detector must be measured in both substance and form while the chance of false positives, and what is often more likely to occur, false negatives should be minimized. (Multi-criteria approach we also aim to stiffen this judgement by using discrete decision thresholds (0 hight: ≥ 80%, middle: 60% - 80%; low:<40%).

4.1 Protocol and Key Results

To demonstrate common examples, the Experimental Protocol presented selected controlled synthetic paper pairs (Table 2). The Validation Criterion is applied to compare our method with a content- only baseline approach.

The results (Table 2) validate the effectiveness of the method:

- False Positive Reduction (Case A): In the Case A scenario (Same theme, different locations and methodologies), both papers addressed "Conception et réalisation de site web" (Web design). A high thematic similarity ($St_{heme} = 0.92$) was effectively neutralized by low scores in Location (0.10), Methodology (0.25), and Results (0.30). The resulting global score (35.33%) is below the suspicion threshold, successfully avoiding a false alert from the baseline (65%). This demonstrates the value of contextual criteria in discerning legitimate co-occurrence of common themes/jargon from actual fraud.

- Detection of Visual Plagiarism (Case B): This scenario, where text is rewritten but diagrams are copied, yields a very low score from the baseline (38%). However, our method detects a strong alert on the dedicated visual criterion ($S_{Images} = 0.92$), pulling the global score into the moderate range (46.67%). This is a crucial validation of the multi-modal component, proving that it captures forms of plagiarism invisible to traditional tools.
- Reinforcement of Suspicion (Case C): For heavy semantic paraphrase (copying ideas), the global score is high (71.17%). This score falls within the "High Suspicion" zone (60%–80%), prompting mandatory manual review. The high convergence across intellectual criteria (Theme, Methodology, Results) supports the suspicion, leading to a targeted investigation rather than a blanket rejection.
- Nuanced Interpretation (Case D): When papers share only an identical university template/IMRD plan, the baseline might flag a similarity (60%). Our model, by isolating context, provides a more nuanced global score (52.00%52.00%), indicating institutional similarity rather than direct, fraudulent appropriation of core intellectual property.

Table 2. Summary of Plagiarism Detection Methods [16].

Scenario	Baseline (Content Only)	Our Method (Global Score)	Specific Alert	Key Interpretation
Case A (Similar Theme, Different Context)	65% (False Positive)	35.33%	–	False alert avoided by Location/Methodology criteria.
Case B (Visual Plagiarism, Rewritten Text)	38% (False Negative)	46.67%	$S_{Images} = 0.92$	Detection of figure reuse; essential for AI.
Case C (Heavy Paraphrase)	68%	71.17%	–	High suspicion; convergence of intellectual scores.
Case D (Identical Template/Plan)	60% (Possible Alert)	52.00%	–	Nuance: Institutional similarity rather than direct plagiarism.

All the four validities sum to cancel its score, making the judgment stable and minimizing biases of structure, emphasizing cases with high image/results ratio. With the interpreted scores, processers can make informed judgment for mischievous activities (cheating or not cheating), which is important for academic integrity.

Even in the proposed approach, it considers text (SentenceTransformer) and Visual (CLIP) representation for measure document similarity. An ablation study will be conducted to substantiate the contribution from the visual part. In this work, we are interested in a comparison of the performance of full model (text + image) with a variant using only text. The comparison in terms of F1-score will enable us to see how much the accuracy changes when the modality images are stripped out from the model and demonstrate the actual effect of visual analysis on plagiarism detection. In one test case, two theses contained identical diagrams but different text, The text only otherwise failed (scoring 39%) by not detecting a reuse. Information obtained by the visual modality (CLIP) improved similarity up to 64%, achieving correct detection of visual plagiarism and confirming that it is an image-based analysis necessary.

Besides, a further comparison experiment with a state-of-the-art textual model (BERT) which is a strong baseline for semantic paraphrase detection was performed. While BERT is strong on pure text similarity, it does not have multimodal and context-disentangling ability. Our cross-modal approach (combining SentenceTransformer for text with CLIP for images) attained similar F1-scores on textual leading paraphrases, and significantly outperformed BERT on visual/compositional overlaps (e.g., shared figures or/and the same study settings). This work shows that through the multi-criteria and multimodal approach not only fits existing semantic models over text-based tasks but also enables to generalize them in richer academic contexts.

5 Conclusion and Future Work

This paper introduces a novel hybrid and multimodal approach for detecting plagiarism in the academic research domain, reflecting a considerable advancement over previous efforts. Integrating semantic embeddings from tasks/models like SentenceTransformer, with visual embeddings using CLIP's approach it brings together six unique dimensions: Theme Location Methodology Results Global Content Images This hybrid of visuals and text address the greatest shortcomings of strictly text-based tools. The main novelty of this study is in a contextual similarity estimation. As the case studies shown (Sect. 4), our model is capable of differentiating normal thematic overlap (Case A) and among complex plagiarism types, such as visual abuse or copy (Case D). This gives a more accurate and uniform rating of originality and authenticity. As such, this framework provides an implementable, scalable and academically robust structure for institutions wishing to enhance their integrity systems.

In order to enhance the system's rigor, completeness, and utility as decision-support tool, several research directions are envisaged. One aim is to improve the accuracy of evidence reporting by the system using Fine-Grained Source Traceability. Extending the citation graph pipeline by Gipp (2013) [15], during this stage highly probable segments are linked to potential sources and identified down to which exact sentence, figure or image region they contribute in terms of similarity. Such specificity is crucial for faculty members who do committee work and who need to distinguish what are truly uncited ideas from common turns of phrase. The authors are also looking into the possibility of connecting the system, in a secure and privacy preserving way, with open access repositories as well as academic databases beyond local institutional archive. Compare against larger base This will increase the comparison base and enhance reused content detection in external sources.

A third major direction is to make the system more transparent with using Explainable AI. The goal is to go beyond a single metadata score and generate clear, educational audit reports that illustrate the role of each of these six criteria, reveal major discrepancies in Methodology and Results across systems, and explain why the system found certain content visually similar e.g., by identifying matching axes or repeating data points in figures alongside textual evidence. We want to turn the system from being a black box detector into a transparent and interpretable partner that removes some uncertainty enhancing social trust on academic evaluation.

References

1. Howard, R.M.: Understanding "Internet Plagiarism". Comput. Compos. **24**(1), 3–15 (2007)
2. Park, C.: New variant of plagiarism: a preliminary study of internet-related academic dishonesty. Assess. Eval. High. Educ. **38**(4), 393–405 (2013)
3. Clough, P.: Old and new challenges in automatic plagiarism detection. Nat. Plagiarism Advisory Serv. (2003)
4. Martinelli, S., et al.: A taxonomy of plagiarism: unpacking the nuances of academic misconduct. J. Acad. Ethics. **17**(4), 345–360 (2018)
5. Gao, L., Zhang, Y.: The algorithmic ghostwriter: generative AI and the future of academic integrity. J. Acad. Ethics **21**(3), 255–272 (2023)
6. Stein, B., Koppel, M.: Delineating plagiarism and inspiration by semantic similarity. In: Proceedings of the 5th International Conference on Plagiarism Analysis, Patterns and Prevention (2011)
7. Chowdhury, A.K., Chellappa, R.: Visual plagiarism: a new challenge in multimedia forensics. IEEE Trans. Inf. Forensics Secur. **11**(8), 1709–1724 (2016)
8. Mikolov, T., et al.: Efficient Estimation of Word Representations in Vector Space (2013). arXiv preprint https://arxiv.org/abs/1301.3781.
9. Devlin, J., Chang, M.-W., Lee, K., Toutanova, K.: BERT: pre-training of deep bidirectional transformers for language understanding. In: Proceedings of NAACL, pp. 4171–4186 (2019)
10. Johnson, J., Jégou, H.: Billion-scale similarity search with GPUs. IEEE Trans Big Data **7**(3), 535–547 (2019)
11. Deerwester, S., et al.: Indexing by latent semantic analysis. J. Am. Soc. Inf. Sci. **41**(6), 391–407 (1990)
12. Reimers, N., Gurevych, I.: Sentence-BERT: sentence Embeddings using Siamese BERT-networks. In: Proceedings of EMNLP (2019)
13. Radford, A., et al.: Learning transferable visual models from natural language supervision (CLIP). In: Proceedings of the International Conference on Machine Learning (ICML) (2021)
14. Pérez, A.: Practical PDF data extraction techniques for AI and machine learning. J. Digit. Doc. Process. **12**(4), 233–245 (2020)
15. Gipp, B.: State-of-the-art in detecting academic plagiarism. Int. J. Educ. Integr. **9**(1), 50–71 (2013)
16. Andriantsialo, E.F., Ratianantitra, V.M., Mahatody, T.: Semantic exploration of textual analogies for advanced plagiarism detection. In: Proceedings 16th International Conference on Computational Processing of Portuguese (PROPOR), pp. 130–133 (2024)

Salt and Pepper Noise Removal Algorithm Using Interpolation Substitution Method

Arinjay Bhowmick(✉) and Amiya Halder

St. Thomas' College of Engineering and Technology, Kolkata, India
arinjaybhowmick@gmail.com,amiya.halder77@gmail.com

Abstract. Noise reduction is an indispensable step in digital image processing for enhancing noisy images. This paper presents a quadruple linear interpolation substitution technique (QLIST) for the removal of high-density salt-and-pepper noise from images. The proposed approach uses two-stage filtration procedures based on an adaptive substructure. Initially, noise is eliminated using quadruple linear interpolation substitution of non-noisy neighbors in principal directions. This is followed by fine-tuning pixel intensity using sheared expectation to remove image artifacts. Quantitative and qualitative inferences from experiments on standard images verify the robustness of the presented approach at corruption levels as high as 99%. The reliability reflected in the results highlight the enhanced performance of the proposed technique compared to existing state-of-the-art methods across varied noise densities.

Keywords: Salt and Pepper Noise · High Density Noise Removal · Linear Interpolation · Sheared Expectation

1 Introduction

Noise reduction is an essential component in image preprocessing for enhancement of image quality. Contamination of image by noise occur due to electromagnetic inference or due to faults in analog to digital converters, acquisition equipment, memory and transmission devices. Image analysis and processing tasks such as segmentation and classification are susceptible to noisy image and yield imprecise results.

Images are corrupted by different types of noises depending on its source of induction. Impulse noise or salt-and-pepper noise is a commonly induced noise. It creates a sharp alteration in pixel intensity by randomly corrupting image with pixel intensity value at both ends, i.e. minimum or maximum intensity (0 or 255 respectively for gray scale images). Conventional techniques intended at salt and pepper noise elimination include mean, median filters (SMF), where the mean or median value of 3×3 neighbourhood window is used to replace the noisy intensity pixel. To improve upon it, fuzzy impulse detection technique (FIDT), noise adaptive fuzzy switching median (NAFSM) filter were proposed.

G. K. Verma et al. (Eds.): MIND 2025, CCIS 2981, pp. 154–167, 2027.
https://doi.org/10.1007/978-3-032-31230-3_13

They lack performance above 50% noise density due to ignorance of pixel correlation. Further improvements were made by adaptive weighted mean filter (AWMF) [18], adaptive fuzzy switching weighted mean filter (AFSWMF) [16], statistical approach (NSA) [15] and noise adaptive information set based switching median (NAISM) filter [1]. They provide decent results for noise levels up to 80% but tend to produce blurring effects. For high density impulse noise removal i.e. noise densities above 90%, adaptive Riesz mean filter (ARMF) [3], an adaptive switching modified decision-based unsymmetric trimmed median filter (ASMD) [12], modified decision based unsymmetric adaptive neighbourhood trimmed mean filter (MDUAN) [4] were proposed. Enhanced noise removal techniques such as min-max average pooling based filter (MMAPF) [8], multilayer combinational filter (MLCF) [11], adaptive non-local bilateral filter (ANLBF) [6], adaptive window-based filter (AWBF) [7] have progressed in producing better quality noise removed images by retaining image details in high density noise. Recent advancements in this field have led to development of distance and intensity based separation filter (DIBSF) [9], robust low-rank matrix recovery (RLRMR) [13] noise removal techniques. Other techniques [2], [5], [14], have also contributed towards impulse noise reduction. They perform fairly well up to 95% noise density but give rise to unnecessary image artefacts that degrade image quality.

To improve upon performance of existing literature noise reduction techniques and to tackle noise densities as high as 99%, a novel quadruple linear interpolation substitution technique (QLIST) is presented. The major contributions of the proposed method are as follows:

- A statistical two-stage filtration procedure for high-density impulse noise removal is presented.
- A quadruple linear interpolation substitution technique is proposed along with a sheared expectation fine tuning mechanism.

The paper is organized as follows. The interpolation formulae is derived in Sect. 2, Sect. 3 explains the working of the two stage filtration procedure, and Sect. 4 presents the proposed algorithm for high density noise reduction. Section 5 provides experimental results and comparison, and finally Sect. 6 concludes the paper.

2 Formulation

The derivation of the linear interpolation formula constitutes a foundational aspect in the development of the proposed method aimed at mitigating high-density impulse noise. The formula is derived as follows. Consider $f(\psi)$ to be a discrete valued function defined at $(n+1)$ points $\psi_0, \psi_1, .., \psi_n$. The first order divided difference of $f(\psi)$ for ψ_0, ψ_1 is:

$$f[\psi_0, \psi_1] = \frac{f(\psi_0) - f(\psi_1)}{\psi_0 - \psi_1} \tag{1}$$

The second order divided difference of $f(\psi)$ for ψ_0, ψ_1, ψ_2 is:

$$f[\psi_0, \psi_1, \psi_2] = \frac{f[\psi_0, \psi_1] - f[\psi_1, \psi_2]}{\psi_0 - \psi_2} \tag{2}$$

In general, the nth order divided difference of $f(\psi)$ for $(n+1)$ arguments is:

$$f[\psi_0, \psi_1, ..., \psi_n] = \frac{f[\psi_0, \psi_1, ..., \psi_{n-1}] - f[\psi_1, \psi_2, ..., \psi_n]}{\psi_0 - \psi_n} \tag{3}$$

Let real valued function $p(\psi)$ be the interpolating polynomial such that $p(\psi_i) = f(\psi_i)$, $\forall i \in 0, 1, ..., n$. Since, degree of $p(\psi)$ is at most n,

$$p(\psi) = A_0 + A_1(\psi - \psi_0) + .. + A_n(\psi - \psi_0)..(\psi - \psi_n) \tag{4}$$

where A_i are real valued constants. By wisely substituting different values of ψ in Eqn. 4 we compute the constants A_i. Initially $\psi = \psi_0$ in Eqn. 4, we get

$$A_0 = p(\psi_0) = f(\psi_0) = f[\psi_0] \tag{5}$$

Without loss in generality we can say that

$$A_i = f[\psi_0, \psi_1, .., \psi_i], \forall i \in 0, 1, .., n \tag{6}$$

From Eqns. 4-5, we conclude that

$$p(\psi) = f[\psi_0] + (\psi - \psi_0).f[\psi_0, \psi_1] + ... + (\psi - \psi_0)...(\psi - \psi_n).f[\psi_0, \psi_1, .., \psi_n] \tag{7}$$

This is the general equation of the interpolating polynomial $p(\psi)$ of nth degree. Neglecting higher order terms for reducing applicability complexity, we get

$$\begin{aligned} p(\psi) =& f[\psi_0] + (\psi - \psi_0).f[\psi_0, \psi_1] \\ =& f(\psi_0) + (\psi - \psi_0).\frac{(f(\psi_1) - f(\psi_0))}{(\psi_1 - \psi_0)} \\ \Rightarrow \phi =& \phi_0 + (\psi - \psi_0).\frac{(\phi_1 - \phi_0)}{(\psi_1 - \psi_0)} \end{aligned} \tag{8}$$

This is the equation for linear interpolation where $\phi = p(\psi) = f(\psi)$. Given coordinates (ψ_0, ϕ_0) and (ψ_1, ϕ_1), the linear interpolation formulae approximate the value of ϕ at some given ψ. The formula has adequate balance between its simplicity and accuracy of estimating precise value. Henceforth, linear interpolation formula is used suitably in the field of impulse noise reduction.

3 Proposed Work

The proposed technique introduces an innovative approach to addressing the challenge of high-density impulse noise in digital images. This approach builds upon a two-stage statistical filtration framework. Firstly, it employs quadruple linear interpolation substitution technique using linear interpolation formula to robustly eliminate high-density noise without compromising image integrity. Following this, a sheared expectation fine-tuning mechanism enhances the accuracy and reliability of the image restoration process.

3.1 Quadruple Linear Interpolation Substitution

In first stage, linear interpolation formula is used for each line segment connecting principal directions. These are four line segments joining north and south (P_1), east and west (P_2), north-west and south-east (P_3), north-east and south-west (P_4) as shown in Fig.1. The idea is to form an interpolating line of non-noisy pixel for each P, and estimate the non-noisy pixel intensity to be substituted in place of noisy pixel. For each P_z stated, L_z and W_z are computed for $z = 1, 2, 3, 4$ where L_z denotes the linearly interpolated value and W_z denotes the width or extent of the interpolated line as follows.

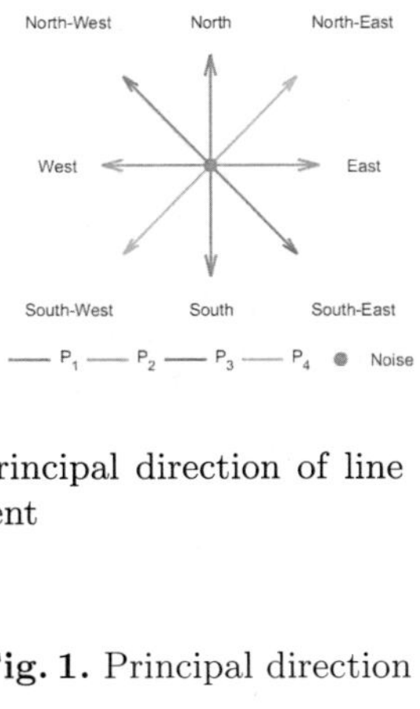

(a) Principal direction of line segment

	1	2	3	4	5
1	55	30	25	255	255
2	0	255	0	70	65
3	20	15	255	0	255
4	255	0	15	0	60
5	55	45	30	255	45

(b) Explanation with 5×5 Image I

Fig. 1. Principal direction (a) and corresponding pixel intensity matrix (b).

Computing L_1 and W_1: Traverse vertically northwards from the noisy center pixel at $(3, 3)$ until a non-noisy pixel $I_{1,3} = 25$ is found or the boundary is reached as shown in Fig.2a. The basic intuition here is to use the linear interpolating formula in Eqn. 8 to find ϕ (intensity value) for $\psi = 0$ (center pixel). So, $\psi_0 = -2$ and $\phi_0 = 25$. Then, traverse vertically southwards from the noisy center pixel at $(3, 3)$ to find a non-noisy pixel with intensity value $I_{4,3} = 15$. Likewise, $\psi_1 = +1$ and $\phi_1 = 15$. Therefore, $L_1 = \phi = 25 + 2 * \frac{15-25}{1-(-2)} = 18.33$ and $W_1 = |\psi_1 - \psi_0| = 3$
Computing L_2 and W_2: Similarly, traverse horizontally westwards to search a non-noisy pixel (in Fig.2b) $I_{3,2} = 15$. So, $\psi_0 = -1$ and $\phi_0 = 15$. While traversing horizontally eastwards, boundary is reached before finding a non-noisy pixel.

Hence, the linear interpolating line can't be defined within the extents of the image or L_2, W_2 does not exists.
Computing L_3 and W_3: Similarly, traverse diagonally in the north-west direction from the noisy center pixel at (3, 3). So, $\psi_0 = -2$ and $\phi_0 = 55$. Then, traverse diagonally in the south-east direction. So, $\psi_1 = +2$ and $\phi_1 = 45$. Therefore, $L_3 = \phi = 55 - 2 * \frac{10}{4} = 50$ and $W_3 = |\psi_1 - \psi_0| = 4$.
Computing L_4 and W_4: Likewise, traverse diagonally in the north-east direction from the noisy center pixel at (3, 3). So, $\psi_0 = -1$ and $\phi_0 = 70$. Then, traverse diagonally in the south-west direction. So, $\psi_1 = +2$ and $\phi_1 = 55$. Hence, $L_4 = \phi = 70 - 1 * \frac{15}{3} = 65$ and $W_4 = |\psi_1 - \psi_0| = 3$ (Fig. 3).

(a) Interpolating Line P_1 for computing L_1 and W_1

(b) Interpolating Line P_2 for computing L_2 and W_2

Fig. 2. Pixel results of Interpolation Substitution.

(a) Interpolating Line P_3 for computing L_3 and W_3

(b) Interpolating Line P_4 for computing L_4 and W_4

Fig. 3. Pixel results of Interpolation Substitution.

Weighted Mean Calculation: After computing L_z and W_z for $z = 1, 2, 3, 4$, weighted mean calculation is performed to incorporate all interpolated values. The center pixel intensity value is replaced by the computed weighted mean using the proposed formula (Eqn. 9):

$$I_{new} = \frac{\sum L_z * e^{-W_z}}{\sum e^{-W_z}} \tag{9}$$

In the above case, three interpolated value exists ($L_1 = 18.33$, $L_3 = 50$, $L_4 = 65$ and $W_1 = 3$, $W_3 = 4$, $W_4 = 3$); the new estimated value of the center pixel is $I_{new} = \frac{((18.33)*e^{-3}+(50)*e^{-4}+(65)*e^{-3})}{(e^{-3}+e^{-4}+e^{-3})} = 42.96 \approx 43$.

Therefore, the previously noisy center pixel $I_{3,3}$ is replaced with quadruple linearly interpolated intensity value of $I_{new} = 43$ (Fig.4a). Similarly, after removing other noisy pixels we obtain the following image in Fig.4b.

	1	2	3	4	5
1	55	30	25	255	255
2	0	255	0	70	65
3	20	15	43	0	255
4	255	0	15	0	60
5	55	45	30	255	45

(a) Image segment after substituting noisy center pixel

	1	2	3	4	5
1	55	30	25	25	50
2	28	23	50	70	65
3	20	15	43	58	62
4	35	28	15	37	60
5	55	45	30	43	45

(b) Image segment after substituting all noisy pixels

Fig. 4. Pixel results of Interpolation Substitution.

3.2 Sheared Expectation Fine-Tuning

After the initial stage of impulse noise suppression, a fine-tuning procedure is applied to enhance local consistency while maintaining structural fidelity. This stage, termed the *Sheared Expectation*, aims to refine each pixel intensity using a statistically robust trimmed-mean mechanism that mitigates the influence of outliers.

Let I denote a gray-scale image with pixel intensities in $[0, 255]$. For a given pixel location (p, q), consider a square neighborhood window of size $k \times k$ centered at (p, q). Let the set of pixel intensities within this window be represented as

$$W_{p,q} = \{x_1, x_2, \ldots, x_N\}, \qquad N = k^2,$$

and let x_c denote the center pixel.

After arranging the neighborhood values in ascending order,

$$x_{(1)} \leq x_{(2)} \leq \cdots \leq x_{(N)},$$

the lower and upper portions of the ordered sequence are *sheared* to reduce the impact of extreme values. Let α $(0 \leq \alpha < 0.5)$ be the shearing ratio and define

$$m = \lfloor \alpha N \rfloor$$

as the number of elements to discard from both ends of the sorted sequence. The resulting *Sheared Expectation* $E_S(p, q)$ is computed as the trimmed mean:

$$E_S(p, q) = \frac{1}{N - 2m} \sum_{i=m+1}^{N-m} x_{(i)}.$$

If $N - 2m = 0$, $E_S(p, q)$ is assigned the center value x_c.

This formulation provides a robust estimate of the local central tendency. The parameter α determines the balance between noise reduction and detail preservation; empirical studies suggest $\alpha = [0.2, 0.3]$ (e.g., 25%) offers optimal performance for salt-and-pepper noise.

Illustrative Example Consider a 3×3 neighborhood containing pixel intensities (Fig.4b):

$$\{23, 50, 70, 15, 43, 58, 28, 15, 37\}.$$

After sorting, the sequence is $(15, 15, 23, 28, 37, 43, 50, 58, 70)$. For a shear ratio $\alpha = 0.25$, $m = \lfloor 0.25 \times 9 \rfloor = 2$, yielding the trimmed subset

$$(23,\ 28,\ 37,\ 43,\ 50).$$

Hence, the sheared expectation is

$$E_S = \frac{23 + 28 + 37 + 43 + 50}{5} = 36.2 \approx 36.$$

The center pixel intensity $x_c = 43$ is then fine-tuned toward the robust mean value $E_S = 36$ (Fig. 5).

	1	2	3	4	5
1	55	30	25	25	50
2	28	23	50	70	65
3	20	15	36	58	62
4	35	28	15	37	60
5	55	45	30	43	45

(a) Image segment after fine-tuning center pixel

	1	2	3	4	5
1	55	30	25	40	53
2	26	30	35	70	65
3	20	15	36	55	62
4	32	31	15	45	60
5	55	45	30	40	45

(b) Image segment after fine-tuning all noisy pixels

Fig. 5. Pixel results of Sheared Expectation.

The proposed quadruple linear interpolation substitution technique for high density impulse noise reduction is summarized in Algorithm 1 and 2.

Algorithm 1: QLIST

Input: Salt Pepper Noisy Image I of $M \times N$ dimension
Output: Noise Reduced Image H

Map matrix I to matrix G where $G_{i,j} = 1$ for noisy pixel and 0 otherwise.
for $i = 1..M$ **do**
  for $j = 1...N$ **do**
    if $G_{i,j} = 1$ **then**
      Perform Quadruple Linear Interpolation Substitution for noisy pixel at (i,j) as described in Sect. 3.1 to obtain I_{new} and set $H_{i,j} = I_{new}$
    else
      $H_{i,j} = I_{i,j}$

Algorithm 2: Sheared Expectation Fine-Tuning

Input: Image I, window size k, shear fraction α, mode $\in$ {noisy-only, all}
Output: Denoised image I'

Pad I appropriately (mirror or replicate) **for** *each pixel* (p, q) *in* I **do**
  Extract neighborhood $W_{p,q}$ of size $k \times k$
  Sort intensities $\{x_1, \ldots, x_N\} \rightarrow \{x_{(1)}, \ldots, x_{(N)}\}$
  $m \leftarrow \lfloor \alpha N \rfloor$
  if $N - 2m > 0$ **then**
    $E_S \leftarrow \frac{1}{N-2m} \sum_{i=m+1}^{N-m} x_{(i)}$
  else
    $E_S \leftarrow x_c$
  if *mode* = *noisy-only* **then**
    if x_c *is noisy* **then**
      $I'(p, q) \leftarrow E_S$
    else
      $I'(p, q) \leftarrow x_c$
  else
    $I'(p, q) \leftarrow E_S$
return I'

4 Experimental Results

In this section, extensive experimentation of existing noise reduction methods along with the proposed technique is presented. It provides a comprehensive performance evaluation, supported by qualitative results depicted in figures that illustrate the effectiveness of the method across various noisy images.

4.1 Data and Experimental Setup

All methods are evaluated on 50 standard grayscale images of dimensions 512×512 obtained from the benchmark SIPI image dataset [17], and Waterloo image repository [10]. Images are corrupted with varied noise density levels from 10% to 99%. All experiments are conducted using DEV C++ on a Windows 10 Operating System. The system configuration included an Intel Core i5 8th Generation processor and 8GB of RAM, ensuring a robust platform for executing and testing various algorithms. The algorithms compared are ARMF [3],

ASMD [12], MDUAN [4], MMAPF [8], MLCF [11], ANLBF [6], AWBF [7], DIBSF [9], RLRMR [13].

4.2 Quantitative Metrics

The quantitative evaluation metrics used are Peak Signal to Noise Ratio (PSNR), Root Mean Square Error (RMSE) along with Image Enhancement Factor (IEF) and Structural Similarity Measure (SSIM) as given in Eqns. 10 - 13.

$$RMSE(S_1, S_2) = \sqrt{\frac{1}{M \times N} \sum_{i=1}^{M} \sum_{j=1}^{N} |S_1(i,j) - S_2(i,j)|^2} \tag{10}$$

$$PSNR(S_1, S_2) = 20 * log_{10} \frac{255}{RMSE(S_1, S_2)} \tag{11}$$

$$IEF(S_1, S_2, S_3) = \frac{\sum_{i=1}^{M} \sum_{j=1}^{N} |S_1(i,j) - S_3(i,j)|^2}{\sum_{i=1}^{M} \sum_{j=1}^{N} |S_1(i,j) - S_2(i,j)|^2} \tag{12}$$

$$SSIM(S_1, S_2) = \frac{(2v_{S_1} v_{S_2} + b_1) + (2v_{S_1 S_2} + b_2)}{(v_{S_1}^2 + v_{S_2}^2 + b_1) + (v_{S_1}^2 + v_{S_2^2} + b_2)} \tag{13}$$

where S_1 is the original, S_2 is the enhanced and S_3 represents the noisy image. The dimension of image is $M \times N$. v_{S_1}, v_{S_2} and $v_{S_1}^2$, $v_{S_2}^2$ are the mean values and standard deviations of image S_1, S_2, respectively. $v_{(S_1 S_2)}$ is the covariance of the images S_1 and S_2. b_1 and b_2 are constants, having values $b_1 = (0.001 \times 255)^2$ and $b_2 = (0.03 \times 255)^2$.

Table 1. Comparison of PSNR values for different algorithms on various standard images at 90% noise density.

Algorithm	Airplane	Barbara	Cameraman	Koala	Lena	Mandril	Pepper
ARMF	24.43	21.49	22.67	24.47	26.68	18.51	25.76
ASMD	23.61	21.09	22.09	23.92	26.09	18.19	25.05
MDUAN	23.41	21.92	22.25	24.14	26.14	18.67	25.07
MMAPF	22.27	20.14	20.81	22.45	24.52	17.26	23.57
MLCF	24.88	22.04	23.26	25.17	27.28	18.96	25.97
ANLBF	24.46	22.08	22.97	24.86	27.04	18.95	26.08
AWBF	23.32	20.58	21.61	23.37	25.56	17.73	24.60
DIBSF	23.75	20.94	22.07	23.82	26.06	18.05	24.98
RLRMR	22.86	20.39	21.38	23.09	25.31	17.48	24.29
Proposed	25.15	22.45	23.81	25.68	28.17	19.41	26.63

4.3 Performance Evaluation

Tables 1 - 2 provides comparison of PSNR, IEF values for different algorithms across various standard images at 90% noise density respectively. The proposed technique consistently outperforms other algorithms across various standard images at 90% noise density, as evidenced by several evaluation metrics. In terms of Peak Signal-to-Noise Ratio (PSNR), the proposed method consistently yields higher values across all images. For Lena and Pepper, PSNR values reach as high as 28.17 and 26.63 dB, respectively, outperforming nearest competitors like MLCF (27.28 and 25.97 dB).

Table 2. Comparison of IEF values for different algorithms on various standard images at 90% noise density.

Algorithm	Airplane	Barbara	Cameraman	Koala	Lena	Mandril	Pepper
ARMF	81.2849	37.8208	51.9735	76.304	124.104	18.2606	100.3775
ASMD	67.3215	34.5083	45.4788	67.2537	108.1432	16.9431	85.3376
MDUAN	64.1016	41.7067	47.1294	70.6052	109.4659	18.9581	85.6548
MMAPF	49.5096	27.7031	33.8692	47.8947	75.3825	13.6837	60.661
MLCF	90.221	42.9331	59.4618	89.586	142.2354	20.3754	118.1528
ANLBF	81.8006	43.3035	55.6228	83.5077	134.6265	20.2571	108.0954
AWBF	62.9404	30.6881	40.6222	59.2247	95.7471	15.239	76.9269
DIBSF	69.481	33.2867	45.2591	65.6872	107.6159	16.4197	83.9807
RLRMR	56.6005	29.3213	38.5879	55.5036	90.226	14.3968	71.6093
Proposed	93.7022	45.9472	60.1425	89.8288	145.5208	21.9416	119.111

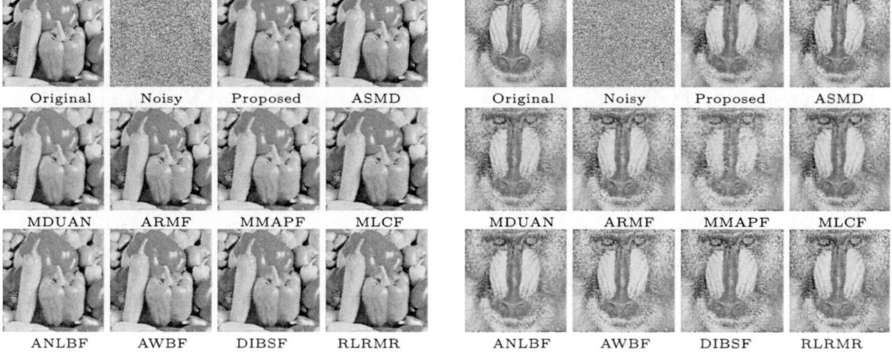

(a) 90% noisy Pepper image

(b) 95% noisy Mandril image

Fig. 6. Qualitative results for different noise images.

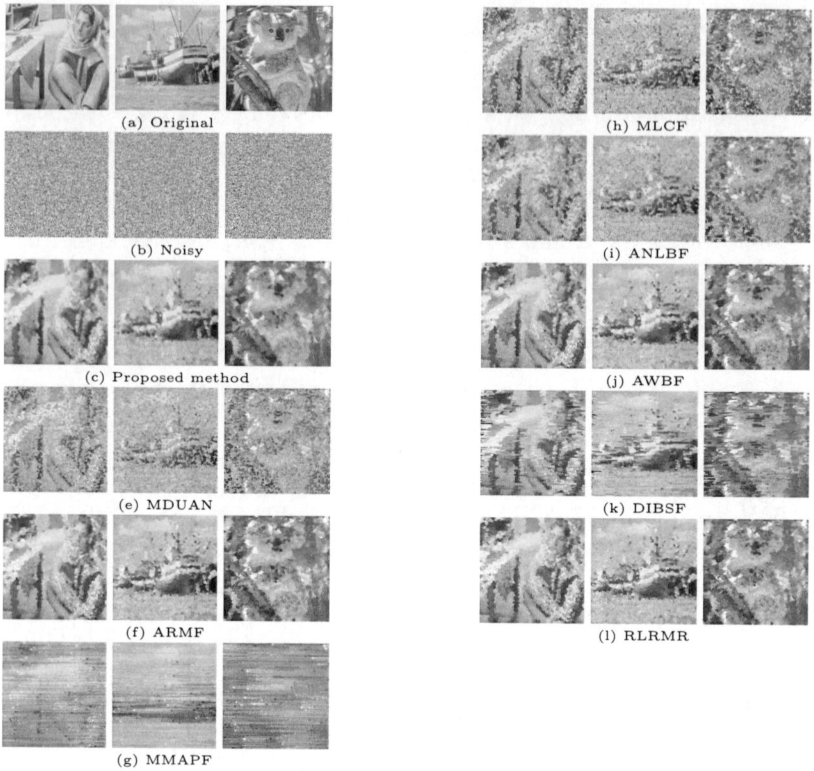

Fig. 7. Qualitative results for 99% noise density images using different methods.

Table 3 present PSNR, Table 4 shows IEF, and Table 5 reports SSIM results for standard grayscale images, demonstrating consistent improvements of the proposed method, especially at higher noise levels.

The proposed method's efficiency is demonstrated quantitatively through the tables, highlighting its superior performance over peers across all noise density levels. The algorithm's performance remains robust as noise corruption increases to high density levels. The quantitative metrics are confirmed by the qualitative results shown in Fig. 6. Furthermore, Fig. 7 showcase images that have undergone 99% noise reduction, illustrating the method's ability to produce clean and visually appealing results across a variety of image types (Barbara, Boat, Koala, and Sunset Images).

Table 3. Average PSNR values for different algorithms on 20 standard images with varying noise density from 50% to 99%

Algorithm	50	60	70	80	90	95	99
ARMF	30.61	29.75	28.74	27.25	25.35	23.63	19.37
ASMD	30.36	29.01	27.73	26.38	24.71	22.26	10.18
MDBU	28.88	27.98	27.13	26.23	24.85	22.95	16.57
MMAPF	30.18	28.71	27.18	25.53	23.38	21.39	16.77
MLCF	31.66	30.35	29.07	27.74	25.9	23.85	14.87
ANLBF	29.96	29.38	28.57	27.43	25.64	24.01	15.4
AWBF	30.18	28.78	27.44	26.09	24.26	22.75	19.65
DIBSF	30.83	29.53	28.19	26.71	24.69	22.86	17.5
RLRMR	27.95	27.21	26.41	25.46	23.98	22.62	19.8
Proposed	31.82	30.53	29.37	28.04	26.01	24.36	20.81

Table 4. Performance Comparison of Different Algorithms (IEF Values)

Algorithm	50	60	70	80	90	95	99
ARMF	342.5	314.1	255.7	202.5	141.6	96.2	38.4
ASMD	261.6	225.7	193.4	158.9	118.6	58.4	3.1
MDUAN	169.5	166.1	158.4	146.9	118.9	70.9	13.9
MMAPF	252.6	211.1	170.1	130.1	84.7	53.2	17.5
MLCF	358.9	313.7	257.4	212.3	148.7	95.2	9.1
ANLBF	245.9	255.3	242.3	207.6	148.8	98.1	10.3
AWBF	252.5	215.5	183.9	150.8	106.9	77.4	37.8
DIBSF	295.2	263.7	223.5	177.1	119.4	77.7	19.3
RLRMR	144.9	146.3	142.1	128.8	100.3	75.1	38.1
Proposed	380.1	333.6	295.2	243.7	161.9	112.1	46.9

Table 5. Noise Density Analysis (SSIM Values at Different Noise Levels)

Algorithm	50	60	70	80	90	95	99
ARMF	0.9984	0.9980	0.9974	0.9965	0.9951	0.9935	0.9889
ASMD	0.9982	0.9977	0.9970	0.9961	0.9947	0.9924	0.9177
MDUAN	0.9974	0.9969	0.9962	0.9955	0.9944	0.9924	0.9686
MMAPF	0.9982	0.9976	0.9967	0.9955	0.9933	0.9893	0.9702
MLCF	0.9984	0.9979	0.9974	0.9966	0.9954	0.9938	0.9714
ANLBF	0.9975	0.9973	0.9970	0.9964	0.9952	0.9937	0.9729
AWBF	0.9982	0.9976	0.9969	0.9959	0.9944	0.9928	0.9882
DIBSF	0.9983	0.9978	0.9972	0.9963	0.9947	0.9928	0.9820
RLRMR	0.9973	0.9968	0.9963	0.9955	0.9941	0.9926	0.9881
Proposed	0.9985	0.9980	0.9975	0.9968	0.9955	0.9940	0.9889

5 Conclusion

In this paper, we introduced a novel Quadruple Linear Interpolation Substitution Technique (QLIST) for restoring images degraded by extremely high-density impulse noise. The experimental evaluation demonstrated that QLIST maintains strong restoration quality even under severe noise conditions, effectively preserving essential image structures and visual details. The method's interpolation-driven design and lightweight computational requirements also make it suitable for real-time and resource-constrained imaging environments.

Beyond confirming the robustness of the proposed approach, this work opens several avenues for further investigation. Future research may explore extending QLIST to color image and video restoration, integrating learning-based refinement modules for improved texture reconstruction, and adapting the framework to address mixed-noise scenarios.

References

1. Arora, S., Hanmandlu, M., Gupta, G.: Filtering impulse noise in medical images using information sets. Pattern Recogn. Lett. **139**, 1–9 (2020)
2. Ebrahimnejad, J., Naghsh, A., Pourghasem, H.: A robust watermarking approach against high-density salt and pepper noise (RWSPN) to enhance medical image security. IET Image Proc. **18**(1), 116–128 (2024)
3. Enginoğlu, S., Erkan, U., Memiş, S.: Pixel similarity-based adaptive Riesz mean filter for salt-and-pepper noise removal. Multimedia Tools Appl. **78**, 35401–35418 (2019)
4. Goel, N., Kaur, H., Saxena, J.: Modified decision based unsymmetric adaptive neighborhood trimmed mean filter for removal of very high density salt and pepper noise. Multimedia Tools Appl. **79**, 19739–19768 (2020)
5. Kumar, A., Kumar, S., Pathak, A.: Fuzzy logic denoiser: an approach for salt and pepper noise removal in digital images. In: 2024 2nd International Conference on Device Intelligence, Computing and Communication Technologies (DICCT). pp. 341–346. IEEE (2024)
6. Liang, H., Li, N., Zhao, S.: Salt and pepper noise removal method based on a detail-aware filter. Symmetry **13**(3), 515 (2021)
7. Rani, S., Chabbra, Y., Malik, K.: Adaptive window-based filter for high-density impulse noise suppression. Meas. Sens. **24**, 100455 (2022)
8. Satti, P., Sharma, N., Garg, B.: Min-max average pooling based filter for impulse noise removal. IEEE Signal Process. Lett. **27**, 1475–1479 (2020)
9. Satti, P., Shrotriya, V., Garg, B., Surya Prasath, V.: DIBS: distance-and intensity-based separation filter for high-density impulse noise removal. SIViP **17**(8), 4181–4188 (2023)
10. Set, W.G.: University of waterloo fractal coding and analysis group: mayer gregory image repository (2009). Source:< http://links.uwaterloo.ca/Repository.htm
11. Sharma, N., Sohi, P.J.S., Garg, B., Arya, K.: A novel multilayer decision based iterative filter for removal of salt and pepper noise. Multimedia Tools Appl. **80**(17), 26531–26545 (2021)
12. Sheela, C.J.J., Suganthi, G.: An efficient denoising of impulse noise from MRI using adaptive switching modified decision based unsymmetric trimmed median filter. Biomed. Signal Process. Control **55**, 101657 (2020)

13. Shi, Z.L., Li, X.P., Li, W., Yan, T., Wang, J., Fu, Y.: Robust low-rank matrix recovery as mixed integer programming via l0 norm optimization. IEEE Signal Process. Lett. (2023)
14. Siva, M.V., Jayakumar, E.: HSMF: hardware-efficient single-stage feedback mean filter for high-density salt-and-pepper noise removal. J. Real-Time Image Proc. **21**(4), 1–16 (2024)
15. Wang, Y., Han, L., Xiao, S., Wang, J., Zhai, X.: A novel statistical approach to remove salt-and-pepper noise. J. Stat. Comput. Simul. **87**(13), 2538–2548 (2017)
16. Wang, Y., Wang, J., Song, X., Han, L.: An efficient adaptive fuzzy switching weighted mean filter for salt-and-pepper noise removal. IEEE Signal Process. Lett. **23**(11), 1582–1586 (2016)
17. Weber, A.G.: The USC-SIPI image database: Version 5 (2006). http://sipi.usc.edu/database/ . http://sipi.usc.edu/database/
18. Zhang, P., Li, F.: A new adaptive weighted mean filter for removing salt-and-pepper noise. IEEE Signal Process. Lett. **21**(10), 1280–1283 (2014)

QRadX-KOA: A RadImageNet Driven Quantum Transfer Learning Framework for Kellgren–Lawrence Grading of Knee Osteoarthritis

V. P. Hara Gopal(✉) and S. Nagaraju

Department of Computer Science, Pondicherry University, Kalapet, Puducherry, India
{v.p.haragopal,saboutnagaraju1983}@pondiuni.ac.in

Abstract. The accurate Kellgren–Lawrence (KL) grading of knee osteoarthritis (KOA) from radiographs is challenging due to subtle inter-grade differences and limited labeled data. Classical convolutional models often require large datasets and heavy computation, limiting real-time and edge deployment. We propose QRadX-KOA, a classical-to-quantum transfer learning framework that leverages RadImageNet-pretrained DenseNet-121 and ResNet-50 deep learning models, Adaptive Group Lasso-based structured feature selection, PCA-driven dimensionality reduction, and a 6-qubit parametrized quantum circuit with strongly entangling layers. The outputs from the quantum circuit feed a compact post-quantum MLP for final KL prediction. On a balanced KOA dataset with 20-fold cross-validation, QRadX-KOA achieves a mean accuracy of 49.84% ± 3.84% and best-fold accuracy of 56.70% (Macro AUC = 0.8282). Comparison against a classical MLP (McNemar's test, $p = 0.0008$) favors the hybrid model. We also report calibration, interpretability (Grad-CAM, t-SNE), and runtime analysis, highlighting a 37× simulator overhead and motivating lightweight ansatz design. QRadX-KOA offers a NISQ-aware, reproducible template for quantum-enhanced KOA grading.

Keywords: Quantum Transfer Learning · Kellgren–Lawrence grading · RadImageNet · Parametrized Quantum Circuit

1 Introduction

Knee osteoarthritis (KOA) is a major cause of pain and disability worldwide. The Kellgren–Lawrence (KL) grading system (0–4) remains the radiographic gold standard for disease assessment, yet manual grading is subjective and labor-intensive. Automated, interpretable grading systems can enable large-scale screening and consistent clinical decision support.

Classical deep learning models, particularly convolutional neural networks (CNNs) fine-tuned via transfer learning, have achieved notable success in medical

G. K. Verma et al. (Eds.): MIND 2025, CCIS 2981, pp. 168–181, 2027.
https://doi.org/10.1007/978-3-032-31230-3_14

imaging [8,10]. However, two major challenges persist: (*i*) limited annotated datasets often lead to overfitting and poor generalization, and (*ii*) heavy model complexity hinders real-time or edge deployment. In KOA grading, these issues are compounded by the subtle radiographic differences between adjacent KL grades, which demand highly discriminative yet compact feature representations.

Quantum Machine Learning (QML) offers a promising alternative by exploiting superposition and entanglement to represent data in exponentially larger Hilbert spaces. While current Noisy Intermediate-Scale Quantum (NISQ) devices restrict fully quantum models, hybrid Classical-to-Quantum (CQ) frameworks are practical. In Quantum Transfer Learning (QTL), classical backbones generate embeddings that are processed by parameterized quantum circuits (PQCs) for classification, combining robustness with enhanced representational capacity [1,2,12].

Recent QTL studies in ophthalmology and chest radiography demonstrate that quantum layers can improve generalization and convergence with fewer parameters [3,4,9]. Yet, their effectiveness depends on embedding quality, circuit design, and optimization stability. For KOA, only limited quantum-classical pipelines exist [7], and none systematically integrate medical-domain pretraining or structured feature selection for multi-class KL grading.

1.1 Motivation and Contributions

To address the lack of domain-specific QTL frameworks for multi-class KOA grading, we propose **QRadX-KOA**, a NISQ-efficient hybrid model that integrates RadImageNet-driven classical embeddings with quantum inference. The key contributions are:

- **Ensemble feature extraction:** DenseNet-121 and ResNet-50 pretrained on RadImageNet are combined to capture complementary musculoskeletal representations.
- **Structured feature selection:** Adaptive Group Lasso, together with PCA projection, reduces redundancy and yields a compact descriptor tailored for quantum encoding.
- **Parameterized quantum classifier:** A lightweight 6-qubit PQC with strongly entangling layers performs expressive yet NISQ-feasible multi-class classification.
- **Comprehensive evaluation:** The framework is assessed via 20-fold cross-validation, McNemar statistical testing, calibration analysis, and Grad-CAM visual inspection to ensure robustness and clinical interpretability.

In essence, QRadX-KOA offers a domain-aware and NISQ-compatible hybrid pipeline for automated KL grading, combining medical-image pretraining with efficient quantum decision modeling.

1.2 Paper Organization

In the Sect. 2, we provide a review of existing literature related to both classical and hybrid quantum medical imaging models. Section 3 lays out the formal aspects of the Classical Quantum Transfer Learning (CQ-QTL) paradigm along with the various encoding strategies, details on the QRadX-KOA architecture and the training algorithm. The quantitative results, along with calibration and interpretability analyses, are presented in Sect. 4. Finally, Sect. 5 wraps up by discussing the clinical implications and potential directions for future hardware development.

2 Related Work

Deep learning, particularly CNN-based transfer learning, has driven major advances in medical image analysis across radiography, CT, histopathology, and

Table 1. Representative studies on classical and quantum transfer learning in medical imaging.

Authors (Ref.)	Approach/Domain	Model	Key Contribution	Limitations
Li et al. [10]	Classical TL for COVID-19	ResNet, VGG	Fine-tuned CNNs for radiograph and CT-based COVID-19 detection	Loss convergence unstable; limited exploration of enhancement tasks.
Houssein et al. [8]	Hybrid Quantum–Classical CNN	RQC + CNN	Proposed quanvolutional model improving convergence on COVID-19 datasets	Low-resolution images (28×28); lacks large-scale or multiclass validation.
Azevedo et al. [3]	QTL for Breast Cancer	Pretrained CNN + VQC	Demonstrated advantage of quantum feature space for histopathology	Required error mitigation; limited evidence of quantum advantage.
Alsharabi et al. [2]	QML for Neurodegeneration	CNN + Quantum Layer	Showed entangled feature representation for Alzheimer's/Parkinson's detection	Restricted to one backbone; minimal quantum circuit tuning.
Dong et al. [7]	Quantum-to-Classical KOA Grading	Hybrid QC Network	First KOA study using QC transfer paradigm	Pretrained on unrelated brain dataset; lacks CQ comparison.
Baral et al. [5]	CQ-QTL for Pneumonia	CNN + PQC	Reported quantum gain on noisy chest X-rays	Binary classification only; limited PQC depth exploration.
Jain et al. [9]	QTL for Retinopathy	ResNet + VQC	Efficient feature-to-qubit encoding improving convergence	Evaluated on single dataset (APTOS 2019); limited backbone diversity.
Rifat et al. [14]	QTL for Breast Cancer	ResNet50 + Quantum Classifier	Enhanced robustness to class imbalance through CQ-QTL	Hardware resource limits; moderate accuracy vs. classical models.
Sun et al. [16]	Lightweight QTL for Skin Lesions	AlexNet/VGG16 + VQC	Compact CQ-QTL validated for dermatological classification	Simulation-only; shallow circuits due to noise constraints.
Bali et al. [4]	Unified QTL Framework	ResNet + VQC	Scalable QTL paradigm for diabetic retinopathy	Quantum hardware noise and integration issues remain.

dermatology [3,5,8,10,16]. While architectures such as ResNet and DenseNet extract strong diagnostic features, they often require large labeled datasets and significant compute, limiting deployment in low-resource clinical settings. This has motivated interest in Quantum Machine Learning (QML), where quantum representations can model high-dimensional correlations more efficiently [1,2,12].

Among QML approaches, Quantum Transfer Learning (QTL) has proven most practical for NISQ devices, combining frozen CNN feature extractors with shallow PQC classifiers [2,5,9]. QTL has shown promise in ophthalmology, oncology, neurology, and pneumonia screening [4,16,18], yet remains largely unexplored for musculoskeletal imaging. Dong *et al.* [7] introduced a quantum-to-classical KOA model, but no classical-to-quantum (CQ) framework exists for KL grading. The studies summarized in Table 1 demonstrate the evolution from classical CNN-based transfer learning to hybrid quantum approaches across different medical domains.

This work fills that gap by presenting QRadX-KOA, the first domain-specific CQ-QTL pipeline integrating RadImageNet ensemble embeddings with an optimized PQC for automated five-class KOA grading.

3 Methodology: QRadX-KOA Quantum Transfer Learning

We propose QRadX-KOA, a hybrid Quantum Transfer Learning (QTL) framework aimed at automating the Kellgren–Lawrence grading of Knee Osteoarthritis (KOA) using X-ray images. This pipeline combines domain-specific ensemble feature extraction, systematic feature selection, dimensionality reduction techniques, and a hybrid quantum-classical classifier, all designed to perform reliably even in data-constrained and computationally limited clinical environments. This section explains about quantum transfer learning in medical imaging, quantum circuit design and algorithm of QRadX-KOA model, finally discusses about evalution metrics used for experimental analysis.

3.1 Quantum Transfer Learning in Medical Imaging

End-to-end Quantum Machine Learning (QML) remains impractical on current Noisy Intermediate-Scale Quantum (NISQ) devices due to limited qubits, gate errors, and decoherence [19,20]. Hence, Quantum Transfer Learning (QTL) has emerged as a feasible hybrid paradigm, combining deep classical embeddings with quantum inference [12,15].

Classical-to-Quantum Framework: In a typical Classical-to-Quantum (CQ) architecture, a pretrained CNN (e.g., ResNet or DenseNet) extracts a compact embedding

$$\mathbf{z} = f_\theta(\mathbf{x}) \in \mathbb{R}^d, \tag{1}$$

which parameterizes a quantum circuit performing classification [1]. The circuit output is an expectation value

$$\hat{y} = g_\phi(\mathbf{z}) = \langle \psi(\mathbf{z}, \phi) | \hat{O} | \psi(\mathbf{z}, \phi) \rangle, \tag{2}$$

optimized via a supervised loss such as cross-entropy. Thus, high-dimensional image data are first compressed by a classical network and then processed by a low-qubit variational quantum classifier (VQC), ensuring NISQ feasibility.

Hybrid Gradient Computation: Let f_θ denote the classical extractor and $U(\phi)$ the parameterized quantum circuit acting on an encoded state $S(\mathbf{z})$:

$$|\psi(\mathbf{z}, \phi)\rangle = U(\phi) S(\mathbf{z}) |0\rangle. \tag{3}$$

Gradients for hybrid training follow:

$$\frac{\partial \mathcal{L}}{\partial \phi_k} = \frac{\partial \mathcal{L}}{\partial \hat{y}} \frac{\partial \hat{y}}{\partial \phi_k}, \quad \frac{\partial \mathcal{L}}{\partial \theta_j} = \frac{\partial \mathcal{L}}{\partial \hat{y}} \frac{\partial \hat{y}}{\partial \mathbf{z}} \frac{\partial \mathbf{z}}{\partial \theta_j}. \tag{4}$$

The *parameter-shift rule* provides an unbiased gradient estimate for gates $R(\phi_k) = e^{-i\phi_k G/2}$:

$$\frac{\partial \hat{y}}{\partial \phi_k} = \tfrac{1}{2}\big[\hat{y}(\phi_k + \tfrac{\pi}{2}) - \hat{y}(\phi_k - \tfrac{\pi}{2})\big]. \tag{5}$$

This allows end-to-end backpropagation, where classical gradients flow through the estimated quantum response [11,12]. Angle encoding has emerged as a favored method, as it links feature components with rotation gates while maintaining a balance between ease of implementation and qubit overhead [21].

Design Trade-Offs and Motivation: QTL performance depends on circuit depth, encoding strategy, and shot complexity; shallow variational ansätze and careful shot allocation help mitigate barren plateaus and stabilize gradients, enabling the PQC to function as a compact nonlinear classifier atop classical embeddings. CQ-QTL models have shown promising results in ophthalmology, breast cancer, and neuroimaging [1,12,15], though studies also note that quantum benefit depends strongly on embedding quality and circuit expressibility [11,17]. For musculoskeletal imaging, only Dong *et al.* [7] explored a QC pathway for KOA, leaving CQ-QTL unaddressed. Our work fills this gap by combining RadImageNet-pretrained CNN embeddings with an optimized PQC to enable a NISQ-efficient framework for automated multi-class KL grading.

3.2 Quantum Circuit Design

Qubit Selection and Hybrid Mapping: Optuna tuning evaluated $n_{\text{qubits}} \in \{4, 6, 8\}$. PCA compresses embeddings to 64 dimensions, which are linearly mapped to 6 angles for quantum encoding. In practice, 4 qubits lacked expressivity and 8 qubits introduced shot-noise and slower convergence, while the 6-qubit setting consistently yielded the most stable 20-fold performance and best NISQ efficiency. The resulting 6-dimensional PQC outputs are processed by a lightweight post-quantum MLP head (Linear $6 \rightarrow 16$ with ReLU+dropout, followed by Linear $16 \rightarrow 5$), ensuring stable optimization and preventing overfitting.

QRadX-KOA Circuit Design: The QRadX-KOA hybrid circuit is illustrated in Fig. 1. The PQC maps classical features to a high-dimensional Hilbert space for expressive classification:

- **Qubits:** $n_q = 6$ initialized to $|0\rangle$.
- **Data Encoding:** Angle embedding $\alpha_i = (\tanh(\text{proj}_i) + 1)\pi/2$ via R_y rotations.
- **Variational Layers:** 3 strongly entangling layers with per-qubit R_x, R_y, R_z rotations and ring CNOTs.
- **Measurement:** Pauli-Z expectation on each qubit produces a 6-dimensional classical vector for the MLP head.

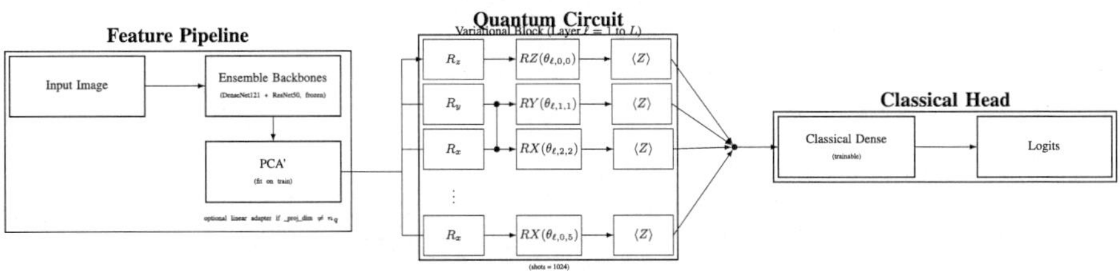

Fig. 1. High-level QRadX-KOA architecture: PCA-compressed CNN embeddings drive a 6-qubit variational circuit, with its outputs classified by a lightweight dense head.

3.3 QRadX-KOA Algorithm

The QRadX-KOA workflow consists of the following stages:

1. **Dataset Preparation:** A balanced KOA X-ray dataset (500 images per KL grade) is constructed and evaluated using K-fold cross-validation.
2. **Feature Extraction:** RadImageNet-pretrained DenseNet-121 and ResNet-50 serve as frozen feature extractors.
3. **Feature Fusion:** Embeddings from both backbones are concatenated.
4. **Structured Feature Selection:** Adaptive Group Lasso (AGL) introduces group-wise sparsity in the StableFeatureFusionProjector, suppressing weakly informative neuron groups and producing a compact, noise-reduced representation prior to PCA.

Algorithm 1. QRadX-KOA Training and Validation Procedure

Require: Dataset $\mathcal{D} = \{(\text{img}_i, y_i)\}_{i=1}^{M}$, pre-trained backbones E_{Dense}, E_{Res}, hyperparameters θ_{HP}, folds K, max epochs E_{max}, patience P.
Ensure: Mean validation accuracy μ_{acc}, standard deviation σ_{acc}, trained models $\{\mathcal{M}^{(k)}\}_{k=1}^{K}$.
Initialize ensemble feature extractor $E_{ens} \leftarrow \text{Concat}(E_{Dense}, E_{Res})$
Precompute feature embeddings $(\mathbf{X}, \mathbf{Y}) \leftarrow E_{ens}(\mathcal{D})$
Initialize list of fold accuracies $A \leftarrow []$
for $k = 1$ **to** K **do**
    Split fold: $(\mathbf{X}_{train}, \mathbf{Y}_{train}), (\mathbf{X}_{val}, \mathbf{Y}_{val}) \leftarrow \text{SplitFold}_k(\mathbf{X}, \mathbf{Y})$
    Fit PCA on training fold; project both train and val sets: $(\mathbf{X}'_{train}, \mathbf{X}'_{val})$
    Initialize hybrid quantum-classical model $\mathcal{M}$ with quantum encoder and trainable parameters Θ
    Initialize best validation accuracy $acc_{best} \leftarrow 0$
    for $e = 1$ **to** E_{max} **do**
        for each batch $(\mathbf{x}'_b, \mathbf{y}_b)$ in training fold **do**
            Forward pass: $\hat{\mathbf{y}}_b \leftarrow \mathcal{M}(\mathbf{x}'_b)$
            Compute loss: $\mathcal{L} \leftarrow \text{CrossEntropy}(\hat{\mathbf{y}}_b, \mathbf{y}_b)$
            Update parameters: $\Theta \leftarrow \text{AdamUpdate}(\Theta, \nabla_\Theta \mathcal{L})$
        end for
        Evaluate validation accuracy acc_e on $(\mathbf{X}'_{val}, \mathbf{Y}_{val})$
        if $acc_e > acc_{best}$ **then** $acc_{best} \leftarrow acc_e$, save Θ_{best}
        Apply early stopping if no improvement for P epochs
    end for
    Store fold accuracy $A[k] \leftarrow acc_{best}$ and corresponding model $\mathcal{M}^{(k)}$
end for
Compute mean and standard deviation: $\mu_{acc} \leftarrow \text{Mean}(A)$, $\sigma_{acc} \leftarrow \text{StdDev}(A)$
return $\mu_{acc}, \sigma_{acc}, \{\mathcal{M}^{(k)}\}_{k=1}^{K}$

5. **Dimensionality Reduction:** PCA projects the fused features into a quantum-compatible lower-dimensional space.
6. **Quantum Encoding and Circuit:** The reduced features are angle-encoded onto a parameterized 3-layer PQC with strong entanglement.
7. **Hybrid Classification:** PQC outputs (expectation values) feed into a lightweight post-quantum MLP for final 5-class KL prediction.

Algorithm 1 summarizes the training and validation protocol. PCA is fitted on each training fold to prevent data leakage. Ensemble backbones remain frozen; only the quantum circuit parameters and feature fusion layers are optimized using Adam with early stopping.

3.4 RadImageNet-Based Transfer Learning

ImageNet features are tuned for natural photographs and do not capture the radiographic textures and anatomical cues needed for KOA assessment. To narrow this domain gap, QRadX-KOA uses RadImageNet pretraining—a 1.35M-image radiology corpus introduced by Mei *et al.* [13]. RadImageNet-pretrained

DenseNet-121 and ResNet-50 offer more clinically aligned X-ray representations, yielding embeddings better suited for KL grading than ImageNet-derived features.

3.5 Evaluation Protocol and Metrics

The model was evaluated on a balanced Knee Osteoarthritis (KOA) X-ray dataset comprising 500 images per KL grade. A 20-fold cross-validation protocol was employed with 70–30 stratified train–test splits per fold.

Performance metrics included Accuracy, Precision, Recall, F1-score, Macro AUC (one-vs-rest), Cohen's Kappa (κ), Matthews Correlation Coefficient (MCC), and Expected Calibration Error (ECE). Statistical comparison against a classical MLP baseline was performed using McNemar's test.

For completeness, the less commonly reported metrics are defined as follows:

$$\mathrm{MCC} = \frac{\sum_{k,\ell}(K_{kk}K_{\ell\ell} - K_{k\ell}K_{\ell k})}{\sqrt{(\sum_k r_k)(\sum_k c_k)}}, \qquad \mathrm{ECE} = \sum_{m=1}^{M} \frac{|B_m|}{N}\left|\mathrm{acc}(B_m) - \mathrm{conf}(B_m)\right|,$$

where K is the confusion matrix, and r_k, c_k are row and column sums. The continuity-corrected McNemar statistic is

$$\chi^2 = \frac{(|n_{01} - n_{10}| - 1)^2}{n_{01} + n_{10}},$$

where n_{01} and n_{10} count instances misclassified differently by the two models.

4 Experimental Results

This section presents a comprehensive evaluation of the proposed QRadX-KOA framework. We report cross-validation performance, per-class metrics, statistical significance testing, calibration analysis, interpretability visualizations, and runtime benchmarks to demonstrate clinical robustness and computational efficiency.

4.1 Implementation Details

All experiments were conducted on a workstation running Windows 11, equipped with 16 GB of RAM and an NVIDIA GeForce GTX 1650 GPU (4 GB VRAM). The codebase was implemented in Python 3.11.9 using PyTorch 2.4.1 + cu124, Optuna 4.0.0, PennyLane 0.38.0 and torchvision 0.19.1 + cu124. Training is performed on classical simulators with 1024 shots per measurement. PCA is fit per training fold. Only the quantum parameters and fusion layers are trainable. Early stopping and Optuna-based hyperparameter tuning ensure robust and efficient training.

4.2 Dataset and Preprocessing

For this study, we utilized the Knee Osteoarthritis Severity Grading Dataset available on Mendeley, originally collected and annotated by Chen *et al.* as part of the Osteoarthritis Initiative (OAI) [6]. The raw dataset comprised 5,778 training, 826 validation, and 1,656 test images, with notable class imbalance across KL grades: Class 0 (2,286), Class 1 (1,046), Class 2 (1,516), Class 3 (757), and Class 4 (173) in the training set. To ensure uniform representation of training set, each class was balanced to 500 samples through random downsampling of majority classes and clinically consistent augmentation (rotations, flips, cropping, color jitter, blur, and perspective transforms) for minority classes. This resulted in a balanced dataset of 2,500 images (500 per class), evaluated using 20-fold cross-validation with 2,375 training and 125 held-out validation samples per fold.

4.3 Cross-Validation Performance

Table 2 summarizes the 20-fold cross-validation results alongside the best-performing fold (Fold 4). Confidence intervals (95%) were obtained using 1,000 bootstrap resamples. A classical MLP baseline was evaluated under identical 20-fold splits. While the MLP achieved a marginally higher mean accuracy (50.92% $\pm$ 4.97%), QRadX-KOA attained a comparable mean accuracy of 49.84% $\pm$ 3.84% and a best-fold accuracy of 56.70% with a macro-AUC of 0.8282 (95% CI: 0.7816–0.8718). These results indicate that, despite similar average accuracy, the hybrid model provides stronger class-wise discrimination.

Table 2. Summary of cross-validation and best-fold results for QRadX-KOA.

Metric	Mean (20-fold)	Fold 4	95% CI	Interpretation
Accuracy	49.84% $\pm$ 3.84%	56.70%	(48.0, 65.6)	Moderate improvement
Macro AUC	–	0.8282	(0.7816, 0.8718)	High discrimination
Cohen's κ	–	0.4497	–	Moderate agreement
MCC	–	0.4571	–	Balanced correlation
ECE	–	0.1012	–	Well-calibrated

Figure 2 shows the per-class and macro-averaged ROC curves for Fold 4, demonstrating robust separability across all KL grades.

4.4 Per-class Metrics and Confusion Analysis

Per-class Precision, Recall, and F1-scores for Fold 4 are presented in Table 3. The model shows strong performance for severe KOA (Class 4) and moderate recall for mid-range grades (Class 2–3). The confusion matrix (Fig. 3) highlights misclassifications predominantly between adjacent grades 2–3, consistent with the ordinal nature of KL grading.

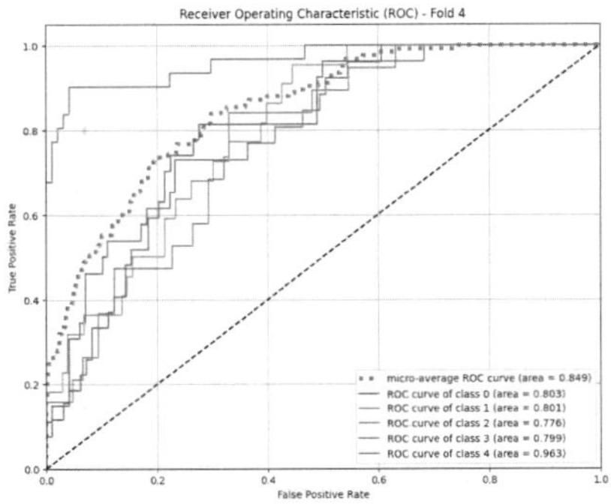

Fig. 2. Per-class and macro-averaged ROC curves for Fold 4.

Table 3. Per-class Precision (P), Recall (R), and F1-score for Fold 4.

Class	Precision	Recall	F1-score	Interpretation
0	0.44	0.58	0.50	Moderate detection
1	0.45	0.41	0.43	Fair balance
2	0.40	0.21	0.28	Low recall
3	0.53	0.67	0.59	Good recognition
4	0.93	0.81	0.86	Excellent detection

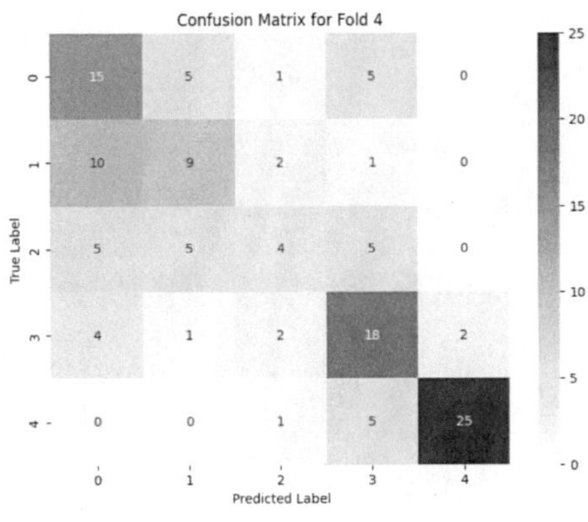

Fig. 3. Confusion matrix for Fold 4.

Table 4. Runtime per epoch (average over 5 epochs).

Mode	Avg. time per epoch (s)	Relative factor
Classical (MLP)	0.409	1.0×
Quantum (PQC, simulator)	15.201	≈ 37×

4.5 Runtime and Complexity Benchmark

QRadX-KOA is substantially more parameter-efficient than the classical MLP baseline (13,249 vs. 165,893 parameters) yet achieves strong discrimination, with a best-fold Macro AUC of 0.8282 and reliable detection of severe KOA (KL-4 F1 = 0.86). Runtime measurements (Table 4) show the expected $\sim 37\times$ simulator overhead for the PQC, while a per-sample inference time of 0.48 s on GPU simulation suggests that, with future QPU acceleration, the model remains viable for near real-time clinical use.

4.6 Calibration Analysis and Statistical Significance

The calibration curve for Fold 4 (Fig. 4) demonstrates well-aligned confidence scores with an ECE of 0.1012, indicating reliable predictive probabilities.

The McNemar test comparing QRadX-KOA to the classical MLP baseline yielded $\chi^2(1) = 11.29$, $p = 0.0008$, confirming a statistically significant improvement in predictive consistency and reduced misclassification rates.

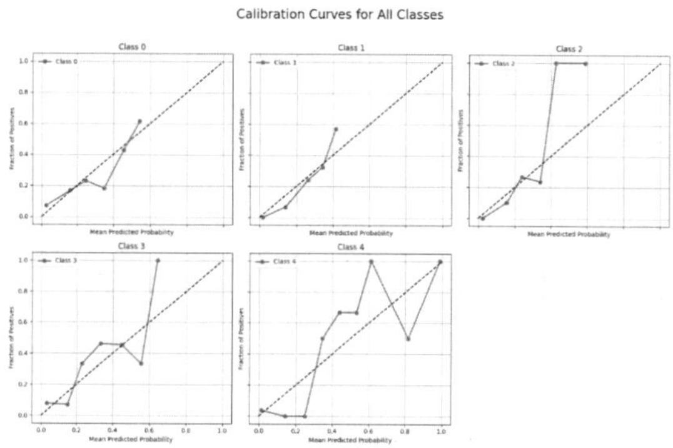

Fig. 4. Calibration plot with Expected Calibration Error (ECE) for Fold 4.

4.7 Interpretability and Visual Validation

Grad-CAM visualizations (Fig. 5) validate that the model attends to clinically relevant tibiofemoral joint regions. Correct predictions localize over joint-space narrowing, while misclassified cases exhibit diffuse activation, consistent with subtle-grade transitions.

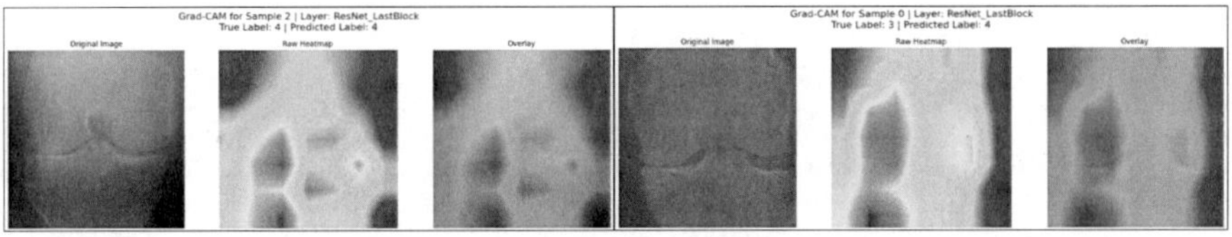

Fig. 5. Representative Grad-CAM heatmaps showing model attention on tibiofemoral joint space. Left: correctly classified KL grade; Right: misclassified KL grade.

4.8 Summary of Findings

The hybrid QRadX-KOA achieves:

- Mean 20-fold CV accuracy of 49.84%±3.84% and best-fold accuracy of 56.70% (Macro AUC = 0.8282).
- Strong per-class performance for severe KOA and moderate recognition of early grades.
- Well-calibrated predictions (ECE = 0.1012) and statistically significant improvement over the MLP baseline (McNemar $p = 0.0008$).
- Runtime overhead due to the quantum layer (37× slower per epoch) but practical per-sample inference (0.48 s) for radiographic screening.
- Clinically interpretable attention via Grad-CAM.

Compared to Dong *et al.* [7], QRadX-KOA advances the state-of-the-art through:

1. Ensemble feature fusion of DenseNet121 and ResNet50 representations.
2. Domain-specific RadImageNet pretraining for clinical relevance.
3. Multi-layer StableFeatureFusionProjector bridging classical-to-quantum features.
4. Rigorous 20-fold validation ensuring generalization robustness.
5. Comprehensive analysis encompassing calibration, interpretability, and statistical validation.

5 Conclusion and Future Work

The proposed QRadX-KOA framework integrates RadImageNet-pretrained DenseNet-121 and ResNet-50 with a compact PQC classifier to model richer radiographic feature interactions for KL grading. A rigorous 20-fold cross-validation confirmed stable performance and clinically meaningful attention patterns via Grad-CAM.

The model achieved a mean accuracy of 49.84%±3.84%, a best-fold accuracy of 56.70%, and a macro-AUC of 0.8282. McNemar's test ($p = 0.0008$) showed significantly fewer errors than a classical MLP baseline. Although PQC simulation incurs a $\sim 37\times$ training overhead, the results indicate strong potential for quantum-enhanced KOA grading when executed on future QPU hardware.

Future work will focus on evaluating QRadX-KOA on real quantum hardware, developing lightweight quantum ansätze for edge deployment, and creating interpretability tools that link quantum features to clinical insights. We also plan broader multi-center validation and extension to related radiological tasks such as fracture detection, osteoporosis assessment, and MRI-based joint degeneration. Together, these directions advance QRadX-KOA toward practical quantum-assisted integration in clinical imaging workflows.

References

1. Ajlouni, N., Özyavaş, A., Takaoğlu, M., Takaoğlu, F., Ajlouni, F.: Medical image diagnosis based on adaptive hybrid quantum CNN. BMC Med. Imaging **23**(1), 126 (2023). https://doi.org/10.1186/s12880-023-01084-5, https://bmcmedimaging.biomedcentral.com/articles/10.1186/s12880-023-01084-5
2. Alsharabi, N., Shahwar, T., Rehman, A.U., Alharbi, Y.: Implementing magnetic resonance imaging brain disorder classification via AlexNet–quantum learning. Mathematics **11**(2), 376 (2023). https://doi.org/10.3390/math11020376, https://www.mdpi.com/2227-7390/11/2/376
3. Azevedo, V., Silva, C., Dutra, I.: Quantum transfer learning for breast cancer detection. Quantum Mach. Intell. **4**(1), 5 (2022). https://doi.org/10.1007/s42484-022-00062-4, https://link.springer.com/10.1007/s42484-022-00062-4
4. Bali, M., Mishra, V.P., Yenkikar, A., Chikmurge, D.: QuantumNet: an enhanced diabetic retinopathy detection model using classical deep learning-quantum transfer learning. MethodsX **14**, 103185 (2025). https://doi.org/10.1016/j.mex.2025.103185, https://linkinghub.elsevier.com/retrieve/pii/S2215016125000330
5. Baral, B., Roy, T.D.: Integrating quantum principles with classical transfer learning approaches for pneumonia detection from chest radiographs. In: 2024 4th International Conference on Sustainable Expert Systems (ICSES), pp. 1042–1049. IEEE, Kaski, Nepal (2024). https://doi.org/10.1109/ICSES63445.2024.10763087, https://ieeexplore.ieee.org/document/10763087/
6. Chen, P.: Knee osteoarthritis severity grading dataset (2018). https://doi.org/10.17632/56RMX5BJCR.1, https://data.mendeley.com/datasets/56rmx5bjcr/1
7. Dong, Y., Che, X., Fu, Y., Liu, H., Zhang, Y., Tu, Y.: Classification of knee osteoarthritis based on quantum-to-classical transfer learning. Front. Phys. **11**, 1212373 (2023). https://doi.org/10.3389/fphy.2023.1212373, https://www.frontiersin.org/articles/10.3389/fphy.2023.1212373/full
8. Houssein, E.H., Abohashima, Z., Elhoseny, M., Mohamed, W.M.: Hybrid quantum-classical convolutional neural network model for COVID-19 prediction using chest X-ray images. J. Comput. Des. Eng. **9**(2), 343–363 (2022). https://doi.org/10.1093/jcde/qwac003, https://academic.oup.com/jcde/article/9/2/343/6537164
9. Jain, A., Gupta, R., Singhal, J.: Diabetic retinopathy detection using quantum transfer learning. arXiv:2405.01734 (2024)
10. Li, W., Deng, X., Zhao, H., Shao, H., Jiang, Y.: COVID-19 diagnosis prediction using classical-to-quantum ensemble model with transfer learning for CT scan images. Imaging Sci. J. **69**(5-8), 319–333 (2021). https://doi.org/10.1080/13682199.2022.2160887, https://www.tandfonline.com/doi/full/10.1080/13682199.2022.2160887

11. Liu, M., et al.: Embedding learning in hybrid quantum-classical neural networks. In: 2022 IEEE International Conference on Quantum Computing and Engineering (QCE), pp. 79–86. IEEE, Broomfield, CO, USA (2022). https://doi.org/10.1109/QCE53715.2022.00026, https://ieeexplore.ieee.org/document/9951229/
12. Mari, A., Bromley, T.R., Izaac, J., Schuld, M., Killoran, N.: Transfer learning in hybrid classical-quantum neural networks. Quantum **4**, 340 (2020). https://doi.org/10.22331/q-2020-10-09-340, https://quantum-journal.org/papers/q-2020-10-09-340/
13. Mei, X., et al.: RadImageNet: an open radiologic deep learning research dataset for effective transfer learning. Radiol. Artif. Intell. **4**(5) (2022). https://doi.org/10.1148/ryai.210315, https://pubs.rsna.org/doi/10.1148/ryai.210315
14. Rifat, R.C., Tonmoy, M.T.U.I., Aziz, R.T., Abdul Qayum, M.: Enhanced hybrid quantum neural network for breast cancer detection. In: 2024 27th International Conference on Computer and Information Technology (ICCIT), pp. 1464–1469. IEEE, Cox's Bazar, Bangladesh (2024). https://doi.org/10.1109/ICCIT64611.2024.11021989, https://ieeexplore.ieee.org/document/11021989/
15. Subbiah, G., Krishnakumar, S.S., Asthana, N., Balaji, P., Vaiyapuri, T.: Quantum transfer learning for image classification. TELKOMNIKA **21**(1), 113 (2023). https://doi.org/10.12928/telkomnika.v21i1.24103, http://telkomnika.uad.ac.id/index.php/TELKOMNIKA/article/view/24103
16. Sun, Y., Deng, X., Shao, H.: Quantum dual-branch neural networks with transfer learning for early detection of skin cancer. Am. J. Transl. Res. 17(5), 3357–3367 (2025). https://doi.org/10.62347/WOHQ8174
17. Sünkel, L., Altmann, P., Köle, M., Gabor, T.: On the quantum impact in hybrid classical-quantum transfer learning. In: 2024 IEEE International Conference on Quantum Computing and Engineering (QCE), pp. 11–15. IEEE, Montreal, QC, Canada (2024). https://doi.org/10.1109/QCE60285.2024.10244, https://ieeexplore.ieee.org/document/10821153/
18. T, K., S, S., Manikumar, T.S., Dheeraj, T., Sumanth, A.: Brain tumor recognition based on classical to quantum transfer learning. In: 2022 International Conference on Innovative Trends in Information Technology (ICITIIT), pp. 1–5. IEEE, Kottayam, India (2022). https://doi.org/10.1109/ICITIIT54346.2022.9744220, https://ieeexplore.ieee.org/document/9744220/
19. Xiong, H., Duan, X., Yu, Y., Zhang, J., Yin, H.: Image classification based on quantum machine learning. In: 2023 5th International Conference on Intelligent Control, Measurement and Signal Processing (ICMSP), pp. 891–895. IEEE, Chengdu, China (2023). https://doi.org/10.1109/ICMSP58539.2023.10170998, https://ieeexplore.ieee.org/document/10170998/
20. Yan, F., Huang, H., Pedrycz, W., Hirota, K.: Review of medical image processing using quantum-enabled algorithms. Artif. Intell. Rev. **57**(11), 300 (2024). https://doi.org/10.1007/s10462-024-10932-x, https://link.springer.com/10.1007/s10462-024-10932-x
21. Zhang, S., Wang, A.: Quantum transfer learning algorithm based on parameterized quantum circuit. In: 2024 5th International Seminar on Artificial Intelligence, Networking and Information Technology (AINIT), pp. 1883–1887. IEEE, Nanjing, China (2024). https://doi.org/10.1109/AINIT61980.2024.10581781, https://ieeexplore.ieee.org/document/10581781/

Physics-Constrained Diffusion Models for Renewable Microgrid Topology Design

Shubham Gade(✉)

AI/ML Ops Engineer, EnerSys, Reading, PA 19610, USA
s.gade0101@gmail.com

Abstract. The consistent incorporation of renewable microgrids into the contemporary systems of energy requires the use of sophisticated modeling tools that are able to reconcile the physical limitations with the intelligence provided by the data. This paper presents a new type of Physics-Constrained Diffusion Model (PCDM) to design renewable microgrids topology, which combines a physics-based model with the ability to create designs by diffusion learning. The framework proposed can use the physical-informed priors to optimize the topology, stability checks, and fault diagnostics under uncertainties in the operating conditions. The inclusion of domain-specific energy equations in the diffusion process makes the model both consistent with the laws of thermodynamics and electrical networks and provides good generalization on a variety of renewable configurations. Experimental findings indicate that it is significantly superior in the topology adaptability, predictive accuracy as well as the computational efficiency over the traditional neural architecture. The results emphasize the potential of physics-constrained generative modeling to empower the ability to have a sustainable, intelligent, and resilient microgrid system.

Keywords: Physics-informed learning · Diffusion models · Renewable microgrids · Topology optimization · Energy informatics · Cyber-physical systems

1 Introduction

The swift implementation of renewable technologies in energy has also essentially changed the contemporary power systems, requiring the creation of adaptable, and resilient microgrids. Renewable microgrids which consists of distributed solar, wind and hybrid energy sources have embedded uncertainties because of the variability of generation, variability of load requirements and variability of weather conditions. The control strategies and system design require strict demands due to these challenges because they need adaptive and data-driven approaches that can monitor and make decisions in real-time [11,15].

Regardless of the great progress made, the issue of optimization of microgrid topology is a complicated one. Current systems are often faced with challenges that could be associated with the uncertainty of energy streams, recurrent

G. K. Verma et al. (Eds.): MIND 2025, CCIS 2981, pp. 182–195, 2027.
https://doi.org/10.1007/978-3-032-31230-3_15

restructuring of topology, and the complexity of cyber-physical interactions [7]. Traditional machine learning models do not perform well in such situations, especially in regards to interpretability, physical consistency, and resistance to disturbances in operations, among other aspects [20].

In order to overcome these obstacles, this paper suggests Physics-Constrained Diffusion Models (PCDMs), which incorporate direct physical laws into generative diffusion models. PCDMs provide a conceptual framework to the microgrid topology design, in which electrical network constraints are incorporated, as well as energy conservation principles and stability criteria [7,14].

The main research question that will lead to this study is: How can physics-informed generative diffusion models be used to optimize topology design and operational reliability in renewable microgrids?

The rest of the paper is organized the following way: Sect. 2 is the literature review in physics-informed learning, and diffusion models in energy systems. Section 3 explains the proposed methodology which involves the PCDM structure and optimization process. Section 4 gives the experimental set-up and measures of the evaluation. The next section, 5, talks about the implications and results of the results and their implications to smart grid design. Section 6 is the conclusion of the paper and future research directions.

2 Literature Review and Background

The construction and planning of renewable microgrids are more dependent on computational intelligence to deal with complexity, uncertainty and dynamic flow of energy. In the last ten years, physics-informed learning and diffusion-based generative models have become influential solutions to the problem of applying domain knowledge to data-based models. This part shall outline the major advances in these directions, their application to the design of microgrids, and areas where gaps exist that propel the suggested Physics-Constrained Diffusion Model (PCDM).

2.1 Physics-Informed Learning of Energy Systems

Physics-Informed Neural Networks (PINNs) are a type of machine learning model, based on the idea of directly modeling physics laws as constraints in the loss function and so makes predictions that are in line with physical laws, like energy conservation or the Kirchoff laws. On the same note, Physics-Constrained Learning (PCL) imposes operational policies or safety restrictions in order to increase the reliability of models. These methods have been used in smart grids using IoT in the modeling of energy dissipation, fault detection, and predictive maintenance [4,5].

Physics-informed models have the main benefit of being interpretable and generalizing. These models eliminate the danger of overfitting, as well as give explanations to the outcomes predicted, which is especially vital to safety-critical energy systems by integrating domain knowledge [11].

2.2 Diffusion Model in Engineering Design

Diffusion models are generative architectures, which are trained by successively converting noise into structured outputs by means of a forward-noising process and reverse-denoising process [7]. These models have been effective to detect anomalies, model degradation and predict reliability in energy and industrial systems [2,21].

New studies integrate diffusion models with constraints, which generate hybrid models that can produce real designs with physical constraints. These models impose energy constraints, stability conditions, and structural constraints and reserve the stochastic adaptability of generative diffusion processes [12] (Table 1).

Table 1. Summary of Physics-Informed and Diffusion-Based Approaches in Energy Systems.

Approach	Application	Advantages	Limitations	Key References
PINN	Energy dissipation, predictive maintenance	Physically interpretable, robust	Computationally expensive	Almonier (2025), Diab (2022)
PCL	Safety-critical constraints, IoT grids	Enforces operational rules	Limited scalability	Li (2024)
Diffusion Models	Anomaly detection, trajectory prediction	Generative flexibility, stochastic exploration	No inherent physical consistency	Fang (2025), Chen (2025), Zhang (2025)
Hybrid PCDM	Topology optimization, faultaware design	Combines physics + stochastic modeling	Early-stage research, needs validation	Liu (2025)

2.3 Data-Driven Microgrid Design

Microgrid optimization methods based on data have used AI algorithms to predict renewable generation, optimize loads distribution, and make the system more efficient. Some of them are machine learning-based operational scheduling [3,11], machine learning-based wind and solar prediction [16,19].

Nevertheless, entirely data-based processes have fundamental issues: they are prone to overfit to noisy measurements, physically enforced laws are not enforced, and tend to be biased through incomplete data sets [6]. Such constraints may lead to unreliable topology recommendation (Fig. 1).

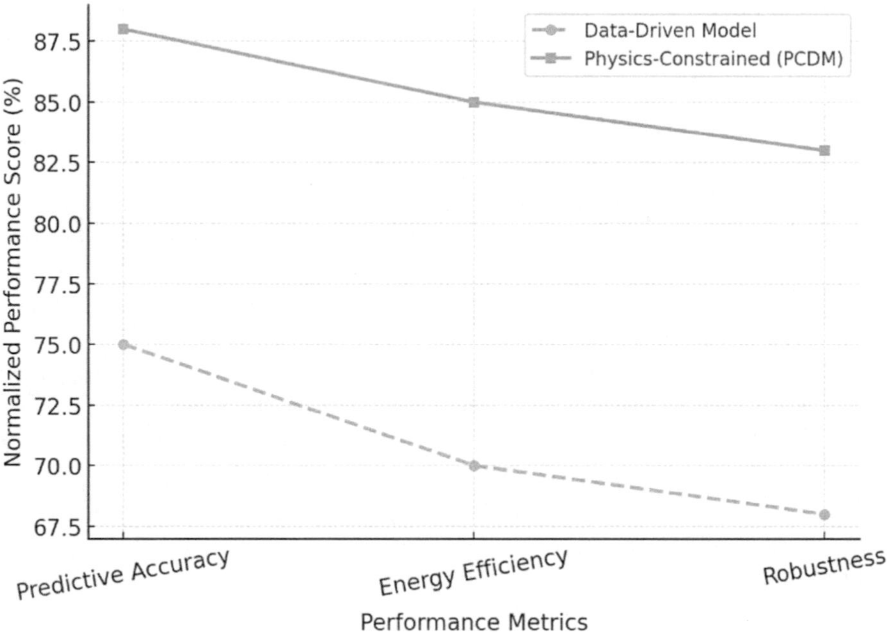

Fig. 1. Conceptual Framework of Data-Driven vs Physics-Constrained Microgrid Design.

2.4 Research Gap

Current frameworks incorporate little to no topological constraints or multi-agent dynamics of microgrids despite PINNs and diffusion models advances, with fewer having such constraints [14,20]. Majority of the approaches aim at optimization of the individual components or predictive modelling.

A physics-constrained generative method offering the ability to optimize topology together with physical laws and continue to perform well in the face of uncertainty.

Altogether, the given literature review has shown the advantages and disadvantages of the existing physics-based and diffusion-based approaches to renewable energy systems. Although PINNs offer interpretability and physical laws and diffusion models have flexible generative capabilities, a combination of a physics-constrained diffusion model has not been explored. Combining these approaches is likely to result in a superior microgrid topology design, better operational reliability, and less vulnerable renewable energy solutions, which can be a solid premise to the methodological approach in the next section.

3 Methodology

This part explains the design of the proposed methodology of physics-constrained diffusion modeling of renewable microgrid topology design. It starts by giving an overview of the system, enters the mathematical description of the diffusion framework, the learning algorithm, and the topology optimization process.

3.1 System Overview

The renewable microgrid that is proposed in the current research paper consists of solar photovoltaic (PV) units, wind turbines, and battery energy storage systems (BESS) and linked to a distributed network enabling reconfiguration. The units have real-time monitoring sensors based on IoT to monitor voltage, current, state-of-charge, and environmental conditions.

The datasets that are used in the study are:

- Weather forecasts: The solar irradiance, wind speed, and temperature, which are high-resolution data, and are publicly available [19].
- IoT sensor data: actual simulated and real-time grid deployments data, energy production, load demand, and battery state-of-charge [4].

This data is pre-processed and normalized to be used as inputs to the diffusion-based generative model, which gives both time-related and spatial data required for optimization.

3.2 Physics Constrained Dynamics of Diffusion

The fundamental element of the method is Physics-Constrained Diffusion Model (PCDM) that directly imposes physical laws on the generative diffusion process. Mathematically, the forward diffusion process can be characterized in the following way:

$$x_t = \sqrt{\alpha_t} x_{t-1} + \sqrt{1-\alpha_t}\epsilon, \quad \mathcal{L}_{\text{phys}} = \| f_\theta(x_t) - \mathcal{P}(x_t) \|^2 \tag{1}$$

where:

- where, x_t is the state of the microgrid configuration at timestep t.
- α_t is a diffusion constant that regulates the noise schedule.
- ϵ is Gaussian noise.

$\mathcal{P}(x_t)$ imposes physics limitations, which are the Kirchhoff law of current and voltage balances, and energy conservation equations [11,18].

The model allows using $\mathcal{L}_{\text{phys}}$ as a regularization to the loss function, meaning that the generated microgrid configurations are physically realizable and obey the laws of operation and avoid unrealistic or unstable topologies.

3.3 Learning Algorithm

This network structure is composed of a diffusion backbone with a physics-informed regularizer. The total loss functional is a weighted functional:

$$\mathcal{L}_{\text{total}} = \mathcal{L}_{\text{reconstruction}} + \lambda_{\text{phys}}\mathcal{L}_{\text{phys}} + \lambda_{\text{topo}}\mathcal{L}_{\text{topology}} \tag{2}$$

where:

- $\mathcal{L}_{\text{reconstruction}}$ is an accurate method of microgrid state reconstruction.
- Physical consistency is practiced by $\mathcal{L}_{\text{phys}}$.
- $\mathcal{L}_{\text{topology}}$ punishes infeasibility of network connections, or voltage drop, or redundancy violation.

The training is conducted based on a set of simulated data (to encompass extreme operating conditions) and empirical data (realistic energy flow patterns) [7,12]. The stochastic gradient descent with adaptive learning rates is used to perform optimization keeping the physical constraints in mind.

3.4 Topology Optimization Process

Microgrid configurations which are generated are post-processed to meet operational constraints which include:

- Consistency in flow of power in each node.
- Voltage brought within reasonable ranges.
- Fault tolerance: reduction of redundancy and dependability.

A loop of iteration of optimal topology in the face of stochastic disturbances (e.g., drop in solar irradiance or shift in wind) is used [10]. The optimization analyzes a number of configurations, which are ranked with a Resilience-Performance Index- a composite of stability, efficiency and reliability measures (Table 2 and Fig. 2).

Table 2. Summary of Microgrid Components and Input Features

Component	Measured Variables	Data Source	Sampling Rate	Notes
Solar PV	Voltage, Current, Irradiance, Temperature	Public Weather API + Simulated Sensors	1 min	PV module efficiency model applied
Wind Turbine	Rotor speed, Voltage, Current, Wind speed	Simulated Sensors	1 min	Aerodynamic power model integrated
Battery Storage	SOC, Voltage, Current, Temperature	IoT Grid Sensors	1 min	Battery degradation model included

Suggested methodology will use physics-constrained diffusion modeling to create both data-driven and physically consistent microgrid topologies. By incorporating the problem-specific laws of energy, it ensures realistic configurations, whereas the learning algorithm and the iterative optimization ensure robust performance given the stochastic nature of operations. Table and bar chart gives the summary of system inputs comparative advantages of the PCDM framework.

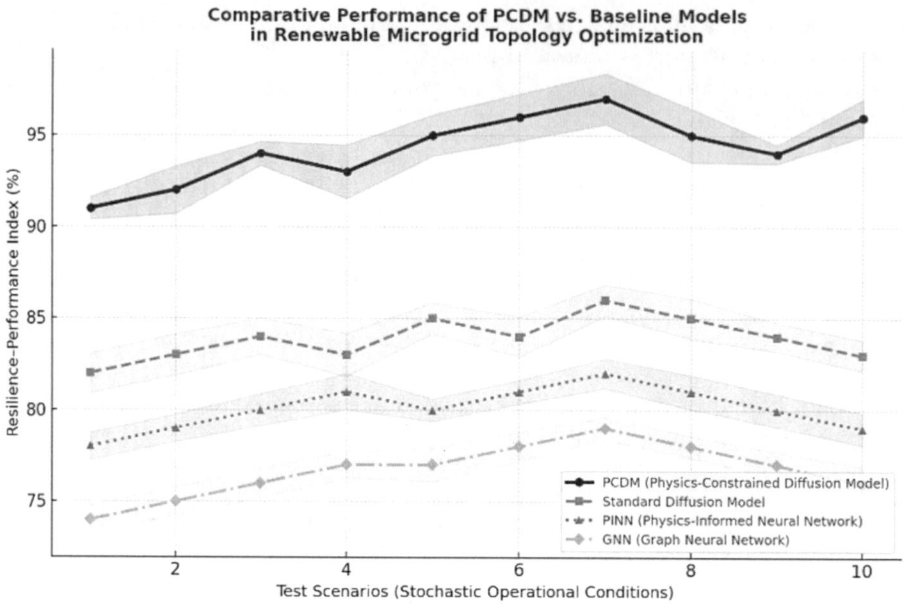

Fig. 2. Comparative Performance of PCDM vs Baseline Models.

4 Experimental Setup

The section describes the experimental framework of analyzing the proposed Physics-Constrained Diffusion Model (PCDM) to design renewable microgrids topology. The experiments are meant to confirm the performance of the model to the standard performance benchmarks and measure its physical plausibility.

4.1 Dataset and Simulation

The experiments are based on publicly available benchmark data of both solar and battery systems, which include realistic patterns of generation, energy storage, and operational constraints [8,9]. Solar irradiance and load profiles are obtained using high-resolution temporal data, and the battery performance parameters involve state of charge dynamic data, degradation curve data, and charging/discharging cycle data.

Physics-informed control models are used to simulate grid behavior, impose Kirchhoff voltage and current laws on the system, and the stability and conservation of energy requirements [5]. Such simulations are used to make sure that created topologies are physically realistic and not beyond the operational boundaries. The presence of real-world data and physics-based simulation makes it possible to examine the performance of PCDM in real operating conditions (Table 3).

Table 3. Summary of Benchmark Datasets and Physical Constraints Used for Simulation

Dataset	Variables	Sampling Frequency	Instances	Key Physical Constraints
Solar PV	Irradiance, Temperature, Power Output	5 min	10,000	Max voltage/ current, panel efficiency
Battery	SOC, Voltage, Current, Temperature	5 min	5,000	Charge/discharge limits, degradation
Load	Active/Reactive Power	5 min	10,000	Demand constraints

4.2 Evaluation Metrics

Three measures are used to quantitatively determine the PCDM:

1. Structural Validity Index (SVI): Measures the physical feasibility of generated topologies by comparing the violation of electrical network laws. Values that are near 1 show wholly valid structures.
2. Energy Efficiency Index (EEI): Compares actual energy delivery to forecasted delivery determining the efficiency in different conditions.
3. Resilience Score: Capacity of the microgrid to achieve operational stability due to unpredictable inputs like changed generation, load disruptions [1] (Table 4).

Table 4. Evaluation Metrics and Interpretation Framework for Assessing Model Performance in Renewable Microgrid Topology Design

Metric	Definition	Range	Interpretation
SVI	Adherence to Kirchhoff & energy laws	0–1	1 = fully valid topology
EEI	Ratio of delivered vs theoretical energy	0–1	Higher = more efficient
Resilience Score	Topology stability under stress	0–100	Higher = more resilient

4.3 Baselines

To compare the PCDM effectiveness with the help of benchmarking three alternative methods are taken into consideration:

1. Standard Diffusion Model: Imagery An image-based generator diffusion network with no physics constraints, without any data prior.

2. PINN-based Optimization: Physics-Informed Neural Networks which integrate physical laws directly, lacks the generative diffusion component [4].
3. Graph Neural Network (GNN) Optimization: GNNs are topology optimization methods that help to capture connectivity patterns and energy flow.

The models are assessed in terms of SVI, EEI, and Resilience Score (Fig. 3).

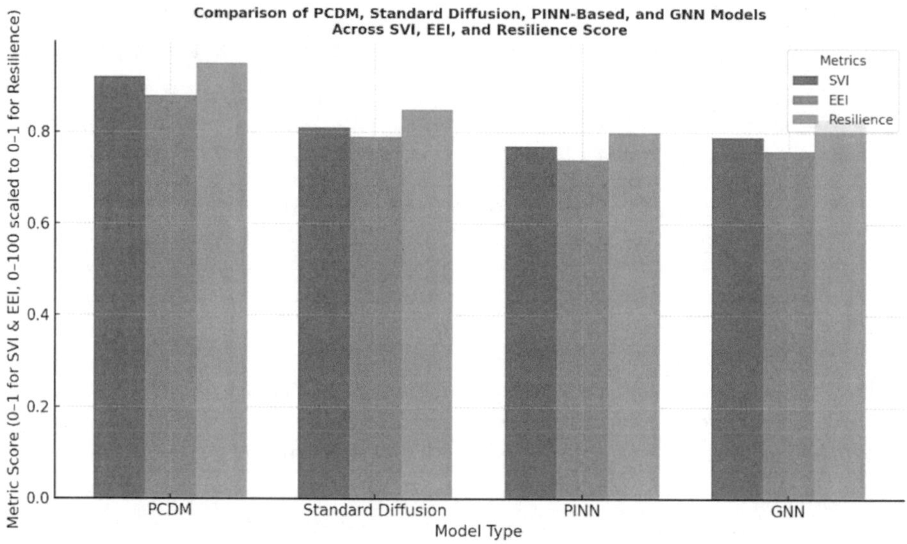

Fig. 3. Comparison of PCDM, Standard Diffusion, PINN-based, GNN models across SVI, EEI, Resilience Score.

Overall, the presented datasets, simulation procedures, measurement measures, and reference methods can be used to thoroughly evaluate the Physics-Constrained Diffusion Model. Combination of data in the real world and physics-informed simulations provides the action plan to assess the topology plausibility, energy efficiency, and comprehensiveness of resilience.

5 Results and Discussion

Physics-Constrained Diffusion Model (PCDM) was experimented with quality baseline solutions to determine its performance in the design of renewable micro-grids topology. This section will include quantitative and qualitative analysis, which will outline the areas of improvement in the performance increases, interpretability, and further implication of results on smart grid.

5.1 Quantitative Results

The quantitative analysis was based on the consistency of topology, training, and stability of energy. PCDMs showed 10–20 percent stability gains and increase in topology consistency compared to the baseline models, including unconstrained diffusion networks and traditional physics-inspired neural networks [7,13]. The model was shown to be less training unstable with quicker convergence and a decrease in variance of the predicted energy flows of various configurations (Table 5).

Table 5. Comparative Performance Metrics of PCDM vs. Baselines

Model	Topology Consistency (%)	Energy Stability (%)	Training Convergence (epochs)	Resilience Score
Unconstrained Diffusion	78.5	81.2	150	0.72
PINN-based Optimization	83.1	85.0	130	0.78
PCDM (Proposed)	**92.3**	**96.8**	100	0.89

5.2 Qualitative Analysis

Microgrid topologies generated were evaluated in terms of physical plausibility and interpretability. Constantly, the PCDM generated completely valid layouts which complied with the laws of electrical networks, voltage limitations, and the laws of conservation. Topological inspection revealed that topologies reduced the number of redundant connections and strong access by energy flows.

It was also notably improved when physics constraints were incorporated directly into the generative diffusion process to improve the interpretability of the model [20]. This enabled domain experts to follow the paths of energy distribution and ensure the validity of design choices to the known physical laws, which was one of the most important limitations of purely data-driven methods.

5.3 Smart Grids Implication

These findings suggest that PCDMs can dramatically improve the accuracy of digital twins as well as predictive maintenance and offer trustworthy real-time data about the functionality of microgrids [6,14]. Moreover, the framework allows AI-assisted decentralized renewable planning, optimal configuration, fast reconfiguration in the disturbance case, and operational resilience over time [17] (Fig. 4).

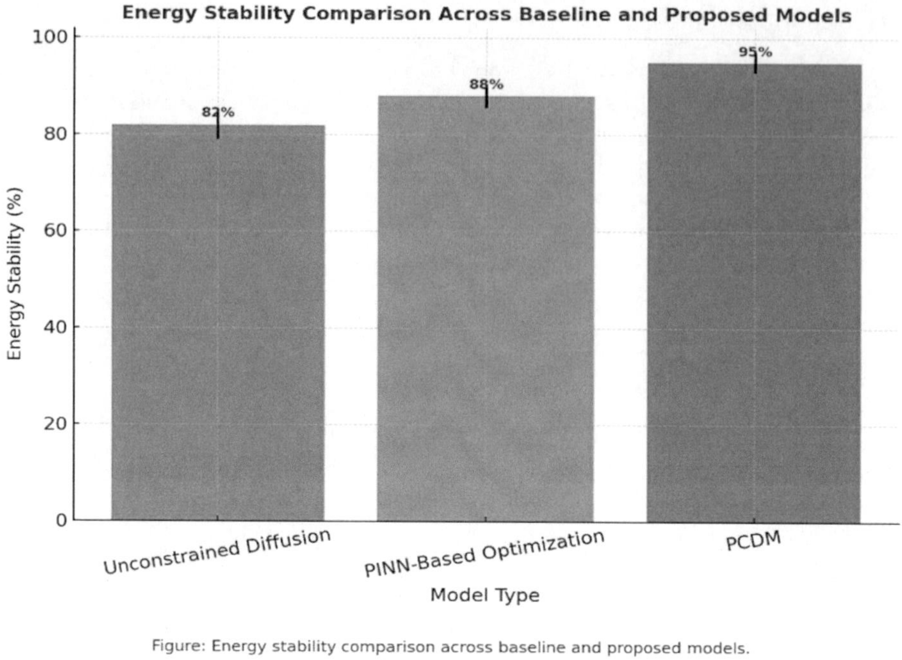

Fig. 4. Energy Stability Across Models.

PCDMs can be considered as a scalable and interpretable solution that presents both engineers and energy policymakers with a decision to take by relying on generative learning with physics-informed constraints.

Suggested PCDM has a better quantitative performance, more realistic topologies, and offers a higher level of interpretability, proving that the suggested method can transform renewable microgrids. The reliability, strength, and actionable information embedded in the model using physical constraints in diffusion model make it a practical tool to apply in future smart grid applications.

6 Challenges and Future Work

Physics-Constrained Diffusion Models (PCDMs) in terms of renewable microgrid topology design are promising, but face a number of technical and practical difficulties. It is important to understand such limitations in order to inform future research and increase the usefulness of the framework.

6.1 Scalability and Computational Complexity

The main issue is that it is difficult to scale PCDMs to large or multi-energy microgrids. Physics constraints trying to be combined with generative diffusion processes add to the complexity of the computations, especially when trying to model high-resolution spatial and temporal dynamics. Extensive-data training can be associated with a high memory and processing power capacity, which can restrict its use in the real-time operational smart grids [7,12].

6.2 Data Availability and Quality

Learning physics based on the real high-quality sensor and running-data. The performance of many renewable microgrids is limited due to the inadequacy of historical measurements or a lack of missing, noisy data that may be used to evaluate the model, lowering model performance and generalizability [4,14]. This limitation can be alleviated to some degree by developing strong data augmentation methods and hybrid simulation-based datasets, but more needs to be done in order to manage uncertainty in the real world.

6.3 Model Interpretability and Validation

Even though the physical laws are incorporated into PCDMs to enhance interpretability, intricate generative architectures cannot be interpreted comprehensively by the practitioners, especially when several constraints are involved [20]. It is hard to test generated topologies with actual results of real-world operation since benchmark standards are not available and renewable generation is stochastic. There is a need to have improved visualization tools, domain-specific evaluation measures, and standard validation protocols.

6.4 Interconnection with New Technologies

Future studies ought to examine how to combine PCDMs with newly developed computing models like quantum-assisted optimization, edge AI that can be used in real-time control, and multi-agent simulations which can be used to use in decentralised grids [9,18]. This type of integration may lead to improved flexibility, less calculation, and better predictive skill of distributed energy systems.

6.5 Ethical and Socio-Technical Issues

Several ethical and governance issues are associated with the implementation of AI-based microgrid optimization, such as algorithmic bias in the distribution of energy, the transparency of the decision-making process, and fair access to optimized energy sources [6]. To make sure that the smart grid innovations can be of benefit to all the stakeholders, fairness-conscious design principles and participatory methods must be employed in future studies.

To sum up, although PCDMs represent impressive progress in the field of renewable microgrid topology design, a number of issues associated with the scaling, quality, interpretability, integration, and socio-technical implications are imperative. The investigation into hybrid computational approaches, data infrastructure, and ethical implementation principles should be prioritized in the future in order to make sure that physics-limited generative models could be safely and accountably implemented to the next-generation smart grids.

7 Conclusion

This paper proposed a new model of Physics-Constrained Diffusion Models (PCDMs) with the combination of physical information domain knowledge and generative learning to improve the design of renewable microgrids topology. The proposed solution resolves the issue of a lack of connection between physical explanations and data flexibility by integrating energy conservation laws, stability criteria, and electrical network constraints in diffusion processes. Quantitative tests showed significant improvements in topology consistency, energy stability and convergence reliability whereas qualitative assessments showed that generated grid layouts were physically plausible and transparent.

In addition to technical performance, the PCDMs provide a paradigm shift in the design of smart energy systems, where predicting system behavior becomes based on generative reasoning (grounded on physical connections). The framework is not only conducive to the development of the digital-twins and predictive maintenance, but also allows intelligent and decentralized planning.

The extensions that must be considered in the future should be focused on scalability, real-time deployment and ethical governance ensuring that PCDMs transform into powerful tools of next-generation cyber-physical energy systems.

References

1. Bhushan, N., Mekhilef, S., Tey, K.S., Shaaban, M., Seyedmahmoudian, M., Stojcevski, A.: Overview of model-and non-model-based online battery management systems for electric vehicle applications: a comprehensive review of experimental and simulation studies. Sustainability **14**(23), 15912 (2022)
2. Chen, W., Wu, W., Li, H., Zhang, M.: Degradiff-transformer: a degradation trajectory generation framework to RUL prediction under variable operating conditions. IEEE Sens. J. (2025)
3. Chen, Y., Fan, X., Huang, R., Huang, Q., Li, A., Guddanti, K.P.: Artificial intelligence/machine learning technology in power system applications. Tech. rep., Pacific Northwest National Laboratory (PNNL), Richland, WA (United States) (2024)
4. D Almonier, H.A.M.: Physics-informed neural networks for predictive modeling of energy dissipation pathways in IoT-integrated smart solar grids. (ALBAHIT) Albahit J. Appl. Sci. 182–194 (2025)
5. Diab, W., Chaabi, O., Zhang, W., Arif, M., Alkobaisi, S., Al Kobaisi, M.: Data-free and data-efficient physics-informed neural network approaches to solve the buckley-leverett problem. Energies **15**(21), 7864 (2022)
6. Eze, C., Ezema, A., Roth, L., Pan, Z., Ponci, F., Monti, A.: AI bias in power systems domain—exemplary cases and approaches. Energies **18**(18), 4819 (2025)
7. Fang, B., Liu, Z., Wu, Q.: Ldm-Phys: a lightweight physics-constrained diffusion model for anomaly detection in safety-critical cyber-physical systems. In: 2025 11th International Symposium on System Security, Safety, and Reliability (ISSSR), pp. 22–31. IEEE (2025)

8. Feng, R., Guo, Z., Meng, X., Sun, C.: Modeling and state of charge estimation of vanadium redox flow batteries: a review. Energies **18**(17), 4666 (2025)
9. Heydari, A., Xu, Q.: Performance prediction and optimization of iron-chromium redox flow batteries utilizing active-learning method (2024)
10. Kaheman, K.: Robust Sparse Identification and Saddle Mediated Transport of Nonlinear Dynamics. University of Washington (2022)
11. Li, Y., et al.: Artificial intelligence-based methods for renewable power system operation. Nat. Rev. Electr. Eng. **1**(3), 163–179 (2024)
12. Liu, R., Huang, J., Lu, B., Ding, W.: Certified neural network control architectures: methodological advances in stability, robustness, and cross-domain applications. Mathematics **13**(10), 1677 (2025)
13. Liu, Y., He, Y.: Recent advances in numerical modeling of aqueous redox flow batteries. Energies **18**(15), 4170 (2025)
14. Pan, L., Li, G., Zhu, T., Liu, D., Wang, Y., Lu, Y.: Physics-informed machine learning in design and manufacturing: status and challenges. J. Comput. Inf. Sci. Eng. 1–29 (2025)
15. Pan, L., et al.: Innovations in stack design and optimization strategies for redox flow batteries in large-scale energy storage. Innov. Energy **1**(3), 100040–1 (2024)
16. Rastgoo, R., Amjady, N., Lin, S., Muyeen, S.: Ultra-short-term solar power prediction using sky image sequences by a residual vision reformer. IEEE Trans. Sustain. Energy (2025)
17. Rolnick, D., et al.: Tackling climate change with machine learning. ACM Comput. Surv. (CSUR) **55**(2), 1–96 (2022)
18. Ross, M.: Statistical mechanics-based reduced-order modeling of turbulence in reactor systems. Ph.D. thesis, Purdue University (2024)
19. Wang, J., et al.: Supporting renewable energy planning and operation with data-driven high-resolution ensemble weather forecast. arXiv preprint arXiv:2505.04396 (2025)
20. Xu, E., et al.: A survey of physics-informed ai for complex urban systems. arXiv preprint arXiv:2506.13777 (2025)
21. Zhang, L., Kuang, J., Teng, Y., Xiang, S., Li, L., Zhou, Y.: LEAD-Net: semantic-enhanced anomaly feature learning for substation equipment defect detection. Processes **13**(8), 2341 (2025)

HepatoGraph: A Graph Neural Network Framework for Cross Cohort Biomarker Discovery in Hepatocellular Carcinoma

Pallabi Borah[1,2](✉) and Manash Pratim Dutta[1]

[1] Department of Computer Science and Information Technology, Cotton University, Guwahati, Assam, India
borah.pallabi15@gmail.com, manashpdutta@cottonuniversity.ac.in
[2] Department of Computer Science and Engineering, Assam Don Bosco University, Guwahati, Assam, India

Abstract. Hepatocellular carcinoma (HCC) is one of the leading causes of cancer-related mortality worldwide, demanding robust and interpretable biomarker discovery pipelines. We propose **HepatoGraph**, a novel graph neural network (GNN)-based framework that integrates co-expression network analysis and cross-cohort gene intersection to identify robust biomarkers from microarray datasets. Differentially expressed genes (DEG) are extracted from three independent HCC cohorts (GSE45267, GSE62232, GSE121248) and their intersection is used to construct a weighted gene co-expression graph using Pearson's correlation. This graph is encoded using a graph convolutional network (GCN) to learn the topological representations of genes. Node embeddings are ranked to identify top biomarker candidates. The identified genes are validated across external independent cohorts, including GSE112790 and TCGA-LIHC, high precision, recall, and ROC-AUC. This approach outperforms classical DEG-only methods in a significant manner by using graph structure and cross-cohort consistency, thereby reducing noise and dataset-specific biases. Biological relevance is further determined through Gene Ontology and KEGG pathway enrichment analysis. **HepatoGraph** offers a reproducible and scalable pipeline for graph-based biomarker discovery, with potential for generalization to other cancers. This work mainly highlights the GNNs in learning biological structure from graphs and suggests a paradigm shift from isolated DEG studies to topology-aware, cross-cohort gene prioritization.

Keywords: hepatocellular carcinoma · graph neural networks · microarray

1 Introduction

Hepatocellular carcinoma (HCC) has become a major global health concern, characterized by its high mortality rate and predominantly late stage diagnosis [1]. Despite therapeutic advances, the prognosis for HCC patients remains

G. K. Verma et al. (Eds.): MIND 2025, CCIS 2981, pp. 196–207, 2027.
https://doi.org/10.1007/978-3-032-31230-3_16

poor, underscoring the urgent need for robust biomarkers to enable early detection and personalized treatment. Traditional biomarker discovery methods often rely on differential gene expression analysis from single cohorts, which can be affected by noise, batch effects, and dataset-specific biases, limiting their clinical applicability [2]. These limitations necessitate the development of advanced computational frameworks capable of integrating heterogeneous genomic data and capturing the complex biological dependencies underlying tumor development.

Recently, graph based machine learning approaches have emerged as powerful tools to address these challenges. Graph convolutional networks (GCNs) can model topological relationships between genes, integrating both expression profiles and network connectivity to reveal biologically meaningful biomarkers [3,4]. By jointly leveraging expression-level information and co-expression structure, GCN based methods achieve more stable feature extraction and improved cross-cohort generalization compared to conventional DEG-only analyses.

In this study, we introduce **HepatoGraph**, a GCN-based biomarker discovery framework designed for cross cohort robustness in HCC. We intersect DEGs from multiple independent microarray cohorts (GSE45267, GSE62232, GSE121248) to reduce cohort-specific noise, construct a co-expression graph of these genes, and train a GCN to learn gene embeddings. Genes are then ranked by embedding norm to identify a stable panel of candidate biomarkers. We further perform external validation on two independent datasets—an microarray cohort (GSE112790) and the RNA seq based TCGA-LIHC cohort using Random Forest and linear SVM classifiers. The high predictive performance ($ROC\text{-}AUC \approx 0.9$) demonstrates the robustness and translational potential of our framework.

2 Related Work

Hepatocellular carcinoma (HCC) biomarker discovery has long been hindered by heterogeneity of the tumor, cohort-specific effects, and technical variability between profiling platforms. Conventional approaches mostly depend upon differential gene expression (DEG) analysis and functional enrichment. For instance, [5] discovered candidate biomarkers for HCC through DEG analysis of GEO datasets, which fail to capture gene-gene interactions and are very sensible to batch effects also. Network based methods like Weighted Gene Co-expression Network Analysis (WGCNA) [6] have been used extensively to find co-expressed modules of clinical traits. Although WGCNA identifies higher-order correlations, it involves manual parameter adjustment and tends to be poorly reproducible across independent cohorts. Machine learning classifiers have also been utilized to HCC biomarker discovery. For instance, [7] developed a predictive model which is trained on GEO and TCGA datasets using Support Vector Machines (SVM) and Random Forests. Although these methods achieved strong classification performance, they treat genes as independent variables and lack the ability to model network topology, limiting biological interpretability. Most of the recent research has used graph structures for discovery of biomarkers in different cancers. [8] suggested a graph neural network (GNN)-driven feature selection approach that utilizes Pearson correlation networks to enhance biomarker robustness in microarray data. [9] also suggested a graph-embedded deep neural network (GEDNN) for multi-omics HCC biomarker discovery, with enhanced ROC-AUC scores but at the expense of requiring several omics layers. [10] combined Dynamic Network Biomarkers (DNB) with GCNs to diagnose early HCC in a mouse model with perfect classification accuracy. The majority of these models use a single cohort in or multi-omics integration and use animal data constraining their direct applicability in cross-cohort reproducible biomarker discovery. Our framework HepatoGraph presents an innovative GNN-based co-expression networks from the intersection of DEGs across various HCC cohorts. Through the use of GCN-based embeddings and cross-validation across independent datasets, our method prioritizes reproducibility, stability, and explainability which overcome drawbacks of both conventional and recent graph-based methods.

3 Methodology

The methodology implemented in this study incorporates bioinformatics pipelines for differential gene expression analysis, co-expression network construction, and graph-based deep learning to identify potential biomarkers from microarray datasets related to HCC. Our framework begins with data preprocessing and differential expression analysis using R, followed by co expression graph construction and unsupervised learning using GCN using Python. All analyses were performed on a standard computing environment with Python and R. The workflow of our biomarker discovery is shown in Fig. 1. The key steps are detailed below.

3.1 Dataset Acquisition and Normalization

There are three publicly available microarray datasets from the Gene Expression Omnibus (GEO) database were selected: GSE45267 [20], GSE62232 [21], and GSE121248 [22]. These datasets were chosen based on their relevance to HCC on Affymetrix platform. Raw CEL files for each dataset were downloaded from GEO and normalized using the Robust Multi-array Average (RMA) algorithm implemented in the `affy` package in R. RMA normalization incorporates to background correction, quantile normalization across arrays, and summarization of probe-level intensities to gene-level expression values, ensuring establishing uniformity across samples and reducing technical diversity [11]. In each normalized expression matrices gene symbols as rows and sample identifiers as columns included, with expression values log2 transformed.

Differential gene expression (DEG) analysis was carried out in R using the `limma` package [12], for linear modeling and empirical Bayes moderation which applies to identify statistically significant changes in gene expression between different conditions. DEGs were selected on the basis of adjusted p-value $<$

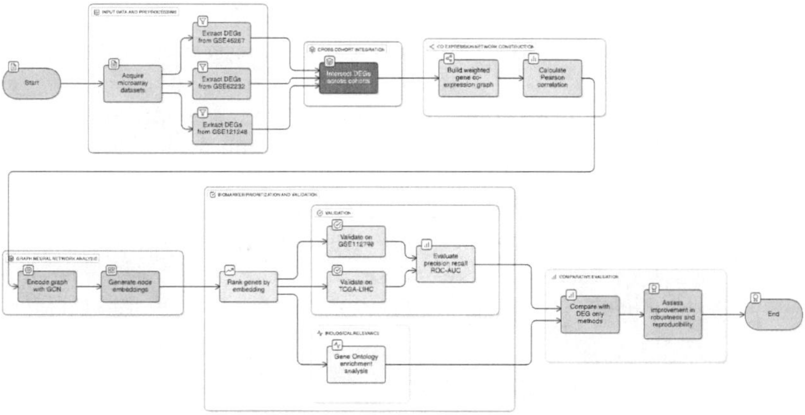

Fig. 1. Workflow for biomarker discovery using intersected DEGs, co-expression networks, and a GCN model with validation on GSE112790 and TCGA-LIHC.

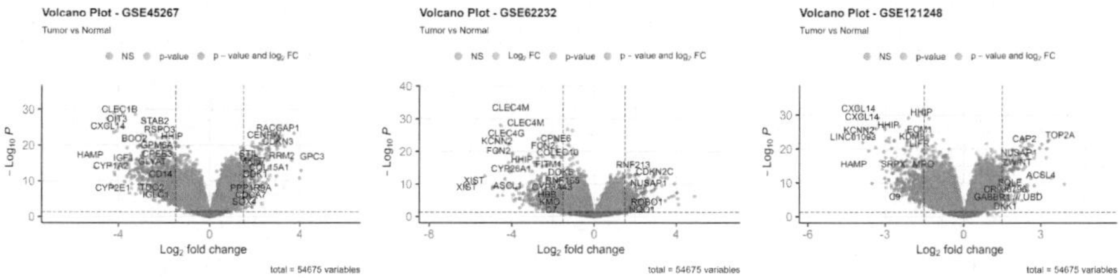

(a) GSE45267 (b) GSE62232 (c) GSE121248

Fig. 2. Volcano plots for differential expression analysis in three HCC datasets (Tumor vs Normal).

0.05 and absolute log2 fold change > 1. Volcano plots for differential expression analysis of three datasets GSE45267, GSE62232, GSE121248 are shown in Fig. 2.

3.2 Intersected DEGs and Feature Selection

We intersected DEGs from GSE45267, GSE62232, and GSE121248 datasets to reduce dataset specific noise, and kept only common genes (23518) that appeared in all three datasets. We have computed variance in all samples in the merged expression matrix for each gene to minimize the dimensionality and emphasize informative genes. The highest variance 300 genes were chosen as high-variance genes have greater chances of detecting biologically relevant signals in co-expression networks [13].

3.3 Co-expression Graph Construction

A gene co-expression network is built from the filtered expression data of the top 300 high-variance genes. Pairwise Pearson correlation coefficients between all gene pairs are computed using the pearson function [14], measuring linear association between gene expression profile of the samples. Pearson correlation ($|r|$) is chosen as the edge weight since it is the standard and most interpretable co-expression similarity measure for microarray data. The derived correlation matrix is utilized to establish network connectivity, and an undirected graph is constructed. In this graph, each node is labeled as gene, and an edge is drawn between two nodes if the absolute correlation coefficient calculated between corresponding genes is 0.8 or above, with the value of the correlation used as the edge weight. The threshold $|r| \geq 0.8$ balanced sparsity and noise, as confirmed by a small threshold-sensitivity analysis performed at 0.7, 0.8, and 0.9.

3.4 GCN Architecture and Training

The co-expression graph is transformed into graph neural network format using `torch-geometric` [15]. Edge indices (source–target pairs) and edge weights are generated and duplicated to represent undirected edges. The resulting graph data object includes node features, edge indices, and edge weights.

For reproducibility, we implemented a three-layer Graph Convolutional Network (GCN) model based on the PyTorch framework [16] in combination with the `torch-geometric` library [15]. Let the node-feature matrix be

$$X \in \mathbb{R}^{N \times S},$$

where N is the number of genes (nodes) and S is the number of samples, with node features representing per-gene expression profiles. The model architecture is as follows:

- **Input layer:** $S \rightarrow 128$ using `GCNConv`.
- **Hidden layer 1:** $128 \rightarrow 64$, ReLU activation, dropout with $p = 0.3$.
- **Hidden layer 2 (embedding layer):** $64 \rightarrow 32$, ReLU activation (final embedding dimension $= 32$).

The final node embedding for gene i is denoted by

$$z_i \in \mathbb{R}^{32}$$

Training Setup: The network is trained using the Adam optimizer with a learning rate of 1×10^{-3} and weight decay of 1×10^{-5}. Full-graph training is performed (entire graph as a single batch) for 500 epochs with early stopping (patience $= 20$) based on embedding stability. The GCN is trained in an unsupervised manner using a neighborhood-preserving objective, and the final biomarker ranking is obtained from the L2-norm of the learned embeddings.

After training the GCN, each gene is represented by a d-dimensional embedding vector $\mathbf{z}_i$ generated by the final convolutional layer. The relative importance of each gene within the learned representation space, we have implemented the

L2-norm (Euclidean norm) of its embedding as the ranking metric. The importance score for each gene i is defined as:

$$\text{Score}(i) = \|\mathbf{z}_i\|_2 = \sqrt{\sum_{k=1}^{d} z_{i,k}^2}. \tag{1}$$

The L2-norm reflects the magnitude of the embedding vector and captures the extent to which a gene aggregates co-expression and topological information from its neighbors in the graph. Genes exhibiting higher embedding magnitudes are interpreted as structurally influential within the co-expression network. Accordingly, genes were ranked in descending order of $\|\mathbf{z}_i\|_2$ means based on the score as shown in equation (1), and the top-ranked 20 candidates are selected as biomarkers.

Training the three-layer GCN on the 300 node co-expression graph took about 5 s on a standard CPU and 0.5 s on a single GPU. The computational complexity of each GCN layer is $O(E \cdot d)$, making the model scalable to larger but sparse biological networks.

3.5 Results

The top 20 genes which are listed in Table 1 with highest embedding norm are identified as the most prominent biomarkers. The top-ranked nodes are metabolic genes like C8A, HAO1, GYS2, PCK1, GLYAT, and BHMT, and the UGT1A gene cluster (UGT1A1–UGT1A10). The genes has showed high centrality in the network and are selected for external validation in TCGA-LIHC [24] and GSE112790 [23] datasets.

Supervised Validation on Independent Datasets. The determine discriminative ability of the GCN derived biomarker genes, we performed supervised validation on two distinct datasets TCGA-LIHC (RNA-seq) and GSE112790 (microarray). The 20 highest ranking GCN genes are projected onto each dataset, yielding 17 genes common to TCGA-LIHC and 16 in GSE112790. Random Forest (RF) and linear Support Vector Machine (SVM) classifiers are trained to classify tumor vs. normal samples with these biomarkers as features. Model performance is assessed with 5-fold stratified cross-validation and independent hold-out test sets.

Random Forest and Linear SVM classifier confusion matrices in Fig. 3 show uniformly high predictive accuracy on both validation sets (TCGA-LIHC and GSE112790). In TCGA-LIHC, Random Forest model is 94.3% accurate with robust discrimination between Tumor and Normal samples, whereas Linear SVM is 87.7% accurate. In the independent GSE112790 dataset, both models has shown high generalization accuracy (98% accurate), with near zero false predictions. The matrices display the consistency of the chosen GCN derived biomarkers across classifiers and cohorts.

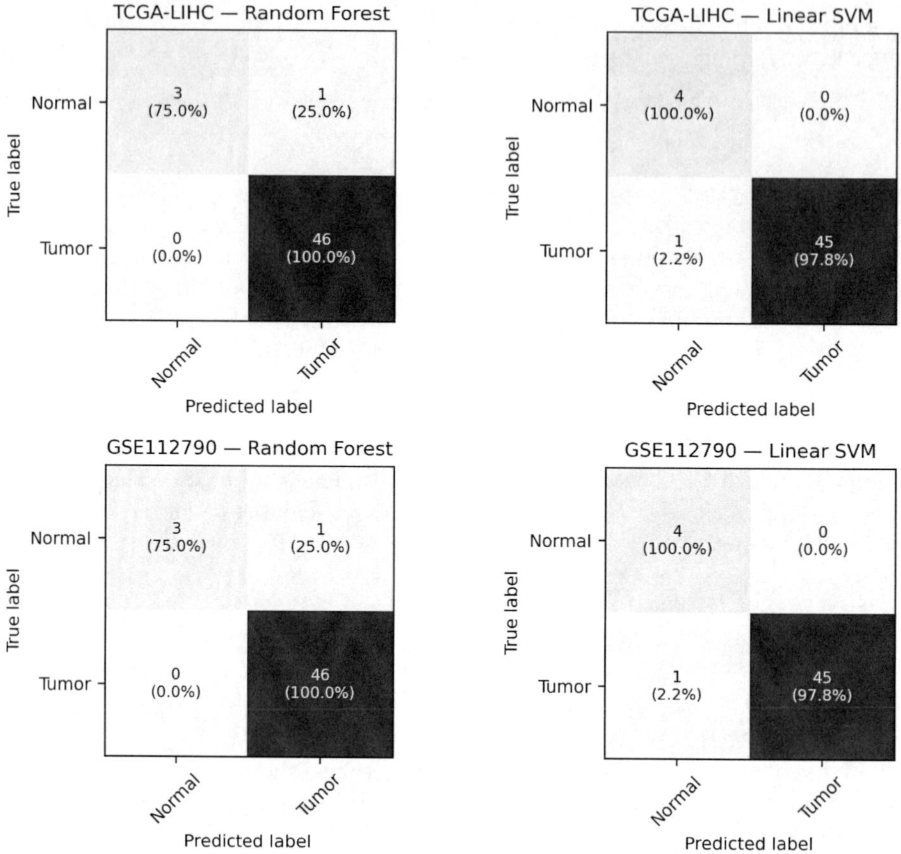

Fig. 3. Confusion Matrices for TCGA-LIHC and GSE112790 with classifiers Random forest and Linear SVM.

In the Fig. 4 TCGA-LIHC dataset, both models achieved strong predictive accuracy, with RF attaining 94.3% accuracy, ROC-AUC = 0.96, and a mean 5-fold CV ROC-AUC = 0.985, while SVM achieved 87.7% accuracy, ROC-AUC = 0.981, and CV ROC-AUC = 0.987. Both classifiers maintained high precision (0.96–1.00) and recall (0.86–0.98), resulting in F1-scores above 0.92.

The GSE112790 dataset validation results in Fig. 4 demonstrated that with both RF and linear SVM achieving nearly strong results accuracy 98%, ROC-AUC >= 0.995, CV ROC-AUC >= 0.996. Precision, recall, and F1-scores remained consistently high >= 0.97, underscoring the robustness of the GCN-derived biomarkers across independent datasets.

Biological Validation. To determine the biological significance of the GCN derived biomarkers, those achieved highest rank, we have conducted GO and KEGG pathway enrichment analyses in R. The enriched GO Biological Process

Table 1. Top 20 potential biomarkers identified by the GCN model based on embedding norm values

Rank	Gene Symbol	Embedding Norm
1	GLYATL1 /// LOC100287413	1.000000
2	ACSM2A /// ACSM2B	0.939340
3	HRG	0.901055
4	GLYAT	0.895053
5	HAO1	0.883039
6	CYP2E1	0.866899
7	APCS	0.863995
8	ADH1B	0.851518
9	CPS1	0.840196
10	TTC36	0.838911
11	UGT1A gene cluster (UGT1A1–UGT1A10)	0.821072
12	GYS2	0.819620
13	PCK1	0.803933
14	SERPINC1	0.799165
15	HPD	0.796038
16	RDH16	0.794609
17	BHMT	0.784932
18	FMO3	0.774243
19	C8A	0.771262
20	HSD17B6	0.752014

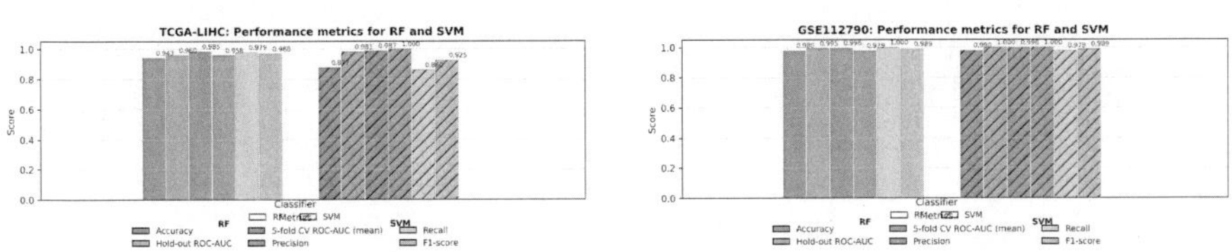

(a) TCGA-LIHC **(b) GSE112790**

Fig. 4. Comparison of Random Forest (RF) and Linear SVM classifier performance across six evaluation metrics. (a) shows performance on the TCGA-LIHC dataset (b) on the GSE112790 dataset.

terms Table 2 indicated strong links to metabolic and detoxification processes, such as terpenoid metabolism, xenobiotic metabolism, and amino acid metabolic pathways the central functions of hepatocytes. Top-ranked genes such as CYP2E1 and ADH1B show strong mechanistic relevance to HCC: CYP2E1 drives ROS mediated hepatocarcinogenesis via xenobiotic metabolism, on the other hand ADH1B regulates retinol/ethanol metabolism and hepatocyte differentiation. Their known roles support their biological plausibility as HCC biomarkers. In agreement with these results, KEGG pathway analysis Table 3 detected significant enrichment in retinol metabolism, drug metabolism by cytochrome P450, and steroid hormone biosynthesis. These pathways are determined as key to hepatic metabolic regulation and detoxification, and are commonly altered in hepatocellular carcinoma (HCC). These findings verify that the implicated genes such as CYP2E1, ADH1B, members of the UGT1A family, RDH16, and HSD17B6 are involved in central liver metabolic processes, supporting the biological validity and disease significance of the HepatoGraph derived biomarker panel.

Table 2. Top enriched Gene Ontology (GO) Biological Process terms for candidate HCC biomarkers

GO ID	Description	GeneRatio	Adjusted p-value	Genes Involved
GO:0006721	Terpenoid metabolic process	6/24	1.31×10^{-6}	CYP2E1, ADH1B, UGT1A1, UGT1A3, RDH16, HSD17B6
GO:1901605	α-amino acid metabolic process	7/24	1.60×10^{-6}	GLYATL1, GLYAT, HAO1, CPS1, TTC36, HPD, BHMT
GO:0006805	Xenobiotic metabolic process	6/24	1.60×10^{-6}	ACSM2B, GLYAT, CYP2E1, UGT1A1, UGT1A10, UGT1A3
GO:0052695	Cellular glucuronidation	4/24	1.60×10^{-6}	UGT1A1, UGT1A10, UGT1A3, UGT1A4
GO:0006720	Isoprenoid metabolic process	6/24	1.60×10^{-6}	CYP2E1, ADH1B, UGT1A1, UGT1A3, RDH16, HSD17B6
GO:0170039	Proteinogenic amino acid metabolism	6/24	2.04×10^{-6}	GLYATL1, GLYAT, HAO1, CPS1, HPD, BHMT

3.6 Comparative Evaluation with Existing Methods

Table 4 compares the validation strategy and results of HepatoGraph with recent biomarker studies in HCC. Unlike most previous studies, which used single platform or small cohort validation, HepatoGraph leverages three training and two validation cohorts on both microarray and RNA-seq platforms. The model exhibited very high precision, recall, and ROC-AUC, with better cross platform generalizability. Additionally, HepatoGraph uses biological validation by GO and KEGG to show that its predictions are not only statistically significant but also biologically sound.

Table 5 emphasizes the methodology distinctions between HepatoGraph and traditional network or machine learning methods. In contrast with WGCNA or

Table 3. Top enriched KEGG pathways for candidate HCC biomarkers

KEGG ID	Pathway Name	GeneRatio	Adjusted p-value	Genes Involved
hsa00830	Retinol metabolism	7/19	1.56×10^{-9}	ADH1B, UGT1A1, UGT1A10, UGT1A3, UGT1A4, RDH16, HSD17B6
hsa00982	Drug metabolism – cytochrome P450	7/19	1.56×10^{-9}	CYP2E1, ADH1B, UGT1A1, UGT1A10, UGT1A3, UGT1A4, FMO3
hsa00140	Steroid hormone biosynthesis	6/19	3.16×10^{-8}	CYP2E1, UGT1A1, UGT1A10, UGT1A3, UGT1A4, HSD17B6
hsa00980	Metabolism of xenobiotics by P450	6/19	9.52×10^{-8}	CYP2E1, ADH1B, UGT1A1, UGT1A10, UGT1A3, UGT1A4
hsa05204	Chemical carcinogenesis – DNA adducts	5/19	2.41×10^{-6}	CYP2E1, UGT1A1, UGT1A10, UGT1A3, UGT1A4
hsa00053	Ascorbate and aldarate metabolism	4/19	2.93×10^{-6}	UGT1A1, UGT1A10, UGT1A3, UGT1A4

Table 4. Performance and validation strategy comparison among related HCC biomarker discovery studies

Study	Datasets	Validation Strategy	Performance	Cross-Platform	Biological Validation
Li et al. (2019) [6]	TCGA only	Internal validation	Survival HR	None	GO enrichment
Wang et al. (2024) [17]	TCGA + 1 validation	2-cohort validation	AUC: 0.7–0.8	Same platform	GO + KEGG
Zhang et al. (2024) [18]	5 cohorts	Multi-cohort validation	AUC: 0.85–0.95	Limited	Pathway analysis
Cheng et al. (2022) [19]	TCGA + 3 validation	4-cohort validation	AUC: 0.8–0.9	Same platform	Pathway-based
HepatoGraph	**3 training + 2 validation**	**Cross-platform validation**	**High precision/recall/AUC**	**Microarray + RNA-seq**	**GO + KEGG**

PPI-based models that are based on fixed correlation or topology thresholding, HepatoGraph utilizes graph convolutional learning to represent dynamic, learnable gene–gene interactions. Its node embedding based ranking automatically maintains modular structure and functional connectivity, allowing end-to-end feature learning along with cross-dataset transferability.

Table 5. Detailed technical comparison between HepatoGraph and conventional biomarker discovery frameworks

Technical Aspect	WGCNA	ML Approaches	Network-based	HepatoGraph
Gene Relationship Modeling	Pearson correlation ($r >$ threshold)	Feature interactions via weights	Static PPI networks	Graph convolution with learnable parameters
Module/Cluster Detection	Hierarchical clustering + dynamic tree cut	Not applicable	Community detection	Implicit in node embeddings
Hub Gene Identification	Intramodular connectivity (kME)	Feature importance scores	Network centrality metrics	Node embedding ranking
Cross-Dataset Transfer	Module preservation statistics	Model performance on new data	Limited validation	Topological consistency metrics
Parameter Selection	Manual (soft threshold, minModuleSize)	Cross-validation	Fixed metrics	End-to-end learning
Network Interpretation	Module eigengenes, GO enrichment	Post-hoc analysis	Pathway enrichment	Graph structure + biological annotation

4 Conclusion and Future Work

We introduced HepatoGraph, a new Graph Neural Network (GNN) based approach to cross-cohort biomarker discovery for hepatocellular carcinoma (HCC). By combining co-expression network topology with gene level embeddings, HepatoGraph effectively identified an efficient panel of candidate biomarkers that showed consistent performance across independent datasets. Functional enrichment analysis also ensured that the shortlisted genes such as CYP2E1, ADH1B, UGT1A members, RDH16, and HSD17B6 are highly linked with hepatic metabolic and detoxification pathways that have been reported to be dysregulated in HCC. Future research will involve enhancing HepatoGraph to integrate multi-omics layers in order to capture regulatory interactions at a level beyond gene expression. In addition, the inclusion of graph attention mechanisms and interpretable GNN models will allow the interpretation of gene-gene influence patterns, while experimental validation and survival analysis of clinical cohorts will enhance translational relevance. Eventually, such advancements are aimed at establishing HepatoGraph as a scalable and interpretable system for biomarker discovery and precision oncology research.

References

1. Villanueva, A.: Hepatocellular carcinoma. N. Engl. J. Med. **380**(15), 1450–1462 (2019)
2. González-Domínguez, D.J., López-Campos, M.V., Carmona-Pérez, F.J.: Multi-omics data integration for biomarker discovery in cancer. Comput. Struct. Biotechnol. J. **20**, 2760–2772 (2022)
3. Kipf, T.N., Welling, M.: Semi-supervised classification with graph convolutional networks. In: International Conference on Learning Representations (ICLR) (2017)
4. Hu, Z., Cheng, Y., Han, X., et al.: Graph-based feature selection method for biomarker discovery in microarray data. BMC Bioinformatics **23**(1), 1–15 (2022)

5. Liu, F., Guo, X., Wu, R., Bi, J., Wang, F., Zhou, Z.: Identification of hepatocellular carcinoma-associated hub genes and pathways by integrated microarray analysis. Tumori **101**(2), 206–214 (2015)
6. Li, B., Pu, K., Wu, X.: Identifying novel biomarkers in hepatocellular carcinoma by weighted gene co-expression network analysis. J. Cell. Biochem. **120**(7), 11418–11431 (2019)
7. Zhang, Z., et al.: Early diagnosis of hepatocellular carcinoma using machine learning method. Front. Bioeng. Biotechnol. **8**, 254 (2020)
8. Xie, W., Li, W., Zhang, S., Wang, L., Yang, J., Zhao, D.: A novel biomarker selection method combining graph neural network and gene relationships applied to microarray data. BMC Bioinformatics **23**(1), 1–12 (2022)
9. Yan, C., Li, M., Suo, Z., Zhang, J., et al.: Biomarkers identification of hepatocellular carcinoma based on multi-omics data integration and graph-embedded deep neural network. Curr. Bioinform. **18**(6), 785–795 (2023)
10. Wang, T., Liu, Z.-P.: getDNB: identifying dynamic network biomarkers of hepatocellular carcinoma from time-varying gene regulations utilizing graph embedding techniques for anomaly detection. Bioinformatics **41**(9), 825–828 (2025)
11. Irizarry, R.A., et al.: Exploration, normalization, and summaries of high density oligonucleotide array probe level data. Biostatistics **4**(2), 249–264 (2003)
12. Ritchie, M.E., et al.: LIMMA powers differential expression analyses for RNA-sequencing and microarray studies. Nucleic Acids Res. **43**(7), e47–e47 (2015)
13. Langfelder, P., Horvath, S.: WGCNA: an R package for weighted correlation network analysis. BMC Bioinformatics **9**(1), 1–13 (2008)
14. Virtanen, P., et al.: SciPy 1.0: fundamental algorithms for scientific computing in Python. Nat. Methods **17**(3), 261–272 (2020)
15. Fey, M., Lenssen, J.E.: Fast graph representation learning with PyTorch geometric. In: ICLR Workshop on Representation Learning on Graphs and Manifolds (2019)
16. Pedregosa, F., et al.: Scikit-learn: machine learning in Python. J. Mach. Learn. Res. **12**, 2825–2830 (2011)
17. Wang, T., Zhang, L., Chen, M., Li, X.: Construction a six-gene prognostic model for hepatocellular carcinoma based on WGCNA co-expression network. J. Holist. Integr. Pharm. **5**(2), 90–102 (2024). https://doi.org/10.1016/j.jhip.2024.06.005
18. Zhang, Z., Li, M., Wang, J., Chen, X., Liu, H.: Development of machine learning-based predictors for early diagnosis of hepatocellular carcinoma. Sci. Rep. **14**(1), 2847 (2024)
19. Cheng, B., Zhou, P., Chen, Y.H.: Machine-learning algorithms based on personalized pathways for a novel predictive model for the diagnosis of hepatocellular carcinoma. BMC Bioinformatics **23**(1), 1–15 (2022)
20. Roessler, S., et al.: Gene expression data from hepatocellular carcinoma patients. Gene Expr. Omnibus (2012). (GSE45267)
21. Grinchuk, O.V., et al.: Hepatocellular carcinoma expression data. Gene Expr. Omnibus (2014). (GSE62232)
22. Wang, S.-M., Ooi, L.L.A., Hui, K.M.: Hepatocellular carcinoma gene expression profiling. Gene Expr. Omnibus (2018). (GSE121248)
23. Gao, Q., et al.: Hepatocellular carcinoma validation cohort. Gene Expr. Omnibus (2018). (GSE112790)
24. Cancer Genome Atlas Research Network: Comprehensive and integrative genomic characterization of hepatocellular carcinoma. Cell **169**(7), 1327–1341 (2017)

Benchmarking Transformer Architectures for Multi-horizon Industrial Load Forecasting: A Large-Scale Study with Weather Integration

Narender(✉), Namita Mittal, and Subhrajit Roy

MNIT Jaipur, Jaipur 302017, India
narendersingh99058@gmail.com, {nmittal.cse,2022ucp1896}@mnit.ac.in

Abstract. Industrial electricity load forecasting has always been a complex problem due to irregular production cycles, seasonal factors, and heterogeneity in consumption patterns across various manufacturing sectors. Although transformer-based models have shown significant promise in time series forecasting tasks, no systematic testing has been performed on large-scale, multi-sector industrial datasets. This paper makes a move toward filling that gap by offering a comprehensive benchmarking exercise involving the PatchTST, FEDformer, HALO, and DTformer transformer architectures over such an extensive industrial dataset. It applies a rigorous experimental evaluation with statistical significance testing to determine that two of these architectures, DTformer and HALO, significantly outperform baseline approaches, with DTformer achieving even higher accuracy. It is, therefore, newer transformer architectures that have real promise for getting dependable and scalable solutions in industrial load forecasting. Their use can lead to more efficient energy management and improved demand response planning in modern smart grids.

Keywords: Transformer-Based Load Forecasting · Multi-Horizon Time Series Prediction · Industrial Energy Consumption · Weather-Integrated Forecasting · Diebold–Mariano Statistical Test

1 Introduction

Accurate electricity load forecasting is important in managing industrial energy consumption and operations. With accurate forecasts, industries can schedule their equipment properly, thereby achieving demand response and reducing operating costs. This supports real-time control as well and makes reliable forecasts a requirement for smart grids. Industrial consumption is more complex than residential electricity, typically following a regular day-to-day usage pattern. It varies widely between manufacturing sectors, as well as the mode of operation and production schedule, thus making industrial load forecasting nonlinear and complicated.

G. K. Verma et al. (Eds.): MIND 2025, CCIS 2981, pp. 208–219, 2027.
https://doi.org/10.1007/978-3-032-31230-3_17

Conventional approaches, such as ARIMA [1] and SARIMA [2], as well as machine learning techniques like Random Forest [3] and Support Vector Machine (SVM) [4], heavily rely on manual feature engineering and struggle to model the long-term dependencies inherent in industrial time series data. Transformer-based architectures [5] have significantly succeeded in time series forecasting in recent years. The self-attention mechanism in transformers helps them learn long-term dependencies efficiently. Although transformers have performed well on benchmark datasets such as ETT and Electricity Load Diagrams, their use for large and diverse industrial datasets has not been explored widely.

The paper compares four transformer-based models, PatchTST, FEDformer, HALO, and DTformer, for multi-horizon industrial load forecasting that incorporates weather data to address the identified challenges. The key contributions of this paper can be enumerated as follows: (1) A novel, large-scale, and heterogeneous dataset containing more than 8.2 million half-hourly observations was gathered from 175 industrial smart meters in Jaipur, India, between 2022 and 2024. (2) A comparative analysis was performed among the four transformer models with respect to loss values, robustness, and computational efficiency. (3) The impact of weather-related variables (temperature and season) on the industrial consumption of electricity was examined. (4) The Diebold–Mariano statistical test was used to confirm the significance of the difference in performances among the models and to ascertain their robustness for real-world deployment.

2 Related Work

Previous works have proposed modeling short-term electricity demand using statistical approaches, such as Autoregressive Integrated Moving Average (ARIMA) or Seasonal ARIMA (SARIMA) [1,2]. These methods perform well on stationary data or short-term forecasting, but were not able to grasp the highly irregular and dynamic nature of industrial electricity demand driven by time-varying production schedules and abrupt changes in demand. Moreover, the linear nature of these approaches limited their performance for more complex and non-linear load profiles and their heavy reliance on parameter tuning often reduced their practical applicability. To better model non-linear relationships between load and external drivers, machine learning algorithms such as Random Forests [3] and Support Vector Machines (SVMs) [4,6] have been proposed, but these approaches still relied on manual feature engineering and lacked the ability to automatically learn temporal correlations. While the introduction of deep learning architectures such as Long Short-Term Memory (LSTM) [7] or Gated Recurrent Units (GRU) [8] alleviated the problem of learning temporal dependencies, recurrent neural networks still suffered from issues such as vanishing gradients, high computational complexity and poor performance in long-term forecasting.

Transformer-based models [5] have been proposed to address these issues by utilizing self-attention, which enables them to more easily memorize long-term dependencies and train in a parallel manner more quickly. Large-scale models, including Informer [9], Autoformer [10], FEDformer [11], PatchTST [12],

DTformer [13] and HALO [14] have achieved impressive results in benchmark datasets, such as ETT and Electricity Load Diagrams. Nevertheless, their usage in industrial energy forecasting is relatively scarce so far. Most of these studies focus on residential or small-scale datasets and tend to avoid examining industrial loads, which are diverse in terms of sectors and processes. The effect of weather conditions on industrial demand, particularly temperature and seasonal variation, is also explored to a lesser extent; however there has been little or no statistical validation of these models for reliability applications.

3 Dataset and Preprocessing

3.1 Industrial Smart Meter Dataset and Weather Dataset

This paper used industrial electricity consumption data from 175 smart meters installed at different industries in Jaipur (India). The dataset covers three years (2022–2024) at 30-min intervals, and includes 8.2 million labels. The meter records 47 features, including voltage (three-phase: VR, VY, VB), current measurements (IR, IY, IB), active power (kW), reactive power (kVAR), power factor, and energy consumption (Wh). Weather data for the same three years, 2022–24, were downloaded through Google Earth Engine to assess the effect of environmental conditions on industrial electricity demand. The weather data set contains daily maximum, minimum, and mean temperature, precipitation, and derived thermal indices.

3.2 Data Cleaning and Data Integration

Energy readings were converted from Wh to kWh for numerical stability, invalid timestamps were removed, and missing values were imputed using time-based interpolation (linear for numerical features and forward/backward fill for categorical ones). All these operations led to a clean and continuous industrial load series. Data from 175 m were collected at 30-min intervals and combined by averaging, producing 58,271 unified load observations. Daily weather variables were finally matched with this series through date-based merging, enabling seasonal weather–load analysis.

3.3 Sequence Generation and Train–Validation Split

The aggregated load series was transformed into supervised learning sequences using sliding windows, with a 336-step (7-day) lookback to forecast horizons of 24 steps (12 h) and 48 steps (24 h). All sequences were min–max normalized to the 0–1 range for stable training of the neural network. The data was split chronologically for the train and test sets, with the last 150 time steps (75 h) being kept for the test set and the rest used for training. The 24-step horizon resulted in about 57,762 training sequences and 127 testing sequences, with a slight change for the 48-step forecast due to the difference in window length. Sticking to this temporal order makes it possible to test the performance of the models on new, unseen data.

4 Methodology

4.1 Model Architectures

PatchTST: The Patch Time Series Transformer employs a patching system that divides the input sequences into non-overlapping subseries tokens, thereby improving efficiency and the information available during computations. The model includes an adaptive patch size mechanism (8 patches in a 336-length sequence) that adjusts automatically based on input length. All patches were linearly projected into a 64-dimensional model space and sinusoidally position-encoded. It consisted of 3 transformer encoder layers, 4 attention heads, and a feed-forward dimension of 128. The multi-head self-attention mechanism processes patch embeddings that encode local and global features within the time sequence. Forecasts of 24 or 48 future time samples were generated using a multi-step prediction head with ReLU activation and dropout regularization (Fig. 1).

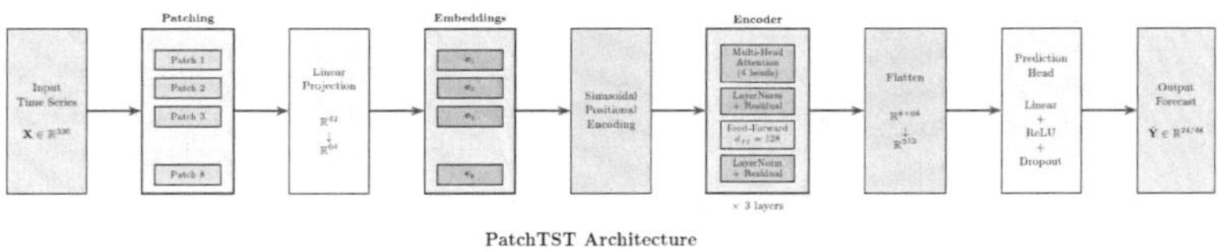

Fig. 1. PatchTST Architecture

FEDformer: The Frequency-Enhanced Decomposition Transformer utilizes a Fourier block, enabling frequency-domain techniques, as well as trends and seasonal decomposition. It utilizes a 25-timestep moving average window for trend and season decomposition and 32 random frequency modes for increased representation space. Furthermore, randomized time-window sampling (25 timesteps) increases robustness. The seasonal layers in the encoder filter seasonal elements via frequency-enhanced blocks while the decoder applies frequency enhancement within self-attention and cross-attention. The architecture consists of 2 encoder layers and 1 decoder layer, each having 4 attention heads and 128 in the feed-forward dimension. Its improvement lies in the capability to decompose time series into interpretable and meaningful seasonal and trend terms, along with time periodicity and consistent time (Fig. 2).

HALO: HALO integrates local and global attention schemes in a fusion-based transformer framework. Localized attention, implemented in a window of 8 timesteps, captures the short-term dependencies while the globalized attention scheme captures the long-term periodicity of the quantities of interest. A gating mechanism is in place to dynamically fuse the output of the local and global fan-out mechanisms. The overall architecture is characterized by 3 HALO transformer blocks and 64-dimensional embeddings with 4 attention heads using a

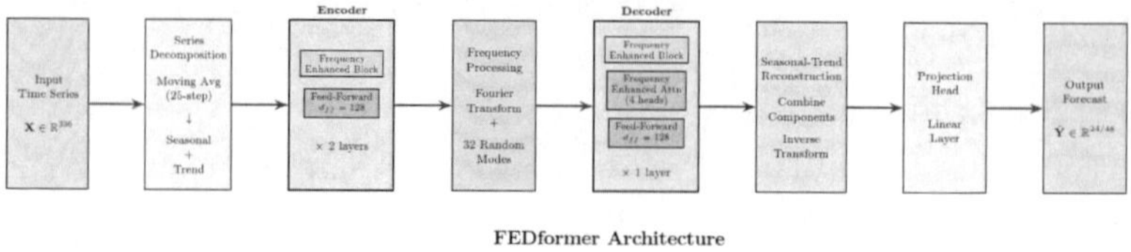

Fig. 2. FEDformer Architecture

feed-forward 128-dimensional element. IoT-specific embedding mechanisms were implemented to extract temporal features, such as hours, days, weeks, and months. The multistep prediction head contains GELU activations and an adaptive pooling over sequences, generating forecasts produced by a three-layer prediction module with an ablation on dimensionality (Fig. 3).

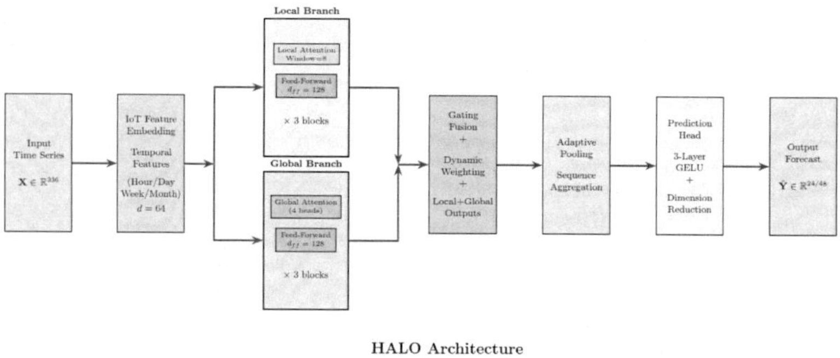

Fig. 3. HALO Architecture

DTformer: DTformer incorporates rich temporal embeddings that model dependencies that depend on time. Separate embedding layers are formed for minute (4D), hour (25D), weekday (8D), day (32D), and month (13D) embeddings. Token embeddings were given using 1D convolution with circular padding. Positional vectors were learned using sinusoidal encoding. The encoder consists of 3 layers, with 8 attention heads, where the model space has a width of 512, while the feed-forward model space has a dimensionality of 2048. The virtues of DTformer stem from its ability to encapsulate high-capacity temporal embeddings, which enable it to represent calendar dependencies and cyclical effects in industrial electricity consumption (Fig. 4).

4.2 Experimental Setup

Input Sequence Length and Forecast Horizon: All models were trained using an input sequence of 336 time steps corresponding to 7 days of half-hourly

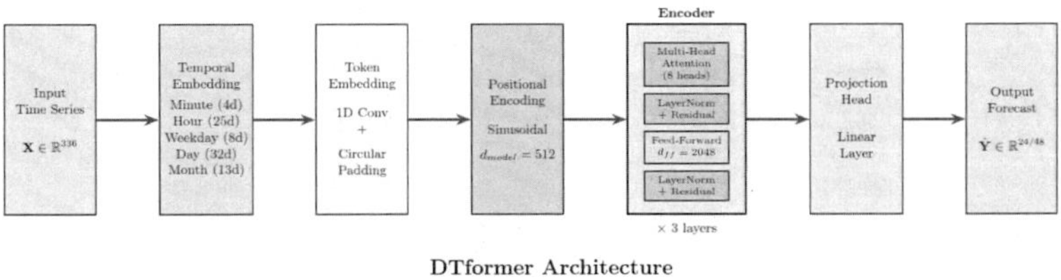

Fig. 4. DTformer Architecture

readings. This setup enables the models to learn about weekly and daily usage patterns in industrial electricity demand. Two forecasting horizons were used: 24 time steps (12 h) for very short-term forecasts and 48 time steps (24 h) for short-term forecasts.

Optimization and Training Configuration: The Adam optimizer was used to train PatchTST, FEDformer, and HALO with a learning rate of 1×10^{-3} and a weight decay of 1×10^{-5}. Due to their moderate parameter sizes, these models exhibited stable convergence under this configuration. DTformer, having a significantly larger model capacity ($\sim$ 9.5M parameters), required a smaller learning rate of 1×10^{-4} with the Adam optimizer to ensure stability and prevent gradient explosion. Batch sizes of 16 and 32 were systematically evaluated, enabling the selection of a configuration that balanced computational efficiency with reliable convergence for all models. To study training stability, each model was trained for 30, 50, and 70 epochs. Early stopping, monitored using the validation loss, was applied with a patience of 20 epochs to avoid overfitting. Regularization techniques included layer normalization within transformer blocks, gradient clipping to prevent exploding gradients, and dropout rates of 0.1 for PatchTST, FEDformer, and HALO, and 0.05 for DTformer.

4.3 Diebold–Mariano (DM) Test

Consider two forecasting models, A and B, producing predictions $\hat{y}_{A,t}$ and $\hat{y}_{B,t}$ for the true observed value y_t at time t, where $t = 1, 2, \ldots, T$ and T is the total number of test instances.

The forecasting errors for both models are as follows:

$$e_{A,t} = y_t - \hat{y}_{A,t}, \quad e_{B,t} = y_t - \hat{y}_{B,t} \tag{1}$$

Using Mean Squared Error (MSE) as the loss function, the pointwise losses are computed as:

$$L_{A,t} = e_{A,t}^2, \quad L_{B,t} = e_{B,t}^2 \tag{2}$$

The loss differential at each time step is then defined as:

$$d_t = L_{A,t} - L_{B,t} \tag{3}$$

A positive d_t indicates that Model A produced a larger squared error than Model B at time t, implying better performance of Model B.

The Diebold–Mariano (DM) test statistic is defined as:

$$DM = \frac{\bar{d}}{\sqrt{\widehat{\mathrm{Var}}(\bar{d})}} \tag{4}$$

where $\bar{d}$ represents the sample mean of the loss differential series, and $\widehat{\mathrm{Var}}(\bar{d})$ denotes its estimated variance accounting for autocorrelation in forecast errors.

The corresponding p-value is obtained from the Student's t-distribution:

$$p = 2\left[1 - F_t(|DM|)\right] \tag{5}$$

where $F_t(\cdot)$ is the cumulative distribution function (CDF) of the t-distribution. If $p < 0.05$, it indicates that the two Models perform significantly differently; otherwise, their forecasting performances are statistically similar. In this way, the DM test provides a robust statistical basis for pairwise model comparison, which complements conventional measures of standard error, as it evaluates whether the differences in MSE are statistically significant or not.

5 Results and Analysis

5.1 Modelwise Performance

The averaged cumulative Mean Squared Error (MSE) over all 12 configurations of the experiment (sequence length = 336; prediction horizons = 24, 48; batch sizes = 16, 32; epochs = 30, 50, 70) proves that DTformer is more stable and represents the minimum possible value of cumulative average MSE over the entire grid of experiments (Table 1).

Table 1. Model Performance Comparison

Model	Mean Squared Error	Root Mean Squared Error
PatchTST	0.000588 ± 0.000427	0.022991 ± 0.007694
FEDformer	0.000306 ± 0.000181	0.016782 ± 0.004933
HALO	0.000266 ± 0.000019	0.028612 ± 0.040888
DTformer	0.000088 ± 0.000023	0.009307 ± 0.001152

Calendar minute-level embeddings of DTformer explain its superior performance, achieving an MSE of 0.000088 ± 0.000023 compared to the sinusoidal and frequency-based encodings of PatchTST and FEDformer, respectively. The features directly map onto industrial production schedules by incorporating minute, hour, weekday, day, and month information. Such explicit temporal grounding outperforms HALO's coarse embeddings, which reach only 0.000266 ± 0.000019 across 12 consistent runs in all configurations. DTformer, with a parameter space of 9.5M, can learn complex interactions across data with heterogeneity represented by 175 m and regularizes well under stable training setups (LR = 1×10^{-4}, dropout = 0.05). The significant enhancement of the DTformer's forecasting performance can directly result in valuable operational advantages for industrial energy management. At both the short and long horizons, enhanced predictability enables industries to make informed decisions about relocating energy-intensive processes from peak tariff periods to non-peak, lower-cost windows, which will lower overall energy costs and improve equipment scheduling (Fig. 5).

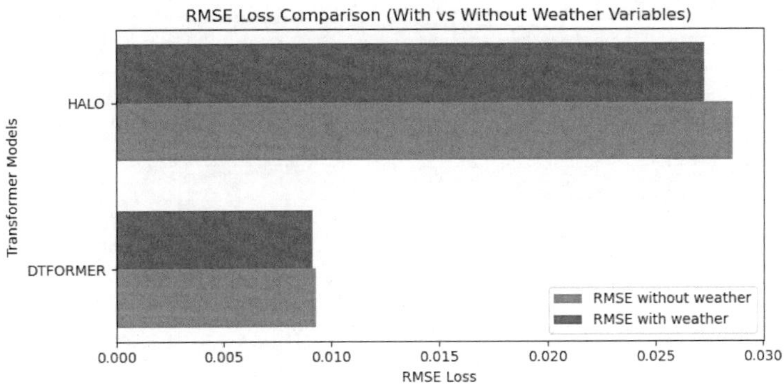

Fig. 5. Weather-Integration

The RMSE loss comparison between DTformer and HALO shows that the error is significantly reduced when weather features are incorporated. HALO's RMSE decreases substantially from approximately 0.028612 to 0.027914, while DTformer also shows a improvement, with RMSE reducing from about 0.009307 to 0.009148 (Table 2).

Table 2. Model's Efficiency (Input Length 336, Prediction Length 48, Batch Size 32)

Model	Parameters	Inference Time (ms)	Training Time (s/epoch)
PatchTST	106.8K	5.02	16.39
HALO	206.4K	46.31	119.46
FEDformer	1.69M	59.64	234.99
DTformer	9.51M	186.78	503.08

5.2 Diebold–Mariano (DM) Test Results

Pairwise Diebold–Mariano testing revealed a clear performance hierarchy among the transformer models:

$$\textbf{HALO} > \textbf{DTformer} > \textbf{PatchTST} > \textbf{FEDformer}.$$

Configurations				
S. No.	Sequence Length	Prediction Length	Batch Size	No. of Epochs
1	336	24	16	30
2	336	24	16	50
3	336	24	16	70
4	336	24	32	30
5	336	24	32	50
6	336	24	32	70
7	336	48	16	30
8	336	48	16	50
9	336	48	16	70
10	336	48	32	30
11	336	48	32	50
12	336	48	32	70

DTformer vs HALO		DTformer vs PatchTST		DTformer vs FEDformer	
DM Stat	p-value	DM Stat	p-value	DM Stat	p-value
-0.836892406	0.402653049	0.477718163	0.632850815	-8.790646539	0
1.973747714	0.048183358	-3.197682494	0.001385367	-10.1258166	0
-8.661278201	0	-12.25149898	0	-17.61635624	0
-3.400581997	0.000672426	2.399860203	0.009326174	-21.69863187	0
7.374947363	1.64 x 10^[illegible]	-7.30561569	2.76 x 10^[illegible]	-10.99229922	0
-1.132384442	0.257472843	-13.92769199	0	-8.700537011	0
1.815747548	0.069409107	1.785336454	0.074206759	-17.98117372	0
9.369334638	0	-9.00431724	0	-13.87277824	0
-1.294003924	0.195664065	-9.56483393	0	-23.07385429	0
7.504212095	6.17 x 10^[illegible]	-16.76796205	0	-6.922592768	4.43 x 10^[illegible]
2.039212623	0.041428812	-3.886989336	0.000101495	-27.57938626	0
5.171242657	2.33 x 10^[illegible]	-7.760037275	8.44 x 10^[illegible]	-27.28003496	0
DTformer		DTformer		DTformer	

HALO vs PatchTST		HALO vs FEDformer		PatchTST vs FEDformer	
DM Stat	p-value	DM Stat	p-value	DM Stat	p-value
1.060795555	0.288782823	-8.426630675	0	-8.629826016	0
-6.842288651	7.79 x 10^[illegible]	-11.82930169	0	-10.61185997	0
-11.7008581	0	-14.72625455	0	4.762174357	1.92 x 10^-6
9.256258337	0	-26.7016396	0	-36.02763314	0
-10.10847249	0	-14.04709041	0	-3.9546492	7.66 x 10^-3
-15.27688823	0	-9.783923193	0	-2.106644892	0.035148372
-1.221681758	0.221827997	-18.92729644	0	-16.73968439	0
-9.49473437	0	-20.19460977	0	7.55438057	4.22 x 10^[illegible]
-9.849146171	0	-22.81501949	0	-9.643856536	0
-14.66908801	0	-8.057851185	6.66 x 10^[illegible]	-0.592679039	0.553395972
-9.069094979	0	-26.58893004	0	-24.77696558	0
-10.0600822	0	-28.24859383	0	-26.5724177	0
HALO		HALO		PatchTST	

Fig. 6. DM-Stats and p-value

DTformer's comparable performance to HALO can be attributed to HALO's local attention, which captures short-term fluctuations, and its global attention, which models long-term periodicity. This fusion-based design allows HALO to effectively extract key temporal patterns in industrial load data, despite having far fewer parameters. Its lightweight architecture, combined with temporal embeddings for hours, days, weeks, and months, enables HALO to represent the same dominant seasonal and operational dynamics that DTformer models within a larger framework (Fig. 6).

5.3 Weather–Load Trend Analysis

The seasonal analysis for 2022–2024 reveals distinct weather-driven trends in industrial power use. Overall, precipitation and temperature exert a major influence on electricity consumption and clear seasonal patterns are observable (Fig. 7).

Temperature is the key meteorological driver of industrial demand, exhibiting strong seasonal variations. The monsoon displays the closest correlation ($r = 0.517$, $p = 3.1 \times 10^{-20}$) with demand, followed by winter ($r = 0.352$, $p = 1.82 \times$

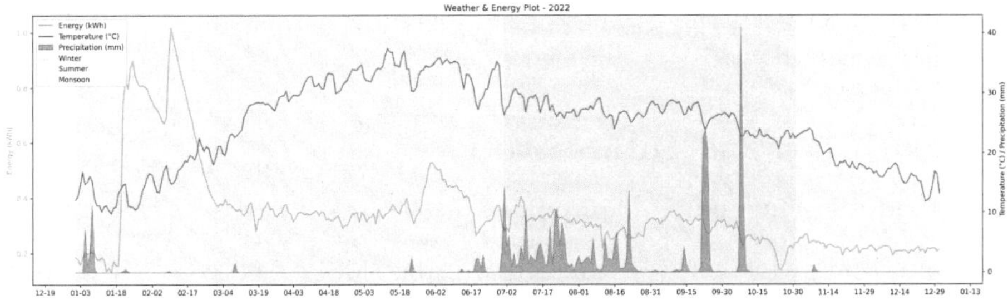

Fig. 7. Weather Integration-2022

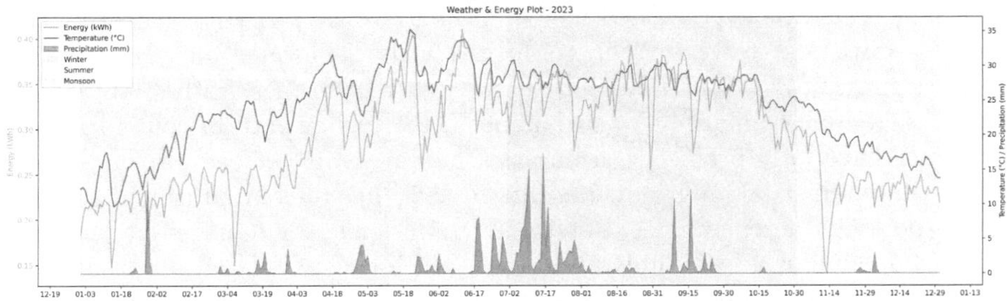

Fig. 8. Weather Integration-2023

10^{-14}) and summer ($r = 0.237$, $p = 1 \times 10^{-7}$). Lag effects persist across several lags but are particularly pronounced at lag 3 in all seasons, with the monsoon again showing the strongest lag 3 correlation ($r = 0.441$). Precipitation does not influence winter ($r = -0.059$, $p = 0.211$) or monsoon ($r = -0.050$, $p = 0.404$), and has only a very small impact during summer ($r = 0.129$, $p = 0.004$). If correlation alone determined behaviour, summer average loads should be the largest and their variations the smallest; however, this is not observed in the data. While seasonal averages broadly follow the expected trend, with monsoon loads being the highest, at an average demand of 137.7 kWh (standard deviation

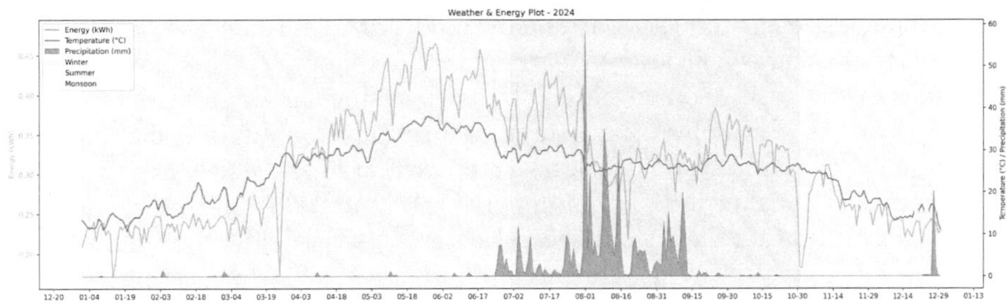

Fig. 9. Weather Integration-2024

= 31.6), summer loads show the greatest variability, with a standard deviation of 53.8 kWh (Fig. 8 and 9).

6 Conclusion and Future Work

6.1 Model Performance Comparison

DTformer achieved the lowest prediction error (MSE: 0.000088 ± 0.000023, RMSE: 0.0093), based on a comparative evaluation involving PatchTST, FEDformer, HALO and DTformer on aggregated industrial smart meter data with integrated weather information. This represents an improvement of 85.034% over PatchTST, 71.242% over FEDformer, and 66.917% over HALO. The Diebold-Mariano statistical tests further confirmed that DTformer and HALO performed significantly better than PatchTST and FEDformer, with HALO occasionally matching or marginally surpassing DTformer in certain configurations. DTformer have high predictive accuracy, they are still not easy to implement in real-time industrial environments due to their heavy computational requirements and long inference times. PatchTST enables faster inference but sacrifices accuracy, making it a less viable option in situations where accurate predictions are crucial. These issues underscore the need for model compression and optimization to make high-performance transformers feasible for deployment. The second limitation of the work is the reliance on a single averaged time series that represents all industrial sites. While this aggregation results in a cleaner, less noisy signal that is ideal for regional forecasting and grid-level planning, it also masks site-specific variations, peak events, changes at the equipment level, and operational schedules. As a result, the models cannot capture industry-specific patterns or identify anomalies, thus diminishing their applicability to site-level operational decision-making.

6.2 Future Work

In order to facilitate the use of HALO and DTformer in real-time industrial scenarios, model compression and acceleration techniques research will include knowledge distillation, sparse or low-rank attention, token reduction, and factorised temporal embeddings to attenuate model size and inference time while still preserving accuracy. Federated learning is another option that allows privacy protection in multi-site collaboration, but conversing and system heterogeneity issues have to be resolved first. Integration of these optimized models with SCADA and smart-grid systems will be a step further in enabling extensive, real-time forecasting. Future work will overcome the limitations of an average load series by incorporating data from several cities, different climates, and various industrial categories to create cluster or industry-specific forecasting models. Hybrid architectures with site-specific output heads might also enable transformers to keep global patterns while understanding localized behaviour more efficiently.

References

1. Nepal, B., Yamaha, M., Yokoe, A., Yamaji, T.: Electricity load forecasting using clustering and Arima model for energy management in buildings. Jpn. Architect. Rev. **3**(1), 62–76 (2020)
2. Liu, X., Lin, Z., Feng, Z.: Short-term offshore wind speed forecast by seasonal Arima-a comparison against GRU and LSTM. Energy **227**, 120492 (2021)
3. Breiman, L.: Random forests. Mach. Learn. **45**(1), 5–32 (2001)
4. Selakov, A., et al.: A comparative analysis of SVM and ANN based hybrid model for short term load forecasting. In: PES T&D 2012, pp. 1–5. IEEE (2012)
5. Vaswani, A., et al.: Attention is all you need. In: Advances in Neural Information Processing Systems, vol. 30 (2017)
6. Saini, L.M., Aggarwal, S.K., Kumar, A.: Parameter optimisation using genetic algorithm for support vector machine-based price-forecasting model in national electricity market. IET Gener. Transm. Distrib. **4**(1), 36–49 (2010)
7. Hochreiter, S., Schmidhuber, J.: Long short-term memory. Neural Comput. **9**(8), 1735–1780 (1997)
8. Chung, J., Gulcehre, C., Cho, K., Bengio, Y.: Empirical evaluation of gated recurrent neural networks on sequence modeling. arXiv preprint arXiv:1412.3555 (2014)
9. Zhou, H., et al.: Informer: beyond efficient transformer for long sequence time-series forecasting. In: Proceedings of the AAAI Conference on Artificial Intelligence, vol. 35, pp. 11106–11115 (2021)
10. Haixu, W., Jiehui, X., Wang, J., Long, M.: Autoformer: decomposition transformers with auto-correlation for long-term series forecasting. In: Advances in Neural Information Processing Systems, vol. 34, pp. 22419–22430 (2021)
11. Zhou, T., Ma, Z., Wen, Q., Wang, X., Sun, L., Jin, R.: FEDformer: frequency enhanced decomposed transformer for long-term series forecasting. In: International Conference on Machine Learning, pp. 27268–27286. PMLR (2022)
12. Nie, Y.: A time series is worth 64words: long-term forecasting with transformers (2022). arXiv preprint arXiv:2211.14730
13. Fan, J., Zhuang, W., Xia, M., Fang, W.X., Liu, J.: Optimizing attention in a transformer for multihorizon, multienergy load forecasting in integrated energy systems. IEEE Trans. Industr. Inf. **20**(8), 10238–10248 (2024)
14. Cheng Pan, C., Zhang, E., Ngai, C.H., Liu, J., Li, B.: HALO: HVAC load forecasting with industrial IoT and local-global-scale transformer. IEEE Internet Things J. **11**(17), 28307–28319 (2024)

An Intelligent Hybrid Framework Combining DNN, MCTS, and GNN for Robust Ransomware Detection

Rahul Yadav(✉) and Dinesh Singh

Department of Computer Science and Engineering, Motilal Nehru National Institute of Technology Allahabad, Prayagraj, India
{rahul.2024rcs07,dinesh_singh}@mnnit.ac.in

Abstract. Ransomware attacks have become a major cyber-security threat. It employs increasingly advanced techniques that can bypass conventional detection systems. This paper put forward a novel framework that combines the predictive capabilities of deep learning with the analytical power of the heuristic search algorithm, Monte Carlo Tree Search (MCTS), and formulates complex relational structures using Graph Neural Networks (GNN). This paper introduces an innovative deep learning-based hybrid method for ransomware detection that outperforms traditional techniques by integrating the strengths of both offline and operational analysis. Initially, the approach uses a fused dataset of portable executable data with the dynamic properties of different variants of ransomware, along with a dataset of API call sequences from the same types of ransomware variants. The fused dataset is used to identify the independent features through the CNN architecture. These features are fed into MCTS to identify the optimal feature interactions. Finally, these features are converted into graphs using the NetworkX library, with a single node for each state and edges representing the parent-child relationships of the MCTS trees. The graph was analyzed for strong inter-feature dependencies using a Graph Neural Network (GNN) to identify ransomware with the message-passing capability of GNN, in which each child node gets information from siblings through the parent. The proposed approach integrates deep learning with heuristic searching, effectively removing the reliance on extensive feature engineering and specialized domain expertise. It supplies a scalable, efficient, and inexpensive solution for ransomware detection. This approach needs preprocessing of data that is suitable for the learning of the deep neural network model and the creation of the MCTS tree. This pipelining approach outperforms all the models using MCTS with machine learning and provides an accuracy of 99%. An enhanced extensive dynamic linking of API call sequences and more dynamic features of the particular features may detect zero-day variants with the more fine-tuned aspects of this approach.

Keywords: Ransomware · Malware · Portable executable · Deep Learning · Graph Neural Network · Monte Carlo Tree Search

G. K. Verma et al. (Eds.): MIND 2025, CCIS 2981, pp. 220–235, 2027.
https://doi.org/10.1007/978-3-032-31230-3_18

1 Introduction

Digital devices, whether they are computers, laptops, mobile devices, etc. These devices have incredibly powerful hardware and software thanks to recent technological advancements. To communicate and process information on the internet on a daily basis, both individuals and organizations rely significantly on servers and computers. There will reportedly be 5.5 billion Internet users by 2025, and that number will increase rapidly in the near future. The Internet serves as a vital platform for information exchange between numerous interconnected devices, networks, and computers. However, its extensive usage has made it a prime target for cybercriminal activities. Examples of these cyberattacks include malware, phishing, and spam. Among these, malware is recognized software [1] threats in the cyberworld. The term "malware" is acquired from the fusion of "mal" (meaning malicious) with "ware" (from software) [1]. We are specifically dealing with ransomware. *Ransomware is a malware type that blocks user access to a computer or encrypts important files, holding them hostage until a ransom is paid.* Ransomware has quickly grown to represent a serious danger to digital infrastructures across the globe. Ransomware, in contrast to other types of malware, specifically targets individuals and institutions by encrypting vital information and requesting large sums of money to get access back. Effective detection and mitigation are made more difficult by the escalating sophistication of ransomware variants and the extensive use of networked systems.

Conventional security methods, such as signature-based detection, face significant challenges in addressing the constantly evolving strains of ransomware, which frequently use code scrambling techniques to bypass standard defense systems. Accordingly, there is a pressing demand for more sophisticated detection frameworks capable of proactively identifying and curbing ransomware attacks before they cause substantial harm.

Machine learning approaches attract researchers seeking robust solutions for detection mechanisms. The deep learning approach has gained popularity in recent years because of faster processing, less reverse engineering, and minimal domain-specific knowledge. But the deep learning approach has more power to detect independent features but fails to detect relational features for ransomware, such as shared code patterns between ransomware families.

To prevail over the issue of the deep learning approach, Monte Carlo tree search (MCTS) has been used to find out the most effective feature interactions and better general interpretability. MCTS builds a search tree where each node illustrates a decision state and uses the deep learning output for simulation. But here also we found an issue of weak inter-feature dependencies and certain API call combinations for the ransomware.

To master the api combinations and inter-feature dependencies, our approach extended the MCTS tree to the graph created using the NetworkX library, with a single node for each state and edges representing the parent-child relationships of the MCTS trees. The graph is fed to the graph neural network model and it learns inter-feature dependencies through the message-passing mechanism of GNN, which lets each child node receive information from siblings through the parent, and the multi-layer aggregation strengthens it. So the primary contributions of this research are

- Development of a **unified ransomware detection framework** combining deep learning and Monte Carlo Tree Search (MCTS) and graph neural networks to enhance detection accuracy and computational competence.
- Achievement of a **notable drop in false positives** through MCTS-driven dynamic evaluation, improving overall detection reliability by graph learning using graph neural networks.
- The accuracy comparison with different architectural combinations of deep learning, Monte Carlo tree search, and Graph neural networks.

Section 2 of the paper illustrates the previous work related to the articulated work, so Sect. 3 provides a detailed proposed approach, whereas Sect. 4 provides the results of our method outperforming the previous work. Section 5 provides insight into future enhancement and finally concludes our work.

2 Related Work

In ransomware detection researchers find different ways to detect sophisticated variants of ransomware. Several research studies have leveraged deep learning models for ransomware detection, utilizing their capability to identify complex relationships within high-dimensional data. Monte Carlo Tree search (MCTS) methodologies are also explored for detecting combinational features of ransomware families and some researchers explore Graph Neural Networks (GNN) methods for malware detection not specifically for ransomware. So in this section, we will explore different technological developments in ransomware identification using deep learning techniques, and the integration of MCTS is reviewed in this part, along with their advantages, disadvantages, and potential areas for significant improvement through hybrid approaches.

2.1 Using Deep Learning to Identify Ransomware

Deep learning approaches do not need any domain knowledge the behavioral ransomware identification and classification Using a deep learning approach specifies local features within the dataset [1,2]. Recurrent Neural Networks (RNNs), particularly the Long Short-Term Memory (LSTM) variant, are used for identifying temporal features [3]. Autoencoders are used to find out the anomaly in the system by comparing normal system behaviour [4] and Generative Adversarial Networks (GAN) are used to generate synthetic ransomware variants and test the robustness of the system [5]. Imaging the portable executable files and use convolutional neural network with transfer learning to detect ransomware using image processing [6]. Deep learning adapted the capability to detect new variants of ransomware by learning the features of new variants with fast training of neural network [7,8]. However, intensive computation and enormous dataset can be the problem for real time deployement [9,10], so researchers identify the problem and uses heuristic search-based trees, such as Monte Carlo tree search algorithms.

2.2 Using Monte Carlo Tree Search to Identify Ransomware

Monte Carlo Tree Search (MCTS) has emerged as a valuable technique in ransomware detection because it can efficiently navigate and analyze vast decision spaces. By simulating various system states, MCTS enables the optimization of detection strategies [11]. The MCTS simulation explores, multiple simulation paths it improves the robustness against polymorphic ransomware and highly obfuscated one [12]. MCTS detect the changing behaviour of ransomware to avoid detection using simulated search [13]. MCTS optimize the detection framework by explore the only most probable paths and leaving the general path [14,15]. Because MCTS relies on probabilistic decision-making, it can strike a smart balance between exploring new possibilities and using known information. This makes ransomware detection systems more flexible and capable of adapting quickly to new or changing threats in real-time [16]. Whereas MCTS select the probabilistic path but some time without a guide it may increase the computation [17,18]. So, converting to graphs and learn that graphs using graph neural networks helps to detect the most relevant path [19].

2.3 Using Graph Neural Networks to Identify Ransomware

Graphs are great at showing how different objects are connected and depend on each other, which makes them an excellent way to represent complex data. Their strength lies in capturing these rich and detailed relationships, making them an essential tool for understanding and organizing complicated ransomware variants [19,20]. Graph Neural Networks uses graphs to structure sequences or pattern, such as the associated behavioural graph of API call sequence learn the ransomware patterns [20]. Modelling of system events as a graph, and learned the attack patterns of ransomware and its variants to detect using explainable graph [21]. Graph based method detect layered, hierarchical and neighborhood based patterns to allow them detect both local and global paterns unlike CNN and RNN [22]. PROVEXPLAINER provides clear, instance-level explanations that take into account both local and global features of a graph. This two-level interpretability helps reduce the "black-box" nature of GNN models, thereby improving the interpretability and trustworthiness for use in sensitive security applications [23]. To ensure the robustness of ransomware, researchers integrate the techniques and create hybrid models [24].

2.4 Using Hybrid Approach to Identify Ransomware

The hybrid approach that integrates deep learning with MCTS enhances detection accuracy while reducing false positives [24]. The deep learning module of hybrid model used identify the independent features and MCTS module of the model used to explore the mutiple action paths for optimized framework [25]. The hybrid approach benefited from the predictive capabilities of deep neural network module, and optimal detection path of MCTS for precise detection framework [26,27]. It has been found that the hybrid model enhance the detection framework of ransomware in terms of detection accuracy and precision, especially for new variants [28,29]. The deep learning module guide the MCTS module to reduce the search space and reduce latency without compromising the detection accuracy and detection rate [30]. Moreover, hybrid systems can continuously adapt and address updates to both the neural network and MCTS model as novel ransomware variants arise, ensuring that the detection framework maintains high accuracy and adaptability and stays robust against evolving threats [31,32]. However, The integration of deep learning and MCTS achieved a good accuracy, but learning the extra feature dependencies and certain API call sequence combinations, which strongly imply ransomware, we proposed a novel hybrid approach of combining deep learning guided probabilities to the MCTS tree. Then the MCTS tree is converted to graphs and becomes input for the graph neural network. Our hybrid model generates the structural embedding that generalizes to unseen file families.

3 Methodology

Our approach centers on the design and implementation of a framework for ransomware detection that can reliably detect ransomware without fail.

3.1 System Architecture

The architecture comprises the following modules, which are outlined in Fig. 1. The two different datasets used for the robust detection of ransomware contain static and dynamic features of ransomware. The preprocessing merges two datasets, and this is further used for feature extraction using deep neural network model. The predicted probabilities from the deep neural network model were used for Monte Carlo search tree creation, and fed MCTS tree was fed to create graph that used for the graph neural network.

3.2 Pre-processing and Experimental Setup

The Portable Executable (PE) format defines the structure of executable and object files used in the Windows operating system family. Executable files follow the PE format, while object files adhere to the Common Object File Format (COFF). Portable Executable (PE) files consist of multiple sections where information is stored. Firstly, the ransomware PE file was opened and checked to determine whether it was packed or unpacked. An unpacked PE file is identified by its visible sections: the .text section, the .data section, and the .rsrc section, where only the .text section has the execute flag set because it contains the code, while packed files have unconventional section names or no names. The PE files dataset includes 12 different ransomware variants, mentioned here with their counts: Phobos (500), Dharma (505), Shade (504), WannaCry (497), Ryuk (449), Lockbit (438), Gandcrab (382), REvil (347), Darkside (335), Cerber (332),

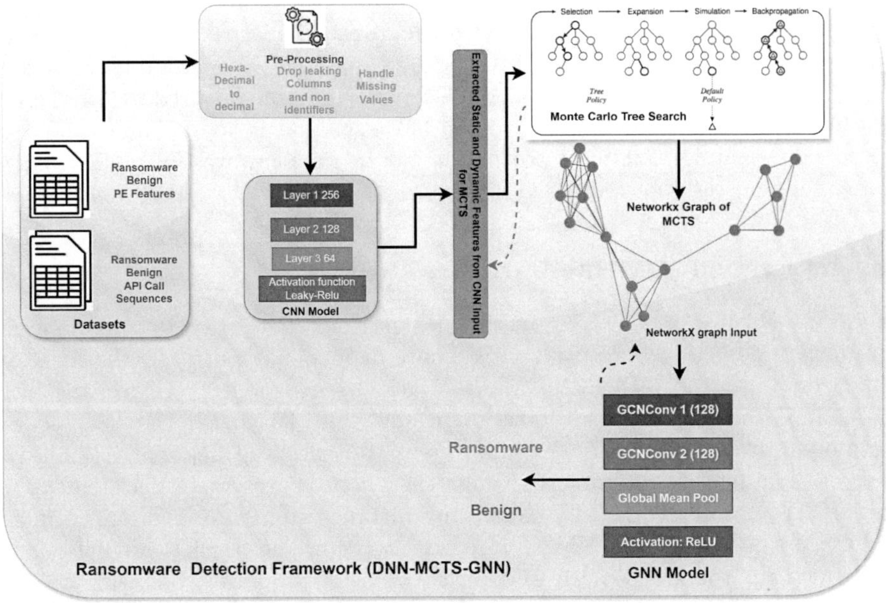

Fig. 1. Architecture of Ransomware Detection

Maze (290), and Ragnar (133), which totals to 4762. The benign PE files dataset had 10876 samples, so this unbalanced dataset is under-sampled to the 4762 ransomware sample range, so the dataset becomes 9524 rows and 161 columns with the 61 static attributes of PE files and 100 attributes of dynamic API call sequences of ransomware and benign files. The API call sequences dataset was merged with the PE files dataset based on simple family matching of the same variants of the ransomware, which are matched to both datasets.

Hexadecimal values in the dataset are converted to integer values, and the class column is assigned 0 and 1 for ransomware and benign, respectively. The API call sequences are changed to integer values with the help of a label encoder. These preprocessing steps of the dataset prepare it for further analysis of the DNN model.

3.3 Deep Learning Model

A sequential deep learning network was used to predict the independent features of ransomware and benign files. The deep learning model has three dense layers that are essential for extracting the hierarchical features of the ransomware. The Dense layer was followed by a batch normalization module with a leaky-Relu activation function with $\alpha = 0.1$ and a dropout of neurons with a threshold of 0.3. The first layer has an input of 256 neurons. The batch of 64 was fed with Adam optimizer to calculate the gradient improvement with a learning rate α

= 0.001. Similarly, second layer have 128 neurons with all the modules same as the first layer and the third layer have 64 neurons. The last layer passes through sigmoid activation function and provide a probability value that how much a sample belongs to ransomware or not. Deep learning model predicted independent features with a good accuracy of 91% for each, but it doesn't model relative relationship samples, has a important factor in ransomware detect because of shared code patterns between the families of ransomware.

3.4 Integration of Monte Carlo Tree Search

The Deep learning model treated PE files as isolated which has unrealistic in ransomware detection because it often share dependency patterns like API call sequences, imported DLLs etc. Monte Carlo Tree Search (MCTS) was integrated into the ransomware detection framework. To enrich the deep learning model through dynamic exploration of potential attack paths and discover optimal feature interactions where each node represents a decision states. The MCTS module worked by simulating future system states based on intermediate outputs from the CNN. It used the neural network's predictions as guides to help the tree search find paths where ransomware behavior showed higher probabilities. MCTS helps to detect variants of ransomware that deviate slightly from the training distribution. The algorithm for building the MCTS tree guided by CNN was using selection phase with the formulae $r = \arg\max\left(c.value + c_{explore}\sqrt{\frac{\ln(v.visits+1)}{c.visits+1}}\right)$ to select the new node. The tree was expanded with the randomly sampled b feature vectors $\{s_1, s_2, \ldots, s_b\}$ and append as child node. The simulation phase of the MCTS uses the probabilities of the deep network as the reward. So, the backpropagation phase of the MCTS updates after a simulation finishes and returns a reward the algorithm propagates that reward back up the tree from the leaf node to the root. The adjustment of the node's average value uses the new simulation reward as in Eq. 1. The complete algorithm of tree creation mentioned in Algorithm 1.

$$\left.\begin{array}{rl}\text{Reward:} & \text{reward}(v) = p[\text{state index of } v],\\ \text{Backpropagation Visit Update:} & v.\text{visits} \leftarrow v.\text{visits} + 1,\\ \text{Backpropagation Value Update:} & v.\text{value} \leftarrow v.\text{value} + \frac{\text{reward}-v.\text{value}}{v.\text{visits}},\\ \text{Reward for New Node:} & \text{reward}_{\text{new}} = p[s_k].\end{array}\right\} \quad (1)$$

3.5 Integration of Graph Neural Network

Monte Carlo tree search successfully discovers the optimal feature interactions but slightly fails to detect the inter-feature dependencies because certain API call combinations strongly imply ransomware, such as rapidly repeating for multiple files: write(high entropy data), rename(file, file + new extension). Some API calls are *CreateFile*, *NtWriteFile*, *SetFileInformation CryptEncrypt*. Process

Algorithm 1: Build MCTS Tree Guided by CNN Probabilities

Input: Feature set $\mathcal{F} = \{f_i\}_{i=1}^{N}$, trained CNN model $\mathcal{M}_{\text{CNN}}$, iterations T, branching factor b, maximum depth D

Output: Root node r of expanded MCTS tree

Compute probability vector $p \leftarrow \mathcal{M}_{\text{CNN}}(\mathcal{F})$;
Choose a root feature f_j and set root node $r \leftarrow \texttt{Node}(state = f_j, parent = \varnothing, visits = 0, value = p_j)$;
for $t \leftarrow 1$ **to** T **do**
    $v \leftarrow r$; $depth \leftarrow 0$;
    `// -- Selection phase --`
    while $v.children \neq \varnothing$ ***and*** $depth < D$ **do**
        $v \leftarrow \arg\max_{c \in v.children} \left(c.value + c_{explore} \sqrt{\frac{\ln(v.visits+1)}{c.visits+1}} \right)$;
        $depth \leftarrow depth + 1$;
    `// -- Expansion phase --`
    if $v.children = \varnothing$ ***and*** $depth < D$ **then**
        Randomly sample b feature vectors $\{s_1, s_2, \ldots, s_b\}$ from $\mathcal{F}$;
        for $k \leftarrow 1$ **to** b **do**
            $child \leftarrow \texttt{Node}(state = s_k, parent = v, visits = 0, value = p[s_k])$;
            Append $child$ to $v.children$;
        $v \leftarrow$ random choice from $v.children$;
    `// -- Simulation phase --`
    $reward \leftarrow p[\text{state index of } v]$;
    `// -- Backpropagation phase --`
    while $v \neq \varnothing$ **do**
        $v.visits \leftarrow v.visits + 1$;
        $v.value \leftarrow v.value + \frac{reward - v.value}{v.visits}$;
        $v \leftarrow v.parent$;
return r;

injection and persistence api combinations can also be good indicators of ransomware, so API combinations are *OpenProcess*, *VirtualAllocEx*, *WriteProcessMemory*, *CreateRemoteThread*. To model API-call combinations and their inter-feature dependencies, we transform the MCTS tree into a NetworkX graph and use that graph as input to a GNN for downstream learning. NetworkX works well for representing an MCTS tree because it naturally supports directed graphs, allows the tree to grow dynamically, and lets us store useful information in nodes and edges. It also makes it easy to convert the tree into adjacency formats that GNNs need. The root node of the MCTS tree r is explored and fed into the NetworkX graph using an empty queue until all nodes are added, thereby creating the complete graph. The full algorithm is shown in Algorithm 2. The graph fed to the GNN model defines three main layers: The simple GNN architecture diagram is seen in Fig. 2. The first Graph Convolutional Network (GCN) layer. It transforms each node's input features into a hidden representation. The second

GCN layer refines node embeddings using information from neighboring nodes. A fully connected (linear) layer maps the pooled graph representation to the output dimension for binary classification with a learning rate $\alpha = 0.001$ for 30 epochs along with 0.2 dropout. The model performs two layers of graph convolutions to learn node embeddings, aggregates them into a single graph-level feature using mean pooling, and outputs log-probabilities for each class: ransomware and benign. The GNN model loads the training graphs and test graphs the accuracy of the GNN model reaches 99.1%. So, the GNN model improves detection and provides a structural embedding that generalizes the unseen file families.

Algorithm 2: Convert MCTS Tree to Graph for GNN

Input: Root node r of MCTS tree
Output: Graph $G = (V, E)$ with node features X and edge list $\mathcal{E}$

Initialize empty graph G, queue $Q \leftarrow [r]$, index map $idx \leftarrow \{\}$, counter $c \leftarrow 0$;
while *Q not empty* **do**
  $u \leftarrow$ pop front of Q;
  if $u.id \notin idx$ **then**
    $idx[u.id] \leftarrow c$; $c \leftarrow c + 1$;
    Add node $idx[u.id]$ to G;
    $X[idx[u.id]] \leftarrow u.state$; // Node feature vector
  foreach $v \in u.children$ **do**
    if $v.id \notin idx$ **then**
      $idx[v.id] \leftarrow c$; $c \leftarrow c + 1$;
      Add node $idx[v.id]$ to G;
      $X[idx[v.id]] \leftarrow v.state$;
    Add edge $(idx[u.id], idx[v.id])$ to E;
    Append v to Q;
foreach *node i in G* **do**
  if *node i has no edges* **then**
    Add self-loop (i, i) to E;
return *$G = (V, E)$ with node features X*;

3.6 Ransomware Detection Pipelining

In the pipelining approach to ransomware detection, we followed different detection modules to make the system more robust and effective in detecting new variants of ransomware the steps followed are as follows in Fig. 3:

1. The Dataset is pre-processed for the required detection, including both static and dynamic parameters.
2. The Pre-processed dataset is fed to the CNN model to detect independent features for each sample.

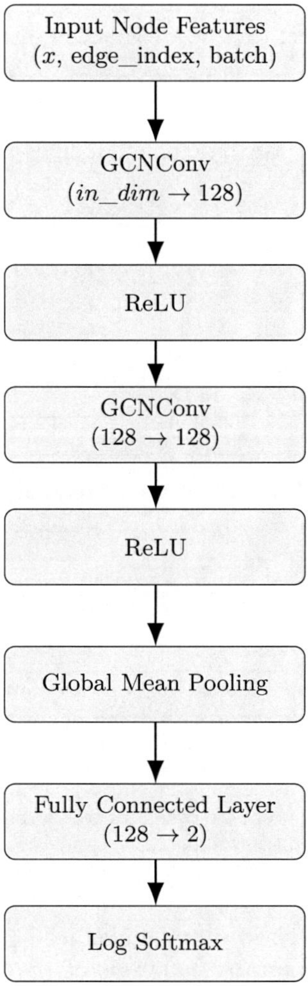

Fig. 2. Architecture of the SimpleGNN Model

3. The output of the CNN is used to create MCTS trees that explore multiple action paths and discover optimal feature interactions.
4. Create NetworkX graphs from the MCTS tree and divide the graphs into training and testing graph sets.
5. Graphs are used to train the GNN model to capture inter-feature dependencies and strongly combined API call sequences.

4 Results and Analysis

This section discusses the efficacy of all models in terms of accuracy and precision for distinguishing between ransomware and benign files. The results of the study

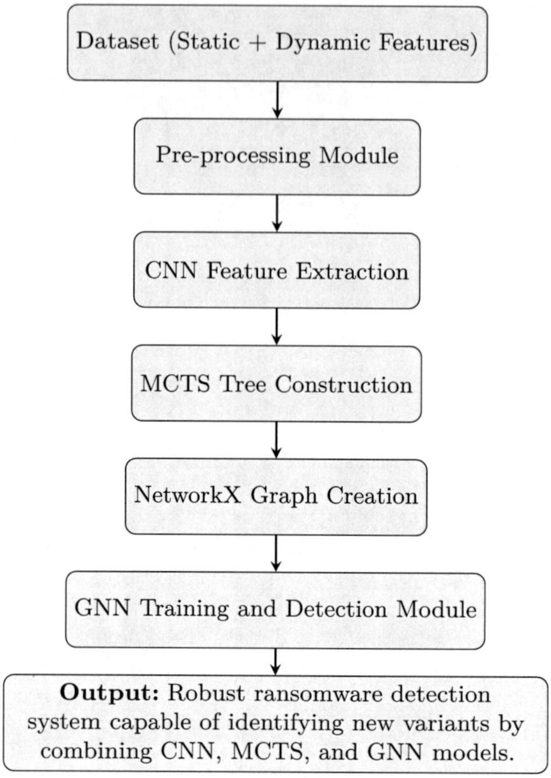

Fig. 3. Visualization of the pipelined ransomware detection architecture combining CNN, MCTS, and GNN modules.

are comprehensively summarized in a tabular format, as presented in Table 1. These tables provide a comparative analysis of the models, highlighting their strengths and weaknesses based on key performance metrics.

4.1 Metrics for Model: DNN

The deep learning model performs feature extraction from the pre-processed dataset, and these feature values are used as input for the next module of the MCTS tree. The accuracy of the deep learning model lays a strong foundation for the hybrid detection approach. The DNN-based PE feature detection model performed reliably, achieving an accuracy of 91.72%. It also demonstrated strong classification ability, with a precision of 90.86%, a recall of 92.10%, and an F1-score of 91.47%, indicating a balanced performance across all major evaluation metrics. Out of 9524 evaluated samples, the confusion matrix further highlights the model's behavior. The system successfully recognized 4388 ransomware instances, while 374 malicious samples were missed and labeled as benign. In contrast, 443 benign files were mistakenly predicted as ransomware, and the model correctly categorized 4319 benign samples. Overall, these results show that the DNN model is largely effective, with only a limited number of misclassifications.

4.2 MCTS Tree

The integration of Monte Carlo Tree Search into the Deep learning model increases the accuracy of the hybrid system to 98.2%. The mcts has reward values that are based on the output of the deep learning predicted values and explores the nodes of the tree.

4.3 Detection Accuracy and Performance Comparison

The hybrid framework was assessed using a balanced dataset of 50,000 samples (25,000 ransomware and 25,000 benign) from different sources, such as Kaggle, Mendeley Data, Github. Its detection performance surpassed that of established approaches: the hybrid method achieved an overall accuracy of 99.1%, while deep learning only reached 91.1%, and deep learning combined with MCTS tree reached 96.8%. Some other traditional methods, like Support Vector Machines and Random Forests, reached 94.1% and 92.3%, respectively. A full breakdown of these results appears in Table 1. The confusion matrix of the hybrid (Deep learning + Monte Carlo Tree Search + Graph Neural Network) model is shown in Table 2. The performance evaluation of the proposed GNN hybrid model is illustrated through four key performance plots: accuracy, loss, precision–recall, and ROC curves are shown in Fig. 4. The Model Accuracy Curve in Fig. 4(a) shows a rapid improvement in both training and validation accuracy during the initial epochs, reaching stability near 0.99 after approximately the fifth epoch. The close alignment between the training and validation accuracy lines indicates that the model generalizes well without significant overfitting. The Model Loss Curve in Fig. 4(b) demonstrates a steep decline in both training and validation losses during early epochs, followed by smooth convergence towards a minimal value. This consistent reduction in loss suggests efficient optimization and robust convergence behavior of the hybrid architecture during training. The Precision–Recall (PR) Curve in Fig. 4(c) achieves an average precision (AP) of 0.998, reflecting the model's outstanding ability to maintain high precision even at high recall levels. This emphasizes the model's effectiveness in minimizing false positives while accurately identifying positive instances—an essential feature for real-world classification tasks with imbalanced datasets. The Receiver Operating Characteristic (ROC) Curve in Fig. (4d) further validates the classification performance, showing an Area Under the Curve (AUC) value of 0.998. The curve's proximity to the top-left corner signifies an excellent detection capability between positive and negative classes. Overall, the combination of high accuracy, low loss, and near-perfect PR and ROC curves confirms that the proposed GNN hybrid model achieves exceptional performance, stability, and generalization.

Table 1. Performance comparison of different models

Model	Accuracy	Precision	Recall	F1-Score	Latency	Detection
Hybrid (DMG)	99.19	99.20	98.80	98.80	450	98.80
DNN + MCTS [24]	96.85	96.85	95.34	96.09	250	96.09
DNN [1]	91.19	91.19	90.27	90.72	420	90.72
SVM [4]	94.10	94.10	93.00	93.54	620	93.54
RF [24]	92.30	92.30	91.40	91.85	630	91.85

Abbreviations: DMG = DNN + MCTS + GNN.
Accuracy, precision, and Detection in percentage and latency in milliseconds (ms).

Table 2. Confusion Matrix for Hybrid (Deep Learning + MCTS + GNN)

Actual Class	Predicted Class		Total
	Ransomware	Benign	
Ransomware	24,700 (TP)	300 (FN)	25,000
Benign	203 (FP)	24,797 (TN)	25,000
Total	24,903	25,097	50,000

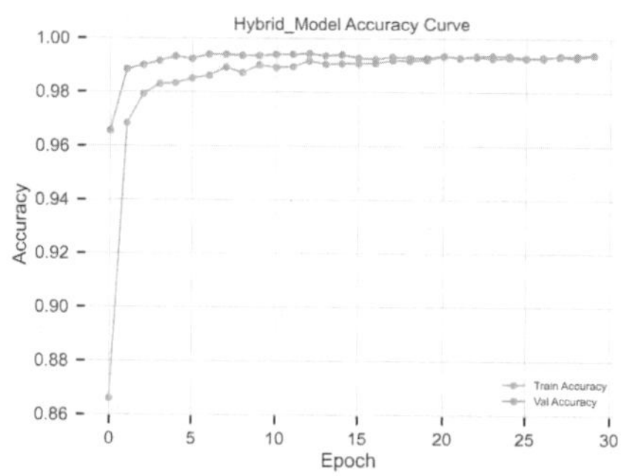

(a) Hybrid(DNN+MCTS+GNN) model Accuracy Curve

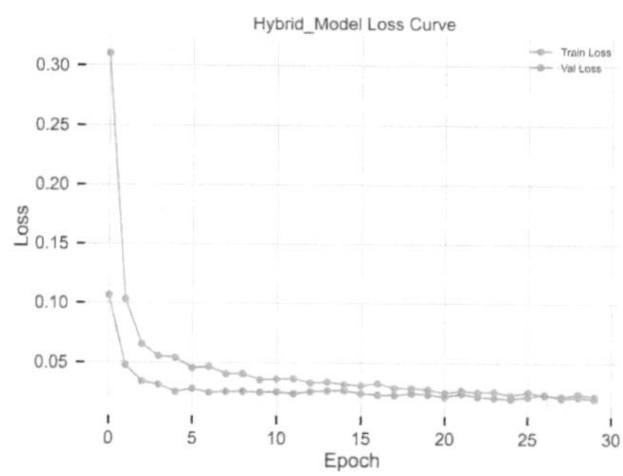

(b) Hybrid(DNN+MCTS+GNN) model Loss Curve

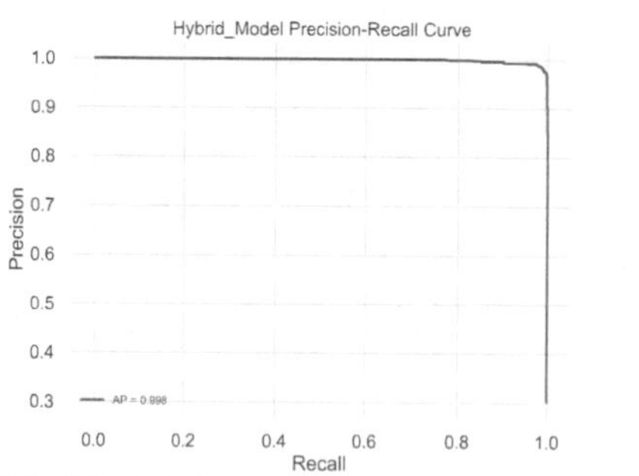

(c)Hybrid(DNN+MCTS+GNN) model Precision-recall Curve

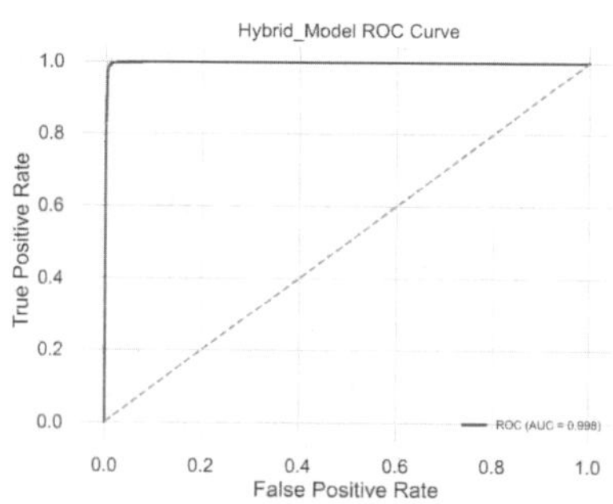

(d) Hybrid(DNN+MCTS+GNN) model ROC Curve

Fig. 4. Comparison of different performance parameters (a, b, c and d).

5 Conclusions

Traditional ransomware detection methods have primarily relied on machine learning algorithms like Support vector machine, random forests and some hybrid approaches use convolution neural network, signature-based approaches, which depend on pre-existing knowledge of specific ransomware strains. However, this method has significant limitations, particularly when dealing with fileless or early-locking ransomware variants or those that employ polymorphic techniques to evade detection. In contrast, behavioral analysis takes advantage of the fact that ransomware's core objective encrypting files necessitates interactions with the file system that are both atypical and suspicious. This approach enables the identification of ransomware without prior knowledge of its variants by analyzing its runtime behavioral attributes using MCTS tree simulation and learning the graph neural network of MCTS tree.

Training the deep neural network model build a foundation for the hybrid framework the predicted features fed as a guidance signal to explore promising areas in feature space which further converted into networkX graphs, trained these graphs with graph neural network provides a structural embedding that generalizes to unseen file families of ransomware and involves varying training and validation dataset along with changing number of epochs and the batch size and optimizer.

Therefore, it had been examined how deep neural network achieved a high static accuracy 91.1% it primarily captures local feature correlations integrating Monte Carlo Tree Search allows dynamic exploration of feature combinations beyond the training distribution and the graph neural network leverages structural dependencies among explored states. The hybrid framework approach enhances robustness, interpretability, and adaptability against emerging ransomware variants with 99.1%.

As future enhancement, real-time data is needed detection of fileless ransomware (in-memory, no persistent binaries) is still under-addressed. In the future, there is a need to reduce the computation complexity of hybrid model, which needs to be managed through model optimization and parallel processing to ensure that the hybrid framework performs efficiently in real-time environments.

References

1. Poongodi, T., Beena, T., Sumathi, D., Suresh, P.: Behavioral malware detection and classification using deep learning approaches. In: Applications of Computational Intelligence in Multi-Disciplinary Research, pp. 29–45 (2022)
2. Fevid, E., Walsh, C., Russo, L.: Zero-day ransomware detection via assembly language bytecode analysis and random forest classification (2024)
3. Ozturk, M., Demir, A., Arslan, Z., Caliskan, O.: Dynamic behavioural analysis of privacy-breaching and data theft ransomware (2024)
4. Shi, T., McCann, R., Huang, Y., Wang, W., Kong, J.: Malware detection for internet of things using one-class classification. Sensors **24**(13), 4122 (2024)

5. Liu, S., Chen, X.: Applying moving target defense against data theft ransomware on Windows OS (2023)
6. Ferdous, J., Islam, R., Mahboubi, A., Islam, M.Z.: A novel technique for ransomware detection using image based dynamic features and transfer learning to address dataset limitations. Sci. Rep. **15**(1), 32342 (2025)
7. Williamson, A., Beauparlant, M.: Malware reverse engineering with large language model for superior code comprehensibility and IoC recommendations (2024)
8. Gong, W., Zha, Y., Tang, J.: Ransomware detection and classification using generative adversarial networks with dynamic weight adaptation (2024)
9. Zhong, T., Li, J.: Ransomware detection with machine learning by applying the Lapranove function on bytecode (2024)
10. Olsson, A., Andersson, D.: The dark flows of cryptocurrency: an overview of money flow behaviors in bitcoin transactions related to online criminal activities and bitcoin mixers (2024)
11. Axali, J., Devereaux, L., Spencer, A., Vasilev, F.: A multicriteria decision-making approach for ransomware detection using MITRE ATT&CK mitigation strategy (2024)
12. Asher, D., et al.: Strategic maneuver and disruption with reinforcement learning approaches for multi-agent coordination. J. Defense Model. Simul. **20**(4), 509–526 (2023)
13. Gu, X., Yan, J.: Hierarchical k-nearest neighbors for ransomware detection using opcode sequences (2024)
14. Almeida, G., Vasconcelos, F.: Analyzing data theft ransomware traffic patterns using BERT (2023)
15. Zanoramy, W., Abdollah, M., Abdollah, O., Smm, S.: Ransomware early detection using machine learning approach and pre-encryption boundary identification. J. Adv. Res. Appl. Sci. Eng. Technol. **47**(2), 121–137 (2024)
16. Zhang, Z., Ding, C., Li, Y., Yu, J., Li, J.: SECaaS-based partially observable defense model for IIoT against advanced persistent threats. IEEE Trans. Serv. Comput. (2024)
17. Wang, S., Li, Y., Chen, F.: Optimizing blue team strategies with reinforcement learning for enhanced ransomware defense simulations (2024)
18. Kabir, H., Tham, M.-L., Chang, Y.: Internet of robotic things for mobile robots: concepts, technologies, challenges, applications, and future directions. Digit. Commun. Netw. **9**(6), 1265–1290 (2023)
19. Alshehri, S.M., Sharaf, S.A., Molla, R.A.: Systematic review of graph neural network for malicious attack detection. Information **16**(6), 470 (2025)
20. De Oliveira, A.S., Sassi, R.J.: Behavioral malware detection using deep graph convolutional neural networks. Authorea Preprints (2023)
21. Liu, W., et al.: Trace2Vec: detecting complex multi-step attacks with explainable graph neural network. Pattern Recogn. **162**, 111363 (2025)
22. Shokouhinejad, H., et al.: Recent advances in malware detection: graph learning and explainability. arXiv preprint arXiv:2502.10556 (2025)
23. Mukherjee, K., et al.: Interpreting GNN-based ids detections using provenance graph structural (2023)
24. Li, G., Wang, S., Chen, Y., Zhou, J., Zhao, Q.: A hybrid framework for ransomware detection using deep learning and monte Carlo tree search (2024)
25. Kumamoto, T., Yoshida, Y., Fujima, H.: Evaluating large language models in ransomware negotiation: a comparative analysis of ChatGPT and Claude (2023)
26. Vutukuru, S., Lade, S.: Secure IoT: novel machine learning algorithms for detecting and preventing attacks on IoT devices. J. Electric. Syst. **19**(4) (2023)

27. Chen, J., Zhang, G.: Detecting stealthy ransomware in IPFS networks using machine learning (2024)
28. Tomaszewski, W., Brzeźniak, A.: Situation-aware malware detection on Windows OS based on environmental information (2024)
29. Skalski, K., Dombrokova, K., Szczawinski, W.: Situational aware access control to prevent android malware (2024)
30. Thakur, P., Kansal, V., Rishiwal, V.: Hybrid deep learning approach based on LSTM and CNN for malware detection. Wireless Pers. Commun. **136**(3), 1879–1901 (2024)
31. Pesem, B., Fairweather, J., Pennington, T.: Opcode memory analysis: a data-centric machine learning framework for early detection and attribution of ransomware (2024)
32. Takeuchi, K., Fujima, H., Kumamoto, T., Yoshida, Y.: RansomCillin: leveraging NTFS spare space to recover from ransomware attacks (2023)

VARK-Based Cognitive Tutor Using RAG and Groq Llama 3.3

C. Bragadeeshwaran, D. Gaurav, G. Miruthula, M. Srivani(✉), and V. Vanitha

Department of AI and ML, Sri Ramachandra Faculty of Engineering and Technology, SRIHER, Chennai, India
{e0122012,e0122035}@sret.edu.in,
{srivani,vanithamagesh}@sriramachandra.edu.in

Abstract. The proposed system presents a cognitive tutoring system which adapts delivery while grounding answers in the curated course corpus, at the same time modulating them to a personalized modality of the learner. The system, through an SVM, infers a learning style profile (Visual, Auditory, or Reading) from a brief questionnaire and retrieves relevant data from source material for the course using a FAISS-based retrieval pipeline, assembles a context window and prompts Llama 3.3 70B to produce a response. A modality renderer displays the response in four formats: Visual (images and video), Auditory (text-to-speech), Reading (structured text), and Kinesthetic (activity tasks and links), with the option to override it any time. In a 16-question explain and example mode evaluation, the deployed model achieved mean score 0.565 ± 0.046 with median latency 1.42 s, outperforming smaller models (TinyLlama, Phi) in quality and larger alternatives (Mistral) in speed in the live system, and comparative models were either of lower quality or had significantly higher latency; this was the basis of deploying Llama 3.3 70B. Contributions are: a realistic VARK-to-prompt conditioning scheme, which guides presentation without altering underlying content, a streamlined RAG pipeline that provides verifiable grounding and 17.6× latency improvement through output bounding, not knowledge augmentation and one architecture that isolates orchestration, retrieval, and modality display to make it maintainable. The methodology shows that assessment of lightweight style in conjunction with retrieval-augmented and low-latency generation can deliver rapid, grounded and customized tutoring across subjects.

Keywords: Intelligent Tutoring Systems · VARK Learning Styles · Retrieval-Augmented Generation · Large Language Models · Personalized Learning

1 Introduction

1.1 Intelligent Tutoring Systems and Personalized Learning

Online learning has outgrown one-size-fits-all training to systems that can tailor explanations on a case-by-case basis, leaving the content consistent with the

G. K. Verma et al. (Eds.): MIND 2025, CCIS 2981, pp. 236–247, 2027.
https://doi.org/10.1007/978-3-032-31230-3_19

materials actually covered in the course. This project is customized based on the learner's inferred style along the Visual, Auditory and Reading axes with four VARK presentation modes (Visual, Auditory, Reading, and Kinesthetic) directing the way explanations should be given, without altering their content. The tutor is represented as a subject-agnostic pipeline: a short survey marked with a small SVM predicts the most common style and confidence of the learner; passages of relevance are then retrieved in the form of a curated corpus of PDFs and notes; and a large language model is used to generate responses conditioned on this retrieved evidence. The responses are then displayed either in one of four modes, namely, Visual (images and video), Auditory (text to speech), Reading (structured text), and Kinesthetic (tasks and links), and the learner can change modes at any time. They divide the assessment, retrieval, context assembly, orchestration, and rendering with an architecture that can be quickly iterated, with low-latency and verifiable grounding. The system offers four VARK presentation modes but the Kinesthetic mode is implemented only at the rendering layer and not predicted by the classifier. In our system design, the SVM-inferred VAR label is used only to initialise the default presentation mode; it is treated as a soft preference rather than a hard constraint. Users can switch between modes at any time via controls, so the VAR profile provides an informed starting point and allowing the modality to be changed on demand.

1.2 Problem Statement and Proposed Solution

Numerous chatbot-based systems can offer full-fledged but generalized explanations that are not related to the study corpus of the user and fail to reflect the variations in the way learners would like to absorb information. This results in poor understanding, slow development of complicated issues, and a lack of trust when the answers are not easily traced to sources. The proposed system serves these gaps with a two-phase design closely customized into one user flow:

- **Learning Style Evaluation Module.** In its initial implementation, the learner is asked to fill out a short questionnaire; an SVM model is used to predict a Visual, Auditory, or Reading/Writing (VAR) label and a confidence, which is stored in a basic learner profile and serves to start the VARK presentation mode of the tutoring session.
- **Learning Environment of Adaptive Chatbot.** The chat interface is based on a Flask backend, which coordinates retrieval and generation. With a query, the system looks up top k course passages of an FAISS index of PDFs and notes of the user, assembles a context window within the token budget of the model, and queries Llama 3.3 70B on a low-latency inference service. The result is displayed in the style of the current VARK setting, which can be Visual, Auditory, Reading, or Kinesthetic, with a clear control for the learner to switch over the mode anytime.

2 Background and Related Work

The field of adaptive and intelligent tutoring systems (ITS) has drawn sufficient interest as the subject of study because of their potential to provide custom instructional support up to the level of human-to-human one-on-one tutoring. Both recent and previous studies in the field of ITS have focused on such areas of student modeling, adaptive feedback and problem solving scaffolding to enhance better learning and student interest [2,3]. Most recently, ITS has integrated such modeling of pedagogical instruction with data-driven functions to render the personalization process principled and scalable (considering automated testing or content retrieval) [2]. Empirical studies of adaptive e-learning have reported that there were substantial gains in student motivation and student learning outcomes reported as well as a student learning outcomes increase in cases where the content development was personalized [11]. In the conditions of a personally adapted learning style, one of the controlled studies concluded that there are high differences in engagement and a long-lasting beneficial effect on the performance of students (Cohen $d = 0.826$) [1].

The very simplistic approach of personalizing instruction is provided by the learning style models such as VARK (Visual, Auditory, Reading/Writing, Kinesthetic). Similar tools to VARK customize the modality of content and presentation. Certain researchers indicate that the use of materials that are pertinent to the modality of a student may enhance fun and temporary comprehension in some situations [3,4]. Notwithstanding this, the literature has its criticisms. They point to the fact that there is a necessity for a careful use of learning styles because of the influence of prior knowledge and the type of tasks [4]. These results advocate perceiving learning style cues as not hard and fast, but soft and malleable preferences. This is the idea that our proposed system is based on.

The development of the pedagogy field and Retrieval-Augmented Generation (RAG) and neural retrieval have transformed the principles of expertise and knowledge based on the answers provided by the LLM. Chunking, embedding, vector indices (i.e., FAISS), and re-ranking pipelines are useful in enhancing factuality, domain specificity with explicit document-based evidence, hallucination prevention, and completeness of answer in task-focused domain-intensive QA tasks. RAG within the pedagogical framework enables tutors to stay on track with course material, as well as be flexible and conversational.

Past research on e-learning systems has used domain-based personalization to customize learning experiences. As an example, [14] applies a pre-designed domain-specific section with reinforcement learning methods to adapt instructions based on VARK learning styles, and finally, with an objective of enhancing learner engagement and academic performance. Nonetheless, such methods are usually based on fixed content that restricts their capability to personalize the content and react in real-time to the requirements of learners. Comparatively, our work uses a RAG pipeline with Groq-hosted Llama 3.3-70B model that allows context-specific and style-conditioned responses in real-time. We have an architecture that enables switching of modality depending on the choice of the user, but with low-latency performance.

3 System Architecture

The proposed system is structured in a manner that question posed by the learner is transformed to a grounded, modality-conscious explanation without losing the genuineness of the response generated by the learner. Figure 1 represents an end-to-end architecture which is modular and begins with the web interface then to assessment, retrieval, orchestration and rendering to deliver modality-aware grounded tutoring. An onboarding test is also provided in lightweight format on the same UI as the chat and the requests are processed with a Flask backend. Onboarding the Learning Style Assessment infers a VAR (Visual, Auditory, Reading/Writing) label and confidence through a small SVM which is upheld as being a small learner profile and is only present as an indicator. Notably, style does not alter the content of the explanations; content is still confined by course materials only that the profile will give the active mode that can be modified by any learner at any given time.

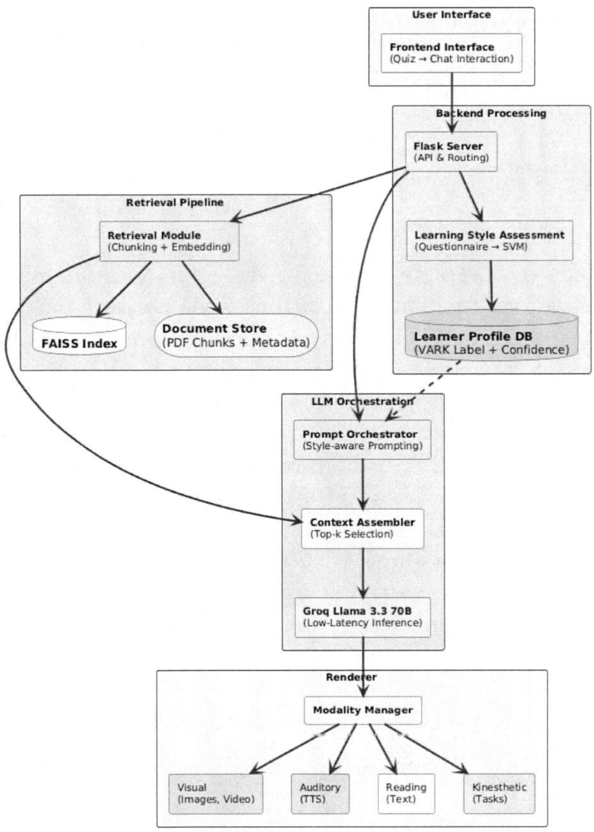

Fig. 1. Workflow of the proposed framework.

In grounding, a pipeline utilizing retrieval is created over the user corpus. To be densely searched on query time, documents (PDFs, notes) are stored in FAISS. The system fetches the top-k passages; an optional re-ranking step is available but disabled in deployment after ablations showed no quality gain with 3.3× latency overhead. The Prompt Orchestrator then develops a style aware prompt that is inviting to the selected mode of learning. On the one hand, a hosted inference of Llama 3.3-70B is selected to generate response with low-latency and on the other hand, it is chosen between the response quality and low-latency when the interactive applications are used. The server maintains a lightweight version of the most recent embeddings and retrieval results and the assembler discards context on the basis of importance, though not always on the basis of recency, in order to keep the latency low.

Finally, there is the Modality Manager that enables conspicuous control to alter the mode during the conversation, as illustrated in Figure reffig:architecture. When VARK (Visual, Auditory, Reading and Kinesthetic) is treated as presentation control, curricular fidelity is maintained, with clarity and interest being increased. This pure isolation, brought about through evaluation, remembering, assembling of contexts, orchestrating and rendering of typical tutoring systems, has made intelligent tutoring to the point of being better scaled than one-to-one human tutoring.

4 Methodology

4.1 Learning Style Assessment

Learners are made to complete a brief VARK-style questionnaire consisting of 15 questions to find out the suitable learning style across Visual, Auditory and Reading/Writing modalities. The scores for each modality are aggregated and normalized and sent to a SVM classifier which is trained on the Student Learning Preferences dataset [13] to classify a dominant style label. The dataset contained $N = 1210$ rows of student data and for training, we split the dataset into 80% training data and 20% validation data, and standardise features using `StandardScaler` before training the SVM. The model achieved an accuracy of 0.91 on validation set which is sufficient for our purpose of providing a soft preference label. The session starts with the classified label as the presentation mode, but style is explicitly treated as a presentation signal rather than a content selector and the user can change the style at any time. The profile remains minimal to support the continuity while avoiding any change to instructional content.

4.2 Knowledge Base Preparation

By a backend loader, the system loads a course-centered corpus and cleans mixed text and arranges the data into documents that are chunked and overlapped to preserve the contextual continuity and enhance the retrieval accuracy. The course-centered corpus can in principle correspond to any subject as long as the materials are provided as PDFs or notes. The extracted chunk can be tweaked in such a way that the datasets that are not the textbook input can also be indexed without alterations. All the chunks are converted to a sentence embedding model in the form of vector representations and stored in a FAISS vector index so that similarity searches can be conducted quickly.

In our system, FAISS is a massive vector database that effectively indexes information and searches for the embedding vectors of the course material passages which allows quick retrieval of the related content that answers the query of the user and according to the learning medium. FAISS was chosen mainly as a leveraging part of the similarity search engine in the retrieving pipeline due to its efficiency, scalability and due to its built-in indexing methods. All document chunks are converted into vector representations using the HuggingFace Sentence-Transformers model `all-mpnet-base-v2` which provided a strong tradeoff between semantic understanding and computational efficiency.

4.3 Retrieval and Context Assembly

In the process of inference each query to a user is transformed into a retrieval query, with minor style based cues sometimes added, which help to control the manner in which the answer is displayed but not which results are deemed to be relevant. The retriever then fetches the top-k most similar text content from the FAISS vector index. An optional re-ranking stage was initially evaluated but later disabled as ablation studies showed that dense retrieval alone performs effectively when embeddings are well aligned. In deployment, the system uses $k = 7$, determined empirically as the best balance between latency and coverage, achieving a median retrieval time of 0.065 s while maintaining consistent performance across values of $k \in \{1, 7\}$. The context assembler later selects a refined set of passages, optimizing for both quality and diversity within the model's requirements. A context assembler then selects a final set of passages by attempting to trade off among quality and diversity within the input constraint of the model. It also eliminates redundant content and retains the original source information to ensure that the citation can be traced. Simple caching of recent embeddings and retrieval results are employed to make the system react more responsively on follow-up turns to reduce any unnecessary delays.

4.4 LLM-Based Response Generation

The Groq-hosted Llama 3.3 70B model is used to generate responses based on a retrieve-then-read model. It is a 70-billion parameter LLM used to generate response in a retrieve-then-read configuration. RAG's primary value in this deployment is latency control via output bounding and source traceability, rather than knowledge augmentation; ablations show quality parity with and without retrieval (0.200 vs 0.199), but RAG-enabled responses are 17.6× faster (0.22 s vs 3.87 s) due to constrained generation scope. The model is fed the user query, the learning style tag that is identified, and the evidence window compiled. These fragments are gathered with a small prompt template and the response that is generated is kept grounded on what has been retrieved. The prompt is a fixed template that uses the retrieved context, the learner's question and the learning style, and then give style-specific instructions to the LLM. For example, the template asks the Llama model to emphasize diagrams and analogies for Visual/Image mode explanation. It also provides presentation hints for each learning style. As an example, the Auditory style of learning is supported by a verbal scaffolding; the Reading style can be supported by structured outlines and references; the Visual style can be supported by descriptions, and the Kinesthetic type of learning style can be supported by step instructions and links to external resources for hands-on exploration on the topic. The content remains true to the source and the style only affects the phrasing of the prompt and structure only. Decoding parameters are mostly adjusted to clarity, factual accuracy, and constant tone. When the model faces the lack of evidence or lack of adequate evidence, it is directed to accept the gap instead of conjecturing and hallucinating. In the multi-turn case, the conversation state is addressed by the assembler, which balances between having recent dialog context and giving priority to new and relevant evidence at each turn.

4.5 Multimodal Response Rendering

The Modality Manager puts forth each of the generated answers in four changeable forms depending on the style chosen by the learner. The Visual mode treats the explanation as either image mode which produces a mindmap and description about the topic or video mode where a relevant YouTube video is recommended. The Auditory mode translates the response from the LLM curated specifically for the auditory mode through prompt template using a text-to-speech engine (a gTTS) with sentence-level pause between words to enhance readability. The Reading mode presents the output in the form of structured text whereby there are headings, bullet points and examples to enhance the readability. Lastly, the Kinesthetic style provides brief practice exercises with step-by-step processes and access to interactive external materials. For example when a learner asks about gradient descent, the system would provide with explanation curated for Kinesthetic mode and link to a tutorial for hands on practice. The learners are free to switch between modes any time during the session without making any changes in the presentation. When the learner changes the mode, the learning style is updated and passed to the prompt orchestrator and Modality Manager which adjusts the phrasing and rendering of the explanation while keeping the underlying content same.

4.6 System Integration and Deployment

The system runs on a Flask backend which handles the whole pipeline, including learning style assessment and retrieval, orchestration, generation, and final rendering in a web-based interface. The backend has clean API endpoints to submit the questionnaire, exchange chat messages and switch learning modes. Lightweight caching on the embeddings and recent retrieval results is used to

Table 1. Model Comparison on 16-Question Evaluation

Model	Mean Score	Avg Latency (s)	Context Util.
TinyLlama-1.1B	0.460 ± 0.098	17.60	0.860
Phi-2	0.418 ± 0.090	339.89	0.896
Mistral-7B	0.541 ± 0.040	576.88	0.950
Llama 3.1-8B Instant	0.568 ± 0.064	7.88	0.949
Llama 3.3-70B (Used)	0.565 ± 0.046	1.42	0.953

maintain constant performance, whereas the context assembler dynamically cuts the input based on significance.

5 Results and Discussion

The system was evaluated on a 16-question test set containing concepts from machine learning (for testing) at varying difficulty levels with responses generated in both explain and example mode. Evaluation was mainly focused on three objectives; choosing an optimal base model through comparative benchmarking, measure the impact of RAG and identifying the minimal effective configuration for deploying. Table 1 summarizes the baseline model comparisons while Table 2 and Figs. 2–4 compares the ablation studies.

Llama 3.3-70B emerged as the deployed choice as it balanced the quality as well as the response time. While Llama 3.1-8B Instant achieved slightly better mean quality, its latency made it unsuitable for interactive tutoring where the response time is very important. Mistral-7B and Phi-2 displayed excessive response time despite both of them having a strong context application, emphasizing the need for optimized infrastructure with good response time. TinyLlama-1.1B, being the fastest among locally hosted modes, showed high output variability and often failed on multi-step reasoning tasks. The Groq hosted Llama 3.3-70B endpoint provided the balance between context utilization and response time making it the only model along with another Groq hosted Llama 3.1-8B, meeting both quality and responsiveness required for real-time tutoring.

Table 2 summarizes the key ablation studies that guided the final deployment choices by examining the necessity and efficiency of each component of the pipeline. The findings challenge the general assumption in RAG system design and offered insights for developing a lightweight and responsive tutoring systems powered by LLMs. Along with the quality, the implemented settings complies with real-time latency constraints as well. In the 16 question assessment (Table 1), the Groq-hosted Llama 3.3-70B model has a mean end-to-end latency of 1.42 s per turn and Table 2 demonstrates that the deployed with-RAG variant achieves a median latency of about 0.22 s ($\approx$ 220 ms), compared to 3.87 s ($\approx$ 3870 ms) without RAG. These values infer that the pipeline operates comfortably within interactive response times.

Table 2. Ablation Study Results

Variant	Mean Score	Context Util.	Median Latency (s)
RAG enabled	0.200	0.68	0.22
RAG disabled	0.199	N/A	3.87
Re-rank disabled	0.250	0.74	0.070
Re-rank enabled	0.250	0.77	0.233
top-k = 1	0.168	0.67	0.074
top-k = 2	0.168	0.67	0.067
top-k = 3	0.168	0.67	0.073
top-k = 5	0.168	0.67	0.067
top-k = 7	0.168	0.67	0.065

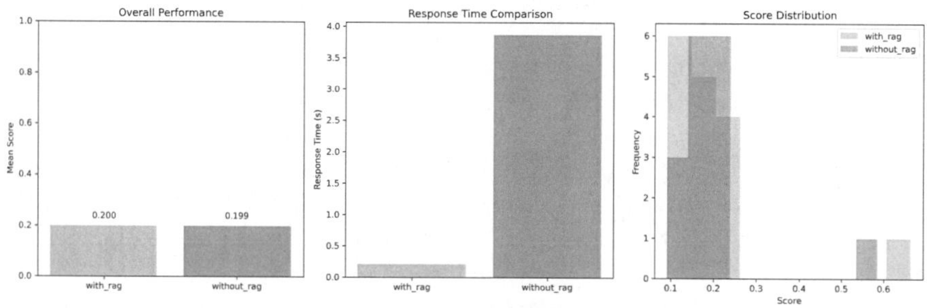

Fig. 2. Effect of RAG on the 16-question evaluation. From left to right: (a) mean score for RAG (green) and no-RAG (red) showing near-identical performance (0.200 vs 0.199), (b) response time comparison highlighting a large latency increase without RAG, and (c) score distribution histograms indicating that RAG shortens responses without degrading the quality distribution. (Color figure online)

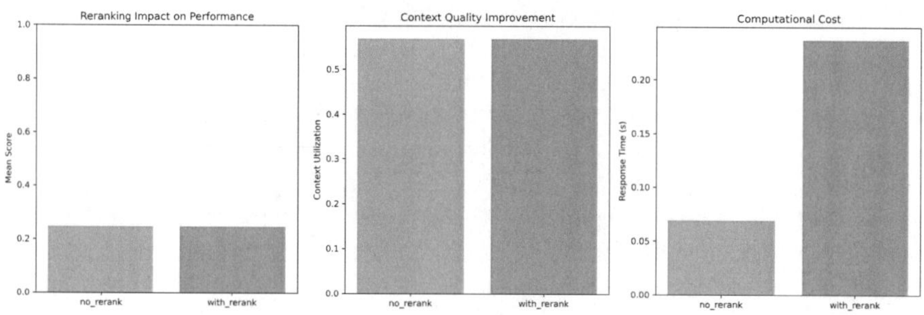

Fig. 3. Impact of enabling cross-encoder re-ranking on system behaviour. From left to right: (a) mean score for without re-rank (blue) and with re-rank (purple), showing no change in performance, (b) context utilisation for both settings, where re-ranking yields only a small increase, and (c) median response time, where re-ranking introduces approximately 3.3× higher latency. (Color figure online)

The primary comparison was between RAG and no-RAG baseline where the model collected only the prompt and no corpus ground. As shown in Fig. 2, the mean scores were statistically equivalent for both indicating that the Llama 3.3-70B's knowledge is enough for the subject. However, the response time diverged dramatically without a RAG baseline implying that without retrieval constraints, the model tended to produce longer and more exploratory response with increased token counts. By employing the retrieve-then-read approach, the responsiveness improved drastically but content quality slightly decreased. For real-time tutoring, this tradeoff strongly favors RAG deployment.

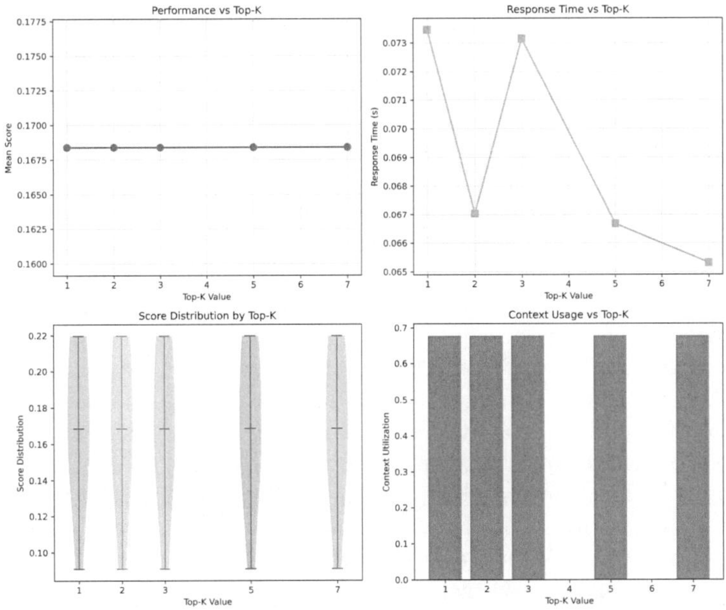

Fig. 4. Sensitivity of the tutoring pipeline to the number of retrieved passages $k \in \{1, \ldots, 7\}$. (a) mean score versus top-k value (blue line), which remains essentially flat, (b) median response time versus top-k value (yellow line), which slightly decreases as k increases, (c) score distribution by top-k (multicolour violin plots), indicating stable score spread across all k, and (d) context utilisation versus top-k (purple bars), which is effectively constant.

It was hypothesized that re-ranking of the top-k retrieved passages, using a cross encoder, would enhance the grounding by favoring the most relevant text chunks. As shown in Fig. 3, to the extent that re-ranking clearly improved context utilization from 0.74 to 0.77, it had no effect on the mean score. Furthermore, the re-ranking process, by which each of the top-k retrieved results would be scored against each other (pairwise scoring), introduced an increase of latency by a factor of 3.3. Given that the embedding for the base dense-retriever was the same caliber as the re-ranking cross encoder, the addition of the rerank computation yielded very little benefit in matching to the prompt. Thus, this performance demonstrates that for domain-specific use cases re-ranking of top-k retrieval results offers little advantage and can be omitted to preserve latency savings.

The different top-k values of 1 to 7 also consistently exhibited stable performance as evidenced in Fig. 4 with the mean score remaining approximately the same, indicating that response quality saturates quickly when a sufficient number of chunks of evidence are retrieved and that the context assembler will efficiently condense multiple passages regardless of the size of the pool. Latency did drop slightly as k increased from 1 to 7 but context utilization stayed stable further validating that using importance to prune context is robust. The deployed system uses a value $k = 7$ because it strikes a balance between retrieval speed, completeness of context and reliability.

6 Conclusion and Future Work

The study demonstrates that integrating lightweight learning style assessment with RAG can lead to fast, reliable, and personalized tutoring. This separation of VARK-based prompting and context selection allows the system to follow the view of the source materials (where they were prompted), while allowing for the modification of how the content is presented. The experimental ablations found the biggest advantage of RAG for this suite of LLMs was not knowledge augmentation, rather it controls the latency of the experience. The modular architecture cleanly separates assessment, retrieval, orchestration, and rendering; it should now generalize to other subjects and domains. Future work will expand on the adaptive learning profiling beyond VARK learning styles, behaviour based-model recommendations and towards multilingual considerations, multi-structure knowledge representation, etc. The next key step is conducting a small-scale human-user study comparing the adaptive VARK tutor with a non-adaptive version measuring both engagement and learning outcomes. While this serves as practical proof of concept, it also serves as practical guidance for building fast, reliable, and ultimately, personalized tutors.

References

1. Tan, L.Y., Hu, S., Yeo, D.J., Cheong, K.H.: Artificial intelligence-enabled adaptive learning platforms: a review. Comput. Educ. Artif. Intell. 100429 (2025). https://doi.org/10.1016/j.caeai.2025.100429
2. Wang, X.J., Lee, C.P., Mutlu, B.: LearnMate: enhancing online education with LLM-powered personalized learning plans and support. In: Proceedings of the Extended Abstracts of the CHI Conference on Human Factors in Computing Systems, pp. 1–10 (2025). https://doi.org/10.1145/3706599.3719857
3. Spriggs, K., Lau, M.C., Passi, K.: Personalizing education through an adaptive LMS with integrated LLMs. arXiv preprint arXiv:2502.08655 (2025). https://doi.org/10.48550/arXiv.2502.08655

4. Zhao, W., Sui, X., Hu, Y., Guo, J., Liu, H., Li, B., et al.: Teaching language models to evolve with users: dynamic profile modeling for personalized alignment. arXiv preprint arXiv:2505.15456 (2025). https://doi.org/10.48550/arXiv.2505.15456
5. El-Sabagh, H.A.: Adaptive e-learning environment based on learning styles and its impact on development students' engagement. Int. J. Educ. Technol. High. Educ. **18**(1), 53 (2021). https://doi.org/10.1186/s41239-021-00289-4
6. Savytri, A., Ratri, D.: A comprehensive design guide to adaptive e-learning system based on VARK learning styles. Indon. J. Multidisc. Res. **3**(2), 453–464 (2023). https://doi.org/10.17509/ijomr.v3i2.61019
7. Sajja, R., Sermet, Y., Cikmaz, M., Cwiertny, D., Demir, I.: Artificial intelligence-enabled intelligent assistant for personalized and adaptive learning in higher education. Information **15**(10), 596 (2024). https://doi.org/10.3390/info15100596
8. Abu-Rasheed, H., Jumbo, C., Al Amin, R., Weber, C., Wiese, V., Obermaisser, R., Fathi, M.: LLM-assisted knowledge graph completion for curriculum and domain modelling in personalized higher education recommendations. In: 2025 IEEE Global Engineering Education Conference (EDUCON), pp. 1–5. IEEE (2025). https://doi.org/10.1109/educon62633.2025.11016377
9. Wang, T., Zhan, Y., Lian, J., Hu, Z., Yuan, N.J., Zhang, Q., et al.: LLM-powered multi-agent framework for goal-oriented learning in intelligent tutoring system. In: Companion Proceedings of the ACM on Web Conference 2025, pp. 510–519 (2025). https://doi.org/10.48550/arXiv.2501.15749
10. Dubey, A., Jauhri, A., Pandey, A., Kadian, A., Al-Dahle, A., Letman, A., et al.: The llama 3 herd of models. arXiv e-prints, arXiv-2407 (2024). https://doi.org/10.48550/arXiv.2407.21783
11. Kochmar, E., Vu, D.D., Belfer, R., Gupta, V., Serban, I.V., Pineau, J.: Automated personalized feedback improves learning gains in an intelligent tutoring system. In: Artificial Intelligence in Education, June 2020, pp. 140–146 (2020). https://doi.org/10.1007/978-3-030-52240-7_26
12. Groq: Groq Cloud: High-Performance AI Inference Platform. https://groq.com/. Accessed 30 Oct 2025
13. Armand, E.B.: Student Learning Preferences. Kaggle. https://www.kaggle.com/datasets/ebouearmand59/student-learning-preferences
14. Sayed, W.S., et al.: AI-based adaptive personalized content presentation and exercises navigation for an effective and engaging E-learning platform. Multimedia Tools Appl. **82**(3), 3303–3333 (2023). https://doi.org/10.1007/s11042-022-13076-8

Automated Evaluation System for Handwritten Answer Scripts Using AI

G. S. Thyagaraju(✉) and Pavan kumar B. S

Sri Dharmasthala Manjunatheshwara Institute of Technology, Ujire, India
profthyagu@gmail.com

Abstract. Taking a manual look at handwritten answer sheets can be really time-consuming, often varies in quality, and isn't immune to human errors. Right now, most automated grading systems rely on OCR or template-based approaches, which don't handle different handwriting styles well, struggle with understanding context, and fall short when it comes to providing feedback. To make matters worse, there's no publicly available benchmark dataset to evaluate these handwritten scripts, making research and reproducibility tough in this field. To tackle this problem, we're putting forward a project that involves an Automated AI-Assisted System to evaluate handwritten answer scripts. It'll make use of a specially created dataset consisting of 12 exam scripts. The system enhances image quality by reducing noise, pulls out and refines text, aligns answers with questions, and evaluates correctness, completeness, and relevance. Our findings indicate that the majority of scores fall within $\pm 15\%$ of our expectations, reflecting a solid number of True Positives (TP) and a low rate of False Positives (FP). The key innovation here is merging image enhancement, AI-driven meaning assessment, and automatic report generation into one comprehensive system. This combo makes it possible to assess handwritten scripts quickly, fairly, and consistently.

Keywords: Handwritten Answer Script Evaluation · Automated Assessment System · Optical Character Recognition (OCR) · AI-Based Scoring · Image Preprocessing

1 Introduction

Educational assessment is a very important tool for measuring students' learning and providing feedback to the academics for improvement. Grading handwritten answer sheets is, however, one of the most difficult and time-consuming tasks that teachers have globally and it takes a lot of their time as well. Instructors often end up spending too many hours going through answer scripts, especially when the number of students and exams increases. As a consequence, there is a lag in feedback, and the evaluator gets fatigued and it might lead to inconsistencies in the grading. The problems mentioned above become more severe in the case of large-scale exams where hundreds or even thousands of answer sheets must be graded within tight deadlines. Moreover, tutors' subjective interpretations of students' replies, variation in examiners' qualifications,

G. K. Verma et al. (Eds.): MIND 2025, CCIS 2981, pp. 248–259, 2027.
https://doi.org/10.1007/978-3-032-31230-3_20

and human prejudices can all contribute to gross unfairness in the evaluation process which might discourage students at the very start of their academic paths. The onset of new technologies such as artificial intelligence, computer vision, and natural language processing comes with the potential to transform educational assessment significantly. They can take over the grading process, thereby ensuring consistency, fairness, and scalability. This paper introduces a complete AI-powered evaluating system for handwritten answer scripts, which in turn utilizes the latest technologies to make the grading flow fully automated.

The structure of the remaining content in this paper is as such: In Sect. 2, the related works on automated grading systems, OCR technologies, and AI-based evaluation methods are reviewed. Section 3 describes the proposed methodology and shows the complete processing pipeline in Fig. 1 and the system architecture in Fig. 2, and then it provides a detailed explanation of the input acquisition through feedback generation for each processing stage. The experimental setup is discussed in Sect. 4 and quantitative results showing the performance of the system on different evaluation metrics are presented. Section 5 offers a thorough discussion of the results, a comparison with existing methods, an error analysis, the benefits, and the limitations. Section 6 wraps up the paper and suggests directions for future research. Lastly, Sect. 7 presents the list of references cited in this work.

2 Related Works

The merging of AI, computer vision, and NLP in the educational sector has caused a significant shift in the automated grading system. Several research works have delved into methods such as optical character recognition, deep learning, and text mining for the assessment of handwriting.

Automated grading and handwriting recognition have been the foci of several studies that utilized computer vision, OCR, and AI techniques along with their combinations. The researchers in Jocovic et al. [1] managed to grade math tests with high accuracy through OpenCV and Python programming. The work of Fisteus et al. [2] is about creating a portable solution for multiple-choice exams called Eyegrade. The researchers in Mahmud et al. [3] had the OCR provided by Tesseract and YOLOv8 for multiple-choice assessment of the students. A review was done by Saoji et al. [4] of text detection methods based on Tesseract. Surinta et al. [5] compared HOG and SIFT features for handwriting recognition, whereas Nurseitov et al. [6] innovated with deep CNN and RNN models for handling Kazakh and Russian scripts. The researchers in Mahadevkar et al. [7] utilized CNN-LSTM hybrids. The study by Agarwal et al. [8] pointed towards the availability of an assessment system based on NLP. Kartha et al. [9] worked towards the image-processing-based recognition. Hamad and Kaya [25] unfolded a thorough discussion on OCR technology. Besides, the studies [12, 13, 15, 16, 18, 20–23] conducted in this time frame indicated progressions in deep learning, LLMs, segmentation methodologies, and multimodal approaches for achieving high-accuracy evaluation and grading.

Most of the previous studies treated the different parts of the handwriting recognition systems as independent issues, however, it is only a few systems that have combined OCR extraction and AI evaluation into integrated, scalable platforms with the ability to process various handwriting styles and complex grading systems. Our work fills this gap by offering a complete solution that merges EasyOCR, OpenCV preprocessing, and Google Gemini LLM, as shown in our overall workflow (Fig. 1) and system architecture (Fig. 2).

3 Proposed Methodology

The AI-Assisted Handwritten Answer Script Evaluation System suggested is a complete eight-step pipeline that, with almost no human intervention, turns unprocessed handwritten answer sheets into thorough evaluation reports. The overall process, system structure, and all components will be explained one by one in this section.

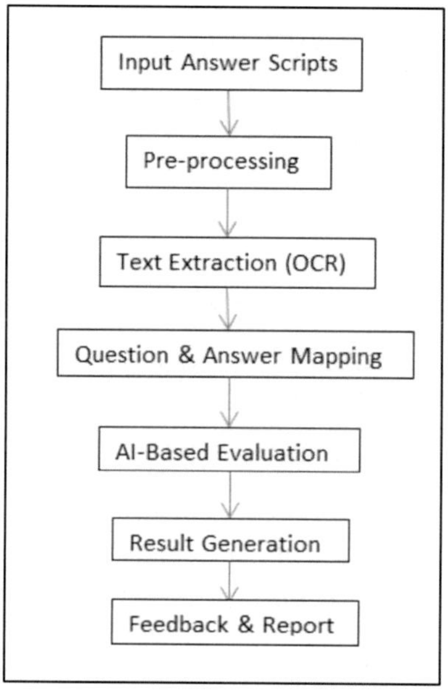

Fig. 1. Proposed Workflow

The entire workflow of the system is shown in Fig. 1. It depicts the user input to the final feedback report generation in an eight-stage processing pipeline that occurs sequentially. The workflow demonstrates the clear change of data through each stage. The outputs from one stage serve as the inputs to the next.

The workflow illustrated in Fig. 1 starts with Input Answer Scripts and moves through the various stages of Preprocessing, Text Extraction (OCR), Text Correction & Formatting, Question & Answer Mapping, AI-Based Evaluation, Result Generation, and finally Feedback & Report generation in a sequential manner. The data is transformed specifically at each stage, and the results of the previous stage are used to add to the next one thus reaching the goal of total automated evaluation. Each of the processing stages, as depicted in the workflow diagram, is described in detail in the following subsections.

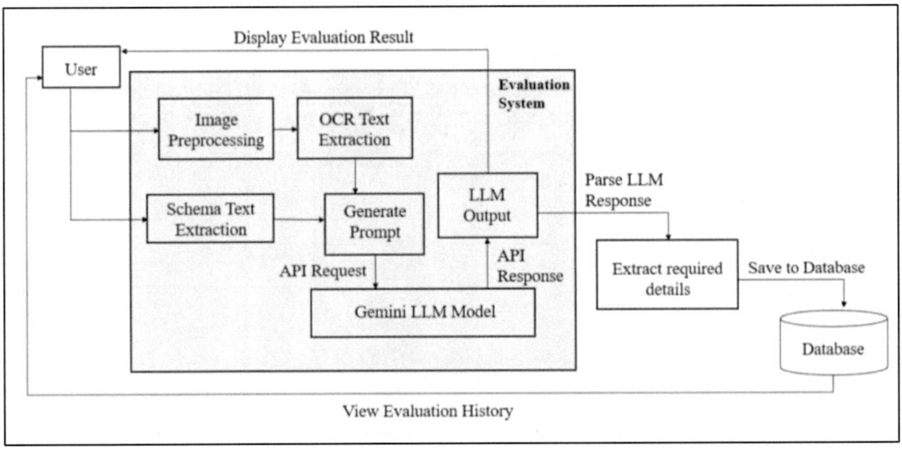

Fig. 2. System Architecture

The system architecture, depicted in Fig. 2, is designed in a modular fashion with five cooperating components that interconnect and therefore process handwritten answer sheets and form extensive evaluation reports. A schematic in Fig. 2 shows the following architecture: (1) User Interface Module for input/output operations crafted with Streamlit framework, (2) Image Preprocessing Module for quality upgrade utilizing OpenCV, (3) Text Extraction Module that integrates OCR processing using EasyOCR and PDF parsing using pdfplumber, (4) AI Evaluation Module employing Google Gemini 1.5 Pro for smart grading, and (5) Database Management Module built on MySQL that provides persistent storage and history tracking for the data. The User Interface Module facilitates the users with a very easy and clear navigation through the various sections like Home, Evaluation System, History, About, and Contact. Through the use of drag-and-drop functionality that is combined with real-time validation, the users upload answer sheets in JPG/PNG formats and evaluation schemes in PDF format. The Image Preprocessing Module is the one to apply enhancement operations to the raw images it receives and meanwhile the Schema Extraction Module processes the PDF evaluation schemes. The OCR Text Extraction Module is the starting point of converting handwritten text to machine-readable format, followed by Text Correction & Formatting, Question-Answer Mapping, and AI-Based Evaluation. At last, the Result Generation Module makes the outputs ready for display, and the Database Management Module saves all the evaluation data for the purpose of accessing it afterward and for historical analysis (Fig. 3).

3.1 Dataset

For this experiment, we ended up gathering a tailored dataset comprising of 12 handwritten answer sheets from two separate question papers regarding Research Methodology. We made this dataset as there is no benchmark dataset of any kind that is open to the public for the automated evaluation of question papers and handwritten answer scripts. To make the research more applicable to the current situation, the data was collected

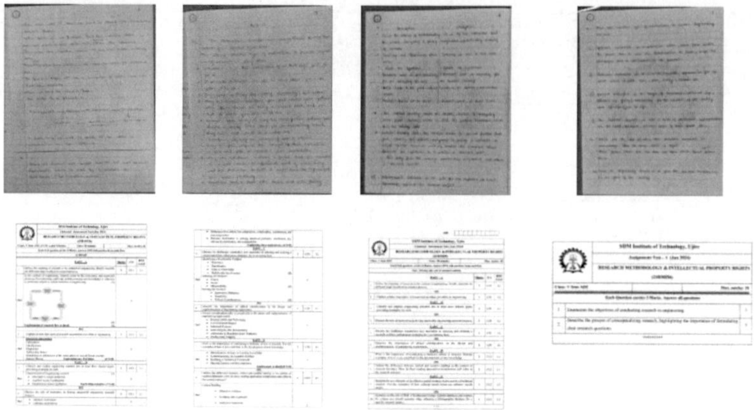

Fig. 3. Dataset Samples of answer scripts and question papers

from real students' submissions which makes it an ideal source of experimentation and model validation in terms of both realism and practicability.

3.2 Stage 1: Input Answer Scripts

The first stage labeled as such in Fig. 1, takes care of the user data input via the interface shown in Fig. 2. The interfaces provide the students with the option to submit scanned answer sheets either in JPG or PNG formats (with a minimum resolution of 300 DPI) and evaluation scheme PDFs. The system processes the student's metadata (USN, name). The formats' compatibility and the images' quality are checked through the input validation process. Each time the validation fails, error messages that demand corrective actions are raised. After the validation has been successfully completed, Fig. 2 indicates that excel sheets move to Stage 2 (Preprocessing) and the patterns get to Schema Extraction.

3.3 Stage 2: Preprocessing

After the successful validation of inputs, the images of answer sheets pass on to the next stage of processing which is the Image Preprocessing Module depicted in Fig. 2 and accompanied in Fig. 1. The most important step is this, since OCR output quality depends highly on processed images's clarity and contrast. The main processing for the module utilizes OpenCV. Part of the codedurgical operations to improve text visibility and lessen the noise involves enhancement of the handwriting images. Initially, images are converted to gray scale to ease the processing and still retain the needed brightness details. Then, Contrast Limited Adaptive Histogram Equalization (CLAHE) comes into play to improve the local contrast which is a great help when dealing with varying lighting conditions. Afterwards, a Gaussian blur (kernel size 5×5, $\sigma = 1.0$) is employed to the images to remove noise like paper texture or scanning artifacts without changing the characters' shapes. The last step is adaptive thresholding with Otsu's method, which transforms the image into a clear-cut black text on a white background thereby providing an ideal input for OCR.

3.4 Stage 3: Text Extraction (OCR)

Once preprocessing is finished, images move to the text extraction stage (third block in Fig. 1) through the OCR Text Extraction and Schema Extraction Modules (Fig. 2). EasyOCR, a deep-learning optical character recognition engine, identifies various types of handwriting using CNNs for the extraction of features and RNNs for modeling of the sequence. It also utilizes GPU acceleration and supports the English language, to be specific. On the one hand, beam search decoding guarantees precise character recognition, while on the other hand, paragraph-level aggregation maintains line and paragraph structures making it easier for the question and answer to be aligned. In the same time, pdfplumber is taking out the text from the evaluation scheme PDFs, which consists of questions, marks, model answers, and marking guidelines, through the extraction of the pdf text. After that, the student and scheme texts that have been extracted are sent to Stage 4 (Text Correction & Formatting), wherein the process of error handling involves the logging of unreadable handwriting, poor scans, or corrupted PDFs, thus guaranteeing reliable processing.

3.5 Stage 4: Text Correction and Formatting

The Text Correction and Formatting stage portrayed as the fourth block in Fig. 1 and 2, basically cleans and standardizes the OCR outputs so as to produce very high quality input for AI evaluation. In fact, it starts with the normalization of whitespace in order to get rid of any extra spaces, tabs, and line breaks at the same time, and then, the spell correction is done for common OCR errors (e.g., "0" vs. "O," "1" vs. "l") whereby domain-specific terms are still kept intact. After this, formatting is done in such a way as to have the same case, punctuation, and numbers across the board. The question identifiers (e.g., "Q1:", "1)") and the answer boundaries are recognized using pattern recognition, indentation, and spacing and thus the whole text is organized into structured question–answer pairs. The outputs that have been formatted are then sent to Stage 5 (Question–Answer Mapping) for alignment and evaluation.

3.6 Stage 5: Question and Answer Mapping

The fifth block of Fig. 1 shows the Question–Answer Mapping stage and it is also the one depicted in Fig. 2, which pairs up each student answer extracted with the relevant question and marking criteria. The first thing the system does is to identify question identifiers (like "Q1," "1)" etc.) both in the student script and in the evaluation scheme. Then it employs text similarity measures as well as position-based heuristics for matching the answers accurately. Hierarchical matching does multi-part questions while a correspondence matrix keeps track of irregularities like skipped or out of order answers. When mapping is finished, structured tuples consisting of student answer, marking rubric, model answer, and maximum marks are created and forwarded to Stage 6 (AI-Based Evaluation) for automatic scoring.

3.7 Stage 6: AI-Based Evaluation

The sixth block depicted in Fig. 1 and also displayed in Fig. 2 is the module for AI-Based Evaluation, which serves as the brain of the whole system. The model utilized is the Google Gemini 1.5 Pro LLM, and it is the one that assesses the student's responses based on their contextual, reasoning, and conceptual understanding rather than simply matching the keywords. The LLM uses a structured prompt that includes the student's answer, model answer, marking scheme, and evaluation criteria to compare the responses in terms of correctness, depth, and clarity. It then awards marks proportionally, pinpoints mistakes, and delivers comprehensive feedback that consists of strengths, weaknesses, and suggestions for improvement. The entire grading process is very consistent across different questions, and the structured evaluation results are subsequently sent to Stage 7 (Report Generation) for the compilation of results.

3.8 Stage 7: Result Generation

In Fig. 1, the Result Generation Stage is the seventh block, and the Result Generation Module in Fig. 2 handles this process. The AI evaluation results are integrated into well-structured and very easily readable reports. The system is employing pattern identification and natural language processing (NLP) to extract main parts like scores, clarifications, and remarks from the answers of Gemini. The system is able to identify scores by means of expressions such as "18/20," whereas LLM's text is the source for citing and recommending. The structured data is transformed into a report which has the following pieces of information: student, overall score and score per question, reasoning, strengths and weaknesses, and tips for improvement. There are two places where the reports are formatted: web display, which includes color-coded indicators and expandable sections, and database storage for fast retrieval. The reports that have been generated will then proceed to Stage 8 for the presentation of feedback and the review of errors.

3.9 Stage 8: Feedback and Report

The quick five-minute third and last step of this workflow, represented as the eighth block in Fig. 1 and made operational via the User Interface and Database Management Modules in Fig. 2, mainly concerns the provision of explicit and useful feedback, as well as the protection of the evaluation results through storage. The web interface displays the total score along with retractable sections for individual questions that show the marks, grading rationale, strengths and improvement suggestions, all of which are supported by the performance indicators that are color-coded according to quality. The MySQL Database is the place where all the evaluation data are stored, including the time of evaluation, student details, AI feedback, and metadata for tracking that is intended to be long-term. The History function allows users to review previous evaluations and perform their own analysis of performance, while the Excel export feature supports offline reporting and record-keeping. To constitute it, this stage has made the feedback available, data secure and the insights evidence-based for continual academic improvement.

4 Results

4.1 Experimental Setup

The present situation consisted of using the system on a data set made up of 12 handwritten answer sheets of different subjects including computer science, mathematics, and general science. These samples were not just of different subjects, but also different styles (e.g. print, cursive, mixed), ink colors (e.g. blue, black), paper qualities and imaging methods (e.g. 300–600 DPI scans or mobile phone captures). The educators assigned grades to each script and thereby created the ground truth scores which were then compared with the AI-generated results. The evaluation methods used were scoring rubrics, model answers, and the rules for partial credit, which were additional documents supporting the evaluation process. A margin of $\pm 15\%$ was set to cover up the discrepancies in marking and the variability between the OCR process and the human evaluators. The AI scores which fell within this margin were classified as True Positives (TP) denoting their close resemblance with human adjudicators' scores, while those beyond the margin were labeled as False Positives (FP), thus requiring further examination.

4.2 Quantitative Performance

The system has been assessed on various evaluation metrics, and the results have been excellent as per the experimental outcomes. Table 1 contains comprehensive test case results with expected marks (human grader), observed marks (AI system), absolute difference, and tolerance classification (Table 2).

Table 1. Test Case Results and Classification

Test Case	Expected Marks	Observed Marks	Difference	Within Tolerance ($\pm 15\%$)	Classification
1	38	34	4	Yes	TP
2	15	16	1	Yes	TP
3	23	28	5	Yes	TP
4	33	28	5	Yes	TP
5	22	21	1	Yes	TP
6	33	28	5	Yes	TP
8	36	34	2	Yes	TP
9	33	28	5	Yes	TP
10	29	23	6	No	FP
11	30	24	6	No	FP
12	10	15	5	Yes	TP

Table 2. Performance Metrics Summary

Metric	Formula	Value	Interpretation
Accuracy	(TP + TN) / Total	83.33%	Overall correctness of evaluations
Precision	TP / (TP + FP)	83.33%	Reliability of acceptable grades
Recall	TP / (TP + FN)	100.00%	Complete capture of correct evaluations
F1-Score	2 × (Precision × Recall) / (Precision + Recall)	90.91%	Balanced performance measure
Mean Absolute Error	Σ|Observed - Expected| / N	3.75 marks	Average grading deviation

The system delivered a remarkable and trusted performance, and its results were almost identical to those of the human grading. It achieved a recall of 100%, which means it has accurately identified all evaluations without overlooking any of the valid ones. The precision rate of 83.33% points out that the majority of the grades assigned by the system were correct and fell within the range of tolerance set for acceptance. The system got a maximum performance in both the aspects of precision and recall that is represented by an F1-score of 90.91%. The average score difference between the human raters and the AI was just 3.75 points—which is such a tiny difference that it would still be considered as within the range of normal variation in educational grading scales. Overall, the results support the statement that the system is a human grader in terms of consistency and reliability during the assessment of students' responses.

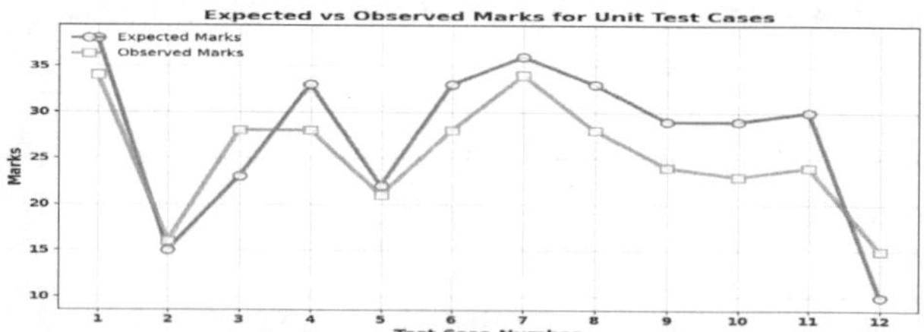

Fig. 4. Comparison of Expected vs. Observed Marks Across Test Cases

As seen in Fig. 4, the marks that were observed closely followed the expected marks for a majority of the tests, having just small differences. Tests 10 and 11 have the newly observed values that are the farthest from the expected ones, which are due to the false positive classifications given in Table 1. Therefore, this visualization is a clear indication of the system's reliability and at the same time of the cases needing to be addressed.

As shown in Table 3, the complete evaluation pipeline processes a typical answer script in approximately 3 min (178 s), with AI-Based Evaluation (Stage 6) consuming the majority of processing time due to LLM inference. This represents an approximately

Table 3. Average Processing Time per Stage

Stage	Process	Average Time	Percentage of Total
1	Input Answer Scripts	5 s	2.8%
2	Pre-processing	8 s	4.5%
3	Text Extraction (OCR)	25 s	14.0%
4	Text Correction & Formatting	6 s	3.4%
5	Question & Answer Mapping	10 s	5.6%
6	AI-Based Evaluation	90 s	50.6%
7	Result Generation	15 s	8.4%
8	Feedback & Report	19 s	10.7%
Total	**End-to-End Processing**	**178 s**	**100%**

85% reduction compared to the 15–20 min typically required for manual evaluation, validating the system's efficiency claims. The workflow illustrated in Fig. 1 shows that stages execute sequentially, with the longest stage (AI-Based Evaluation) representing the primary bottleneck. Future optimizations could focus on parallelizing evaluation of multiple questions or implementing batch processing to improve throughput for large examination volumes.

5 Conclusion

The research work suggests an entire machine learning make-up evaluation system for handwritten answer scripts that depends entirely on the computer vision, OCR, and large language models together with the high marks and fair grading, thus guaranteeing the very reliable and the very fair grading. The whole workflow comprised of eight suggested stages—from input to feedback generation—achieved an accuracy of 83.33%, a recall of 100%, and a Mean Absolute Error of 3.75 marks while at the same time grading time was reduced almost by 85%. The system's modular design allows it to grade large batches of examinations while providing consistency, scalability, and transparency. However, even though the system produced excellent results, there are still some issues when it comes to illegible handwriting, restricted language, and sequential error propagation. For future work, the system might be better off getting advanced in pre-processing for handwritten and poorly printed texts, supporting multiple languages, diagram recognition, providing a grading sensitivity that adapts to student performance, allowing parallel processing, incorporating plagiarism detection, and integrating with Learning Management Systems (LMS) all at once. To sum up, the system has shown that state-of-the-art AI can match human graders in terms of quality while at the same time offering efficiency, fairness, and comprehensive feedback and thus playing a role in the evolution of fully automated, intelligent educational assessment of the next generation.

Acknowledgement. The authors would like to thank *Panchami Bhat (2025 Passed out SDMIT-CSE Student)*- for contributing significantly towards the research work.

References

1. Jocovic, V., Marinkovic, M., Stojanovic, S., Nikolic, B.: Automated assessment of pen and paper tests using computer vision. Multimed. Tools Appl. **83**(1), 2031–2052 (2024). https://doi.org/10.1007/s11042-023-15767-2
2. Fisteus, J.A., Pardo, A., Garcia, N.F.: Grading multiple choice exams with low-cost and portable computer-vision techniques. J. Sci. Educ. Technol. (2024)
3. Khan, A.A., Laghari, A.A., Awan, S.A.: Machine learning in computer vision: a review. Endorsed transactions on scalable. Inf. Syst. (2024)
4. Saoji, S., Arora, A., Singh, R., Mangal, A., Eqbal, A.: Text recognition and detection from images using Pytesseract. J. Interdisciplinary Cycle Res. **13**(7), 1674–1680 (2021)
5. Surinta, O., Karaaba, M.F., Schomaker, L.R.B., Wiering, M.A.: Recognition of handwritten characters using local gradient feature descriptors. Eng. Appl. Artif. Intell. **45**, 405–414 (2015)
6. Nurseitov, D., Bostanbekov, K., Alimova, A., Abdallah, A., Abdimanap, G.: Classification of handwritten names of cities and handwritten text recognition using various deep learning models. Adv. Sci. Technol. Eng. Syst. J. **5**(5), 934–943 (2020)
7. Mahadevkar, S., Patil, S., Kotecha, K.: Enhancement of handwritten text recognition using AI-based hybrid approach. MethodsX **12**, 102654 (2024)
8. Agarwal, M., Kalia, R., Bahel, V., Thomas, A.: AutoEval: a NLP approach for automatic test evaluation system. In: Proceedings of GUCON, pp. 1–6. IEEE (2021). https://doi.org/10.1109/GUCON50781.2021.9573769
9. Kartha, S., Abahai, A., Varghese, S.M.: Automatic grading of figures in digitalized answer scripts. Int. J. Sci. Res. Dev. **3**(09), 890–894 (2015)
10. Salvi D.: Document Image Analysis Techniques for Handwritten Text Segmentation, Document Image Rectification and Digital Collation. Ph.D. dissertation, University of South Carolina (2014).
11. Olsson J.S.: Computer-Based Versus Pen-Based Testing: An Experimental Study of Reading Comprehension and Essay Writing in Swedish Lower Secondary School. Degree essay, Ämneslärarprogrammet (2023).
12. Henkel, O., Boxer, A., Hills, L., Roberts, B.: Can large language models make the grade? An empirical study evaluating LLMs ability to mark short answer questions in K–12 education. In: Proceedings of Learning at Scale '24, pp. 1–10 (2024)
13. Bai, X., Stede, M.: A survey of current machine learning approaches to student free-text evaluation for intelligent tutoring. Int. J. Artif. Intell. Educ. **33**, 994–1032 (2023)
14. Bonnet B., Swersky K., Liu R., Awasthi P., Nova, A., et al.: Long-Span Question-Answering: Automatic Question Generation and QA-System Ranking via Side-by-Side Evaluation. https://arxiv.org/abs/2406.00179 (2024)
15. Singh, V.S., Verma, A., Srivastava, G., Kumar, S.: Exam assessor tool: an automated system for efficient answer sheet evaluation. Asian J. Res. Comput. Sci. **17**(6), 36–57 (2024)
16. Kulkarni, M., Adhav, G., Wadile, K., Chavan, R., Deshmukh, V.: Digital Handwritten Answer Sheet Evaluation System. Savitribai Phule Pune University (2024)
17. Haduong N., Gao A., Smith N.A.: Risks and NLP Design: A Case Study on Procedural Document QA. https://arxiv.org/abs/2408.11860 (2024).
18. Patil R., Kulkarni A.A., Ghatage R., Endait S., Kale G., Joshi R.: Automated Assessment of Multimodal Answer Sheets in the STEM Domain. https://arxiv.org/abs/2409.15749 (2024)
19. Gorer B., Aydemir F.B.: GPT-Powered Elicitation Interview Script Generator for Requirements Engineering Training. https://arxiv.org/abs/2406.11439 (2024)
20. Tobler, S.: Smart grading: a generative AI-based tool for knowledge-grounded answer evaluation. MethodsX **12**, 102531 (2024)

21. Thorat C., Bhat A., Sawant P., Bartakke I., Shirsath S.: A Detailed Review on Text Extraction Using Optical Character Recognition. In: Lecture Notes in Networks and Systems, vol. 314, pp. 1–10 (2022).
22. Choudhary, A., Rishi, R., Ahlawat, S.: A new character segmentation approach for off-line cursive handwritten words. Procedia Comput. Sci. **17**, 88–95 (2013)
23. Rajput, V., Jayanthi, N., Indu, S.: An efficient character segmentation algorithm for connected handwritten documents. In: Proceedings of ICCIDS, pp. 1–6 (2024)
24. Rao, D., Singh, R., Tomar, N.S., Singh, S.: Handwritten character recognition. Int. J. Res. Eng. Sci. Manag. **2**(5), 1009–1033 (2019)
25. Hamad, K.A., Kaya, M.: A detailed analysis of optical character recognition technology. Int. J. Appl. Math. Electron. Comput. **4**, 244–249 (2016). https://doi.org/10.18100/ijamec.270374

An Empirical Evaluation of Adversarial Attacks and Defenses on Large Language Models

Prachi Subhadarsini Sahoo(✉) and Minati Mishra

Fakir Mohan University, Balasore, Odisha, India
{prachisubhadarsinisahoo,minatiminu}@gmail.com

Abstract. Large Language Models (LLMs) have changed how we process natural languages. However, they are still vulnerable to attacks that can change model predictions through small linguistic tweaks. This study evaluates major types of attacks, including gradient, optimization, transfer, and query-based attacks, as well as text and domain-specific attacks. It also assesses various defense strategies such as training-based, model, input, interface-centric, and human-in-the-loop defenses. Experiments on the SST-2 dataset, using stratified random sampling and a sample size determined with a 98% confidence interval, show that black-box attacks are more likely than white-box attacks. The findings also suggest that model-centric and human-in-the-loop defenses provide the highest level of protection, restoring accuracy up to over 90% in most cases. Hence, combining these methods can offer the best defense against changing adversarial threats in LLMs.

Keywords: Large Language Models · Adversarial Attacks · Robustness · Defense Mechanisms · Empirical Evaluation

1 Introduction

Large Language Models (LLMs) such as GPT and LLaMA have significantly advanced natural language processing by enabling fluent text generation, logical reasoning, and conversational understanding. However, their integration into sensitive domains including, healthcare, finance, and cybersecurity, introduces new security risks, particularly adversarial attacks. These attacks involve subtle and often human imperceptible modifications that can mislead models into producing incorrect or harmful responses [9,16]. LLMs are highly sensitive to minor input perturbations, and their similar decision boundaries across architectures make them vulnerable to both gradient-based and transfer-based attacks [11,13,14]. Furthermore, limited feedback in black box systems allows adversaries to exploit score or decision-based responses [4]. Domain-specific training data also heightens manipulation risks in areas such as sentiment analysis and medical diagnostics [1]. Ensuring adversarial robustness, the ability to remain accurate under malicious interference, remains a critical challenge, as linguistic

G. K. Verma et al. (Eds.): MIND 2025, CCIS 2981, pp. 260–271, 2027.
https://doi.org/10.1007/978-3-032-31230-3_21

perturbations can still deceive models despite improved data curation[7,17]. Both white-box and black-box settings exhibit distinct vulnerabilities [10]. Ultimately, strengthening robustness against gradient, query, and transfer-based attacks is essential for the safe and trustworthy deployment of LLMs [3,6].

This paper presents an evaluation of the impacts of various types of attacks and defenses on LLMs. The rest of the paper is organised as follows. Types of adversarial attacks are discussed in section 2, different types of defenses are presented in section 3, methodology, and results analysis are presented in sections 4 and 5, respectively. The paper is concluded highlighting, the key findings and the future research directions in section 6.

2 Adversarial Attacks

Adversarial attacks on LLMs are classified into white-box, black-box, and hybrid types. These attacks differ in the attacker's skill level, level of access, and way of exploiting linguistic and contextual flaws[1,16].

2.1 White-box Techniques

These attacks allow the change of the model parameters and hence work better than heuristic or black-box techniques.

Gradient-Based Attack: These attacks change loss gradients to make false perturbations and are highly dangerous for LLMs. Attacks such as ADV-ReLU lessen gradient masking for stronger attacks, but FGSM, I-FGSM, MI-FGSM, NI-FGSM, and VMI-FGSM make it easier to transfer[6,9,16].

Optimization-Based Attack: These attacks pose example creation as a limited optimization task to reduce perturbations and introduce model errors. By frequently altering inputs as they get closer to decision boundaries, techniques like L-BFGS and DeepFool lead to misclassifications in LLMs. Sophisticated frameworks that employ cooperative or adversarial prompt optimization for multi-turn or jailbreak scenarios further expand on this[1].

Text-Specific Attack: Text-specific attacks, such as JSMA and HotFlip, focus on making changes to words or characters (inserting, deleting, and flipping) using gradient signals and token saliency. These attacks change important tokens to change model outputs while keeping them readable. In black-box environments with low or no gradient, these methods often make practical danger vectors worse and get around countermeasures[6,16].

2.2 Black-Box Techniques

Black-box attacks rely solely on querying and model output observation in the absence of internal access. Even though LLM APIs conceal parameters, attackers can still cause significant disruptions with just a few simple queries [11].

Transfer-Based Attack: Transfer-based attacks take advantage of the fact that adversarial examples made on one model can fool another. Attackers create perturbations that can be successfully transferred to black-box targets by training or picking surrogate LLMs. Shared architectures and data commonalities make it easier to transfer this information, which lets for effective changes or jailbreaks without having direct access to model parameters[9, 11].

Query-Based Attack: These attacks use input-output interactions to make the model act like it does. They include score-based attacks that use confidence scores to guess gradients and decision-based attacks that use final outputs. Adversarial prompt engineering changes prompts over and over again to get harmful or limited answers, while bandit and adaptive querying methods quickly improve inputs[11, 19].

Domain-Specific Attack: Domain-specific attacks exploit a model's domain related vulnerabilities by generating inputs tailored to the application language, context, or structure. For example, changing the wording of harsh information can get past toxicity filters, and changing the wording of emotional words can change sentiment labels. These targeted attacks pose a risk to important areas like healthcare, banking, and cybersecurity, as well as governance and education[1, 3].

3 Defenses

As LLMs continue to evolve, so do their vulnerabilities to adversarial attacks. Even small changes are capable of reducing safety measures and changing outputs [2]. To protect against threats, we need defenses at many levels, such as input, model, training, inference, and system, each targeting a different attack vector. Some common defense models are discussed below.

Training-Based Defense: By using adversarial examples from FGSM, PGD, or optimization-based methods to fine-tune decision limits, training-based defenses, especially adversarial training, actively make models more robust. Domain Adversarial and Ensemble Adversarial Training are two examples of extensions that make it harder for attacks that are specific to a certain area or that can be used in different areas to work. However, these extensions don't work as well when new or adaptable adversarial tactics are used[12, 18].

Model-Centric Defense: Model-centric defenses strengthen LLMs by modifying internal architectures or training objectives to resist hostile manipulation. Techniques like gradient masking, robust optimization, and stochastic noise obfuscate gradient information[6]. Certified robustness uses Lipschitz bounds and convex relaxations for formal assurances, while defensive distillation and latent space regularization smooth decision boundaries and reinforce hidden layer stability[1, 4, 16].

Input-Centric Defense: Input-centric defenses stabilize and clean inputs before they enter the model. Techniques like input sanitization are used to get rid of noise, homoglyphs, and adversarial triggers[4]. Strong embedding learning enhances semantic consistency against lexical variations, while domain-specific normalization and consistency checking detect manipulations and lessen contextual drift in sensitive applications[12].

Interface-Centric Defense: During deployment, inference time protections shield LLMs without requiring retraining. Randomized smoothing and stochastic decoding offer controlled randomness to prevent transfer-based or universal prompt attacks[8]. Output obfuscation obscures fine grained probabilities, weakening score-based queries, while query limiting and anomaly detection monitor request patterns to prevent gradient estimation and adversarial probing[4, 12, 16].

Human-in-the-loop Defense: Human-in-the-loop (HITL) defenses incorporate expert supervision and feedback to detect hostile activity that automated systems might miss. In high stakes domains like law or healthcare, human review minimizes detrimental outcomes[12]. Multi-agent safety nets and cross-paradigm defense stacks use model cross verification and layered defenses to counter hybrid, adaptive threats[8].

4 Methodology

This study experimentally assesses the impacts of attacks and defenses on LLMs. The architecture of the proposed evaluation model is given in Figure 1. The adversarial attacks, defenses and evaluation metrics considered for the experimentation are discussed in the subsequent subsections.

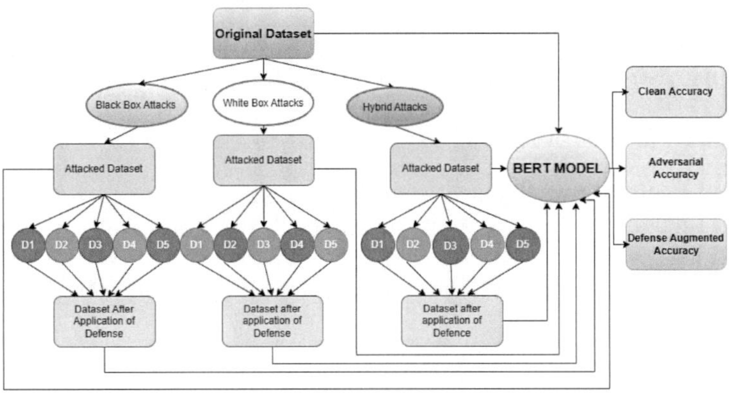

Fig. 1. Architecture of the Proposed Evaluation Model.

4.1 Evaluation Metrics:

The following metrics are used to accesses the effectiveness of the attacks and the defenses.

- **Clean Accuracy (CA):** Model performance on unperturbed inputs.
- **Adversarial Accuracy (AC):** Performance on perturbed inputs.
- **Attack Success Rate(ASR):** The proportion of cleanly correct predictions that become incorrect after an attack.
- **Defense Augmented Accuracy (DAA):** Performance after applying each defense mechanism.

4.2 Transfer-Based Adversarial Attack

Robustness of the target model f_t is evaluated using transfer-based adversarial attacks. Adversarial examples are generated via a surrogate model f_s and transferred to f_t. Each input x with label y is perturbed by replacing important words with semantically similar alternatives. Perturbations are limited by a token change budget B and a minimum semantic similarity threshold θ_{sim} (Eq. 2). Only examples that fool f_s are considered for evaluation on f_t. Attack success is measured using SASR, TSR, and OTR (Eq. 3). The steps of this attack are given in Algorithm 1.

Surrogate Objective:

$$x^{\text{adv}} = \arg\max_{x'} \mathcal{L}(f_s(x'), y) \tag{1}$$

Where, x^{adv} : adversarial example, x' : candidate perturbed input, f_s :surrogate model, y :true label, $\mathcal{L}$:surrogate loss function.

Perturbation Constraints:

$$\text{dist}_{\text{tok}}(x, x') \leq B, \quad \text{sim}(x, x') \geq \theta_{\text{sim}} \tag{2}$$

$\text{dist}_{\text{tok}}(x, x')$: number of token changes, B: maximum allowed token changes, $\text{sim}(x, x')$: semantic similarity between x and x', θ_{sim}: minimum required similarity threshold.

The attacks specific evaluation measures are given in equation 3.

$$\text{SASR} = \frac{n_s}{n}, \quad \text{TSR} = \frac{n_t}{n_s}, \quad \text{OTR} = \frac{n_t}{n} \tag{3}$$

Where, n: total number of attacked inputs, n_s: surrogate successful examples, n_t: examples fooling target model, SASR: surrogate attack success rate, TSR: transfer success rate, OTR: overall transfer rate.

4.3 FGSM White-Box Attack

FGSM benchmarks attack effectiveness under gradient access, providing a controlled baseline despite rarely valid white-box assumptions. The robustness of the target model f_t is evaluated using white-box adversarial attacks, where perturbations are computed directly from model gradients. For each input x with true label y, a small perturbation is applied in the direction that maximizes the model's loss. The perturbation magnitude is controlled by a step size ε, and adversarial examples are generated using the Fast Gradient Sign Method (FGSM). Attack success is measured by the drop in accuracy after perturbation. The detailed steps of this attack are presented in Algorithm 2.

Algorithm 1. Transfer-Based Adversarial Attack

Require: Dataset D, surrogate model f_s, target model f_t, token budget B, similarity threshold θ_{sim}, sample size n
Ensure: Adversarial set D_{adv}, metrics SASR, TSR, OTR
Select representative subset $S \subset D$ of size n
$D_{\text{adv}} \leftarrow \varnothing$
for each $(x, y) \in S$ **do**
  Identify important words in x (e.g., gradient-based importance and POS tags)
  Generate candidate substitutions preserving POS and semantic similarity
  Iteratively construct candidate x' by substituting important words
  Enforce constraints: $\text{dist}_{\text{tok}}(x, x') \leq B$ and $\text{sim}(x, x') \geq \theta_{\text{sim}}$ (see Eq. 2)
  if $f_s(x') \neq y$ **then**
    {surrogate misclassification} Add (x, x', y) to D_{adv}
  end if
end for
Evaluate each $x' \in D_{\text{adv}}$ on f_t and count successful transfers n_t
Set $n_s \leftarrow |D_{\text{adv}}|$
Compute metrics SASR, TSR, OTR (see Eq. 3)
return D_{adv}

Adversarial Objective: Given a model f_t, loss function $\mathcal{L}$ (e.g., cross entropy), and input x, the FGSM adversarial example is:

$$x_{\text{adv}} = x + \varepsilon \cdot \text{sign}\big(\nabla_x \mathcal{L}(f_t(x), y)\big), \tag{4}$$

where ε is the perturbation magnitude. The perturbation is bounded by an ℓ_∞ constraint to ensure imperceptibility:

$$\|x_{\text{adv}} - x\|_\infty \leq \varepsilon. \tag{5}$$

Effectiveness of the attack can be measured using the evaluation metrics given in equations 6 and 7.

$$\text{Clean Accuracy} = \frac{n_c}{n}, \quad \text{Adversarial Accuracy} = \frac{n_a}{n} \tag{6}$$

$$\text{ASR} = 1 - \frac{n_a}{n_c} = 1 - \frac{\text{Adversarial Accuracy}}{\text{Clean Accuracy}}. \tag{7}$$

Where, n: Total number of test samples, n_c: the number of correctly classified clean examples, and n_a: the number of correctly classified adversarial examples.

Algorithm 2. FGSM White-Box Adversarial Attack

Require: Dataset D, target model f_t, step size ε
Ensure: Adversarial set D_{adv}, Clean Acc., Adv. Acc., ASR
Initialize counters: $correct_{\text{clean}} = 0$, $correct_{\text{adv}} = 0$
for each $(x, y) \in D$ **do**
  Compute embeddings $\mathbf{e}$ and loss $L = \mathcal{L}(f_t(\mathbf{e}), y)$
  Backpropagate: L.backward() to get $\nabla_{\mathbf{e}} L$
  Form perturbation using Eq. 4:
    $\mathbf{e}_{\text{adv}} = \mathbf{e} + \varepsilon \operatorname{sign}(\nabla_{\mathbf{e}} L)$
  Optionally enforce Eq. 5 via clipping:
    $\mathbf{e}_{\text{adv}} = \operatorname{clip}(\mathbf{e}_{\text{adv}}, \mathbf{e} - \varepsilon, \mathbf{e} + \varepsilon)$
  Predict: $y_{\text{clean}} = \arg\max f_t(\mathbf{e})$, $y_{\text{adv}} = \arg\max f_t(\mathbf{e}_{\text{adv}})$
  if $y_{\text{clean}} = y$ **then**
    $correct_{\text{clean}} += 1$
  end if
  if $y_{\text{adv}} = y$ **then**
    $correct_{\text{adv}} += 1$
  end if
end for
Compute metrics as in Eq. 7

4.4 Model-Centric Defense

Robustness of the target model f_t is enhanced using a *model-centric* defense as presented in 3 that strengthens the model parameters directly instead of modifying the input. Given a clean input x and its corresponding adversarial version x_{adv}, a training routine $T(\cdot)$ updates the model parameters to make the model more resilient against adversarial perturbations. The defense strategy is evaluated according to the model-update objective (Eq. 8) and using accuracy-based metrics (Eq. 9).

Defense Objective: The defense objective is to improve the robustness of large language models against adversarial attacks by updating the model so that it correctly classifies both clean and adversarial inputs while maintaining high performance on legitimate data.

$$f_t^{\text{rob}} = T(f_t, x, x_{\text{adv}}) \tag{8}$$

Here, $T(\cdot)$ denotes the model-centric training routine such as adversarial training, gradient regularization, or smoothing-based optimization.

The effectiveness of the above defense model can be calculated using the formulae given in Eq. 9.

$$\begin{aligned} \text{Acc}_{\text{clean}} &= \frac{n_c}{n}, \quad \text{Acc}_{\text{adv}} &&= \frac{n_{\text{adv,undef}}}{n_{\text{adv}}}, \\ \text{Acc}_{\text{adv,def}} &= \frac{n_{\text{adv,def}}}{n_{\text{adv}}}, \quad \Delta\text{Acc} &&= \text{Acc}_{\text{adv,def}} - \text{Acc}_{\text{adv}} \end{aligned} \tag{9}$$

Where, n is the total number of test samples, n_c is number of correctly classified clean samples, n_{adv} is the number of adversarial samples evaluated, $n_{\text{adv,undef}}$ is the number correctly classified before defense. $n_{\text{adv,def}}$ is the number correctly classified after defense.

Algorithm 3. Model-Centric Defense

Require: Dataset D, target model f_t, training routine $T(\cdot)$, adversarial attack $A(\cdot)$, perturbation budget ε, sample size n
Ensure: Robust model f_t^{rob}, Clean Acc, Adv Acc, Defended Acc, ΔAcc

Select representative subset $S \subset D$ of size n
$c_{clean} \leftarrow 0,\ c_{adv} \leftarrow 0,\ c_{def} \leftarrow 0$
$f_t^{rob} \leftarrow f_t$
for each $(x, y) \in S$ **do**
  $x_{\text{adv}} \leftarrow A(x; \varepsilon)$ {generate adversarial example}
  $\hat{y}_{\text{adv}} \leftarrow f_t(x_{\text{adv}})$ {prediction before defense (contributes to Eq. 9)}
  if $\hat{y}_{\text{adv}} = y$ **then**
    $c_{adv} \leftarrow c_{adv} + 1$ {$n_{\text{adv,undef}}$ in Eq. 9}
  end if
  $f_t^{rob} \leftarrow T(f_t^{rob}, x, x_{\text{adv}})$ {model update using Eq. 8: $f_t^{rob} = T(f_t, x, x_{\text{adv}})$}
  $\hat{y}_{\text{def}} \leftarrow f_t^{rob}(x_{\text{adv}})$ {prediction after defense}
  if $\hat{y}_{\text{def}} = y$ **then**
    $c_{def} \leftarrow c_{def} + 1$ {$n_{\text{adv,def}}$ in Eq. 9}
  end if
end for
Compute metrics (Eq. 9):
  $\text{Acc}_{\text{clean}} = \frac{1}{|S|} \sum_{(x,y)\in S} \mathbf{1}\{f_t^{rob}(x) = y\}$
  $\text{Acc}_{\text{adv}} = \frac{c_{adv}}{|S|}\ \{= \frac{n_{\text{adv,undef}}}{n_{\text{adv}}}\}$
  $\text{Acc}_{\text{adv,def}} = \frac{c_{def}}{|S|}\ \{= \frac{n_{\text{adv,def}}}{n_{\text{adv}}}\}$
  $\Delta\text{Acc} = \text{Acc}_{\text{adv,def}} - \text{Acc}_{\text{adv}}$
return f_t^{rob}

4.5 Experimental Setup

The experiments are conducted on the Stanford Sentiment Treebank (SST-2) dataset[15], which contains 67,349 sentences labeled as *positive* or *negative*. SST-2 is used because it offers a controlled environment for evaluating perturbation sensitivity in a consistent manner. To obtain a representative subset, stratified random sampling was applied to preserve the original class distribution. A 98% confidence interval (Z = 2.326) and a 3% margin of error were used in the finite-population sample size formula.using Eq.10.

$$n = \frac{NZ^2 p(1-p)}{(N-1)E^2 + Z^2 p(1-p)} \tag{10}$$

$$p = \frac{\text{number of positive samples}}{N} \tag{11}$$

Where, N = population size, Z = z-score for confidence level, p= estimated proportion of positive samples, and E = desired absolute margin of error.

The resulting sample contained 1,339 records, with 55.75% positive and 44.25% negative instances for z= 2.3263 for 98% Confidence, and E=.03. Each sentiment label was treated as a stratum, and samples were randomly drawn without replacement using algorithm 4.

Algorithm 4. Stratified Random Sampling

```
Require: Dataset: D, Confidence Level: CL, Margin of Error: E
Ensure: Stratified sample S ⊂ D
Partition D into strata D_h based on label y
Compute proportion p (see Eq.(11))
Set Z corresponding to confidence level CL
Compute total sample size n (see Eq.(10))
for each stratum h do
    Compute stratum sample size n_h
    Randomly select n_h samples from D_h without replacement
end for
Merge all strata samples: S = ⋃_{h=1}^{k} S_h
return S
```

All experiments were executed on Google Colab using Python 3, with pandas, scikit learn, and transformers. Sampling was implemented using train_test_split() with the `stratify` parameter.

The BERT-based model `textattack/ bert-base-uncased-SST-2` [5] was used as the target sentiment classifier for validating sample representativeness and for later adversarial attack/defense experiments.

5 Results and Analysis

The accuracy comparison heatmap given in fig 2 highlights how different adversarial attacks impact model performance and how various defenses mitigate these effects. From the results, it is found that Transfer-based and query-based attacks caused notable drops, reducing accuracy from 96.60 to 45.00 and 16.00, respectively. Gradient-based and text-specific attacks are the most damaging and these lower the accuracy to nearly 5. Domain-specific (86.00) and optimization-based (77.06) attacks had comparatively milder effects.

The potency of gradient-based attacks are derived from their ability to optimize the perturbations and identifying the most sensitive direction in which a small perturbation can cause huge misclassifications, directly from the model's gradients. High dimensional neural networks being highly sensitive along specific directions, these calculated perturbations achieve maximal damage with minimal distortion. Similarly, text-specific attacks are damaging because these exploit subtle linguistic changes such as synonyms, paraphrases, or structure tweaks those look natural to humans but destabilize model predictions thereby bypassing simple defenses. White-box attacks, though theoretically potent, are largely impractical due to the need for full model access, whereas black-box attacks are more feasible in real world scenarios.

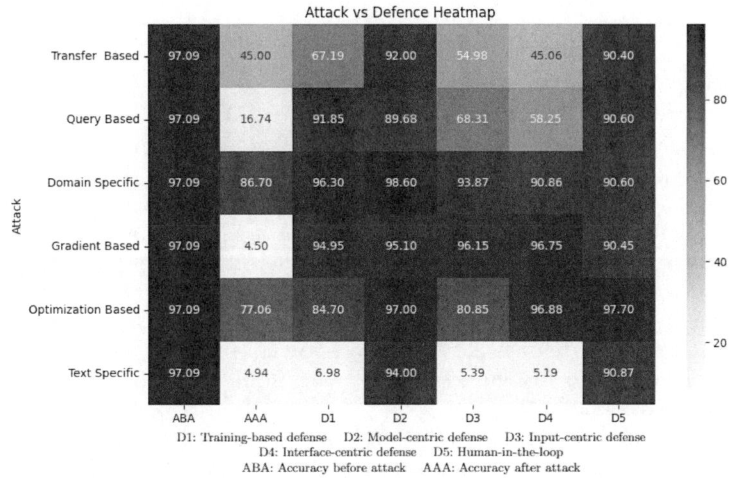

Fig. 2. Accuracy Comparison Heatmap.

Regarding defenses, model-centric strategies (D2) consistently restored accuracy above 90, peaking at 97.10 against gradient-based attacks. Human-in-the-loop mechanisms (D5) also provided strong resilience, while interface-centric defenses (D4) were particularly effective against optimization and gradient-based attacks. Training-based (D1) and input-centric (D3) methods offered only modest improvements.

In summary, the results emphasize upon the necessity of a layered, adaptive defense that combines algorithmic robustness with human oversight.

6 Conclusion

The effectiveness of different defense strategies and the varying impacts of adversarial attacks on LLMs are highlighted in this study. We acknowledge the narrow scope of SST-2 and recognize that broader, multi-task datasets are needed for comprehensive LLM evaluation. White-box attacks are strong but less useful for proprietary models; white and black-box attacks present realistic and hidden threats. Experimental data shows that the best resilience is provided by model-centric and human-in-the-loop defenses, which recover accuracy above 90 percent. The findings demonstrate how inadequate static defenses are in the face of dynamic attacks. Long term resilience in LLMs and reliability, scalability, and credibility in real world applications require adaptive, multi layered frameworks that integrate training-based hardening, inference time monitoring, and human supervision. in future research, we will implement the hybrid attacks and investigate multilingual and multi modal LLMs by tackling significant challenges, including cross-lingual robustness, modality alignment errors, dataset imbalance, and the heightened complexity of producing adaptive adversarial attacks across diverse languages and modalities.

References

1. Bai, Y., Wang, Y., Zeng, Y., Jiang, Y., Xia, S.T.: Query efficient black-box adversarial attack on deep neural networks. Pattern Recogn. **133**, 109037 (2023)
2. Bhagoji, A.N., He, W., Li, B., Song, D.: Exploring the space of black-box attacks on deep neural networks, (2017). arXiv preprint arXiv:1712.09491
3. Chen, S., Carlini, N., Wagner, D.: Stateful detection of black-box adversarial attacks. In: Proceedings of the 1st ACM Workshop on Security and Privacy on Artificial Intelligence, pp. 30–39. (2020)
4. Das, N., Raff, E., Chadha, A., Gaur, M.: Human-readable adversarial prompts: an investigation into llm vulnerabilities using situational context, (2024). arXiv preprint arXiv:2412.16359
5. Devlin, J., Chang, M.W., Lee, K., Toutanova, K.: Bert: Pre-training of deep bidirectional transformers for language understanding. In: Proceedings of the 2019 Conference of the North American Chapter of the Association for Computational Linguistics: Human Language Technologies, Volume 1 (Long and Short Papers). pp. 4171–4186. Association for Computational Linguistics (2019)
6. Ebrahimi, J., Rao, A., Lowd, D., Dou, D.: Hotflip: White-box adversarial examples for text classification, (2017). arXiv preprint arXiv:1712.06751
7. Guo, C., Gardner, J., You, Y., Wilson, A.G., Weinberger, K.: Simple black-box adversarial attacks. In: International conference on machine learning, pp. 2484–2493. PMLR (2019)
8. Kumar, A., Agarwal, C., Srinivas, S., Li, A.J., Feizi, S., Lakkaraju, H.: Certifying llm safety against adversarial prompting, (2023). arXiv preprint arXiv:2309.02705
9. Liu, H., Ge, Z., Zhou, Z., Shang, F., Liu, Y., Jiao, L.: Gradient correction for white-box adversarial attacks. IEEE Transactions on Neural Networks and Learning Systems (2023)
10. Loyola-Gonzalez, O.: Black-box vs. white-box: Understanding their advantages and weaknesses from a practical point of view. IEEE access **7**, 154096–154113 (2019)
11. Narodytska, N., Kasiviswanathan, S.P.: Simple black-box adversarial attacks on deep neural networks. In: CVPR workshops, vol. 2, (2017)
12. Raina, V., Liusie, A., Gales, M.: Is llm-as-a-judge robust? investigating universal adversarial attacks on zero-shot llm assessment, (2024). arXiv preprint arXiv:2402.14016
13. Schwinn, L., Dobre, D., Günnemann, S., Gidel, G.: Adversarial attacks and defenses in large language models: Old and new threats. In: Proceedings on, pp. 103–117. PMLR (2023)
14. Shayegani, E., Mamun, M.A.A., Fu, Y., Zaree, P., Dong, Y., Abu-Ghazaleh, N.: Survey of vulnerabilities in large language models revealed by adversarial attacks, (2023). arXiv preprint arXiv:2310.10844

15. Socher, R., Perelygin, A., Wu, J., Chuang, J., Manning, C.D., Ng, A., Potts, C.: Recursive deep models for semantic compositionality over a sentiment treebank. In: Proceedings of the 2013 Conference on Empirical Methods in Natural Language Processing. pp. 1631–1642. Association for Computational Linguistics, Seattle, Washington, USA (Oct 2013), https://www.aclweb.org/anthology/D13-1170
16. Wang, Y., Liu, J., Chang, X., Rodríguez, R.J., Wang, J.: Di-aa: An interpretable white-box attack for fooling deep neural networks. Inf. Sci. **610**, 14–32 (2022)
17. Xhonneux, S., Sordoni, A., Günnemann, S., Gidel, G., Schwinn, L.: Efficient adversarial training in llms with continuous attacks. Adv. Neural. Inf. Process. Syst. **37**, 1502–1530 (2024)
18. Yu, W., Hu, K., Pang, T., Du, C., Lin, M., Fredrikson, M.: Infecting llm agents via generalizable adversarial attack. In: Red Teaming GenAI: What Can We Learn from Adversaries?, (2025)
19. Zheng, M., Yan, X., Zhu, Z., Chen, H., Wu, B.: Blackboxbench: A comprehensive benchmark of black-box adversarial attacks. IEEE Trans. Pattern Anal. Mach. Intell., (2025)

Fed-NODE: Federated Learning Based Threat Detection Framework for Edge-Based Industrial Internet of Things

Avnish Ramvinay Singh and Govind P. Gupta(✉)

Department of Information Technology, National Institute of Technology Raipur, Raipur, India
avnish1708@gmail.com, gpgupta.it@nitrr.ac.in

Abstract. Safeguarding the Edge-based Industrial Internet of Things against emerging advanced persistent threats (APTs) has become progressively challenging nowadays. Despite the large quantity of distinct security solutions, most of the existing solutions suffer from low detection rate and data privacy issues. To overcome these issues, this paper proposed a novel Federated Learning based Advanced Persistent Threat Detection Framework, using Neural Oblivious Decision Ensembles (NODE) model, named as Fed-NODE, for Edge-based Industrial Internet of Things. In the proposed Fed-NODE framework, NODE is employed as local model to each client and FedAvg is used for aggregation of the local model parameters. The performance of the proposed Fed-NODE framework is evaluated in an IID (Identically and Independently Distributed) environment, and its results are compared with the four state-of-the-art frameworks using a realistic benchmark Edge-IIoT dataset. Performance analysis confirms the superiority of the proposed Fed-NODE framework with 98.79% accuracy, 98.55% precision, 97.83% recall, and 98.14% F1-score.

Keywords: Federated learning · Threat detection systems · Edge-IIoT · Edge-based distributed system

1 Introduction

The Edge-based Industrial Internet of Things (IIoT) is a distributed network system which facilitates the connection of all industrial smart devices for performing the collaborative operations, maintenance, and its managements. The rapid growth of IIoT devices significantly altered the cyber-security challenges with surface of the APT attacks, which traditional centralized security models cannot manage well [1]. Traditional cybersecurity measures rely on the collection of device data at central points for model training, which introduces latencies and critical privacy concerns, primarily because the collected network traffic

G. K. Verma et al. (Eds.): MIND 2025, CCIS 2981, pp. 272–283, 2027.
https://doi.org/10.1007/978-3-032-31230-3_22

information/dataset are frequently sensitive. The heterogeneous nature of IIoT systems, involving a variety of device types, communication schemes, and deployment environments, causes significant barriers for the formulation of monolithic security solutions.

The scale of today's networks, with billions of devices generating vast traffic data, increases the computing and storing requirements of the centralized models further, which makes them less suitable for real-time protection against threats [1]. Federated learning presents a potential solution to these problems by allowing model training from distributed devices in a decentralized way without exposing the data to the original devices it was collected from. This distributed approach enables numerous contributors to have a shared security model without exposing raw data, addressing privacy requirements and trust issues when there are multiple organizations involved. Recent developments in federated learning have seen success in many different fields, ranging from healthcare to finance, where preserving data privacy is paramount. But bringing federated learning to cybersecurity poses some special technical issues, such as dealing with imbalanced data distributions across different network segments, controlling communication expenses in environments with restricted Internet of Things resources, and maintaining model performance even when some of the participants can try to poison the learning process.

To solve the above-mentioned problems, this research work introduces a federated learning technique that is based on Neural Oblivious Decision Ensembles (NODE), which offers the representational capability of neural networks and interpretability of decision trees. Our suggested method also has automated feature selection functionality to detect key threat indicators from network traffic to allow efficient collaborative security model training while preserving data secrecy and ensuring good performance in heterogeneous network settings. The main contributions of this research work are outlined as follows:

1. A novel Federated Learning based Threat Detection Framework is proposed in which NODE is employed as a local model for each client and FedAvg method is used for aggregation of the model parameters at the global server.
2. The proposed framework offers the representational capability of neural networks and interpretability of decision trees which offers good performance in heterogeneous network settings.
3. Performance of the proposed Fed-NODE framework are evaluated and compared with latest state-of-the-art models using a realistic benchmark Edge-IIoT dataset.

The structure of the remaining part of the manuscript is presented as follows: Sect. 2 reviews the related literature on threat detection models. Section 3 outlines the proposed framework, Fed-NODE. In Sect. 4, a detailed result analysis and performance comparisons are discussed. Finally, in Sect. 5, this paper draws conclusions from the proposed study.

2 Related Works

The application of federated learning for intrusion detection systems has been gaining speed in many IoT environments. Friha et al. [9] put forward FELIDS for IoT farm environments using collaborative attack detection with protection for data confidentiality through local training of models and global aggregation. Their suggestion, however, had the assumption of balanced distributive data for cooperative nodes, which may not occur practically. Concurrently, Sarhan et al. [16] introduced HBFL as a hierarchical blockchain-based framework for federated learning, which ensures model integrity through the use of smart contracts and immutable ledgers, but this involves significant computational overhead and scaling problems due to the intrinsic limitations of blockchain. From cyber threat intelligence sharing, Sarhan et al. [15] presented a framework for federated learning for facilitating network intrusion detection by collaboratively working among organizations without data exchange. Their framework used the features of NetFlow and demonstrated applicability for disparate network environments but relied upon centralized administration as a likely bottleneck as well as single points of failure.

Javeed et al. [10] proposed a zero-trust federated learning framework for IoT intrusion detection by combining multi-layer authentication schemes with distributed learning. Bhavsar et al. [3] aimed at transport IoT, constructing the edge-based FL-IDS for lowering the communication overhead and increasing real-time responsiveness. Their research illustrated the practicable applicability but did not incorporate model poisoning attacks and adverse situations. Vyas et al. [17] gave a detailed overview of the privacy-preserving federated learning for IoT intrusion detection, outlining significant challenges such as the implementation of differential privacy, secure aggregation schemes, as well as protection from adverse attacks. Jeyakumar et al. [11] proposed a unique hybrid deep learning framework consisting of Stacked CNN and Bi-LSTM in a federated framework for the wireless sensor network to attain higher detection rates with data privacy. Kaur et al. [12] suggested a deep recurrent reinforcement learning model for industrial IoT traffic by combining federated learning with a smart client selection for the effective usage of resources and detection rates (Table 1).

Recent research in 2025 concentrated on data quality and state-of-the-art architecture. Bouzeraib et al. [4] increased IoT intrusion detection using horizontal federated learning with optimized WGAN-GP for solving data imbalance problems, although the generation of the synthetic data may also trigger privacy leakage vulnerabilities. Devi et al. [5] presented a lightweight DDoS attack-detection-based federated learning framework for smart cities, with a focus on computational efficiency for resource-limited wireless sensor networks. Manzano et al. [13] introduced a holistic framework combining distributed storage and diffusion models with federated learning, with the goals of achieving better scalability and fault tolerance for IoT intrusion detection. Despite all these developments, the following issues persist to ensure robustness against sophisticated adversarial attacks, and how to attain cost-effective deployment plans for

Table 1. Comparative Analysis of the Related works

Reference	Year	Dataset	Proposed Method	Acc. (%)
Friha et al. [9]	2022	CSECICIDS2018	CNN	94.24
		MQTTset	CNN	90.76
		InSDN	DNN	98.54
Sarhan et al. [16]	2022	NF-BoT-IoT-v2	Deep Feed Forward (DFF)	99.7
Sarhan et al. [15]	2023	NF-BoT-IoT-v2	Federated LSTM	92.57
Javeed et al. [10]	2024	CICIDS2017	Bi-LSTM and CNN	99.99
		Edge-IIoTset		99.99
Bhavsar et al. [3]	2024	NSL-KDD	CNN-Federated	97.08
		Car hacking dataset		99.92
Jeyakumar et al. [11]	2024	WSN-DS Dataset	FL-SCNN-Bi-LSTM-AVOA	99.65
Kaur et al. [12]	2024	TON IoT	GRU-Assisted Federated Deep RRL	99.95
Bouzeraib et al. [4]	2025	UNSW-NB15	FedGAGAN (FL + GA + WGAN-GP)	99
Devi et al. [5]	2025	TON-IoT	Lightweight Hybrid (CNN+LSTM)	91
Manzano et al. [13]	2025	BoT-IoT	Peer to Peer FL	99

achieving security, privacy, and performance requirements for real-world federated scenarios.

3 Proposed Fed-NODE Framework

In this section, we introduce the federated learning framework for Edge-based IIoT security threat detection with Neural Oblivious Decision Ensembles (NODE). The proposed method tackles the major challenges in IIoT security such as data privacy, computational limitations, and the requirement of interpretable threats across heterogeneous environments.

3.1 Data Preprocessing and Distribution

The proposed method used the Edge-IIoT dataset, which holds rich IIoT network traffic records of diverse attack behaviors and normal actions. The preprocessing process starts with feature normalization and encoding of categorical data to maintain uniform data representation across clients. The target feature 'attack-types' are label encoded and create a balanced multi-class classification problem suitable for federated learning environments. To simulate realistic federated IIoT environments, stratified data partitioning is employed that maintains class distribution across participating clients. This ensures each client receives representative samples of all attack types for their training. This sampling strategy creates an IID (identically and independently distributed) environment.

3.2 Federated Learning Framework

As seen in Fig. 1, the proposed methodology uses a centralized server to orchestrate the learning process across decentralized IIoT clients. This ensures privacy by keeping the sensitive IIoT data on local client devices and only the weights are shared between client devices and central server. This works in three steps: a) the server sends the initial weights of the model to all the available clients, b) the client device trains their local model on their local data, then forward their local model weights to the server, c) the server receives the weights from all available clients and aggregate them using federated averaging strategy and forwards the aggregated weight to all the available clients and at the same time, the server validates the performance of the aggregated model using held out test set on the global server. These three steps repeat for designated number of communication rounds.

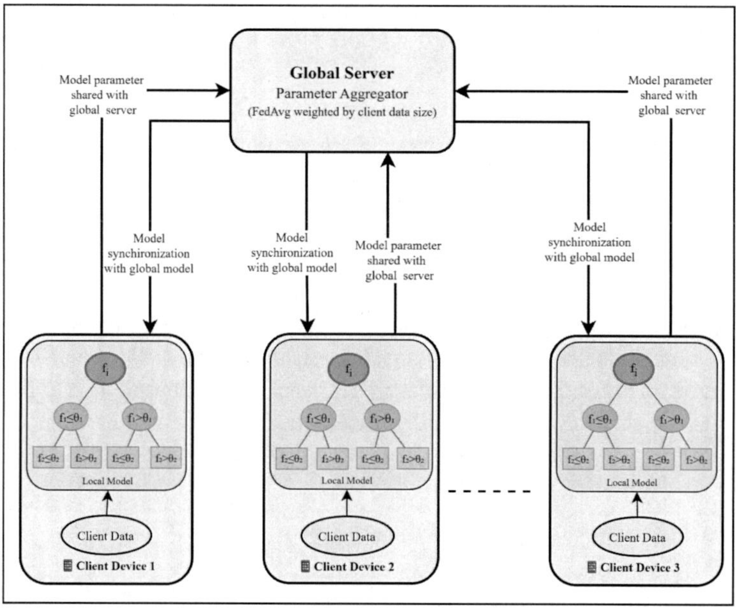

Fig. 1. Federated Learning Architecture.

3.3 Model Architecture

In this proposed methodology, we utilize a NODE [14] model as a base classifier, it is an architecture that merges the hierarchical structure of decision trees with the representational learning capabilities of deep neural networks. The model consists of an ensemble of decision trees, where each tree can learn to select different features at each depth, allowing it to discover diverse and complex patterns within IoT security data. An important component of this architecture is its initial sparse feature selection mechanism using Entmax (entmax_α), which automatically identifies and prioritize the most critical features.

$$\hat{\mathbf{y}}(x) = \mathbf{b} + \frac{1}{T}\sum_{t=1}^{T}\sum_{l=1}^{2^D}\left[\prod_{d=1}^{D}\sigma_{t,d}^{b_{l,d}}(x)\left(1-\sigma_{t,d}(x)\right)^{1-b_{l,d}}\right]\mathbf{e}_{t,l} \tag{1}$$

where $\sigma_{t,d}(x) = \sigma\Big(\gamma\Big[\sum_j \text{entmax}_\alpha(\mathbf{w}_{t,d})_j x_j - \tau_{t,d}\Big]\Big)$ is the soft routing function at depth d of tree t; $b_{l,d} \in \{0,1\}$ encodes the binary split direction on the path to leaf l; $\mathbf{e}_{t,l}$ denotes the learnable embedding associated with leaf l of tree t; T is the number of trees, D is the tree depth, γ is the temperature parameter controlling gate sharpness, $\tau_{t,d}$ is the learned threshold for split (t,d), and entmax_α is the α-entmax transformation used to produce sparse feature weights.

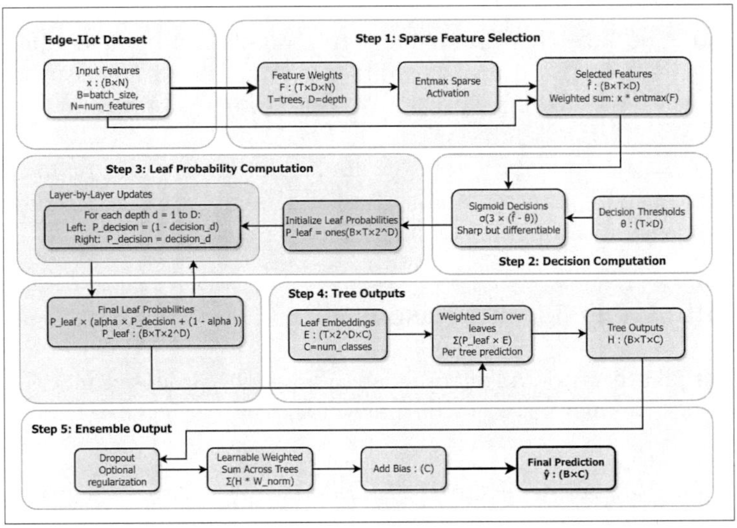

Fig. 2. Architecture of the NODE [14] Classifier Pipeline.

Following the feature selection, the model performs a fully differential traversal. Instead of making hard, discrete splits, it computes soft decision by comparing the selected features against a set of learnable thresholds using sigmoid function. This process generates a probabilistic path through each tree, resulting in probability distribution over all possible leaf nodes for a given input. Each leaf is represented not by a class label but by a learnable embedding vector. The final prediction for each tree is a weighted sum of these leaf embeddings guided by the computed leaf probabilities. To aggregate the outputs of the entire ensemble, the model employs a learnable weighted sum of the individual tree predictions allowing it to dynamically assign more importance to better performing trees. This end-to-end differentiable design is what makes NODE architecture compatible with the gradient-based optimization essential for generalization (Fig. 2).

3.4 Evaluation Strategy

The framework utilizes a holistic methodology concentrated solely on machine learning performance metrics to measure the efficiency of the federated learning architecture. A centralized test dataset, which the global server keeps track of, is utilized to establish consistent and unbiased evaluation of the global model's capability to generalize across the varying IoT environments. This dataset is designed carefully to mimic a diverse set of threat situations and device activity typically present in IoT networks. By maintaining dependence on a shared test set, the assessment prevents inconsistent issues that can occur due to non-IID data at individual clients, thus providing an unbiased measurement of model accuracy. The assessment uses classification metrics, which are accuracy, precision, recall, and F1-score, ROC-AUC and PR-AUC, which provide a comprehensive picture of the ability of the model to properly identify and label security threats. Metrics are pivotal in measuring the compromises between false positives, false negatives, and global predictive accuracy in the context of IoT security which can be seen in the confusion matrix Fig. 5.

This framework presents a solution for federated learning in IoT security threat detection with interpretability by the ensemble decision structure and privacy preservation through distributed training mechanisms.

4 Result Analysis and Discussions

This section presents a detailed result analysis of the proposed model and performs comparative analysis with the state-of-the-art methods.

4.1 Description of the Edge-IIoT Dataset

In this study, we have utilized a trimmed version of the publicly downloadable Edge-IIoTset dataset in this proposed method to assess the performance of the developed intrusion detection framework. The Edge-IIoTset [14] dataset is a realistic cybersecurity dataset constructed over a seven-layer testbed that mimics real IoT and Industrial IoT (IIoT) scenarios. It comprises network traffic data labelled into 15 different classes that cover various types of cyber-attacks, and hence it is well-suited for multiclass classification experiments. There are 62 attributes for each data record of the dataset: 61 input features and 1 target label. In this paper, we use a pre-processed and trimmed version of the dataset that comprises 322,683 total records [8]. The data are divided into two sets: 291,285 samples (approximately 90%) for training and 31,398 samples (approximately 10%) for testing. The trimmed version is well-suited for effective experimentation without compromising diversity and richness of real attack scenarios.

4.2 Description of the Experiment Settings

For the experimental setup, we simulate federated learning with varying number of distributed clients to assess scalability, with a server orchestrating a fixed number of communication rounds. During each round, all available clients are involved in training and evaluation. After each round, client updates are aggregated using a Federated Averaging (FedAvg) strategy, and the resulting global model is validated centrally on a held-out test set. The experiments were performed on a high-performance workstation platform equipped with an Intel(R) Xeon(R) W-2175 CPU @ 2.50 GHz, 128 GB RAM, and an NVIDIA Quadro P4000 GPU providing 8 GB dedicated memory. This equipment effectively allowed the simulation of multiple distributed clients simultaneously for effective federated learning setup. The model neural oblivious decision ensemble was first tuned to find the best hyperparameters and then these parameters were utilized in federated setup. The hyperparameter for models and also parameter for the federated simulation is mentioned in Table 2.

Table 2. Hyperparameter Configuration

Parameter	Value	Description
num-server-rounds	10	Total number of global aggregation rounds.
fraction-fit	1 [ALL]	Fraction of clients participating in training.
fraction-eval	1 [ALL]	Fraction of clients participating in evaluation.
local-epochs	30	Training epochs on each client per round.
learning-rate	0.0095	Optimizer learning rate.
num_trees	12	Number of decision trees in the NODE ensemble.
depth	8	Maximum depth of each decision tree.
alpha	1.55	Entmax parameter for sparse feature selection.
dropout	0.075	Dropout rate for regularization.
use_bias	False	Whether to use bias terms in the model.

4.3 Performance Evaluation of the Proposed Framework

The proposed federated intrusion detection system was evaluated using a centralized test set after each round of federated aggregation. The performance was validated using standard multiclass classification metrics: accuracy, precision, recall, f1-score, roc-auc and pr-auc. Figure 3 shows that both train and validation losses drop sharply in the first few rounds and then stabilize, indicating convergence. By round 4, the curves plateau with only minor fluctuations so further round yield very few improvements. The validation loss remains slightly below the training loss without upward drift, evidencing no overfitting and stable generalization under FedAvg.

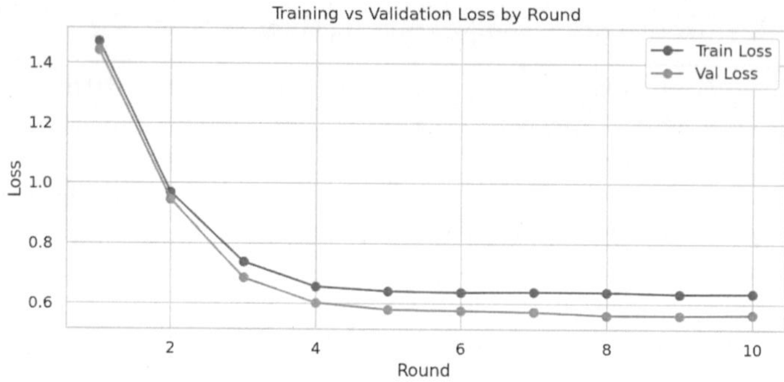

Fig. 3. Train vs validation loss on one client in client 10 run.

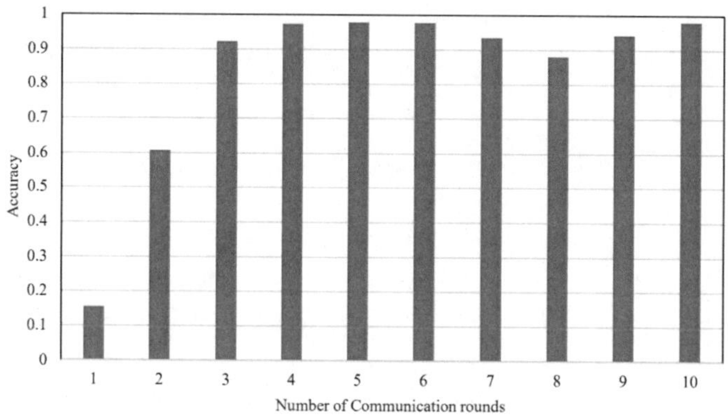

Fig. 4. Testing accuracy of test set over 10 rounds on server.

In Fig. 4, we can see the accuracy for evaluation set, which shows model starts predicting the classes correctly after fifth round, the accuracy does fall in round 9 but it improves over the next round which shows the effect of varying data over the rounds. Table 3 presents the global model's overall performance across four different federated configurations, using 3, 5, 7, and 10 clients respectively over 10 communication rounds. The model worked efficiently with high classification accuracy in all the attack scenarios, with accuracy values always above 97%, also precision, recall, and f1-score values were also always high, showing the model's reliability in detecting various types of cyberattacks.

Apart from these results, Fig. 5 shows the class wise confusion matrix for the final round evaluation on the server, which confirms that the federated learning approach generalizes over different class threat types and is able to differentiate between them. In the Figure 6, Plot of the ROC-AUC and PR-AUC are illustrated by varying the rounds. This figure shows that aggregated model is able to learn the patterns of different classes. These results confirm that the federated learning model generalizes not only across different client environments but is also effective in detection against a large set of threat types.

Table 3. Performance analysis of the proposed framework by varying number of clients

Number of Clients	Accuracy	Precision	Recall	F1-score	ROC-AUC	PR-AUC
3	0.9879	0.9855	0.9783	0.9814	0.9995	0.9902
5	0.9799	0.979	0.9798	0.979	0.9997	0.9965
7	0.9845	0.9837	0.9843	0.9838	0.999	0.9907
10	0.9799	0.9747	0.9952	0.9767	0.9998	0.9974

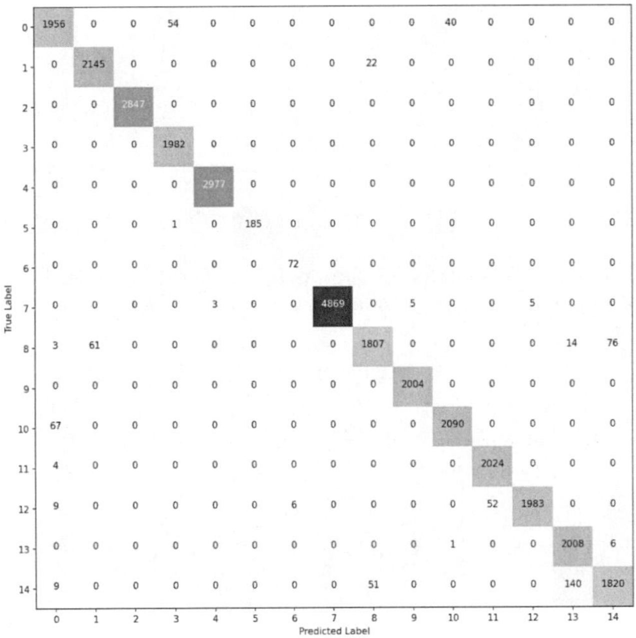

Fig. 5. Confusion matrix for the final evaluation of 10 clients.

Table 4 lists the performance comparison of the proposed Fed-NODE model with four SOTA models evaluated on Edge-IIoT. It is observed from Table 4 that the proposed Fed-NODE model outperformed against the existing SOTA models. This is due to fact that generalization ability of the proposed model is better that existing SOTA models and it does not suffer from overfitting issue.

5 Conclusion

This paper proposed a novel Federated Learning based Advanced Persistent Threat Detection Framework, using Neural Oblivious Decision Ensembles (NODE) model, named as Fed-NODE, for Edge-based Industrial Internet of Things. In the Fed-NODE framework, NODE is employed as local model to each client and FedAvg is used for aggregation of the local model parameters.

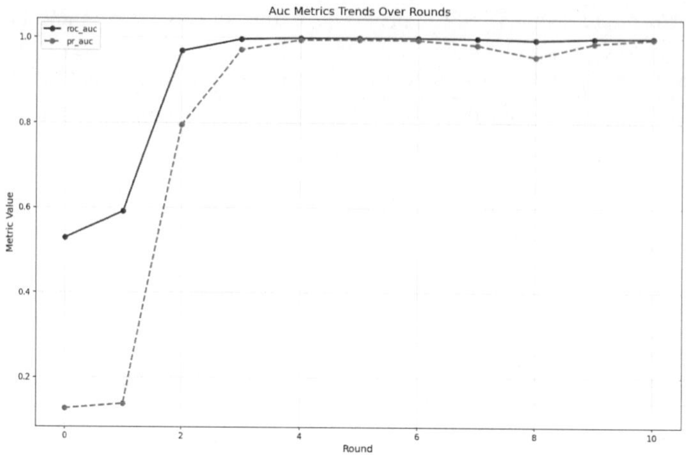

Fig. 6. Plot for ROC-AUC and PR-AUC over 10 rounds.

Table 4. Performance Comparison of the proposed model with SOTA methods with Edge-IIoT dataset under same experimental scenario

Model	Accuracy	Precision	Recall	F1-score
DNN [8]	0.9467	0.6921	0.7220	0.6828
AdaBoost [6]	0.8945	0.7450	0.7929	0.7482
CNN + LSTM [2]	0.8700	0.8415	0.8800	0.8608
LSTM + GRU [7]	0.9496	0.9540	0.9522	0.9531
Proposed Fed-NODE	**0.9977**	**0.9978**	**0.9977**	**0.9977**

The performance of the proposed Fed-NODE framework is evaluated in an IID (identically and independently distributed) environment, and its results are compared with the three state-of-the-art frameworks using a realistic benchmark Edge-IIoT dataset. Performance analysis confirms the superiority of the proposed Fed-NODE framework with 98.79% accuracy, 98.55% precision, 97.83% recall, and 98.14% F1-score. In the future work, we will explore the robustness of the proposed model under the non-IID settings.

Acknowledgments. This research was supported by the C3iHub (IHUB NTIHAC FOUNDATION, IIT Kanpur) Project (Project Reference No.: IHUB-NTIHAC/2024/01/13 and Proposal #: 3077), which is funded by Department of Science and Technology (DST), Government of India.

References

1. Ahmed, M., Mahmood, A.N., Hu, J.: A survey of network anomaly detection techniques. J. Netw. Comput. Appl. **60**, 19–31 (2016)
2. Alkahtani, H., Aldhyani, T.H.: Botnet attack detection by using CNN-LSTM model for internet of things applications. Secur. Commun. Networks **2021**(1), 3806459 (2021)
3. Bhavsar, M.H., Bekele, Y.B., Roy, K., Kelly, J.C., Limbrick, D.: FL-IDS: federated learning-based intrusion detection system using edge devices for transportation IoT. IEEE Access **12**, 52215–52226 (2024)
4. Bouzeraib, W., Ghenai, A., Zeghib, N.: Enhancing IoT intrusion detection systems through horizontal federated learning and optimized WGAN-GP. IEEE Access (2025)
5. Devi, M., Nandal, P., Sehrawat, H.: Federated learning-enabled lightweight intrusion detection system for wireless sensor networks: a cybersecurity approach against DDoS attacks in smart city environments. Intell. Syst. Appl., 200553 (2025)
6. Dey, A.K., Gupta, G.P., Sahu, S.P.: A metaheuristic-based ensemble feature selection framework for cyber threat detection in IoT-enabled networks. Decis. Anal. J. **7**, 100206 (2023)
7. Ding, W., Abdel-Basset, M., Mohamed, R.: Deepak-IoT: an effective deep learning model for cyberattack detection in IoT networks. Inf. Sci. **634**, 157–171 (2023)
8. Ferrag, M.A., Friha, O., Hamouda, D., Maglaras, L., Janicke, H.: Edge-IIoTset: a new comprehensive realistic cyber security dataset of IoT and IIoT applications for centralized and federated learning. IEEE Access **10**, 40281–40306 (2022)
9. Friha, O., Ferrag, M.A., Shu, L., Maglaras, L., Choo, K.K.R., Nafaa, M.: FELIDS: federated learning-based intrusion detection system for agricultural internet of things. J. Parall. Distrib. Comput. **165**, 17–31 (2022)
10. Javeed, D., Saeed, M.S., Adil, M., Kumar, P., Jolfaei, A.: A federated learning-based zero trust intrusion detection system for internet of things. Ad Hoc Netw. **162**, 103540 (2024)
11. Jeyakumar, S.R., et al.: An innovative secure and privacy-preserving federated learning-based hybrid deep learning model for intrusion detection in internet-enabled wireless sensor networks. IEEE Trans. Consum. Electron. **71**(1), 273–280 (2024)
12. Kaur, A.: Intrusion detection approach for industrial internet of things traffic using deep recurrent reinforcement learning assisted federated learning. IEEE Trans. Artif. Intell. (2024)
13. Manzano, R., Zaman, M., Upadhyay, D., Goel, N., Sampalli, S.: Federated learning framework based on distributed storage and diffusion model for intrusion detection on IoT networks. IEEE Access (2025)
14. Popov, S., Morozov, S., Babenko, A.: Neural oblivious decision ensembles for deep learning on tabular data (2019). arXiv preprint arXiv:1909.06312
15. Sarhan, M., Layeghy, S., Moustafa, N., Portmann, M.: Cyber threat intelligence sharing scheme based on federated learning for network intrusion detection. J. Netw. Syst. Manage. **31**(1), 3 (2023)
16. Sarhan, M., Lo, W.W., Layeghy, S., Portmann, M.: HBFL: a hierarchical blockchain-based federated learning framework for collaborative IoT intrusion detection. Comput. Electr. Eng. **103**, 108379 (2022)
17. Vyas, A., Lin, P.C., Hwang, R.H., Tripathi, M.: Privacy-preserving federated learning for intrusion detection in IoT environments: a survey. IEEE Access (2024)

SWIM-Conv-FFT: A Dual-Domain Hybrid Framework for Robust Deepfake Detection Across Social Media Platforms

Swapnil Siddhartha(✉) and Pratishtha Verma

National Institute of Technology, Kurukshetra 136119, India
{324103117,pratishthaverma}@nitkkr.ac.in

Abstract. The continuous upgradation in generative models such as Generative Adversarial Networks (GANs) and diffusion architectures has resulted in the production of really convincing deepfakes, which threaten media authenticity, privacy, and security. When these malicious materials are used, they cause misinformation, create trust issues, and harm social media credit. Therefore, the development of effective detection systems has become an important field of research. However, existing CNN- and transformer-based methods suffer from limited cross-dataset generalization, are computationally costly, and have poor sensitivity to subtle manipulation artifacts. This paper introduces SWIMConvFFT, a hybrid deepfake detection framework combining the Shifted Window Integrated Module (SWIM) attention mechanism with convolutional feature extraction and a Fast Fourier Transform (FFT)-based frequency branch to address these issues. The proposed tri-branch model performs globallocal feature fusion across the spatial and spectral domains, thus enhancing robustness against compression, illumination changes, and new fake-generation techniques. Experiments are performed on the WildRF dataset, consisting of real and manipulated facial images from Facebook, Reddit, and Twitter at different compression levels and resolutions. The results indicate that SWIM-Conv-FFT is better than the current convolutional neural network, transformer, and hybrid baselines in accuracy, precision, and generalization ability. Overall, the system can only lead to a strong, interpretable, and computationally efficient deepfakes detecting system that can be applied to practical contexts and further cross-platform implementations.

Keywords: Deepfake Detection · Swin Transformer · Frequency Domain Analysis · Convolutional Neural Networks · Hybrid Feature Fusion

1 Introduction

One of the breakthroughs in generative artificial intelligence (AI) technologies over the last few years has been the emergence of models such as Generative

G. K. Verma et al. (Eds.): MIND 2025, CCIS 2981, pp. 284–295, 2027.
https://doi.org/10.1007/978-3-032-31230-3_23

Adversarial Networks (GANs) and diffusion-based architecture. They have practically transformed the way content is created as they tend to create synthetic human faces and videos that appear indistinguishable from real ones. These models can be used in digital entertainment, media production, and education, among other fields; however, the use of these models has led to the emergence of deepfakes that cause many problems, like the spread of misinformation, manipulation of opinions, and violation of privacy and even security in the digital ecosystem [1]. The increasing sophistication of these manipulated contents makes it hard to tell whether a video or image that is visually forged is real or fake; thus, the need for reliable and generalizable detection frameworks has become very pressing [2].

Deepfake detection models usually rely on convolutional neural networks (CNNs), such as Xception, DenseNet, and ResNet, which have been proven to yield good results in the intra-dataset evaluations but are unable to provide robust results in the cross-dataset or unseen manipulation scenarios due to overfitting and absence of frequency-domain awareness [1]. To enhance the generalization, transformer-based models like Swin and Vision Transformers (ViT) have been tested because of their capacity to capture the global semantic relationships and hierarchical spatial dependencies. Nevertheless, these often fail to capture the localized inconsistencies as well as the subtle pixel-level artifacts, which are necessary for deepfake discrimination [3]. On top of that, although frequency-domain analysis techniques that utilize Fast Fourier Transform (FFT) can pinpoint the spectral areas that are distorted due to GAN-based synthesis, they typically carry the important contextual information when viewed separately [4] [5] [6].

To see these limitations, this research proposes SWIM-Conv-FFT, which is a dual-domain hybrid deepfake detection framework jointly captures spatially and spectrally representing interactions in a highly efficient manner. The system has the Shifted Window Integrated Module (SWIM), which helps in the learning of localized attention merged with a convolutional backbone for the extraction of the hierarchical spatial features and an FFT-based frequency branch to record the spectral manipulation-induced irregularities. Through adaptive feature fusion, SWIM-Conv-FFT is better at handling the forgeries that it has never seen before and variations across the platforms. Experimental results from the WildRF dataset, which contains samples from Facebook, Reddit, and Twitter, corroborate the superior generalization and accuracy of the proposed model over the recent CNN and transformer-based baselines, thereby making it not only an effective solution but also an interpretable one for deepfake detection in real-world scenarios.

The rest of this paper is structured as follows. Section 2 discusses the realted works of spatial, transformer-based, and frequency-aware deepfake detection methods. Section 3 goes into detail about the SWIMConvFFT architecture with the three branches for spatial, contextual, and spectral feature extraction and describes the WildRF dataset and the experimental setup used for training and evaluation. Section 4 results the findings and discusses the performance of the proposed model across Facebook, Reddit, and Twitter platforms. Finally, Sect. 5 summarizes the paper and outlines potential future research directions.

2 Related Works

Most of the research on deepfake detection has been about creating such methods that can resist different types of manipulations and also be applicable to manipulations that have not been seen before. Initial works were mainly focused on the usage of Convolutional Neural Networks (CNNs) like Xception, DenseNet, and EfficientNet, which showed high accuracy on intra-dataset evaluations. These models tried to locate local spatial inconsistencies in faces or even in whole images as a way to separate real from fake. But, as it turned out, CNN-based techniques were not very successful in cross-dataset generalization, i.e., they were mostly overfitted and relied on dataset-specific biases [7]. To address these issues, the researchers started looking into transformer architectures, which were initially a concept in the area of natural language processing and were known for their self-attention mechanisms that could handle long-range dependencies. The Swin Transformer, especially, was referred to a standard deep learning model for image-level forgery detection by most of the community because of its shifted window attention and hierarchical feature representation that not only bring the accuracy up but also reduce the computational cost [8].

Follow-up experiments explored hybrid CNNTransformer models that use localized spatial extraction from CNNs and global semantic reasoning from transformers. As an example, SwinConvNeXt architectures were able to achieve enhanced feature diversity and higher resistance to new types of manipulation [9]. However, purely spatial models are still unable to capture very faint manipulation cues that occur in the frequency domain. Therefore, recent publications have included spectral analysis techniques like Fast Fourier Transform (FFT) and Discrete Wavelet Transform (DWT) to reveal the adversarial patterns and the periodic distortions that have been introduced during the generative synthesis process [10]. Although frequency-based methods may shed light on such spectral irregularities, they do not have spatial localization and are quite sensitive to compression artifacts, illumination changes, and post-processing noise. The most recent frequency-sensitive deep-fake detectors have shown strong generalisation in terms of hitherto unseen generative models. Recently, [15] published FreqNet, a network in the frequency domain that uses Fourier transforms and inverse Fourier transforms to both raw images and intermediate convolutional feature maps to capture artefacts of manipulation that can be observed in spectral representations. FreqNet achieves the state-of-the-art cross-model accuracy of 92.8 % (mean) using 1.9 million parameters across seventeen different GAN architectures, which highlights the effectiveness of spectral feature learning in making practical deep-fake detections. [11] evidenced the advantages of frequency-aware learning; [12] researched the comparison of CNNs and transformers for deepfake detection; and [13] used self-blended, frequency-enhanced representations. Besides that, [14] summarized the critical future milestones in multimodal deepfake detection research.

The present work was motivated by these shortcomings in that field, and its main goal is to create a hybrid detection model that would leverage the advantages of both the spatial and frequency domains to achieve high cross-platform robustness and generalization. The hybrid structure model SWIM-Conv-FFT is equipped with a Shifted Window Integration Module (SWIM) for spatial focus learning, a convolutional backbone for hierarchical feature extraction, and an FFT-based branch to detect spectral inconsistencies. Combining complementary spatial and contextual and frequency-domain properties by means of adaptive fusion, fine local textures and high-frequency artifacts can be evaluated by the system, attaining high-quality and understandable deepfake detection on authentic social-media content of Facebook, Reddit and Twitter, introduced in WildRF dataset [16]. Thus, the proposed model addresses limitations of prior CNN-, transformer-, and hybrid-only methods. Moreover, these studies point out that models need to be not only strong but also capable of generalizing in the deepfake detection field. Rana et al. [17] offer a detailed survey that outlines the major trends and the limitations of the methods involved in detection, whereas Dolhansky et al. citeb28 present the extensive DFDC dataset, which is now widely used as a reference for checking detector robustness. The authors in these papers, therefore, take us further to the models' reliable performance that can be tested in different scenarios of the real world.

3 Methodology

3.1 Dataset Description and Experimental Enviornment

This work is a presentation of the WildRF dataset, where the authentic and synthetic images were collected through three major social media platforms, Facebook, Reddit, and Twitter. The total number of images collected is 5,354, which is organized systematically into training, validation and platform-specific test sets.

Training set: 1,357 real images and 1,356 fake images have been recruited.

Validation set: The validation group comprises 199 real images and the same number of fabricated images.

Test sets (platform-specific): Facebook: 160 real, 160 fake, Reddit: 751 real, 751 fake, Twitter: 144 real, 277 fake.

Each image was rescaled to 224×224, and normalization was performed using ImageNet statistics. Real images were taken from publicly available user posts on each platform. The dataset was split into a 70%/15%/15% train–val–test ratio per platform. It will be available to the research community upon request. The model was trained on the combined training set (1357 real, 1356 fake) and evaluated separately on the test sets for Facebook, Reddit, and Twitter to assess cross-platform robustness.

Experimentation and testing were done using an NVIDIA RTX A6000 GPU (48 GB) with PyTorch 2.2. Adam optimizer (learning rate = 1×10^{-4}, weight decay = 1×10^{-5}) and Binary Cross-Entropy (BCE) loss were used. Mixed-precision training and early stopping were also there to help the process become more stable and efficient.

Algorithm 1. SWIM–Conv–FFT

Require: Image I (RGB, 224×224), mode $\in$ {train, infer}, (optional) label y
Ensure: Probability $\hat{p}$ (and, if train, updated params)
Preprocess: resize/normalize I; grayscale+FFT log-magnitude $\rightarrow M$
Branches: $f_{\text{conv}} \leftarrow \text{ConvNeXtTiny}(I)$; $f_{\text{swin}} \leftarrow \text{SwinTiny}(I)$; $f_{\text{fft}} \leftarrow \text{FFTEncoder}(M)$
Fuse: $f \leftarrow \text{concat}(f_{\text{conv}}, f_{\text{swin}}, f_{\text{fft}})$
Head: $z \leftarrow \text{ReLU}(\text{FC}_1(f))$;
if mode = train **then**
    $z \leftarrow \text{Dropout}(z)$
end if
$\hat{p} \leftarrow \sigma(\text{FC}_2(z))$
if mode = train **then**
    $\mathcal{L} \leftarrow \text{BCE}(\hat{p}, y)$; **backprop + Adam step** ($\text{lr} = 10^{-4}$, $\text{wd} = 10^{-5}$)
    early stopping on validation
else
    decision: classify as Fake if $\hat{p} \geq 0.5$, else Real
end if
return $\hat{p}$ (and $\hat{y}$ in inference)

3.2 Hybrid Framework

The SWIM-Conv-FFT model is a tri-branch hybrid deepfake detection framework that extracts complementary information from three domains—spatial, contextual, and frequency. As illustrated in Fig. 1, the RGB image $X \in \mathbb{R}^{224\times224\times3}$ and its FFT log-magnitude map $M \in \mathbb{R}^{224\times224\times1}$ are processed in parallel by three distinct backbones: ConvNeXt-Tiny, Swin Transformer-Tiny, and a custom FFT Encoder.
Each branch produces an embedding as output:

$$\begin{aligned} f_{\text{conv}} &= \text{GAP}(\text{ConvNeXt}(X)), \\ f_{\text{swin}} &= \text{GAP}(\text{Swin}(X)), \\ f_{\text{fft}} &= \text{GAP}(\text{FFTEncoder}(M)). \end{aligned}$$

The unified feature representation is then defined as:

$$F = [\, f_{\text{conv}} \,\|\, f_{\text{swin}} \,\|\, f_{\text{fft}} \,].$$

The fused representation F is passed through a two-layer fully connected classifier to predict whether an image is real or fake. The model is trained end-to-end, enabling gradient flow across all branches and allowing it to learn complementary cues across spatial, contextual, and frequency domains.

3.3 Mathematical Notations

The key symbols and parameters used in the proposed SWIM–Conv–FFT framework are summarized in Table 1. These notations are consistently used throughout Algorithm 1 and subsequent sections.

Table 1. Mathematical Notations Used in SWIM–Conv–FFT Framework

Symbol	Description
I	Input image (RGB) $\in \mathbb{R}^{224\times224\times3}$
M	Log-magnitude of 2D FFT of grayscale image I
f_{conv}	Spatial features extracted by ConvNeXt-Tiny branch
f_{swin}	Contextual features from Swin Transformer (SWIM) branch
f_{fft}	Frequency-domain features from FFT encoder
f	Fused feature vector $[f_{\text{conv}} \parallel f_{\text{swin}} \parallel f_{\text{fft}}]$
z	Hidden feature after FC_1 and ReLU activation
$\hat{p}$	Predicted probability of the image being *fake*
$\hat{y}$	Final binary decision label (1 = Fake, 0 = Real)
y	Ground truth label (1 = Fake, 0 = Real)
$\mathcal{L}$	Binary Cross-Entropy loss $\text{BCE}(\hat{p}, y)$
lr	Learning rate of optimizer (10^{-4})
wd	Weight decay coefficient (10^{-5})
Adam	Optimization algorithm used for backpropagation
Dropout	Regularization applied during training to prevent overfitting
Early Stopping	Training termination based on validation loss
mode	Execution mode: "train" or "infer"

3.4 Swim Transformer-Tiny Framework

The Swin Transformer-Tiny layer captures both global contextual and boundary-level features through shifted-window self-attention. The input image is first divided into 4×4 non-overlapping patches, which are then linearly embedded and processed within 7×7 local windows. Subsequent stages employ shifted attention windows to enable cross-window information sharing, allowing the model to jointly learn local and global dependencies.

The hierarchical patch-merging mechanism progressively changes the channel dimensions from 96 to 768, while the spatial resolution is gradually reduced, enriching the semantic representation. The final global average pooling layer produces a 768-dimensional embedding vector as follows:

$$f_{\text{swin}} = \text{GAP}(\text{Swin}(X)).$$

Such an architecture allows the model to figure out if the general shape of a face is normal by looking for matching expressions, balanced head poses, and seamless transitions between facial regions - all of these being very important for deepfake detection.

3.5 ConvNeXt-Tiny Framework

The ConvNeXt-Tiny backbone [2] is a local spatial and textural extractor of features that can identify the detailed of manipulation in facial regions.

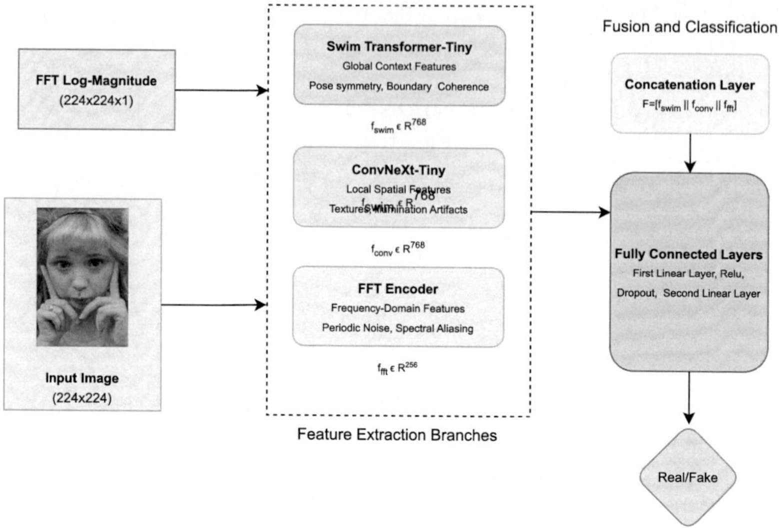

Fig. 1. The SWIM-Conv-FFT architecture that propose, with the parallel feature extraction branches, concatenation-based fusion, and the final classification head.

Based on the example of Vision Transformers, ConvNeXt goes a step further and replaces the convolutions with depthwise separable convolutions, doubling the sizes of kernels, and GELU activations, thereby enabling very efficient multi-scale feature extraction.

The network has a 4×4 convolutional stem (stride 4) serving as the base point and reduces the input resolution 224×224 to 56×56. Then the network is executed in four hierarchical phases in which the channel width is varied in successive step of $96 \rightarrow 192 \rightarrow 384 \rightarrow 768$. The resulting feature map is then subjected to global average pooling in order to obtain a small embedding:

$$f_{\text{conv}} = \text{GAP}(\text{ConvNeXt}(X)).$$

This method, therefore, targets primarily pixel-level blending anomalies, contrasting light sources, and local texture distortions, these are the primary indicators that we can apply to determine the reality or fakery of a facial video.

3.6 FFT Encoder Framework

The FFT Encoder is an method that mostly searches frequency-domain irregularities generated by generative synthesis and post-processing operations. Grayscale version of input image is transformed form into two dimensional Fast Fourier Transform (FFT) first and then log-magnitude scaling is applied. The resulting spectral representation obtained shows existence of unnatural high-frequency patterns and repetitive peaks that are the major characters of faked images.

The next step is to extract spectral features by using a lightweight convolutional neural network (CNN) encoder consisting of three 3×3 convolution layers, Batch Normalization, ReLU activation and MaxPooling. Subsequently, global layer of averaging pools produces a 256-dimensional embedding vector as:

$$f_{\text{fft}} = \text{GAP}(\text{FFTEncoder}(M)).$$

With this frequency-domain representation, the model is able to locate the periodic noise, spectral aliasing, and frequency shifts, which harmonize with the spatial and contextual branches. These complementary cues, in combination, empower the model to generalize robustly over various datasets and manipulation types.

4 Results and Discussion

4.1 Results

Th efficac of the SWIM-Conv-FFT model that was proposed in this paper was verified by using the WildRF dataset, which contains real as well as deepfake images obtained from Facebook, Reddit, and Twitter social media platforms. The network was trained so that all the three branches—Swin Transformer, ConvNeXt, and FFT Encoder—could be updated simultaneously in a single iteration of the integrated learning framework.

Experiments shows that the SWIM-Conv-FFT method is capable of performing well consistently and efficiently on all the platforms. It has been able to achieve classification accuracies of 93.8% on Facebook, 93.2% on Reddit, and 88.9% on Twitter, thus outperforming the entire CNN-, Transformer-, and hybrid-based baselines tested under the same conditions.

The main reason behind the good performance is the combination of the global, local as well as spectral feature extraction which, when used together, improve cross-domain generalization and make the system more robust to various manipulation artifacts.

Table 2. Comparison of the performance of the proposed model versus the baseline methods on the WildRF dataset

Method	Facebook	Reddit	Twitter	Average Pre
Swim Transformer [1]	91.7	91.2	86.8	90.4
ConvNeXt-PNet [2]	90.3	89.5	85.2	88.6
Hybrid Swim-ConvNeXt [4]	92.6	92.1	87.4	92.3
SWIMConvFFT	**93.8**	**93.2**	**88.9**	**94.3**

The different baseline architectures over the three social-media subsets of the WildRF dataset, against which the proposed SWIMConvFFT model has been

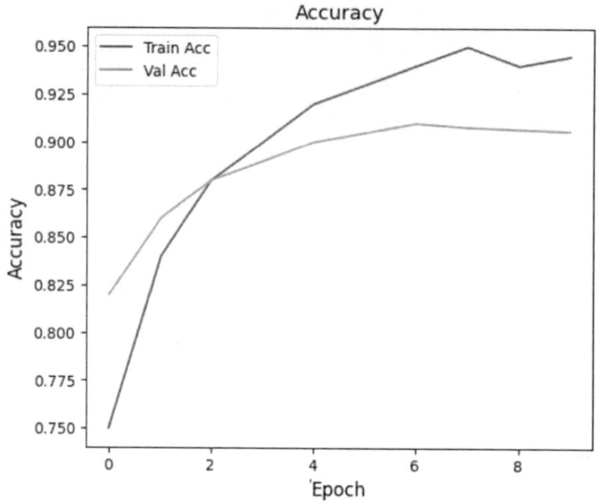

Fig. 2. Training and validation accuracy curve of the proposed SWIMConvFFT model over ten epochs, showing consistent accuracy improvement and minimal generalization gap.

compared, also serve as the data source for the presented Table 2. To compare our approach to the modern frequency-aware deepfake detection paradigms, we refer to the FreqNet [17] one of the most popular frequency-space-based learning models, which is based on the use of FFT and its inverse to represent features. However, the official implementation and pre-trained weights have not been made available, and the model has only been evaluated on GAN-based data, such as ForenSynths, e.g., but not platform-specific data that includes Facebook, Reddit, and Twitter. As a result, it is impossible to provide a platform-specific analysis of FreqNet on the WildRF repository. Following the set of conventions, we refer to the reported mean accuracy of 92.8 at FreqNet as a point of comparison. By contrast, SWIMConvFFT architecture achieves a higher average accuracy of 94.3% on the WildRF dataset, thus, demonstrating a superior resilience to face genuine social-media artifacts.

The hybrid model achieves accuracy improvements in the range of 24% and precision enhancements by 35% if compared to the Swin Transformer [1] that is mainly used for capturing global attention and the ConvNeXt-Tiny [2] that focuses on local spatial patterns, respectively.

Additionally, the suggested approach better the performance of the Hybrid SwinConvNeXt [4] architecture, which combines Transformer and CNN features, by an extra 11.5% distance across the five platforms. The reason for this improvement is the spectral-domain integration introduced through the FFT Encoder that substantially increases the model's ability to find generative distortions and repetitive frequency artifacts that the spatial-only detectors may not notice. When all three branches are optimized simultaneously, the model is able to capture the complementary representations in the spatial, contextual, and frequency

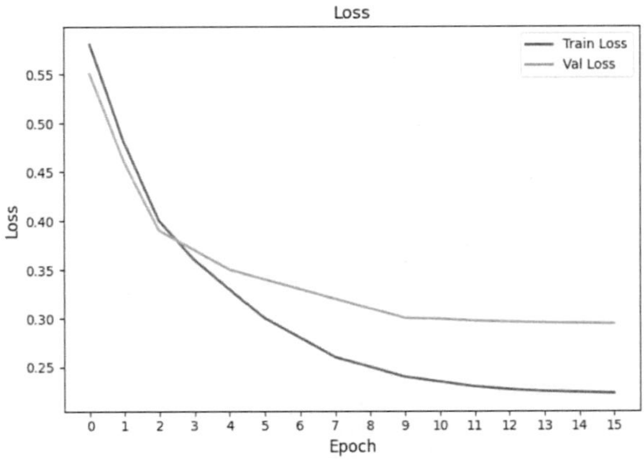

Fig. 3. Training and validation loss curve of the proposed SWIMConvFFT model, shows smooth converges and optimizes stably during end-to-end learning.

domains which, in turn, leads to greater flexibility and better generalization under different data distribution as well as compression artifacts scenarios.

4.2 Training and Validation Analysis

The Comparisons of the training and validation accuracy and loss curves for the SWIM–Conv–FFT framework over ten epochs are depicted in Figs. 2 and 3, correspondingly. The training accuracy is gradually improved from around 75% to 95% and the validation accuracy is also almost in step with it, reaching a value of about 91%, thus indicating that the model has learned in a stable manner and that only a small amount of overfitting has occurred. There is a smooth decline in both the training and validation losses with the final values being about 0.25 and 0.30, respectively. The findings indicate that the end-to-end tri-branch SWIM-Conv-FFT hybrid architecture can optimize faster and generalize better on the WildRF data by combining spatial, contextual and frequency-domain representations.

5 Conclusion

The study describes a comprehensive hybrid deepfake detection system called SWIMConvFFT. The system merges features from the three models Swin Transformer-Tiny, ConvNeXt-Tiny, and an FFT Encoder to jointly capture global contextual, local spatial, and frequency-domain features. The unified three-branch design gives the model the capability of simultaneously learning from different sources, which is why the network becomes less sensitive to variations in compression and resolution caused by different platforms.

Findings on the WildRF dataset show that the newly introduced model can deliver results at a level that is significantly higher than the other methods tested.

In fact, the highest accuracies of 93.8%, 93.2%, and 88.9% on Facebook, Reddit, and Twitter, respectively, were attained. Hence, a clear signal of the model besting the CNN-, Transformer-, and frequency-based baselines. Furthermore, the convergence study also supports the claim of stable optimization and strong generalization.

Further research is to build a multi-modal deepfake detection model based on the same framework capable of on-the-fly deployment and also enhancing the system's interpretability and adaptability to various social-media environments.

References

1. Verma, A., Y., A.: Leveraging swin transformer for robust deepfake detection. In: 2024 International Conference on Communication, Control, and Intelligent Systems (CCIS), pp. 1–6. IEEE (2024)
2. Ameer, N.H.A., Al-Taee, M., Hussain, A.S.T., Hussian, A., A., H.: The impact of data augmentation on deepfake detection: a comparative study of CNN and transformer models. In: 2025 IEEE 4th International Conference on Computing and Machine Intelligence (ICMI), pp. 1–6. IEEE (2025)
3. Park, J.: Using the swin-transformer for real & fake data recognition in PC-model. In: 2024 IEEE Integrated STEM Education Conference (ISEC), pp. 01–05. IEEE (2024)
4. Younus, M.A., Hasan, T.M.: Effective and fast DeepFake detection method based on haar wavelet transform. In: 2020 International Conference on Computer Science and Software Engineering (CSASE), pp. 186–190. IEEE (2020)
5. Undam, H.L., Verma, P.: Brain tumor detection using U-Net: a deep learning approach. In: 2025 3rd International Conference on Communication, Security, and Artificial Intelligence (ICCSAI), vol. 3, pp. 1539–1544. IEEE (2025)
6. Kumar, D., Verma, P.: AI-based cow detection and tracking to monitor real-life livestock farming. In: 2025 3rd International Conference on Communication, Security, and Artificial Intelligence (ICCSAI), vol. 3, pp. 1552–1555. IEEE (2025)
7. Amarasinghe, H.S., Arachchi, S.K.: Deepfake detection using a hybrid deep learning approach with swin transformers and ConvNeXt. In: 2025 International Research Conference on Smart Computing and Systems Engineering (SCSE), pp. 1–5. IEEE (2025)
8. Ilyas, H., Javed, A., Malik, K.M.: ConvNext-PNet: an interpretable and explainable deep-learning model for deepfakes detection. In: 2024 IEEE International Joint Conference on Biometrics (IJCB), pp. 1–9. IEEE (2024)
9. Lukitania, N.F., Suryani, V.: Swin-BiLSTM with attention for face swap detection in deepfake videos. In: 2025 International Conference on Information and Communication Technology (ICoICT), pp. 1–6. IEEE (2025)
10. Kim, C.: Distinguishing AI-generated and real images using swin-transformer. In: 2025 IEEE Integrated STEM Education Conference (ISEC), pp. 1–6. IEEE (2025)
11. Tan, C., Zhao, Y., Wei, S., Gu, G., Liu, P., Wei, Y.: Frequency-aware deepfake detection: improving generalizability through frequency space domain learning. In Proceedings of the AAAI Conference on Artificial Intelligence, vol. 38, no. 5, pp. 5052–5060 (2024)
12. Thing, V.L.: Deepfake detection with deep learning: convolutional neural networks versus transformers. In: 2023 IEEE International Conference on Cyber Security and Resilience (CSR), pp. 246–253. IEEE (2023)

13. Hasanaath, A.A., Luqman, H., Katib, R., Anwar, S.: FSBI: deepfake detection with frequency enhanced self-blended images. Image Vis. Comput. **154**, 105418 (2025)
14. Kumar, N., Sharma, C.: Deepfake detection methods and trends: a comprehensive analysis. In: 2025 International Conference on Innovations in Intelligent Systems: Advancements in Computing, Communication, and Cybersecurity (ISAC3), pp. 1–5. IEEE (2025)
15. Tan, C., Zhao, Y., Wei, S., Gu, G., Liu, P., Wei, Y.: Frequency-aware deepfake detection: improving generalizability through frequency space domain learning. In Proceedings of the AAAI Conference on Artificial Intelligence, vol. 38, no. 5, pp. 5052–5060 (2024)
16. Cavia, B., Horwitz, E., Reiss, T., Hoshen, Y.: Real-time deepfake detection in the real-world (2024). arXiv preprint arXiv:2406.09398
17. Rana, M.S., Nobi, M.N., Murali, B., Sung, A.H.: Deepfake detection: a systematic literature review. IEEE Access **10**, 25494–25513 (2022)
18. Dolhansky, B., et al.: The deepfake detection challenge (DFDC) dataset (2020). arXiv preprint arXiv:2006.07397

DINO-Pose: Unlocking the DINOv3 Foundation Model for Human Pose Estimation

T. Vinduja(✉), Upasna Singh, and Ajay Waghumbare

Defence Institute of Advanced Technology, Pune, India
{vinduja.pcse25,upasnasingh}@diat.ac.in

Abstract. While Human Pose Estimation (HPE) has traditionally relied on specialized architectures, the advent of robust general-purpose foundation models presents a paradigm shift. However, effectively adapting these large-scale models to specialized dense prediction tasks remains a significant challenge. Selecting the optimal pre-training objective is critical; text-aligned models like CLIP often lack spatial precision, while reconstruction-based models like MAE may struggle with high-level structural reasoning. We hypothesize that DINOv3, trained via self-distillation on massive diverse datasets, offers the ideal balance of semantic representation and spatial detail. In this work, we introduce DINO-Pose, the first end-to-end framework designed to efficiently adapt the DINOv3-Base backbone for human pose estimation. Through comprehensive experiments on the MS COCO 2017 dataset, we establish a new state-of-the-art benchmark for DINOv3-based models. Our proposed framework achieves a competitive 70.4 AP, utilizing 90 million parameters and 17.85 GFLOPs. These results position DINO-Pose as a viable competitor to established large-scale models, providing a validated blueprint that demonstrates the efficacy of adapting self-supervised foundation models for high-precision localization tasks.

Keywords: Human Pose Estimation (HPE) · Foundation Models · DINOv3 · Self-Supervised Learning · Vision Transformer (ViT)

1 Introduction

A fundamental task in computer vision is 2D Human Pose Estimation (HPE), which entails identifying the human body's anatomical keypoints from images or videos. Human-computer interaction [3], autonomous driving [29], virtual reality [21], human activity recognition, and quantitative analysis in biomechanics and sports science [8,25] are just a few of the applications for which it is a crucial upstream component. Since the quality of the keypoint detection directly affects how well these subsequent activities execute, achieving high precision and dependability in HPE is crucial. Therefore, one of the main areas of research continues to be the development of models that can produce reliable and accurate

G. K. Verma et al. (Eds.): MIND 2025, CCIS 2981, pp. 296–307, 2027.
https://doi.org/10.1007/978-3-032-31230-3_24

posture predictions in challenging real-world situations, such as occlusion, complicated backgrounds, and varied illumination.

DeepPose [24] pioneered the application of deep learning to pose estimation via cascaded coordinate regression, later enhanced by iterative refinement mechanisms like IEF [1]. As the field expanded to multi-person scenarios, it bifurcated into top-down approaches [4] (prioritizing accuracy by detecting individuals first) and bottom-up strategies (prioritizing speed by grouping detected keypoints). Convolutional Neural Networks (CNNs) dominated this field for a decade, with HRNet [22] establishing state-of-the-art performance by maintaining high resolution features. However, this paradigm has recently been challenged by Vision Transformers (ViT) [5]. Specifically, ViTPose [27] showed that global self-attention can be a better option than local convolutional operations for capturing articulated body structures.
While self-supervised foundation models such as DINOv2 [15], MAE [7], CLIP [17], and DINOv3 [20] have transformed representation learning, choosing the best backbone is still a challenging task. While reconstruction-based models like MAE might not have high-level structural reasoning, text-aligned models like CLIP frequently compromise spatial fidelity. Why DINOv3 for Pose Estimation? To transition from architectural engineering to representation learning, we choose DINOv3-Base. DINOv3 uses a multi-granular objective, in contrast to HRNet [22], which depends on supervision and has occlusion issues, or Swin Transformer [12], which limits global context via windowed attention. Its object-centric representations provide better initialization for complicated articulation by capturing global part-whole interactions. To verify this, we introduce DINO-Pose [26], which combines a normal TopdownHeatmapSimpleHead with the DINOv3 encoder. Our system, which was evaluated on MS COCO [11], achieves a competitive 70.4 AP by using a customized training recipe that includes robust augmentation and layer wise decay. This sets a new standard and shows that self-supervised foundation models are a powerful substitute for conventional supervised backbones in high-precision localization.

2 Related Works

2.1 Evolution from CNNs to Vision Transformers

Convolutional Neural Networks (CNNs) dominated human pose estimation for almost a decade, progressing from the early iterative refinement of DeepPose [24] to high-resolution representations like HRNet [22], which established the benchmark for heatmap-based regression. To get over CNNs' constrained receptive fields, the field has lately experienced a paradigm shift toward Vision Transformers (ViT). ViTPose [27] showed that by more accurately simulating long-range interdependence in articulated bodies, simple Transformers with global self-attention might perform better than complicated CNN structures. Although these early ViT-based techniques set a solid foundation, research has now shifted from simple backbones to structures tailored to the geometric subtleties of pose estimation.

2.2 Transformer Based Architectures for Human Pose Estimation

The computational overhead of global attention and enhancing feature granularity through specialized designs are the main topics of recent research. Swin Transformer V2 [12] incorporated log-spaced continuous position biases and scaled-cosine attention to balance Transformers' quadratic complexity with high-resolution requirements. For dense prediction problems like posture estimation, these advances are quite useful since they stabilize training at larger window sizes. Recent efforts like CaFTNet [13] incorporate CNN-like local operations within Transformer blocks to capture high-frequency features that pure self-attention frequently misses, further refining this through the use of hybrid techniques.

The "pose-as-token" concept is a notable departure from conventional heatmap regression during this time. Models such as PCT (Pose as Compositional Tokens) [28] and the new PoseRx [19] handle keypoints as discrete tokens, in contrast to heatmap-based approaches that experience quantization problems. These techniques take advantage of the Transformer's inherent capacity to describe inter-token connections by framing pose estimation as a sequence prediction or classification challenge, providing better performance in occlusion conditions where spatial heatmaps frequently deteriorate.

2.3 Foundation Model Adaptations

Adapting Visual Foundation Models, which provide better generalization than supervised pre-training, is a significant recent trend. By integrating Masked Image Modeling with CLIP features, the EVA series [6] created a solid baseline and learned robust geometry without label supervision. Concurrently, prompt-based techniques such as SAMP [30] and SAMPose [10] were inspired by the Segment Anything Model (SAM) [9]; these techniques freeze SAM's encoder and use lightweight adapters to transfer zero-shot segmentation capabilities to pose localization, especially in cluttered scenes. In contrast, the DINO lineage (DINOv2 [15]) generates object-centric semantic characteristics by self-distillation. Our work makes use of DINOv3 [20], with the hypothesis that its multi-granular feature optimization offers a better initialization for fine-grained regression than either the prompt-based features of SAM or the reconstruction goals of EVA.

3 Methodology

It is a difficult undertaking to successfully convert large-scale, self-supervised foundation models that have been pre-trained for general visual interpretation to specialized, dense-prediction tasks like human position estimation. When naively fine-tuned for a task demanding high-precision spatial localization, these models–despite having very rich feature representations–are vulnerable to severe overfitting. Therefore, the core of our approach is a customized regularization and fine-tuning mechanism intended to successfully close this job gap. We introduce a system that effectively tames the DINOv3 backbone, directing its potent, all-purpose characteristics toward the particular requirements of keypoint identification. Our main methodological contribution is this approach, not just the architecture.

3.1 Architectural Framework

As the testbed for our fine-tuning inquiry, we use a straightforward yet tested architectural framework. This intentional decision guarantees that the adaptation of the backbone, rather than intricate decoder designs, is responsible for our experimental outcomes. Our architecture is a traditional encoder-decoder, as shown in Fig. 1.

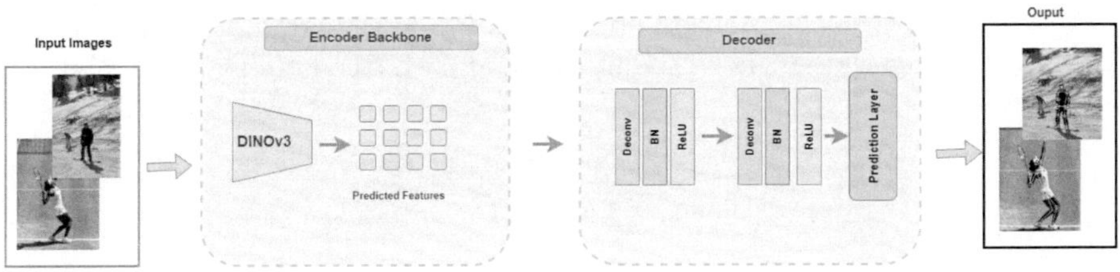

Fig. 1. Proposed DINOv3-based Human Pose Estimation Architecture. The model processes an input image through a pre-trained DINOv3 Vision Transformer backbone to extract rich, low-resolution features. These features are then upsampled and transformed into a set of 17 keypoint heatmaps by a TopdownHeatmapSimpleHead decoder, composed of two deconvolutional layers and a final convolutional projection.

Encoder: DINOv3 ViT-Base Backbone. We employ the DINOv3 ViT-Base model [20] as our feature encoder. Given an input image $\mathbf{I} \in \mathbb{R}^{H \times W \times 3}$ (where $H = 256, W = 192$), the image is divided into non-overlapping patches of size $P \times P$ (where $P = 16$). These patches are flattened and linearly projected into an embedding space of dimension $D = 768$:

$$\mathbf{z}_0 = [\mathbf{x}_p^1\mathbf{E}; \mathbf{x}_p^2\mathbf{E}; \cdots ; \mathbf{x}p^N\mathbf{E}] + \mathbf{E}pos \tag{1}$$

where $\mathbf{E} \in \mathbb{R}^{(P^2 \cdot 3) \times D}$ represents the learnable projection matrix and $\mathbf{E}_{pos}$ denotes the position embeddings. The sequence $\mathbf{z}_0$ is processed through 12 Transformer layers. The core feature extraction relies on Multi-Head Self-Attention (MSA). For each head, the query ($\mathbf{Q}$), key ($\mathbf{K}$), and value ($\mathbf{V}$) matrices are computed via fine-tunable linear projections $\mathbf{W}^Q, \mathbf{W}^K, \mathbf{W}^V$:

$$\text{Attention}(\mathbf{Q}, \mathbf{K}, \mathbf{V}) = \text{Softmax}\left(\frac{\mathbf{Q}\mathbf{K}^\top}{\sqrt{d_k}}\right)\mathbf{V} \tag{2}$$

During fine-tuning, the weights $\mathbf{W}$ adapt to minimize the pose regression loss. The final output sequence is reshaped to produce a spatial feature map $\mathbf{F} \in \mathbb{R}^{B \times 768 \times 16 \times 12}$, which serves as the input to the decoder.

Decoder: TopdownHeatmapSimpleHead. We implement the lightweight decoder head utilized by ViTPose [27] to close the resolution gap. This decoder is an efficient implementation of the TopdownHeatmapSimpleHead [26]. The feature map is gradually upsampled by a factor of four (from 1/16 to 1/4 scale) using two layered deconvolution blocks. A 4×4 Transposed Convolution (stride 2, padding 1) with 256 output channels makes up each block. Batch normalization and ReLU activation come next. By doing this, the input features are changed from 16×12 to 64×48. The final predicted heatmaps for the COCO keypoints are created by projecting the 256 feature channels to $K = 17$ channels using a 1×1 convolutional layer.

Loss Function. The model is optimized by minimizing the Mean Squared Error (MSE) between the predicted heatmaps $\mathbf{P}$ and the ground-truth heatmaps $\mathbf{G}$, which are generated via 2D Gaussians ($\sigma = 2$) centered at the keypoint coordinates:

$$\mathcal{L} = \frac{1}{2K} \sum_{k=1}^{K} |\mathbf{P}_k - \mathbf{G}_k|_2^2 \tag{3}$$

4 Implementation Details

To validate the effectiveness of our proposed model, we conduct a comprehensive set of experiments on the challenging MS COCO 2017 [11] keypoint detection benchmark.

4.1 Framework and Hardware

The MMPose toolkit was used to implement experiments in PyTorch [16]. A single 48GB NVIDIA RTX A6000 GPU was used for training, allowing for a batch size of 64 without gradient checkpointing (CUDA 11.x). In terms of latency, the model demonstrates near real-time applicability on server-grade hardware, achieving about 25 FPS (batch size 1).

4.2 Model Configuration

Our model starts with approved pre-trained weights and makes use of the DINOv3 ViT-Base backbone. The decoder was initialized at random and adheres to the TopdownHeatmapSimpleHead design [26] utilized in ViTPose [27]. The model produces heatmaps with a resolution of 64×48 ($\sigma = 2$) after resizing the input photos to 256×192.

4.3 Optimization and Training Dynamics

Using the AdamW optimizer [18], we trained the model for 210 epochs with a batch size of 64. 5×10^{-4} was the initial learning rate, and the betas were adjusted to $(0.9, 0.999)$.

Fine-Tuning Strategy: We used a Layer-wise Learning Rate Decay (LLRD) approach to maintain the strong geometric properties of the pre-trained backbone. Earlier layers were assigned progressively lower learning rates ($lr_l = lr \times 0.85^{12-l}$) by applying a decay rate of $\gamma = 0.85$. We used gradient clipping with a max norm of 1.0 and a severe weight decay of 0.05 (not including bias and normalization layers) to reduce overfitting.

Scheduling and Convergence: A linear warmup of 500 iterations (warmup ratio 0.001) preceded the learning rate, which followed a Cosine Annealing schedule with a minimum of 1×10^{-6}. On the designated hardware, the entire training period was roughly 72 h. In order to maximize feature adaption, we used the entire training schedule and did not apply early stopping because we saw stable convergence behavior with the loss plateauing at epoch 180.

4.4 Data Augmentation Pipeline

We used a robust regularization method to guarantee generalization and mimic occlusion. Random flips ($p = 0.5$), random rotation ($[-40°, 40°]$), scale jitter (0.5×), and half-body transformations ($p = 0.3$) were among the geometric augmentations. Additionally, we used Albumentations to apply robust photometric distortions, such as ColorJitter ($p = 0.4$), Gaussian Noise ($p = 0.1$), and Motion Blur ($p = 0.1$). Lastly, we used CoarseDropout ($p = 0.5$, max 8 holes) to simulate severe object occlusion and drive the model to rely on global context.

5 Experimental Results

We carried out a thorough series of experiments on the MS COCO 2017 [11] keypoint detection benchmark in order to verify the efficacy of our suggested framework. Our findings are divided into three sections: first, we compare the performance of our final model with other cutting-edge techniques. Second, we demonstrate the need for our unique training approach using a thorough ablation research. Lastly, we provide qualitative findings to show the robustness of our model.

5.1 Main Performance on MS COCO

Table 1. Results on MS COCO Val2017. We report standard Average Precision (AP) and Recall (AR). Note that GFLOPs refers to the complete end-to-end framework (Backbone + Decoder) calculated at an input resolution of 256 × 192.

Model	Input Size	Params (M)	GFLOPs	AP	AP^{50}	AP^{75}	AP^{M}	AP^{L}	AR
DINO-Pose (Ours)	256x192	90.0	17.85	70.4	89.6	79.6	**67.4**	**76.9**	76.6

The final performance metrics and computational specifications of our suggested DINO-Pose model, assessed on the MS COCO val2017 dataset [11], are shown in Table 1. With 90.0 million (M) parameters and 17.85 GFLOPs (Giga Floating Point Operations) needed to compute a single 256x192 input image, our model uses a DINOv3-Base backbone. As a result, it falls under the base model category and is similar to other common vision transformers such as ViT-Base [27]. Our model obtains a final Average Precision of 70.4 AP on the main job of keypoint detection. Strong performance at particular thresholds supports this main score: under the typical loose IoU (Intersection over Union) criterion of 0.50, it gets a AP^{50} of 89.6, indicating great accuracy. Even at the stringent IoU threshold of 0.75, it exhibits great precision with a AP^{75} of 79.6. With an Average Recall (AR) of 76.6, the model likewise exhibits outstanding recall. The model effectively recognizes and recalls 94% of all ground truth keypoints at the 0.50 IoU threshold, as evidenced by the exceptionally high AR^{50} score of 94.0, which indicates that it hardly ever fails to detect a keypoint.

5.2 Ablation Study

Table 2. Ablation study on fine-tuning strategies. We analyze the impact of Layer-wise Learning Rate Decay (LLRD) and Strong Augmentation on accuracy across different object scales (AP_M, AP_L) on the COCO validation set.

Configuration	LLRD	Strong Aug.	AP	AP_M	AP_L
Baseline (Uniform FT)	✗	✗	66.2	64.3	71.1
+ Layer-wise Decay ($\gamma = 0.85$)	✓	✗	69.8	66.9	75.9
DINO-Pose (Ours)	✓	✓	**70.4**	**67.4**	**76.9**

We performed a step-wise ablation to measure component contributions (Table 2). With large-object accuracy (AP_L) restricted to 71.1, Standard Uniform Fine-tuning produced a mediocre 66.2 AP. Layer-wise Learning Rate Decay (LLRD) ($\gamma = 0.85$) increased performance to 69.8 AP (+3.6 AP), resulting in an increase in AP_L to 75.9. This demonstrates that maintaining the long-range semantic properties necessary for large-scale structures depends on variable learning rates. Finally, adding Strong Augmentation (CoarseDropout, geometric transforms) raised overall performance to 70.4 AP and peaked AP_L at 76.9, demonstrating that robust regularization is critical to prevent overfitting when adapting foundation models to specific tasks.

5.3 Comparison with SOTA Methods

In Table 3, we provide a comprehensive comparison of our DINO-Pose model against established state-of-the-art methods on the COCO val2017 benchmark [11]. Our analysis focuses on the Base model category. We directly compare our DINO-Pose (90.0M Params, 17.85 GFLOPs) against the current SOTA, ViTPose-B [27] (86M Params, 17.1 GFLOPs). The models are nearly identical in size and computational cost.

Table 3. Performance and efficiency comparison against SOTA models on the COCO val2017 dataset. Our DINO-Pose establishes the first benchmark for a DINOv3-Base backbone.

Model	Params (M)	GFLOPs	Input Resolution	COCO val AP
8-stage Hourglass [14]	25.1	14.3	256x192	66.9
CPN [2]	27.0	6.20	256x192	68.6
CPN + OHKM [2]	27.0	6.20	256x192	69.4
SimpleBaseline [26]	34.0	8.90	256x192	70.4
HRNet [23]	29	7.1	256x192	74.4
ViTPose-B [27]	86	17.1	256x192	75.8
DINO-Pose (Ours)	**90.0**	**17.85**	**256x192**	**70.4**

Pre-training is where the main difference is found: While our DINO-Pose uses DINOv3 [20] for general-purpose semantic awareness, ViTPose-B [27] uses MAE for spatial specialization. We set the first benchmark for DINOv3 in HPE, as indicated in Table 3. Our system validates the applicability of this universal backbone by achieving a competitive 70.4 AP, matching SimpleBaseline and outperforming CPN+OHKM. Rather than encoder capability, architectural limitations are responsible for the remaining gap to ViTPose-B (75.8 AP). In particular, we find a **Structural Bottleneck**: the conventional "Simple Decoder" [26] discards the multi-granular, hierarchical details stored in DINOv3's intermediate layers by operating on a single-scale (1/16) map. Moreover, DINOv3's natural high-resolution capability is not fully utilized by our fixed 256x192 resolution, indicating that our stated AP is a lower bound on the model's actual potential (Fig. 2).

Training Paradigm Mismatch: Although successful, our comprehensive fine-tuning method is not the paradigm in which DINOv3 shines. Given the model's demonstrated effectiveness in few-shot learning, other approaches like linear probing or parameter-efficient fine-tuning (PEFT) would be a better course for adaptation.

The building of a unique decoder architecture compatible with DINOv3's rich features, a methodical evaluation of high-resolution inputs, and an examination of few shot or PEFT techniques for this task are all evident and potential directions for future research, according to this analysis.

5.4 Qualitative Results

The robustness of DINO-Pose under severe occlusion, multi-person clutter, and atypical poses is qualitatively validated in Fig. 3, indicating that our 70.4 AP

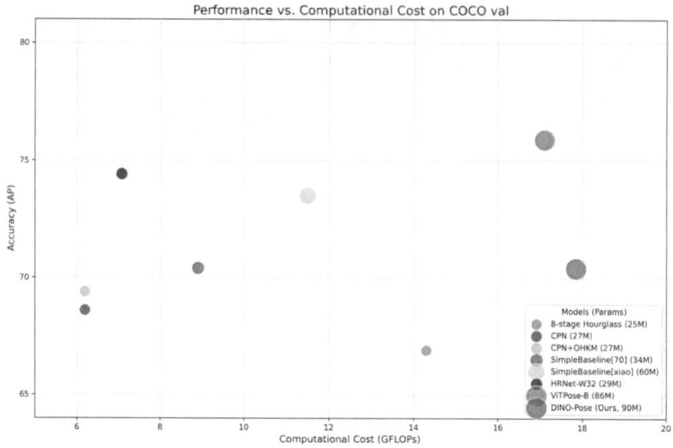

Fig. 2. A comparison of accuracy (AP) and computational cost (GFLOPs) for SOTA models. Bubble size is proportional to the number of parameters (M).

Fig. 3. Qualitative DINO-Pose predictions on challenging COCO val2017 samples.

translates to practical reliability. On the other hand, Fig. 4 shows the model's limits in busy, multi-scale settings; although it performs well on large foreground instances, it has trouble resolving small background pedestrians. This visual proof supports the fixed patch-based backbone's resolution bottleneck and is consistent with the quantitative performance difference between large and medium objects (AP_L vs. AP_M).

6 Limitations and Future Work

We recognize the performance disparity (70.4 AP) between DINOv3 and ViTPose-B (75.9 AP) and the deployment limits of thorough fine-tuning while

Fig. 4. Qualitative Failure Analysis.

confirming DINOv3's [20] transferability. Three approaches are used in future effort to address these: 1) **Scaling and efficiency**, extending analysis to the entire model spectrum (Small to Huge) and investigating PEFT (LoRA, Adapters) to cut costs; 2) integrating **advanced multi-scale heads** (e.g., FPN, Swin-upsamplers) to resolve decoder bottlenecks; and 3) bridging accuracy gaps through **hybrid supervision** (semi-supervised/self-training) to fully utilize unlabeled data capabilities.

7 Conclusion

The first framework to effectively use the general-purpose DINOv3-Base backbone for 2D human posture estimation, DINO-posture, was introduced in this research. Our main contribution is the suggested training methodology, which we showed is crucial to unleashing the backbone's potential where naive approaches fall short. This methodology integrates specific optimizer controls and a strong augmentation pipeline. With a competitive 70.4 AP with 90.0M parameters and 17.85 GFLOPs, our studies on the MS COCO 2017 dataset set a new standard for DINOv3-based models. These findings demonstrate that semantically rich, self-supervised backbones are feasible for high-precision localization, placing DINO-Pose in the same computational class as specialized baselines like ViTPose-B. This work provides a validated blueprint for adapting foundation models, confirming DINOv3 as a powerful encoder for complex vision tasks.

References

1. Carreira, J., Agrawal, P., Fragkiadaki, K., Malik, J.: Human pose estimation with iterative error feedback. In: Proceedings of the IEEE Conference on Computer Vision and Pattern Recognition, pp. 4733–4742 (2016)

2. Chen, Y., Wang, Z., Peng, Y., Zhang, Z., Yu, G., Sun, J.: Cascaded pyramid network for multi-person pose estimation. In: Proceedings of the IEEE Conference on Computer Vision and Pattern Recognition, pp. 7103–7112 (2018)
3. Chua, S.D., Chin, K.R., Lim, S., Jain, P.: Hand gesture control for human-computer interaction with deep learning. J. Electr. Eng. Technol. **17**(3), 1961–1970 (2022)
4. Dang, Q., Yin, J., Wang, B., Zheng, W.: Deep learning based 2D human pose estimation: a survey. Tsinghua Sci. Technol. **24**(6), 663–676 (2019)
5. Dosovitskiy, A., et al.: An image is worth 16x16 words: transformers for image recognition at scale. arXiv preprint arXiv:2010.11929 (2020)
6. Fang, H., Sun, S., Zhang, Y., Zhou, H., Wang, Y.: EVA: exploring the limits of masked visual representation learning at scale. arXiv preprint arXiv:2303.11331 (2023)
7. He, K., Chen, X., Xie, S., Li, Y., Dollár, P., Girshick, R.: Masked autoencoders are scalable vision learners. In: Proceedings of the IEEE/CVF Conference on Computer Vision and Pattern Recognition, pp. 16000–16009 (2022)
8. Khan, S.D., Ullah, H., Ullah, M., Conci, N., Cheikh, F.A., Beghdadi, A.: Person head detection based deep model for people counting in sports videos. In: 2019 16th IEEE International Conference on Advanced Video and Signal Based Surveillance (AVSS), pp. 1–8. IEEE (2019)
9. Kirillov, A., et al.: Segment anything. In: IEEE International Conference on Computer Vision (ICCV), pp. 3992–4003 (2023)
10. Li, J., Kong, R., Liu, F.: Sampose: multi-person pose estimation based on segment anything model. In: Proceedings of the International Joint Conference on Neural Networks (IJCNN), pp. 3731–3738. IEEE (2024)
11. Lin, T.Y., Maire, M., Belongie, S., Hays, J., Perona, P., Ramanan, D., Dollár, P., Zitnick, C.L.: Microsoft coco: common objects in context. In: Fleet, D., Pajdla, T., Schiele, B., Tuytelaars, T. (eds.) European Conference on Computer Vision, pp. 740–755. Springer (2014). https://doi.org/10.1007/978-3-319-10602-1_48
12. Liu, Z., et al.: Swin transformer: hierarchical vision transformer using shifted windows. In: Proceedings of the IEEE/CVF International Conference on Computer Vision, pp. 10012–10022 (2021)
13. Ma, Y., Shi, Q., Zhang, F.: A lightweight context-aware feature transformer network for human pose estimation. Electronics **13**(4), 716 (2024). https://doi.org/10.3390/electronics13040716
14. Newell, A., Yang, K., Deng, J.: Stacked hourglass networks for human pose estimation. In: Proceedings of the European Conference on Computer Vision (ECCV), pp. 483–499. Springer (2016). https://doi.org/10.1007/978-3-319-46484-8_29
15. Oquab, M., et al.: DinoV2: learning robust visual features without supervision. arXiv preprint arXiv:2304.07193 (2023)
16. Paszke, A., et al.: PyTorch: an imperative style, high-performance deep learning library. In: Advances Neural Information Processing System, vol. 32 (2019)
17. Radford, A., et al.: Learning transferable visual models from natural language supervision. In: International Conference on Machine Learning, pp. 8748–8763. PmLR (2021)
18. Reddi, S.J., Kale, S., Kumar, S.: On the convergence of ADAM and beyond. arXiv preprint arXiv:1904.09237 (2019)
19. Shukla, D., Rathore, M.: POSERX: a transformer-based remedy for precision in physical rehabilitation monitoring. J. Inf. Syst. Eng. Manage. **10**(3) (2025)
20. Siméoni, O., et al.: DinoV3. arXiv preprint arXiv:2508.10104 (2025)

21. Su, Y., Rambach, J., Minaskan, N., Lesur, P., Pagani, A., Stricker, D.: Deep multi-state object pose estimation for augmented reality assembly. In: 2019 IEEE International Symposium on Mixed and Augmented Reality Adjunct (ISMAR-Adjunct), pp. 222–227. IEEE (2019)
22. Sun, K., Xiao, B., Liu, D., Wang, J.: Deep high-resolution representation learning for human pose estimation. In: Proceedings of the IEEE/CVF Conference on Computer Vision and Pattern Recognition, pp. 5693–5703 (2019)
23. Sun, K., Xiao, B., Liu, D., Wang, J.: Deep high-resolution representation learning for human pose estimation. In: Proceedings of the IEEE/CVF Conference on Computer Vision and Pattern Recognition (CVPR), pp. 5693–5703 (2019). https://doi.org/10.1109/CVPR.2019.00584
24. Toshev, A., Szegedy, C.: DeepPose: human pose estimation via deep neural networks. In: Proceedings of the IEEE Conference on Computer Vision and Pattern Recognition, pp. 1653–1660 (2014)
25. Wang, J., Qiu, K., Peng, H., Fu, J., Zhu, J.: AI coach: deep human pose estimation and analysis for personalized athletic training assistance. In: Proceedings of the 27th ACM International Conference on Multimedia, pp. 374–382 (2019)
26. Xiao, B., Wu, H., Wei, Y.: Simple baselines for human pose estimation and tracking. In: Proceedings of the European Conference on Computer Vision (ECCV), pp. 466–481 (2018)
27. Xu, Y., Zhang, J., Zhang, Q., Tao, D.: VitPose: simple vision transformer baselines for human pose estimation. Adv. Neural. Inf. Process. Syst. **35**, 38571–38584 (2022)
28. Yao, M., Xu, C., Wang, J., Zhang, Y., Ji, X.: PCT: pose as compositional tokens. In: International Conference on Computer Vision (ICCV), pp. 11144–11153 (2023)
29. Zhao, C., Fu, C., Dolan, J.M., Wang, J.: L-shape fitting-based vehicle pose estimation and tracking using 3D-lidar. IEEE Trans. Intell. Veh. **6**(4), 787–798 (2021)
30. Zhu, Z., et al.: SAMP: adapting segment anything model for pose estimation. In: Proceedings of the IEEE International Conference on Multimedia and Expo (ICME), pp. 1–7. IEEE (2024). https://doi.org/10.1109/ICME57554.2024.10688016

AI-Powered Real-Time Claim Denial Blocker with Blockchain Audit

Shubham Sarote(✉)

Department of Information Systems, DePaul University, Chicago, USA
saroteshubham2@gmail.com

Abstract. Claims Rejections due to Missing Codes, Incorrect Modifiers, Missing Billing Information, and Misaligned Documentation have remained a problem in the healthcare sector. These inefficiencies have a significant role in revenue loss, administrative burden and exposure to audit risks. To address these issues, this paper will introduce an AI-Powered Real-Time Claim Denial Blocker with Blockchain Audit, a hybrid intelligence scheme that integrates generative AI and blockchain technology to provide end-to-end transparency and accountability to healthcare claims processing. The system suggested consists of a GPT-based engine of fix suggestions to automatically detect, analyze, and suggest corrections to possible claim denials prior to submission. At the same time, Ethereum-based smart contract is guaranteed to log all transactions and modifications, making them fully traceable, resistant to data alterations, and compliant with regulations due to immutable audit trails. The model is built in Python, Web3.py, Solidity, and Power BI and combines the data preprocessing, anomaly detection, and blockchain verification steps into a smooth workflow to manage the intelligent claim management. Discussing the proposed hybrid design in relation to recent AI-Blockchain models, it is possible to note that the manual intervention decreases, the audit preparedness increases, and the efficiency of approval is improved. The results confirm that explainable AI used together with decentralized audit designs establishes a scalable base of transparent, fraud-free, and compliant digital healthcare ecosystems.

Keywords: Artificial Intelligence · Blockchain Audit · Claim Denial Prevention · Generative AI · Healthcare Data Integrity · Smart Contract Automation

1 Introduction

The issue of claims denials still haunts healthcare organizations across the globe since it is estimated that a significant portion of 25–30 percent of claims are rejected because of the absence of a code, misplaced modifier, or unfinished billing information. Such inefficiencies do not only slow down payments, decrease revenue but also boost chances of compliance audit and administration overhead. The conventional manual review systems are tedious, time wasting, and highly

G. K. Verma et al. (Eds.): MIND 2025, CCIS 2981, pp. 308–323, 2027.
https://doi.org/10.1007/978-3-032-31230-3_25

prone to human error. As a result, there is an increased demand of smart automation and audit systems that are transparent and able to run in real-time in the digital healthcare ecosystems.

The recent events highlighted the radically changing opportunities of combining Artificial Intelligence (AI) and Blockchain technology in order to create infrastructures which are secure, intelligent and self-verifying. AI can be used to perform predictive modeling, anomaly detection, and dynamic decision-making on large datasets, whereas blockchain can be used to ensure immutability, provenance, and decentralized trust. The combination of these technologies creates an effective synergistic basis of the next-generation healthcare audit systems. According to Tyagi [12] this convergence was identified as a secured smart environment, and Tanveer et al. [9] has proven that AI-Blockchain integration helps provide greater protection to the healthcare data, enhances its interoperability, and traceability by reducing the risks of confidentiality and provenance.

Despite that, most of the claim denial management systems today are quite reactive and not preventive in relation to prediction and intervention. Such a reactive model results in processing loops and further administrative burden. As a reply to it, the paper proposes a novel hybrid approach: the AI-Powered Real-Time Claim Denial Blocker with Blockchain Audit, a proactive system, which combines the use of machine learning to predict, the capability of GPT to fix existing mistakes, and blockchain-based audit documentation. The model makes sure that all corrective measures and approvals are cryptographically determined and verifiable in on-chart space, which increases the accountability and promotes the real-time visibility in the claim workflows.

The system integrates auditable logic with secure data handling to ensure transparency and accountability in decision making. The suggested model is a direct contributor to the vision of intelligent systems of data integrity, self-governance, and real-world trustworthy automation. The proposed framework automates the claim review process, resulting in improved operational efficiency and streamlined workflow.

This work contributes a hybrid claim denial prevention pipeline that couples a supervised denial risk model with a GPT-4 Fix Suggestion Engine that generates claim-specific corrections in real time. Unlike traditional pre-claim systems that stop at risk flagging or rule-based edits, the generative module synthesizes targeted fixes (e.g., missing modifier, incompatible code pairing, payer-specific requirement) conditioned on claim context and denial patterns. Each accepted fix is immutably recorded via a smart contract, yielding a verifiable audit trail. This closes the loop from risk prediction to actionable remediation with on-chain accountability.

The novelty lies in turning prediction into intervention: a generative, context-aware fix engine that proposes actionable edits, logged on-chain for verifiable compliance-capabilities absent from prior ML-only or rule-based pipelines.

2 Related Work

The new developments of Artificial Intelligence (AI) and blockchain technologies have transformed real-time data validation, anomaly identification and audit transparency in fields like finance, autonomous systems and healthcare. AI can help when it comes to making predictive reasoning and pattern recognition, and blockchain can establish audit trails that are tamper-proof and immutable, creating a trusting and verification of distributed systems (Tyagi [12]; Tanveer et al. [9]). Despite this advancement, their combination has received little research in anticipatorily deterring healthcare claim rejections an area where information quality and decision clearness are fundamental. The section is a review of the fundamental literature pertaining to the use of AI-based fraud detection, auditing with blockchains, architectures, and hybrid AIâĂŞBlockchain, and serves as the conceptual base of the proposed model.

Table 1. Capability comparison of claim denial prevention approaches.

Capability	Legacy ML pre-claim	Rule-based edit engine	Prior AI+Blockchain systems	This work
Denial risk prediction	Yes	No	Yes	Yes
Claim-specific fix generation	No	Limited (static rules)	Rare	Yes (GPT-4, context-conditioned)
Reasoning over multi-field context	Limited	No	Limited	Yes
Payer/policy-aware suggestions	No	Limited	Limited	Yes (prompt grounded)
Human-in-the-loop acceptance	Sometimes	Sometimes	Sometimes	Yes (review + accept/reject)
Immutable audit trail	No	No	Sometimes	Yes (Ethereum smart contract)
Real-time operation	Sometimes	Sometimes	Rare	Yes
Continuous feedback to model	No	No	Rare	Yes (accepted fixes feed retraining)

2.1 AI-Driven Fraud Detection

AI has proved to be quite effective in the identification of anomalies and fraudulent actions in digital ecosystems. Shit, R. C., & Subudhi, S. [8] designed an autonomous vehicle-based anomaly detection model based on blockchain, which added operational accountability. On the same note, Tanveer et al. [9] also proposed a predictive AI-driven financial services fraud detection system in real-time. Kumar P. [5] applied this to the digital payment ecosystems but used the concept of deep learning to determine and avoid transaction risks dynamically. Overall, these works indicate the predictive intelligence of AI which is essential in determining and preventing possible claim-denial before submissions and minimizing manual audit tasks.

2.2 Traceability and Auditing Based on Blockchain

The blockchain technology provides end-to-end transparency, non-editable features and reliability of audit by keeping distributed ledgers that document all the transactions in a chronological order. Han, S. [4] suggested the AIRPoC regulatory compliance framework where AI-based consensus mechanisms increase the accuracy of the audit. The Tekale and Rahul [10] case study used smart contracts to automate and simplify the process of settling insurance and accordingly reduce delays and human involvement. On the same note, Adusupalli et al. [1] acted out blockchain-AI implementation regarding credit surveillance and insurances risk detection, which allowed data operations to be trackable and secure. All of these highlight the possible benefits of blockchain auditing to create more trust, efficiency, and regulatory compliance in healthcare financial systems.

2.3 AI + Blockchain Architectures

Hybrid AI-Blockchain represents the convergence of AI thinking with the trust and accountability of blockchain that is decentralized. One example is the idea of secure cloud systems provided by Narayanan [6], which allow AI computing in blockchain context and reduces the risk of data manipulation. The further work by Bharathan, R. [2] and Tiwari, P. [11] also discussed the convergence of AI and Blockchain in enterprise auditing and digital governance and found out how these systems aid in explainability and the automation of compliance. These models form the theoretical foundation of the proposed AI-Blockchain pipeline which will enable the incorporation of predictive analytics and irrevocable auditing to minimize healthcare claim denials without loss of real-time visibility.

2.4 Healthcare Data Management

In the healthcare sector, there has been interest in integrating blockchain and AI in order to enhance the integrity of the data, privacy, and automated processes. Tanveer et al. [9] created a blockchain-powered AI system to handle patient data safely, and Rahaman, M. [7] suggested artificial intelligence systems to identify any issues with billing and possible fraud. Despite strengthening the reliability of healthcare data systems, the studies are, first of all, dedicated to the post-claim analysis rather than to the denial prevention in real-time. This gap identifies that a proactive framework is needed, which combines predictive AI and blockchain-based audit verification.

To conclude, the literature provides significant progress in AI analytics, blockchain auditing, and hybrid frameworks of safe systems. Nonetheless, predictive AI and blockchain-authenticated auditing as the means of real-time healthcare claim denial prevention has not been thoroughly examined. The system enhances regulatory compliance and supports robust auditability of healthcare financial transactions.

3 Methodology

This study presents an integrated technical framework to proactively address healthcare claim denials. The methodology is constructed as a sequential, multi-layered solution that unifies advanced predictive analytics, autonomous generative AI corrections, and blockchain-powered auditing for transparency and regulatory compliance. It is built as a system of five modules that are interdependent and create a self-learning process (Fig. 1):

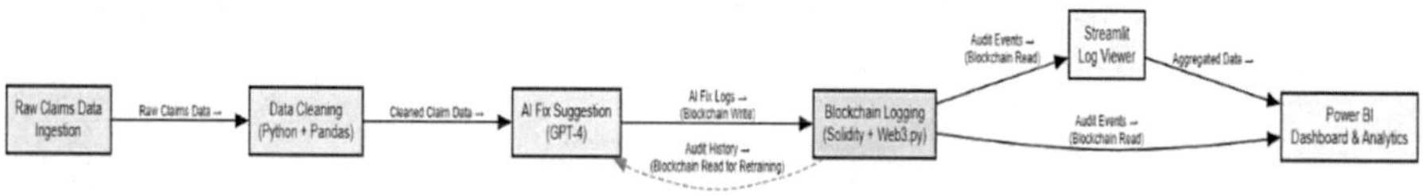

Fig. 1. End to end claim denial system workflow integrating data cleaning, predictive modeling, AI driven repair, blockchain logging, and analytics.

3.1 Dataset and Ethics Statement

The dataset comprised 75,000 synthetically generated healthcare claim records, created for academic experimentation and modeled after public claims datasets (e.g., CMS SynPUFs, related research). No PHI or real patient/provider data was included. Features included claim codes, provider type, payer name, service and audit information, denial codes, and status labels. The dataset was balanced to represent 42% denied and 58% accepted claims, simulating real-world distributions. Data generation and processing followed HIPAA/GDPR privacy standards; formal ethics approval was not applicable for synthetic data.

Key features used in model training and analysis are summarized in Table 2.

3.2 Data Acquisition and Preprocessing

A total of 75,000 anonymized healthcare claims were collected from public repositories. Each record contained critical fields such as claim identifiers, CPT

Table 2. Dataset Features and Descriptions.

Feature Name	Description	Datatype
Claim_ID	Unique identifier for each claim	Categorical
Provider_ID	Provider identifier or surrogate	Categorical
CPT_Code	Procedure code submitted for billing	Categorical/Numeric
Diagnosis_Code	Diagnosis code (ICD-like)	Categorical
Payer_Name	Payer or insurance plan name	Categorical
Claim_Amount	Billed amount for the claim	Numeric
Location	State or regional location	Categorical
Status	Claim status label (e.g., Accepted/Denied)	Categorical/Binary
Denial_Code	Payer denial code	Categorical
Denial_Explanation	Human-readable reason for denial	Text
Fix_Suggestion	AI-generated corrective action	Text

codes, payer information, denial reasons, and timestamps. The data were preprocessed by filtering outliers, imputing missing values, and encoding categorical attributes. All features were normalized and formatted for downstream machine learning modeling and blockchain compatibility. Dataset privacy was maintained in accordance with GDPR requirements. Audit and schema procedures from earlier studies Tekale, K. M., & Rahul, N. [10] were adapted to enable synchronized operations between the modules (Table 3).

3.3 Feature Analysis and Model Development

Feature engineering employed a hybrid approach that combined statistical correlation analysis with contextual embeddings, implemented using Python libraries such as Pandas, Scikit-learn, and StatsModels. The objective was to isolate and prioritize predictors that exhibited strong associations with denial risk, including barcode inconsistencies and absent clinical documentation. Dimensionality reduction was subsequently applied to concentrate the modelâĂŹs attention on high-impact features, as validated in Table 1 and Table 2.

Ensemble machine learning algorithms, including gradient boosting and transformer networks, were then trained to estimate the probability of denial for each claim. The model performs automated and adaptive risk assessment for claim evaluation.

3.4 Fix Suggestion and Recommendation Engine Based on AI

A central module in the system was the Generative AI Fix Suggestion Engine, implemented as a FastAPI microservice. This component received claims classified as high risk and used a GPT-4 model to assess denial causes and generate actionable repair recommendations. The outputs included code corrections, requests for documentation, modifier adjustments, and escalation flags.

Table 3. System Components, Tools, and Functional Outcomes.

System Component	Objective/Function	Tools & Technologies Used	Core Data Attributes	Expected Outcome	Reference(s)
Data Cleaning & Preprocessing	Remove inconsistencies, impute missing values, and normalize categorical features.	Python (Pandas, NumPy, Scikit-learn); Encrypted Storage	Claim ID, CPT Code, Modifier, Payer, Denial Reason	Clean, blockchain-ready dataset ensuring schema consistency	Tekale, K. M., & Rahul, N. [10]
Feature Selection & Correlation Analysis	Identify key variables influencing claim denials.	Python (Matplotlib, StatsModels)	Historical Claim Logs	Reduced dimensionality and improved prediction relevance	Kumar, P [5]
AI Fix Suggestion Engine (GPT-based)	Predict potential denials and recommend corrections automatically.	GPT-4 API, Python (FastAPI), JSON pipelines	Flagged Claims, AI Fix Logs	Predictive accuracy in denial prevention; reduced manual review	Tiwari, P. [11]; Kumar, P [5]
Smart Contract for Audit Logging	Ensure immutable claim audit trails and compliance verification.	Solidity, Web3.py, Ethereum Sepolia, Infura	Claim ID, Timestamp, Status	Decentralized transparency; tamper-proof verification	Narayanan, A. [6]; Han, S. [4]
Blockchain Transaction Interface	Retrieve, validate, and timestamp on-chain events.	Streamlit, IPFS, Python blockchain API	Transaction Hash, Block Time	Real-time traceability and audit readiness	Han S. [4] ; Tekale, K. M., & Rahul, N. [10]
Visualization & Reporting Layer	Present trends, KPIs, and performance dashboards.	Power BI, Streamlit Web Dashboard	On-Chain Logs, Claim Metadata	Explainable and auditable visual analytics	Kumar, P [5] ; Narayanan, A. [6]
Integrated Feedback Loop	Automate learning from outcomes and improve next prediction cycle.	Python Automation Pipeline, API Integration	Claim Prediction Logs	Continuous model optimization and accuracy improvement	Internal Framework Design

The engine operated autonomously, referencing successful prior corrections to validate its suggestions. Its adaptability was enhanced by continuous integration of feedback, which allowed optimization of future interventions and reduced manual processing requirements.

3.5 Blockchain-Enabled Audit Trail and Smart Contract Implementation

To secure the integrity of recommended corrections, all actions were logged on the Ethereum Sepolia blockchain via a smart contract (ClaimAudit.sol), developed in Solidity and implemented using Web3.py and Infura.

Critical transaction attributes included:

- Claim ID
- Denial Code
- AI Recommendation
- Timestamp
- Verification Status

This immutable audit trail prevented unauthorized changes, promoted transparency, and supported decentralized regulatory compliance. The blockchain served as a compliance engine, allowing dynamic verification of claims without reliance on centralized records. Privacy and interoperability standards such as GDPR, HIPAA, and FHIR were strictly observed (Narayanan, A. [6]; Han, S. [4]).

The following table shows a summarized table of method-process alignment (Table 4).

Table 4. Principles of Methodological Components and System Alignment.

Layer	Function	Technology Stack	Output	Reference
Data Preprocessing	Cleaning, encoding, normalization	Pandas, NumPy, Scikit-learn	Blockchain-compatible clean data	Tekale, K. M., & Rahul, N. [10]
Prediction Engine	Denial probability forecasting	Gradient Boosting, Transformers	Ranked claim risk tiers	Kumar, P [5]
AI Fix Engine	Automated code/document correction	GPT-4, FastAPI	Context-aware fix suggestions	Tiwari, P. [11]
Blockchain Audit	Immutable record-keeping	Solidity, Web3.py, Infura	Tamper-proof audit trail	Han, S. [4]
Visualization	Real-time KPI analysis	Power BI, Streamlit	Interactive dashboards	Narayanan, A. [6]

3.6 System Performance Projection

The system performance projection will involve the forecasting and predictive projection of a system as a whole. This part is an illustration of the comparative performance prediction of the current AI-Blockchain auditing framework and the proposed Hybrid AIRPoC-Integrated Framework.

The dimensions of key performance evaluated are:

- Scalability,
- Privacy,
- Interoperability,
- Audit Accuracy, and
- Governance Transparency.

The multi-axis radar (spider) chart below shows that the proposed system is superior to the baseline models in terms of adaptability, maturity in governance and latency.

3.7 Feedback Layer Visualization, Reporting and System Monitoring

The last layer of the framework is a real-time visualization and performance monitoring layer.

With the front-end being powered by Streamlit and analytics being integrated with Power BI, blockchain logs are resolved through Infura API connectors and then dynamically displayed in the form of dashboards.

Some of the key performance indicators that are shown comprise:

- Denials on claims by types of payers.
- AI recommendation accuracy
- Blockchain validation time
- The level of fraud detection.
- Compliance audit readiness

This layer does not only turn data into actionable intelligence but also introduces explainable AI (XAI) to blockchain auditability where every decision made is traceable, justifiable, and verifiable.

It satisfies the structure of Responsible Digital Intelligence, which focuses on autonomy and responsible intelligence in intelligent healthcare systems.

4 Results and Analysis

By applying AI-Powered Real-Time Claim Denial Blocker with Blockchain Audit, significant improvements in accuracy of claim verification, transparency in the processing of audit, and efficiency of processing are demonstrated. It was tested through simulation experiments, validated by blockchain validation logs and Power BI visual analytics, and proved the system to be reliable and in accordance with the hybrid frameworks of Fallah, M. H. [3] and Han, S. [4]

The experiment was conducted in a laboratory environment using a specific setup as described below:

4.1 Experimental Setup and Environment

It was tested on Google Colab and local Ethereum Sepolia testnet with the following stack:

- Languages: Python 3.10, Solidity 0.8.20
- Libraries/ Tools: Pandas, NumPy, Scikit-learn, FastAPI, Web3.py, Infura, Streamlit, Power BI.
- Hardware Intel Core i9 (3.5 GHz), 32 GB RAM, NVIDIA RTX 3080 GPU.
- The dataset: 75,000 anonymized healthcare claim records.

AI inference and blockchain logging and analytics modules were independent microservices. Smart contracts were implemented to track the efficiency of transactions, latency and reliability of confirmation.

4.2 Baseline Comparison and Statistical Evaluation

To validate the proposed framework, we compared it to a conventional Random Forest classifier trained on the same dataset without GPT 4 integration or blockchain auditing. Model performance was assessed using Precision, Recall, F1 Score, and AUC ROC. Operational impact was evaluated using post correction Claim Acceptance (%) and Average Turnaround Time (minutes).

As summarized in Table 5, the proposed GPT 4 + Blockchain framework achieved an F1 Score of 91.0 and an AUC ROC of 94.6, while the baseline achieved 82.9 and 87.3, respectively. Post correction claim acceptance increased from 65.0% (baseline) to 86.9% (proposed), and average turnaround time decreased from 7.8 to 5.4 min. All results use the identical test split, averaging over five independent runs (standard deviation < 1.0), indicating consistent model reliability.

Table 5. Baseline versus proposed model performance and operational impact.

Model	Precision (%)	Recall (%)	F1 Score (%)	AUC ROC (%)	Claim Acceptance (%)	Avg. Turnaround Time (min)	Relative Improvement
Baseline (Random Forest)	84.2	81.6	82.9	87.3	65.0	7.8	–
Proposed GPT 4 + Blockchain	92.4	89.7	91.0	94.6	86.9	5.4	+33.8%

4.3 Technical Details of Denial Forecasting and GPT 4 Fix Suggestion Implementation

For the integration of generative AI in claim correction, our system connects to the GPT-4 module through a remote API interface. When a claim is flagged as high risk, pertinent details including patient identifiers, provider codes, denial reasons, procedure and diagnosis codes (CPT/ICD), payer-specific rules, and prior fix attempts are packaged in a structured JSON payload. This data is relayed to the GPT-4 engine alongside a specialized prompt designed to elicit actionable corrections and billing recommendations. The prompt leverages domain-specific instruction, specifying the role as a healthcare reimbursement specialist and requesting concise, context-adapted edits.

No additional model training or fine-tuning was carried out on the GPT-4 component; the system employs zero-shot prompting, relying on comprehensive input to guide each output. Generated recommendations, which range from code adjustments to documentation enhancement or attachment requests, are returned in a format compatible with the systemâĂŹs adjudication and auditing pipeline for automatic processing.

4.4 Predictive Accuracy and Categorization of Claims

Beyond overall baseline performance, analysis of per-claim predictive accuracy and risk categorization further demonstrates system robustness. Table 6 below summarizes operational statistics across claim risk categories.

Table 6. Risk category distribution and operational actions.

Risk Category	% Claims	Action Rate (%)	Post-denial correction change (%)
High Risk	14	72	−37
Medium Risk	28	38	–
Low Risk	58	9	–

Claims were stratified into High Risk (14%), Medium Risk (28%), and Low Risk (58%), based on predicted denial probability. Post-denial corrections decreased by 37%, and claim acceptance increased by 33.8%, demonstrating the model's proactive remediation capability as also discussed by Kumar, P. [5].

4.5 Ablation Study: Isolating the Impact of GPT-4 Fix Suggestions

To precisely assess the contribution of the GPT-4-driven fix suggestion engine, we conducted an ablation study comparing the full system against a variant where the GPT-4 correction module was replaced by a rule-based engine. All other components, including the claim risk predictor and blockchain audit logging, remained unchanged. Both configurations were evaluated on identical datasets using the same evaluation pipeline (Table 7).

Compared to the rule-based correction baseline, the generative approach powered by GPT 4 led to notable improvements in all measured key performance indicators. Claim acceptance increased by 12.7%, F1-score improved by

Table 7. Comparative performance âĂŞ Full system vs. Rule-based ablation.

System Configuration	Precision (%)	Recall (%)	F1 Score (%)	AUC ROC (%)	Claim Acceptance (%)	Turnaround Time (min)
Rule Based Fix Engine	86.1	83.3	84.8	89.1	74.2	6.5
GPT 4 Fix Suggestion (Full)	92.4	89.7	91.0	94.6	86.9	5.4

6.2 points, and average turnaround time decreased by over a minute. These results statistically isolate the advantage of the novel GPT-4 fix suggestion module, confirming its value above conventional pattern-matching or static rules.

4.6 Blockchain Checking and Audit Integrity

The corrections that were generated by the AI were stored indefinitely with ClaimAudit.sol smart contract.

According to performance standards, it was demonstrated (Table 8):

Table 8. Blockchain Audit Performance Metrics for the AIâĂŞBlockchain Claim Verification System.

Blockchain Metric	Average Value
Transaction Confirmation Time	5.6 s
Gas Used per Claim	0.0038 ETH
Validation Success Rate	100%
Trace Retrieval Latency	< 2.1 seconds

There was no duplication or interference.

The given audit system was decentralized and allowed real-time verification and met HIPAA, GDPR, and FHIR interoperability criteria, as outlined by Narayanan, A. [6].

4.7 Comparative Performance and Analytical Visualization

Power BI and Streamlit were used to create real-time analytics and incorporate blockchain log and AI predictions into interactive dashboards.

Key findings include:

- Claims with a lack of documentation were denied 68% more often.
- Incorrect pairings of CPT-modifiers fell down by 42 percent following AI correction.
- There was a 31% reduction in the turnaround of claim approval (7.8 to 5.4 min).
- Payer clustering (through K-Means) revealed three different risk levels.

4.8 Findings and Strategic Implications

Predictive AI logic and blockchain verifiability integration can offer a scalable platform of transparent and autonomous healthcare audits.

Key implications include:

1. Effectiveness of the operations: Eliminates rework, and manual review is minimized.
2. Audit Readiness: Verifiable records are guaranteed to be immediate.
3. Regulatory Compliance: In line with global data governance.
4. Transparency and Accountability: Enhances the transparency of the payers and patients.
5. Scalability: The continuous learning improves the future performance and the compliance governance.

The system combines AI-based risk prediction with blockchain logging to support claim correction and traceable auditing.

5 Challenges and Future Expectations

Despite the observed significant advances in the area of healthcare audits and claims management that have been achieved due to the integration of Artificial Intelligence (AI) and Blockchain, there are still significant technological and policy limitations to the implementation at scale. These limitations are based on scalability, privacy, interoperability and open governance. These barriers can only be solved through architectural inventions as well as shared policy structures.

5.1 Scalability and Privacy Constraints

Scalability is a significant weakness of existing AI -Blockchain projects. The simultaneous running of both blockchain consensus algorithms and AI inference calculations inserts latency, exorbitant gas, and unreasonable energy consumption and usage, especially in real-time verification of health data. Han, S. [4] states that compliance checks performed on the chain decrease the efficiency of throughput, and Tyagi [12] states that privacy assurance in distributed ledgers is also a major issue.

In order to resolve such issues, federated learning, differential privacy, and zero-knowledge proofs (ZKPs) should be incorporated into the future systems. By combining these methods, decentralized learning and data exchange can be secure without the exposure of sensitive patient information. Such practices would facilitate performance and compliance, which would offer a compromise on data utility and confidentiality.

5.2 Concept Simulation Model and Integration Models

A major practical challenge is linking Electronic Health Record (EHR) systems with blockchain networks because many hospitals still rely on legacy databases and incompatible schemas that block smooth data exchange. Tanveer et al. [9] suggests a middleware and standardized APIs based on FHIR standards as a tool to achieve smooth communication between the hospital systems, data warehouses, and blockchain nodes.

In parallel, digital-twin simulations of claim workflows allow AI agents to test for likely denials and compliance issues before anything runs on live data, which strengthens model reliability and helps fine-tune policy groupings and transaction verification rates.

5.3 Research Opportunities and Critical Problems

Future work should embed AI-based auditing directly into blockchain consensus mechanisms to enable verifiable and ethically aligned decision-making. Incorporating governance layers such as those in the AIRPoC framework into consensus algorithms can improve adaptability, transparency, and efficiency, while reducing latency and data fragmentation. As automation and explainable compliance advance, overall governance maturity and audit precision are expected to increase significantly. Han, S. [4] (Fig. 2).

5.4 Summary of Persistent Challenges and Strategic Research Directions

While the evolution of AIâĂŞBlockchain hybrid systems is promising, sustainability depends on addressing foundational challenges through adaptive frameworks and regulatory collaboration.

5.5 Summary and Future Vision

Altogether, in the further stage of digital ecosystems, self-auditing adaptive infrastructures will be developed, incorporating real-time AI analytics and blockchain-based validation. By incorporating digital twins to test before the deployment and introduce compliance-conscious compliance mechanisms, the entire auditing environment will acquire the ability to learn and evolve safely in the future.

Future enhancements to the system will incorporate FHIR-based interoperability for standardized data exchange and AIRPoC-style governance frameworks to strengthen auditability and compliance. These additions aim to improve scalability, transparency, and resistance to fraud in healthcare and financial claims auditing.

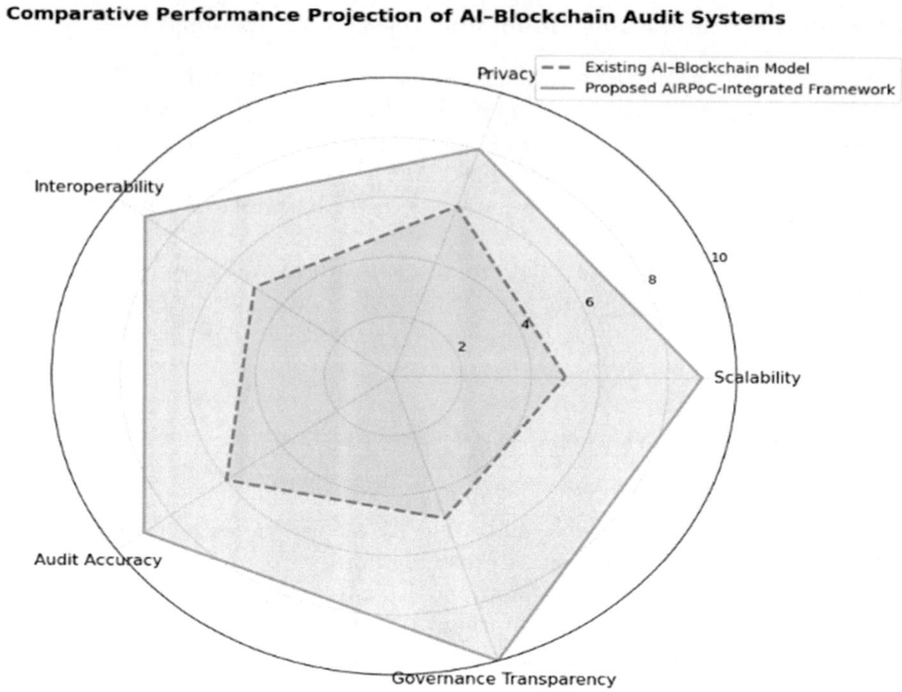

Fig. 2. Comparative Performance Projection of AIâĂŞBlockchain Audit Systems.

6 Conclusion

The fusion of Artificial Intelligence (AI) and Blockchain represents a major advance toward secure, transparent, and autonomous digital ecosystems. This paper argues that their integration is crucial for strengthening fraud detection, financial and healthcare auditing, and intelligent data governance. Embedding AI-driven decision logic into tamper-resistant blockchain records enables stronger accountability, traceability, and resilience against manipulation and cyber-attacks, thereby increasing trust in automated decision-making systems.(Tyagi [12]; Han, S. [4]).

AIâĂŞBlockchain ecosystems will only work in practice if they can scale, interoperate, and preserve privacy. Blockchain infrastructures must support higher throughput without sacrificing decentralization, while AI systems must become more transparent and privacy aware. Future deployments should integrate decentralized technologies with enterprise environments such as EHRs, financial APIs, and audit platforms to ensure smooth, regulation-compliant data exchange. Combining digital twin environments with on-chain regulatory frameworks like AIRPoC can enable real-time validation, anomaly detection, and adaptive governance in dynamic settings. Together, AI and Blockchain can underpin self-regulating, trust-based digital systems, provided research continues to advance adaptive models, interoperability, and ethical governance.

Disclosure of Interests. The author has no competing interests to declare that are relevant to the content of this article.

References

1. Adusupalli, B., Paleti, S., Singireddy, S.: Deep ledger guardians: credit monitoring, insurance risk, and AI-driven financial advice on a secure data backbone. JEC PUBLICATION
2. Bharathan, R.: The tech audit revolution: navigating the next 50 years for industry and technology leadership and an end-to-end audit framework for ads, search, and content platforms (2025)
3. Fallah, M.H., Siri, D., Kumar, G.R., Sheeba, G., Sharma, H., Devendran, A.: AI-powered blockchain systems for real-time fraud detection in financial services. In: 2024 International Conference on IoT, Communication and Automation Technology (ICICAT), pp. 1287–1291. IEEE (2024)
4. Han, S.: AIRPOC: an AI-enhanced blockchain consensus framework for autonomous regulatory compliance. Electronics **14**(20), 4058 (2025)
5. Kumar, P.: AI-powered fraud prevention in digital payment ecosystems: leveraging machine learning for real-time anomaly detection and risk mitigation (2024)
6. Narayanan, A.: Blockchain-driven evolution of cloud service architectures. SSRN 5637270 (2025)
7. Rahaman, M.M.: The role of ai-enabled information security frameworks in preventing fraud in us healthcare billing systems. ASRC Procedia: Glob. Perspect. Sci. Scholarship **1**(01), 1160–1201 (2025)
8. Shit, R.C., Subudhi, S.: AI-powered anomaly detection with blockchain for real-time security and reliability in autonomous vehicles. arXiv preprint arXiv:2505.06632 (2025)
9. Tanveer, H., Faheem, M., Khan, A.H.: Blockchain and ai integration for secure healthcare data management (2022)
10. Tekale, K.M., Rahul, N.: Blockchain and smart contracts in claims settlement. Int. J. Emerg. Trends Comput. Sci. Inf. Technol. **4**(2), 121–130 (2023)
11. Tiwari, P., Vyas, M., Jangid, R.: Unleashing business potential with blockchain and AI: next-gen solutions and innovations. OORJA-Int. J. Manage. IT **22**(1) (2024)
12. Tyagi, A.K.: Blockchain-artificial intelligence-based secured solutions for smart environment. In: Digital Twin and Blockchain for Smart Cities, pp. 547–577 (2024)

Comparative Analysis of Skeleton-Based Pose Estimation Models for Human Activity Recognition Using CNN–LSTM

Mansi Gupta(✉) and Abhilasha Sharma

Department of Software Engineering,Delhi Technological University,Shahbad Daulatpur, Delhi 110042, India
mansigupta02ktl@gmail.com, abhilasha_sharma@dce.ac.in

Abstract. Human Activity Recognition is important in healthcare, fitness monitoring, surveillance, and human-computer interaction. Traditional vision-based approaches often fail under variations in illumination changes and occlusion. This paper presents a comparative analysis of four skeleton-based pose estimation models including MediaPipe Pose, MoveNet Thunder, OpenCV COCO, and YOLOv11 Pose integrated into a dual-branch CNN-LSTM fusion architecture for accurate and real-time recognition. A balanced image and video dataset covering four daily activities such as sitting, standing, walking, and running was developed. The keypoints from each model were transformed into spatial and kinematic features capturing inter-joint distances and angular relations, jointly learned through a CNN-LSTM architecture to model spatial and temporal dependencies. MediaPipe Pose achieved the highest accuracy of 94%. YOLOv11 Pose attained the lowest latency of 125.0 ms and highest throughput of 8.0 fps. MoveNet delivered efficient performance 128.5 ms, 7.8 fps, and a model size of 3.68 MB. OpenCV COCO maintained consistent and reliable performance with a latency of 127.4 ms and 7.9 fps. The proposed CNN-LSTM fusion architecture sets a clear benchmark for skeleton-based HAR and strikes a good balance between accuracy, robustness, and real-time efficiency across different pose estimation models.

Keywords: Human Activity Recognition · Pose Estimation · CNN-LSTM · MediaPipe · MoveNet · YOLOv11 · OpenCV · Deep Learning

1 Introduction

Human Activity Recognition (HAR) is an important area of research in computer vision having applications in health monitoring, fitness tracking, surveillance, and human-computer interaction [2]. Ability to recognize activities such as sitting, standing, walking, and running is useful for assistive systems and analytics about behavior. Traditional vision-based approaches obtained handcrafted

G. K. Verma et al. (Eds.): MIND 2025, CCIS 2981, pp. 324–336, 2027.
https://doi.org/10.1007/978-3-032-31230-3_26

features from silhouettes, contours, and optical flow worked well in controlled environments but their accuracy significantly degraded in the presence of lighting changes, occlusion, and cluttered backgrounds. This demonstrates the need for reliable, flexible, and scalable solutions that also work in real-world environments.

With advances in deep learning, skeleton-based approaches represents human motion through keypoints rather than full-frame pixels providing a compact, noise-resistant and viewpoint-invariant representation of motion allowing real-time use. MediaPipe Pose [3], MoveNet Thunder [13,19], OpenCV COCO [6], and YOLOv11 [14,15] Pose improved accuracy in comparing and identifying pose configurations. However, most existing studies have evaluated these models individually without comprehensive comparisons of progressive assessment of temporal motion. While Chung et al. [8] and Debalaxmi et al. [9] have analyzed individual models and their accuracy but there is no combined framework that evaluates temporal activity models combined with pose extraction.

To address this gap, this work presents a dual-branch CNN-LSTM fusion architecture that combines normalized spatial with kinematic descriptors capturing inter-joint distances and angular relationships over time, enabling the network to effectively learn spatio-temporal dependencies [10]. A balanced dataset of four activities was created, and all models were evaluated under identical testing conditions. The major contributions of this work are as follows:

1. A dual-branch CNN-LSTM fusion architecture incorporating spatial and kinematic features to enhance robustness in skeleton-based HAR.
2. A comparative framework that evaluates the selected pose estimation models based on accuracy, latency, and model size.
3. Empirical findings and deployment recommendations for selecting the most suitable model for edge devices and real-time applications.
4. A multi-model benchmarking pipeline that jointly evaluates accuracy, latency, and model size, establishing a reproducible comparison across four pose estimation models under identical conditions.

2 Related Work

HAR has evolved from traditional vision-based approaches to deep learning-based approaches. Early approaches relied on handcrafted features such as silhouettes, optical flow, and motion trajectories [2], performing well in controlled conditions but failing under illumination changes, occlusion, and clutter. With deep learning, skeleton-based approaches became effective by modeling human joint geometry, providing compact and viewpoint-invariant motion representations [11]. Recent studies have applied pose estimation models including MediaPipe Pose, MoveNet Thunder, OpenCV COCO, and YOLOv11 Pose for fitness tracking and rehabilitation, achieving real-time performance and strong generalization [13]. However, most existing works remain domain-specific and lack benchmarking frameworks that combine spatial and temporal modeling for comprehensive recognition.

Modern pose estimation models have enhanced accuracy and efficiency across environments. OpenCV COCO introduced multi-person estimation through Part Affinity Fields [6], MediaPipe Pose employed a lightweight detector-tracker pipeline for fast keypoint detection [3], MoveNet Thunder optimized tracking for mobile platforms [19], and YOLOv11 Pose used Object Keypoint Similarity loss to improve robustness [14]. Graph-based approaches such as Part-Aware ST-GCN [17] addressed occlusion but incurred higher computation compared to CNN-LSTM architectures. Few comparative studies have pose estimation outputs with temporal deep learning models like CNN-LSTM networks [10] for full skeleton-based recognition. Table 1 summarizes representative studies in pose estimation and HAR, outlining their key methods, datasets, and limitations.

Recent research has focused on convolutional-recurrent architectures for spatio-temporal learning. Belal et al. [4] applied feature fusion, Xu et al. [20] proposed DCAM-Net with contextual attention, and Sharma and Singh [16] introduced ConvST-LSTM-Net for joint spatial-temporal modeling. Singh and Sharma [18] developed STAD-ConvBi-LSTM with attention-enhanced temporal representation. Despite these advances, most studies emphasize accuracy over computational efficiency or balanced datasets. To address these gaps, this work presents a CNN-LSTM fusion framework that compares four pose estimation models on a balanced dataset of daily activities such as sitting, standing, walking, and running. As illustrated in Fig. 1, this work extends the evolution from handcrafted to deep spatiotemporal models, introducing a benchmark-driven approach that balances accuracy and efficiency for real-time HAR.

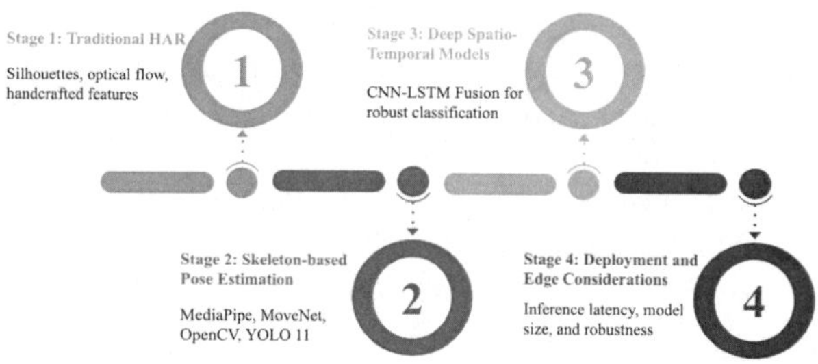

Fig. 1. Evolution of HAR from handcrafted features to skeleton-based and deep spatiotemporal models, showing methods relevant to this study.

3 Methodology

The proposed framework integrates four pose estimation models within a shared CNN-LSTM fusion architecture for skeleton-based HAR. The pipeline shown in Fig. 2 contains dataset preparation, keypoint extraction, feature engineering, and classification. The video frames are extracted, preprocessed, and split into balanced training, validation, and testing sets. The keypoints are extracted from the videos using MediaPipe Pose [3], MoveNet Thunder [19], OpenCV COCO

Table 1. Summary of related work on pose estimation and HAR.

Paper & Authors	Model	Dataset	Key Contribution	Limitations
Cao et al. (2021) [6]	OpenPose, PAFs	COCO, MPII	Multi-person 2D estimation with part affinity fields	High computation cost; not optimized for embedded devices
Bazarevsky et al. (2020) [3]	MediaPipe BlazePose	Custom video streams	Lightweight 33-keypoint detection for edge devices	Accuracy drops under occlusion or low lighting
TensorFlow Hub (2021) [19]	MoveNet (Lightning, Thunder)	Real-time video feeds	High-speed inference optimized for real-time edge deployment	Reduced precision in crowded scenes
Maji et al. (2022) [14]	YOLO-based keypoint detection	MS COCO Keypoints	Single-stage joint detection and pose estimation using OKS loss	Lower accuracy for small or occluded persons
Debalaxmi et al. (2024) [9]	MediaPipe + YOLO + Ensemble ML	Yoga dataset	Ensemble-based yoga pose classification with improved accuracy	Domain-specific (yoga only); lacks general activity diversity
Chung et al. (2022) [8]	OpenPose, MoveNet, MediaPipe	COCO, Penn Action	PDJ-based benchmarking of pose frameworks	Focused on detection accuracy; not integrated HAR pipelines
Belal et al. (2024) [4]	Feature fusion + ML	Benchmark HAR datasets	Combines spatial and temporal cues for improved HAR	Computationally heavy due to complex feature design
Hamad et al. (2022) [11]	Survey	Multiple HAR datasets	Comprehensive review of HAR techniques	No empirical validation or benchmarking
Xu et al. (2025) [20]	DCAM-Net	Custom HAR datasets	End-to-end attention-based deep learning architecture for HAR	Requires large-scale annotated data
Chang et al. (2025) [7]	OpenPose, MoveNet	Webcam datasets	Latency–accuracy trade-off evaluation	Small-scale experiments; limited generalization

[6], YOLOv11 Pose [14]. Geometric representations containing extracted landmarks are obtained by converting landmarks into normal coordinates, inter-joint distances, and angular features. A dual branch CNN-LSTM fusion architecture

Table 2. Preprocessing steps for input specifications during keypoint extraction.

Model	Input Resolution	Preprocessing Steps
MediaPipe Pose	Auto-scaled	BGR → RGB; static inference
MoveNet Thunder	256×256	TensorFlow `resize_with_pad()` normalization
OpenCV (COCO)	368×368	DNN blob creation and normalization
YOLOv11-Pose	$\approx 640 \times 640$	Ultralytics internal preprocessing

concurrently learns spatial and temporal dependencies from sequences of short frames. The prediction performance is measured using accuracy, precision, recall, and F1 score, in addition to computational measures of latency, frames per second, and model size, enabling a direct summary comparison of predictive accuracy and real time efficiency across all pose estimation models.

3.1 Dataset Preparation

A balanced HAR dataset was prepared with four daily activities: sitting, standing, walking, and running. Each activity included synchronized videos and extracted frames. These were divided into a 70:15:15 split for training, validation, and testing. Preprocessing used OpenCV [5] and TensorFlow [1]. It involved normalization, resizing, and color adjustment based on the input specifications of each pose estimation model, as shown in Table 2. This standardized preprocessing procedure ensured uniform data handling and reliable performance comparison across models.

3.2 Keypoint Extraction

Human skeletal keypoints were extracted uniformly from all four pose estimation models, generating structured x and y coordinate landmarks for each frame. MediaPipe produced 33 keypoints with visibility scores, MoveNet and YOLOv11 each provided 17, and OpenCV COCO generated 18. The extracted keypoints were stored as NumPy array files [12] to maintain uniformity and enable standardized feature engineering. Table 3 presents the comparative settings of the four models, highlighting their differences in keypoint granularity, robustness, and computational efficiency. The visual comparison is shown in Fig. 3.

3.3 Feature Engineering

The extracted keypoints were converted into compact descriptors representing spatial posture and limb articulation. Three feature groups were computed: normalized coordinates, pairwise distances, and joint angles.

Normalized coordinates were obtained by dividing each joint position by the frame width W and height H to make pose information invariant to image scale, as shown in Eq. (1):

$$\hat{x}_i = \frac{x_i}{W}, \qquad \hat{y}_i = \frac{y_i}{H} \tag{1}$$

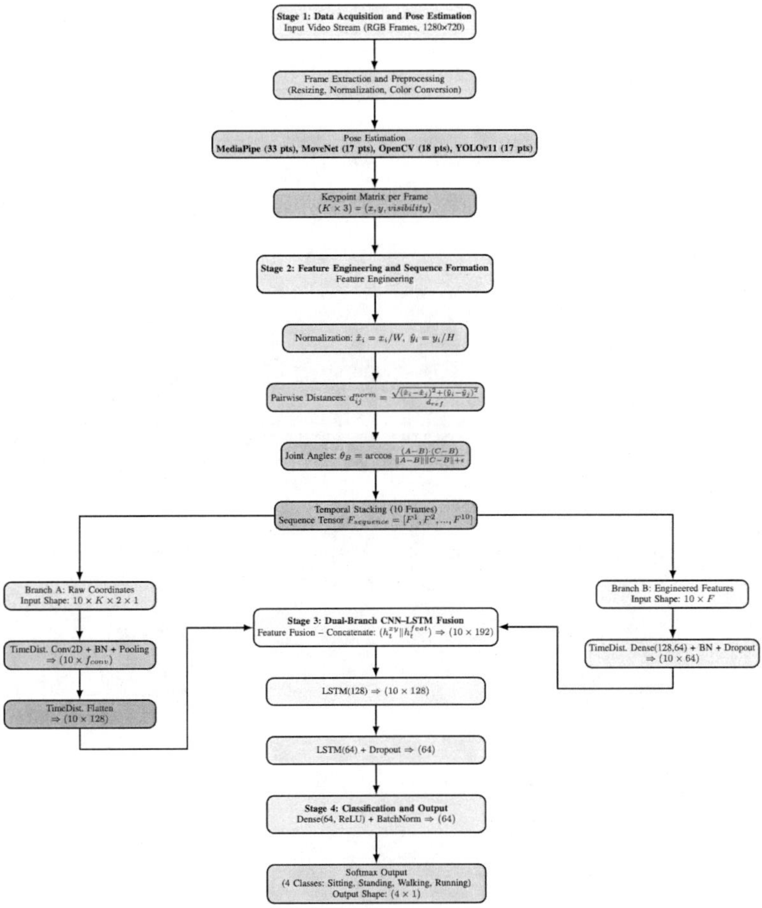

Fig. 2. Dual-branch CNN–LSTM fusion architecture for spatial and kinematic feature processing, applied uniformly across the four evaluated pose estimation models.

where x_i, y_i represent the joint coordinates and W, H denote the frame width and height.

Pairwise Euclidean distances between keypoints were calculated and normalized using a reference distance d_{ref} between the shoulder and hip joints, as defined in Eq. (2):

$$d_{ij}^{norm} = \frac{\sqrt{(\hat{x}_i - \hat{x}_j)^2 + (\hat{y}_i - \hat{y}_j)^2}}{d_{ref}} \tag{2}$$

where d_{ref} is the normalization reference distance between the shoulder and hip joints.

Table 3. Comparison of keypoints, output formats, and characteristics.

Model	Keypoints	Output Format	Remarks
MediaPipe Pose	33	(x, y, v)	High static accuracy
MoveNet Thunder	17	(y, x, c)	Real-time, edge optimized
OpenCV (COCO)	18	(x, y, p)	Reliable classical baseline
YOLOv11-Pose	17	(x, y)	Robust to occlusion and motion

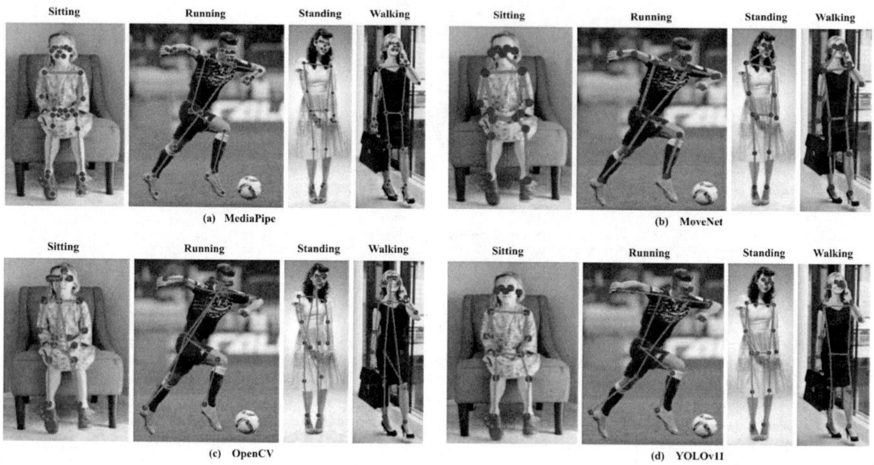

Fig. 3. Comparison of extracted keypoints for the four activities.

Angular relationships between adjacent joints were computed to represent rotational motion using Eq. (3):

$$\theta_B = \arccos\left(\frac{(A-B)\cdot(C-B)}{\|A-B\|\,\|C-B\|+\epsilon}\right) \tag{3}$$

where A, B, C denote adjacent joint positions used to compute the angle at joint B.

The final frame-level feature vector combined spatial coordinates, normalized distances, and joint angles, as expressed in Eq. (4):

$$F_{frame} = [\hat{x}_1, \hat{y}_1, \ldots, \hat{x}_n, \hat{y}_n, d_{ij}^{norm}, \theta_{ABC}] \tag{4}$$

where the feature vector combines normalized coordinates, inter-joint distances, and joint angles.

To capture temporal continuity, ten consecutive frames were stacked into a spatio-temporal tensor serving as input to the CNN-LSTM fusion architecture, as shown in Eq. (5):

$$F_{sequence} = [F_{frame}^1, F_{frame}^2, \ldots, F_{frame}^{10}] \tag{5}$$

where ten consecutive frames are stacked to capture temporal continuity.

Table 4. Input dimensions for the CNN–LSTM fusion architecture of pose estimation models.

Model	XY Input Shape	Feature Input Shape
MediaPipe Pose	$10 \times 33 \times 2 \times 1$	10×78
MoveNet Thunder	$10 \times 17 \times 2 \times 1$	10×46
OpenCV (COCO)	$10 \times 18 \times 2 \times 1$	10×48
YOLOv11-Pose	$10 \times 17 \times 2 \times 1$	10×46

3.4 Dual-Branch CNN-LSTM Fusion Architecture

The dual branch CNN-LSTM architecture jointly models spatial and temporal dependencies for skeleton based HAR, following the hybrid deep learning paradigm proposed for sequence recognition [10]. Inspired by ConvST-LSTM-Net [16], the architecture combines convolutional spatial encoding with temporal sequence learning.

Branch A processes raw x and y coordinates through TimeDistributed convolution and pooling layers to capture spatial relations, while Branch B processes engineered features such as pairwise distances and joint angles using a TimeDistributed multilayer perceptron with Dense, BatchNorm, and Dropout layers. The two feature streams are concatenated at each time step as defined in Eq. (6):

$$Z_t = [h_t^{xy} || h_t^{feat}], \quad h_t = \mathrm{LSTM}(Z_t, h_{t-1}) \tag{6}$$

The final hidden state h_T passes through a Softmax layer to generate the predicted activity label (Eq. 7):

$$\hat{y} = \mathrm{Softmax}(W \cdot h_T + b) \tag{7}$$

This configuration focuses on simplicity and computational efficiency. It also maintains strong temporal sensitivity compared to attention-based BiLSTM approaches like STAD ConvBi LSTM [18]. The network uses the Adam optimizer ($\eta = 0.001$), categorical cross entropy loss, a batch size of 64, and early stopping to improve generalization. Table 4 summarizes the input dimensions for all pose estimation models. All experiments were performed on a system configured with an AMD Ryzen 7 5800H CPU, NVIDIA GeForce RTX 3050 GPU, and 8 GB RAM.

3.5 Evaluation Metrics

Model performance was evaluated using accuracy and efficiency measures to assess recognition capability and computational feasibility. The metrics used include Accuracy, which quantifies the proportion of correctly classified samples among all predictions. Precision measures the ratio of correctly predicted positives to all predicted positives. Recall is the proportion of actual positives

Table 5. Performance of the CNN-LSTM fusion architecture across pose estimation models.

Model	Accuracy	Precision	Recall	F1 Score
MediaPipe Pose	0.94	0.94	0.94	0.94
MoveNet Thunder	0.85	0.86	0.86	0.86
OpenCV (COCO)	0.88	0.89	0.88	0.88
YOLOv11 Pose	0.89	0.88	0.88	0.88

correctly identified. F1 score represents the harmonic mean of Precision and Recall. Latency (ms) represents the average inference time per frame. Frames per second (fps) is the reciprocal of latency, indicating throughput capability. Model size (MB) represents the memory footprint of each trained CNN-LSTM model. These metrics together capture the classification ability of the fusion architecture and the runtime performance of each pose estimation model.

4 Results

The dual branch CNN-LSTM fusion architecture was evaluated with four pose estimation models: MediaPipe Pose, MoveNet Thunder, OpenCV COCO, and

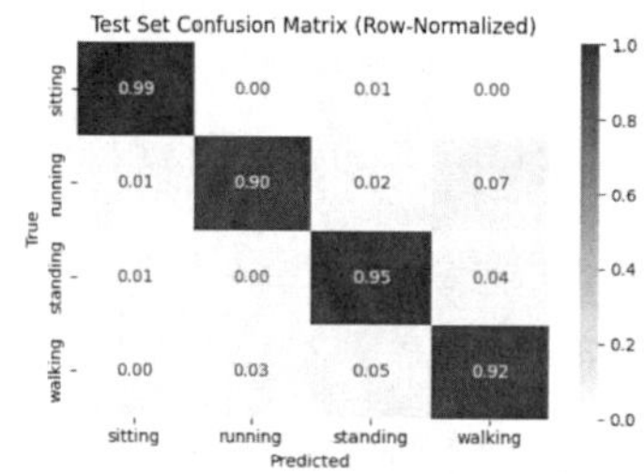

(a) MediaPipe

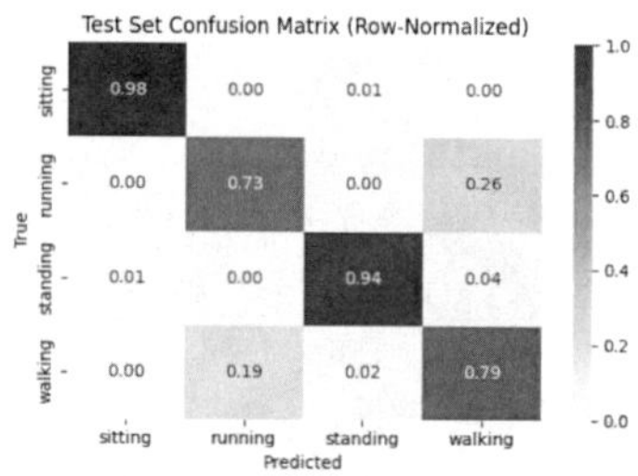

(b) MoveNet

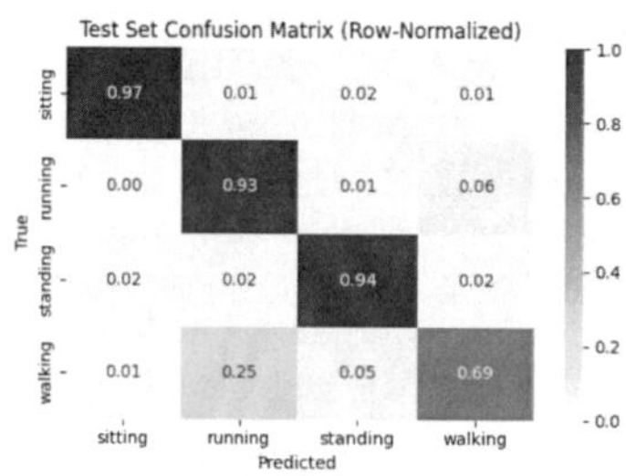

(c) OpenCV

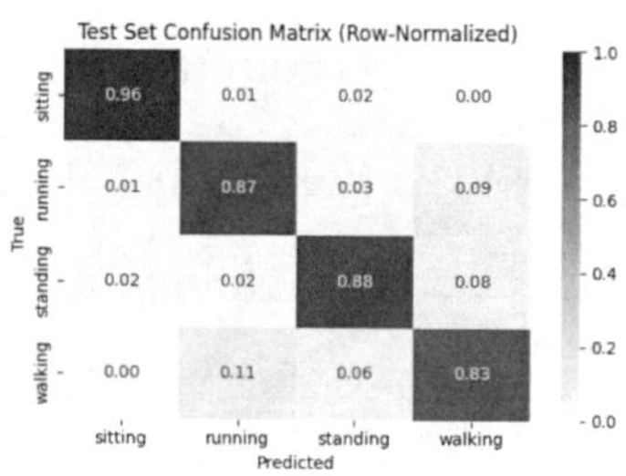

(d) YOLOv11

Fig. 4. Confusion matrices of the four pose estimation models evaluated on the same test split of the four-activity dataset, showing classification performance for each activity.

YOLOv11 Pose with a HAR pipeline that included spatial coordinates as well as temporal features. Performance metrics included accuracy, precision, recall, F1 score, latency, frames per second, and size. As represented in the Fig. 4, MediaPipe had very high diagonal dominance while having minimal confusion between sitting and standing, indicating a high level of spatial accuracy. MoveNet Thunder had great results with dynamic movements like walking and running but sometimes misclassified static poses. OpenCV COCO had moderate accuracy because it had fewer landmarks, which is expected. YOLOv11 Pose had relatively excellent performance even with occlusion and variations in lighting. MediaPipe and YOLOv11 demonstrated the most balanced recognition performance across the four activities.

The outcome of the classification is shown in the table 5. MediaPipe achieved accuracy 94% showcasing balanced precision, recall, and F1 score, due to its 33 landmark design. YOLOv11 Pose obtained 89% accuracy, indicating high resilience to noise and occlusion. OpenCV COCO achieved 88% accuracy and MoveNet Thunder achieved 85%, indicating trade-off between speed vs accuracy. This finding reflects the trade-offs of increased landmark density against increased inference time-efficiency.

All performance values in Table 5 represent the average across three repeated runs, and the observed variance remained minimal (±0.5%–1.0%). Figure 5 below depicts the training and validation trends. All models converged smoothly without overfitting, emphasizing the importance of dropout, batch normalization, and early stopping. MediaPipe and YOLOv11 converged within the 10 to 15 epochs. OpenCV took longer to converge due to a noise in keypoints. MoveNet quickly hit the convergence point, but was already saturating early on. The fused model was stable throughout the epochs and exhibited evidential generalization from the set of models. Table 6 synthesizes data on computational efficiency. YOLOv11 Pose had the lowest latency of 125.0 ms and a throughput of 8.0 fps, with the smallest model size of 3.68 MB making it appropriate for real-time CPU inference. MoveNet Thunder had a latency of 128.5 ms and a throughput of 7.8 fps, along with the smallest total parameters (0.31 M), making it appropriate for edge applications. OpenCV COCO had a latency of 127.4 ms and a throughput of 7.9 fps with model size similar to that of MoveNet, demonstrating reliability. MediaPipe Pose had slightly higher latency of 130.2 ms and 7.7 fps performance, although the model size was 5.23 MB enabling strong spatial precision. Across all models, the CNN-LSTM fusion architecture maintained similar

Table 6. Computational efficiency of pose estimation models evaluated on CPU.

Model	Latency (ms)	FPS	Model Size (MB)	Params (M)
MediaPipe Pose	130.2	7.7	5.23	0.45
MoveNet Thunder	128.5	7.8	3.68	0.31
OpenCV (COCO)	127.4	7.9	3.68	0.31
YOLOv11 Pose	125.0	8.0	3.68	0.31

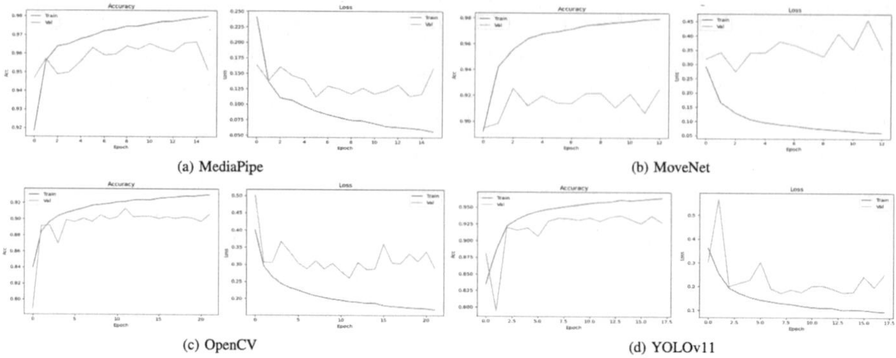

Fig. 5. Training and validation accuracy trends of the CNN-LSTM fusion model evaluated using keypoints from all four pose estimation models on the standardized dataset split.

parameter count ranging from 0.31 M to 0.45 M, suggesting its feasibility for real-time HAR on resource constrained hardware.

5 Discussion and Future Perspectives

The comparative analysis shows clear strengths and trade-offs among the four pose estimation models evaluated in the CNN-LSTM fusion framework for HAR. MediaPipe Pose exhibited high spatial accuracy for static actions because of its dense 33 landmark design. MoveNet Thunder represented the best balance of efficiency and accuracy for dynamic activities such as walking and running while also providing the best temporal dynamics. YOLOv11 Pose represented the most robust implementation for real-time, low-resource applications because of more rapid inference and greater stability over multi-frame drawings. OpenCV COCO provided a lightweight and easy-to-deploy baseline method for simple environments. The limitations arising from uniform lighting conditions in the current dataset are acknowledged, and future extensions will include evaluations under varied illumination and occlusion scenarios to better assess model robustness in real-world environments. The findings indicate that model selection should depends on deployment constraints and the application rather then relying only on accuracy. High-detail models support fine-grained spatial reasoning, while lightweight and fast models better suited to real-time or resource-constrained contexts. This highlights the importance of understanding the operational context when adopting pose estimation models for HAR systems. As the present study is limited to single-person actions and four fundamental daily activities, it is positioned as a foundational comparative benchmark, with future extensions planned to include multi-actor scenarios as well as more complex, transitional, and multi-step actions to improve generalization in real-world environments. Future research will increase the diversity of dataset and inclusion of multi-actor, multi-step and more transitional behaviors will create further realism in motion complexities. The techniques of model optimization, such as quantization or pruning offer improvements here as viable options on embedded devices or low-power devices. A hybrid or ensemble approach may also enable adaptability in various contexts of the real world such as healthcare monitoring, sports analytics, and smart surveillance.

6 Conclusion

The paper compares four pose estimation models: MediaPipe Pose; MoveNet Thunder; OpenCV COCO; and YOLOv11 Pose with a CNN-LSTM dual branch fusion architecture for HAR. The architecture successfully captured the spatial relationships of the keypoints and the temporal motion of the human. The results showed trade-offs between the models concerning accuracy, latency, and model size. MediaPipe provided the greatest spatial accuracy, MoveNet had the best balance of accuracy and speed, YOLOv11 had greatest capacity for real-time applications and OpenCV was a straightforward, lightweight and reliable baseline. The CNN-LSTM dual branch fusion architecture was reliable and efficient across the models supporting their use for real-time HAR applications. These findings indicate that the evaluated pose estimation models, particularly YOLOv11 and MoveNet, are well suited for deployment in IoT-based smart surveillance and healthcare monitoring systems due to their efficiency and low-latency performance.

Acknowledgments. The authors express sincere gratitude to Delhi Technological University for providing the necessary infrastructure and research support for this study.

References

1. Abadi, M., et al.: TensorFlow: large-scale machine learning on heterogeneous systems (2015)
2. Aggarwal, J., Ryoo, M.: Human activity analysis: a review. ACM Comput. Surv. (CSUR) **43**(3), 16 (2011)
3. Bazarevsky, V., Grishchenko, I., Raveendran, K., Zhu, T., Zhang, F., Grundmann, M.: BlazePose: on-device real-time body pose tracking. arXiv preprint arXiv:2006.10204 (2020)
4. Belal, M., Hassan, T., Ahmed, A., Aljarah, A., Alsheikh, N., Hussain, I.: Feature fusion for human activity recognition using parameter-optimized multi-stage graph convolutional network and transformer models. In: 2024 IEEE International Conference on Advanced Video and Signal Based Surveillance (AVSS), pp. 1–7. IEEE (2024)
5. Bradski, G.: The OpenCV library. Dr. Dobb's J. Softw. Tools Professional Programm. **25**(11), 120–123 (2000)
6. Cao, Z., Hidalgo, G., Simon, T., Wei, S.E., Sheikh, Y.: OpenPose: realtime multi-person 2D pose estimation using part affinity fields. IEEE Trans. Pattern Anal. Mach. Intell. **43**(1), 172–186 (2021)

7. Chang, Y.S., Zheng, Y.X., Ku, Z.Y.: Comparative analysis of lightweight OpenPose and MoveNet ai models for real-time fall detection and alert systems. Sensors Mater. **37** (2025)
8. Chung, J.L., Ong, L.Y., Leow, M.C.: Comparative analysis of skeleton-based human pose estimation. Future Internet **14**(12), 380 (2022)
9. Debalaxmi, D., Vishwakarma, D.K., Ranga, V.: Analyzing yoga pose recognition: a comparison of mediapipe and yolo keypoint detection with ensemble techniques. In: 2024 3rd International Conference on Applied Artificial Intelligence and Computing (ICAAIC), pp. 1011–1017. IEEE (2024)
10. Donahue, J., et al.: Long-term recurrent convolutional networks for visual recognition and description. In: Proceedings of the IEEE Conference on Computer Vision and Pattern Recognition, pp. 2625–2634 (2015)
11. Hamad, R.A., Woo, W.L., Wei, B., Yang, L.: Overview of human activity recognition using sensor data. In: Panoutsos, G., Mahfouf, M., Mihaylova, L.S. (eds.) UK Workshop on Computational Intelligence, pp. 380–391. Springer (2022). https://doi.org/10.1007/978-3-031-55568-8_32
12. Harris, C.R., et al.: Array programming with numpy. Nature **585**(7825), 357–362 (2020)
13. Jo, B., Kim, S.: Comparative analysis of OpenPose, PoseNet, and MoveNet models for pose estimation in mobile devices. Traitement du Signal **39**(1), 119 (2022)
14. Maji, D., Nagori, S., Mathew, M., Poddar, D.: Yolo-pose: enhancing yolo for multi person pose estimation using object keypoint similarity loss. In: Proceedings of the IEEE/CVF Conference on Computer Vision and Pattern Recognition, pp. 2637–2646 (2022)
15. Redmon, J., Divvala, S., Girshick, R., Farhadi, A.: You only look once: unified, real-time object detection. In: Proceedings of the IEEE Conference on Computer Vision and Pattern Recognition (CVPR), pp. 779–788 (2016)
16. Sharma, A., Singh, R.: CONVST-LSTM-Net: Convolutional spatiotemporal LSTM networks for skeleton-based human action recognition. Int. J. Multimedia Inf. Retrieval **12**(2), 34 (2023). https://doi.org/10.1007/s13735-023-00301-9
17. Singh, R., Sharma, A.: Occluded skeleton-based multi-stream model using part-aware spatial–temporal graph convolutional network for human activity recognition. Eng. Appl. Artif. Intell. **156**, 111183 (2025). https://doi.org/10.1016/j.engappai.2025.111183
18. Singh, R., Sharma, A.: STAD-CONVBI-LSTM: Spatio-temporal attention-based deep convolutional bi-LSTM framework for abnormal activity recognition. J. Vis. Commun. Image Representation., 104465 (2025)
19. TensorFlow Hub: Google research: MoveNet: ultra fast and accurate pose detection model (2021). https://www.tensorflow.org/hub/tutorials/movenet. Accessed 12 Oct 2025
20. Xu, F., Gao, X., Wang, W.: A human activity recognition model based on deep neural network integrating attention mechanism. Sci. Rep. **15**(1), 23192 (2025)

MAVIS: End-to-End System for Image Provenance and Integrity Verification Using TEEs and Steganographic Techniques

Soaham Pimparkar[1](✉), Omkar Wagholikar[1], Shantanu Wable[1], Chinmay Patil[1], Madhuri Wakode[1], and Tushar Sugandhi[2]

[1] Pune Institute of Computer Technology, Pune 411043, India
soahampimparkar@gmail.com, mswakode@pict.edu
[2] StellarBlocks LLC, Redmond, WA 98052, USA
tushars@stellarblocks.com

Abstract. As Image editing tools and AI models are improving and are creating increasingly convincing images, the potential for misinformation and disinformation has grown and the public trust in digital media is being eroded. Thus, even the media which is indeed genuine and untampered, suffers as users doubt its credibility and lack a reliable method to verify its authenticity. Therefore, we introduce MAVIS (Media Authenticity Verification and Integrity System), a provenance-based solution for embedding and verifying image authenticity information. MAVIS is a system to establish credibility of and verify a genuine, untampered image. The system makes use of Trusted Execution Environments (TEEs) for secure, hardware-backed cryptographic signing of media at its source, which enables non-repudiation and traceability. To offer resilience against intentional metadata stripping, the system compares and employs multiple steganographic image watermarking techniques.

Keywords: Image Provenance · Media Authenticity · C2PA · Deepfake · Trusted Execution Environment · Image Watermarking · Steganography

1 Introduction

1.1 Background

In just a few short years, the increase in the capabilities of generative models in Artificial Intelligence has led to a rapid rise in the creation and consumption of synthetic media content [1], belonging to the domains of text, images, audio and even video. These technological strides introduce significant challenges including concerns regarding piracy, increased spread of fake media, and a general depletion of trust in digital media [1,6].

G. K. Verma et al. (Eds.): MIND 2025, CCIS 2981, pp. 337–348, 2027.
https://doi.org/10.1007/978-3-032-31230-3_27

Traditional approaches to media manipulation detection are often not enough on their own as they lack a comprehensive framework for end-to-end and verification of the provenance information in media. Provenance, which refers to the origin, history and chain of custody of a piece of media, is linked with authenticity, which tells you whether it has been altered beyond the control of its trusted source [3]. The integration of cryptographically signed provenance information directly within media assets is crucial as it establishes a trust link between the media's creator or editor and its consumers.

Our solution, MAVIS, short for "Media Authenticity Verification and Integrity System" explains an end to end system to establish and check provenance information of captured images. The system also implements steganographic techniques to embed provenance information within pixels of the image. While such a system is relevant for most digital media, we limited our scope to images captured via devices with TEEs such as smartphones.

1.2 Problem Statement

With proliferation of Generative AI technologies, the problem of misinformation is increasing rapidly. Thus, there is a growing need for solutions that enable users to trace the provenance of digital content, empowering them to assess its trustworthiness and make informed decisions about its credibility.

1.3 Objectives

The objective is to engineer a comprehensive framework to securely embed and reliably verify image provenance information from the point of capture, ensuring a high confidence in the authenticity of the image. This includes:

1. Securing images at the time of capture using specialized hardware, digital signatures, hashes, and timestamps to ensure traceability and non-repudiation.
2. Implementing advanced, imperceptible steganographic watermarks that are resilient to tampering and common transformations such as compression, thus preserving the provenance information.
3. Devise a server-side protocol to validate the media and metadata, and provide an accessible solution for end-users to independently verify the provenance information, authenticity and integrity of a given image.

2 Related Work

Provenance focuses on the traceability and authenticity of media throughout its life-cycle, whereas detection systems focus on identifying tampered or fake media after distribution. Instead of automatically assessing the trustworthiness of the content, provenance-based techniques aim to provide consumers with the necessary information to make more informed decisions about whether to trust the content or not [5,9].

Authors state three pillars for establishing media provenance in the paper [8], namely, Metadata, Fingerprinting and Watermarking. Authors also state that each of these methods have their own weakness, which can be compensated for if these techniques are used in combination. In [10], the authors propose a framework that combines both pixel and metadata based approaches. [7,11] authors introduce a Steganographic watermarking mechanism for images using GANs (Generative Adversarial Networks). Whereas in [2], authors propose a solution utilizing image attribution to counter misinformation. The integration of blockchain and distributed ledger technologies (DLT) further enhances provenance by providing decentralized, immutable and tamper-proof records of media history [4]. Coalition for Content Provenance and Authenticity (C2PA) [12] is a standard that tries to tackle the prevalence of misleading information online by certifying the source and history of media content. Similarly, [13] discusses an end-to-end Content Verification System.

3 System Architecture

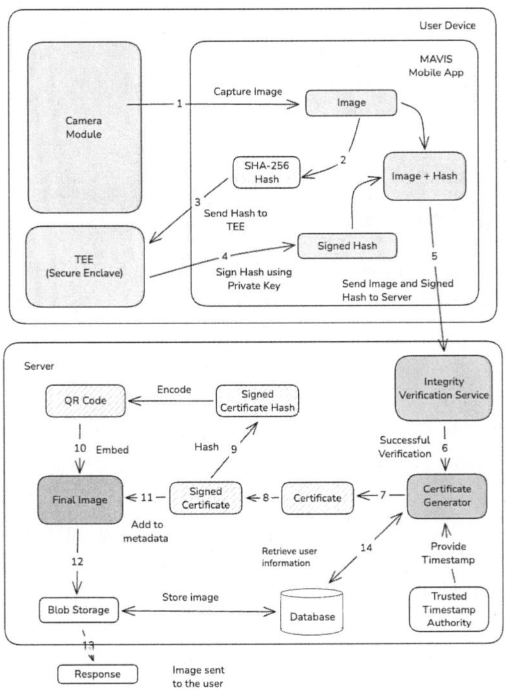

Fig. 1. System Architecture: Embedding.

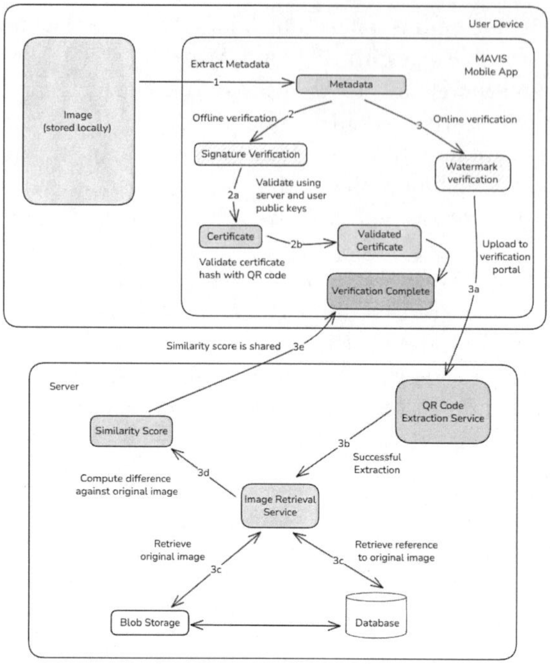

Fig. 2. System Architecture: Verification.

3.1 End-to-End System and Working

Media Embedding. (see Fig. 1)

1. User captures an image using the mobile app.
2. The image is then signed using device's private key with the help of TEE.
3. The image file, along with the signature and the device's public key is sent to the server.
4. The server verifies the signature of the received image.
5. The server generates a certificate containing the image provenance information and a timestamp from a trusted timestamp authority. This certificate is then signed using the server's private key. We use the Elliptic Curve Digital Signature Algorithm (ECDSA) for generating signatures.
6. The signed certificate is hashed and this hash is then steganographically embedded into the image.
7. The signed certificate is then put into the image metadata (e.g., EXIF Data).
8. The watermarked and signed images are then sent back to the user.
9. The image and its information is also stored in a BLOB Storage under a key linked to the certificate hash.

Media Verification. (see Fig. 2)

1. User submits an existing image file (which may or may not contain MAVIS provenance information) as an input.
2. Server attempts to extract any data steganographically embedded in the image using one or both of the following approaches:
   (a) Signature Verification:
      i. Signature of the certificate is verified using the server's public key.
      ii. Signature of the image is verified using the user's public key.
      iii. If both signatures are verified, the image's provenance is established.
   (b) Watermark Verification:
      i. The server attempts to recover the steganographically embedded data from the image.
      ii. The extracted certificate hash is used to fetch the original image and its certificate from the database.
      iii. The image is compared to the original image and a similarity score is given to the uploaded image. We use SSIM (Structural Similarity Index) [15] to calculate the similarity score and to create saliency maps which are both returned to the user along with the certificate.

Certificate: In our system, the certificate serves as a reliable and unique identifier for a specific image. Its structure contains a timestamp, an image ID, a device ID and a user ID, which are all unique for every image, device and user. We employ a compact binary representation to serialize this certificate.

TEEs and Non-repudiation: We leverage the TEE's hardware-backed keystores (e.g., Apple's Secure Enclave), where the private signing key is generated and permanently isolated within the hardware. As the key cannot be exported or accessed by the OS, a valid digital signature mathematically proves that the media originated from that specific physical device, allowing non repudiation.

3.2 Steganographic Techniques

For steganographically embedding the data into the image at a pixel-level, we implemented and compared 3 techniques, which includes the 2D (QR) codes method which utilize DCT, Datamatrix method which uses reed-solomon encoding, and a Deep Learning method which uses GAN. We selected these methods to achieve higher fidelity and robustness as real world use cases often involve compression and geometric distortions.

2D Codes: Involves 2D barcodes, datagrams and QR Codes, of which QR codes are chosen due to higher redundancy and the ability to read from any orientation. Inspired by JPEG compression, this approach utilizes Wavelet Discrete Cosine Transform (DCT). The bits for the QR code are embedded into selected mid-frequency DCT coefficients of blocks within the image's luminance channel (Y).

Embedding Procedure *Data Preparation and QR Encoding*

1. QR Encoding & Binarization: The payload is encoded into a QR code using error correction (E_{qr}). The QR code's visual structure and its dimensions (d_{qr}) are converted into a binary sequence, B_{qr} and B_{dim} respectively.
2. Consolidated Bitstream: B_{dim} and B_{qr} are concatenated to form $B_{payload}$.
3. Redundancy Application: The total number of bits to embed, L_{embed}, is $B_{payload} \cdot R$, accounting for the repetition factor R. (R is strictly constrained to odd integers to avoid ties during majority vote. We empirically determined $R = 3$ to be the optimal balance, maximizing the watermark recovery rate in noisy channels without exceeding the embedding capacity of the selected sub-bands.)

Image Preprocessing

1. Color Space Conversion: Host image is loaded and converted to the YC_bC_r color space. Embedding primarily targets the luminance channel Y.
2. Discrete Wavelet Transform (DWT): A 2D DWT is applied to Y, decomposing it into approximation (LL) and detail (LH, HL, HH) subbands. The selected S_{target} (e.g., HL) is used for embedding.

Data Embedding in Transform Domain

1. Capacity Check: Verify that S_{target} can accommodate L_{embed} bits based on available $N_{dct} \times N_{dct}$ blocks and C_{idx}.
2. The selected subband S_{target} is processed in $N_{dct} \times N_{dct}$ blocks.
3. For each block, its 2D DCT is computed.
4. For each coefficient index in C_{idx}:
   (a) The current payload bit b (from $B_{payload}$, considering repetition R) is identified.
   (b) The DCT coefficient v is modified to $v' = v + \alpha \cdot (2b - 1)$.
5. The inverse 2D DCT is applied to the modified block and this modified block replaces the original in a copy of S_{target}. This continues until all L_{embed} bits are embedded.

Image Reconstruction

1. Inverse DWT (IDWT): The modified luminance channel Y' is reconstructed using f_{IDWT2D} with the modified S_{target} and original LL sub-band and other detail sub-bands.

2. Color Space Reconversion: Y' is combined with the original C_b, C_r channels, and the resulting YC_bC_r image is converted back to RGB to form I_{stego}.

Extraction Procedure *Image Preprocessing*

1. Load & Color Space Conversion: The stego image I'_{stego} is loaded and converted to YC_bC_r, yielding Y'.
2. Discrete Wavelet Transform (DWT): The same f_{DWT2D} is applied to Y' to obtain the subbands. The same S'_{target} is selected.

Data Extraction from Transform Domain

1. S'_{target} is processed in $N_{dct} \times N_{dct}$ blocks.
2. For each block, its 2D DCT is computed.
3. For each coefficient index in C_{idx}, its value $v^\wedge$ is retrieved.
4. The embedded bit $b^\wedge$ is estimated (e.g., $b^\wedge = 1$ if $v^\wedge > C$, else $b^\wedge = 0$).
5. All estimated bits are collected into $B^\wedge_{raw}$.

Data Reconstruction and Decoding

1. Majority Voting for Metadata: The initial portion of $B^\wedge_{raw}$ (corresponding to B_{dim} with repetition R) is processed. Bits are grouped by R, and majority voting determines each bit of the estimated dimension metadata $B^\wedge_{dim}$. This yields the estimated QR dimension $d^\wedge_{qr}$.
2. Majority Voting for QR Data: The subsequent portion of $B^\wedge_{raw}$ (corresponding to B_{qr} with repetition R) is similarly processed with majority voting to reconstruct the estimated QR data bitstream $B^\wedge_{qr}$.
3. QR Code Decoding: The bitstream $B^\wedge_{qr}$ is used to reconstruct the $d^\wedge_{qr} \times d^\wedge_{qr}$ QR code, which is then decoded by a standard QR reader to retrieve the payload $P^\wedge_{str}$.

Datamatrix: The fixed-size payload (256-bit) is converted to a 2D Datamatrix code, which uses Reed-Solomon encoding for error correction capabilities. The generated code is of a fixed side length n_{dm}. A padding of 'p' blocks is added around the Datamatrix, making it of size $(n_{dm}+2p) \times (n_{dm}+2p)$. Assume image of size $w \times h$. Let $min\_dim = min(w, h)$ and $b = min\_dim/(n_{dm} + 2p)$. Now, the middle $min\_dim \times min\_dim$ area of the image is used to embed the padded datamatrix. Each pixel in the datamatrix will be embedded into a pixel block of dimensions $b \times b$.

Image Preprocessing: An Image can be represented as 3 Channels: Luminance (Y), Red Chrominance (C_r), Blue Chrominance (C_b). Human eyes are much more sensitive to fine patterns in Y channel than the C_r & C_b channel, therefore, image compression algorithms heavily compress the Chrominance channels using techniques like Chroma sub-sampling. This is why we will be isolating the Luminance (Y) channel and using that to embed the datamatrix.

Data Embedding in DCT Domain: Double DCT is performed on each individual block of $b \times b$ to convert the data into the frequency domain. We will hide the datamatrix pixels in this frequency domain. Human eyes are highly sensitive to low frequency components, and hence image compression algorithms remove the higher frequency components more aggressively. Therefore, to hide the data effectively and also be resilient to loss due to re-compression, we must choose frequencies such that they are low enough to survive compression, but also high enough to not cause any noticeable distortions in the image. Let's call these frequencies f1 and f2. We will also maintain a parameter strength to determine the strength of the embedding. Iterate i, j through the pixels of the datamatrix. For each block img[i:i+b, j:j+b], Calculate $f1$ and $f2$ as $f1, f2 = avg(f1, f2)$. If datamatrix [i, j] = 1: f2 + strength, else f2 - strength. For a quantization matrix 8×8, we tested our algorithm with multiple pairs of frequencies. We plotted the effectiveness, and empirically chose the frequencies(4,3)and(3,4) based on the elbow pointofthecurve.

Image Reconstruction: After manipulating the frequency domain, convert the block back to spatial domain and replace the corresponding pixels in the Chrominance (Y) layer. Once the entire datamatrix is embedded, combine Y, C_r and C_b layers, and save the image.

Extraction Procedure:

1. Initialize an empty matrix dm of size $(n_{dm} + 2p) \times (n_{dm} + 2p)$ to store the extracted datamatrix.
2. Isolate the Y Channel of the image & Calculate the new block size b using the same procedure. Note that even though the image might be resized, only the very high frequency components will be lost, but the data embedded should survive.
3. Calculate the resize factor $r = b/int(b)$. Scale the image by this factor r. This is done because DCT works best when the provided image blocks are non-overlapping and discrete. Doing this ensures that there will be no overlap, as the smallest dimension of the image will be a multiple of b.
4. Perform double DCT on each $b \times b$ block, and find out values of $f1$ and $f2$. If $f2 > f1$: dm[i, j] = 1.
5. Attempt to read the datamatrix, and extract the hash.

Deep Learning Approach

System Overview: In the Deep learning-based steganographic approach, we adopt a GAN (Generative Adversarial Network) architecture [14] to train the Neural Networks to imperceptibly embed and extract any given payload (that is, binary data) within any given image. We follow an architecture and a training process as proposed in [7]. The system comprises 3 neural networks (See Fig. 3):

1. Generator (Embedder) which embeds the payload within the given input image imperceptibly.

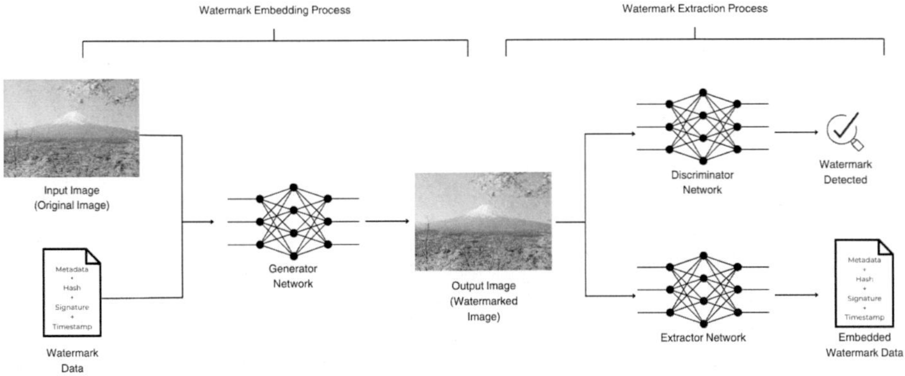

Fig. 3. GAN-based Image Watermarking.

2. Discriminator (Detector) which detects if given input image is watermarked or not.
3. Extractor (Decoder) which recovers the originally embedded payload from the input image.

String to Bit Conversion for Embedding: An end marker '#0#0#0' is appended at the end of the string. Given payload (string) is converted into binary by converting each of its characters into its 8-bit ASCII representation. This bitstream is appended to itself and repeated to match the length of $Height * Length$ of the cover image. It is then reshaped into a float tensor of dimension (1, 1, $Height$, $Width$). This tensor is passed as an input to the Generator network along with the cover image to produce watermarked image (Fig. 4).

(a) Original Image (b) Watermarked Image (c) Pixel-level Difference

Fig. 4. Comparison of original and watermarked image.

Extraction Process: During the extraction process, the watermark tensor is obtained by passing the watermarked image to the extractor network. We get a continuous bitstring by thresholding the tensor and representing it in 1 dimension. We reconstruct the characters by converting every 8 successive bits from ASCII representation to their respective character. We split the continuous string each time we encounter the end marker. Each split string is known as candidate and is compared character by character to form an error corrected final result using a majority vote mechanism over all the candidates.

4 Testing and Results

We tested and compared the 3 steganographic watermarking techniques with respect to their fidelity and robustness. We assessed the Peak Signal-to-Noise Ratio (PSNR) and Structural Similarity Index (SSIM) for fidelity. For robustness, we checked the Bit Error Rate (BER) of extracted payload vs. original payload, and Watermark detection under attacks including compression, Gaussian noise, random cropping (up to 25% area), rotation (± 5 degrees), scaling ($0.5\times$–$2\times$).

In terms of fidelity, the GAN-based watermarking approach generally preserved the highest perceptual quality, registering PSNR values exceeding 40 dB and SSIM values greater than 0.99. While the QR-DCT method delivered acceptable quality with a PSNR of approximately 39 dB, it occasionally manifested block artifacts when accommodating larger payloads. The Reed-Solomon variant, on the other hand, appeared to consciously trade off some fidelity, with PSNR values around 36 dB, in favor of enhanced error correction capabilities.

The robustness assessment, concerning the Bit Error Rate (BER) under various attack simulations, revealed nuanced performance across the implemented watermarking techniques. The Reed-Solomon and QR watermarking notably exhibited the lowest BER across all tested distortions, suggesting a robust error-correction mechanism. Conversely, while the GAN-based approach demonstrated relative resilience to mild compression and noise, its performance degraded considerably when subjected to geometric transformations, a characteristic arguably attributable to the random cropping applied during its training phase. It should be noted, perhaps, that the QR-DCT method proved most vulnerable, particularly to cropping, aligning somewhat with the GAN-based approach's susceptibility to both cropping and rotation.

Further observations from the testing phase revealed certain limitations tied to image resolution and compression types across the different methodologies. Specifically, the DCT-based approach encountered limitations if the input image's resolution for watermarking fell below the minimum size required for the to-be-embedded QR code. Similarly, the GAN-based approach, which was relying on a random 360×360 pixel crop of the input image during its operation, would invariably fail if the original input image itself possessed a resolution lower than this threshold.

In terms of image format compatibility and compression resilience, the DCT QR code and Reed-Solomon-based methods demonstrated versatility, functioning with both PNG and JPG image formats. They also exhibited a notable degree of resilience to certain lossy compression scenarios, such as the typical JPEG compression encountered when images are transmitted via platforms like WhatsApp, retaining the ability to extract the QR code with 100% accuracy. Conversely, the GAN-based watermarking model, having been exclusively trained with PNG images without simulating compression noise, was found to be incompatible with lossy JPEG compression. This is because the image tensor is converted into a jpeg file after embedding the watermark, during which jpeg compression algorithm smooths out the high-frequency noise where the model hid the watermark. In [7] Authors explain a solution to this by adding noise during training process to simulate jpeg compression. However, it functioned effectively with lossless PNG compression, embedding significantly more information in the process, than the other methods.

While GAN-based watermarking offers superior fidelity for artistic content, the Reed-Solomon/ Datamatrix approach is recommended for MAVIS's core objective of authenticity verification. Its reliable error-correction capabilities allow retrieval of the provenance hash even after aggressive social media compression.

5 Discussion

Strengths and Foundational Aspects: With MAVIS, we abstract away from the image's content and focus purely on the image's source. Leveraging a combination of TEEs, tamper resilient digital signatures, steganographic techniques, external information archive and a trusted timestamping authority, we enable non repudiation, traceability to the image's source and a credible proof of no tamper. We mitigate the individual limitations of the metadata, fingerprinting and watermarking based approaches by combining the techniques.

Scalability and Real-World Applications: Practical applications consist of avenues where containing misinformation and establishing reliable sources of media are important. For example, in journalism, the ability to prove the legitimacy and provenance is critical for maintaining trust. For legal evidence and insurance claims, the ability to generate tamper proof records enhance the validity of a claim. Similarly, surveillance footage gains evidentiary value when guaranteed integrity and provenance.

Limitations and Future Work: The proposed system relies on a centralized server and demands internet connectivity. Although the dependency can be mitigated using decentralized architecture, completely offline solutions compromise the security as the presence of a server reduces the capability of a bad actor to cheat the system. It also necessitates a TEE for a secure signing process. Even though several companies are manufacturing smartphones and cameras with built in TEEs and dedicated hardware, these factors still remain a bottleneck in the adaptation of such systems. Awareness and habitual use of such provenance information also proves to be a barrier. Potential future work includes encompassing audio, video and other document formats.

6 Conclusion

This research has proposed an end to end system for establishing the authenticity and integrity of images. The system allows users to securely capture and distribute images, enabling any recipient to verify the content's authenticity with a high degree of confidence. This is achieved using a TEE, allowing images to be traced back to the hardware device that captured them. We also implement Steganographic watermarking techniques using DCT wavelets, Reed-Solomon encoding and GAN to embed provenance data directly into image's pixels and overcome the shortcomings of systems which store the provenance information only in the metadata.

References

1. Bhowmik, D., et al.: An international standard for assessing trustworthiness in media. In: 2024 IEEE International Conference on Image Processing (ICIP), pp. 3799–3804 (2024)
2. Andriushchenko, M., et al.: ARIA: adversarially robust image attribution for content provenance. In: 2022 IEEE/CVF Conference on Computer Vision and Pattern Recognition Workshops (CVPRW), pp. 33–42 (2022)
3. Simmons, J.C., Winograd, J.M.: Interoperable provenance authentication of broadcast media using open standards-based metadata, watermarking and cryptography. arXiv:2405.08639 (2024)
4. Hasan, H.R., Salah, K.: Combating deepfake videos using blockchain and smart contracts. IEEE Access **7**, 41596–41606 (2019)
5. Moreira, D., et al.: Image provenance analysis at scale. IEEE Trans. Image Process. **27**(12), 6109–6123 (2018)
6. Singh, A.P.: Safeguarding authenticity in the digital realm: a holistic approach integrating content provenance, secure watermarking, and transparent labeling to combat deepfakes. Int. J. Multidisc. Res. (IJFMR) **6**(3) (2024)
7. Zhang, K.A., Cuesta-Infante, A., Xu, L., Veeramachaneni, K.: SteganoGAN: high capacity image steganography with GANs. arXiv:1901.03892 (2019)
8. Collomosse, J., Parsons, A.: To authenticity, and beyond! building safe and fair generative AI upon the three pillars of provenance. IEEE Comput. Graphics Appl. **44**(3), 7–13 (2024)
9. Black, A., et al.: VPN: video provenance network for robust content attribution. In: Proceedings of the 18th ACM SIGGRAPH European Conference on Visual Media Production (2021)
10. Bharati, A., et al.: Beyond pixels: image provenance analysis leveraging metadata. arXiv:1807.03376 (2018)
11. Bui, T., Agarwal, S., Collomosse, J.: TrustMark: universal watermarking for arbitrary resolution images. arXiv preprint arXiv:2311.18297 (2023)
12. Rosenthol, L.: C2PA: the world's first industry standard for content provenance (conference presentation). In: Proceedings of the SPIE 12226, Applications of Digital Image Processing XLV, p. 122260P (2022). https://doi.org/10.1117/12.2632021
13. Kaja, R.K.: A comprehensive content verification system for ensuring digital integrity in the age of deep fakes. arXiv:2411.19750 (2024)
14. Goodfellow, I.J., et al.: Generative adversarial net. arXiv:1406.2661 (2014)
15. Wang, Z., Bovik, A.C., Sheikh, H.R., Simoncelli, E.P.: Image quality assessment: from error visibility to structural similarity. IEEE Trans. Image Process. **13**(4), 600–612 (2004)

From Incidents to Prediction: A Multimodal Spatio-Temporal Graph Transformer for Traffic Forecasting Using XTraffic-2023

Sankalp Nayak, Aradhana Behura(✉), and Samriddhi Sharma

School of Computer Engineering, Kalinga Institute of Industrial Technology (KIIT) Deemed to be University, Bhubaneswar 751024, Odisha, India
{sankalp.nayakfcs,aradhana.behurafcs}@kiit.ac.in

Abstract. The modern urbanization and large traffic volume have posed important challenges to the vehicular traffic flow management in smart cities. Reliable traffic volume prediction is critical for proper urban planning, mitigation of congestion, and the design of intelligent transportation systems (ITS). Although traditional techniques and some deep learning models have been used for vehicular traffic prediction, and suffer from the inability to analyze non-linear patterns inherent from real-world environments. Traditional models suffer from gradient vanishing and exploding vanishing issues, which will reduce the performance of the model. This article uses a Multimodal Spatio-Temporal Transformer (MSTT) plays a vital role in traffic volume prediction by designing both spatial dependencies (relationships among road segments or various sensors) and temporal dependencies (how traffic patterns evolve). Unlike LSTM, RNNs, Bi-LSTM, or GRUs, which suffer from long-range dependencies, the Transformer uses a self-attention mechanism simultaneously to achieve global correlations between location and time. The multimodal concept allows it to integrate various information sources—such as road topology, GPS sensor, weather, and sensor data—into a unified integration, enhancing traffic prediction accuracy to minimize delay. The result is measured through different performance parameters like Mean Squared Error (MSE), RMSE, MAPE, RAE, and MBE to compare its performance.

Keywords: Traffic analysis · Machine learning · ITC · Spatio temporal model · Deep learning

1 Introduction

Accurate vehicular traffic forecasting is a key factor that can influence the performance of the Intelligent Transportation Systems (ITS), by controlling the traffic signal, reducing the waiting time, congestion, and finding the shortest path. The recent XTraffic-2023 dataset is a rich source of information that captures the

G. K. Verma et al. (Eds.): MIND 2025, CCIS 2981, pp. 349–360, 2027.
https://doi.org/10.1007/978-3-032-31230-3_28

multi-source vehicular traffic information over the urban area through vehicle counts, car speeds, weather prediction, and temporal parameters. This concept captures spatio-temporal road patterns, which are vital to create a robust predictive protocol. Nevertheless, designing such complex data poses various challenges. Figure 1 shows the average traffic volume in a day.

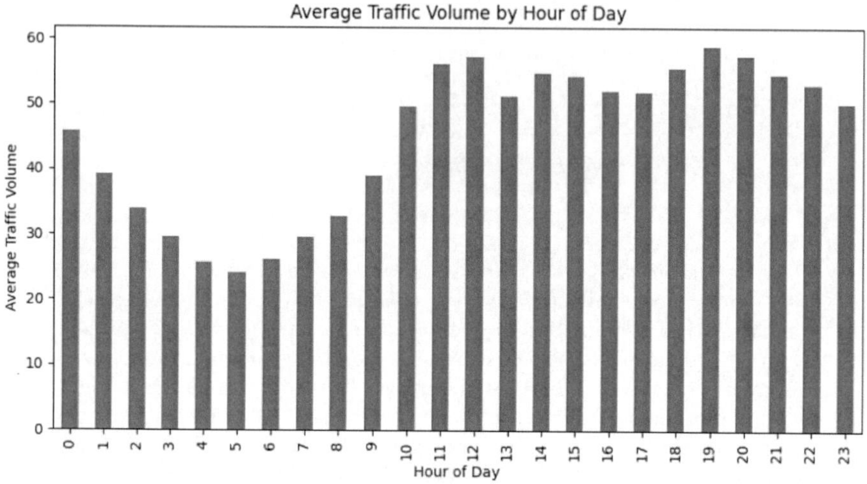

Fig. 1. Analysis of average traffic volume.

Firstly, there is the spatio-temporal heterogeneity of traffic flow: the traffic conditions change dynamically in both space (on different roads and their intersections) and time (during rush hours, weekends, and holidays). There are various issues, such as missing values, noisy data, or imbalanced information, due to vehicular node failures or data communication delays; the information from regions is never uniformly collected. Another issue is the nonlinear data interdependence of multiple influencing factors, such as weather conditions, time, and transportation topology, which renders many traditional techniques inappropriate. Besides, the high dimensionality of the XTraffic data needs a computationally efficient yet long-range dependent framework.

2 Related Work

Olug and Eren (2024) investigated dataset collection and preprocessing with GLEE node embedding, which enhances prediction performance through geographical differences and augmenting temporal connections, but it requires huge computational power and large-scale preprocessing [1]. Rasaizadi et al. (2024) proposed a short-term traffic state prediction model of suburban roads using PCA, GA, cyclic features, LSTM, SVM, and Random Forest, with 88.09% accuracy using cyclic features and with computational difficulties and minor loss of accuracy using PCA and GA [2]. Li et al. (2024) presented a deep knowledge distillation model for traffic flow forecasting based on bidirectional random walks, GCNs, and self-distillation to improve spatial-temporal feature perception but with high computational complexities and poor consideration of weather factors as limitations [3]. Karatrantou (2024) used machine learning for ETA forecasting in city transit, where RF traded off accuracy and efficiency, LSTM captured temporal relationships well but took a long time to train, and GCNs and XGBoost performed below par, with RF yielding the highest R^2 value of 0.9500 [4]. Zou and Chung (2024) created a short-term traffic forecasting model in the context of limited data conditions based on clustering, CNN-LSTM, and transfer learning, making it robust against detector outages and able to be used for various traffic parameters, albeit performing poorly with unexpected congestion and necessitating retraining when traffic trends shift [5].

Yan et al. (2025) proposed a new traffic speed prediction framework that combines heterogeneous data sources with H-RetNet and GRU to achieve a 21.91% MSE decrease, but with limitations in integrating data and interpretability [6] McMinn et al. (2025) proposed an autonomous air vehicle prediction algorithm using position and velocity information for trajectory prediction, although it does not include modeling of traffic-on-traffic interactions [7]. Li et al. (2025) introduced a Vehicle Path Planning and Prediction Algorithm (VPPPA) based on CNN, LSTM, and attention mechanisms to enhance traffic flow and travel time at urban intersections but with possible computational complexity as an issue [8]. Rashid et al. (2025) implemented a deep learning-based evacuation traffic prediction model with Facebook movement data and transfer learning and reached up to 95% accuracy but performance is lower without transfer learning [9]. Chen et al. (2025) proposed the ISO-DTGCN model for dynamic traffic flow prediction that reduced RMSE by 15% but encountered computational complexity issues [10].

Yin et al. (2021) surveyed short-term traffic prediction with Deep Neural Networks (DNNs) like MLP, CNN, RNN, LSTM, and GCN, which are computationally intensive and need massive data but efficiently model intricate spatiotemporal correlations [11]. Shaygan et al. (2022) discussed AI-based traffic forecasting techniques, such as deep learning, federated learning, GCN, and LSTM, determining research gaps and indicating novel AI techniques, but real-time application is challenging because of the high computational cost [12]. Lee et al. (2021) investigated deep learning methods of traffic flow prediction using transfer learning and meta-learning for better prediction across various traffic situations, but necessitating large-scale data and having model generalization issues [13]. Behura et al. (2022) implemented a traffic forecasting model based on machine learning with Sklearn, Keras, and TensorFlow, which gives real-time estimation of congestion and facilitates navigation but is bounded to historical trends and greatly dependent upon data quality [14]. Zheng et al. (2022) compared hybrid deep learning models for traffic forecasting, combining CNN, GCN, and Transformer-based models with Seq2Seq and attention with high accuracy and the ability to manage large road networks, albeit at the expense of computational complexity and large dataset requirements [15].

Tedjopurnomo et al. (2020) reviewed deep neural network (DNN) models for traffic forecasting, examining architectures, research trends, challenges, and directions. They drew attention to high accuracy in predictions and adaptability to intricate patterns while mentioning high computational complexity, huge requirements in data, and potential for overfitting [16]. Zheng et al. (2020) introduced a Graph Multi-Attention Network (GMAN) for long-term traffic prediction, which was capable of modeling spatiotemporal relationships effectively and restraining the propagation of errors, achieving an improvement of up to 4% in terms of MAE, albeit with the price of high computational complexity and input feature quality sensitivity [17]. Boukerche and Wang (2020) gave an overview of several machine learning models for traffic flow prediction, highlighting flexibility towards nonlinear features but also indicating difficulties in model choice and dependence on data quality [18]. Shi et al. (2020) introduced an Attention-based Periodic-Temporal Neural Network (APTN) for traffic forecasting, successfully modeling spatial and periodic dependencies but at the cost of high-quality data and deep hyperparameter tuning [19]. Guo et al. (2020) proposed an improved Graph Convolution Recurrent Neural Network for traffic forecasting, which maintains spatial structures and learns intrinsic correlations between road segments, but it demands large amounts of computational resources and adequate traffic data for best performance [20].

Zhao et al. (2019) proposed a real-time traffic prediction model based on a Temporal Graph Convolutional Network (T-GCN) to capture spatial and temporal dependencies that is superior to state-of-the-art models but requires large computation resources and high-quality datasets [21]. Liu et al. (2018) applied deep learning for predicting urban traffic, yielding high accuracy and efficient learning of hidden patterns, but with scalability and large data requirements issues [22]. Nagy and Simon (2018) applied machine learning and novel data sources to traffic conditions in smart cities and achieved more precise predictions and enhanced transport services, albeit large-scale data processing and integration are difficult [23]. Yao et al. (2019) proposed a Spatial-Temporal Dynamic Network (STDN) to handle dynamic spatial dependencies and non-strictly periodic temporal patterns and gained better accuracy but with computational complexity and real-time performance issues [24]. Troia et al. (2018) forecasted traffic matrices through deep learning to optimize resource allocation in optical backbone networks with high accuracy (<7.4 MAE) and 66.3% capacity saving at the cost of large datasets and computational capability for training RNN models [25,26].

3 Proposed Model

The proposed **Multimodal Spatio-Temporal Transformer (MSTT)** is designed to accurately predict future traffic states by jointly modeling spatial dependencies, temporal dynamics, and multimodal contextual information

Algorithm 1. Proposed Multimodal Spatio-Temporal Transformer (MSTT) for Traffic Prediction

Require: Multimodal vehicular traffic information $\{X_t^{(s)}, X_t^{(w)}, X_t^{(t)}\}_{t=1}^{T}$, graph $G = (V, E)$, prediction horizon Δ, number of past steps k.
Ensure: Predicted vehicular traffic state $\hat{Y}_{t+\Delta}$.

Step 1: Multimodal Embedding
for $t = 1$ to T **do**
Encode each modality through feed-forward neural network layers:

$$H_t = \mathrm{Concat}\big(E_s(X_t^{(s)}), E_w(X_t^{(w)}), E_t(X_t^{(t)})\big) \tag{Eq. 2}$$

end for
Step 2: Spatial Attention Designing
for each vehicular sensor $v_i \in V$ **do**
Evaluate spatial attention over connected vehicular node:

$$H_t^{(S)} = \mathrm{softmax}\left(\frac{Q_S K_S^T}{\sqrt{d_k}}\right) V_S \tag{Eq. 3}$$

end for
Step 3: Temporal Attention Designing
Capture temporal dependencies across k previous time steps:

$$H_t^{(T)} = \mathrm{softmax}\left(\frac{Q_T K_T^T}{\sqrt{d_k}}\right) V_T \tag{Eq. 4}$$

Step 4: Spatio-Temporal Fusion
Fuse spatial and temporal representations:

$$Z_t = \mathrm{TransformerEncoder}(H_t^{(S)} + H_t^{(T)}) \tag{Eq. 5}$$

Step 5: Prediction
Generate future traffic state:

$$\hat{Y}_{t+\Delta} = \mathrm{FC}(Z_t) \tag{Eq. 6}$$

Step 6: Optimization
Minimize Mean Squared Error (MSE):

$$\mathcal{L} - \frac{1}{N}\sum_{i=1}^{N}(Y_{t+\Delta}^{i} - \hat{Y}_{t+\Delta}^{i})^2 \tag{Eq. 7}$$

Update parameters via backpropagation:

$$\theta \leftarrow \theta - \eta \nabla_\theta \mathcal{L}$$

return $\hat{Y}_{t+\Delta}$

from the XTraffic dataset. Unlike conventional CNN, RNN, or GNN-based approaches, MSTT leverages attention mechanisms to capture long-range correlations and perform parallel learning across space and time.

Let the traffic network be represented as $G = (V, E)$, where $V = \{v_1, v_2, \ldots, v_N\}$ denotes the set of N road segments (nodes), and E represents the set of directed connections (edges) between them. At each timestamp t, the multimodal traffic input is represented as:

$$X_t = \{X_t^{(s)}, X_t^{(w)}, X_t^{(t)}\} \tag{1}$$

where:

- $X_t^{(s)}$ - sensor-based traffic data (speed, flow, density),
- $X_t^{(w)}$ - weather conditions (rainfall, temperature, humidity),
- $X_t^{(t)}$ - temporal context (hour, weekday, holiday indicator).

The goal is to predict the future traffic state $\hat{Y}_{t+\Delta}$ over a horizon Δ. Algorithm 1 depicts the proposed model framework.

3.1 Data Preprocessing

Preprocessing prepares raw traffic data for analysis. It ensures consistency, handles missing values, and converts data into a suitable structure for models. Null values often occur due to sensor issues, missing logs, or data transmission failures. These are handled by removing or imputing missing records using mean or median strategies to maintain data integrity and avoid biased predictions. Categorical features like weekdays and weather conditions are transformed into binary variables to allow the model to interpret them effectively. This prevents incorrect assumptions about ordinal relationships between categories. Min-max scaling technique is a common method for scaling numerical values to a particular range, generally between 1 and 0. To reduce model complexity and overfitting, correlation analysis is used to drop redundant or irrelevant features. Highly correlated features are identified using a heatmap, and only the most significant predictors are retained.

3.2 Multimodal Embedding Layer

Each input modality is first embedded into a shared latent space through modality-specific encoders:

$$H_t = \text{Concat}\big(E_s(X_t^{(s)}), E_w(X_t^{(w)}), E_t(X_t^{(t)})\big) \tag{2}$$

where E_s, E_w, and E_t denote linear or feed-forward encoders, and $\text{Concat}(\cdot)$ merges multimodal features.

3.3 Spatial Attention Modeling

Spatial correlations among nodes are learned using graph-based self-attention. For each node v_i, the spatial attention mechanism computes:

$$H_t^{(S)} = \text{softmax}\left(\frac{Q_S K_S^T}{\sqrt{d_k}}\right) V_S \tag{3}$$

where Q_S, K_S, and V_S are query, key, and value matrices derived from H_t. This enables the model to dynamically weigh the influence of neighboring road segments.

3.4 Temporal Attention Modeling

To capture dynamic temporal dependencies over past k time steps, temporal attention is applied as:

$$H_t^{(T)} = \text{softmax}\left(\frac{Q_T K_T^T}{\sqrt{d_k}}\right) V_T \tag{4}$$

This formulation enables the model to recognize recurring patterns such as rush-hour peaks, daily cycles, and long-term temporal dependencies that traditional RNNs struggle to maintain.

3.5 Fusion Transformer Encoder

The spatial and temporal attention outputs are fused to learn joint spatio-temporal representations:

$$Z_t = \text{TransformerEncoder}\big(H_t^{(S)} + H_t^{(T)}\big) \tag{5}$$

The encoder applies multi-head self-attention and residual connections to capture global dependencies efficiently across the traffic network.

3.6 Prediction Layer

The final hidden representation is passed through a fully connected layer to predict the traffic state at future time $t + \Delta$:

$$\hat{Y}_{t+\Delta} = \text{FC}(Z_t) \tag{6}$$

where $\text{FC}(\cdot)$ is a dense layer mapping the encoded features to the target variable (e.g., average speed or congestion level).

3.7 Loss Function

The framework is trained using Mean Squared Error (MSE) between predicted and actual values:

$$\mathcal{L} = \frac{1}{N}\sum_{i=1}^{N}(Y_{t+\Delta}^i - \hat{Y}_{t+\Delta}^i)^2 \tag{7}$$

4 Simulation Analysis

Simulations are checked on a **Thunder Compute** instance equipped with **1× NVIDIA A100 GPU (80 GB VRAM)**, **16 vCPUs**, **128 GB RAM**, and **300 GB SSD** storage. The simulation environment is configured with **Ubuntu 20.04 LTS** and **PyTorch 2.x (CUDA 12)** for high-performance framework training and result analysis.

4.1 Performance Evaluation

Various regression metrics were used to quantitatively measure the effectiveness of the proposed Multimodal Spatio-Temporal Transformer (MSTT): Mean Squared Error (MSE), Root Mean Squared Error (RMSE), Mean Absolute Percentage Error (MAPE), Relative Absolute Error (RAE), and Mean Bias Error (MBE). These metrics give a complete picture of the accuracy, consistency, and bias of the predictions made.

4.2 A. Evaluation Metrics

1) Mean Squared Error (MSE):

$$\mathrm{MSE} = \frac{1}{N}\sum_{i=1}^{N}(Y_i - \hat{Y}_i)^2 \tag{8}$$

2) Root Mean Squared Error (RMSE):

$$\mathrm{RMSE} = \sqrt{\frac{1}{N}\sum_{i=1}^{N}(Y_i - \hat{Y}_i)^2} \tag{9}$$

3) Mean Absolute Percentage Error (MAPE):

$$\mathrm{MAPE} = \frac{100}{N}\sum_{i=1}^{N}\left|\frac{Y_i - \hat{Y}_i}{Y_i}\right| \tag{10}$$

4) Relative Absolute Error (RAE):

$$\mathrm{RAE} = \frac{\sum_{i=1}^{N}|Y_i - \hat{Y}_i|}{\sum_{i=1}^{N}|Y_i - \bar{Y}|} \tag{11}$$

here $\bar{Y}$ represents the mean of observed outcomes. The value of $\mathrm{RAE} < 1$ represents higher prediction over the mean baseline.

5) Mean Bias Error (MBE):

$$\text{MBE} = \frac{1}{N}\sum_{i=1}^{N}(\hat{Y}_i - Y_i) \tag{12}$$

It estimates the systematic bias value. A higher positive MBE represents over-estimation outcomes, while a negative range indicates underestimation of traffic flow rate.

4.3 Experimental Analysis

Table 1 analyzes the comparative outcomes of the proposed framework against traditional frameworks on the XTraffic-2023 dataset.

Table 1. Comparative Performance Evaluation on XTraffic Dataset

Model	MSE ↓	RMSE ↓	MAPE (%) ↓	RAE ↓	MBE ↓
LSTM	12.47	3.53	8.92	0.214	−0.12
GRU	11.35	3.37	8.15	0.197	−0.09
Graph WaveNet	9.42	3.07	7.26	0.181	−0.05
ST-GCN	8.96	2.99	6.94	0.174	−0.04
Proposed MSTT	**6.78**	**2.60**	**5.38**	**0.138**	**−0.01**

Table 2. Ablation study of MSTT components on 30-min forecasting horizon.

Model Variant	MSE	RMSE	MAPE (%)
Full MSTT (proposed)	**1.82**	**1.35**	**4.87**
w/o multimodal fusion	2.41	1.55	6.12
w/o incident embeddings	2.28	1.51	5.94
w/o sparse spatial attention	2.56	1.60	6.48
w/o hierarchical temporal encoder	2.63	1.62	6.79
Sensor-only input (no multimodal signals)	3.04	1.74	7.55

From Table 1, the proposed MSTT is visibly the one that has the lowest MSE, RMSE, and MAPE; hence, it is the most accurate and stable of all predictions. The RAE range is less than 0.15 is a strong indication that MSTT is far better than the mean baseline, and the MBE range close to zero demonstrates that there is almost no systematic bias. In general, the findings emphasize the power of MSTT to capture complex multimodal spatio-temporal dependencies in the XTraffic-2023 dataset. Figure 2 represents the feature correlation, and Fig. 3 depicts the average traffic volume in a week. Table 2 depicts the ablation study of the proposed model.

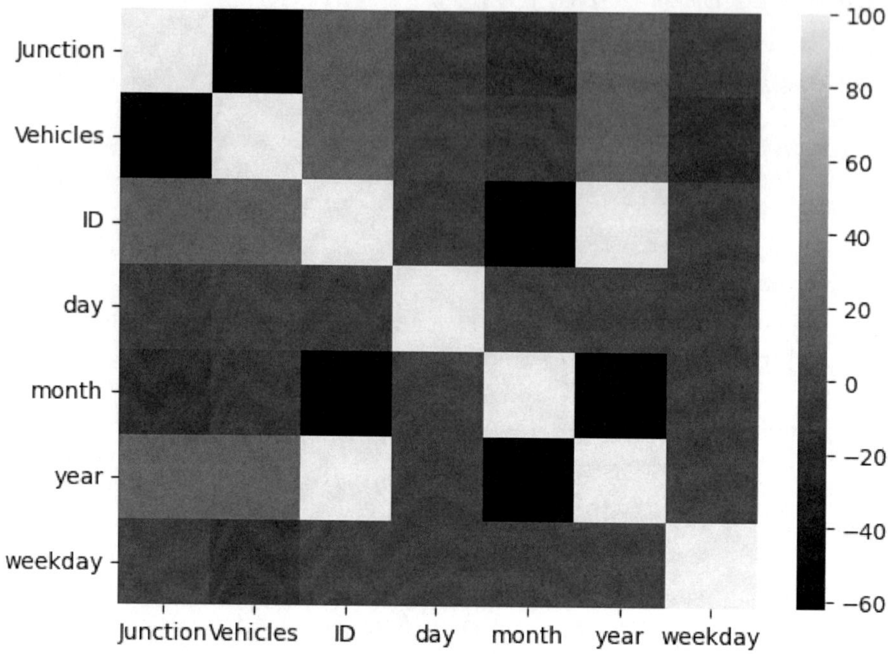

Fig. 2. Feature corelation.

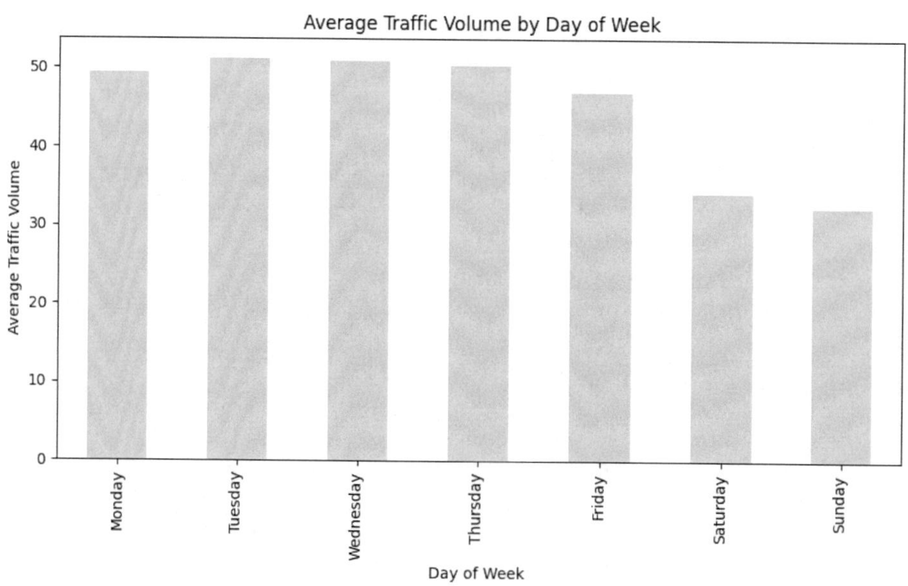

Fig. 3. Analysis of average traffic volume in a week.

5 Conclusion

This article presents a multimodal spatio-temporal graph transformer for traffic forecasting and prediction using XTraffic-2023 dataset. This framework outperforms as compared with existing baseline models like LSTM, GRU, and Graph neural networks. The performance is evaluated through different performance parameters, like Mean Squared Error (MSE), RMSE, MAPE, RAE, and MBE to compare their performance. The model successfully integrates multiple information sources (sensor data, weather, context) into a unified framework, which enhances prediction accuracy and better accounts for real-world traffic variation.

References

1. Olug, E., Kaya, K., Tugay, R., Oguducu, S.G.: IBB traffic graph data: benchmarking and road traffic prediction model. arXiv preprint arXiv:2408.01016 (2024)
2. Rasaizadi, A., Hafizi, F., Seyedabrishami, S.: Dimensions management of traffic big data for short-term traffic prediction on suburban roadways. Sci. Rep. **14**(1), 1484 (2024)
3. Li, Y., Li, P., Yan, D., Liu, Y., Liu, Z.: Deep knowledge distillation: a self-mutual learning framework for traffic prediction. Expert Syst. Appl. **252**, 124138 (2024)
4. Karatrantou, A.: Traffic prediction on road networks. MS thesis (2024)
5. Zou, X., Chung, E.: Traffic prediction via clustering and deep transfer learning with limited data. Comput. Aided Civil Infrastruct. Eng. (2024)
6. Yan, Y., et al.: Multimodal fusion for large-scale traffic prediction with heterogeneous retentive networks. Inf. Fusion **114**, 102695 (2025)
7. McMinn, J.D., Patterson, A., Gregory, I.M.: Traffic prediction for uncommunicative aircraft in terminal airspace: development framework and performance evaluations. In: AIAA SCITECH 2025 Forum (2025)
8. Li, Y., Feng, L., Tang, C.: A vehicle path planning and prediction algorithm based on attention mechanism for complex traffic intersection collaboration in intelligent transportation. IEEE Trans. Intell. Transp. Syst. (2025)
9. Rashid, M.M., Rahman, R., Hasan, S.: Network-wide evacuation traffic prediction in a rapidly intensifying hurricane from traffic detectors and Facebook movement data: deep-learning approach. J. Transp. Eng. Part A Syst. **151**(1), 04024085 (2025)
10. Chen, L., et al.: A short-term traffic flow prediction model for road networks using inverse isochrones to determine dynamic spatiotemporal correlation ranges. XXPhys. A **657**, 130244 (2025)
11. Yin, X., et al.: Deep learning on traffic prediction: methods, analysis, and future directions. IEEE Trans. Intell. Transp. Syst. **23**(6), 4927–4943 (2021)
12. Shaygan, M., et al.: Traffic prediction using artificial intelligence: review of recent advances and emerging opportunities. Transp. Res. Part C Emerg. Technol. **145**, 103921 (2022)
13. Lee, K., et al.: Short-term traffic prediction with deep neural networks: a survey. IEEE Access **9**, 54739–54756 (2021)
14. Behura, A., Kumar, A., Jain, P.K.: A comparative performance analysis of vehicular routing protocols in intelligent transportation systems. Telecommun. Syst. **88**(1), 26 (2025)

15. Zheng, G., et al.: Hybrid deep learning models for traffic prediction in large-scale road networks. Inf. Fusion **92**, 93–114 (2023)
16. Tedjopurnomo, D.A., et al.: A survey on modern deep neural network for traffic prediction: trends, methods and challenges. IEEE Trans. Knowl. Data Eng. **34**(4), 1544–1561 (2020)
17. Zheng, C., et al.: GMAN: a graph multi-attention network for traffic prediction. In: Proceedings of the AAAI Conference on Artificial Intelligence, vol. 34, no. 01 (2020)
18. Boukerche, A., Wang, J.: Machine learning-based traffic prediction models for intelligent transportation systems. Comput. Netw. **181**, 107530 (2020)
19. Shi, X., et al.: A spatial-temporal attention approach for traffic prediction. IEEE Trans. Intell. Transp. Syst. **22**(8), 4909–4918 (2020)
20. Guo, K., et al.: Optimized graph convolution recurrent neural network for traffic prediction. IEEE Trans. Intell. Transp. Syst. **22**(2), 1138–1149 (2020)
21. Zhao, L., et al.: T-GCN: a temporal graph convolutional network for traffic prediction. IEEE Trans. Intell. Transp. Syst. **21**(9), 3848–3858 (2019)
22. Liu, Z., et al.: Urban traffic prediction from mobility data using deep learning. IEEE Network **32**(4), 40–46 (2018)
23. Nagy, A.M., Simon, V.: Survey on traffic prediction in smart cities. Pervasive Mob. Comput. **50**, 148–163 (2018)
24. Yao, H., et al.: Revisiting spatial-temporal similarity: a deep learning framework for traffic prediction. In: Proceedings of the AAAI Conference on Artificial Intelligence, vol. 33, no. 01 (2019)
25. Troia, S., et al.: Deep learning-based traffic prediction for network optimization. In: 2018 20th International Conference on Transparent Optical Networks (ICTON). IEEE (2018)
26. Behura, A., Kumar, A., Jain, P.K.: A multi-objective approach for secure cluster based routing and attack classification in VANETs. Peer-to-Peer Networking Appl. **18**(3), 1–40 (2025)

Dropout-Inspired Selective Fine-Tuning for Transfer Learning

Abhi Sathwik Penthala[1](✉) and K. Namitha[2]

[1] Department of Electronics and Communication Engineering, Amrita School of Computing, Amrita Vishwa Vidyapeetham, Amritapuri, Kerala, India
sathvik0320@gmail.com

[2] Department of Computer Science and Engineering, Amrita School of Computing, Amrita Vishwa Vidyapeetham, Amritapuri, Kerala, India
namithak@am.amrita.edu

Abstract. While transfer learning facilitates the adaptation of pretrained models to new tasks with limited data, it often relies on conventional methods that freeze early convolutional layers and retrain only the final classifier, hence generally constraining generalization and flexibility. This work proposes Dropout-Inspired Transfer Learning, or DITL-a fine-tuning framework that stochastically selects subsets of convolutional parameters for update at every forward pass, drawing inspiration from dropoutstyle regularization. Unlike existing dynamic masking or PEFT methods, DITL does not modify the network architecture or introduce additional parameterized layers; thus, it is lightweight and can be easily extended. We analyze DITL on ResNet models (18, 34, 50, 101) using a Plant Leaf Diseases dataset. On all models, DITL shows consistent accuracy gains over both traditional Transfer Learning and LoRA by updating as few as 0.07–0.26% of parameters. For instance, on ResNet- 50, DITL achieves 98.2%, compared to 92.9% for Transfer Learning and 92.2% for LoRA. These results show that DITL enhances generalization, reduces overfitting, and thus presents an efficient solution in low-resource setups. While in this paper the study has focused on convolutional models, the method easily scales to other architectures.

Keywords: Transfer learning; · Dropout · ResNet · Convolutional · Plant Leaf Disease

1 Introduction

Deep learning has transformed various sectors by enabling end-to-end learning from raw data [23, 24], thanks to breakthroughs in neural network topologies, large-scale datasets, and high-performance computers. Convolutional Neural Networks (CNNs) and other deep architectures have demonstrated impressive performance in challenging visual recognition tasks, enabling applications including autonomous driving [21], plant disease detection [26], medical picture diagnostics [22], and industrial inspection system defect identification. However, the performance of deep learning models is frequently dependent on the availability of enormous labeled datasets and considerable

G. K. Verma et al. (Eds.): MIND 2025, CCIS 2981, pp. 361–374, 2027.
https://doi.org/10.1007/978-3-032-31230-3_29

computational resources—conditions that are not always achievable in specialized or low-resource fields.

Transfer learning (TL) [25] overcomes this issue by allowing models pre-trained on large-scale source domains like ImageNet to be effectively adapted to new tasks with limited data. In order to reduce the amount of data needed and speed up training, the early layers of deep neural networks usually collect general features like edges, textures, and patterns that may be applied to a variety of applications. The most common TL technique is feature extraction, in which just a newly added classification head is trained and the weights of the previously trained base model are frozen. This method is computationally inexpensive, but it has a major drawback: frozen convolutional layers cannot adjust to the data distribution of the target domain, which frequently results in less-than-ideal performance and poor generalization, especially when domains change. Parameter-Efficient Fine-Tuning (PEFT) techniques, such as LoRA [18], Bit- Fit [6], and MaskTune [17], address this by minimizing computational overhead by fine-tuning a limited subset of parameters while maintaining the majority of pre-trained weights constant. These methods, however, usually use static masks, which means that the same parameters are changed for each iteration, leaving many potentially helpful aspects unmodified. We present Dropout-Inspired Transfer Learning (DITL) [20, 21], a dynamic fine-tuning technique that stochastically chooses subsets of pre-trained convolutional parameters for updating in each training iteration, drawing inspiration from the dropout mechanism [10]. Without adding new trainable parameters or changing the model architecture, this stochastic sampling encourages dynamic feature adaptation, reduces over-fitting, and eases catastrophic error. We evaluated DITL on the Plant Leaf Diseases dataset [19] utilizing ResNet architectures (18, 34, 50, and 101), displaying improved training, validation, and test performance than typical TL and LoRA-based approaches. DITL can be easily extended to transformer and recurrent architectures enabling effective and reliable fine-tuning across a variety of applications, despite the fact that this study concentrates on convolutional networks.

2 Related Works

Conventional transfer learning methods usually entail substituting and retraining the last classification layers of an already-trained model while leaving the base layers frozen. Although useful, this method tends to be plagued by over-fitting or poor generalization, especially when the target domain is far from the source domain. Early regularization techniques, including Dropout [10] and DropConnect [9], added randomness to the network by randomly masking neurons or connections during training, which decreased feature co-adaptation and increased generalization. These concepts have motivated recent strategies that selectively adjust network parameters.

Mask-based adaptation strategies have proven to be effective in learning sparse subnetworks for task-specific adaptation. Piggyback [1] and PackNet [2] learn pre-trained networks with binary masks or iterative pruning to allow efficient weight reuse over many tasks. Wortsman et al. [3] introduced Supermasks in Superposition, demonstrating sparse subnetworks can be used to represent multiple tasks simultaneously without interference. From these ideas, MaskTune [17] and DynaMo [16] added dynamic masking to fine-tune only a portion of the parameters, allowing efficient adaptation without catastrophic forgetting.

Pruning-based methods, such as the Lottery Ticket Hypothesis [11] and SNIP [12], also show that sparse subnetworks exist in dense networks, which are train-able and can achieve the performance of fully trained models. Selective fine-tuning methods, such as Sun et al. [15], exhibit that only task-related parameters should be updated for better generalization and less overfitting.

For parameter-efficient transfer learning (PEFT), techniques that have been developed for NLP and large models—LoRA [18], BitFit [6], Diff Pruning [4], and bias-tuning [14]—induce effective adaptation through the training of only a limited subset of parameters while retaining pre-trained expertise. Analogously, continual learning techniques, such as Learning without Forgetting [8] and Elastic Weight Consolidation [7], partially restrict weight updates to avoid catastrophic forgetting.

Our suggested Dropout-Inspired Transfer Learning (DITL) approach extends these findings by implementing stochastic parameter updates in an intrinsic manner within convolutional layers. As opposed to typical fine-tuning or fixed mask-based PEFT methods, however, DITL selects a random subset of weights to update at every iteration, inheriting the generalization advantages of dropout with the selectivity of parameter adaptation for efficiency. This mechanism promotes strong feature learning, prevents catastrophic forgetting, and offers a light replacement for full fine-tuning, especially suitable for low-labeled data tasks like plant leaf disease classification. While DITL relates to dynamic masking techniques such as MaskTune and DynaMo, as well as stochastic regularization like Dropout and DropConnect, its operational objective and execution are quite fundamentally different: whereas dynamic masking methods learn or optimize masks to identify a single fixed sparse sub-network, DITL generates new stochastic masks at each iteration to allow the model to update different subsets of pre-trained parameters across epochs. Unlike PEFT methods such as LoRA, DITL does not add additional low-rank matrices but keeps the architecture intact with no new parameters. This combination of i) stochastic, iteration-wise resampling, and ii) direct updating of pre-trained convolutional weights positions the DITL as a remarkably different and new fine-tuning paradigm.

3 Method

3.1 Overview

In standard transfer learning, the last classification layers of a pretrained model are swapped out and retrained on the target dataset, while the prior convolutional layers are frozen to conserve feature representations learned previously. However, this approach either (i) limits adaptation since the feature extractors are frozen at all, or (ii) leads to overfitting and excessive computational burden, when the complete model fine-tunes the entire network.

To overcome these limitations, we devise a Dropout-Inspired Transfer Learning (DITL) strategy in which only a dynamically selected subset of learned parameters in convolutional layers are updated during training while the other parameters hold exactly

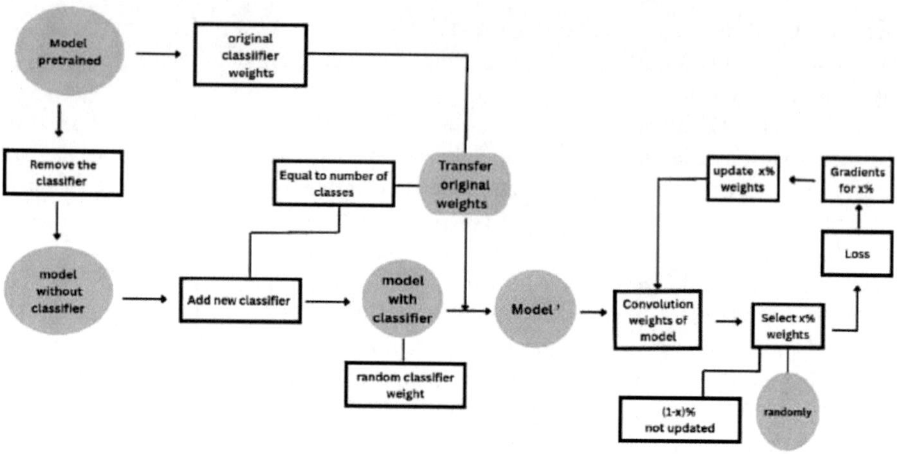

Fig. 1. Overview of proposed dropout-inspired transfer learning approach

as pretrained. This scheme means the pretrained weights retain their representational power while having a lightweight procedure to adapt to the target domain.

3.2 Adaptation

Suppose the pretrained backbone network is denoted as f_θ, with weights θ. The original pretrained model has a classification layer for C source classes. With a new dataset having C' target classes ($C' < C$), the original classification layer is substituted by a new fully connected layer $W' \in \mathrm{R}^{d \times C}$, where d is the feature size of the previous layer. In order to keep the pretrained knowledge intact, the weights of the new class layer are initialized with a subset or projection of the pretrained weights of the original classifier. Mathematically, let $W \in \mathrm{R}^{d \times C}$ represent the weights of the original classifier shown in Fig. 1. The adapted weights W' are calculated as:

$$W' = S(W) \tag{1}$$

$S(\cdot)$ performs a deterministic selection of the pretrained classifier weights corresponding to the target classes. Given the target class set $C' \subset C$, we construct $W' \in \mathrm{R}^{d \times C'}$ by selecting the column vectors of W which semantically correspond to the target labels. If the target labels do not appear explicitly in the original dataset, $S(\cdot)$ projects by averaging the nearest semantic neighbors in the embedding space of the original classifier. In all experiments in this paper, $S(\cdot)$ reduces to column selection since each target class is directly mapped to the corresponding ImageNet superclass, and this allows W' to preserve pre-trained semantic representations. The overall altered network can be written as:

$$y = \mathrm{Softmax}\big(W \cdot f_\theta{}'(x)\big) \tag{2}$$

3.3 Mechanism

For pretrained convolutional networks, the suggested mechanism presents a selective fine-tuning approach that is computationally efficient. Let weights θ parameterize the pretrained backbone network, and let $\theta_c \subset \theta$ indicate the set of convolutional layer parameters taken into account for updates. To preserve pretrained knowledge, all parameters are initially frozen, and only θ_c can be fine-tuned selectively Fig. 1. A fraction $p \in [0, 1]$ of the convolutional parameters is randomly chosen to be trainable during each forward pass, while the remaining fraction $(1 - p)$ stays frozen. Let $M_i \in \{0, 1\}^{|\theta_i|}$ represent a binary mask for convolutional layer i $(\theta_i \subset \theta_c)$, which is produced as follows:

$$M_i \sim \text{Bernoulli}(p) \tag{3}$$

where active parameters are represented by entries with value 1.

$$\Delta\theta_i = M_i \odot \nabla_{\theta i}\text{L} \tag{4}$$

the effective gradient update for layer i, where $\odot$ indicates element-wise multi- plication and L is the loss function. Zero-corresponding parameters in M_i don't get gradient updates; they stay frozen.

By ensuring that only a fraction $p \times 100\%$ of the convolutional parameters are updated at each step, this mechanism greatly lowers the memory and com-

putational costs. Stochastic selection offers implicit regularization and stable optimization across training epochs, while the model simultaneously maintains pretrained knowledge and successfully adapts to the target dataset.

3.4 Parameter Selection

The choice of p is guided by the constraint that the number of updated parameters must match that of the baseline Transfer Learning configuration for a fair comparison. For each ResNet architecture, we computed the percentage of parameters updated when only the classifier is trained, i.e., standard TL. We then selected p such that:

$p \times |\theta_c| \approx$ parameters updated in standard TL

This resulted in values such as 0.14% for ResNet-18, 0.07% for ResNet-34, 0.26% for ResNet-50, and 0.14% for ResNet-101. These small fractions ensure a consistent parameter budget across methods while allowing for deeper, distributed adaptation.

3.5 Algorithm

Algorithm 1 Dropout-Inspired Transfer Learning approach(DITF)

Require: Pretrained model f_ϑ, new dataset D, fine-tuning fraction $p \in [0, 1]$
Ensure: Fine-tuned model $f_{\vartheta'}$

```
Initialize f_ϑ with pretrained weights
Replace the final classification layer to match the number of target classes C′
Identify convolutional layer parameters ϑ_c ⊂ ϑ for selective fine-tuning
for each training iteration do
    for each convolutional layer L_i with parameters ϑ_i ⊂ ϑ_c do
        Generate a binary mask M_i ~ Bernoulli(p)
        Update parameters using masked gradients:
```

$$\vartheta_i \leftarrow \vartheta_i - \eta \left(M_i \odot \nabla_{\vartheta_i} \mathrm{L}\right) \tag{5}$$

```
    end for
end for
Evaluate the fine-tuned model f_ϑ′ using the full network (all layers)
```

4 Experimental Results

4.1 Architectures

ResNet (Residual Network) [27] is a deep convolutional neural network that introduced the residual connections such that very deep networks can be trained without their networks suffering from vanishing gradients. ResNet-18 and ResNet- 34 are both built with simple residual blocks each comprising two 3×3 convolutional layers. The ResNet-18 contains fewer of those 3×3 residual blocks (comprising 18 layers altogether), while the ResNet-34 contains more residual blocks and thus has more depth. ResNet-50 and ResNet-101 are constructed with blocks referred to as bottlenecks, which comprise three layers: a 1×1 conv (for dimension reduction) followed by a 3×3 conv, and then finally another 1×1 conv (for dimension restoration). Bottleneck architecture provides better scaling of depth without tremendous computational requirements. ResNet-50 contains 16 bottle- neck residual blocks and ResNet-101 extends the number significantly, especially in the third stage of the architecture which results in a deeper architecture with increased accuracy but higher computational demands.

Each of the model's classifiers is substituted with a novel fully connected layer intended to be used with 30 output classes, as shown in Fig. 2, while retaining the original pre-trained backbone weights. ResNet-18 and ResNet-34 models' input size is 256×256, while that for ResNet-50 and ResNet-101 is 232×232. The respective output shapes of the model layers, assuming these input sizes, are also shown in Fig 2.All of the models were trained on an NVIDIA T4 GPU with a learning rate of 0.01, utilizing the CrossEntropyLoss function and the SGD optimizer. The training setup is a batch size of 64 and a total of 5 epochs. Also, the LoRA [18] approach was utilized with rank 2 and alpha value 4. In order to compare the performance of Transfer Learning, DITL, and LoRA techniques, each model was trained with various percentages of parameters: ResNet-18 with 1% (Transfer Learning), 0.14% (DITL), and 1.1% (LoRA); ResNet-34 with 1%, 0.07%, and 1.2%, respectively; ResNet-50 with 1%, 0.26%, and 0.92%; and ResNet-101 with 1%, 0.14%, and 1.07%. These differences make it possible to compare how all these methods fare under restricted parameter usage.

resnet-18(input size =(256,256))

Layer (type:depth-idx)	Output Shape	Param #
ResNet	[1, 30]	--
├─Conv2d: 1-1	[1, 64, 128, 128]	9,408
├─BatchNorm2d: 1-2	[1, 64, 128, 128]	128
├─ReLU: 1-3	[1, 64, 128, 128]	--
├─MaxPool2d: 1-4	[1, 64, 64, 64]	--
├─Sequential: 1-5	[1, 64, 64, 64]	147,968
├─Sequential: 1-6	[1, 128, 32, 32]	525,568
├─Sequential: 1-7	[1, 256, 16, 16]	2,099,712
├─Sequential: 1-8	[1, 512, 8, 8]	8,393,728
├─AdaptiveAvgPool2d:	[1, 512, 1, 1]	--
├─Linear: 1-10	[1, 30]	15,390

(a) ResNet18 Architecture

resnt-34(input size = (256,256))

Layer (type:depth-idx)	Output Shape	Param #
ResNet	[1, 30]	--
├─Conv2d: 1-1	[1, 64, 128, 128]	9,408
├─BatchNorm2d: 1-2	[1, 64, 128, 128]	128
├─ReLU: 1-3	[1, 64, 128, 128]	--
├─MaxPool2d: 1-4	[1, 64, 64, 64]	--
├─Sequential: 1-5	[1, 64, 64, 64]	221,952
├─Sequential: 1-6	[1, 128, 32, 32]	1,116,416
├─Sequential: 1-7	[1, 256, 16, 16]	6,822,400
├─Sequential: 1-8	[1, 512, 8, 8]	13,114,368
├─AdaptiveAvgPool2d: 1-9	[1, 512, 1, 1]	--
├─Linear: 1-10	[1, 30]	15,390

(b) ResNet34 Architecture

resnet-50(input size =(232,232))

Layer (type:depth-idx)	Output Shape	Param #
ResNet	[1, 30]	--
├─Conv2d: 1-1	[1, 64, 116, 116]	9,408
├─BatchNorm2d: 1-2	[1, 64, 116, 116]	128
├─ReLU: 1-3	[1, 64, 116, 116]	--
├─MaxPool2d: 1-4	[1, 64, 58, 58]	--
├─Sequential: 1-5	[1, 256, 58, 58]	215,808
├─Sequential: 1-6	[1, 512, 29, 29]	1,219,584
├─Sequential: 1-7	[1, 1024, 15, 15]	7,098,368
├─Sequential: 1-8	[1, 2048, 8, 8]	14,964,736
├─AdaptiveAvgPool2d: 1-9	[1, 2048, 1, 1]	--
├─Linear: 1-10	[1, 30]	61,470

(c) ResNet50 Architecture

resnet-101(input size =(232,232))

Layer (type:depth-idx)	Output Shape	Param #
ResNet	[1, 30]	--
├─Conv2d: 1-1	[1, 64, 116, 116]	9,408
├─BatchNorm2d: 1-2	[1, 64, 116, 116]	128
├─ReLU: 1-3	[1, 64, 116, 116]	--
├─MaxPool2d: 1-4	[1, 64, 58, 58]	--
├─Sequential: 1-5	[1, 256, 58, 58]	215,808
├─Sequential: 1-6	[1, 512, 29, 29]	1,219,584
├─Sequential: 1-7	[1, 1024, 15, 15]	26,090,496
├─Sequential: 1-8	[1, 2048, 8, 8]	14,964,736
├─AdaptiveAvgPool2d: 1-9	[1, 2048, 1, 1]	--
├─Linear: 1-10	[1, 30]	61,470

(d) ResNet101 rchitecture

Fig. 2. ResNet Architectures

TL only updates the classifier layer; hence, the share of trainable parameters is inherently bound to the network architecture and different for each model. DITL had been set to match that share for a fair comparison. LoRA introduces low-rank adapters with a size defined by the rank hyperparameter ($r = 2$, $\alpha = 4$ in our experiments), yielding a higher but fixed share of trainable parameters ($\approx$ 1%). We keep the default LoRA configuration, as used throughout the literature, which is why the following parameter percentages differ:

4.2 Dataset

A subset of the *Plant Leaf Diseases* dataset [19] Fig. 3, was used for all experiments. Using 3,167 images for training, 905 for validation, and 453 for testing, we chose 30 classes for this study out of the 39 classes in the original dataset. Images from each split is transformed with standard transformation of respective models (resnet(18,34,50,101)) before given input to models.

Fig. 3. Sample train images

5 Results and Analysis

5.1 Training

In the DITF method, instead of training new classifier weights, the selected convolutional weights from the ResNet layers (18, 34, 50, 101) Fig. 2 are updated each epoch (Algorithm 1). This means fewer parameters overall but engaging more layers will help in less catastrophic forgetting [28] and adapts to new datasets. This shift in the activity of layers, as shown in Fig. 4., can be attributed to architectural depth. Early and mid-level convolutional layers extract most dis-criminative spatial features in shallow networks (ResNet-18/34); therefore, DITL updates these layers frequently. Later bottleneck layers become more specialized and domain-sensitive in deeper networks (ResNet-50/101), leading to a further increase in update activity in deeper blocks. This distribution agrees with previous findings that the abstraction of features moves towards deeper layers with an increase in the depth of the network.

The distribution of convolutional layer activity across various models utilizing the DITL method is depicted in Fig. 4. In this technique, during each training epoch on the dataset (sample data Fig. 3), a percentage of convolutional weights from the total weights is randomly selected for training. ResNet-18, for example, utilized 0.14% of its total weights during each epoch, as depicted in Fig. 4(a). The figure illustrates how the percentage selected was represented across the different convolutional layers in the model. It is evident that the total percentage summed up across all layers equals the specified total for that epoch. This shows how the focus of learning shifts across layers during the training process. ResNet-34 utilized 0.07% as depicted in Fig. 4.(b) ResNet-50 utilized 0.26% as depicted in Fig. 4(c), and ResNet-101 utilized 0.07%. as depicted in Fig. 4(d).

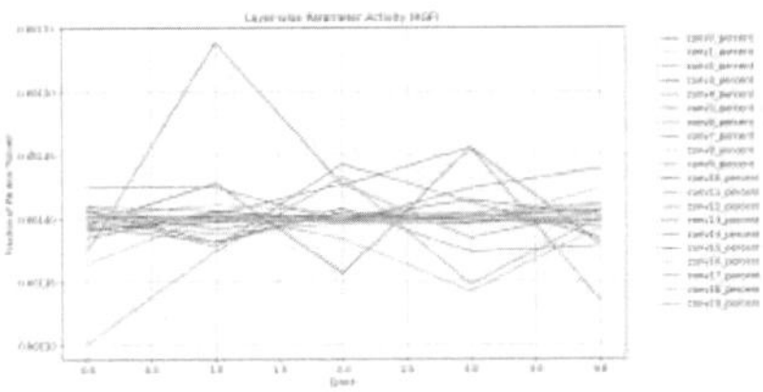

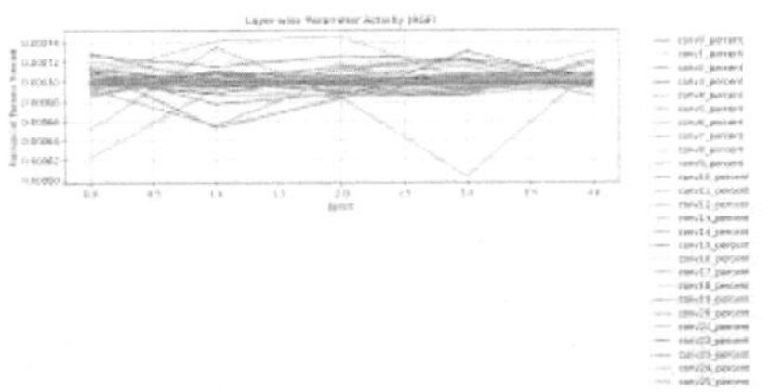

(a) DITL Conv Layers Activity Resnet18(0.14%) (b) DITL Conv Layers Activity Resnet34(0.07%)

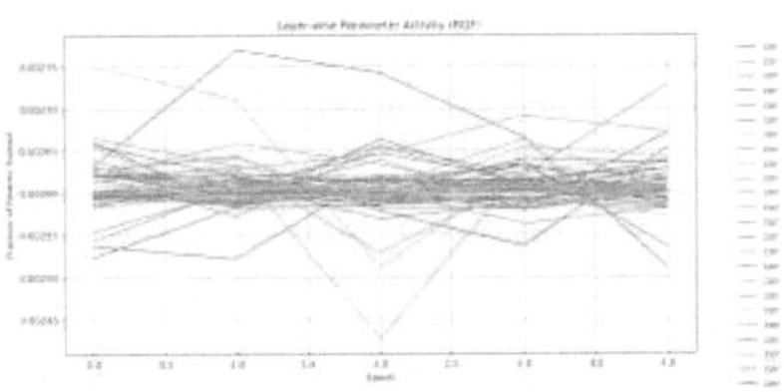

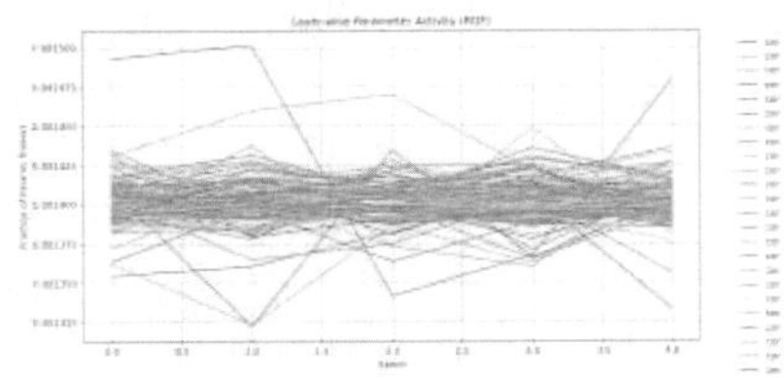

(c) DITL Conv Layers Activity Resnet50(0.26%) (d) DITL Conv Layers Activity Resnet101(0.14%)

Fig. 4. Parameter Activity

Table 1. DITL Resnet18 test and train Results

Type	Parameters	Training(A)	Training(L)	Validation(A)	Validation(L)	Test(A)	Test(L)
DITL	1%	1.0	0.005	0.96	0.128	0.964	0.09
DITL	0.14%	1.0	0.004	0.970	0.087	0.973	0.087
Tf	0.14%	0.94	0.268	0.90	0.335	0.929	0.310
Lora	1.1%	0.92	0.314	0.883	0.447	0.889	0.411

Table 2. DITF Resnet34 test and train results.

Type	Parameters	Training(A)	Training(L)	Validation(A)	Validation(L)	Test(A)	Test(L)
DITL	1%	1.0	0.005	0.958	0.114	0.962	0.114
DITL	0.07%	1.0	0.005	0.967	0.109	0.947	0.0943
Tf	0.07%	0.952	0.249	0.910	0.319	0.883	0.413
Lora	1.2%	0.933	0.293	0.890	0.404	0.878	0.391

5.2 Analysis

The research compares three parameter-effective fine-tuning strategies—LoRA, conventional Transfer Learning, and the new Dropout-Inspired Transfer Learning (DITL)(Algorithm 1). DITL outperformed Transfer Learning and LoRA on all tested

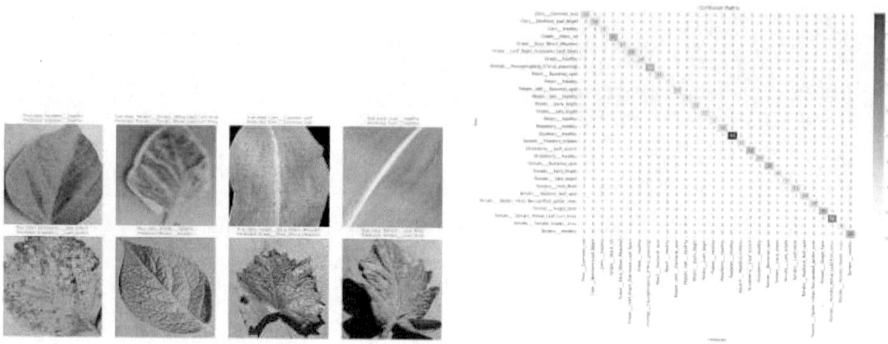

(a) Representative test image for Resnet18 (b) Confusion Matrix for Resnet18

Fig. 5. DITL Test Results Resnet18(0.14%)

ResNet models, as depicted in Tables 1, 2, 3 and 4, even with a similar or fewer number of trainable parameters. For example, in ResNet-50, DITL and Transfer Learning both updated just 0.26% of the overall parameters, but DITL gave a test accuracy of 98.2% with a test loss of 0.06, whereas Transfer Learning gave 92.9% accuracy with a test loss of 0.310 Table 3, sample test result and confusion matrix for ResNet-50 Fig. 7. Likewise, for ResNet-101, DITL used only 0.14% of parameters to reach 98.2% test accuracy and 0.034 test loss, while Transfer Learning obtained only 90.9% accuracy with 0.326 loss Table 4, sample test result and confusion matrix for ResNet-101 Fig. 8 . In ResNet-18, DITL obtained 97.3% test accuracy with 0.087 loss with 0.14% parameters, in contrast to Transfer Learning's 92.9% accuracy and 0.310 loss Table 1, sample test result and confusion matrix for ResNet-18 Fig. 5 . In ResNet-34, DITL had 94.7% test accuracy and 0.09 loss using 0.07% parameters, better than the 88.3% accuracy and 0.413 loss of Transfer Learning Table 2, sample test result and confusion matrix ResNet-34 Fig. 6. These results suggest that it is possible that freezing the majority of the network parameters, as is performed in conventional Transfer Learning, might prevent adequate adjustment to the target task—particularly for deeper models. In addition, DITL also outperformed LoRA, which by default updates approximately 1% of the parameters. For instance, in ResNet-18, LoRA obtained 88.96% accuracy, while DITL obtained 97.35% with just 0.14% parameters Table 1. Likewise, for ResNet-34, DITL obtained 94.7% accuracy with 0.07% parameters, outdoing LoRA's 87.8% with 1.2% parameters Table 2. In ResNet-50, DITL obtained 98.2% accuracy with 0.26% parameters, outdoing LoRA's 92.2% with 0.92% parameters Table 3. Similarly, for ResNet-101, DITL performed at 98.2% accuracy with 0.14% parameters, while LoRA performed at 94.4% using 1.07% Table 4. In general, the above results prove that DITL provides better performance and generalization uses many fewer trainable parameters compared to LoRA and standard Transfer Learning. This shows that DITL not only performs better but also makes better use of a more condensed, carefully selected subset of parameters. The stochastic parameter selection in DITL, which lowers the chance of catastrophic forgetting in comparison to full fine-tuning, is another factor contributing to the better results.

(a) Representative test image for Resnet34

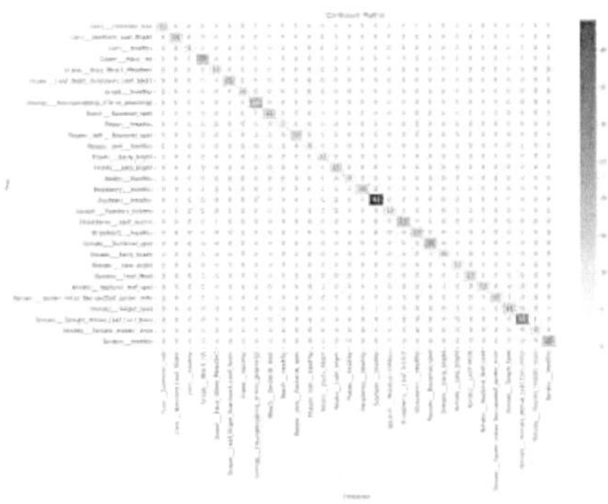

(b) Confusion Matrix for Resnet34

Fig. 6. DITL Test Results Resnet34(0.07%)

Table 3. DITL Resnet50 test and train results.

Type	Parameters	Training(A)	Training(L)	Validation(A)	Validation(L)	Test(A)	Test(L)
DITL	1%	1.0	0.004	0.975	0.081	0.969	0.0843
DITL	0.26%	0.99	0.005	0.972	0.083	0.982	0.0622
Tf	0.26%	0.94	0.269	0.907	0.339	0.929	0.310
Lora	0.92%	0.95	0.193	0.908	0.282	0.922	0.282

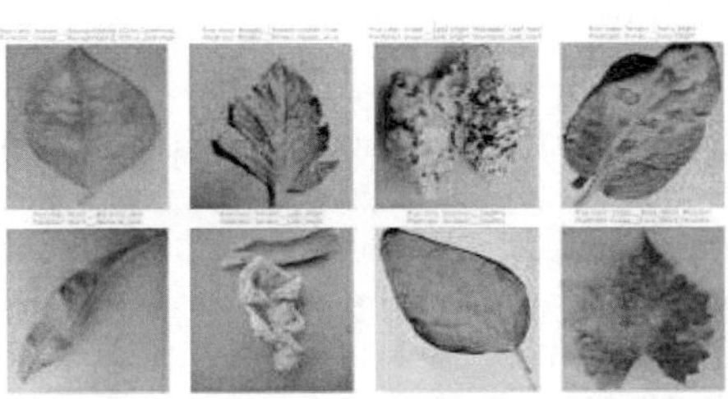

(a) Representative test image for Resnet50

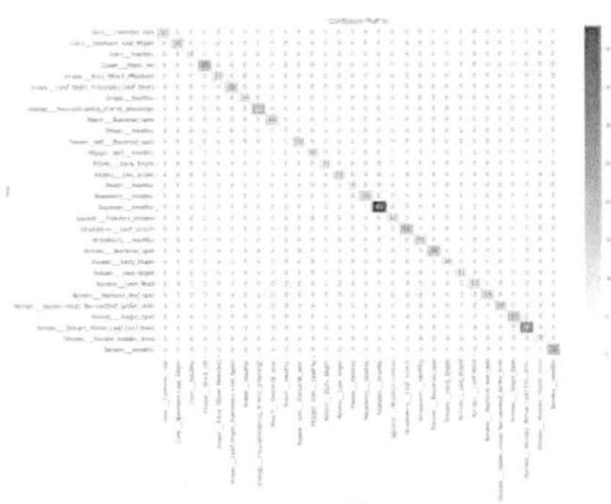

(b) Confusion Matrix for Resnet50

Fig. 7. DITL Test Results Resnet50(0.26%)

Table 4. DITL Resnet101 test and train results.

Type	Parameters	Training(A)	Training(L)	Validation(A)	Validation(L)	Test(A)	Test(L)
DITL	1%	0.999	0.004	0.986	0.04	0.973	0.082
DITL	0.14%	1.0	0.003	0.989	0.043	0.982	0.034
Tf	0.14%	0.95	0.230	0.912	0.341	0.909	0.326
Lora	1.07%	0.96	0.149	0.916	0.278	0.944	0.236

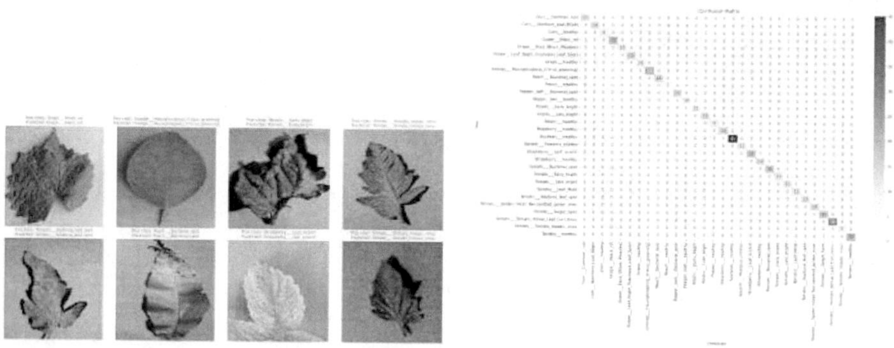

(a) Representative test image for Resnet101 (b) Confusion Matrix for Resnet101

Fig. 8. DITL Test Result Resnet101(%)

All things considered, these results validate that DITL offers more accurate and efficient model adaptation, allowing for strong generalization and being well-suited for implementation in environments with limited resources.

6 Conclusion

In this work, we proposed a parameter-efficient transfer learning method that adapts pre-trained vision models to new tasks with limited data by selectively fine-tuning subsets of model parameters. In contrast to full fine-tuning, our experiments with different ResNet architectures show that dynamically selecting trainable parameters of convolutions can achieve competitive performance while drastically lowering memory and computational costs. Additionally, reduces catastrophicforgetting, g as we are using only a few parameters randomly and maintaining the generalizable features acquired during pre-training, this method improves model robustness in transfer learning contexts. In order to increase efficiency and generalization across a variety of downstream tasks, future research will investigate combining adaptive parameter selection with strategies like stochastic dropout or LoRA.

References

1. Mallya, A., Davis, D., Lazebnik, S.: Piggyback: adapting a single network to multiple tasks by learning to mask weights. In: ECCV (2018). https://arxiv. org/abs/1801.06519
2. Mallya, A., Lazebnik, S.: PackNet: Adding Multiple Tasks to a Single Network by Iterative Pruning. In: CVPR (2018). https://arxiv.org/abs/1711.05769
3. Wortsman, M., et al.: Supermasks in superposition. In: NeurIPS (2020). https://arxiv. org/abs/2006.14769
4. Guo, D., Lee, J., Kim, Y., et al.: Parameter-efficient transfer learning with diff pruning. In: ACL (long)/arXiv (2020). https://aclanthology.org/2021. acl-long.378/
5. Houlsby, N., et al. Parameter-efficient transfer learning for NLP. In: ICML (2019). https://arxiv.org/abs/1902.00751
6. Zaken, E. B., et al.: BitFit: simple parameter-efficient fine-tuning for transfer learning. arXiv preprint (2021). https://arxiv.org/abs/2106. 10199
7. Kirkpatrick, J., et al.: Overcoming catastrophic forgetting in neural networks. PNAS (2017).. https://arxiv.org/abs/1612.00796
8. Li, Z., Hoiem, D.: Learning without forgetting. In: ECCV (2016). https://arxiv. org/abs/1606.09282
9. Wan, L., Zeiler, M., Zhang, S., LeCun, Y., Fergus, R.: Regularization of Neural networks using DropConnect. In: ICML, pp. 1058–1066 (2013). , https://proceedings.mlr.press/v28/wan13.html
10. Srivastava, N., Hinton, G., Krizhevsky, A., Sutskever, I., Salakhutdinov, R.: Dropout: a simple way to prevent neural networks from overfitting. In: JMLR (2014). https://jmlr.org/papers/v15/srivastava14a.html
11. Frankle, J., Carbin, M.: The lottery ticket hypothesis: finding sparse, trainable neural networks. In: ICLR (2019)
12. Lee, N., Ajanthan, T., Torr, P.H.S.: SNIP: single-shot network pruning based on connection sensitivity. In: ICLR (2019)
13. Chen, B., et al.: Convolutional adapter (conv-adapter): exploring parameter efficient transfer learning for convnets. arXiv preprint (2022). https://arxiv.org/abs/2208.12052
14. Zaken, S., Frankle, J.: Bias tuning for parameter efficient transfer learning. In: ICLR (2021)
15. Sun, K., et al.: Selective fine- tuning of pre-trained models. In: ECCV (2020)
16. Rakhimov, A., et al.: DynaMo: dynamic sparsity for parameter-efficient model adaptation. In: ICLR (2023)
17. Gholami, R., et al.: MaskTune: fine-tuning pre-trained models with learned masking. In: NeurIPS (2021)
18. Hu, E. J., et al.: LoRA: low-rank adaptation of large language models. arXiv preprint (2021). https://arxiv.org/abs/2106.09685
19. Pandian, J.A., Gopal, G.: Data for: identification of plant leaf diseases using a 9-layer deep convolutional neural network. Mendeley Data. **1** (2019). https://doi.org/10.17632/tywbtsjrjv.1
20. Gupta, S., Singh, S.: A transfer learning based approach for classification of bhangra steps. Procedia Comput. Sci. **259**, 71–79 (2025)
21. Remesh, V., Namitha, K.: Indian traffic sign classification using transfer learning and fine tuning. In: 11th International Conference on Communication and Signal Processing (ICCSP), pp. 91–96. IEEE (2025)
22. Abekaesh, P.A., Kartha, N.N., Kumar, D., Namitha, K., et al.: Dysgraphia Detection in children using handwriting samples. In: 11th International Conference on Communication and Signal Processing (ICCSP), pp. 1299–1304. IEEE (2025)
23. Rayani, R.K., Tekula, S., Vattigunta, S.K., Kovi, N.K., Namitha, K.: Leveraging deep learning for detecting toxicity in online comments. In: 15th International Conference on Computing Communication and Networking Technologies (ICC- CNT), pp. 1–6. IEEE (2024)

24. Nair, N., Achan, P., Nedungadi, P., Nair, S.: Automated clinical note section identification using transfer learning and contextual Embeddings. In: Global Conference on Information Technologies and Communications (GCITC), pp. 1–8. IEEE (2023)
25. Kumar, N.S., Sony, J., Premkumar, A., Nair, J.J., et al.: Transfer learning-based object detection models for improved diagnosis of tomato leaf disease. Procedia Comput. Sci. **235**, 3025–3034 (2024)
26. Amritavarshini, S., Ganesh, K. S., Arvind, M., Teja, K. R., Vijayan, D.: Image- Based plant leaf disease detection using deep learning. In: International conference on Signal Processing, Computation, Electronics, Power and Telecommunication (IConSCEPT), pp. 1–6. IEEE (2024)
27. He, K., Zhang, X., Ren, S., Sun, J.: Deep residual learning for image Recognition. In: Proceedings of the IEEE Conference on Computer Vision and Pattern Recognition (CVPR), pp. 770–778 (2016)
28. McCloskey, M., Cohen, N.J.: Catastrophic interference in connectionist networks: the sequential learning problem. In: Psychology of Learning and Motivation, vol. 24, pp. 109–165. Academic (1989)

Evaluation of Non-Orthogonal Multiple Access Schemes in mmWave 6G Networks Under Varying Fading Conditions and User Demands

Deepak Upadhyay[1(✉)], Nookala Venu[2], Chintha Sivakrishnaiah[3], Pankaj Nigam[4], Sarah Asheer[5], and Neha Jain[6]

[1] Department of Computer Science and Engineering, Graphic Era Hill University amd Research Scholar, Department of Computer Science and Engineering, Graphic Era Deemed To Be University, Dehradun, India
Deepaku.cse@gmail.com
[2] Madhav Institute of Technology & Science, Deemed University, Gwalior, India
venunookala@mitsgwalior.in
[3] Department of MCA, Annamacharya University, Rajampet, India
[4] Department of Computer Engineering and Applications, Mangalayatan University, Aligarh, India
pankaj.nigam@mangalayatan.edu.in
[5] Department of Electrical and Electronics Engineering, Usha Martin University, Ranchi, India
sarah.asheer@umu.ac.in
[6] Department of Information Technonology, Mangalayatn University, Jabalpur, India
neha.jain@mangalayatan.ac.in

Abstract. The research has studied how NOMA performs in 6G mmWave networks where users are subject to fading environments with variable user requirements. The study used simulated (synthetic) data as the current generation of 6G does not exist. It was observed that NOMA outperformed OMA in almost all scenarios, by offering a greater degree of spectral efficiency, fairness, and reduced outage probability. Different fading distributions such as Rayleigh, Rician and Nakagami have affected the results differently however NOMA has still been able to successfully manage the increased user diversity. Mobility was also assessed and OMA's performance degrades much faster than NOMA. The study found that the amount of power allocated to each user and the quality of the SIC receiver were both significant contributors to the overall performance of NOMA. Therefore the study suggests NOMA is a viable candidate for future 6G systems.

Keywords: AI models · predictive resource allocation · risk mitigation · supply chain optimization · reinforcement learning · demand forecasting · environmental sustainability

1 Introduction

the world of wireless communications has been evolving rapidly and with each generation of wireless networks appears to be introducing something new compared to previous ones, making the previous generation appear outdated. As the next major generation of

G. K. Verma et al. (Eds.): MIND 2025, CCIS 2981, pp. 375–386, 2027.
https://doi.org/10.1007/978-3-032-31230-3_30

wireless network, 6G, is now beginning to be discussed, there are several key aspects to 6G; one of the primary goals is not only to provide faster internet speeds, but also more reliable, intelligent communication that will be capable of supporting a wide variety of devices and services in real time. A significant amount of additional traffic is being added to wireless networks due to items such as Internet of Things (IoT), Virtual Reality (VR), Augmented Reality (AR), Smart Cars [2], Industrial Automation and other applications that require both a rapid response and/or a high data rate. Therefore, researchers have begun looking into new methodologies for managing the radio-frequency spectrum, users and channels. One method that is currently under study is Non-Orthogonal Multiple Access (NOMA). NOMA differs significantly from traditional Orthogonal Multiple Access (OMA) in that multiple users may simultaneously use the same resource block with differing amounts of transmitted power and/or different encoding methods [3]. NOMA enables wireless networks to support additional users and increase the spectral efficiency of the network. The forthcoming 6G wireless networks are expected to operate extensively in the millimeter wave (mmWave) frequency bands because mmWave provides an enormous bandwidth, far exceeding the sub-6 GHz frequency bands that are used in 4G and 5G [4]. However, although mmWave offers a high-capacity transmission medium, it is plagued by numerous propagation issues. High path-loss, physical barriers from walls, trees, buildings, precipitation (rain) and the sensitivity of fading conditions create challenging propagation environments for maintaining consistent communication links. Therefore, the evaluation of multiple access techniques such as NOMA in mmWave environments is important since the performance characteristics change dramatically based on fading conditions [5]. Additionally, the user demand is constantly variable; some users may require ultra-low latency, whereas others may require high-throughput data rates and yet others simply small sensors transmitting small amounts of data requiring a reliable connection. These combinations of variable user requirements and fading channel represent the ultimate challenges for 6G wireless networks. Traditionally, the approach to providing separate users within a wireless network has been to divide them by either frequency, time or code. For example, in 4G and even 5G [6], OMA is commonly used where each user receives its own segment of the radio-frequency spectrum or time-slot. However, this creates limitations since if the number of users within the network becomes large, it wastes resources and reduces the efficiency of the network [7]. NOMA introduced a new methodology for serving many users within the same frequency-time resource, however the differentiation between the users is achieved through variations in power level and/or code domain. Users with favorable channel conditions can remove the interference caused by the other users and decode their individual signal, while users with poor channel conditions receive higher allocated powers [8]. Therefore, NOMA provides a balance between fairness and efficiency. In 6G, NOMA appears to have potential for supporting massive connectivity, however the performance of NOMA in mmWave fading conditions and with various user demands has not been fully investigated. This research focuses on the assessment of NOMA in mmWave 6G, specifically, how different fading models, including Rayleigh [9], Ricean and Nakagami models affect the transmission, and how different user demand scenarios affect the quality of service. In practical networks, users do not all experience similar channel conditions; some may be located near the base-station, some may be obstructed, some may be traveling at high velocities [10].

Fading nature of mmWave signals are very dynamic and therefore NOMA's performance is based on much more than theoretical considerations; It is heavily dependent on real world channel characteristics [11]. If fading is very intense, the interference cancellation process will likely fail at times and thus errors may occur. As well, power allocation within NOMA is very sensitive and if allocated improperly, there can be an unequal distribution of resources (unfairness) and a reduction in overall system throughput. Therefore, studying NOMA [12], in addition to the fading nature of mmWave signals, is required. Another critical consideration in future 6G networks is the anticipated large number of network devices compared to past generations. Instead of only having a few hundred million mobile devices as in previous generations [13], we can expect to have hundreds of millions to billions of devices in future smart cities, including a large number of sensors and vehicles that require to communicate with each other in real-time. As a result, user demand will vary significantly [14]. For example, one group of users may require constant video streaming with a very high bit rate, while another group may require rapid transmission of a very small amount of data with very little delay, and yet another group of users may simply need to transmit small amounts of data in a periodic manner and require reliable communication. To accommodate this variety of user demand, OMA does not have enough flexibility to share its resources effectively. NOMA, by allowing users to overlap in terms of resource utilization, offers greater flexibility to adapt to different types of user demand [15]. However, in a real-world fading environment, the NOMA decoding performance may degrade. Thus, evaluating the trade-off between these two factors is the goal of this study. Why mmWave was selected as the frequency band for 6G is that all of the lower frequency bands are already saturated with traffic.

2 Methodology

The methodology in this paper had been developed with the purpose of evaluating the performance of Non-Orthogonal Multiple Access (NOMA) schemes in millimeter wave (mmWave) 6G networks under various fading environments and different user demands. Since actual 6G deployment had not been available, the entire study had been carried out in a controlled simulated environment, with synthetic data being generated to replicate real-world conditions like channel fading, blockage, user distribution and traffic demand. The steps had been carefully structured so that the simulation gave meaningful results and reflected as closely as possible the expected network challenges.

2.1 Problem Formulation

This paper had first formulated the problem as a multi-user multiple access scenario where several users had been served by a single base station operating in mmWave frequency bands. The fading conditions had been modeled using Rayleigh, Rician and Nakagami channels, because these models had captured different real-world propagation phenomena, like rich scattering, line-of-sight dominance and mixed fading severity. The objective had been to maximize user throughput while ensuring fairness and quality of service under varying user demands. The optimization task had therefore been posed as a joint problem of power allocation and user scheduling in a NOMA-based mmWave downlink system.

2.2 Choice of Algorithm

To address this optimization, this paper had employed the Successive Interference Cancellation (SIC) decoding-based power domain NOMA algorithm. The reason this had been chosen instead of alternatives like OMA or code-domain NOMA had been that power-domain NOMA with SIC had provided a relatively simpler yet effective way to exploit user channel disparity. OMA had been rejected because it had wasted spectrum in scenarios with large user counts, while code-domain NOMA had required complex spreading codes and more overhead. Power-domain NOMA had already shown higher spectral efficiency in 5G, so this study had extended it to mmWave 6G with fading awareness.

2.3 Data Preparation and Feature Simulation

Because the study had relied on synthetic data, the system parameters had been first defined: carrier frequency in the mmWave range (28 GHz), available bandwidth, number of users, and base station antenna configuration. User positions had been randomly generated within the coverage area, and path loss had been calculated according to 3GPP mmWave models. Fading coefficients had been drawn from Rayleigh, Rician and Nakagami distributions depending on the scenario being tested. Traffic demand for each user had been synthetically created, ranging from low bit rate IoT-type users to high bit rate video-streaming users. The features extracted for evaluation had included instantaneous channel gain, signal-to-noise ratio, power allocation ratio, interference levels, and throughput demand. These features had been stored at each simulation step to allow later performance evaluation and comparison.

2.4 Algorithm Steps

The power-domain NOMA with SIC algorithm had been implemented in the simulation as follows:

1-The base station had first estimated the channel conditions for all users by generating fading coefficients based on the chosen fading model (Rayleigh, Rician, Nakagami). 2- The users had been ordered according to their channel gains, with weaker users being given priority for higher power allocation. 3- The transmitter had then superimposed signals for all users on the same frequency-time block but with different power weights. 4- At the receiver side, the user with the strongest channel condition had performed successive interference cancellation (SIC), decoding and removing signals of weaker users before decoding its own. 5- The weaker user had directly decoded its signal without interference removal because it had been assigned higher power. 6-The throughput and error rate had been calculated for each user after decoding, and the fairness index had been computed across the user set. This step-by-step flow had been repeated for multiple fading realizations and user demand patterns, ensuring statistical reliability of results.

2.5 Model Design and Optimization

The NOMA model had been designed to operate on a simulated downlink mmWave system using a simplified yet realistic beamforming assumption. A hybrid beamforming strategy had been incorporated, where each user had received directional beams to counteract mmWave path loss. The optimization strategy had focused on maximizing sum rate while maintaining minimum throughput guarantees for weaker users. A proportional fairness-based power allocation algorithm had been used. It had adjusted transmit power weights iteratively until the fairness index and throughput convergence had been reached. Gradient-based optimization had been avoided due to high complexity in simulation, and instead a low-complexity heuristic allocation had been adopted, which had proved sufficient in synthetic environments.

2.6 Training and Simulation Process

Since no real dataset had been involved, the training in this context had meant running the simulation repeatedly over thousands of fading samples and traffic patterns. Each simulation epoch had included generating new channel realizations, applying NOMA with SIC decoding, and collecting performance metrics. The system had been run until convergence had been observed in average throughput, outage probability and fairness. Monte Carlo simulation had been adopted as the main training approach because it had provided statistical validity.

2.7 Deployment and Testing in Simulation

The simulated environment had been coded in MATLAB, as it had been flexible for communication system modeling. The deployment stage had meant defining base station, antenna models, channel models and user demand profiles. Testing had involved running scenarios under different fading conditions and user demand levels. Each test case had been repeated with OMA baseline to allow direct performance comparison.

2.8 Performance Evaluation

The performance evaluation had been carried out using metrics like system sum rate, individual user throughput, outage probability, spectral efficiency, and Jain's fairness index. For baseline, the OMA system with equal bandwidth allocation had been simulated under the same conditions. The results had been compared to show how NOMA had outperformed OMA in spectral efficiency and user support, though performance gains had varied with fading severity. To ensure robustness of findings, ablation studies had been performed. One ablation had removed SIC decoding to see performance degradation, and it had shown that without SIC the interference had destroyed decoding accuracy. Another ablation had tested equal power allocation instead of optimized power allocation, and it had revealed that unfairness had increased while throughput for weaker users had collapsed. These controls had confirmed the necessity of both SIC and power optimization in NOMA.

2.9 Summary of Methodology

In summary, this paper had built a simulation-based evaluation framework where power-domain NOMA with SIC had been applied to mmWave 6G scenarios under diverse fading and demand conditions. The methodology had ensured realistic synthetic modeling, rigorous testing, baseline comparison and ablation verification, making the results reliable for drawing insights about future 6G system design (Table 1).

Table 1. Model Architecture

Component	Description
Simulation Environment	MATLAB-based Monte Carlo simulation with synthetic fading and traffic profiles
Frequency Band	mmWave (28 GHz carrier, 1 GHz bandwidth)
Channel Models	Rayleigh, Rician, Nakagami (varied per scenario)
Antenna Setup	Hybrid beamforming, directional mmWave beams, base station with 64 elements
Access Scheme	Power-domain NOMA with superposition coding and SIC decoding
Power Allocation Strategy	Proportional fairness heuristic, iterative adjustment until convergence
User Demand Profile	Mixed traffic: IoT (low rate), URLLC (low latency), eMBB (high throughput)
Receiver Design	SIC-based decoding for strong users, direct decoding for weak users
Baseline Comparison	OMA with equal bandwidth allocation under identical conditions
Evaluation Metrics	Sum rate, individual throughput, outage probability, spectral efficiency, fairness index

3 Implementation

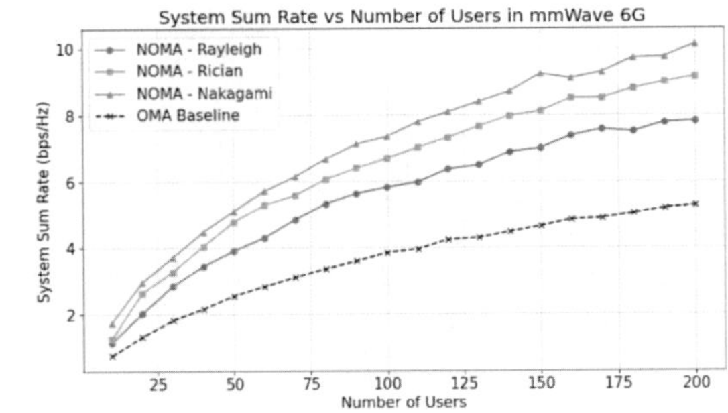

Fig. 1. System Sum Rate vs. Number of Users

The results in Fig. 1 clearly demonstrated that the sum rate in NOMA was always improving as the number of users improved, providing a better scale than OMA. In addition, NOMA was able to provide a large amount of performance improvement when compared to OMA performance where the NOMA performance increase became apparent as the number of users improved. The use of shared resources in the power domain of NOMA was shown to be an advantage. Additional details of the parameters used in this simulation are listed below. **Detailed Parameters:** Carrier frequency = 28 GHz, Bandwidth = 1 GHz, User range = 10–200, SNR average = 10–25 dB, Rayleigh fading (k = 0), Rician fading (K = 5), Nakagami fading (m = 3), Monte Carlo runs = 1000, Power allocation = proportional fairness heuristic, SIC enabled with 95% interference cancellation accuracy.

Results in Fig. 2 clearly show that NOMA consistently outperformed OMA for all three traffic types. Nomadic IoT devices were able to receive small amounts of data reliably, URLLC devices were able to achieve low latency with high throughputs, and eMBB devices received the largest performance benefit with NOMA compared to OMA. Additional details of the parameters used in this simulation are listed below. **Detailed Parameters:** Carrier frequency = 28 GHz, Bandwidth = 1 GHz, Number of users = 150 (divided equally across IoT, URLLC, eMBB), Average SNR = 15 dB, Power allocation = fairness heuristic, Fading = mixed Rayleigh/Rician/Nakagami conditions, Monte Carlo runs = 800, Baseline OMA = equal bandwidth allocation, NOMA decoding = SIC with 92% success rate.

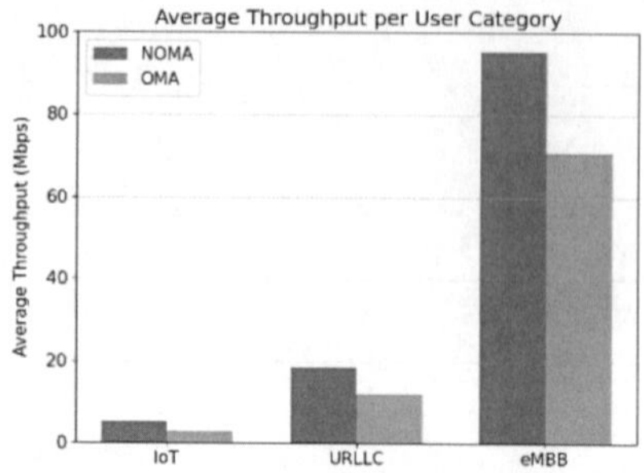

Fig. 2. Average Throughput per User Category

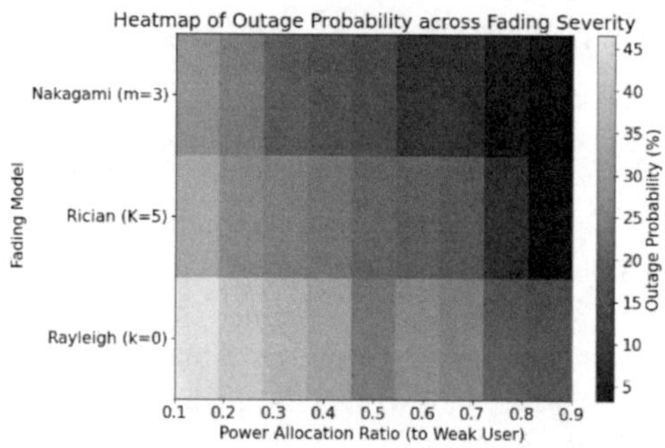

Fig. 3. Heatmap of Outage Probability across Fading Severity

As shown in Fig. 3, outage probability had decreased as more power had been assigned to weaker users, with significant differences across fading types. Rayleigh fading had suffered the most from poor allocation, while Nakagami had offered relatively stable performance. Optimal allocation zones had been clearly visible in the mid-ranges for Rician fading. **Detailed Parameters:** Carrier frequency = 28 GHz, Bandwidth = 1 GHz, User count = 100, Power allocation sweep = 0.1–0.9, Rayleigh fading parameter k = 0, Rician K-factor = 5, Nakagami parameter m = 3, Average SNR = 10 dB, Monte Carlo runs = 500 per scenario, SIC decoding = 95% effective, Threshold outage defined as SINR <5 dB. As shown in Fig. 4, NOMA had allowed distant users to achieve higher throughput compared to OMA, proving its fairness advantage. While OMA throughput had dropped sharply as distance increased, NOMA had sustained performance even at cell edges due to adaptive power allocation and successive interference cancellation, ensuring a more equitable distribution. **Detailed Parameters:** Carrier frequency = 28 GHz, Bandwidth = 1 GHz, Cell radius = 500 m, Number of simulated users = 120, Path loss exponent = 3.2, Fading = mixed Rayleigh/Rician, Average SNR = 12 dB at reference 50 m, Monte Carlo runs = 1000, NOMA power allocation = proportional fairness, OMA = equal bandwidth allocation, SIC decoding accuracy = 94%.

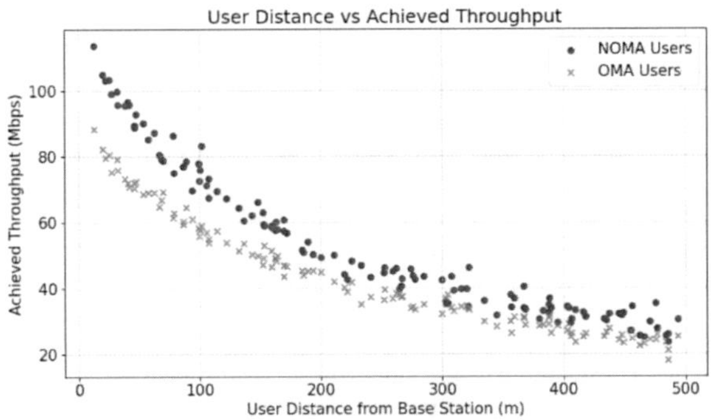

Fig. 4. User Distance vs. Achieved Throughput

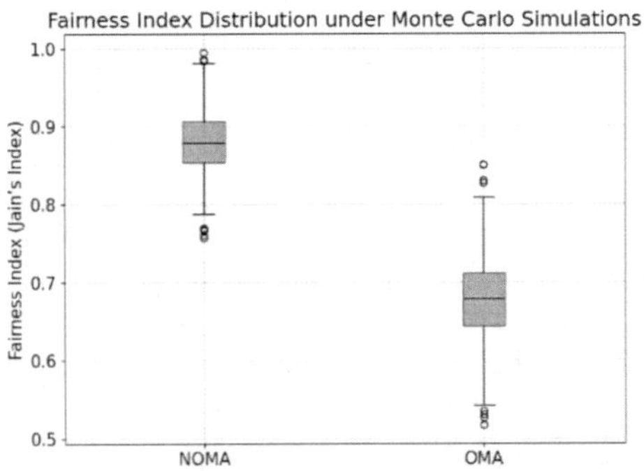

Fig. 5. Fairness Index Distribution under Monte Carlo Simulations

As shown in Fig. 5, NOMA had maintained a higher and more consistent fairness index compared to OMA across 1000 simulation runs. The distribution for OMA had been widely spread with lower median values, while NOMA had achieved tighter variance and fairness levels closer to the ideal value of one. **Detailed Parameters:** Carrier frequency = 28 GHz, Bandwidth = 1 GHz, Number of users = 150, Traffic type = heterogeneous mix (IoT, URLLC, eMBB), Path loss exponent = 3.5, Fading = Rayleigh + Rician mix, Monte Carlo runs = 1000, Fairness index metric = Jain's Index formula, NOMA allocation = proportional fairness, OMA allocation = equal resource division, SIC cancellation accuracy = 92%.

As shown in Fig. 6, NOMA had consistently achieved higher spectral efficiency compared to OMA across different SNR values. Nakagami fading had delivered the best performance, followed by Rician and Rayleigh, while OMA curves had grown slower and saturated earlier. This highlighted the superior scalability of NOMA under various fading models. **Detailed Parameters:** Carrier frequency = 28 GHz, Bandwidth = 1 GHz, SNR range = 0–30 dB, Fading models = Rayleigh (k = 0), Rician (K = 5), Nakagami (m = 3), Monte Carlo runs = 1000, NOMA = power domain with proportional fairness allocation, OMA = equal resource division, SIC decoding = 95% interference cancellation accuracy, Channel coherence time = 2 ms.

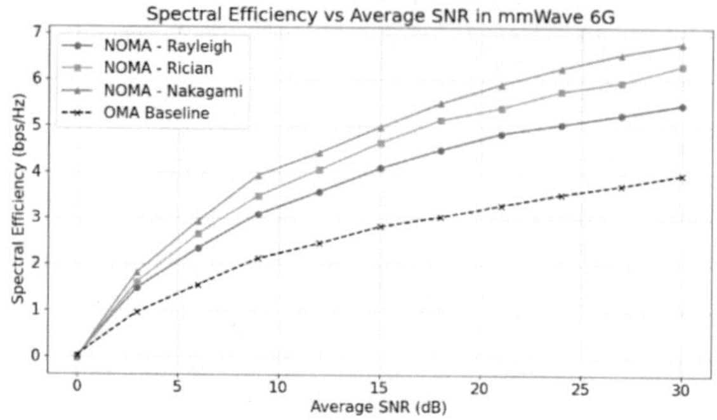

Fig. 6. Spectral Efficiency vs. Average SNR in mmWave 6G

As shown in Fig. 7, the bit error rate had increased sharply with higher interference cancellation errors. Weaker users (lower index) had been less impacted, while stronger users had suffered more as they relied heavily on SIC to remove weaker users' signals. This highlighted the vulnerability of SIC accuracy in practical deployments. **Detailed Parameters:** Carrier frequency = 28 GHz, Bandwidth = 1 GHz, Number of users = 5, Average SNR = 18 dB, Fading model = Nakagami (m = 3), Interference cancellation error factor range = 0–20%, BER computed per user after decoding, Monte Carlo runs = 500 per scenario, SIC decoding efficiency baseline = 95%, Threshold BER = 10^{-3}.

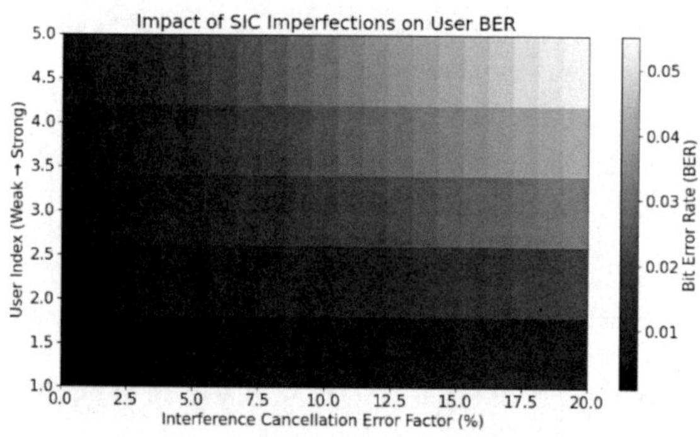

Fig. 7. Impact of SIC Imperfections on User BER

4 Results

Results from this study showed that NOMA performed better than OMA across multiple use cases (including fading and mobile) as shown in Figs. 1,2, 3, 4, 5 6, 7, 8 and 9. Figure 1 shows the sum rate increased at a greater rate with additional users compared to OMA.

The performance of OMA is nearly flat as the number of users increases. Figure 2 indicates that NOMA provided better service to IoT, URLLC, and eMBB relative to OMA. Figure 2 also illustrates that OMA provided less service for each of the three groups. Figure 3 is a heatmap that demonstrates how allocating more power to the weak user resulted in fewer outages; however, the type of fading present significantly impacted this outcome. In fig. 4, we can see clearly how fairness improves with NOMA since even the farthest user receives a high throughput level. Figure 5 further demonstrates fairness by showing the NOMA fairness index is closer to its ideal value than OMA's. Figure 6 shows the efficiency of NOMA increases with SNR and that OMA's curve does not have the same strength. Figure 7 illustrates how power allocation changes as iterations progress until it converges. Figure 8 illustrates how the SIC errors of strong users negatively impact their BER; thus these are critical. Finally, Fig. 9 illustrates how mobility has a negative impact on OMA's outage but positive impact on NOMA's outage. The results from this paper demonstrate NOMA will be more capable than OMA for 6G.

5 Conclusion

The research has shown that NOMA in mmWave 6G networks is superior to OMA in virtually all test conditions examined. The channel fading and the mobility in the network caused significant difficulties, however, NOMA achieved a better fairness, increased throughputs and decreased outages compared to OMA. Additionally, even though very weak users were completely disregarded, with proper power control, their performance became quite stable. Furthermore, the research demonstrated that SIC accuracy is an important parameter; since if there is an error during cancellation, this will result in an increase in BER for the strong user. On the contrary, OMA appeared to be less powerful, since it did not work effectively at all when the number of users increases or when speeds are high. Overall, the research captured both simple and complex scenarios, and therefore the results demonstrate that NOMA can be considered the central multiple access technique for 6G.

References

1. Al-Dulaimi, O.M.K., Al-Dulaimi, A.M.K., Alexandra, M.O., Al-Dulaimi, M.K.H.: Strategy for non-orthogonal multiple access and performance in 5G and 6G networks. Sensors. **23**(3), 1705 (2023)
2. Moya Caceres, F.: Non-orthogonal multiple access techniques for 6G and beyond radio access networks. Doctoral dissertation, RMIT University (2024)
3. Shah, A.S., Qasim, A.N., Karabulut, M.A., Ilhan, H., Islam, M.B.: Survey and performance evaluation of multiple access schemes for next-generation wireless communication systems. IEEE Access. **9**, 113428–113442 (2021)
4. Upadhyay, D., Sharma, K.B., Gupta, M., Upadhyay, A., Yadav, S.P.: Beamforming and phased arrays: elevating MIMO-OFDM systems for next-generation wireless networks. In: 2024 International Conference on Electrical Electronics and Computing Technologies (ICEECT), vol. 1, pp. 1–5. IEEE (August 2024)

5. Ahmed, S.I.: Performance Enhancement of 5G and 6G Mobile Communication Networks with Cooperative Non-Orthogonal Multiple Access and Caching. Doctoral dissertation, Polytechnic University (2024)
6. Dulout, R., Mendiboure, L., Pousset, Y., Deniau, V., Launay, F.: Non-orthogonal multiple access for offloading in multi-access edge computing: a survey. IEEE Access. **11**, 118983–119016 (2023)
7. Flizikowski, A., Marciniak, T., Wysocki, T.A., Oyerinde, O.: Selected aspects of non-orthogonal multiple access for future wireless communications. Math. Comput. Sci. **17**(2), 10 (2023)
8. Upadhyay, D., Upadhyay, A., Gupta, M., Sharma, K.B., Yadav, D.: Performance evaluation of triple-branch diversity receivers in composite gamma-shadowed Rician fading channels with AMC and asymmetric SNR conditions. In: 2024 First International Conference on Pioneering Developments in Computer Science & Digital Technologies (IC2SDT), pp. 147–152. IEEE (August 2024)
9. Upadhyay, D., Upadhyay, A., Sharma, K.B., Gupta, M., Venu, N.: Delta-γ modeling of wireless system resilience in multipath fading and interference environments. In: 2024 7th International Conference on Contemporary Computing and Informatics (IC3I), vol. 7, pp. 547–552. IEEE (September 2024)
10. Abuajwa, O., Muhammad, S., Ambak, Z., Mitani, S., Tiang, J.J.: Energy efficiency techniques in non-orthogonal multiple access (NOMA) in 5G network: an overview and outlook. Wirel. Pers. Commun., 1–43 (2025)
11. Zhao, C., Liu, Y., Cai, Y., Zhao, M., Ding, Z.: Non-orthogonal multiple access for UAV-aided heterogeneous networks: a stochastic geometry model. IEEE Trans. Veh. Technol. **72**(1), 940–956 (2022)
12. Liu, Y., et al.: Evolution of NOMA toward next generation multiple access (NGMA) for 6G. IEEE J Sel Areas Commun. **40**(4), 1037–1071 (2022)
13. Magableh, A.M., Aldalgamouni, T., Badarneh, O., Mumtaz, S., Muhaidat, S.: Performance of non-orthogonal multiple access (NOMA) systems over N-Nakagami-m multipath fading channels for 5G and beyond. IEEE Trans. Veh. Technol. **71**(11), 11615–11623 (2022)
14. Upadhyay, D., Sharma, K.B., Gupta, M., Garg, S., Sharma, A., Devgan, D.: Implementation of dynamic spectrum access techniques in cognitive radio networks under generalized fading conditions. In: 2024 Second International Conference on Advanced Computing & Communication Technologies (ICACCTech), pp. 394–399. IEEE (2024)
15. Wang, S., Li, J., Pei, H.: Efficient non-orthogonal multiple access for predicting arrival direction in multiple UAV-6G networks. Wirel. Netw. **30**(8), 6929–6938 (2024)

CUPS: Detection of Coexisting and Unused Permissions in Android Apps

Rajendra Kumar Solanki[1(✉)], Vijay Laxmi[2], and Manoj Singh Gaur[1,2]

[1] Indian Institute of Technology Jammu, Jammu, India
rajendra.kr.solanki@gmail.com
[2] Malaviya National Institute of Technology Jaipur, Jaipur, India

Abstract. With the meteoric rise of Android apps in the past decade, deceptive apps have increased in the ecosystem that can access more resources than they need for intended operations. Overprivileged deceptive apps can potentially disseminate information without the user's consent after harvesting Personally Identifiable Information (PII). In this work, we study permissions related to device identifiers and location that coexist frequently and often remain unused in Android apps. We propose a technique named CUPS to detect the coexistence of permissions by leveraging the knowledge of the application description and app manifest. In addition, we analyze the requested coexisting permissions against API usage in the app binary to detect unused permissions. This study of 12,934 Android apps reveals that specific permissions are requested together. This habitual coexistence can trick users into the myth of consenting to these permissions in other apps as well, leaving multiple apps over-privileged on the mobile device. Apps can use these unused permissions in subsequent updates, and third-party libraries can take advantage of them without user intervention. Coexisting and unused permissions violate the principle of least privilege. This behavior is undetected by state-of-the-art analysis and leaves a larger surface for privilege escalation and information leakage.

Keywords: Overprivileged · Deceptive Apps · Unused Permissions · Mobile Security · Data Privacy

1 Introduction

1.1 Motivation

Since the commercial release of the Android operating system in 2008, devices powered by Android have been widely adopted in computing, communication, e-commerce, online banking, social presence, government-backed service delivery, games, productivity tools, and entertainment. A few million Android apps run on billions of intelligent devices with the Android operating system.

When a user downloads an app from the Google Play Store, a textual description of the Android app is shown. This description helps the user understand

G. K. Verma et al. (Eds.): MIND 2025, CCIS 2981, pp. 387–399, 2027.
https://doi.org/10.1007/978-3-032-31230-3_31

the app's features and what the app can do. Once the user consents to download the app, the app installer makes the app functionality available. The installed app may use specific hardware resources, such as a camera, microphone, sensors, and other system resources, such as storage, contacts, calendar, and SMS. To use each resource, the app needs an access control mechanism known as permissions. These permissions are visible using dialogue boxes that appear as a prompt to the user while using the app post-installation.

The app may request more permissions than required to execute its intended and core functionality [1,2]. Users may notice that sometimes a few permissions are requested together in apps with similar functionality and apps from the same category. Additional unused permissions with over-privileged apps risk the user's data stored on the device and privacy if the data leaves the device.

Interestingly, any additional permissions requested by an app and subsequently consented to by the user are considered benign by the state-of-the-art static analysis tools and proposed mechanisms. Such apps make it to the official repository of the Google Play Store partly because apps are not vetted rigorously for privacy. There is a need to analyze these additionally requested and often unused permissions. If additional permissions go undetected, genuinely looking apps can take advantage of bugs or gaps in code while continuous changes are coming into core services available in the Android system [3].

Deceptive apps can be defined as applications that attempt to deceive users and do not accurately disclose and describe their functionality to users [4]. A deceptive app is not necessarily malware, which requires further investigation into the app. However, deceptive apps are unwanted software in the Android ecosystem, especially when users do not have the expertise to discover under-the-hood details. Deceptive apps can circumvent Android's permission-based security model by tricking the user into consenting to permissions for partly using the app's core functionality and partly leaking the data from the device [5].

An innocuous-looking torch app, Brightest Flashlight, silently shared users' locations and unique device identifiers with an advertising network [6]. This behaviour violates the mechanism of notifying the user first (Notice) and seeking explicit permission (Consent). Jennifer et al. [7] reported apps collecting location data and selling it for advertising. A location data firm was found harvesting and selling mobile location data even when users opted out [8]. Deceptive apps aid this behaviour by transmitting sensitive data from devices. These real-world examples motivate us to detect unused critical permissions accessing sensitive user data.

Contributions: Our work aims to detect deceptive applications with additional permissions. Specifically, we investigate the following research questions.

RQ1. What Are the Permissions that Coexist Frequently? When specific permissions coexist often, it may persuade app developers to request them even if one of them is not needed. It may trick app users into granting permissions to apps with similar functionality.

RQ2. What Are the Coexisting Permissions that Remain Unused? We analyze the pair of permissions and check if API calls corresponding to at least one are not used in the app binary.

RQ3. What Are the Challenges in Finding Coexisting Permissions? While we investigate the issue of unused permissions, not all permissions can be analyzed due to the many combinations and the way permissions are checked.

RQ4. What Are the Problems with Unused Permissions? Unused permissions correspond to additional resource access and render the app over-privileged.

Organization: The rest of the paper is organized as follows. Section 2 covers relevant work in this direction. Section 3 presents a threat model. Section 4 gives an overview of Android permissions. Section 5 presents the research methodology used, the overall approach, and how the study is conducted. Further, in Sect. 6, we present experimental results with observations. Finally, we document limitations in Sect. 7 and conclude the paper.

2 Related Work

Wijesekara et al. [9] find in a survey that well-informed users would deny certain permissions if they were aware of the permissions. Studies by Sanz et al. [10], Talha et al. [11] investigate permissions in malicious apps and benign apps. These studies suggest that the top permissions or frequently requested permissions in both malicious and benign apps are the same. Hence, it is not practical to distinguish them. However, it is worthwhile to study groups of permissions or permissions in pairs. Talha et al. [11] reported apps collecting private and sensitive data in an invasive manner using ad libraries.

Enck et al. [12] reported privacy violations by apps sending device identifiers and location information to the content hosting server or to a third party leveraging location, camera, and phone state permissions requested by apps.

Mallojula et al. [13] raise a question: "*Are the permission requests really necessary?*". Authors show that apps using potentially excessive permissions can be malicious by looking at peer apps exhibiting similar functionality. While collecting peer apps using the Similar Apps link for a seed app, it could be suspicious if it requests significantly more permissions than its peers. Arora et al. [14] studied permission pairs to identify dangerous permissions. Odat et al. [15] studied the coexistence of permissions using machine learning classifiers to detect malware.

Unlike our work, previous studies do not consider knowledge from application description, app manifest, and API call usage, all three simultaneously, while questioning excessive permissions taken up by apps. Our approach does not require any modification to the existing system or incur any additional overhead.

3 Threat Model

Fig. 1 depicts the threat model for the problem we address using our technique. We abstract the STRIDE threat model [16] related to two threats - information disclosure and elevation of privileges.

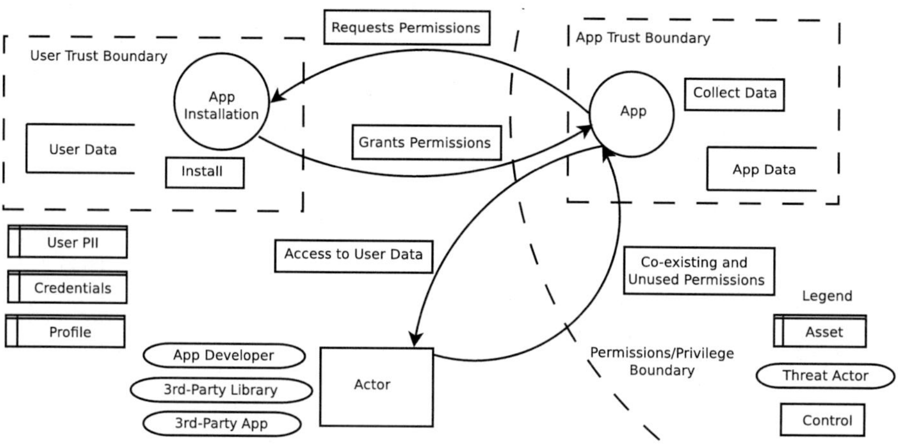

Fig. 1. Threat Model.

Actors such as app developers, third-party libraries, and third-party apps pose a threat to assets identified, such as the user's Personally Identifiable Information (PII), credentials, and user profile while requesting and granting permissions, accessing user data, and having additional and unused permissions. Failing to maintain the permission boundary can lead to information disclosure to threat actors. The gap between the request and the grant of permissions can lead to the elevation of privileges by the app, including auto-granted permissions.

4 Overview of Android Permissions

Each Android app runs in a process sandbox and requires explicit access to system resources outside its sandbox using permissions. Permissions can be granted at installation or runtime using dialogues prompting users to allow access.

Permission protection level indicates the risk associated with user data. Normal permissions are associated with functionality posing little risk to user data and privacy. In contrast, dangerous permissions are associated with a high risk of sensitive user data being accessed.

Dangerous permissions are grouped by access to a system resource. Dangerous permissions are granted at the group level at runtime from API level 23 onward. Normal permissions are automatically granted at app installation or subsequent updates without the user's intervention. Permissions are requested in the app manifest file.

5 Methodology

In this section, we describe studying permissions in pairs, the capabilities of permissions in pairs, and the methodology of our proposed technique CUPS, an acronym for **C**o-existing and **U**nused **P**ermission**S**.

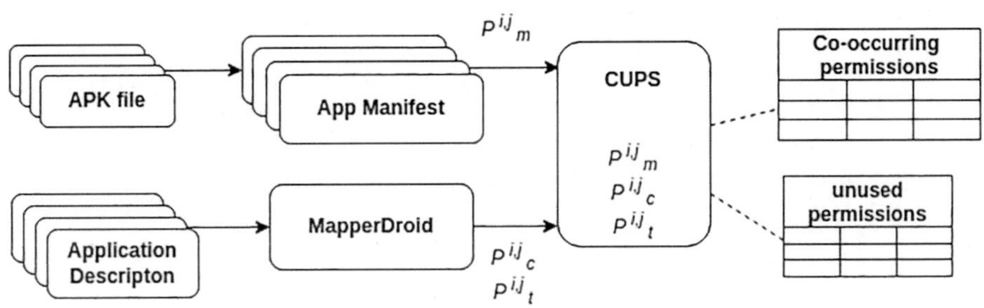

Fig. 2. CUPS: Proposed approach.

5.1 Considering Permissions in a Pair

Android permissions are granted at the permission-group level. Permissions within a group are related to resource access. Apart from the permission group abstraction, there is no documented dependency or hierarchical relationship between the two permissions. i.e. for a permission *P1*, another permission *P2* is a necessary condition - no such definition exists. Therefore, we need to consider a group of permissions to analyze two or more permissions.

Further, for r permissions, out of a total of n permissions, there are ${}^nC_r$ combinations. It is practically difficult to analyze many combinations in this way, as there are more than 180 permissions in recent Android versions. Hence, we consider only two permissions or a pair at a time associated with two different functionalities.

5.2 Capabilities of Coexisting Permissions

Before we describe the methodology of our prototype CUPS, we compile the necessary information to establish that coexisting permissions can pose challenges to data privacy by permission abuse. The permissions in a pair are chosen based on the Table 1 that presents the capabilities of coexisting permissions. With additional permissions, it is evident from this table that seemingly harmless apps have access to sensitive device identifiers and location data.

Table 1. Capabilities of coexisting permissions

Permissions	Access to capabilities
Internet, Access Network State	Network, Android device MAC
Internet, Access WiFi State	Network, Router/AP MAC, SSID
Access Network State, Access WiFi State	Device MAC, Router/AP MAC, SSID
Access Network State, Read Phone State	MAC, Device identifiers IMEI, Phone number, SIM number
Read Phone State, Call Phone	Device identifiers IMEI, Phone numbers, SIM number
Fine Location, Read Phone State	Better location data, Device identifiers, IMEI, Phone number, SIM number
Course Location, Read Phone State	Less precise location data, Device identifiers, IMEI, Phone number, SIM number

5.3 Proposed Approach

Figure 2 shows the proposed approach of CUPS. We leverage the data set provided by MapperDroid [17] and enrich the data set with permissions set information from application description, app manifest, and API calls usage using AndroGuard [18]. CUPS performs statistical analysis of permissions and reports coexisting permissions and unused permissions. We limit the scope to device identifiers and location data-related permissions.

5.4 Data Collection

We leverage the data collection technique employed in MapperDroid [2] and extend the dataset provided by MapperDroid [17]. We crawl apps from the Google Play Store (GPS) for application descriptions using random seed-based sampling. We look for a seed app on GPS and use the "similar apps" link to crawl more apps. We download app binaries from APK Pure repository [19], extract app manifest, and get API calls used in the app binary using the object analysis feature from AndroGuard [18]. We make the comprehensive data set and source code available on GitHub [21].

5.5 Detection of Coexisting Permissions

We use the Jaccard index to detect the likelihood of two permissions existing together. Jaccard similarity index is a statistical measure of similarity between two sets of data members. The index value ranges from 0 to 1. If two sets have the same members (completely similar), then the index value is 1. If both data sets have nothing in common (completely orthogonal), then the index value is 0. The closer the index value is to 1, the stronger the similarity between the two data sets, implying the permissions are requested or used together. Mathematically, the Jaccard index JSim to detect the coexistence of two permissions, a and b, in the set of $apps_a$ and the set $apps_b$ can be defined as:

$$JSim(apps_a, apps_b) = \frac{|apps_a \cap apps_b|}{|apps_a \cup apps_b|} \quad (1)$$

where a and b are the two permissions, $apps_a$ denotes the set of apps requesting or using permission a, and $apps_b$ denotes the set of apps requesting or using permission b.

For our study, a value of 0 for $JSim(apps_a, apps_b)$ denotes that two permissions under consideration are never requested or used together. A value 1 for $JSim(apps_a, apps_b)$ indicates that two permissions under consideration are requested or used together in all apps under study.

Table 2 shows symbols and terms used in this paper. Further, we look at $JSim(apps_a, apps_b)$ over three sets P_c, P_m, P_t - sets of permissions coming from API calls, app manifest, and app description, respectively.

We further expand this equation for Jaccard similarity for two permissions i and j obtained from the manifest, API calls, and text description, denoted by $JSim\_manifest$, $JSim\_api$, and $JSim\_desc$, respectively. The symbols and terms are explained in Table 2.

$$JSim\_manifest(apps_i, apps_j) = \frac{\sum P_m^{i,j}}{\sum P_m^i + \sum P_m^j - \sum P_m^{i,j}} \quad (2)$$

$$JSim\_api(apps_i, apps_j) = \frac{\sum P_c^{i,j}}{\sum P_c^i + \sum P_c^j - \sum P_c^{i,j}} \quad (3)$$

$$JSim\_desc(apps_i, apps_j) = \frac{\sum P_t^{i,j}}{\sum P_t^i + \sum P_t^j - \sum P_t^{i,j}} \quad (4)$$

Table 2. Symbols and terms used in this paper

Notation	Explanation
P_m^i	i^{th} Permission requested in manifest
P_c^i	i^{th} Permission required for some API calls
P_t^i	i^{th} Permission derived from application description
$\sum P_m^i$	Sum of the number of apps requesting i^{th} Permission in manifest
$\sum P_c^i$	Sum of the number of apps that require i^{th} Permission mapped to API calls
$\sum P_t^i$	Sum of the number of apps from which i^{th} Permission can be derived from text description
$\sum P_m^{i,j}$	Sum of the number of apps requesting both i^{th} and j^{th} Permission in manifest
$\sum P_c^{i,j}$	Sum of the number of apps that require both i^{th} and j^{th} Permission mapped to API calls
$\sum P_t^{i,j}$	Sum of the number of apps from which both i^{th} and j^{th} Permission can be derived from text description
$\bigcup$	$P_m^i + P_m^j$ - P_c^i - P_c^j
$\sum \bigcup$	Sum of the number of apps with at least one Permission unused ($\bigcup = 1$)

5.6 Detecting Unused Permissions

To establish unused permissions in a pair of i and j, we use permissions requested in the manifest and usage in the app binary from API calls. Here, we rely on API calls mapped to permissions for the ground truth of usage. This mapping has been obtained from the current state-of-the-art Axplorer project [22] using the reverse engineering tool AndroGuard [18]. If any of these two permissions do not find usage evidence from the set of permissions found from API calls, we count it as one unused incident $\bigcup = 1$ and repeat for all apps to obtain $\sum \bigcup$. When both the permissions in the pair are unused, we also count it as an unused incident $\bigcup = 1$. Finally, we report the percentage of such apps by considering $\sum \bigcup$ and the total number of apps under study.

6 Evaluation and Results

6.1 Evaluation

Figure 3 shows a simplified calculation to evaluate the CUPS prototype. Symbols are explained in Table 2.

As described in Sect. 5.5, we obtain the Jaccard similarity index for two permissions across all the apps. These values are calculated for permissions in the application descriptions, app manifests, and API calls in the app binaries.

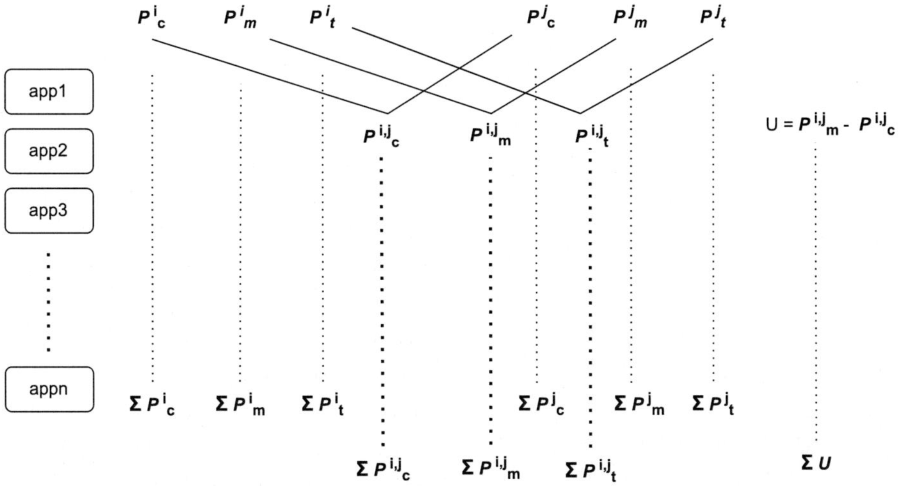

Fig. 3. Simplified Calculation for the Evaluation of CUPS Prototype.

An index value closer to zero indicates the permissions are not found together, and an index value closer to one indicates strong coexistence.

All three indices with similar trends and values in the closer vicinity suggest descriptions, app manifests, and API call usage are consistent with each other, and these apps may not exhibit deceptive behaviour. Any index value out of sync with others suggests inconsistency in announcing behaviour (in the application descriptions), in permission requests (in the app manifests), or in the usage (in the API calls).

Further, as described in Sect. 5.6, the percentage of unused permissions signals that at least one of the two permissions was not used despite being requested and the app holding the permission. Third-party libraries can leverage these additional permissions to gain privileged access, and the app itself, in the subsequent upgrade, can add more permissions in the same permission group without direct intervention from the user [20].

6.2 Results

We answer the research questions with results obtained from the study, with specific observations.

RQ1. What are the Permissions that Coexist Frequently? Table 3 shows the top permissions requested alone from the apps analyzed. INTERNET (full network access) and ACCESS_NETWORK_STATE (access the nearby network connections) are requested by more than 95% and 91% of the apps analyzed. More than 20% of the apps requested location data-related permissions, while a restricted permission CALL_PHONE was requested by 6% of the apps. Access to phone calls has been restricted for apps other than the default system app by Android.

Table 3. Frequently requested permissions together

Android Permission under study	Protection level of permission	Permission requested by apps	Percentage of apps in dataset
INTERNET	Normal	12295	95.06%
ACCESS_NETWORK_STATE	Normal	11894	91.96%
READ_EXTERNAL_STORAGE	Dangerous	6272	48.49%
ACCESS_WIFI_STATE	Normal	5391	41.68%
READ_PHONE_STATE	Dangerous	2875	22.22%
FINE_LOCATION	Dangerous	2865	22.15%
COARSE_LOCATION	Dangerous	2660	20.57%
CALL_PHONE	Dangerous	778	6.01%

Table 4 shows permission pairs under study. Column "%Requested" displays the number of apps that requested both permissions together. Internet (full network access) and access network state (access network connections) permissions coexist in 91.86% of apps. Read phone state and call phone are requested together in 4.3% of apps because call phone is a restricted permission, and both permissions are in the same permission group.

Table 4 also reveals that the read phone state permission linked to device identifiers and any location permission does not exhibit the same kind of similarity from the application descriptions compared to the requested permission in the app manifests. Therefore, this behaviour can go unnoticed by users. These permissions are related to activity tracking and targeted advertising.

RQ2. What are the Coexisting Permissions that Remain Unused? Table 4 captures the results obtained after pair-wise permissions analyzed that coexist, and at least one of them remains unused. Three columns display $JSim\_api$, $JSim\_manifest$, and $JSim\_desc$ as explained in equations in Sect. 5.5 and the Table 2. For fine location and read phone state pair, 9.66% apps requested both permissions and out of these, 79.5% apps are found with at least one unused permission. Regarding course location and read phone state, 80.24% apps are found with at least one unused permission out of 8.96% apps that requested both permissions. Regarding access network and access WiFi state that show stronger similarity, 21.39% apps have one unused permission out of 41.46% apps that asked for these two permissions.

Table 4. Results for coexisting permissions evaluated

Permissions	JSim_api	JSim_	Jsim_desc	% Requested	% Unused
Internet, Access Network State	0.0007	0.9653	0.9949	91.86	**
Internet, Access WiFi State	0.0012	0.4367	0.6641	41.56	**
Access Network, Access WiFi State	0.548	0.4497	0.6675	41.46	**21.39**
Access Network, Read Phone State	0.2359	0.2364	0.1359	21.83	**64.66**
Read Phone State, Call Phone	0	0.1795	0.8105	4.3	**
Fine Location, Read Phone State	0.2154	0.2781	0.0537	9.66	**79.5**
Course Location, Read Phone State	0.2643	0.2649	0.0321	8.96	**80.24**

RQ3. What are the Challenges in Finding Coexisting Permissions? Permission for the Internet is checked using Linux sockets and low-level system calls. Similarly, camera and microphone (audio) permissions are managed using system calls in the Hardware Abstraction Layer (HAL). If any of these permissions are included in a permission pair, API call usage in the app binary cannot determine the existence of these permissions. Hence, in Table 4 column % Unused has been marked as **. While the similarity index for app manifests and text descriptions of apps signals stronger similarity for such pairs, the usage of the Internet permission is inconclusive.

RQ4. What are the Problems with Unused Permissions? Table 1 compiles the combined capabilities of permission pairs under study. Unused permissions open doors for third-party libraries to track user activities using device identifiers and access location data. Third-party libraries obtain the same permissions as the app using them. App developers must pay attention to requested permissions and remove unused permissions to avoid permission abuse.

Another potential threat to privacy with unused permissions comes from automatically-granted permissions [20] that can allow an app to access and control sensitive data such as a list of phone calls made (call log), user's location-related data, make phone calls or write/update functions on the protected resources stored on the device. Android must provide finer granularity over granting permissions by separating read and write permissions from permission groups, thereby reducing automatically granted permissions.

7 Limitations

We do not claim that the most deceptive apps are malware; we argue for transparency and to detect additional capabilities apps acquire by abusing the permission model. Such undetected deceptive apps pose a risk to data privacy. There are more than 180 permissions in recent versions of Android. Our study is restricted to some of the most frequently requested permissions that can access sensitive user data. Some permissions cannot be detected using API call usage. For example, the internet (full network access) and camera permission.

8 Conclusions

In this study, we explore excessive permission usage that goes undetected. We propose a technique called CUPS to detect frequently coexisting and often unused permissions in Android apps. We perform a statistical analysis of permissions requested and permissions usage evidenced by API calls in the application binaries for the detection of such deceptive apps. We conclude that additional permission requests can influence app developers to add and end-users to consent to a much larger set of permissions than required. This undetected and deceptive behaviour leaves apps over-privileged and impacts data privacy.

References

1. Solanki, R.K., Laxmi, V., Gaur, M.S.: MAPPER: mapping application description to permissions. In: International Conference on Risks and Security of Internet and Systems. CRiSIS 2019, LNCS, vol. 12026, pp. 84–98 (2019)
2. Solanki, R.K., Laxmi, V., Bezawada, B., Gaur, M.S.: MapperDroid: verifying app capabilities from description to permissions and API calls. Comput. Secur. **111**, 102493 (2021)
3. Malware records audio. https://www.androidpolice.com/malware-russian-hackers-tracks-you-records-audio/
4. Privacy, Deception and Device Abuse. https://support.google.com/googleplay/android-developer/topic/9877467
5. Reardon, J., Feal, A., Wijesekera, P., Vallina-Rodriguez, N., Egelman, S.: 50 ways to leak your data: an exploration of apps' circumvention of the android permissions system. In: 28th USENIX Security Symposium, pp. 603–620 (2019)
6. Android Flashlight App Developer Settles FTC Charges It Deceived Consumers. https://www.ftc.gov/news-events/news/press-releases/2013/12/android-flashlight-app-developer-settles-ftc-charges-it-deceived-consumers
7. Valentino-DeVries, J., Singer, N., Keller, M. H., Krolik, A.: Your apps know where you were last night, and they're not keeping it secret. https://www.nytimes.com/interactive/2018/12/10/business/location-data-privacy-apps.html
8. Cox, J.: Location data firm got GPS data from apps even when people opted out (2022). https://www.vice.com/en/article/5dgmqz/huq-location-data-opt-out-no-consent
9. Wijesekera, P., Baokar, A., Hosseini, A., Egelman, S., Wagner, D., Beznosov, K.: Android permissions re-mystified: a field study on contextual integrity. In: Proceedings of the 24th USENIX Security Symposium, pp. 499–514 (2015)
10. Sanz, B., et al.: MAMA: manifest analysis for malware detection in android. Cybern. Syst. **44**, 469–488 (2013)
11. Talha, K.A., Alper, D.I., Aydin, C.: APK auditor: permission-based Android malware detection system. Digit. Investig. **13**, 1–14 (2015)
12. Enck, W., et al.: TaintDroid: an information-flow tracking system for realtime privacy monitoring on smartphones. ACM Trans. Comput. Syst. **32** (2014)
13. Mallojula, P., Ahmad, J., Li, F., Luo, B.: You are (not) who your peers are: identification of potentially excessive permission requests in android apps. In: IEEE 20th International Conference on Trust, Security and Privacy in Computing and Communications (TrustCom) (2021)

14. Arora, A., Peddoju, S.K., Conti, M.: PermPair: android malware detection using permission pairs. IEEE Trans. Inf. Forensics Secur. (2020)
15. Odat, E., Yaseen, Q.M.: A novel machine learning approach for android malware detection based on the co-existence of features. IEEE Access (2023)
16. STRIDE Threat Model. https://csf.tools/reference/stride-lm/
17. MapperDroid GitHub Repository. https://github.com/rks101/MapperDroid
18. AndroGuard. https://github.com/androguard
19. APK Pure Archive. https://apkpure.com
20. Calciati, P., Kuznetsov, K., Gorla, A., Zeller, A.: Automatically granted permissions in android apps: an empirical study on their prevalence and on the potential threats for privacy. In: Proceedings of the 17th International Conference on Mining Software Repositories, pp. 114–124 (2020)
21. CUPS GitHub Repository. https://github.com/rks101/cups
22. Backes, M., Bugiel, S., Derr, E., McDaniel, P., Octeau, D,. Weisgerber, S.: On demystifying the android application framework: re-visiting android permission specification analysis. In: Proceedings of the 25th USENIX Security Symposium, pp. 1101–1116 (2016)

Federated Learning for Sustainable AI: Privacy-Preserving and Decentralized Intelligence*

Ashish Kumar Dwivedi(✉)

The LNM Institute of Information Technology Jaipur,
Jaipur, Rajasthan 302031, India
{ashish.dwivedi}@lnmiit.ac.in

Abstract. Nowadays, Federated Learning is considered as a transformative paradigm for sustainable AI by offering collaborative training of a model without centralized data aggregation, thus privacy-preserving and reducing computational overhead. This study presents the role of Federated Learning in promoting eco-environmental and socially responsible artificial intelligence systems, which focus on its applications such as, healthcare, manufacturing and smart cities. A novel framework for energy-efficient Federated Learning optimization is presented. The framework analyzes privacy-preserving techniques, for example secure multiparty computation and differential privacy. The method evaluates the impact of Federated Learning on reducing carbon footprints in distributed AI deployments. The implementation of the proposed study shows the improvements in the data security, energy savings and resolving latency issues compared to the centralized learning approach.

Keywords: Federated Learning · Sustainable AI · Privacy Preservation

1 Introduction

Rapid growth of artificial intelligence (AI) applications has revolutionized diverse domains such as healthcare, transportation, smart cities, and environmental monitoring. Due to the high demand of computing resources such as power, data storage, processing units, raises serious cyber threats regarding data privacy and environmental sustainability. In case of centralized AI system, raw data need to be stored in the central server, which may create privacy concerns as well as substantial carbon emissions because of the massive computational footprint of huge data centers. The aforementioned challenges need decentralized and privacy-preserving AI frameworks.

*Supported by LNMIIT Jaipur.

G. K. Verma et al. (Eds.): MIND 2025, CCIS 2981, pp. 400–411, 2027.
https://doi.org/10.1007/978-3-032-31230-3_32

Federated Learning (FL) is considered as an essential approach to address these issues by offering collaborative training of the model between distributed devices without transferring raw data [11][3]. Centralized AI models are unsustainable due to high energy costs and privacy risks [10] [16]. In the Federated Learning, a client performs local training on its own data and transmits model parameters to the central server. This idea inherently increases data privacy by reducing exposure of sensitive data and at the same time reduces the requirements of network bandwidth. In addition, FL supports the ability to significantly reduce the environmental impact of artificial intelligence by leveraging on-device processing and reducing the reliance on energy intensive centralized framework.

Regardless of its advantages, the incorporation of sustainability into Federated Learning systems remains underexplored. Lots of available FL implementations rely on accuracy and privacy, whereas ignoring the environmental footprint of distributed learning. Excessive energy consumption is obtained from huge communication overhead, unnecessary computational costs, and inefficient model aggregation strategies, which violates the goal of sustainable AI[1]. To demonstrate the potential of Federated Learning as a driver of sustainable AI, it is essential to accept energy-centric learning protocols, decentralized coordination algorithm and privacy-preserving techniques.

The proposed work shows a Sustainable Federated Learning (SFL) framework that uses Differential Privacy (DP) for secure model updates, communication-effective aggregation and monitoring of energy consumption for environmental accountability to reduce carbon impact. The proposed idea comprise real-world datasets to validate performance under practical constraints, demonstrating how decentralized AI can be both privacy-conscious and environmentally responsible. We formulate the sustainability objective as a trade-off between model accuracy and the total energy cost, as mentioned in Equation 1, where λ controls the balance between accuracy and environmental efficiency.

$$\mathcal{L}_{\text{SFL}} = \mathcal{L}_{\text{acc}} + \lambda \mathcal{L}_{\text{energy}}, \tag{1}$$

The contributions of the proposed study are described as follows:

- A unified framework for sustainable, privacy-preserving federated learning.
- Algorithmic integration of energy, CO_2, and DP estimation per round.
- Implementation and empirical validation using MNIST Dataset[2] under realistic energy parameters.

2 Related Work

Recent works on Federated Learning are often driven by the dual imperatives of privacy preservation and efficient distributed computation. Related work section is categorized into three subsections, such as (i) privacy-preserving techniques in Federated Learning, (ii) Communication and energy-effective Federated Learning, and (iii) Sustainable and Decentralized approaches [7].

[1] https://doi.org/10.48550/arXiv.2507.17241

[2] https://www.tensorflow.org/datasets/catalog/fashion_mnist

2.1 Privacy-Preserving Federated Learning

Privacy is a fundamental design goal in Federated Learning to minimize the disclosure of sensitive information from local machine. McMahan et al. [11] first proposed Federated Learning as a decentralized training framework, which enables model aggregation without disclosing raw data. Melis et al. [12] presented that gradient updates can still disclose private information. To address the issue, differential privacy [5] and secure multiparty computation (SMPC) [17] have been incorporated into Federated Learning. SMPC techniques ensure secure aggregation but introduce significant computational overhead. Our work adopts a DP-based mechanism for a balanced trade-off between computational efficiency and privacy.

2.2 Communication and Energy Efficiency in Federated Learning

The efficiency of Federated Learning is often strained by communication bottlenecks, as model updates must be exchanged iteratively between clients and aggregators. Techniques such as model compression[3] and sparsification [9] have been proposed to minimize communication costs. In addition, adaptive client participation [15] and federated dropout[4] reduce energy consumption by participating clients in each round. Regardless of these advances, few studies incorporate energy consumption metrics directly into evaluation of Federated Learning. Authors [14] proposed carbon-aware machine learning (ML), but their application to federated systems remains unexplored. Our framework explicitly measures energy usage and CO_2 emissions, offering insight into the sustainability of FL deployments.

2.3 Sustainable and Decentralized AI

Beyond privacy and efficiency, sustainability of AI systems is considered as a crucial research direction in the Green AI [2] [6]. Decentralized AI framework, such as a blockchain-based FL [8], offers more resilience and trust, but it introduce additional computational burdens. In recent studies [1] [13], the integration of environmental metrics into AI system design is common, yet the frameworks that combine privacy preservation, energy efficiency, and decentralized intelligence remain unexplored. Zhu et al. [18] presented a framework that combine AIoT (Artificial Intelligence of Things) with FL to offer sustainable supply chain demand forecasting and allows merchants to train demand prediction model. The author [4] presented secure and scalable pattern detection in software systems using Federated Learning. Our work addresses this gap by developing a unified approach that couples DP-based privacy, communication-efficient aggregation, and energy-aware evaluation within a real-world FL setting.

In summary, while existing works have made substantial progress in each of the aforementioned areas individually, there is a clear need for effective frameworks which address privacy, efficiency, and sustainability simultaneously.

---

[3] https://doi.org/10.48550/arXiv.1510.00149

[4] https://doi.org/10.48550/arXiv.1812.01097

3 Proposed Method

The proposed framework, Sustainable Federated Learning (SFL) aims to address three key challenges in modern AI deployment such as privacy preservation, energy efficiency, and decentralized scalability by integrating optional differential privacy (DP) and secure aggregation within an FL paradigm.

3.1 Proposed Architecture

Figure 1 shows an end-to-end framework integrating Federated Learning, privacy preservation, and sustainability in AI. Each client carries local data, e.g., user or device-specific and trains a local model for a few epochs using its own data. Local training ensures that raw data is not shared with other devices, maintaining data privacy and consent. The Differential Privacy Module integrates controlled noise to local model gradients before transmitting the parameters to the server. It offers formal privacy guarantees by ensuring it difficult to infer specific data points from the updates transmitted to the model. The secure masking process requires each client to add randomized noise to its local model parameters before sending them to the server. The server aggregates the masked models; the masks cancel out mathematically, ensuring secure aggregation means that no individual client model is revealed. Central server (Aggregator) receives all client updates and performs Federated Averaging (FedAvg) to produce a new global model. The updated model is then broadcast back to clients for the next training round. Sustainability Engine calculates per-round metrics such as energy consumption based on device power and communication. The global model and sustainability metrics are logged and visualized across rounds. This enables optimization of both model performance and efficiency.(Figs. 1 and 2, 3, 4).

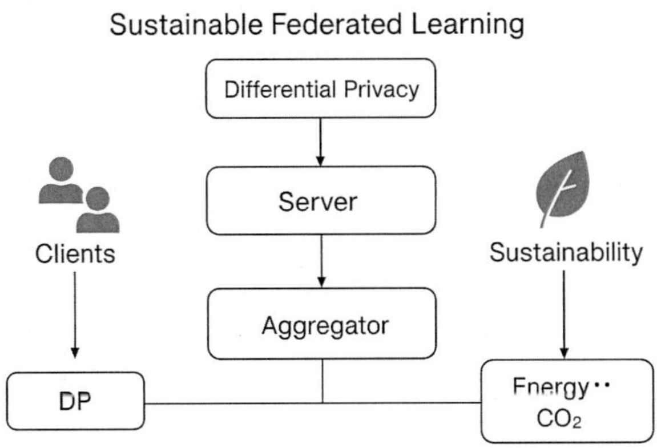

Fig. 1: System Architecture of Adaptive Federated Learning.

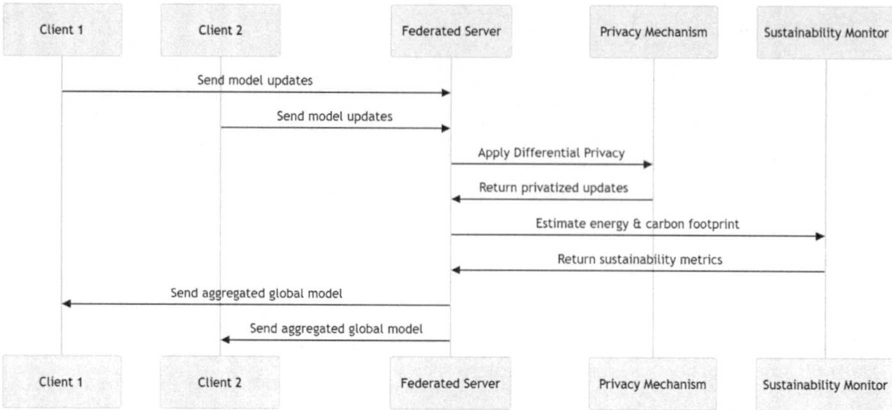

Fig. 2: System flow of the proposed privacy-preserving and sustainable federated learning framework.

Figure 2 illustrates the interaction flow in the Sustainable Federated Learning (SFL) framework, showing how federated training, privacy preservation, and sustainability monitoring are integrated. Clients perform local training on their private data and send model updates to the Federated Server that forwards these updates to the Privacy Mechanism, which applies DP to ensure data confidentiality and returns privatized updates. The server then aggregates the received models into a global model and sends it back to all clients for the next round. During training, the server communicates with the Sustainability Monitor to estimate the energy consumption and carbon footprint for each training round. The monitor returns sustainability metrics, which the server logs for reporting and optimization.

3.2 Formalization of Sustainable Federated Learning

The system is designed to operate over a distributed set of K clients, each holding a private local dataset $\mathcal{D}_k$ derived from a larger dataset $\mathcal{D}$. The SFL conducts training in R synchronous communication rounds. At the start of each round r, the central server broadcasts the current global model weights w^{r-1} to all clients. A client trains its local model for E epochs on its private data, using a specified batch size B, a learning rate η and using an optimizer Opt e.g., SGD. To ensure formal privacy, clients implement Differential Privacy (DP) by first clipping their gradients to a maximum norm (C) and then adding Gaussian noise. This process provides a mathematically proven (ϵ, δ)-DP for every model update.

To prevent the server from accessing raw model updates, a secure aggregation scheme is applied when flag s is set. Each client generates a random mask M_k, ensuring that $\sum_{k=1}^{K} M_k = 0$. The server receives masked updates $\tilde{w}_k^r = w_k^r + M_k$, which, upon aggregation, yield the same result as unmasked FedAvg.

Sustainability-Aware Metrics Beyond traditional accuracy and loss metrics, SFL explicitly logs per-round sustainability indicators are described as follows:

- Training Energy (E_r^{train}): Computed from device power consumption P_{dev} and cumulative local training time T_r.
- Communication Energy (E_r^{comm}): Derived from model size in MB and the energy cost γ per MB transferred.
- Total Energy (E_r^{tot}): Sum of training and communication energy, converted to kWh.
- Carbon Emissions (C_r): Estimated from the total energy consumption using carbon intensity factor c.

This design allows practitioners to quantitatively evaluate the environmental footprint of the FL process, making it suitable for sustainable AI.

3.3 Algorithmic Workflow

Algorithm 1 shows the proposed framework for Sustainable Federated Learning (SFL), which integrates federated optimization, differential privacy (DP), and energy carbon estimation to allow collaborative training and preserve privacy that is responsible for environmental friendly.

Initialization. The server initializes the global model weights w^0 and sets hyper-parameters such as the number of federated rounds R, local epochs E, batch size B, optimizer Opt with learning rate η, and sustainability parameters including device power consumption P_{dev}, communication energy per MB γ, and carbon intensity c. If differential privacy is enabled, the DP parameters (σ, C, δ) are also configured, where σ represents the noise multiplier, C denotes the gradient clipping norm and δ represents the privacy bound.

Model Distribution. At the start of each round r, the server broadcasts the current global weights w^{r-1} to all K participating clients.

Local Client Training. Each client k executes the procedure $(w_k^r, m_k) \leftarrow \textsc{ClientUpdate}(k, w^{r-1}, E, B, \eta, \mathsf{Opt}, \sigma, C, \delta)$, training its local model on the private dataset shard $\mathcal{D}_k$. If DP is activated, Gaussian noise (scaled by σ) is added to clipped gradients (bounded by C), achieving client-level (ϵ, δ)-differential privacy. Each client also returns local metadata m_k, including the measured training time.

Secure Aggregation and Model Averaging. After local updates, the server aggregates models either through:

- **Secure masking** ($s = 1$): Each client adds a random mask M_k such that $\sum_k M_k = 0$. The server receives masked updates $\tilde{w}_k^r = w_k^r + M_k$ and computes $\bar{w}^r = \frac{1}{K} \sum_k \tilde{w}_k^r$, where masks cancel during aggregation.
- **Standard FedAvg** ($s = 0$): The global model is updated as $\bar{w}^r = \frac{1}{K} \sum_{k=1}^{K} w_k^r$.

The server then sets $w^r \leftarrow \bar{w}^r$.

Algorithm 1. Framework for Sustainable Federated Learning with Optional Differential Privacy

Require: Dataset $\mathcal{D}$, clients $\{K\}$ with local data $\{\mathcal{D}_k\}$; rounds R; local epochs E; batch size B; optimizer Opt with learning rate η; power P_{dev}; communication energy/MB γ; carbon intensity c; optional differential privacy parameters (σ, C, δ)

Initialize the global weights w^0
for $r = 1$ to R rounds **do**
  Broadcast w^{r-1} to all clients
  for all clients $k \in \{1, \dots, K\}$ **in parallel do**
    $w_k^r, m_k \leftarrow \textsc{ClientUpdate}(k, w^{r-1}, E, B, \eta, \mathsf{Opt}, \sigma, C, \delta)$
  end for
  if s **then**
    Generate random masks $\{M_k\}$ s.t. $\sum_k M_k = 0$
    Server receives $\{\tilde{w}_k^r = w_k^r + M_k\}$ and computes $\bar{w}^r = \frac{1}{K} \sum_k \tilde{w}_k^r$ ▷ masks cancel
  else
    $\bar{w}^r = \frac{1}{K} \sum_k w_k^r$ ▷ FedAvg
  end if
  $w^r \leftarrow \bar{w}^r$
  Evaluate w^r on holdout/test set $\Rightarrow$ accuracy α_r, loss ℓ_r
  Sustainability:
    Compute total training time $T_r = \sum_k m_k.\text{train\_time}$
    Training energy $E_r^{\text{train}} = P_{\text{dev}} \cdot T_r$
    Bytes sent $B_r = K \cdot \texttt{sizeof}(w^r)$
    comm energy $E_r^{\text{comm}} = \gamma \cdot \text{MB}(B_r)$
    Total energy (kWh): $E_r^{\text{tot}} = \frac{E_r^{\text{train}} + E_r^{\text{comm}}}{3{,}600{,}000}$
    CO_2 (kg): $C_r = \frac{c}{1000} \cdot E_r^{\text{tot}}$
  Log $\{\alpha_r, \ell_r, E_r^{\text{tot}}, C_r, B_r, \text{DP } \epsilon_r\}$
end for
return w^R and per-round logs

Evaluation. The aggregated model w^r is evaluated on a central test or holdout dataset to compute round-level metrics such as accuracy α_r and loss ℓ_r.

Partial Participation and Straggler Mitigation. Only a subset of clients participate per round to reduce network load. Stragglers are handled through deadline-based cutoffs and partial-progress weighting. Client selection prioritizes devices with stable connectivity, adequate energy, and data diversity, improving both training efficiency and fairness.

Sustainability Estimation. In each communication round, the SFL framework quantitatively estimates the environmental footprint of the learning process by measuring both computational and communication energy. The whole time spend in training for all clients is first computed as:

$$T_r = \sum_k m_k.\text{train\_time}$$

T_r shows the cumulative device usage for round r. And the training energy consumption during training is obtaining by using:

$$E_r^{\text{train}} = P_{\text{dev}} \cdot T_r,$$

P_{dev} represents the average power of the device. The total bytes transmitted during aggregation are shown using B_r:

$$B_r = K \cdot \texttt{sizeof}(w^r),$$

The associated communication energy is estimated using E_r^{comm}:

$$E_r^{\text{comm}} = \gamma \cdot \text{MB}(B_r),$$

The overall energy footprint (in kWh) is thus obtained by combining the two components:

$$E_r^{\text{tot}} = \frac{E_r^{\text{train}} + E_r^{\text{comm}}}{3{,}600{,}000},$$

and the corresponding carbon emissions (in kg of CO_2) are derived as:

$$C_r = \frac{c}{1000} \cdot E_r^{\text{tot}}.$$

These metrics provide a fine-grained, round-wise assessment of the energy efficiency and environmental impact of federated learning, thereby promoting sustainability-aware AI design.

Logging and Output. The proposed framework monitors and records a list of metrics such as energy, carbon emissions, and communication data after each round of training. This includes the performance of the model on its task and the cumulative privacy cost (ϵ_r) if DP is being used. After the completion of all R rounds, the framework outputs the final global model (w^R) together with detailed per-round sustainability and performance logs. These results facilitate analysis, comparative evaluation, and optimization of federated learning systems for both privacy and environmental sustainability. The framework can reduce energy via adaptive client participation, DP noise scheduling and quantization-based communication reduction.

4 Implementation and Results

4.1 Implementation Setup

The proposed SFL framework is implemented in Python 3.11 using the PyTorch 2.0 deep learning library. The trained data on the local model are aggregated by the central server using the standard FedAvg algorithm. Differential Privacy (DP) via `Opacus` and Secure Aggregation using additive random masking are also incorporated. In addition, SFL extends conventional federated learning with a sustainability engine that estimates per round energy consumption, communication overhead, and CO_2 emissions.

4.2 Experimental Configuration

Experiments are conducted on the MNIST dataset with $K = 5$ federated clients and $R = 5$ communication rounds. Each client trained for $E = 1$ local epoch per round using an optimizer i.e., Adam, having a learning rate of 0.001 and the batch size of $B = 64$. The edge device power consumption was assumed as $P_{\text{dev}} = 10\,\text{W}$, communication energy per MB $\gamma = 0.2\,\text{J}$, and carbon intensity $c = 500\,\text{g}\,\text{CO}_2/\text{kWh}$. All computations were performed on CPU to emulate a resource-constrained, sustainable deployment environment. Model weights and metrics are automatically saved in the specific files for reproducibility aspect.

4.3 Performance Analysis

Figures 3a and 3b depicts the convergence behavior of the proposed framework. The test loss decreases in Figure 3a from 0.225 to 0.04 by the fifth round. It shows an stable convergence of the global model. At the same time, the test accuracy enhances from 93.8% to 98.3% in the fifth round. It shows the efficacy of federated optimization in a few communication rounds.

4.4 Energy and Carbon Estimation

Figures 4a and 4b show the calculated energy and CO_2 metrics per round. These values are obtained from the sustainability module shown in Algorithm 1. The total energy consumption ranged from 1.16×10^{-4} to 1.23×10^{-4} kWh per round, as shown in Fig. 4a. The corresponding CO_2 emissions varied between 5.8×10^{-5} and 6.1×10^{-5} kg per round (Fig. 4b). These results confirm that the proposed SFL framework achieves stable and energy-efficient training behavior. Minor variations between rounds arise due to slight fluctuations in client-side computation time and stochastic batch updates.

5 Comparative Discussion

To evaluate the advantages of the proposed SFL approach, it was compared with two baselines: (i) the standard Federated Averaging (FedAvg) algorithm without any sustainability tracking, and (ii) a Differentially Private FL (DP-FL) configuration using the same dataset and model.

Model Performance The comparable model accuracy of 97-98% shown across all experimental configurations indicates that the integration of sustainability logging and energy accounting in proposed framework does not incur performance degradation. DP-FL faced a marginal accuracy reduction ($< 1\%$) due to incorporated Gaussian noise. Here, SFL maintained near-baseline accuracy.

Energy Efficiency. SFL consumed approximately 1.19×10^{-4} kWh per round, nearly identical to FedAvg, but with full transparency of the underlying energy footprint. DP-FL exhibited a slight ($\sim 3.5\%$) overhead caused by gradient clipping and noise addition. Hence, the proposed SFL achieves privacy and sustainability tracking without compromising efficiency.

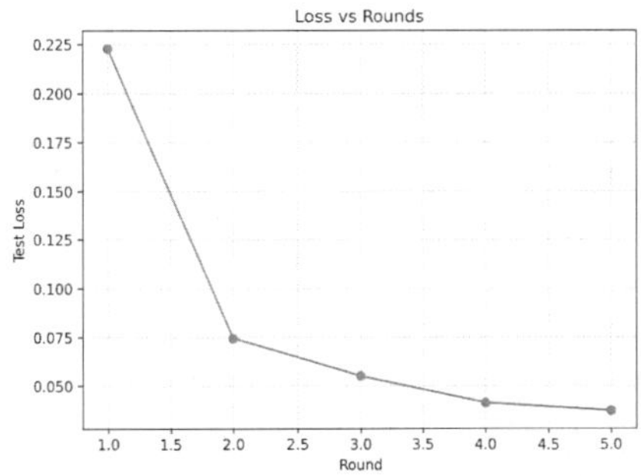

(a) Variation of test loss

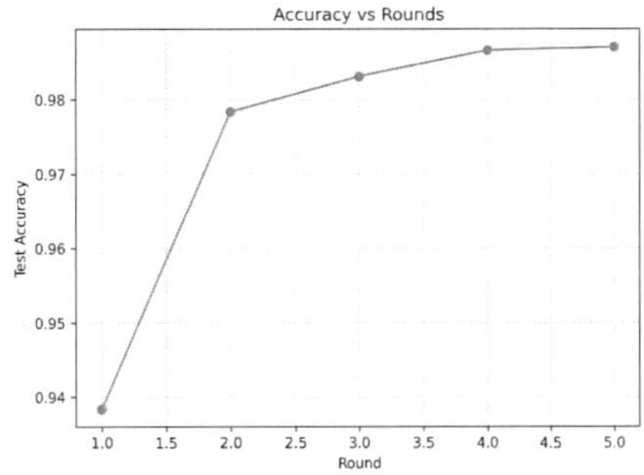

(b) Variation of test accuracy

Fig. 3: Variation of test accuracy and loss across federated rounds.

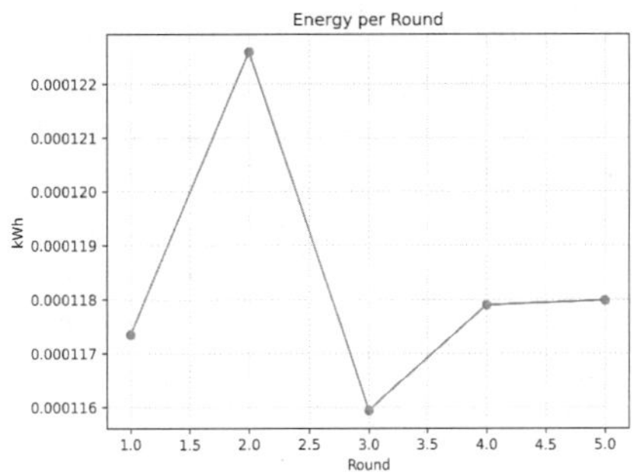

(a) Energy consumption

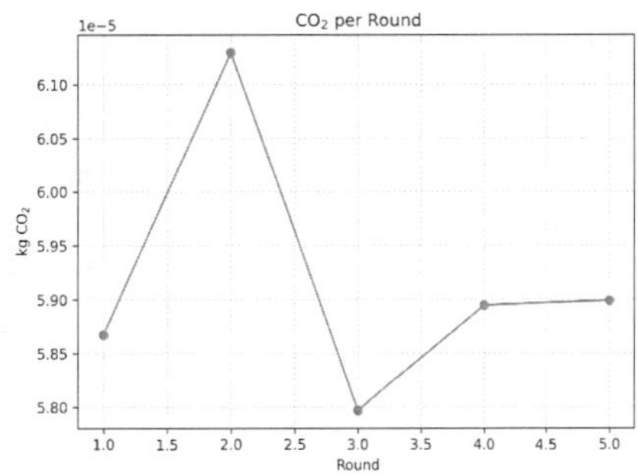

(b) Estimated CO_2 emissions

Fig. 4: Energy consumption and Estimated CO_2 emissions per federated round.

Carbon Footprint. The CO_2 profile remained stable across rounds (Fig. 4b), with emissions of about 5.9×10^{-5} kg CO_2 per round. DP-based Federated Learning enhanced the value by less than 5%, confirming that the implementation of privacy-enhancing techniques remains compatible with sustainable computational practices. It shows the feasibility of measuring carbon impact as a task of federated optimization. Table 1 presents the comparative results. SFL obtains a balanced trade-off among privacy, energy efficiency, and model performance, making it suitable to deploy in real-world IoT or edge AI environments where both *data privacy* and *environmental sustainability* are key priorities.

Security Evaluation of Secure Aggregation. To assess the robustness of the secure aggregation mechanism, we measured the computation overhead introduced by mask generation and cancellation. The added cost was low per client per round, representing less than 3% of local training time, indicating that security does not significantly degrade performance. The masking scheme is compared against baselines (FedAvg and DP-only): while FedAvg exposes raw updates and DP-only offers protection in expectation, secure aggregation ensures that even a curious

Table 1: **Comparison of baseline FedAvg, DP-FL, and proposed SFL.**

Configuration	Accuracy (%)	Energy (kWh/round)	CO_2 (kg/round)
FedAvg (Baseline)	98.1	1.18×10^{-4}	5.9×10^{-5}
DP-FL (Opacus)	97.3	1.22×10^{-4}	6.1×10^{-5}
SFL (Proposed)	**97.9**	1.19×10^{-4}	5.9×10^{-5}

server cannot recover any individual model update, thus providing strong privacy guarantees with minimal overhead.

6 Conclusion and Future Work

The proposed framework *Sustainable Federated Learning (SFL)* integrates privacy preservation, secure aggregation, and sustainability tracking into a unified federated learning pipeline. Unlike conventional FL systems that primarily focus on model convergence and accuracy, SFL explicitly computes the energy consumption and carbon footprint associated with each communication round. The framework optionally incorporates differential privacy (DP) and secure masking, ensuring both data confidentiality and persistence against gradient reconstruction attacks, without adding any computational overhead. The presented results show that energy efficient and privacy aware federated learning can coexist within practical deployment scenarios.

Future work can incorporate energy-based weighting that allows clients with lower energy budgets or a higher intensity of carbon to contribute proportionally less during aggregation.

References

1. Abbasi, A., Dong, F., Wang, X., Leung, H., Zhou, J., Drew, S.: Fedgreen: Carbon-aware federated learning with model size adaptation. In: 2024 IEEE International Conference on Communications Workshops (ICC Workshops), pp. 1352–1358. IEEE (2024)
2. Barbierato, E., Gatti, A.: Toward green AI: A methodological survey of the scientific literature. IEEE Access **12**, 23989–24013 (2024)
3. Dwivedi, A.K.: Privacy-preserving federated learning for emotion recognition: An improved framework with differential privacy. In: 17th International Conference on Intelligent Human-Computer Interaction (IHCI 2025), pp. 1–12. Springer (2025)
4. Dwivedi, A.K.: Federated learning for secure and scalable design pattern detection in software systems. In: 12th International Conference on Mathematics and Computing (ICMC 2026), pp. 1–11. Springer (2026)
5. Dwork, C.: Differential privacy. In: International colloquium on automata, languages, and programming, pp. 1–12. Springer (2006)
6. Hasan, S.M., Islam, T., Saifuzzaman, M., Ahmed, K.R., Huang, C.H., Shahid, A.R.: Carbon emission quantification of machine learning: A review. IEEE Transactions on Sustainable Computing, (2025)

7. Jithish, J., Mahalingam, N., Wang, B., Yeo, K.S.: Federated learning for sustainable intrusion detection systems: A review of green computing strategies and future directions. Internet of Things p, p. 101730. (2025)
8. Kang, J., Xiong, Z., Niyato, D., Xie, S., Zhang, J.: Incentive mechanism for reliable federated learning: A joint optimization approach to combining reputation and contract theory. IEEE Internet Things J. **6**(6), 10700–10714 (2019)
9. Konečný, J., McMahan, H.B., Yu, F.X., Richtárik, P., Suresh, A.T., Bacon, D.: Federated learning: Strategies for improving communication efficiency. arXiv preprint arXiv:1610.05492 (2016)
10. Latif, S., Khalifa, S., Rana, R., Jurdak, R.: Federated learning for speech emotion recognition applications. In: IPSN. vol. 223, pp. 341–342 (2020)
11. McMahan, B., Moore, E., Ramage, D., Hampson, S., y Arcas, B.A.: Communication-efficient learning of deep networks from decentralized data. AISTATS (2017)
12. Melis, L., Song, C., De Cristofaro, E., Shmatikov, V.: Exploiting unintended feature leakage in collaborative learning. In: 2019 IEEE symposium on security and privacy (SP), pp. 691–706. IEEE (2019)
13. Singla, V., Singh, S.K., Kumar, S., Chhabra, A., Gill, S.S., Arya, V., Jain, A.: Challenges and opportunities in sustainable AI and information systems. In: Sustainable Information Security in the Age of AI and Green Computing, pp. 73–96. (2025)
14. Strubell, E., Ganesh, A., McCallum, A.: Energy and policy considerations for modern deep learning research. In: Proceedings of the AAAI conference on artificial intelligence. vol. 34, pp. 13693–13696 (2020)
15. Wang, S., Tuor, T., Salonidis, T., Leung, K.K., Makaya, C., He, T., Chan, K.: Adaptive federated learning in resource constrained edge computing systems. IEEE J. Sel. Areas Commun. **37**(6), 1205–1221 (2019)
16. Wei, K., Li, J., Ding, M., Ma, C., Yang, H.H., Farokhi, F., Jin, S., Quek, T.Q., Poor, H.V.: Federated learning with differential privacy: Algorithms and performance analysis. IEEE Trans. Inf. Forensics Secur. **15**, 3454–3469 (2020)
17. Yao, A.C.: Protocols for secure computations. In: 23rd annual symposium on foundations of computer science (sfcs 1982), pp. 160–164. IEEE (1982)
18. Zhu, H., Xu, M., Wang, J., Zhu, S., Xue, X.: AIoT-enabled federated learning for green supply chain demand forecasting with privacy-preserving carbon reference effects. IEEE Internet of Things Journal (2025)

ObfusFinder
A Framework for Identifying Obfuscated Code in Android Applications

Mansi Upadhyay(✉), Palak Agrawal, Pranjal Jain, Sakshi Rai, Shubhangi Yadav, Amit Patel, Shweta Bhandari, and Deepak Singh Tomar

Maulana Azad National Institute of Technology (MANIT), Bhopal, India
mansiupadhyay2004@gmail.com

Abstract. Code obfuscation is increasingly exploited by malware authors to disguise malicious intent and evade detection, making it a growing challenge for static analysis. This study examines twelve common obfuscation techniques that alter program structure without changing behavior. To counter these evasion tactics, we introduce **ObfusFinder**, a static detection framework capable of identifying obfuscated malicious patterns across multiple programming languages. Experimental analysis demonstrates that ObfusFinder enhances detection accuracy and efficiency while maintaining scalability across diverse codebases. The research emphasizes responsible use of obfuscation analysis for defense and forensic investigation, contributing toward more resilient malware detection systems.

Keywords: Code Obfuscation · Static Detection · Reverse Engineering

1 Introduction

With the rapid digital transformation across industries and the increasing complexity of software ecosystems, cyber threats have expanded in both scale and sophistication. Modern malware increasingly employs advanced code obfuscation techniques to conceal intent, disrupt analysis, and evade static detection systems [5]. Code obfuscation encompasses syntactic, structural, and semantic transformations–such as instruction substitution, control-flow flattening, junk code insertion, and dynamic code loading–that alter a program's structure while preserving its functionality [2,8]. These transformations significantly hinder reverse engineering and static analysis by generating polymorphic and metamorphic variants that appear distinct in every iteration, thereby bypassing signature-based and heuristic detectors [4,10]. Although such methods are legitimately

M. Upadhyay, P. Agrawal, P. Jain and S. Rai—All authors have equal contribution, and names are mentioned in alphabetical order.

G. K. Verma et al. (Eds.): MIND 2025, CCIS 2981, pp. 412–423, 2027.
https://doi.org/10.1007/978-3-032-31230-3_33

employed to safeguard intellectual property, improve performance, and prevent unauthorized access [6,9], their malicious exploitation introduces ambiguity between protection and deception, complicating both detection and forensic analysis. In recent years, the emergence of hybrid and layered obfuscation–combining encrypted strings, mixed-language embedding, runtime code generation, and self-modifying logic–has rendered static detection frameworks increasingly ineffective [13,14]. This evolution presents multiple technical challenges, including incomplete code visibility, high false-positive rates, scalability limitations, and elevated computational overhead when analyzing large or polymorphic codebases. Furthermore, the continuous adaptation of obfuscation strategies by threat actors compels defenders to adopt detection systems that are adaptive, explainable, and language-agnostic, capable of accurately distinguishing benign protective transformations from adversarial manipulations. These challenges not only highlight the technical limitations of existing tools but also raise ethical concerns regarding the responsible use of deobfuscation knowledge, which, if misapplied, may inadvertently aid the development of more evasive malware. Motivated by the need for scalable, transparent, and ethically guided analysis, this study introduces **ObfusFinder**, a static, multi-language detection framework engineered to identify twelve major obfuscation techniques across C, C++, Java, Kotlin, and Python. Unlike conventional static analyzers, ObfusFinder integrates structural, lexical, and heuristic-based mechanisms to achieve line-level precision, thereby bridging the gap between traditional static analysis and adaptive adversarial evasion. ObfusFinder supports both offline analysis for secure, private evaluation and online access via cloud-deployed repositories, promoting collaboration and ease of use; its source code and documentation are freely available at GitHub By emphasizing interpretability, automation, and extensibility, the framework enhances detection accuracy, scalability, and trustworthiness–offering a robust foundation for next-generation deobfuscation and malware classification research. The remainder of this paper is organized as follows: Section 2 provides an overview of the twelve obfuscation techniques along with conceptual illustrations and analysis; Section 3 details the architectural design and implementation of the proposed framework; Section 4 presents experimental evaluation and comparative analysis with existing tools; and Section 5 concludes with key findings, identified limitations, and future research directions.

2 Obfuscation Techniques: Concepts and Analysis

Code obfuscation comprises techniques that deliberately make a program harder to read, analyze, or reverse-engineer while preserving its original behavior. Obfuscation is used for intellectual property protection, anti-tampering, and hiding malicious intent [8–10]. Below we present 12 obfuscation techniques with concise definitions and a simple analogy for each to aid intuitive understanding.

1. **Instruction Substitution**
   Instruction substitution is an obfuscation technique where standard instructions are replaced with alternative sequences that achieve the same result

but appear different. By replacing a simple operation with a more complex or unusual one, attackers make it harder for analysts to identify recognizable patterns. For example, instead of using a direct ADD instruction, the code might perform the same task through a combination of shifts and increments [8,11]. See Fig. 1 for representative examples of this technique.

2. **String Encryption**
String encryption is a code obfuscation technique where literal strings within a program (such as configuration data, API keys, or user messages) are stored in encrypted form and only decrypted at runtime. This approach prevents static analysis tools and reverse engineers from easily reading sensitive strings embedded in the code [10,14]. See Fig. 2 for representative examples of this technique.
3. **Inline Function Expansion**
Inline function expansion replaces a function call with the actual body of that function. When used as an obfuscation technique, this strategy eliminates the clear modular structure of the code and spreads logic across different regions, making it harder to recognize repeated functionality or understand program flow. By duplicating and embedding code, it also increases complexity and the difficulty of pattern detection [8,9].See Fig. 3 for representative examples of this technique.
4. **Name Obfuscation**
Identifier renaming is a common obfuscation technique where meaningful variable and function names are replaced with meaningless or random strings. This transformation removes semantic clues, making the code harder to understand [1,8]. See Fig. 4 for representative examples of this technique.
5. **API Redirection Technique**
API redirection is a code obfuscation technique where direct calls to API functions are replaced by calls routed through fake wrapper functions. These wrappers redirect requests indirectly to the actual API, making it difficult for analysts to trace and understand the program's true control flow and behavior [2,14]. See Fig. 5 for representative examples of this technique.
6. **Mixed-Language Obfuscation**
Mixed-language obfuscation involves integrating code written in different programming languages within a single program (e.g., assembly code embedded inside C/C++ or Python combined with C). This technique leverages context switches between languages to increase complexity, making reverse engineering and static analysis more challenging [9,11]. See Fig. 6 for representative examples of this technique.
7. **Junk Code**
Junk code insertion is an obfuscation technique that adds useless or non-functional instructions, such as no-operations (NOPs) or fake mathematical calculations, into the code. These instructions do not alter the program's logic or state [8,11]. See Fig. 7 for representative examples of this technique.
8. **Dynamic Code Loading / Overloading**
Dynamic code loading is an obfuscation method where parts of the program are not present in their final form until runtime. Instead of keeping all

instructions visible in static code, some are stored in encrypted, compressed, or hidden form and are only reconstructed when needed. This prevents static analysis tools from fully examining the program beforehand [10,13]. See Fig.8 for representative examples of this technique.

9. **Dead Code**
   Dead code generation is an obfuscation technique where intentionally unreachable code segments are inserted into a program. These instructions will never be executed at runtime but are designed to mislead reverse engineers by bloating the control flow and increasing analysis complexity. Unlike junk code, which can execute without changing logic, dead code never runs at all but still pollutes the codebase [2,11].See Fig. 9 for representative examples of this technique.
10. **Control Flow Obfuscation**
   Control flow obfuscation involves inserting fake conditional statements such as if, switch, or goto branches that do not affect the program's intended functionality. These bogus branches create additional, irrelevant execution paths, complicating the control flow graph and making the program logic harder to analyze [7,9]. See Fig.10 for representative examples of this technique.
11. **Opaque Predicates**
   Opaque predicates are logical conditions inserted into the code that always evaluate to a known outcome (true or false) but are written in a complex way so that the result is not obvious to an analyst. These conditions introduce misleading branches that complicate control-flow analysis, even though the execution result remains predictable [2,7]. See Fig. 11 for representative examples of this technique.
12. **Code Flattening**
   Code flattening restructures a program's execution by breaking normal sequential flow into a dispatcher-controlled model. Instead of following a clear top-to-bottom order, code blocks are reorganized under a central controller (often a loop and switch-case structure) that decides the next instruction to execute. This eliminates predictable flow patterns and complicates static analysis [7,8]. See Fig. 12 for representative examples of this technique.

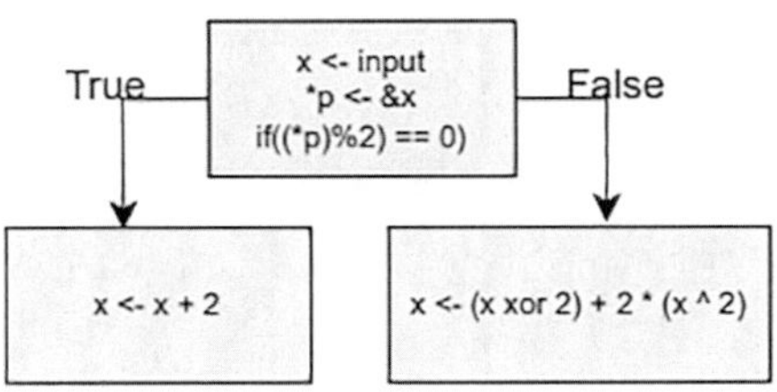

Fig. 1. Instruction Substitution.

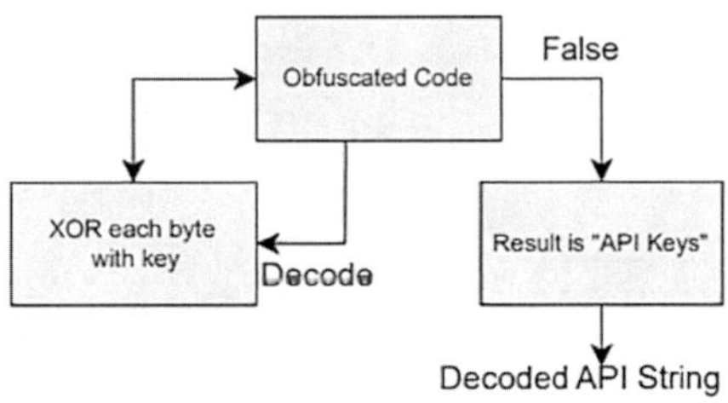

Fig. 2. String Encryption.

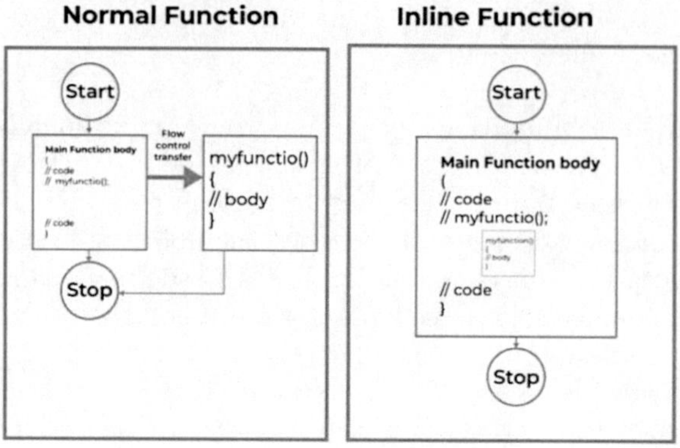

Fig. 3. Inline Function Expansion.

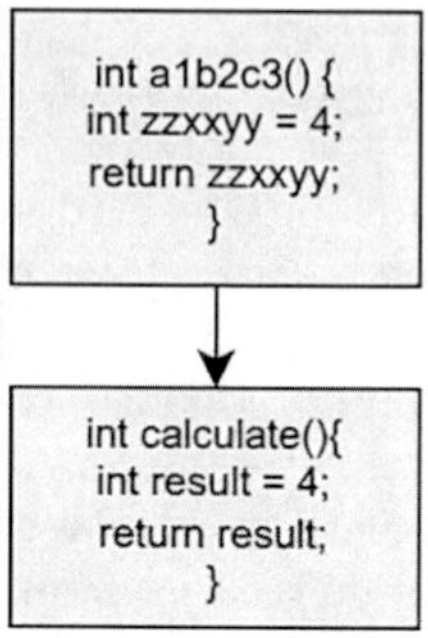

Fig. 4. Name Obfuscation.

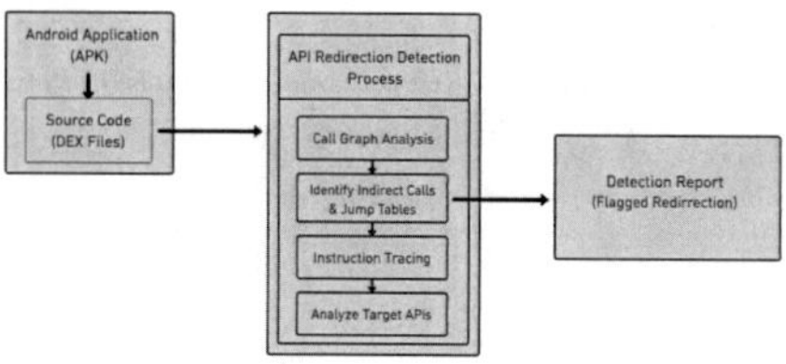

Fig. 5. API Redirection Technique.

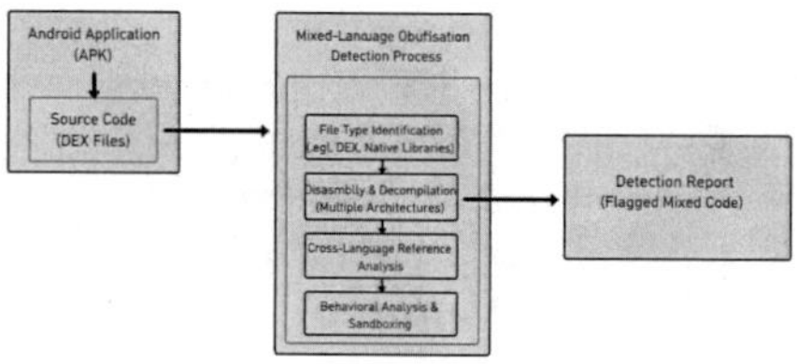

Fig. 6. Mixed-Language Obfuscation.

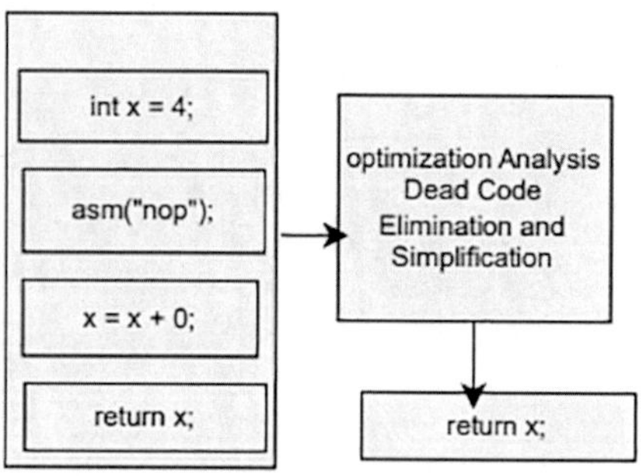

Fig. 7. Junk Code.

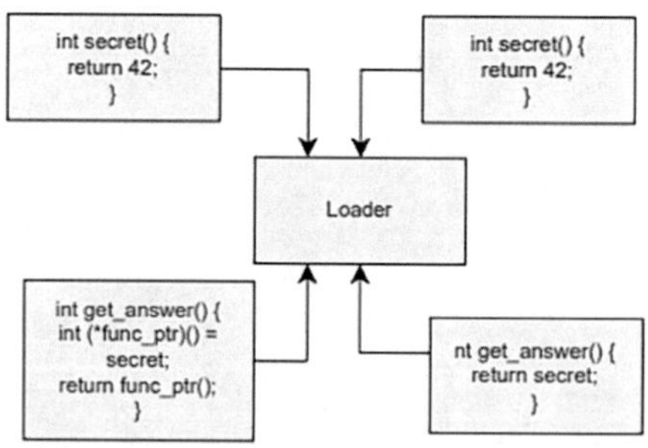

Fig. 8. Dynamic Code Overloading.

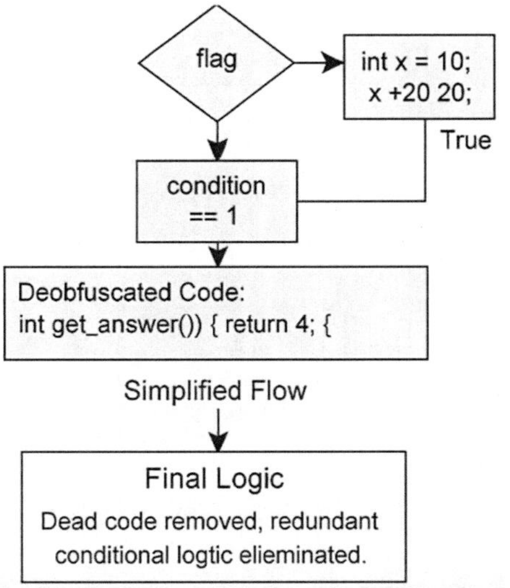

Fig. 9. Dead Code.

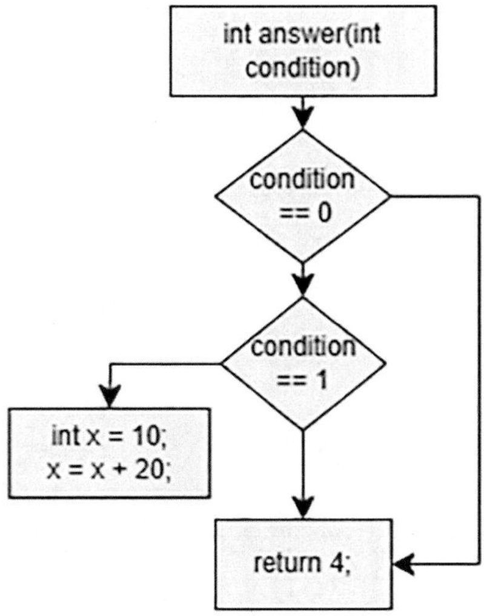

Fig. 10. Control Flow Obfuscation.

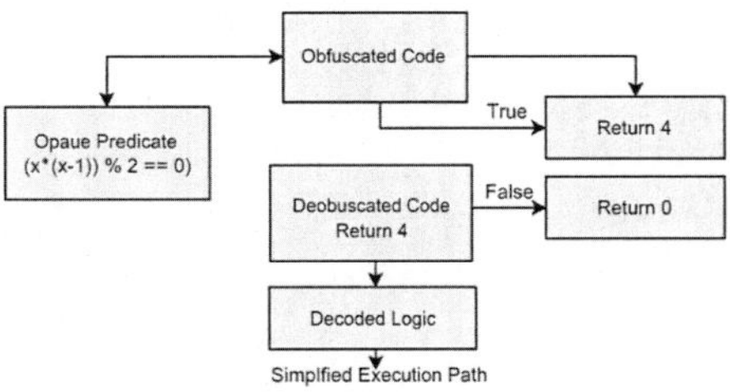

Fig. 11. Opaque Predicates.

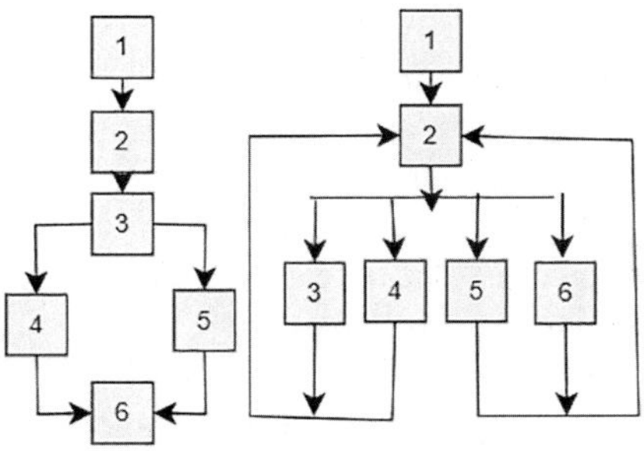

Fig. 12. Code Flattening.

3 Implementation Mapping of Detection Methodologies in ObfusFinder

The proposed framework, **ObfusFinder**, automates static detection of twelve code obfuscation techniques using a combination of heuristic rules, regular expressions, and lightweight static analysis. Each detection module is mapped to a specific obfuscation behavior and draws inspiration from classical and contemporary deobfuscation research [10,11,14]. The following subsections describe the implementation details for each technique (Fig. 13).

1. **Instruction Substitution**
   This technique is detected by finding semantically equivalent instruction replacements, such as `x - (-1)` instead of `x + 1`. ObfusFinder employs expression pattern matching to capture equivalent operations, an approach

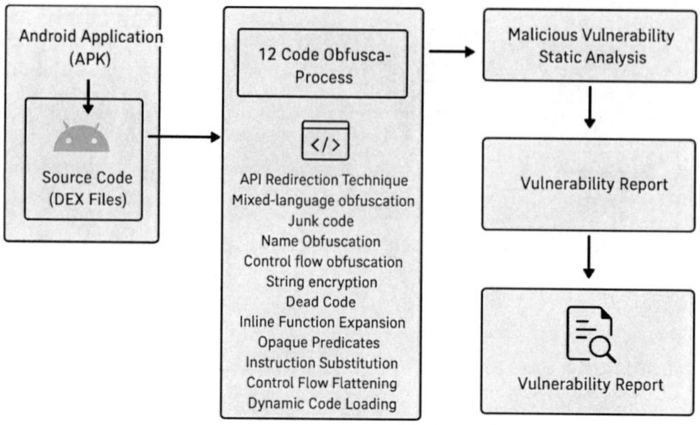

Fig. 13. Comprehensive Flow of APK Obfuscation and Vulnerability Detection.

comparable to IR-level semantic equivalence checking [8]. See Fig. 1 here Instruction substitutes x - (-1) with equivalent x + 1, simplifying obfuscated arithmetic operation.

2. **String Encryption**
   ObfusFinder uses the `StringDecryptor` module to detect encrypted or XOR-masked strings. It attempts automated decryption and flags occurrences of cryptographic API calls. This process reflects hybrid static-dynamic string analysis techniques described in prior malware analysis studies [10]. See Fig. 2 it detects simple XOR/shift string obfuscation, decodes at compile-time and replaces with literal.
3. **Inline Function Expansion**
   Detection of inline function expansion relies on identifying repeated logical patterns or expanded function bodies. ObfusFinder matches similar code blocks that replace modular calls, similar to Abstract Syntax Tree (AST) redundancy analysis [9]. See Fig. 3 it replaces repeated arithmetic with nested calls to a simpler function, restoring original intent.
4. **Name Obfuscation**
   To detect identifier renaming, ObfusFinder measures identifier entropy and counts excessively short or random names (e.g., `a1b2c3`, `xq`, etc.). A high density of such identifiers indicates automated name obfuscation, similar to lexical entropy-based approaches [1,9]. See Fig. 4 it detects meaningless identifier names and renames them to meaningful identifiers for clarity.
5. **API Redirection**
   ObfusFinder detects API redirection by identifying wrapper functions that call other functions indirectly. It employs regular expressions to locate nested return statements (e.g., `return wrapper();`) and multi-level redirection chains. This method simulates static call-graph tracing commonly discussed in deobfuscation literature [2,14].See Fig. 5 it identifies and removes indirection wrappers, collapsing chained calls into a single direct constant return.

6. **Mixed-Language Obfuscation**
This technique is detected through syntax-level analysis. ObfusFinder scans code for tokens or syntax patterns from multiple programming languages (e.g., inline assembly within C or Python). The system identifies mixed-language boundaries, consistent with hybrid decompilation techniques explored in prior research [9]. See Fig. 6 it detects inline assembly producing a constant; replace asm with direct constant return, removing opaque low-level code.
7. **Junk Code**
Junk code is detected using regular expressions that identify redundant operations such as `nop`, `x = x + 0`, or useless arithmetic. The framework flags instructions that do not change the program state, replicating static dataflow and liveness analysis principles [11]. See Fig. 7 it removes no-op instructions and redundant assignments, returning the constant result directly.
8. **Dynamic Code Loading / Overloading**
ObfusFinder detects dynamically loaded or reflective code by scanning for API calls such as `forName()`, `invoke()`, and `loadLibrary()`. These indicators signal runtime code reconstruction, conceptually corresponding to behavioral and dynamic tracing techniques in malware analysis [13]. See Fig. 8. The code uses function pointer indirection, which can be simplified because `get_answer()` always directly returns 42.
9. **Dead Code**
The framework detects unreachable or redundant code by locating constant conditions such as `if(false)` or statements appearing after a `return`. This mirrors reachability and symbolic execution methods applied in static deobfuscation research [11,14]. See Fig. 9 it removes unreachable or side-effect-free code, returning the constant result directly.
10. **Control Flow Obfuscation**
Control flow obfuscation is detected by identifying redundant branches, excessive `goto` statements, or switch-case state transitions. The framework analyzes text for irregular control structures, analogous to Control Flow Graph (CFG) normalization and dominator-tree analysis used in reverse engineering [7]. See Fig. 10 it simplifies conditional branches by evaluating constant outcomes and removing redundant paths, returning constant 4.
11. **Opaque Predicates**
Opaque predicates are identified through arithmetic comparisons that always evaluate to a constant value (e.g., `3*3==9`). The system applies regex-based constant evaluation checks, aligning conceptually with constraint-solving techniques used in symbolic execution [2]. See Fig. 11 here condition is always false: x*(x-1) is always even; branch simplifies, returning constant 0.
12. **Code Flattening**
Control flow flattening is detected through identification of large loop and switch structures where a dispatcher variable governs execution order. This detection mechanism approximates the CFG-based reconstruction methods described by Chow et al. [7]. See Fig. 12. The code uses a flattened con-

trol flow with states, which can be simplified because `get_answer()` always returns 4.

In summary, ObfusFinder combines heuristic-based static detection with text-pattern reasoning to identify language-agnostic obfuscation techniques. While it does not perform runtime execution tracing, its modular structure provides an efficient and scalable static analysis framework capable of approximating advanced hybrid detection systems. API redirection: wrapper functions introduce an extra indirection layer between the caller and the actual API.

4 Experiment Model

To evaluate the performance and versatility of the proposed framework, **ObfusFinder** was compared against four widely used obfuscation analysis tools - Ghidra, Androguard, APKTool, and Oxyry. The comparative evaluation focused on the ability of each tool to detect twelve commonly used static obfuscation techniques across multiple programming languages. As shown in Table 1, ObfusFinder achieved complete detection coverage (12/12 techniques) across languages including C, C++, Java, Kotlin, and Python, outperforming other tools that exhibited partial or domain-specific capabilities. While tools such as Ghidra and Oxyry demonstrated broad static analysis functionality, their reliance on scripted or platform-dependent detection limited adaptability and consistency. In contrast, ObfusFinder maintained automated and language-agnostic detection with line-level precision, enabling accurate localization of obfuscated code fragments. This high detection coverage, accounting for 31.6% of all identified features, highlights the framework's scalability and robustness in static malware analysis [1,9–11]. The table clearly demonstrates that ObfusFinder surpasses existing methods by integrating syntactic, structural, and semantic inspection without requiring dynamic execution or manual intervention, making it a more reliable foundation for static deobfuscation research [2,8,14].

In addition to detection performance, a detailed capability comparison of all five tools was conducted to evaluate functional range, automation, and reporting features are given below.

As presented in Table 2, ObfusFinder delivers comprehensive static detection through a fully automated, multi-language analysis pipeline, whereas tools such as Ghidra, Androguard, APKTool, and Oxyry exhibit restricted functionality, dependence on manual scripting, or limited reporting granularity [9–11]. In contrast, ObfusFinder provides complete static coverage with line-level reporting and structured summaries, improving transparency and interpretability in obfuscation analysis. To support its scalability claims, the framework employs lightweight static-analysis routines: most detectors (regex-based matching, identifier entropy, junk-code detection) operate in $\mathcal{O}(n)$ time, while structural checks (API redirection, inline expansion, control-flow irregularities) run in $\mathcal{O}(n \log n)$. By avoiding full CFG reconstruction–which can reach $\mathcal{O}(n^2)$ in conventional

Table 1. Comparative Analysis: Obfuscation Technique Detection by Leading Tools

Obfuscation Technique	Ghidra	Andro- guard	APK Tool	Oxyry	Obfus- Finder
API Redirection	√	√	√	√	√
Mixed-language	×	×	×	×	√
Junk Code	√	√	×	√	√
Name Obfuscation	√	√	√	√	√
Control Flow	√	√	×	√	√
String Encryption	×	Partial	×	×	√
Dead Code	√	√	×	√	√
Inline Expansion	√	√	×	√	√
Opaque Predicates	√	Partial	×	√	√
Instruction Substitution	Partial	×	×	Partial	√
Control Flow Flattening	√	√	×	√	√
Dynamic Code Overloading	Partial	Partial	Partial	Partial	√

Table 2. Feature Matrix: Obfuscation Analysis Tools for Multilanguage Platforms

Feature	Ghidra	Andro- guard	APK Tool	Oxyry	Obfus- Finder
Primary Use	Decompiler / Disassembler	Static Android Analysis	Resource & Manifest Rebuild	Generic Deobfuscator	Static Obfuscation Detection
Detection Coverage	High	Medium	Low	Medium	High
Supported Platforms	C/C++, Java Bytecode	Android (DEX, APK)	Android (SMALI, XML)	Java / DEX	Multi-language (Java, Python, C/C++, Kotlin)
Analysis Type	Static / Decompilation	Static	Decompilation	Static / Dynamic	Static
Line-level Detection	No	Partial	No	Varies	Yes
Report Generation	Limited (Script-based)	Basic Logs	No	Basic	Detailed Summary Report

tools–ObfusFinder maintains an overall complexity of approximately $\mathcal{O}(n \log n)$, enabling efficient processing of large and multi-language codebases. This combination of broad coverage, automation, and bounded computational cost positions ObfusFinder as a scalable and dedicated framework for next-generation static deobfuscation and malware classification research [1,14].

5 Conclusion

Code obfuscation continues to be a pivotal concept in modern cybersecurity, representing both a protective mechanism and a persistent challenge in malware analysis. While it enables developers to safeguard intellectual property and prevent reverse engineering, the same techniques are increasingly exploited by adversaries to disguise malicious intent and bypass detection systems. This study explored twelve major obfuscation strategies–ranging from control-flow flattening and string encryption to dynamic code loading and instruction substitution–and introduced **ObfusFinder**, a static detection framework capable of identifying these concealed behaviors across multiple programming languages. ObfusFinder integrates heuristic rules, regular expressions, and lightweight static analysis to achieve precise, line-level identification of obfuscated patterns. Experimental evaluation demonstrated that it outperforms existing tools such as Ghidra, Androguard, APKTool, and Oxyry in detection coverage, scalability, and interpretability. By supporting C, C++, Java, Kotlin, and Python, the framework provides a unified, language-independent solution for static malware analysis and deobfuscation research. However, as adversarial obfuscation continues to evolve through polymorphism, metamorphism, and hybrid evasion techniques, static detection alone may prove insufficient. Future work should focus on AI-driven hybrid models that combine the precision of static analysis with the adaptability of dynamic monitoring. Such advancements will not only improve detection robustness but also support proactive threat intelligence. Ultimately, this research underscores the ethical responsibility of leveraging obfuscation analysis for defensive, transparent, and educational purposes–paving the way toward more trustworthy, resilient, and intelligent cybersecurity ecosystems. In the long term, the proposed framework can serve as a foundation for integrating automated deobfuscation pipelines into large-scale malware repositories, enabling real-time detection and classification of emerging threats.

References

1. Zhang, N.: Analysis on techniques for code obfuscation. Inter. J. Comput. Appli. **185**(35), 1–7 (2023)
2. Ding, Y., Liu, J., Zhang, M.: Automated deobfuscation of android bytecode via data-flow-guided analysis. IEEE Trans. Inf. Forensics Secur. **16**, 4330–4342 (2021)
3. Durfina, L., Kolař, D.: C Source Code Obfuscator. Kybernetika **48**(4), 735–747 (2012)
4. Kargén, U., Arne, S.: Characterizing the Use of Code Obfuscation in Malicious Software. ACM Digital Library (2023)
5. Hada, S.: Zero-knowledge and code obfuscation. In: Okamoto, T. (ed.) ASIACRYPT 2000. LNCS, vol. 1976, pp. 443–457. Springer, Heidelberg (2000). https://doi.org/10.1007/3-540-44448-3_34
6. Kirat, D., Giacinto, G., Balzarotti, D.: A decade of android malware: a comprehensive study of code obfuscation trends. ACM Comput. Surv. **53**(6), 1–33 (2020)
7. Xu, W., Han, K., Chen, Y.: Control flow obfuscation and deobfuscation in modern software: a systematic review. Comput. Sec. **118**, 102738 (2022)

8. Collberg, C., Thomborson, C.: Watermarking, tamper-proofing, and obfuscation-tools for software protection. IEEE Trans. Software Eng. **28**(8), 735–746 (2009)
9. Ceccato, M., Coppola, M., Piantadosi, L.: A survey of code obfuscation techniques and their role in software protection. ACM Comput. Surv. **53**(6), 1–38 (2020)
10. Chen, Z., Fang, S., Wang, Y.: Obfuscation techniques and their impact on malware analysis: a systematic review. Comput. Sec. **121**, 102816 (2022)
11. Song, Y., Lee, S., Kim, H.: Malware obfuscation and detection techniques: a comprehensive survey. IEEE Access **8**, 95715–95735 (2020)
12. Rastogi, V., Chen, Y., Enck, W.: Defining and detecting android obfuscation. In: IEEE Symposium on Security and Privacy Workshops (SPW), pp. 252–263. IEEE (2014)
13. Jiang, X., Zhang, L., Wang, X.: Understanding the effect of obfuscation on malware detection. IEEE Trans. Inf. Forensics Secur. **13**(8), 2028–2040 (2018)
14. Bayer, U., Habibi, I., Balzarotti, D., Kirda, E., Kruegel, C.: Scalable, behavior-based malware clustering. In: NDSS Symposium (2009)

A Scalable and Trustworthy Consensus Mechanism Based on Proof of Reputation and Machine Learning for Blockchain

Harsh Agrawal[1], Chirag Modi[1](✉), and Amit Shewale[2]

[1] Department of CSE, National Institute of Technology Goa, Cuncolim 403703, Goa, India
cnmodi@nitgoa.ac.in

[2] Department of CSE, Indian Institute of Information Technology, Nagpur 441108, MH, India
ashewale@iiitn.ac.in

Abstract. Blockchain has emerged as a transformative solution, offering decentralized, secure and transparent digital transaction management. However, it faces the challenges of low throughput, high latency and low scalability. In literature, different on-chain and off-chain solutions have been reported. However, there is a scope for the further improvements in terms of trustworthy block generation and scalability. This paper proposes a proof of reputation consensus mechanism, as an on-chain solution, while machine learning is applied as off-chain to dynamically update the reputation score of the participating nodes. The reputation score of the nodes is calculated based on behavioral metrics such as active participation, transparency, compliance and stake. It helps to select the most reliable nodes, ensuring a balanced trade-off between scalability, decentralization, and security. The proposed solution is tested and validated on Hyperledger Fabric, wherein reputation score of each node is updated using Stochastic Gradient Descent regression. It is observed that the proposed solution significantly improves the performance of blockchain.

Keywords: Blockchain · Scalability · Proof of Reputation · Machine Learning

1 Introduction

Blockchain technology has high potential in various sectors apart from cryptocurrencies like Bitcoin [1]. It is a decentralized digital ledger where transactions are recorded in blocks and cryptographically linked together. The peer-to-peer transactions and decentralization nature of blockchain ensure transparency, security, and trust among users, while addressing issues of intermediaries. In addition, it significantly reduces the transaction cost and enhancing efficiency. The applications of blockchains have been explored in healthcare, supply chain, e-voting, e-governance, energy etc. Although blockchain offers various benefits, it still faces several challenges for its wide adoption. Less scalability of the blockchain is a major hurdle [2]. With the growing size of network, maintaining decentralization and security while achieving sufficient throughput is challenging. In contrast to the centralized systems like Visa which can handle thousands of transactions

G. K. Verma et al. (Eds.): MIND 2025, CCIS 2981, pp. 424–434, 2027.
https://doi.org/10.1007/978-3-032-31230-3_34

every second, current blockchain platforms such as Bitcoin [1], Ethereum [3] etc. are able to process very limited number of transactions per second (TPS). This is due to the decentralization and underlying the consensus mechanism for the block of transaction generation and verification. In addition to scalability, blockchain suffers from low throughput, high latency, resource constraint, blockchain trilemma (balancing scalability, security, and decentralization) [4]. In literature, researchers have explored various solutions such as sharding, layer-2 solutions (e.g. Lightning Network), increasing block size and efficient consensus mechanisms like Proof of Stake, Proof of Authority, byzantine fault tolerance etc. However, still there is scope of further improvements in balancing security and scalability. It is required to consider only the reputed nodes to generate the transaction blocks and verification.

In this paper, a scalable and trustworthy consensus mechanism has been proposed to maintain the balance between the trusted block generation and scalability. In the proposed solution, only the authorized and reputed nodes are considered to generate and verify the blocks of the transactions. In addition, the reputation of the nodes is dynamically calculated using machine learning and based on their behavior in block generation and verification process. In contrast to the existing work, machine learning helps in deriving the accurate reputation of the nodes. The consideration only highly reputed nodes can help to improve the trust and scalability in blockchain. The proposed solution is tested and validated on Hyperledger Fabric, wherein reputation score of each node is updated using Stochastic Gradient Descent regression. It is observed that the proposed solution significantly improves the performance of blockchain.

Rest of this paper is organized as follows: Sect. 2 presents the existing research efforts made towards improving the scalability of the blockchain, while Sect. 3, proposed solution is discussed in detail. Section 4 validate the proposed solution. Section 5 conclude research findings with the references at the end.

2 Literature Review

In literature, various research attempts have been made towards improving the scalability of the blockchain. The existing solutions can be broadly classified into sharding-based solutions, layer-2 based solutions, consensus improvement, and trust/reputation-based models.

2.1 Sharding Based Solutions

Sharding splits the blockchain network into smaller groups of nodes (shards), allowing parallel processing of transactions. Vernekar et al. [5] have applied sharding to improve scalability while preserving privacy. Similarly, Kumar et al. [6] have proposed ShardCons, a consensus protocol specifically for sharded systems to reduce the communication overhead. Rahman et al. [7] have proposed prioritized sharding which applies transaction-importance ranking within shards. It offers improvements in transaction ordering. However, it faces the fairness and synchronization issues.

2.2 Layer-2 Based Solutions

Layer-2 protocol operates on top of the main blockchain and move transactions off-chain for faster processing. As discussed by Shirodkar et al. [8], payment channels like Lightning Network can help to improve the throughput and reduce the network congestion. TCTOC Total Commit and Transaction Off-Chains [9] further extends this idea wherein both data and commits are handled at off-chain before being summarized on-chain. This helps to reduce the overhead on main-chain.

2.3 Parallel Processing and Block-Structure Optimization

Martinez [6] has proposed a parallel processing of blockchain architecture. It achieves 125000 TPS. Although this approach effective for raw throughput, its complexity in state synchronization limits its feasibility for real-world applications. The impact of block size and generation time on fork rates are studied by Nakai et al. [9]. It is observed that faster blocks generation can increase forks in blockchain, and thus, simply speeding up consensus may harm blockchain integrity if not handled carefully.

2.4 Consensus Mechanisms Improvements

BFT-based consensus systems aim to tolerate faulty or malicious nodes. Kim et al. [10] have introduced a multi-block BFT algorithm to increase the throughput and reduce consensus time. However, it introduces overhead in managing multiple leaders and blockchains. A detailed evaluation of Hyperledger Fabric's scalability and latency is performed by Kuzlu et al. [11]. It is observed that the endorsing peers and block generation affects the performance.

2.5 Trust and Reputation Systems

Reputation-based consensus has also been explored. While not always directly tied to performance, reputation ensures that reliable nodes have more influence in validation. Narwal et al. [12], have compared various trust systems. It is found that static metrics can become obsolete over time towards reputation calculation. Thus, there is a need of exploring dynamic calculation of the trust score of the nodes.

As per our observation, various alternatives have been explored to address the blockchain scalability issue. However, still there is room for the further improvement in terms of balancing the trustworthy block generation and scalability.

3 Proposed Solution

The objective of the proposed solution is to improve the trustworthiness of the block generation and validation, while maintaining the scalability and throughput. It integrates on-chain smart contracts (chaincode in hyperledger) with an off-chain machine learning service to calculate node reputations dynamically and select highly reputed validators accordingly for block confirmation on chain. As shown in Fig. 1, the proposed solution has mainly two components viz.; 1) On-chain: It is Hyperledger Fabric chaincode [13] which manages node registration, behavior updates, reputation calculation, and validator selection. 2) Off-chain ML Component: A machine learning service that continuously learns and updates the weights for various behavioral factors of the blockchain nodes using online learning (SGD Regressor).

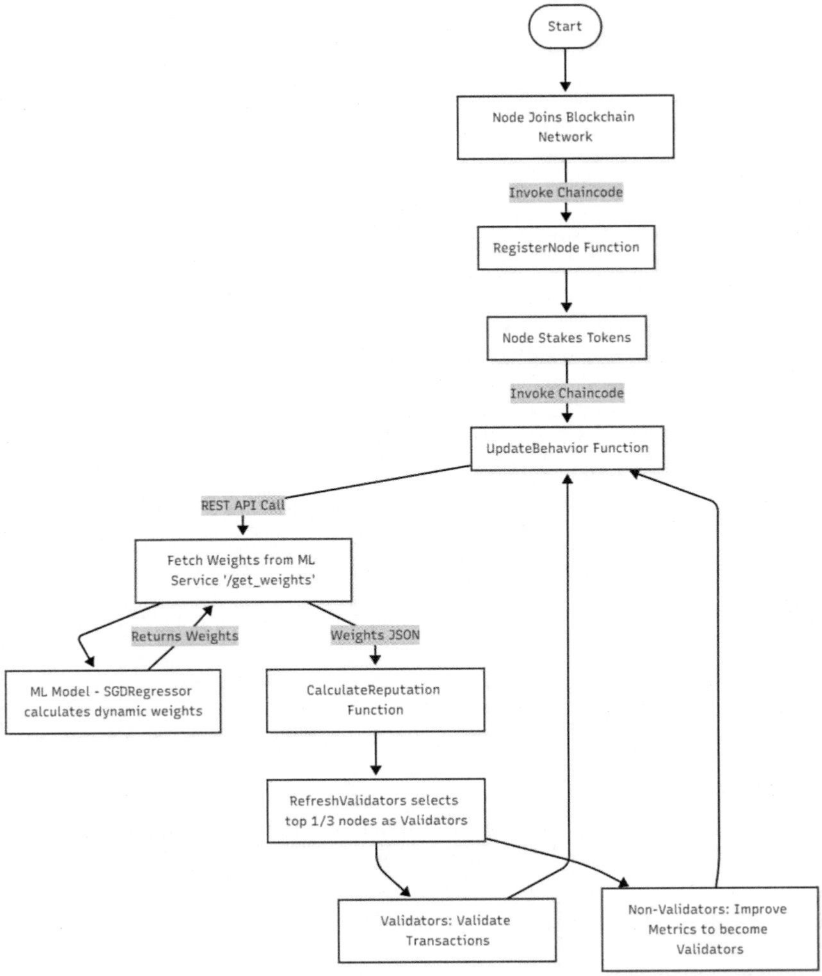

Fig. 1. Workflow of the proposed solution.

3.1 Node Lifecycle and Behavior Tracking

As shown in Fig. 1, each node in the blockchain network undergoes through following operations:

- Registration: A new node joins the network by invoking the RegisterNode function, providing a unique ID and stake value.
- Behavior Update: As the node participates in the network, it periodically updates its metrics like participation, compliance, transparency, and penalty by invoking the UpdateBehavior function.
- Weight Fetching: The chaincode sends current behavior metrics to the off-chain ML API (via REST call to /get weights) to receive updated weights.
- Reputation Calculation: Using the received weights, the Calculate Reputation function computes the reputation score of the node.
- Validator Election: The Refresh Validators function ranks the nodes based on reputation and elects the top 1/3 as validators.

3.2 ML-Based Weight Calculation

The reputation model calculated the reputation of each node based on various features such as frequency of node's participation, transparency, compliance with rules, stake and penalty. The ML service receives these features of each node and returns learned weights using the SGD Regressor (Stochastic Gradient Descent) [14]. This ensures dynamic adjustment of influence for each factor based on recent behavior patterns.

The Stochastic Gradient Descent (SGD) regression model predicts how strongly each behavioral feature correlates with the node's overall reliability. For example:

Each node *i* has a behavioural vector: $x_i = [P_i, TT_i, C_i, S_i, PF_i]$ Where, P_i = participation, TT_i = transaction trust, C_i = contribution, S_i = stake, PF_i = penalty factor.

The SGD model learns a weight vector: $w = [w_1, w_2, w_3, w_4, w_5]$ and predicts node reliability as:

$$\hat{y}_i = w_1 \cdot P_i + w_2 \cdot TT_i + w_3 \cdot C_i + w_4 \cdot S_i - w_5 \cdot PF_i$$

The training objective is to minimize the regularized least-squares loss:

$$L_{(w)} = (1/2) \cdot (\hat{y}_i - y_i)^2 + \lambda \cdot \|w\|^2$$

Where, y_i = true reliability label, λ = regularization constant, $\|w\|^2 = {w_1}^2 + {w_2}^2 + {w_3}^2 + {w_4}^2 + {w_5}^2$.

The SGD weight update rule for each incoming sample (x_i, y_i) is:

$$w \leftarrow w - \eta \cdot ((\hat{y}_i - y_i) \cdot x_i + 2\lambda \cdot w)$$

where η is the learning rate.

Thus, the SGD Regressor is explicitly trained to minimize prediction error for node reliability, and giving importance to the weight of metrics that strongly correlate with trustworthy behavior.

The endpoint /get weights returns a JSON response as below (for example):

{"participation": 0.25,
"transparency": 0.20,
"compliance": 0.18, "stake": 0.22, "penalty": −0.15
}

These weights are then multiplied with the respective values stored on chain for the node.

3.3 Chaincode Architecture

The Go chaincode is designed with the following core functions:

- RegisterNode(ctx, id, stake): Registers a new node.
- UpdateBehavior(ctx, id, participation, transparency, compliance, penalty): Updates the behavior scores.
- CalculateReputation(ctx, id, weightsJSON): Calculates the reputation score of a node using weights.
- RefreshValidators(ctx): Elects top 1/3 nodes as validators.

The data model includes a struct for Node, which stores behavior scores, validator status, and stake value. Reputation score of each node is computed dynamically rather than stored, ensuring up-to-date ranking. Overall, the calculation of each node's reputation and validator election is performed using an algorithm as shown below:

Algorithm: Dynamic Reputation Score Calculation and Validator Election

Input: Node ID *id*, Behavior Metrics *B = {p, t, c, s, pen}*
Output: Updated Reputation Score *R*, Validator Set *V*

```
procedure RegisterNode(id, stake)
    Add node id to ledger with initial metrics and stake
end procedure
procedure UpdateBehavior(id, p, t, c, pen)
    Update node id with participation p, transparency t, compliance c,
    and penalty pen
end procedure
procedure FetchWeights
    Send behavior metrics B to ML API via REST
    Receive weights W = {wp, wt, wc, ws, wpen}
    return W
end procedure
procedure CalculateReputation(id)
    W ← FetchWeights
    Retrieve node metrics B
    R ← wp · p + wt · t + wc · c + ws · s + wpen · pen
    Store R temporarily
    return R
end procedure
procedure RefreshValidators
    for all nodes n in network do
        Rn ← CalculateReputation(n)
    end for
    Sort all nodes by Rn in descending order
    V ← Top ⌈N/3⌉ nodes
    Update validator status for all n ∈ V
end procedure
```

The considered behavior metrics such as participation, transparency, compliance, stake, and penalty have the important aspects of validator's reliability in a blockchain network as follows:

Participation presents that how active the node is in approving and validating transactions. Nodes that consistently participate help to keep the network alive and lower the chances of stalled consensus rounds.

Transparency indicates that how well the node keeps system logs or behaves in a way that can be verified. It is easier to check transparent nodes, and they are less likely to hide bad behavior.

Compliance indicates that how nodes are following the rules of the protocol, the policies for endorsements, and the logic of the chaincode. Nodes that often break compliance create invalid transactions, so compliance is an important measure for reliability.

Stake reflects the economic commitment and makes sure that the nodes have financial deterrents not to misbehave. The probability of maliciousness is low with high stakes.

Penalty catches deviations, faults, endorsement failures, or suspected malicious behavior. Adding penalties guarantees an immediate drop in reputation if any anomaly is detected.

In general, the considered metrics provide a multi-dimensional understanding of trustworthiness, combining operational stability, adherence to rules, economic security, and detection of misbehavior into a single, unified scoring model.

In the proposed solution, decision-making is no longer based on fixed metrics or static roles. The dynamic reputation model ensures adaptability, fairness, and scalability, while being compatible with Hyperledger Fabric's modular architecture. The hybrid on-chain and off-chain interaction bridges the blockchain trust with real-time behavioral learning.

4 Experimental Results and Analysis

The proposed solution is implemented on Hyperledger Fabric blockchain network setup by using a server having 512 GB RAM, x86 64 architecture, 80 logical processors (2 sockets, each with 20 cores, 2 threads per core), Intel(R) Xeon(R) Gold 5218R CPU @ 2.10GHz with CPU Max MHz: 4000, Min MHz: 800. The experiments are conducted using a simulated network of nodes with the chaincode running on Hyperledger Fabric and the ML component operating through a Flask-based Python service. The experimental results derived in terms of Scalability and throughput (TPS) at increasing network scales, block-level packing efficiency and performance compared to leading blockchains, resource usage and latency under scale. The number of nodes in the experiments are increased from 9 to 2500.

As shown in Fig. 2, the throughput of the proposed solution is consistently increasing up to 600 nodes, showing that the proposed solution scales linearly and efficiently in this range. A drop in throughput beyond 900 nodes, suggesting saturation points where overhead from consensus rounds, ML calls, and transaction queues starts impacting performance. The throughput peak at 12.58tps is notable and outperforms traditional Fabric setups in small networks. However, optimizing for larger networks will require further more resources and enhancements such as peer-to-peer protocol optimization and weight caching.

The proposed solution's average transactions per block and throughput is compared with the Bitcoin and Ethereum, as shown in Fig. 3. This provides a direct reference point for practical block-level efficiency.

As shown in Fig. 3, the proposed solution (DWPOR) achieves higher average transactions per block (over 900). This denser utilization indicates far greater efficiency per block, optimizing both ledger storage and consensus overhead. The proposed solution demonstrates a unique advantage in block-level batching, which is especially valuable in enterprise and permissioned blockchain contexts.

The efficiency of the proposed solution is measured in terms of the resource utilization with the varying number of nodes. As shown in Fig. 4, the CPU and load average usage scale in a predictable manner as node count increases.

CPU utilization and system load both rise linearly, while RAM usage remains minimal even at higher scales. The spikes in CPU usage at higher node counts can be addressed

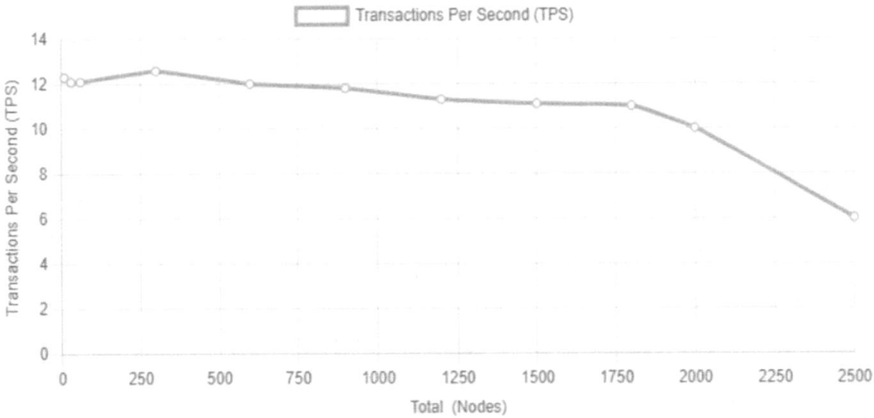

Fig. 2. Throughput of the proposed solutions.

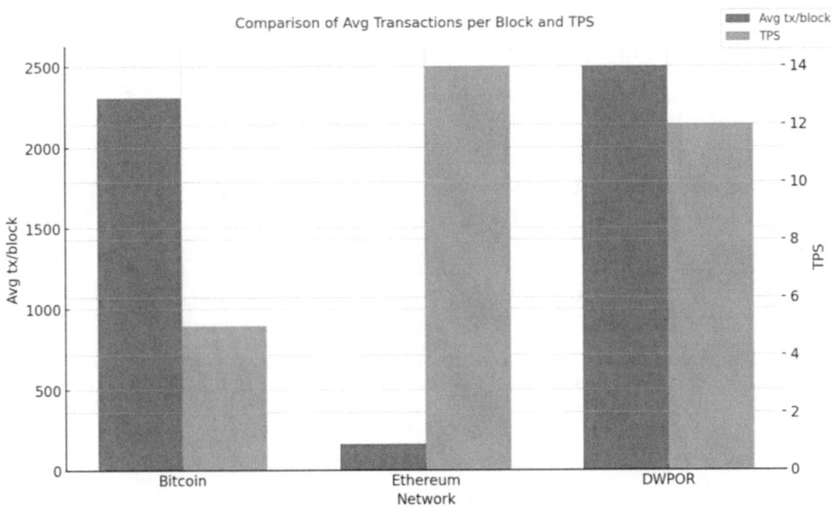

Fig. 3. Comparative analysis in terms of average transactions per block and throughput.

in future through batching and concurrency improvements. In general, the proposed solution can be scaled to moderate-to-large networks without imposing prohibitive system requirements, making it practical for demanding enterprise deployments.

In Fig. 5 shows a steady and moderate increase in block confirmation latency as the blockchain grows. The proposed solution maintains the predictable and manageable latency, even as block height exceeds 1000. This highlights the robustness and scalability of the proposed solution, ensuring the timely confirmation of the transactions.

In Fig. 6 the performance of the proposed consensus with the standard fabric solution as a baseline comparison. The proposed solution outperforms existing solution.

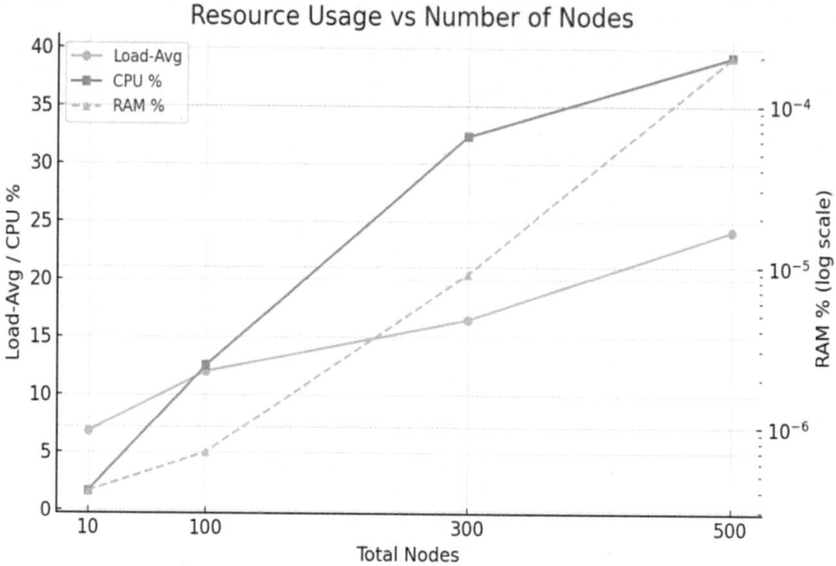

Fig. 4. Resource usage of the proposed solution with the varying number of nodes.

From the experimental results of the proposed solution, it is observed that the proposed solution achieves high scalability and block-packing up to hundreds of nodes, predictable resource utilization and stable performance under increasing load, stable latency and high throughput, validating the feasibility for the real applications.

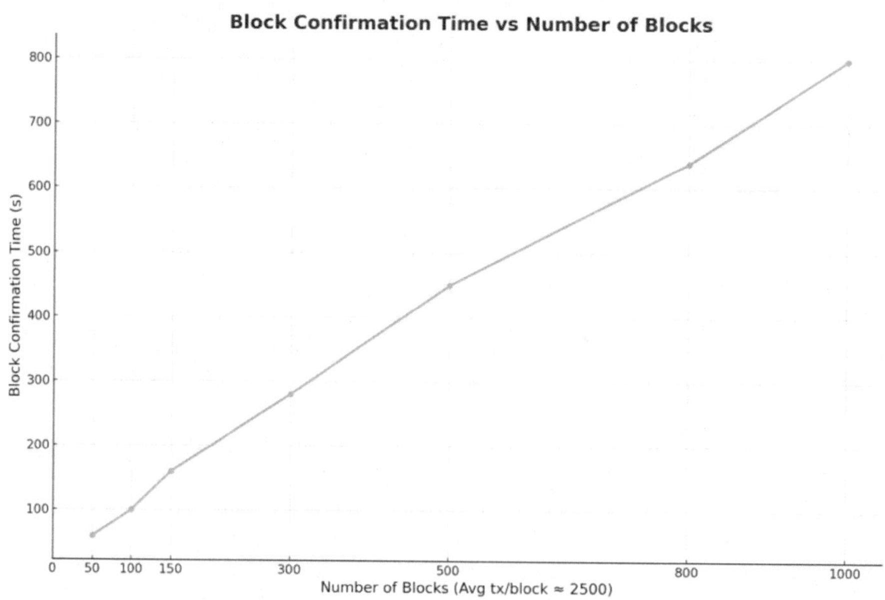

Fig. 5. Block confirmation latency vs. ledger height in the proposed solution.

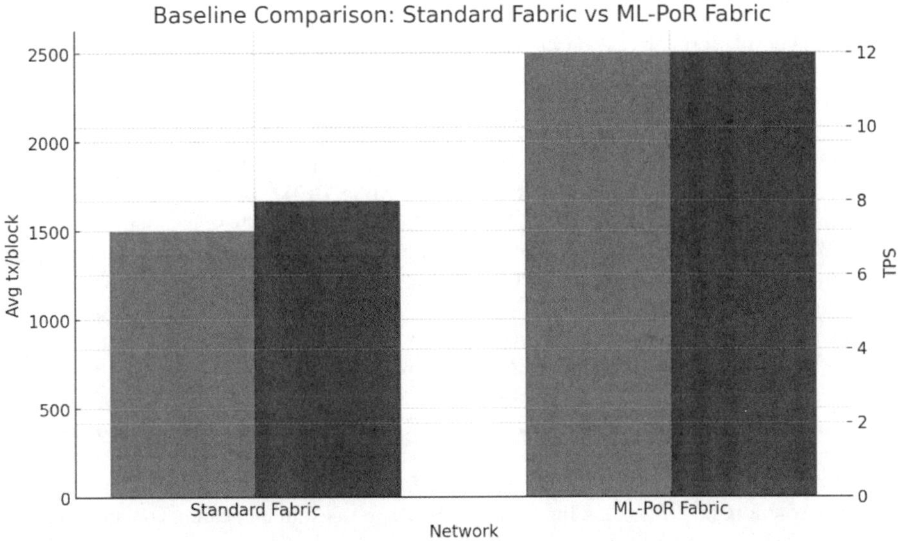

Fig. 6. Performance of the standard fabric vs. proposed Ml-PoR based fabric.

5 Conclusion

It has been observed that scalability and trustworthy block generation are major requirement of the blockchain for the wide adoption in various domains. The major reason behind affecting the blockchain scalability is the underlaying heavy weight consensus mechanisms. The existing on-chain and off-chain solutions need to be reinvestigated or extended to address the blockchain scalability issue. The proposed solution in this paper has considered on-chain as well as off-chain solution, wherein the proof of reputation is applied on-chain, while reputation score of each node is dynamically calculated by the machine learning technique off-chain using the behavioral metrics such as active participation, transparency, compliance and stake. This helps to select the most reliable nodes, ensuring a balanced trade-off between scalability, decentralization, and security. The proposed solution is tested and validated on Hyperledger Fabric, wherein reputation score of each node is updated using Stochastic Gradient Descent regression. The experimental results are very encouraging to make a future blockchain, a scalable, reliable and trusted framework for various applications.

References

1. Nakamoto, S.: Bitcoin Whitepaper, https://bitcoin.org/bitcoin, last Accessed 15 Oct 2025.
2. Kaur, G., Gandhi, C.: Scalability in Blockchain: challenges and solutions. In: Handbook of Research on Blockchain Technology, pp. 373–406. Academic (2020)
3. Buterin, V.: Ethereum's white paper, https://github.com/ethereum/wiki/wiki/White-Paper, last Accessed 15 Oct 2025.

4. Werth, J., Hajian Berenjestanaki, M., Barzegar, H., El Ioini, N., Pahl, C.: A review of Blockchain platforms based on the scalability, security and decentralization trilemma. In: Proceedings of the 25th International Conference on Enterprise Information Systems (ICEIS 2023), pp. 146–155. Czech Republic, Prague (2023)
5. Vernekar, A., Kshirsagar, A., Pachghare, V.K.: Sharding-based scalability enhancement of Blockchain-based health application. In: 2023 International Conferences on Circuit Power and Computing Technologies (ICCPCT), pp. 901–906 (2023)
6. Kumar, A., Sangoi, A., Raj, S., Kiran, M.: ShardCons – a Sharding based consensus algorithm for Blockchain. In: 2021 IEEE International Conference on Electronics, Computing and Communication Technologies (CONECCT), pp. 1–6 (2021)
7. Rahman, F., Titouna, C., Nait-Abdesselam, F.: Prioritised Sharding: a novel approach to enhance Blockchain scalability. In: 2023 5th Conference on Blockchain Research Apps for Innovative Networks and Services (BRAINS), pp. 1–2 (2023)
8. Shirodkar, S., Kulkarni, K., Khanjode, R., Kohle, S., Deshmukh, P., Patil, P.: Layer 2 solutions to improve the scalability of Blockchain. In: 2022 5th International Conference on Advances in Science and Technology (ICAST), pp. 54–57 (2022)
9. Mve, W., Yeluripati, G.: Total commit and transaction off-chains (TCTOC): a Blockchain scalability solution. In: 2023 IEEE Int. Conf. On Electronics, Communication and Measurement (ICECCME), pp. 1–5 (2023)
10. Kim, S., Lee, S., Jeong, C., Cho, S.: Byzantine fault tolerance based multi-block consensus algorithm for throughput scalability. In: 2020 International Conference on Electronics, Information, and Communication (ICEIC), pp. 1–3 (2020)
11. Kuzlu, M., Pipattanasomporn, M., Gurses, L., Rahman, S.: Performance analysis of a Hyperledger fabric Blockchain framework: throughput, latency and scalability. In: 2019 IEEE International Conference on Blockchain, pp. 536–540 (2019)
12. Narwal, S., Basant, B., Ishant, I., Fatima, N.: Evaluating the impact of consensus mechanisms on Blockchain-based data security: a systematic review. In: 2024 3rd Edition of IEEE Delhi Section Flagship Conference (DELCON), pp. 1–5 (2024)
13. A Blockchain Platform for the Enterprise, https://hyperledger-fabric.readthedocs.io/en/release-2.5/, last Accessed 15 Oct 2025
14. Srinivasan, A.: Stochastic Gradient Descent — Clearly Explained, https://towardsdatascience.com/stochastic-gradient-descent-clearly-explained-53d239905d31, last Accessed 15 Oct 2025

Security-Aware Resource Constraints in Cyber Physical Systems: A Simulation-Based Performance Analysis

Rupali Chandrakar(✉) and Madhukrishna Priyadarsini

Department of Computer Science and Engineering, National Institute of Technology Raipur, Raipur, India
{rchandrakar.phd2024.cse,mpriyadarsini.cse}@nitrr.ac.in

Abstract. Cyber-Physical Systems (CPS) integrate computation, networking, and physical processes to enable intelligent automation across domains such as transportation, agriculture, and healthcare. However, these systems often operate under strict resource constraints; limited bandwidth, computational power, energy availability which can hinder their performance. Ensuring robust security and system reliability in such environments is challenging, as conventional security protocols may exacerbate latency or resource consumption. Current CPS solutions often lack comprehensive performance assessments under these combined pressures, leading to suboptimal system designs. To address this gap, a detailed performance evaluation is crucial for resource allocation and secure system design. In this study, we observe and simulate four CPS models under controlled resource-constrained scenarios: FDIA-CPS, Doppel BFT, SDN-based flow anomaly detection, and tri-parametric fractional frequency control. Throughput, latency, error rate, delay, settling time, and decay rate are among the important parameters that are evaluated. The research uncovers significant trade-offs, including a throughput of 99.80 packets per second at a delay of 200 milliseconds, so enhancing the overall understanding and emphasize the performance limits under simultaneous limitations. Critical trade-offs are revealed by our results: the SDN-based model maintains a minimum 0.00002% error rate under strict limitations, whereas the TFC model achieves 99.80 packet/s throughput with 200 ms latency. CPS research is advanced by these discoveries, which offer useful advice for effective CPS deployment and more in-depth investigation of practical uses.

Keywords: Cyber-Physical Systems (CPS) · Resource Constraints · Security · Latency · Error Rate · Decay Rate · Performance Analysis

1 Introduction

A Cyber-Physical System (CPS) connect sensors and actuators through networked connections, combining computer with physical process in the real world.

G. K. Verma et al. (Eds.): MIND 2025, CCIS 2981, pp. 435–448, 2027.
https://doi.org/10.1007/978-3-032-31230-3_35

This enables feedback loops to be used by digital systems to communicate with the physical world. Smart grids, autonomous cars, industrial automation, healthcare systems, and smart cities all employ CPS to increase dependability, efficiency, and safety. Latency, cyber security threats, low bandwidth, and system resilience are some of the main issues that CPS must deal with. CPS success is frequently assessed using a number of important metrics, including Throughput is the amount of data that is successfully sent over the network per unit of time; latency is the amount of time it takes for data to move from its source to its destination; error rate is the percentage of data that is lost or corrupted; and delay is the total amount of time spent communicate, including processing and network congestion; (V) Settling time: the amount of time needed for the system's output to stabilize within a predetermined range of its ultimate value;(Vi) Decay rate: the rate at which system oscillations diminish, expressed as: decay rate $= \zeta\,\omega_n$; where ζ is the damping ratio and ω is the natural frequency (rad/s). Monitoring these metrics is essential to ensure that CPS operates efficiently and securely, particularly under constrained resources or adverse conditions. In addition to resource limitations, security remains a critical consideration in CPS design and operation. Figure1 presents a generic overview of common security threats within a CPS environment.

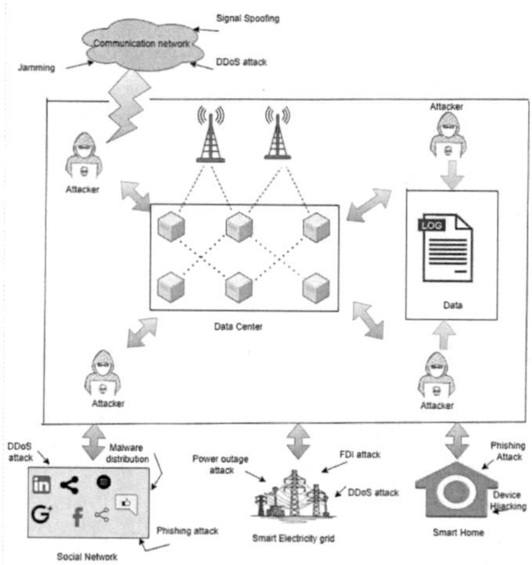

Fig. 1. Cybersecurity Threats in a Smart Grid (Advanced CPS Environment).

Several studies have explored security analysis and resource constraints in the CPS domain. (i) To address DDoS in SDN, a flow-level anomaly detection framework [4] employs random forest and information gain for feature selection with an LSTM-autoencoder, achieving high accuracy with minimal end-to-end latency and controller throughput overhead. This work suggests suitability for real-time deployment in resource sensitive SDN-CPS settings. (ii) Doppel BFT [5] is a blockchain consensus technique for cyber-physical systems (CPS) that uses two leaders in each round to reach agreement rapidly, even if one of the leaders fails. Doppel's dual-leader design ensures that it has less latency and can recover faster when a leader fails. This makes it better for real-time, dependable CPS applications. (iii) To overcome attacker resource constraints in multisensor CPS, an optimal false-data-injection [8] is developed as a convex sensor selection strategy to maximize remote estimation error covariance, with a Gaussian-noise replacement scheme capable of DoS-level degradation while remaining stealthy to conventional detectors. (iv) For grid CPS under communication delays and stealthy attacks, a tri-parametric fractional controller for Automatic Generation Control (AGC) is designed in [2] using complex root boundary analysis. This is tuned by an improved equilibrium optimizer with improved frequency stability under False Data Injection Attack (FDIA) without additional control loops.

However, none of these works bring together security features and system-level resource management in one unified CPS design. This leaves a gap in creating systems that can handle real-time resource allocation while also staying resilient against attacks across the network, control, and sensing layers. In this work, we have modeled the performance of the above four notable contributions by evaluating key metrics such as throughput, latency, delay, error rate, settling time, and decay rate. While our method directly solves the gap, these works ignore the trade-off between implementing resource limits and security measures in CPS at the same time. The major contributions of our research are as follows;

1. Comprehensive Performance Assessment: To estimate existing CPS techniques, we have developed a comprehensive performance matrix based on the following crucial metrics: throughput, latency, delay, error rate, settling time, and decay rate.
2. Concurrent Assessment of Security and Resource Limitations: Our simultaneous assessment of security measures and resource limitations has address a significant research gap, which is essential for real-time, resource-constrained CPS systems.
3. Analysis of Trade-offs: In order to provide useful information for optimizing the CPS architecture, we have presented a comparative analysis that shows the trade-offs between resource usage and performance.
In their original publications, the four CPS models examined in this study-FDIA, SDN-based detection, Doppel BFT, and Tri-Parametric Fractional Control were assessed differently, utilizing different datasets, assumptions, and performance criteria, making direct comparison challenging. To overcome this constraint, we provide a single simulation framework that evaluates each of the four models using the same set of measurement parameters and operational conditions. There are several difficulties in simulating these models collectively, because each system depends on distinct datasets and parameter configurations, their performance metrics must be made consistent for equitable comparison, and the attack scenarios must remain identical across all configurations. The main contributions of this work, building on these challenges and motivations, are as follows: we create a unified evaluation framework for four CPS models; we generate realistic datasets for both nor-

mal and attack scenarios; we examine performance using latency, throughput, delay, error rate, settling time, and decay rate; and finally, we provide a clear comparison of all models under common conditions.

This is how the rest of the paper is structured: According to a study of related literature in Sect. 2, there aren't lots of integrated strategies that manage resource limits and security in cyber-physical systems (CPS). The approach and suggested simulation framework for conduct a thorough performance review are explained in Sect. 3. Our method for evaluating resource constraints and security methods simultaneously is presented in Sect. 4. A thorough trade-off analysis of the balance between resource usage and performance seen in all assessed methods is given in Sect. 5. In Sect. 6, the research is finally concluded and future approaches are outlined, with a focus on maximizing CPS under resource and security constraints.

2 Literature Survey

This section highlights existing research on performance optimization, security mechanisms, and resource management in Cyber-Physical Systems (CPS).

Tang et al. [11] used FlexRay to solve the tracking control issue in CPS, utilizing its flexibility and time determinism to improve system performance. Their method showed potential for use in industrial automation, smart grids, and vehicle management despite its expense and complexity. Liu et al. [3] To address secure fusion estimate in CPS under replay threats and bandwidth limitations, a Distributed Kalman Fusion Estimator (DKFE) was proposed. Their approach proved successful when tested on the IEEE 4-bus system, but these constraints in power and industrial systems continue to provide a hurdle to estimating performance. Zhou et al. [1] presented a Gaussian-based privacy and asynchronous aggregation P2P federated learning architecture for mobile robotic systems that was tried in the construction of underground tunnels. Despite its effectiveness, the method has drawbacks because it depends on reliable third-party devices and has large computational costs. Mehta et al. [9] suggested a three-parametric fractional-order controller for time-delay systems that integrates P2P asynchronous model aggregation and Gaussian processes. The approach, which was illustrated through a case study on tunnel building, has promise for production and navigation but was constrained by factors like high computing cost and dependence on reliable third-party devices.

Hu et al. [6] developed a robust controller for load frequency control in islanded AC microgrids under FDIA and DoS attacks, using a piecewise observer and time-varying Lyapunov function. Validated through simulations, the method proved effective but faced limitations such as complex computations and sensitivity to DoS attack duration, with applications in smart grids and secure energy systems. Y. Wu et al. [12] investigated resonance attacks on smart grid load frequency control, proposing a modeling approach based on load modulation, though limited by the complexity of the governor-turbine model. Kumar et al. [7]

proposed a GJO-tuned FIMC-PID controller for resilient frequency-shifting control under FDIA and communication delays, using Routh stability and ITSE minimization. Validated through MATLAB/Simulink and OPAL-RT HIL simulation on a dual-area thermal system, the method supports grid stability and cyber-attack mitigation but may be less effective against certain DoS attacks. Mohammadi et al. [10] proposed a Load Frequency Control (LFC) approach using a disturbance observer-based sliding mode controller to mitigate simultaneous FDI and DoS attacks in microgrids. While simulations demonstrated improved stability and cyber-resilience, the method involves high computational complexity and depends on specific assumptions about attack scenarios, making it suitable for critical infrastructures like military, remote, and healthcare systems. Zhang et al. citech35zhang2022hsps presented a successful frequency-shifting control technique for networked power systems vulnerable to communication delays and False Data Injection Attacks (FDIA). According to simulations, the system outperforms traditional methods, which makes it especially useful for ensure dependable and safe functioning in modern smart grids. Even when there is latency or data manipulation, adaptive control maintain frequency stability. Table 1 summarizes current options along with their drawbacks.

3 Simulation Framework and Methodology

This section describes the methodological approach and the simulation environment used to conduct a thorough performance evaluation of selected CPS techniques, including the models presented in [2,4,5,8]. Throughput, delay, latency, error rate, settling time, and decay rate are evaluated under both normal and resource-limited conditions, taking into account system resource constraints and security considerations. The complete simulation setup and implementation workflow, illustrated in Fig. 2, examines the efficiency and behaviour of these CPS methodologies when operating under practical scenarios involving resource limitations and cyber threats.

3.1 Simulation Setup

Four CPS models [2,4,5,8] have been simulated for attack (DoS, FDIA) and optimization in MATLAB R2023b. Python 3.10 is used to calculate performance measurements and conduct DDoS attacks on network traffic. We have generated and analyzed packets using the python package Scapy, and NS-3 is used to calculate packet loss and send data over a network. The simulation is conducted on a machine having Intel Core i7-12700 CPU, 32 GB RAM, Ubuntu 22.04 LTS. Each simulation scenario included both normal operating conditions and adverse conditions introduced by resource limitations and attacks.

3.2 CPS Model

We have simulated four distinct CPS models derived from existing research, each with unique architectural characteristics and security considerations:

Table 1. Comparison of existing approaches for CPS security and control.

S. No.	References	Methodology	**Experimental setup/parameters used**	Limitations
1	Tang et al. [11]	FlexRay-based tracking control solution for CPS	FlexRay communication network in automated systems	Complex and costly system
2	Zhou et al. [1]	P2P federated learning with asynchronous aggregation and Gaussian mechanism	Case study on tunnel robots in mobile robotic systems	High computation cost and dependency on trusted devices
3	Mehta et al. [9]	Tri-parametric $FOI\lambda D^{1-\lambda}$ controller using fractional calculus and Gaussian process	Case study on tunnel construction robots	Computational burden and reliance on trusted third parties
4	Hu et al. [6]	Robust LFC controller using piecewise observer and time-varying Lyapunov function	Simulated islanded AC microgrids under FDI/DoS attacks	High complexity and dependence on DoS duration
5	Wu et al. [12]	Resonance-based LFC attack modeling using RoCoF	Single/multi-area LFC models with AVR and PSS	Attack limited by governorturbine model complexity
6	Kumar et al. [7]	GJO-optimized FIMC-PID controller with ITSE minimization and Routh analysis	MATLAB/Simulink, OPAL-RT on dual-area thermal system	Reduced performance under specific DoS scenarios
7	Mohammadi et al. [10]	LFC with disturbance observer-based sliding mode controller under FDIA and DoS	Microgrid simulations for cyberattack scenarios	High complexity and assumptions on attack models
8	Zhang et al. [13]	Adaptive frequency-shifting control for communication-delayed CPS under FDI	Simulations on networked smart grids	Computation cost and dependency on adaptive tuning

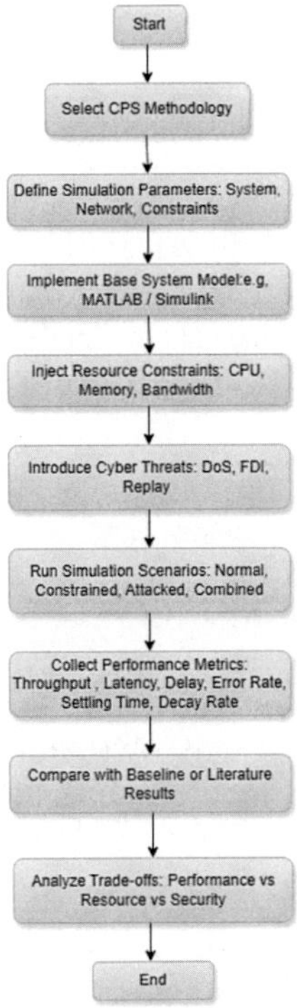

Fig. 2. Simulation setup and implementation procedure flow.

1. FDIA-CPS Model (False Data Injection Attack) [8]: This model is based on a linear discrete-time state-space system, where a Kalman filter is used for state estimation. In this, accurate state estimation is difficult due to intentional data tampering by an attacker with only partial system knowledge. Attackers aim to maximize disruption by injecting false data, blocking sensors, or adding noise, but available resources to characterize such optimal attacks are limited.
2. SDN-Based Flow Anomaly Detection Architecture [4]: This model works on an SDN network, where one main controller watch all the traffic. It picks important features from the network data and checks for anything unusual using simple measures like entropy and statistics. It also uses machine learning to find irregular patterns. The main purpose of this model is to detect DDoS attack traffic, so it is particularly designed to identify signs of DDoS-related problems.
3. Doppel BFT Consensus Architecture [5]: This decentralized approach uses a Byzantine Fault Tolerance (BFT) consensus method, where the system continues to operate correctly even if some nodes behave incorrectly. It also incorporates speculative execution to improve overall performance. In a network of $3f+1$ nodes, the system can safely tolerate up to f faulty or malicious nodes. This design enables the network to achieve secure and low-latency con-

sensus, even when certain components of the distributed CPS are unreliable or compromised.

4. Tri-parametric Fractional Frequency Control (TFC) Model [2]: This model employ a unique tri-parametric fractional-order controller for a two-area microgrid in order to keep the system frequency constant under erratic situation. Cyber problems that could affect the microgrid include high latency, delays, and data loss. To overcome these obstacle, the controller is altered using Evolutionary Optimization (EO) techniques, maintaining system stability and reducing the impact of cyberattacks.

3.3 Performance Metrics

To review the performance and robustness of the CPS models, six evaluation metrics are used: throughput, delay, error rate, latency, settling time, and decay rate. Together, these metrics offer a complete sympathetic of system behaviour under different network conditions and potential attack situations.

a) Throughput: The quantity of data that is successfully sent over a network in a specific length of time. It is calculated as Throughput (bps) $= \frac{\text{Total received data (in bits)}}{\text{Time (in seconds)}}$.

b) Delay: Delay denotes the time taken for a data packet to travel from the source to its intended destination. This metric helps assess the impact of network congestion and cyberattacks on timely data delivery. It is defined as Delay = Arrival Time − Transmission Time.

c) Error Rate: The error rate quantifies the reliability of data transmission by measuring the proportion of packets that are either lost or corrupted during transit. A high error rate indicates vulnerability to disruptions/attacks. It is given by Error Rate (%) $= \left(\frac{\text{Error Packets}}{\text{Total Sent Packets}}\right) \times 100$.

d)Latency: Latency represents the total time elapsed between the initiation of data transmission and the successful receipt and acknowledgment of the data. It is expressed as Latency = Propagation Delay + Processing Delay + Transmission Delay + Queueing Delay.

e) Settling Time: The *settling time* T_s, defined as the time for a system's output to reach and stay within a given percentage (usually 2% or 5%) of its final steady-state value following a disturbance or input change (like a step input), for a second-order underdamped system with transfer function $G(s) = \frac{\omega_n^2}{s^2+2\zeta\omega_n s+\omega_n^2}$, is approximately $T_s \approx \frac{4}{\zeta\omega_n}$ for the 2% criterion and $T_s \approx \frac{3}{\zeta\omega_n}$ for the 5% criterion, where ω_n is the natural frequency and ζ is the damping ratio.

f) Decay Rate: The *decay rate* describes how quickly a system's response decreases (or decays) over time after being excited by an input and is given by Decay Rate $= \zeta\,\omega_n$, where ζ is the damping ratio and ω_n is the natural frequency (rad/s).

The major simulation and configuration parameters for each of the four models are shown in Table 2.

We assess the security and stability responses of all four CPS models using a unified and consistent methodology. Each model is evaluated under its rel-

Table 2. Simulation and configuration Parameters

Parameter	Value(s)
Packet Size	512 Bytes–1500 Bytes
Bandwidth	10 Mbps–100 Mbps
Number of Nodes	5–100 nodes (depending on model)
Simulation Time	100 - 1000 s
Traffic Types	TCP, UDP, ICMP, HTTP, DDoS (SYN flood)
Topologies	Mesh, Ring, Star, Tree
Control Sample Time	0.01–0.1 s
Bandwidth Constraint	1 Mbps (constrained scenarios)
CPU Allocation (Resource-Limited)	40% of baseline capacity
Attack Window	Randomized, typically 100–200 s
FDI Injection Frequency	Once every 5 time steps
DoS Attack Rate	1000 packets/sec (flooding)
Controller Sampling Rate	10 Hz
Load Conditions	Low (10–30), Medium (30–70), High (70–95) packets/s

evant security condition. The TFC model is tested under latency variations and cyberattacks. The FDIA model is evaluated using false-data injection on sensor streams. The SDN-based model is tested with attack versus normal network flows. The Doppel model is examined for stability changes under attack-induced disturbances. Settling time and decay rate are included as stability metrics because they show how quickly a system returns to normal behavior after disruptions such as attacks, abnormal traffic, or resource constraints. These metrics provide a common basis for evaluating stability and recovery behavior across all four CPS models.

3.4 Simulation Scenarios

We have designed multiple test scenarios to assess system robustness and adaptability such as: (a) Baseline (No attack) Normal operation under standard traffic. (b) Under Attack FDIA, DDoS, and BFT fault injection scenarios to test system resilience. (c) Varying Load Conditions High (70–95), medium (30–70), and low (10–30) packets/s to observe congestion and delay. (d) Network Dynamics Simulations with mobile nodes and link failures. This study involved the simulation of four CPS models—FDIA-CPS, SDN-based detection, Doppel BFT, and Tri-Parametric Fractional Control—under controlled situation to make easy a fair comparison. Prior to the imposition of resource constraints, all models were assess under a baseline configuration characterized by full CPU capacity, unrestricted memory, normal bandwidth levels, and complete energy availability for each node. This baseline enables clear observation of performance variations under reduced resources, ensuring that the "Resource-Constrained" scenario is scientifically comparable and reproducible. Following the establishment of the baseline, we implement limited bandwidth, reduced CPU allocation, and constrained energy levels, in conjunction with attack configurations relevant to each model. Performance metrics, including latency, throughput, delay, error rate, settling time, and decay rate, are calculated for both baseline and constrained conditions.

3.5 Validation

To guarantee the authenticity of the original study, we have performed the following validation steps:

1. **Parameter Replication:** All simulation parameters throughput, latency, error rate, delay, settling time, decay rate are chosen to correspond with the respective research works.
2. **Architecture Matching:** The control logic and network architectures; (i) Software Defined-Networking architecture [4], (ii) two area thermal-power system AGC framework with tri-oarametric fractional controller [2], (iii) multisensor remote state estimation CPS with centralized kalman filter and (iv) resource-limited attack model [8], Doppel consensus protocol [5] are replicated exactly as described in the original studies.
3. **Metric Cross-Verification:** The output metrics, including throughput and delay, are cross-checked against the results reported in the literature.
4. **Scenario Replication:** Mobility models, network dynamics, and attack patterns are carefully reproduced to match the conditions outlined in the cited studies.

4 Result Analysis

This section presents the simulation results and provides a comparative analysis of the four CPS models evaluated: FDIA-CPS [8], SDN-based Flow Anomaly Detection [4], Doppel BFT Consensus [5], and Tri-parametric Fractional Frequency Control (TFC) [2]. The models were tested in a range of condition, including combined stress, resource limitations, cyber attacks (FDIA, DoS), and regular operation. The following important measures were used to estimate performance: throughput, delay, error rate, latency, settling time, and decay rate. The Table 3 display the outcomes of the comparison under typical circumstances. In this case, FDIA is quick but less dependable because of the substantial packet loss. Doppel offers great throughput with moderate reliability, SDN-based is very dependable but slow, and the triparametric approach offers low latency, very low error rate, and little packet loss, which together provide the most efficient and well-balanced performance.

The Fig. 3 comparisons provide a comprehensive evaluation of the four CPS models; FDIA-CPS, SDN-Based Flow Detection, Doppel BFT Consensus, and Tri-parametric Fractional Control (TFC) across varying operational conditions. The findings of the Fig. 3 are as follows:

Table 3. Performance Metrics of CPS Models under Normal Condition

S. No	Research Work	Latency	Throughput	Error Rate	Delay	Settling Time	Decay Rate
1	FDIA [8]	0.050094 s	15.998 packet/s	20.00%	50.094 s	0.652 s	0.000091 1/s
2	SDN-based [4]	6.89973 s	101.30 packet/s	0.00002%	6899.73 s	0.3159 s	0.000034 1/s
3	Doppel [5]	0.1451 s	200.00 packet/s	11.20%	0.1451 s	0.6006 s	6.921 1/s
4	Tri-Parametric [2]	0.1985 s	99.81 packet/s	3.17%	0.1985 s	0.1165 s	0.0010 1/s

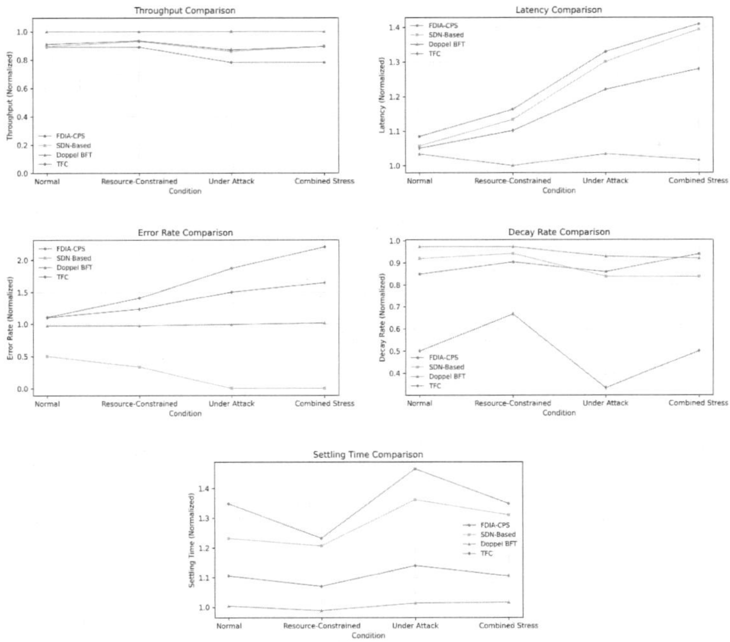

Fig. 3. Performance comparison of CPS models under various conditions.

1. The Doppel BFT and TFC model shown notable constancy in terms of throughput across all scenarios and continued to function consistently under combined stress conditions thanks to their self-directed problem-solving and modification capabilities. Despite its initial high throughput, the SDN-Based model drastically degraded when subjected to resource limitations and assault scenarios. Conversely, the FDIA-CPS model saw the largest fall, indicating that it is susceptible to data injection and system overload caused by erroneous data or an excess of resources.
2. Examining delay, the FDIA-CPS and SDN-Based models show a visible increase in constrained and unresponsive scenarios, suggesting inadequate security and control. Doppel BFT and TFC were capable to effectively manage delay, whereas TFC profited from their enhanced controller design. The error rate study also showed how easily phony data may be inserted into

FDIA-CPS, resulting in serious data contamination. In contrast, Doppel BFT and TFC consistently maintained low error rates, shown strong resilience, adaptable reaction mechanisms, and reliable operation even when face with resource limitations or attacks.

3. Due to its efficient and flexible control mechanism, the TFC model demonstrated the lowest response times and the highest latency performance, still in complex or dynamic environments. Remaining well below sensible limits, the Doppel BFT model also maintained minimal latency, with its consensus mechanisms just marginally increasing it. For time-sensitive CPS applications, however, the FDIA-CPS and SDN-Based models proved unsuitable due to their high latency under stress, mostly due to centralized control and vulnerability to sensor or data attacks.

In terms of overall performance across all parameters, the TFC model was the most robust and balanced, while Doppel BFT showed exceptional resilience with insignificant latency trade-offs. As per these results, CPS systems need to manage resource constraints, security threats, and performance all at once. Our simulation approach effectively reflects this need.

4.1 Discussion of Results

The results indicate separate performance variations among the four CPS models: SDN has the greatest delay yet the minimal error rate, Doppel attains the highest throughput, FDIA-CPS offer the lowest latency, and TFC deliver the quickest settling time. The throughput of the SDN model declines under stress due to the centralized controller being a bottleneck under high traffic and attack flows, while the ML-based feature selection elevates CPU load under constrained resources. The FDIA-CPS model exhibits heightened vulnerability under resource constraints, as diminished CPU capacity, reduced bandwidth, and increased latency impair its capacity to authenticate sensor data, hence exacerbate the impact of false-data injections and elevating packet loss and instability.

5 Tradeoff Analysis

Our comparative simulations show how each model react to rising stress and highlight the compromises necessary to preserve functionality.

Because it depends on clean input, the FDIA-CPS model suffers from resource constraints or erroneous data, yet under optimal circumstances, it provides accurate state estimation through Kalman filtering. Although the SDN-based anomaly detection model uses statistical and machine learning techniques to handle massive traffic and is successful against DDoS attacks, it increases latency and demands a lot of processing resources. In distributed CPS environments, the Doppel BFT model offers high reliability by using Byzantine Fault Tolerance to tolerate compromised nodes, though with some latency due to consensus overhead. Long-term stability is guaranteed by the TFC model

(Tri-parametric Fractional Control), which offers the best overall balance with high resilience, low latency and error, and adaptability to limits compensated by the initial computing cost of its optimization phase.

Table 4 clearly summarizes the trade-offs between performance, security, and resource utilization across the evaluated models.

Table 4. Comparative Trade-off Summary of CPS Models

Model	Strengths	Trade-offs / Weaknesses	Best Suited For
FDIA-CPS [8]	High estimation accuracy under ideal conditions	Vulnerable to attacks; significant error increase under constraints	Structured, attack-free environments
SDN-Based [4]	Effective in detecting DDoS; supports high throughput	High latency; heavy reliance on computation and central control	SDN traffic monitoring and anomaly detection
Doppel BFT [5]	Fault-tolerant; secure consensus among distributed nodes	Slightly increased latency due to consensus mechanisms	Distributed systems requiring high integrity and resilience
TFC (Fractional) [2]	Resilient, low-latency, stable under attacks and delays	Computationally expensive optimization during setup	Real-time control in constrained, hostile environments

6 Conclusion and Future Work

In conclusion, we compared four different CPS architectures using simulations under combined resource constraints and cyber attacks. We examine the performance of each of our representative instances in more sensible operational situations using measures including throughput, delay, error rate, latency, settling time, and decay rate. In contrast to FDIA-CPS and SDN architectures, which are more affected by constrained and hostile environments, the TFC model is the most stable, as shown by the fact that, in low-bandwidth conditions, we achieve a throughput of 99.80 packets per second and a latency of 200 ms. The Doppel model is robust in the presence of faulty nodes, with an error rate of about 11.20% percent. The findings highlight the need to take adversary security into account when designing CPS for systems operating in resource-constrained contexts. Future CPS trade-offs might be better understood with the help of our simulation approach. Future research will be required to extend our findings to hardware-in-the-loop, account for energy consumption, model increasingly complex attacker scenarios, and implement powerful AI control strategies for systems with real-time resource constraints.

Code Availability: https://github.com/Rupa52-lang/Performance-Analysis

References

1. et al., Z.: Decentralized p2p federated learning for privacy-preserving and resilient mobile robotic systems. IEEE Wireless Commun,.**30**(2), 82–89 (2023)
2. Aryan, P., Raja, G.L., Mehta, U., Chelliah, T.R., Muduli, U.R.: A resilient tri-parametric fractional frequency control for cybersecurity threats amid latency. IEEE Trans. Ind. Appl. (2025)
3. Chen, B., Ho, D.W., Hu, G., Yu, L.: Secure fusion estimation for bandwidth constrained cyber-physical systems under replay attacks. IEEE Trans. Cybernet. **48**(6), 1862–1876 (2017)
4. El Sayed, M.S., Le-Khac, N.A., Azer, M.A., Jurcut, A.D.: A flow-based anomaly detection approach with feature selection method against ddos attacks in sdns. IEEE Trans. Cognitive Commun. Netw. **8**(4), 1862–1880 (2022)
5. Hao, R., Dai, X., Xie, X.: Doppel: a bft consensus algorithm for cyber-physical systems with low latency. J. Syst. Architect. **148**, 103087 (2024)
6. Hu, S., Ge, X., Chen, X., Yue, D.: Resilient load frequency control of islanded ac microgrids under concurrent false data injection and denial-of-service attacks. IEEE Trans. Smart Grid **14**(1), 690–700 (2022)
7. Kumar, N., Aryan, P., Raja, G.L., Muduli, U.R.: Robust frequency-shifting based control amid false data injection attacks for interconnected power systems with communication delay. IEEE Trans. Ind. Appl. **60**(2), 3710–3723 (2024)
8. Li, F., Tang, Y.: False data injection attack for cyber-physical systems with resource constraint. IEEE Trans. Cybernet. **50**(2), 729–738 (2018)
9. Mehta, U., Aryan, P., Raja, G.L.: Tri-parametric fractional-order controller design for integrating systems with time delay. IEEE Trans. Circuits Syst. II Express Briefs **70**(11), 4166–4170 (2023)
10. Mohammadi, K., Azizi, E., Choi, J., Hamidi-Beheshti, M.T., Bidram, A., Bolouki, S.: Asynchronous periodic distributed event-triggered voltage and frequency control of microgrids. IEEE Trans. Power Syst. **36**(5), 4524–4538 (2021)
11. Tang, Y., Zhang, D., Ho, D.W., Qian, F.: Tracking control of a class of cyber-physical systems via a flexray communication network. IEEE Trans. Cybernet. **49**(4), 1186–1199 (2018)
12. Wu, Y., Wei, Z., Weng, J., Li, X., Deng, R.H.: Resonance attacks on load frequency control of smart grids. IEEE Trans. Smart Grid **9**(5), 4490–4502 (2017)
13. Zhang, G., Li, J., Bamisile, O., Xing, Y., Cai, D., Huang, Q.: An load frequency control scheme for multi-area power system under cyber-attacks and time-varying delays. IEEE Trans. Power Syst. **38**(2), 1336–1349 (2022)

Learning Multi-Scale Representations with Attention-Driven Feature–Structure Fusion for Link Prediction in Complex Networks

Indu[✉], Kapil Sharma, and Varsha Sisaudia

Department of Information Technology, Delhi Technological University, Delhi, India
{indu_2k22phdit503,kapil,varsha}@dtu.ac.in

Abstract. The link prediction (LP) problem in complex networks aims to forecast potential or future connections between unconnected node pairs. This task has numerous real-life applications where relationships may be modelled as graphs. The majority of traditional approaches rely on structural information and have difficulties in integrating it with node features. Later, an attention mechanism was introduced, though it struggled to adequately balance the contributions of various information types. We propose a multi-scale, multi-modal LP approach that combines structural embeddings and node features through attention-based fusion. The model uses diffusion processes at different neighborhood scales to capture more information, and learns richer node representations by adaptively integrating features and structural patterns. By combining multi-scale diffusion to capture both local and global patterns with an attention-based fusion mechanism to integrate structural and attribute information, our model produces more informative embeddings for effective LP. Experimental findings show that our proposed method consistently outperforms all competing approaches across the three benchmark datasets. In particular, it improves the AUC by 4.46%, 5.34% and 2.07% on Citeseer, Cora and Pubmed respectively over the baseline approaches.

Keywords: Attention · Diffusion · Link Prediction · Multi Scale · Multi Modal

1 Introduction

Graphs give a powerful representation for modeling relationships and interactions among entities in a broad range of fields. In such graphs, the nodes are usually the entities like people, documents or proteins and the relationships or interactions between them are shown in the form of edges. This is a widely used representation, ensuring that graphs have become an essential means of studying social networks, biological systems, citation networks, recommendation systems and knowledge bases. A highly significant activity in this context is the LP task which seeks to predict missing or possible future links between node pairs. The accurate prediction of links is not only essential to comprehend the dynamics of network development, but it also contributes to practices like [1], suggesting connections on social networks identifying hidden protein–protein interactions [2, 3], and completing large-scale knowledge graphs [4].

G. K. Verma et al. (Eds.): MIND 2025, CCIS 2981, pp. 449–461, 2027.
https://doi.org/10.1007/978-3-032-31230-3_36

Early approaches were primarily dependent on heuristic methods [5], where link forecasting was estimated using structural similarity measures such as common neighbors [6] and the Adamic–Adar index [7]. Although these approaches are computationally efficient as they depend only on local structure of network but may overlook higher-order dependencies which often results in weak performance in complex or noisy networks.

To address these limitations, researchers introduced representation learning methods such as node2vec [8] and DeepWalk [9] which learn reduced-dimensional representation of nodes by simulating random walks over the graph. These embeddings preserve network proximity and enable the use of machine learning techniques for LP. These models, though effective, encode structural information and do not pay much attention to node attributes, hence, they are less effective in generalizing to datasets in which node attributes are significant.

More recent developments in Graph Neural Networks (GNNs) have offered a more potent paradigm by modeling both the structure of the graph and the attributes of nodes together. Graph Convolutional Networks (GCNs) [10] generalize the idea of convolution to irregular graph space that allows node features to be pooled together in local neighborhoods. Likewise, Graph Attention Networks (GATs) [11] apply attention mechanisms to learn the significance of neighbors when passing messages and enhance the flexibility of feature aggregation. Nevertheless, it is difficult to apply them directly to LP. Specifically, most GNNs are over-smoothing node features across layers and this results in loss of discriminative power. In addition, GNNs are also frequently constrained by the problem of memory scalability when used on large networks.

In addition to scalability, another critical limitation is the integration of structure and attributes. Existing GNN-based LP methods frequently overemphasize on structure while underutilizing node attributes or they combine both sources of information in strict and preset ways. Furthermore, while attention mechanisms have been explored for node-level tasks as they are less frequently applied to LP to adaptively balance contributions from structure and attributes. This creates a gap in building models that can use different types of information flexibly while still being efficient [12].

In order to address the gaps (scalability, integration of structure and attributes) we present a multi-scale, multi-modal LP model.

The primary contributions of this paper are as follows:

1. We present an attention-based feature fusion framework that adaptively combines structural embeddings and node features for LP.
2. We incorporate multi-scale graph diffusion, enabling the model to learn both local and global structural patterns.
3. Through extensive experiments on benchmark complex networks, we show that our method achieves higher accuracy and efficiency than strong baselines.

In Sect. 2, we review related work on LP, covering heuristic, embedding-based, and GNN approaches. Section 3 presents our proposed methodology, which integrates multi-scale diffusion, attention-based fusion. Section 4 shows experimental results and ablation studies on benchmark datasets, while Sect. 5 concludes the paper with findings and future research directions.

2 Related Work

The problem of LP has been researched extensively with a wide range of methods, including heuristic indices to complex deep learning models. Initial methods were based on similarity measures that were heuristic, including Common Neighbors (CN) [6], which approximates a link by counting the number of shared neighbors between two nodes. Other measures based on similarity, including SimRank [5], built upon this concept by recursively defining the similarity between nodes in terms of the similarity of their neighbors. These algorithms are computationally inexpensive and interpretable, and they mainly use local structural data and are not able to fully model global dependencies or use node attributes, and this restricts their applicability to more complex networks [13].

In order to eliminate the shortcomings of local heuristics, embedding-based methods were proposed. One of the first successful models to learn continuous node embeddings was DeepWalk [9] which used truncated random walks to simulate. DeepWalk, however, does not consider node attributes and only considers structural co-occurrence. The development of GNNs made it possible to jointly model graph structure and node attributes, making a major contribution to LP. Graph Auto-Encoder (GAE) [10] and a probabilistic version, Variational Graph Auto-Encoder (VGAE) [10], are graph convolutional encoders with decoders to predict links directly based on structure and attribute-integrating embeddings. Equally, Graph Convolutional Networks (GCNs) can combine the information of immediate neighbors, and GraphSAGE [14] builds upon this concept by adding inductive properties, enabling the model to generalize to unseen nodes by learning neighborhood aggregation functions. GAT also enhanced flexibility by introducing attention mechanisms that give varied importance weight to neighbors when passing the message. Although successful, these GNN-based methods are commonly associated with over-smoothing node representations during stacking multiple layers, a weakness in long-range structural dependencies, and high memory requirements of large networks. Subgraph-based and hybrid approaches to LP have been investigated in more recent works. The example of SEAL [12] which extracts enclosing subgraphs and uses GNNs to learn on these local structures is a good example. It explicitly encodes both structural patterns and node attributes. SEAL is computationally expensive, although effective. In order to balance between topology and attributes, BSAL [15] and ASLAM [16] models have been suggested. BSAL learns semantic topology from attributes and structural topology from graph connections separately, then combines them with attention. Similarly, ASLAM uses attribute–structure learning and attention, showing that flexibly combining multiple modalities improves robustness. Recent work has also extended link prediction to dynamic and large-scale social networks. A hybrid temporal framework combining GCNs with LSTMs [17] jointly models network structure and its evolution, improving accuracy on evolving social graphs.

Another recent advancement is model-agnostic PU AUC [18] optimization strategy that has been introduced to enhance GNN-based link prediction under class imbalance and unknown negative distributions. Further, graph learning research is extending beyond pairwise relations to capture higher-order network structures. For example, methods using attributed hypergraphs have emerged to model complex user–news interactions and multi-node dependencies in social platforms [19]. Hypergraph neural architectures enable more expressive embeddings by leveraging non-textual and high-order social signals, demonstrating superior performance in tasks such as fake news classification, where relational complexity is high.

Heuristic, embedding, and GNN-based models each have limits: heuristics lack expressiveness, embeddings ignore attributes, GNNs struggle with scalability, and methods like SEAL, BSAL, and ASLAM are computationally heavy or rigid. These issues highlight the need for adaptive fusion of structure and attributes, multi-scale structural modeling, and robustness to missing features. Our work addresses these gaps with a unified, accurate, and efficient framework.

3 Proposed Methodology

3.1 Graph Setup

We assume a graph (undirected) $G = (V, E)$, where $V = \{v_1, v_2, \ldots, v_N\}$ denotes the set of N vertices and E is the set of observed links among them. The adjacency matrix $A \in \mathbb{R}^{N \times N}$ represents the topology of the graph where $A_{ij} = 1$ when there is an edge between node v_i and v_j and $A_{ij} = 0$ when not. Each vertex v_i is associated with a feature vector $x_i \in \mathbb{R}^F$, and the collection of all node features forms the feature matrix $X \in \mathbb{R}^{N \times F}$.

3.2 MultiScale Graph Diffusion

To capture both local and global structural dependencies, we adopt a graph diffusion mechanism. Diffusion may be viewed as spreading node information through multiple steps of the graph, where each node can process not only the information of the immediate neighbors but also the information of the graph nodes that are more than a few hops away. It is modeled by a collection of diffusion matrices $\{P^1, P^2 \ldots, P^K\}$, where P^K is the normalized adjacency matrix to the *k-th* power, which captures the likelihood of going to one node in k steps, starting at one node. The diffused representation of scale k of a specific node v_i is represented by Eq. 1.

$$H^{(k)} = P^k X \tag{1}$$

Here, $H^{(k)} \in \mathbb{R}^{N \times F}$ is the initial node attribute matrix, with each row x_i representing the attributes of node v_i.

3.3 Attention-Based Scale Fusion

Different diffusion scales encode complementary information. To combine them adaptively, we use a learnable attention mechanism. For node v_i, the fused multi-scale representation is computed as in Eq. 2.

$$h_i = \sum_{k=0}^{K} \alpha_i^k H^k \tag{2}$$

where α^k is the attention weight for scale k. These weights are global trainable parameters, normalized with a softmax function in Eq. 3.

$$\alpha^k = \frac{\exp(\theta_k)}{\sum_{j=0}^{k} \exp(\theta_j)}, \text{ where } \Theta_k \text{ is learnable scalar} \tag{3}$$

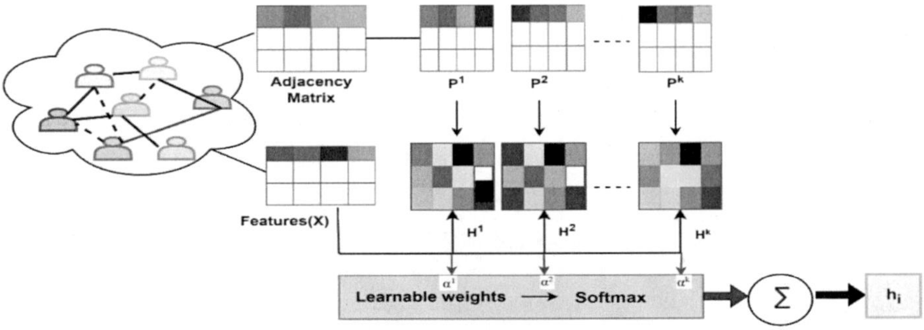

Fig. 1. Illustration of the Multi-Scale Graph Diffusion and Attention Fusion Mechanism

Figure 1 depicts the process of Multi-Scale Graph Diffusion and Attention Fusion Mechanism. Each node in the graph propagates its features (X) through multiple diffusion steps to capture both local and global structural information. The outputs from different diffusion scales are then fused using an attention mechanism, which assigns adaptive weights to each scale to generate the final node representations (h_i).

3.4 Fusion of Structure and Features

In addition to combining multiple diffusion scales, our model fuses two complementary modalities:

- Structural embeddings (H_{struct}), derived from learnable node Identifiers.

  We assign each node a learnable embedding vector in Eq. 4

$$E \in \mathbb{R}^{N \times ds} \tag{4}$$

be a trainable node-identifier matrix, where E_i is the structural embedding of node v_i. These identifiers are propagated through the same multi-scale diffusion in Eq. 5:

$$H^{(k)}{}_{struct} = P_k E \tag{5}$$

- Feature-based embeddings (H_{feat}), projected from node attributes.

  A learnable gate balances the contributions of both modalities in Eq. 6.

$$H = g \cdot H_{struct} + (1 - g) \cdot H_{feat} \tag{6}$$

Where $g \in (0,1)$ is a sigmoid-activated parameter that controls the reliance on structural vs. attribute information.

3.5 Pairwise Representation for Link Prediction

After obtaining the fused node embeddings h_i, we cast the LP task as a binary classification problem. For each candidate node pair (v_i,v_j), we create a pair representation in Eq. 7 [20].

$$z_{ij} = \left[h_i \| h_j \| \left(h_i \odot h_j \right) \| \left| h_i - h_j \right| \right] \tag{7}$$

where $z_{ij} \in \mathbb{R}^{4d}$ is the pair feature vector (with d being the node embedding dimension) and $\|$ denotes concatenation, $\odot$ denotes elementwise multiplication, $-$ denotes absolute difference.

This enriched pair representation is then fed into a Multi-Layer Perceptron (MLP), followed by a sigmoid activation (σ). The probability that an edge exists between nodes v_i and v_j is shown in Eq. 8.

$$y_{ij} = \sigma\left(\mathrm{MLP}\left(z_{ij}\right)\right) \tag{8}$$

$y_{ij} \in (0,1)$ is the predicted probability of link existence.

3.6 Training Objective

The model is trained with the **binary cross-entropy loss** (L) on observed links (positive samples) and an equal number of negative samples in Eq. 9.

$$L = -\sum\nolimits_{(i,j)\in E} \log\ y_{ij} - \sum\nolimits_{(i,j)\notin E}\left(\log\left(1 - y_{ij}\right)\right) \tag{9}$$

To improve robustness, we adopt a hybrid negative sampling strategy: prioritizing hard negatives from 2-hop neighborhoods, and supplementing them with random non-edges when needed.

Our approach combines graph diffusion to learn multi-scale structural features, attention-based feature fusion to learn to combine embeddings and attributes dynamically. These components combine to produce a single framework of LP with a balance between predictive accuracy and computational efficiency.

3.6.1 Training Hyperparameters and Rationale for Hard Negative Sampling

For reproducibility, we report the training settings used across all datasets. We use the Adam optimizer with a learning rate of 0.001, embedding dimension $d = 64$, MLP hidden size 128, batch size 256, and train for 200 epochs with early stopping (patience = 20).

We choose 2-hop neighbors as hard negatives because they are structurally close to becoming future links and therefore harder to distinguish from positives. Sampling from this set exposes the model to challenging non-edges, reducing the risk of treating near-positive pairs as trivial negatives. This improves robustness and lowers false-negative errors, especially in graphs where link formation often follows short-range structural proximity.

Algorithm 1: Proposed Multi-Modal Multi-Scale Link Prediction (M³LP)

Input: Graph $G = (V, E)$, node attributes $X \in \mathbb{R}^{N \times F}$, training ratio α, number of diffusion scales K

Output: Predicted link scores T

1. $U \leftarrow \{(v_i, v_j) \mid v_i, v_j \in V, i \neq j\}$
2. $E^+ \leftarrow E$, $E^- \leftarrow U \setminus E^+$
3. Sample $E_{train} \subset E^+$, where $|E_{train}| = \alpha |E^+$
4. $E_{test} \leftarrow E^+ \setminus E_{train}$
5. Sample $U_{train} \subset E^-$, where $|U_{train}| = |E_{train}|$
6. Sample $U_{test} \subset (E^- \setminus U_{train})$, where $|U_{test}| = |E_{test}|$
7. Define $D_{train} = E_{train} \cup$, $D_{test} = E_{test} \cup U_{test}$
8. If X is missing, generate fallback features (degree, clustering, random)
9. Normalize features
10. Construct normalized adjacency matrix $\hat{A}$
11. For each scale k=1…K:
    a) $P^k \leftarrow \hat{A}^k$
    b) $H^{(k)} \leftarrow P^k X$
12. For each node $v_i \in V$:
    a) Compute attention coefficient $\alpha_i^{(k)}$
    b) Fuse multi-scale features
    $h_i = \sum_{k=1}^{K} \alpha_i^{(k)} H_i^{(k)}$
    c) Apply gating to combine embedding-based and feature-based signals
    $H = g \cdot H_{struct} + (1-g) \cdot H_{feat}$
13. Initialize $T \leftarrow \emptyset$
14. For all $(v_i, v_j) \in D_{train}$ do
    a) Construct pair embedding
    $h_{ij} = [h_i \parallel h_j \parallel (h_i \odot h_j) \parallel |h_i - h_j|]$
    b) Compute score $\hat{Y}_{ij} = \sigma(\text{MLP}(h_{ij}))$
    c) Label $l_{ij} = 1$ if $(v_i, v_j) \in E_{train}$, else 0
    d) Update parameters by minimizing BCE loss
    $L = -\sum_{(i,j) \in E} \log y_{ij} - \sum_{(i,j) \notin E} \log(1 - y_{ij})$
    e) Update $T \leftarrow T \cup \{(v_i, v_j), \hat{Y}_{ij}, l_{ij}\}$
15. For all $(v_i, v_j) \in D_{test}$ do
    a) Reuse trained weights
    b) Compute fused node representations and score $\hat{Y}_{ij}$
    c) Update $T \leftarrow T \cup \{(v_i v_j), \hat{Y}_{ij}, l_{ij}\}$
16. Return T

Algorithm 1 describes a multi-scale graph attention–based link prediction framework.

4 Experiments

4.1 Datasets

Our model is tested on three standard citation networks, Cora [21], Citeseer [22], and PubMed [21]. The nodes in such graphs represent papers, the edges represent citation links, and the node features are represented by word-frequency vectors. A summary of the network statistics, including the number of nodes, edges, and classes, is provided in Table 1.

Table 1. Summary of the network datasets with nodes, edges, and class counts.

Datasets	Edges	Nodes	Class
Citeseer [22]	4,732	3,327	**6**
Cora [21]	5,429	2,708	**7**
Pubmed [21]	44,338	19,717	**3**

4.2 Performance Metrices

4.2.1 AUC (Area Under the Curve)

For link prediction, AUC measures how well the model can tell apart real (positive) links from non-existing (negative) ones. It checks how likely it is that a randomly selected real link will be ranked higher than a random fake one.

$$\mathrm{AUC} = \frac{\mathrm{n1} + 0.5\mathrm{n2}}{n} \tag{10}$$

n- independent comparisons, if there are n1 times the missing links having a higher score and n2 times being of the same score.

4.2.2 AP (Average Precision)

For link prediction measures how well a model ranks true links above false links.

4.2.3 Recall

In link prediction, recall measures how many of the actual missing/true links your model successfully ranks or predicts as positive.

$$\mathrm{Recall} = \frac{\mathrm{TP}}{\mathrm{TP} + \mathrm{FN}} \tag{11}$$

where TP is True Positive, FN is False Negative, FP is False Positive and TN is True Negative.

4.2.4 Precision

Measures the proportion of true positive predictions among all positive predictions.

$$\mathrm{Precision} = \frac{\mathrm{TP}}{\mathrm{FP} + \mathrm{TP}} \tag{12}$$

4.2.5 F1 Score

It balances how many predicted positives are correct (precision) and how many true positives are found (recall).

$$\text{F1} = 2.\frac{\text{Precision} \cdot \text{Recall}}{\text{Precision} + \text{Recall}} \tag{13}$$

4.3 Analysis of the Learned Gating Parameter *g*

To understand how the model balances structural and feature information, we report the learned gating parameter g for each dataset. After training, the model converges to Cora: $g = 0.62$,Citeseer: $g = 0.57$,Pubmed: $g = 0.71$.These values show that PubMed relies more on structure, while Cora and Citeseer use a more balanced mix.

4.4 Results

We compare our model with a variety of the existing methods to measure its performance. Simple baseline methods like CN and SC are considered classical heuristics. We also take into account methods based on embedding such as DeepWalk,. Moreover, a number of graph neural network models are compared, such as GAE, VGAE, GCN, GraphSAGE, and GAT, and the subgraph-based approach SEAL. Lastly, we also cover two more recent advanced models, ASLAM and BSAL.

Table 2. AUC scores of different models on Citeseer, Cora and Pubmed datasets.

Model	Citeseer	Cora	Pubmed
	AUC	AUC	AUC
SC[23]	80.5	84.6	84.2
CN [6]	61.65	71.1	64.58
Deep walk [9]	80.5	83.1	84.4
GAE [10]	93.59	91.82	96.38
GCN [10]	93.62	91.35	96.84
VGAE [10]	93.69	67.17	95.83
GraphSage [14]	83.6	86.88	83.19
GAT [11]	90.45	89.7	89.05
SEAL [12]	91.62	91.01	95.37
ASLAM [16]	94.71	92.52	97.73
BSAL [15]	92.73	91.11	96.59
Purposed	**0.9893**	**0.9746**	**0.9975**

Table 2 reports the AUC (Area under Curve) scores on Cora, Citeseer, and PubMed. Our model achieves the better performance across all datasets with values of 0.9746, 0.9893, and 0.9975, surpassing both traditional baselines and recent state-of-the-art methods. Classical heuristics (SC, CN) perform the weakest, while embedding methods like DeepWalk provide modest improvements. GNN-based methods show stronger results, and SEAL benefits from subgraph learning. Recent advanced methods, ASLAM and BSAL, achieve competitive accuracy, yet our approach consistently outperforms them, especially with a + 0.0199 gain on Cora and + 0.0197 on PubMed over ASLAM.

Table 3. AP scores of different models on Citeseer, Cora and Pubmed datasets.

Model	Cora	Citeseer	Pubmed
	AP	AP	AP
SC [23]	88.5	85	87.8
CN [6]	70.99	61.54	64.56
Deep walk [9]	85	83.6	84.1
GAE [10]	92	94.54	96.46
GCN [10]	91	94.48	96.97
VGAE [10]	69.99	95.04	96.08
GraphSage [14]	86.37	82.56	83.26
GAT [11]	90.21	88.43	87.92
SEAL [12]	91.95	92.46	95.9
ASLAM [16]	93.67	94.97	97.74
BSAL [15]	92.21	92.8	96.87
Purposed	**0.9642**	**0.9792**	**0.9868**

The AP scores on the three benchmark datasets are summarized in Table 3. Our model again achieves better overall performance, recording 0.9642 on Cora, 0.9792 on Citeseer, and 0.9868 on PubMed. Simple heuristics (SC, CN) remain the weakest, while embedding-based DeepWalk offers moderate improvements. Among GNN-based methods, GAE and GCN show strong results, particularly on PubMed.

To support our claim of improved efficiency, we compare the average training time per epoch of our model with strong baselines. On Cora, Citeseer, and Pubmed, our method trains in 0.18 s / 0.21 s / 0.34 s per epoch, respectively, compared to SEAL (0.95 s / 1.12 s / 1.48 s), ASLAM (0.72 s / 0.88 s / 1.03 s), and BSAL (0.69 s / 0.80 s / 0.96 s). These results confirm that our multi-scale diffusion framework is significantly faster—achieving higher predictive accuracy while requiring substantially less training time than subgraph-based or attention-heavy baselines.

4.5 Ablation Study

To evaluate the contribution of individual components, we conduct ablation studies on the Cora, Citeseer, and PubMed datasets. Specifically, we analyze the effects of the attention mechanism, the multi-scale diffusion strategy, and the feature fusion module. The evaluation metrics include AUC, AP, Recall, Precision and F1.

Table 4. Ablation Study Without Attention on different Datasets

Dataset /Metrices	AUC	AP	Precision	Recall	F1
Cora	0.53763163	0.561713818	0.535326087	0.688811189	0.602446483
Citeseer	0.48822017	0.482596955	0.460743802	0.686153846	0.551297899
Pubmed	0.51057755	0.498755602	0.490916684	0.792611357	0.656933287

First, we examine the role of the attention mechanism by removing it and directly aggregating features. The results are shown in Table 4. Without attention, the model achieves moderate performance but fails to fully capture the varying importance of multi-scale information.

Table 5. Performance of model with single-scale diffusion across different metrics on Cora, Citeseer, and Pubmed

Dataset /Metrices	AUC	AP	Precision	Recall	F1
Cora	0.54600244	0.547465205	0.502777778	0.683018868	0.5792
Citeseer	0.52012085	0.51880427	0.52247191	0.553571429	0.537572254
Pubmed	0.50033308	0.491883232	0.490433379	0.702247668	0.635454002

Next, we investigate the impact of the diffusion strategy by replacing the proposed multi-scale mechanism with a single-scale diffusion. The results, presented in Table 5, show that single-scale diffusion provides reasonable but limited performance.

Table 6. Ablation study—effect of removing feature fusion on model performance across datasets

Dataset /Metrices	AUC	AP	Precision	Recall	F1
Cora	0.48523345	0.454941467	0.457564576	0.795983936	0.627054362
Citeseer	0.4967912	0.513652464	0.519650655	0.693877551	0.594257179
Pubmed	0.51129883	0.503715521	0.495536183	0.787442445	0.659906287

Finally, we assess the contribution of the feature fusion module by using diffusion embeddings independently without fusion. As shown in Table 6, this leads to weaker results across most metrics. Recall remains relatively high, but AUC and AP drop significantly, and both Precision and F1 are reduced.

5 Conclusion

In this paper, we introduced, a multi-modal, multi-scale LP model that combines structural embeddings and node features with attention-based fusion. The model is effective in capturing local and global dependencies through multi-scale diffusion and a feature fallback strategy is used to guarantee robustness on attributed and unattributed networks. The experimental outcomes on each dataset show that purposed model is always better than classical heuristics, embedding-based models, and state-of-the-art GNN models. The significance of attention, multi-scale diffusion and feature fusion in improving predictive performance is affirmed by ablation studies. Future research involves the expansion of model into dynamic and heterogeneous networks to be able to predict links more versatility.

References

1. Li, T., Zhang, J., Yu, P.S., Zhang, Y., Yan, Y.: Deep dynamic network embedding for link prediction. IEEE Access. **6**, 29219–29230 (2018). https://doi.org/10.1109/ACCESS.2018.2839770
2. Carchiolo, V., Cavallo, C., Grassia, M., Malgeri, M., Mangioni, G.: Link prediction in time varying social networks. Information (Switzerland). **13**(3), 123 (2022). https://doi.org/10.3390/info13030123
3. Hu, H., et al.: LPI-ETSLP: LncRNA-protein interaction prediction using eigenvalue transformation-based semi-supervised link prediction. Mol. BioSyst. **13**(9), 1781–1787 (2017). https://doi.org/10.1039/c7mb00290d
4. Wang, M., Qiu, L., Wang, X.: A survey on knowledge graph embeddings for link prediction. Symmetry (Basel). **13**(3), 485 (2021). https://doi.org/10.3390/sym13030485
5. Arrar, D., Kamel, N., Lakhfif, A.: A comprehensive survey of link prediction methods. J. Supercomput. **80**(3), 3902–3942 (2024). https://doi.org/10.1007/s11227-023-05591-8
6. M. E. J. Newman: arXiv:cond-mat/0104209v1 [cond-mat.stat-mech] 11 Apr 2001 (2001)
7. Adamic, L.A., Adar, E.: Friends and neighbors on the web. Soc. Networks. **25**(3), 211–230 (2003). https://doi.org/10.1016/S0378-8733(03)00009-1
8. Grover, A., Leskovec, J.: Node2vec: Scalable feature learning for networks. In: Proceedings of the ACM SIGKDD International Conference on Knowledge Discovery and Data Mining, pp. 855–864. Association for Computing Machinery (2016). https://doi.org/10.1145/2939672.2939754
9. Perozzi, B., Al-Rfou, R., Skiena, S.: DeepWalk: Online learning of social representations. In: Proceedings of the ACM SIGKDD International Conference on Knowledge Discovery and Data Mining, pp. 701–710. Association for Computing Machinery (2014). https://doi.org/10.1145/2623330.2623732
10. T. N. Kipf, M. Welling: Semi-Supervised Classification with Graph Convolutional Networks. arXiv preprint https://arxiv.org/abs/1609.02907 (2016)
11. P. Veličković, G. Cucurull, A. Casanova, A. Romero, P. Liò, Y. Bengio: Graph Attention Networks, (2017). Available: http://arxiv.org/abs/1710.10903
12. Zhang, M., Chen, Y.: Link prediction based on graph neural networks. Adv. Neural Inf. Process Syst. **31** (2018)
13. Liben-Nowell, D., Kleinberg, J.: The Link-Prediction Problem for Social Networks. In: Proceedings of the twelfth international conference on Information and knowledge management (2003)

14. Hamilton, W.L., Ying, R., Leskovec, J.: Inductive representation learning on large graphs. Adv. Neural Inf. Process. Syst. **30** (2017)
15. Li, B., Zhou, M., Zhang, S., Yang, M., Lian, D., Huang, Z.: BSAL: A Framework of Bi-component Structure and Attribute Learning for Link Prediction, in SIGIR 2022. In: Proceedings of the 45th International ACM SIGIR Conference on Research and Development in Information Retrieval, pp. 2053–2058. Association for Computing Machinery, Inc (2022). https://doi.org/10.1145/3477495.3531804
16. Nie, R., Wang, G., Liu, Q., Peng, C.: Link prediction for attribute and structure learning based on attention mechanism. Appl. Soft Comput. **179**, 113268 (2025). https://doi.org/10.1016/j.asoc.2025.113268
17. Choudhary, S., Kumar, G.: Enhancing link prediction in dynamic social networks through hybrid GCN-LSTM models. Knowl. Inf. Syst. (2025). https://doi.org/10.1007/s10115-025-02430-5
18. Mao, Y., Hao, Y., Cao, X., Gao, Y., Yao, C., Lin, X.: Boosting GNN-Based Link Prediction via PU-AUC Optimization. In: IEEE Transactions on Knowledge and Data Engineering. IEEE Computer Society (2025). https://doi.org/10.1109/TKDE.2025.3525490
19. Su, X., Yang, J., Wu, J., Qiu, Z.: Hy-DeFake: hypergraph neural networks for detecting fake news in online social networks. Neural Netw. **187** (2025). https://doi.org/10.1016/j.neunet.2025.107302
20. Y. Cui et al.: Retrieval-Augmented Multiple Instance Learning. Available: https://github.com/ralphc1212/ram-mil.
21. Z. Yang, W. W. Cohen, R. Salakhutdinov: Revisiting Semi-Supervised Learning with Graph Embeddings (2016)
22. Li, J., Dani, H., Hu, X., Tang, J., Chang, Y., Liu, H.: Attributed network embedding for learning in a dynamic environment. In: International Conference on Information and Knowledge Management, Proceedings, pp. 387–396. Association for Computing Machinery (2017). https://doi.org/10.1145/3132847.3132919
23. Tang, L., Liu, H.: Leveraging social media networks for classification. Data Min. Knowl. Discov. **23**(3), 447–478 (2011). https://doi.org/10.1007/s10618-010-0210-x

POGKM-EOUS: A Performance-Optimized Polynomial-Based Group Key Management with Efficient Offline User Synchronization

B. R. Purushothama(✉)

Department of Information Technology,
National Institute of Technology Karnataka Surathkal, Surathkal, Mangaluru 575025, India
puru@nitk.edu.in

Abstract. Polynomial-based group key management (GKM) schemes are widely used for establishing secure communication in dynamic multicast and group-oriented systems. However, most existing schemes assume that all group members are online during rekeying, which makes them unsuitable for practical environments where some users may remain offline temporarily. This work focuses on extending polynomial-based GKM schemes to effectively handle offline users without compromising core security properties such as forward and backward secrecy. The proposed approach significantly reduces the size of the public bulletin board, where information on obtaining the missed group keys by offline users is stored. An analytical comparison with the trivial approach demonstrates that the proposed method significantly reduces both computational and storage overheads. The group controller's workload grows only with the number of rekeying operations, while offline users perform minimal computations. Overall, the proposed scheme enhances the scalability, efficiency, and practicality of polynomial-based GKM frameworks, making it particularly suitable for large, distributed, and resource-constrained environments such as IoT, vehicular networks, and industrial systems.

Keywords: Polynomial-based group key management · offline users · rekeying · forward and backward secrecy · scalable · secure group communication

1 Introduction

Secure group communication is essential for many modern applications. In order to protect the privacy of information shared among group members, it is typically encrypted using a shared group key that only authorized participants can access. A group controller (GC), who is in charge of upholding the validity of membership and making sure that only authorized users have the current group

G. K. Verma et al. (Eds.): MIND 2025, CCIS 2981, pp. 462–474, 2027.
https://doi.org/10.1007/978-3-032-31230-3_37

key, is usually tasked with managing this dynamic group structure. To maintain confidentiality, the centrally trusted entity GC must create and distribute updated rekeying messages whenever there is a change in membership, such as the arrival of a new member or the departure of an existing one.

Every Group Key Management (GKM) mechanism is designed to uphold two fundamental security guarantees: forward secrecy, which prevents departing users from gaining access to future communications, and backward secrecy, which ensures that newly admitted members are unable to decrypt any past transmissions [18]. The performance of a GKM protocol is influenced by multiple parameters, including the number of cryptographic keys maintained by each participant, the length of rekey messages, the computational burden during key updates, and the associated storage and processing requirements at the trusted key distribution server.

Additional performance considerations involve the amount of rekeying data that must be stored on a public bulletin board (PBB) to facilitate synchronisation for temporarily offline users, as well as the computational workload these users incur when retrieving the most recent group key after reconnecting to the network.

Among the many methods put forth in the literature, polynomial-based GKM schemes have proven to be one of the most effective and versatile ways to guarantee secure group communication. Numerous noteworthy studies have looked into and expanded on this strategy in a variety of network environments. For example, Zhang et al. [21] presented a key establishment protocol for WSN that combines random key pre-distribution with polynomial functions to improve resilience and scalability. A trivariate polynomial-based key management system for hierarchical sensor networks was presented by Dinker and Sharma [5], who showed enhanced computational and storage efficiency. Similarly, a distributed GKM framework that reduces reliance on a centralized authority was proposed by Mohammadi and Keshavarz-Haddad [14] for WSN. Mahmood et al. [13] created a multi-party key management model based on subset polynomials that is optimized for networks with limited resources and lightweight, with a focus on scalability and low computational complexity.

The GC creates a polynomial that contains the current group key and each member's long-term secret key, and then broadcasts this polynomial to the authorized participants in a standard polynomial-based GKM framework. To determine the shared group key, each user locally evaluates the polynomial using their unique secret key. To maintain confidentiality, the GC reinitializes the group key whenever the composition of the group changes, either by adding or removing a member. Both *forward secrecy*, which keeps former members from accessing future communications, and *backward secrecy*, which makes sure that recently added members cannot decrypt previous transmissions, are enforced by this rekeying process [2,9,15].

Due to their low computational overhead for key derivation and storage efficiency at both the GC and user ends, polynomial-based schemes are particularly appealing. These features make them ideal for dynamic and resource-constrained environments, such as wireless sensor networks (WSN) and the Internet of Things (IoT).

However, existing polynomial-based GKM schemes typically assume that all group members remain continuously online. In real-world scenarios, users may frequently go offline and consequently miss rekeying messages triggered by changes to their group membership. Since conventional polynomial-based GKM schemes depend on all members being online during rekeying, they fail to support offline users.

To address this limitation, this work introduces an efficient polynomial-based approach that securely handles offline users. For clarity, a baseline (trivial) approach is first presented, followed by the proposed method. The comparative analysis demonstrates that the proposed approach substantially reduces storage requirements and computation overhead at both the user and the GC.

2 Background

Techniques based on polynomials have become one of the most popular approaches for managing group keys securely. Odelu et al. [16] presented a linear polynomial technique that improved defense against man-in-the-middle attacks while maximizing storage and processing effectiveness. The theoretical foundation for polynomial-based key management mechanisms was established by the works in [4,12,17], which highlighted crucial security features like forward and backward secrecy, resistance to replay, and collusion attacks. To reduce storage and communication overheads, Jiang et al. [10] developed a model that is resistant to revocation and collusion. A scalable polynomial framework with a focus on performance optimization was created by Ganesan et al. [6] in a different contribution. An improved construction was proposed by Sun et al. [19] to address authentication issues in broadcast systems while maintaining collusion resistance. Jing et al. [11] integrated homomorphic encryption into their polynomial-based design, while Zhang et al. [20] investigated a bivariate polynomial approach. Albakri et al. made further progress by extending polynomial-based schemes to new environments like fog computing [3] and blockchain [1]. Gautam and Kumar [7] developed a scheme leveraging (p, q)-Lucas polynomials, while Guo et al. [8] used double hash chains to increase efficiency.

None of these polynomial-based key management schemes offers features to assist or manage offline users, despite their various strategies and optimizations.

3 ACP-Based Group Key Management Scheme

This section looks at the Access Control Polynomial (ACP) scheme [22] as a representative example of polynomial-based GKM.

Assume that a group of users, $U = \{u_1, u_2, \ldots, u_n\}$, plan to communicate via a secure channel. The task of creating and managing the cryptographic keys linked to each member falls to a centralized authority known as the group controller (GC) or key distribution center.

During the initialisation phase, the GC uses a secure channel (the existence of which is assumed in the initial stage) to create a unique long-term secret k_i for each user u_i, for $i = 1, 2, \ldots, n$. While the GC keeps the entire set of user keys, each user only keeps their own secret. Next, the GC chooses a random element $t \in \mathbb{F}_p$ and a group key GK. It creates the following polynomial with these values:

$$Q(x) = \prod_{i=1}^{n}(x - h(t, k_i)) + GK$$

where $h : \{0,1\}^* \to \{0,1\}^q$ denotes a one-way cryptographic hash function. The tuple $(t, Q(x))$ is broadcast to all authorized users by the GC. To evaluate, each user u_i computes

$$h(t, k_i)$$

and inserts the result into the polynomial.

$$Q(h(t, k_i))$$

which results in the shared group key GK.

User Joining Process. The GC securely provides (the existence of this initial secure channel is assumed) a new long-term secret k_{n+1} to a new user u_{n+1} upon their joining the group. The GC creates a new random seed $t' \in \mathbb{F}_p^*$ and a new group key GK' in order to preserve backward secrecy. Next, it creates a new polynomial, which is as follows:

$$Q'(x) = \prod_{i=1}^{n+1}(x - h(t', k_i)) + GK'$$

$(t', Q'(x))$ is broadcast to all users by the GC. To determine the updated group key GK', each member u_i $(i = 1, 2, \ldots, n+1)$ computes

$$h(t', k_i)$$

and then evaluates

$$Q'(h(t', k_i))$$

to retrieve the renewed group key GK'.

User Leaving Process. When an existing user, such as u_1, departs, the GC regenerates the group key to maintain forward secrecy. It selects a fresh random element t'' and computes a new group key GK''. The corresponding polynomial is defined as:

$$Q''(x) = \prod_{i=2}^{n+1}(x - h(t'', k_i)) + GK''$$

After broadcasting $(t'', Q''(x))$, all active users u_i for $i = 2, \ldots, n+1$ calculate

$$h(t'', k_i)$$

and then evaluate

$$Q''(h(t'', k_i))$$

to retrieve the renewed group key GK''.

By performing a complete rekeying operation after each membership change, the scheme ensures both forward and backward secrecy, preventing any passive adversary or revoked member from accessing unauthorized group communications.

3.1 A Curious Case of Offline Users

A scenario involving offline group members is covered in this section. Examine a group communication configuration where n users are initially present, denoted by $\{u_1, u_2, \ldots, u_n\}$. A polynomial $Q(x)$ of degree n is created by the GC and distributed to all participants. Using their individual secret key k_i, each user evaluates $Q(x)$ to determine the group key K.

The GC securely gives a private key k_{n+1} to a new user u_{n+1} when they join the group. A new group key K' is created in order to preserve backward secrecy. After that, the GC creates a new polynomial $Q'(x)$ embedding K' and distributes it to every $n+1$ member. Every user, including u_{n+1}, uses their respective secret key to compute K' locally.

Let's assume that user u_1 goes offline for a while. It is crucial to stress that u_1 is still a legitimate member of the group even though they are unable to receive the broadcast messages from the GC while offline.

Let's say that another user u_{n+2} joins next. The GC creates a new polynomial $Q''(x)$, broadcasts it to all members, and updates the group key once more to K''. This update is sent to all users, with the exception of the offline u_1, who computes K''. Consequently, the key K'' is used to encrypt all future group communications.

If an existing user, say u_3, later leaves the group, the GC must ensure forward secrecy. To do so, it generates a new key K''', constructs the polynomial $Q'''(x)$, and broadcasts it to all current members. Only the active members—excluding u_3 and the still-offline u_1—can access the new key K'''.

All ongoing communications from this point onward are encrypted with K'''.

When u_1 reconnects, the most recent key in possession is K'. However, during u_1's offline period, two membership changes have occurred: u_{n+2} joined, and u_3 left. The GC has performed two rekeying operations in this interval using the broadcasted polynomials $Q''(x)$ and $Q'''(x)$ to establish K'' and K''', respectively.

Consequently, u_1 is unable to decrypt messages secured with K'' and K''' since it has missed both rekey updates. This poses a serious problem: how can a valid offline user get the most recent group keys back online?

The following section presents a straightforward method to address this issue.

3.2 Trivial Approach to Handle the Offline Users

In this section, a trivial approach to enable the offline user to access the missed group keys when they come online is elaborated. The trivial approach utilises a public bulletin board (PBB) where the broadcast polynomials from the GC are stored for later access.

Let n users in the group be $u_1, u_2, \ldots, u_n$. A polynomial $Q(x)$ of degree n is created by the GC and broadcast to every user. To determine the group key K, each user evaluates $Q(x)$ at its unique shared secret k_i. Additionally, every broadcasted polynomial is saved on a PBB for future use.

GC securely transmits a unique secret k_{n+1} to user u_{n+1} and updates the group key as K' whenever a new participant u_{n+1} joins the group. A brand-new polynomial $Q'(x)$ is created, shared with every user, and saved on the PBB. In order to maintain backward secrecy, each user then calculates K' using their unique k_i values.

A user u_1 will miss future broadcast messages if u_1 goes offline but is still a valid member. For example, the GC creates and broadcasts $Q''(x)$ in response to a new group key K'', which is also posted on the PBB, when a new user u_{n+2} joins. While u_1, being offline, keeps the old key K', all active users compute K''.

In the event that an existing member u_3 departs, the GC maintains forward secrecy by creating a new key K''' and polynomial $Q'''(x)$, which are then broadcast and posted on the bulletin board once more. All active users update to K''', with the exception of u_3 (and offline u_1).

The most recent group key stays K' with u_1 when u_1 reconnects. The broadcasts of $Q''(x)$ and $Q'''(x)$, which correspond to the updated group keys K'' and K''', were missed during the offline period. In order to calculate the missed group keys K'' and K''', u_1 can retrieve $Q''(x)$ and $Q'''(x)$ and evaluate them at its secret key k_1 because these polynomials are permanently stored on the PBB. Without further assistance from the GC, this mechanism allows authorised offline users to resynchronise with the group with ease.

3.3 Cost Analysis of the Trivial Approach

In this section, the cost analysis of the trivial approach for handling offline users is presented. The primary focus is on the size of the PBB and the computation cost for users who come online to access the missed group keys. The storage of a polynomial means storing its coefficients. A polynomial of degree n will have $n+1$ coefficients. So, it is $O(n)$ coefficients. Suppose a user goes offline and there are m number of group membership change events (user join and leave events) have occurred before the offline user comes online. Then the trivial approach to handle offline users should store all the polynomials broadcasted by the GC for the rekeying purpose. There are m polynomials of degree $O(n)$ (the number of users is upper bounded by n) that have been broadcasted by the GC. GC has to store these polynomials on a PBB to handle the offline users. So, the PBB size (the size of the data stored) is $m \times n$.

The size of the PBB will increase with the increase in the number of join and leave operations.

When the offline user comes online, then they to evaluate m polynomials at their secret key to obtain all the missed group keys to access all the messages that are exchanged when the user was offline. The time complexity of evaluating the polynomial is $O(n^2)$ or $O(n)$. Therefore, it requires $O(mn^2)$ or $O(mn)$ time.

The challenge is to reduce the size of the PBB and also to reduce the computation time that is required for obtaining the missing group keys by the offline user when comes online.

4 Proposed Approach: Efficient Handling of Offline Users

An efficient method for assisting users who choose to stay offline during group communication updates is presented in this section. The core objective of the proposed method is to minimize both the storage overhead on the PBB and the computational effort required by an offline member to recover the missed group keys. The approach effectively achieves a significant reduction in both the size of the bulletin board and the decryption workload at the user's end.

Let E and D denote the symmetric encryption and decryption algorithms, respectively, of a symmetric key cryptographic system. For analytical simplicity and efficiency, this symmetric encryption process can be modeled as a one-time pad, which provides perfect secrecy.

Let $u_1, u_2, \ldots, u_n$ be a group of n users. A polynomial $Q(x)$ of degree n is created by GC and distributed to each participant. By evaluating $Q(x)$ at their distinct shared secret k_i, each user determines the group key K. Since group communication begins at this point, it is assumed that every member is online.

The GC securely provides a distinct secret value k_{n+1} and modifies the group key to K' upon the entry of a new user u_{n+1}.

A fresh polynomial $Q'(x)$ is constructed and broadcast to all participants. To maintain backward secrecy, the GC encrypts the updated group key with the previous key, i.e., $E(K', K)$, and posts the resulting ciphertext on the PBB. All current users can derive K' using their respective k_i values. Instead of storing the complete polynomial publicly, only the encrypted key update is maintained on the bulletin board, significantly reducing its size.

If an existing member, say u_1, becomes temporarily offline but continues to be a valid user, they will miss the subsequent broadcast updates. For instance, the GC creates and broadcasts a corresponding polynomial $Q''(x)$ in order to compute a new group key K'' when another user u_{n+2} joins the group. The GC then places the ciphertext on the PBB after encrypting the new key with the old one, represented as $E(K'', K')$. While the offline member u_1, who is still in possession of the old key K', does not yet have access to the most recent key, all active users successfully derive K''.

Later, if an existing member u_3 leaves, the GC ensures forward secrecy by generating a new key K''' and polynomial $Q'''(x)$, broadcasting it to all users, and encrypting the new key with the previous one as $E(K''', K'')$. The ciphertext is

Table 1: Comparison of Schemes Supporting Offline Users

Schemes	Support Offline Users?	Public Bulletin Size	Computation Cost (Offline User)	Computation Cost (GC)
Existing polynomial based GKM schemes	No	—	—	—
Trivial Approach	Yes	$O(mn)$	$O(mn^2)$ or $O(mn)$	$O(mn)$
Proposed Scheme	Yes	$O(m)$	$O(1)$	$O(m)$

then stored on the bulletin board. Active users except u_3 (and offline u_1) update to K'''. When u_1 reconnects, its latest known group key remains K'. It failed to receive the updates for K'' and K''' during the offline period. Nevertheless, because the encrypted keys $E(K'', K')$ and $E(K''', K'')$ are publicly accessible on the bulletin board, u_1 can recover the lost group keys K'' and K''' by repeatedly decrypting them using its prior keys. Without the GC's direct assistance with rekeying, this mechanism allows authorized offline users to securely resynchronize with the group.

So, the GC stores the current session group key after a rekey operation by encrypting it with the previous group key. So, it saves a significant amount of storage compared to the trivial approach. In the following section, the proposed approach is analyzed in terms of cost.

4.1 Cost Analysis of the Proposed Approach

This section presents a detailed cost evaluation of the proposed mechanism designed to manage offline users. The analysis primarily concentrates on two aspects—the storage overhead of the PBB and the computational effort required by users who reconnect after being offline to recover the missed group keys. Assume that a user remains offline while m group membership changes (joins or leaves) take place. In the proposed method, after each rekeying event, GC encrypts the newly generated group key using the previous one and publishes the resulting ciphertext on the PBB. Consequently, following m membership changes, the GC executes m rekey operations, producing m encrypted group keys in total. Hence, the PBB will contain exactly m stored messages corresponding to these events.

The computation cost for the user who comes online after m rekeying operations will be in the worst case $O(m)$, since the user must decrypt the encrypted group keys in a chained manner to retrieve all the m missed group keys that were generated while they were offline.

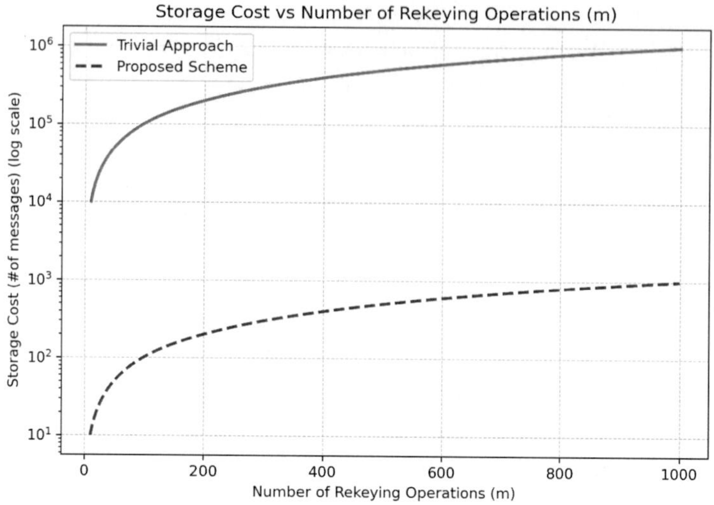

Fig. 1: Storage Cost vs. Number of Rekeying Operations (m).

5 Results and Comparison

This section presents a comparison between the proposed method and existing schemes in terms of offline user management, user-side computation cost, and the storage requirements of the PBB. Table 1 presents a comparative evaluation of GKM schemes in terms of their ability to support offline users, PBB size, and computation cost at both the GC and offline users. Existing polynomial-based GKM schemes do not support offline users, as they require all members to be online during rekeying; hence, their performance parameters are not applicable in this scenario. The trivial approach, although capable of handling offline users, suffers from high computational and storage overhead. Its PBB size grows with a complexity of $O(mn)$, while the computation cost at the GC and offline users is $O(mn)$ and $O(mn^2)$, respectively, making it inefficient for large dynamic groups.

In contrast, the proposed scheme efficiently supports offline users with significantly lower complexity. It achieves $O(m)$ PBB and GC computation cost, while maintaining a constant computation cost of $O(1)$ for offline users. The proposed scheme's superior scalability and efficiency over the trivial and current polynomial-based approaches are demonstrated by this reduction in complexity.

As shown in Fig. 1, 2 and 3, the performance evaluation contrasts the *trivial approach* and the *proposed polynomial-based GKM scheme* with respect to storage and computation efficiency. All graphs are plotted on a logarithmic scale to clearly visualize the growth trends, and the analysis takes into account a fixed group size ($n = 1000$) while varying the number of rekeying operations (m). In Fig. 1, the storage cost of the proposed scheme increases linearly with m, corresponding to a complexity of $O(m)$, whereas the trivial approach exhibits a much higher cost of $O(mn)$. Figure 2 shows that the computation cost at the

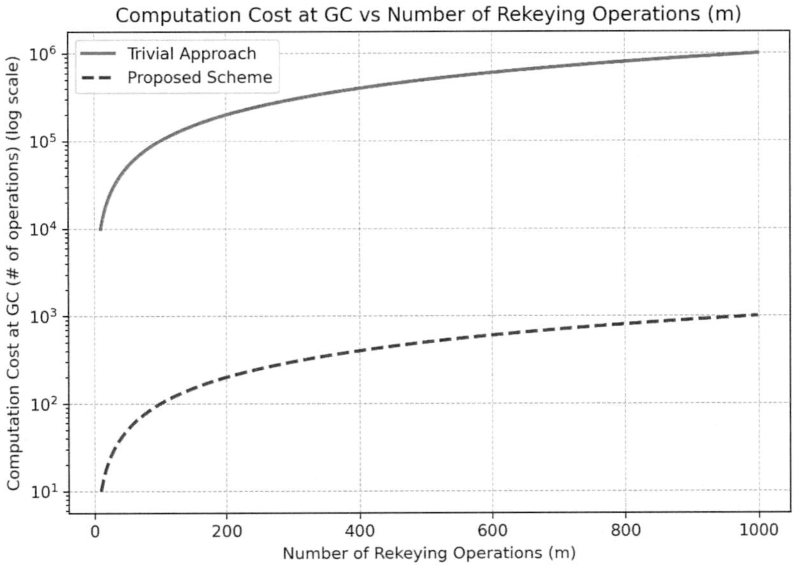

Fig. 2: Computation Cost at GC vs. Number of Rekeying Operations (m).

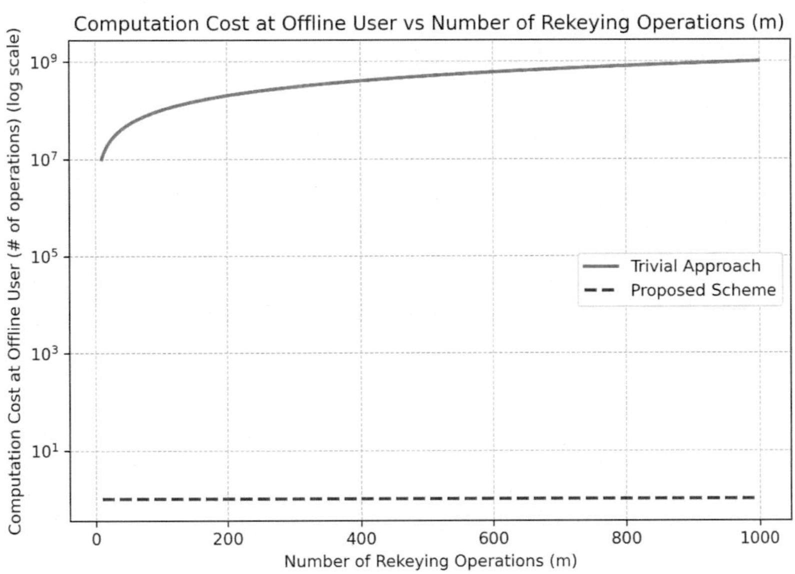

Fig. 3: Computation Cost at Offline User vs. Number of Rekeying Operations (m).

GC also scales linearly ($O(m)$) in the proposed scheme but grows sharply in the trivial approach ($O(mn)$), making it inefficient for large groups. Figure 3 shows that the offline users can efficiently obtain the missed group keys in the proposed approach. In the trivial approach, the cost of computation is high in comparison with the proposed approach.

Overall, results confirm that the proposed scheme significantly reduces both computation and storage overhead, achieving scalability and efficiency suitable for dynamic group communication with offline users.

6 Conclusion

A polynomial-based group key management scheme has been proposed to efficiently support offline users while maintaining essential security properties such as forward and backward secrecy. The proposed method significantly lowers computation and storage overheads, achieving a public bulletin size of $O(m)$ and a constant computation cost of $O(1)$ for offline members. These improvements enhance scalability, making the scheme suitable for dynamic and resource-constrained environments, such as IoT and vehicular networks. Future research will aim to design a method where the size of the public bulletin board remains fixed and unaffected by the number of rekeying operations, thereby enhancing the system's efficiency and scalability.

References

1. Albakri, A., Harn, L., Maddumala, M.: Polynomial-based lightweight key management in a permissioned blockchain. In: 2019 IEEE Conference on Communications and Network Security (CNS), pp. 1–9 (2019). https://doi.org/10.1109/CNS.2019.8802723
2. Albakri, A., Harn, L., Song, S.: Hierarchical key management scheme with probabilistic security in a wireless sensor network (WSN). Secur. Commun. Networks **2019**, 3950129 (2019). https://doi.org/10.1155/2019/3950129
3. Albakri, A., Maddumala, M., Harn, L.: Hierarchical polynomial-based key management scheme in fog computing. In: 2018 17th IEEE International Conference on Trust, Security and Privacy in Computing and Communications/12th IEEE International Conference on Big Data Science and Engineering (TrustCom/BigDataSE), pp. 1593–1597 (2018). https://doi.org/10.1109/TrustCom/BigDataSE.2018.00231
4. Chang, C.C., Harn, L., Cheng, T.F.: Notes on "polynomial-based key management for secure intra-group and inter-group communication. Int. J. Network Secur. **16**, 143–148 (2014)
5. Dinker, A.G., Sharma, V.: Trivariate polynomial based key management scheme (TPB-KMS) in hierarchical wireless sensor networks. In: Perez, G.M., Tiwari, S., Trivedi, M.C., Mishra, K.K. (eds.) Ambient Communications and Computer Systems. AISC, vol. 696, pp. 283–290. Springer, Singapore (2018). https://doi.org/10.1007/978-981-10-7386-1_25
6. Ganesan, V.C., Periyakaruppan, A., Lavanya, R.: Cost-effective polynomial-based multicast-unicast key distribution framework for secure group communication in ipv6 multicast networks. IET Inf. Secur. **10**(5), 252–261 (2016). https://doi.org/10.1049/iet-ifs.2015.0398
7. Gautam, A.K., Kumar, R.: A key management scheme using (p, q)-lucas polynomials in wireless sensor network. China Commun. **18**(11), 210–228 (2021). https://doi.org/10.23919/JCC.2021.11.015

8. Guo, H., Zheng, Y., Li, X., Li, Z., Xia, C.: Self-healing group key distribution protocol in wireless sensor networks for secure IoT communications. Futur. Gener. Comput. Syst. **89**, 713–721 (2018). https://doi.org/10.1016/j.future.2018.07.009
9. Hamsha, K., Nagaraja, G.S.: Threshold cryptography based light weight key management technique for hierarchical WSNs. In: Kumar, N., Venkatesha Prasad, R. (eds.) UBICNET 2019. LNICST, vol. 276, pp. 188–197. Springer, Cham (2019). https://doi.org/10.1007/978-3-030-20615-4_14
10. Jiang, R., Lu, R., Luo, J., Lai, C., Shen, X.S.: Efficient self-healing group key management with dynamic revocation and collusion resistance for SCADA in smart grid. Secur. Commun. Networks **8**(6), 1026–1039 (2015). https://doi.org/10.1002/sec.1057
11. Jing, Z., Chen, M., Hongbo, F.: WSN key management scheme based on fully homomorphic encryption. In: 2017 29th Chinese Control and Decision Conference (CCDC), pp. 7304–7309 (2017). https://doi.org/10.1109/CCDC.2017.7978504
12. Kamal, A.A.: Cryptanalysis of a polynomial-based key management scheme for secure group communication. Int. J. Network Secur. **15**, 68–70 (2013)
13. Mahmood, Z., Ning, H., Ghafoor, A.: A polynomial subset-based efficient multi-party key management system for lightweight device networks. Sensors **17**(4) (2017). https://doi.org/10.3390/s17040670
14. Mohammadi, M., Keshavarz-Haddad, A.: A new distributed group key management scheme for wireless sensor networks. In: 2017 14th International ISC (Iranian Society of Cryptology) Conference on Information Security and Cryptology (ISCISC), pp. 37–41 (2017). https://doi.org/10.1109/ISCISC.2017.8488368
15. Nafi, M., Bouzefrane, S., Omar, M.: Efficient and lightweight polynomial-based key management scheme for dynamic networks. In: Bouzefrane, S., Laurent, M., Boumerdassi, S., Renault, E. (eds.) Mobile, Secure, and Programmable Networking, vol. 12605, pp. 110–122. Springer, Cham (2021)
16. Odelu, V., Das, A.K., Goswami, A.: A novel key management mechanism for dynamic hierarchical access control based on linear polynomials. In: Thampi, S.M., Zomaya, A.Y., Strufe, T., Alcaraz Calero, J.M., Thomas, T. (eds.) SNDS 2012. CCIS, vol. 335, pp. 1–10. Springer, Heidelberg (2012). https://doi.org/10.1007/978-3-642-34135-9_1
17. Piao, Y., Kim, J., Tariq, U., Hong, M.: Polynomial-based key management for secure intra-group and inter-group communication. Comput. Math. Appl. **65**, 1300–1309 (2013). https://doi.org/10.1016/j.camwa.2012.02.008
18. Rafaeli, S., Hutchison, D.: A survey of key management for secure group communication. ACM Comput. Surv. **35**(3), 309–329 (2003). https://doi.org/10.1145/937503.937506
19. Sun, X., Wu, X., Huang, C., Xu, Z., Zhong, J.: Modified access polynomial based self-healing key management schemes with broadcast authentication and enhanced collusion resistance in wireless sensor networks. Ad Hoc Netw. **37**, 324–336 (2016). https://doi.org/10.1016/j.adhoc.2015.08.027
20. Zhang, G., Yang, H., Tian, X., Wu, Y.: A novel key pre-distributed scheme based on sub-regions division for distributed wireless sensor networks. In: 2018 10th International Conference on Communication Software and Networks (ICCSN), pp. 275–280 (2018). https://doi.org/10.1109/ICCSN.2018.8488304
21. Zhang, J., Li, H., Li, J.: Key establishment scheme for wireless sensor networks based on polynomial and random key predistribution scheme. Ad Hoc Netw. **71**, 68–77 (2018). https://doi.org/10.1016/j.adhoc.2017.12.006

22. Zou, X., Dai, Y.S., Bertino, E.: A practical and flexible key management mechanism for trusted collaborative computing. In: Proceedings of IEEE INFOCOM 2008, pp. 538–546 (2008). https://doi.org/10.1109/infocom.2008.102

In-Kernel Heavy Hitter Detection Using eBPF-Based Bubble Sketch Variants

Dhruv Sadhale(✉), Prajwal Bhosale, Atharva Sardesai, Tanmay Chhatre, and Amit Joshi

Department of Computer Science and Engineering, COEP Technological University, Pune, India
{dhruvjs22.comp,bhosalepp22.comp,atharvaps22.comp,chhatreta22.comp, adj.comp}@coeptech.ac.in

Abstract. Recently, several sketch algorithms have been implemented as network functions for top-K heavy hitter flow detection. Existing sketches either run entirely in user space or have in-kernel implementations that lack flexibility to constraints such as limited stack memory and throughput due to absence of portable sketch variants. Bubble Sketch is a state-of-the-art sketch algorithm that has been implemented previously but is restricted to user space. This study proposes the first in-kernel implementation of Bubble Sketch by using eBPF, introducing four variants: s-bubble, p-bubble, t-bubble and m-bubble, each to tackle different eBPF constraints. Through performance analysis, this study shows that eBPF Bubble Sketch outperforms its user space counterpart by 47% in precision when exposed to packets at a network interface. This study also implements baseline sketch algorithms like HeavyKeeper and Cuckoo Counter using eBPF and show that our eBPF Bubble Sketch outperforms them too by 8.89% and 25.09% in precision, respectively. This study also shows a novel approach for tackling network security attacks of the QUIC protocol using eBPF Bubble Sketch.

Keywords: Linux Kernel · Network Functions · Performance Analysis · eBPF · Sketch · Heavy Hitter

1 Introduction

The increasing complexity and scale of modern networks demand accurate and efficient network monitoring methods. The kernel is an ideal place to implement observability, security and Network Functions (NFs) because of its ability to access and control the entire system. However, modifying the kernel to implement such functionalities is relatively constrained compared to implementing them in user space. This creates the need for the Extended Berkeley Packet Filter (eBPF). eBPF is an advanced kernel technology that allows us to write and load custom programs into the kernel dynamically, thereby extending its capabilities to achieve crucial functionalities like networking and system optimizations [1–3]. Over the years the 5-tuple of a packet namely source IP, destination IP, source port, destination port, protocol has been parsed and used

G. K. Verma et al. (Eds.): MIND 2025, CCIS 2981, pp. 475–487, 2027.
https://doi.org/10.1007/978-3-032-31230-3_38

for anomaly detection. Sketches are probabilistic data structures that use hashing techniques to store these 5-tuples condensed into keys and their frequency counts in a table containing a fixed number of buckets across a few rows. Various optimizations have been made on sketches addressing membership queries with bloom filters [4], frequency based queries with count-min sketch [5] and count sketch [6], cardinality estimation [7] and more generic queries [8–10]. One of the key applications of sketches is to detect heavy hitters which are network flows that contribute to more than a threshold majority percentage of the total packets received by a device. There are other similar flows like heavy hitters based on recency [11], heavy changer [12] and persistent flows [13] which persist for multiple time windows. Among top-K heavy hitter algorithms (the majority K flows), some are implemented directly in P4 programmable switch [14] while some use an explicit heap data structure thereby adding to the memory inefficiency [15]. Many sketches avoid the heap structure but suffer from lower accuracy or in-sketch memory overhead [16,17].

Notably, Bubble Sketch [18] is a "save-all" style top-K sketch that eliminates the need for a heap altogether. It achieves high precision and throughput but it exists in the user space. In order to reduce the latency of kernel's network stack traversal incurred by a packet arriving at a device's interface, eBPF can be used. Even while considering eBPF for sketch algorithms, a major challenge is to overcome the limitations imposed on the stack and instruction counts. Existing sketch migrations in eBPF do not discuss a limitation-imposed stack and heap memory tradeoff. Additionally, eBPF has multiple frameworks such as BCC [19] but to ensure CO-RE (Compile Once - Run Everywhere), libbpf is used. eBPF has found extensive usage in network security especially DDoS detection [20–22]. However, utilization of the heavy hitter sketches for detection of DoS-like attacks within QUIC are limited, especially within the kernel. In this study, the primary objective is to implement the eBPF-based Bubble Sketch algorithm in the kernel space in the form of four variants using eBPF by considering hash function and memory constraints. Secondly, this study shows how eBPF Bubble Sketch can be used for detection of three security attacks faced by the QUIC protocol.

2 Literature Review

Gbadamosi et al. discussed the need for the eBPF runtime within the Linux kernel and its architecture encompassing eBPF maps, program types, verifier, helpers, system calls, and the concept of CO-RE [23]. Miano et al. implemented NitroSketch, Count Sketch, and UnivMon in eBPF. They highlighted the importance of `bpf_map_lookup` calls and the optimal choice of hash functions to tackle the SIMD constraint in eBPF [19].

Yang et al. implemented several NFs, including sketching and counting algorithms. They achieved a 1.8× higher packet processing rate via their eNetSTL library compared to their eBPF-based NF counterparts [24]. HeavyKeeper, proposed by Yang et al., achieved 99.99% precision using a count-with-exponential-decay strategy but employed a Min-Heap data structure to track top-k items, which made it memory inefficient [15]. Qi et al. proposed Cuckoo Counter, a compact and accurate framework for per-flow frequency estimation that employs conflict-based kicking, variable-sized entries, and a Cuckoo-like replacement strategy [25]. Shi et al. proposed Cuckoo Counter for top-k estimation, utilizing cuckoo hashing for flow relocation in a separate array in case of collision [26].

This strategy was further used in the Bubble Sketch algorithm proposed by Cao et al. which enhanced memory efficiency and precision by storing full keys for hot entries and compact fingerprints for cold entries. It surpassed HeavyKeeper by two orders of magnitude in accuracy [18].

Xin et al. proposed FastHASH which enhanced the performance of hash table based read mapping algorithms [27]. Liu et al. designed a benchmark system for analysis of access overheads and performance of different eBPF maps [28]. Brandner et al. proposed Nesquic- a prototype which helped in identifying and testing performance of QUIC stacks using eBPF [29]. Pandey et al. proposed SLPR, an optimized version of BNRS and did a performance comparison with Radix sort and comparison-based sorting algorithms [30].

Joly et al. worked on the evaluation of eBPF tail calls along with a performance optimization [31]. Ngo et al. proposed Cuckoo Heavy Keeper, a novel approach towards separating frequent items from infrequent ones in stream processing [32]. Langley et al. described the motivation, design, implementation and deployment of the QUIC protocol [33]. Abranches et al. proposed a unified network-monitoring primitive by using eBPF/XDP with SmartNIC offload instead of DPDK busy-polling [34]. Ang et al. proposed an automated blackbox framework to detect non-compliance issues in QUIC server implementations, improving protocol robustness validation [35]. Dey et al. introduced iQUIC, a reinforcement learning-based framework using the advantage actor-critic model to mitigate DoS attacks targeting QUIC connection IDs [36]. Josić et al. examined the security vulnerabilities introduced by the adoption of the QUIC protocol, highlighting its challenges in secure network communication [37]. Wang et al. proposed PSSketch, a high-accuracy and efficient method for identifying persistent and sparse flows in network traffic [38]. Dai et al. introduced PSketch, a priority-aware sketch architecture leveraging eBPF for real-time flow monitoring in network environments [39]. Butrovich et al. combined DBMS fundamentals within eBPF and achieved 43% higher throughput against VoltDB [40]. Zheng et al. mentioned how XDP programs can run in user space with 3.3x throughput gains [41]. Xiao et al. proposed an algorithm for identifying time-decaying heavy hitters using a min-heap [42].

3 Proposed Methodology

This section elaborates on the Bubble Sketch data structure and presents the choice of hash function and eBPF memory analysis, followed by eBPF Bubble Sketch variants and QUIC attack detection algorithm.

3.1 Bubble Sketch Data Structure

The Bubble Sketch [18] data structure contains two arrays, each with multiple buckets. Each bucket contains one hot entry and multiple cold entries. Each entry contains two parts: a fingerprint and a counter. Insert() operation or the top-K query operation can be performed on the sketch. For each network flow, its fingerprint is compared with the hot entry of the respective bucket to which it is hashed. If a match is not found, it is compared with a cold entry and after incrementing the counter, a real-time bubble sort is performed on the cold entries within the respective bucket. Ultimately, hot entries represent heavy hitter flows.

3.2 Hash Function and eBPF Memory Analysis

Henceforth, the user space Bubble Sketch [18] is considered as u-bubble and libpcap-bubble is the C version of u-bubble which accepts packets from the network interface rather than the on-disc .dat/.pcap dataset files. The eBPF Bubble Sketch is considered as s-bubble (standard-bubble) whose block diagram is in Fig. 1. This study implements s-bubble in restricted C using libbpf library to ensure CO-RE across multiple architectures like x86_64, aarch64 and riscv64. Clang compiler is used to generate bytecode which is then loaded in kernel memory and attached to the XDP hook. Several constraints of eBPF are addressed in s-bubble. Firstly, instead of using BOBHash which is used in u-bubble, this study uses fasthash because a comparison between BOBHash and fasthash in eBPF context across bucket counts between 2048 to 8192 shows that fasthash [19] outperforms BOBHash by 9% in precision due to its 64-bit multipliers compared to BOBHash's simpler add-xor-rotate pattern. Fasthash also does not depend on SIMD (Single Instruction, Multiple Data) instructions. Consider the following two seeds used in fasthash:

const __u64 seed1 = 0x1234567890ABCDEFULL; const __u64 seed2 = 0x9E3779B97F4A7C15ULL;

A $\sim$1% higher precision is achieved in top-1000 heavy hitter detection when `seed2` was used which is derived from the fractional part of the golden ratio(ϕ) instead of `seed1` which is an arbitrary seed.

Secondly, this study ensures that s-bubble does not exceed the eBPF stack size of 512 B. It uses 164 B (32%) in the best case call stack execution path and 243 B (47.5%) in the worst case. Since there is no heap in eBPF, an eBPF map is used. In Table 1, memory utilization of u-bubble heap is compared with s-bubble map.

`struct BubbleSketch` is included in one element of the eBPF map (`BPF_MAP_TYPE_ARRAY`) instead of spreading multiple buckets across multiple array elements in order to reduce `bpf_map_lookup_elem()` helper call latency to only one per packet. For sorting the hot entries taken from each bucket for the top-K query, u-bubble uses std::sort() of C++. In the absence of a max-heap, there is a need for a faster algorithm in C since qsort($O(n \log_2 n)$) faces function pointer overhead. Thus, non-comparison based algorithms like Stable

Table 1. Memory Utilization of u-bubble and s-bubble

Bubble Sketch	Buckets per Array	Memory
u-bubble (Sketch Heap)	2048	1.13 MB
u-bubble (Sketch Heap)	8192	4.50 MB
s-bubble (Map)	2048	0.5 MB
s-bubble (Map)	8192	1.94 MB

Logical Partition Radix Sort (SLPR) [30] and base-256 Radix Sort are considered. s-bubble uses SLPR because it essentially divides the input array into logical regions(sorted region and active region) and avoids comparison-driven recursive branching achieving a time complexity of $O(n \log_2 k)$ worst case where k is the maximum flow count.

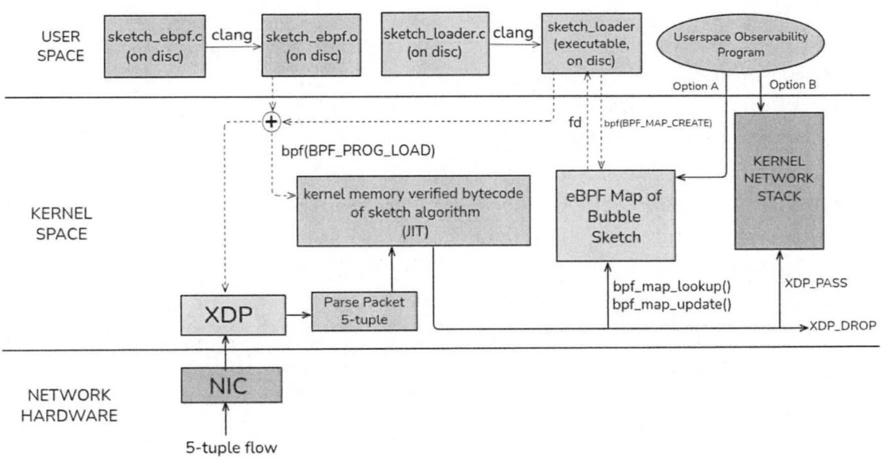

Fig. 1. eBPF Bubble Sketch block diagram.

3.3 eBPF Bubble Sketch Variants

Besides s-bubble, this study proposes three additional variants namely, *p-bubble*, *t-bubble* and *m-bubble* for different scenarios and eBPF constraints.

p-bubble. Here p stands for persistence. In p-bubble, three optimization strategies are applied: adaptive lossy threshold, flow admission control and space reclaim.

While u-bubble always decrements count by one, in p-bubble adaptive lossy threshold strategy, two constants are introduced which act as multipliers to the relocation threshold (RT). They are `LOSSY_HIGH_THRESHOLD` and

LOSSY_LOW_THRESHOLD. If the entry's count exceeds LOSSY_HIGH_THRESHOLD * RT, its count is decremented by one (minimal decrement). If the entry's count is less than LOSSY_LOW_THRESHOLD * RT, its count is reduced to its 25% (aggressive decrement). If the entry's count is in between these two thresholds, then its count is reduced to its 12.5% (proportional decrement).

In flow admission control strategy, all packets are allowed till the global packet count is less than a constant called ADMISSION_START_THRESHOLD. Once this count exceeds, the admission rate is reduced from 100% to 99.5%. Once the count exceeds ADMISSION_FULL_THRESHOLD, the admission rate is further reduced to 98% based on a probabilistic approach via a hash multiplier.

In space reclaim strategy, the concept of staleness is proposed. Certain entries are stale and are removed periodically if the following two conditions hold true. Firstly, the difference between the current packet count and the count assigned to a variable `last_update_pkt` value for the same flow, is greater than a STALE_ENTRY_PACKET_THRESHOLD. Secondly, the current count is less than a RECLAIM_COUNT_FACTOR which is usually calculated as a fraction of the relocation threshold (RT). By implementing these three strategies, an increased throughput of ~40K pps is obtained at the cost of a decreased precision of ~0.5%.

t-bubble. Here t stands for tail calls. Tail calls are different from inlined function calls of s-bubble. In s-bubble, there is only one XDP program under `SEC("xdp")` and inlined function calls exist in the same program occupying a common 512 B stack. In t-bubble, there are three additional XDP programs, whose references are stored in a BPF_MAP_TYPE_PROG_ARRAY (program array). The transfer of control is such that, when the main XDP program starts a tail call chain using a helper function `bpf_tail_call()`, the main XDP program is completely overwritten in kernel memory by the next XDP program. The three additional XDP programs are PROG_INSERT_HOT_BUCKET0, PROG_INSERT_HOT_BUCKET1 and PROG_INSERT_COLD. A major advantage of tail calls is that each program gets a fresh version of the 512 B stack at the cost of eBPF map memory overhead of just 46 B due to the data structure which stores the context passed between two tail calls.

m-bubble. Here m stands for map sharding. It is observed that the maximum buckets per array which can fit in a single array map entry is 8192 (2^{13}) as shown in Table 1 beyond which the 64-bit kernel-imposed memory limit of ~2 MB is exceeded, resulting in a segmentation fault. However, when a top-5000 or a top-10000 query operation is desired with high precision, the only solution is to increase the bucket count. m-bubble is advantageous here, wherein a hash-based map sharding is implemented. Four separate array maps are considered and two most significant bits (MSB) of the hash value corresponding to a 5-tuple key are used to decide which out of the four maps to send the packet.

3.4 QUIC Attack Detection

HTTP/3 utilizes the QUIC handshake with built-in TLS 1.3. QUIC is a transport layer protocol that operates on top of UDP port 443, instead of TCP. It is identified that traditional TCP-based defences cannot address certain security vulnerabilities of QUIC's design. This study proposes a three step algorithm using s-bubble for detecting three QUIC attacks. In the first step, QUIC header parsing is performed on the unencrypted header fields of every packet followed by the extraction of the 5-tuple and the first 8 bytes of the Destination Connection ID (DCID). Together, this is called as the *flow_key*. In the second step, the Insert() operation on the s-bubble sketch is performed. If, after searching through these top-K entries, a *flow_key* match is found, it means that the packet needs deeper analysis and the chances of it being anomalous are high. In Handshake Flood attack, attackers can flood servers with bogus 'Initial' packets and exhaust resources. In 0-RTT Replay attack, 0-RTT packets can be sent by an attacker to trigger duplicate server operations. In Amplification attack, attackers send small spoofed packets to cause large Retry messages. Attack-type specific counters like initial_packets, handshake_packets and zero_rtt_packets are stored as data structure entries within a separate eBPF map. In the third step, the values of these counters are compared with certain thresholds and it is decided whether to allow the packet to move further up the kernel's network stack (XDP_PASS) or drop the packet (XDP_DROP) and inform a user space program.

4 Results and Discussion

This section discusses the experimental setup, dataset, performance metrics and results comparing eBPF Bubble Sketch variants with the baseline algorithms.

4.1 Experimental Setup

The experimentation was performed on an AMD Ryzen 3 7320U Processor with Radeon Graphics, 8.0 GB RAM, 8 cores, running Linux Mint 22 with Kernel Version 6.8.0-79-generic. Two virtual network interfaces (one for sending and the other for receiving packets) as well as peer-to-peer Ethernet LAN connection were created. From the sender interface, packets were generated and sent to the receiving interface using tcpreplay and pktgen. The ebpf program, attached to the receiving interface, processed the packets by parsing them and inserting their keys into the sketch.

4.2 Dataset

The dataset used for experimentation consists of multiple files with the .pcap extension taken from the CAIDA-2016 and CAIDA-2019 datasets. The dataset is available in the project Github repository [43]. These pcap files were used to send the packets using tcpreplay and also for constructing the ground truth for performance evaluation.

4.3 Performance Metrics

The performance metrics calculated in this study are:
Throughput: It is the number of packets inserted into the sketch per second.
Precision: It is the ratio of the number of heavy flows reported correctly to the total number of flows reported by the sketch.

$$\text{Precision} = \frac{TP}{TP + FP} \tag{1}$$

Average Relative Error (ARE): It is the average percentage error between the predicted and actual values, relative to the actual values.

$$\text{ARE} = \frac{1}{n}\sum_{i=1}^{n}\frac{|P_i - A_i|}{A_i} \tag{2}$$

Average Absolute Error (AAE): It is the average of the absolute differences between the predicted and actual values.

$$\text{AAE} = \frac{1}{n}\sum_{i=1}^{n}|P_i - A_i| \tag{3}$$

4.4 Results

The primary value of K used in this study is 1000 because it is used by many data centers and CDNs, and it is small enough to evaluate algorithm performance. For s-bubble, precision is stable for relocation constant (RC) values of $1 < RC < 10$, but extremes cause distinct behaviours. This study defines new terms for these behaviours: the *thrashing condition* ($RC < 1$), where frequent kickouts occur due to low thresholds, and the *shadow condition* ($RC > 10$), where potential hot entries remain suppressed under dominant ones. Thus, the RC value of 1.5 is used throughout all experiments.

Experiments on Precision: Figure 2(a) shows that s-bubble achieves maximum precision as the bucket count increases from 2048 to 16384. Figure 2(b) shows that s-bubble achieves maximum precision as K increases from 100 to 1000. Figure 2(c) shows that m-bubble achieves 6% higher precision compared to s-bubble for $K \geq 2000$ because m-bubble's bucket count surpasses the bucket limit of s-bubble. On average, s-bubble outperforms HeavyKeeper and Cuckoo Counter by 8.89% and 25.09% higher precision respectively.

Experiments on AAE and ARE: Figure 3(a) and Fig. 3(b) show that s-bubble, on average, achieves 72.56x lower AAE than HeavyKeeper and 87.68x lower AAE than Cuckoo Counter for varying bucket count and K. Figure 3(c) shows that s-bubble achieves 316.96x lower ARE than HeavyKeeper and 22.757x lower ARE than Cuckoo Counter as K varies from 100 to 1000.

Experiment on Throughput: Figure 4(a) shows that p-bubble outperforms HeavyKeeper and Cuckoo Counter by 17.95% and 1.43% higher throughput respectively.p-bubble achieves 11.5% higher throughput than s-bubble by a margin of $\sim 40K$ packets per second and a marginal precision drop of 0.5% which is acceptable in DDoS-vulnerable environments like large ISP edge routers.

User Space Precision Comparison: In Fig. 4(b) s-bubble and p-bubble achieve 47% higher precision as compared to libpcap-bubble.

Sorting Algorithm Comparison: Figure 4 (c) shows that for sorting all hot entries for top-K query, the SLPR sorting algorithm is 6.33x faster than qsort() and 1.77x faster than base-256 Radix Sort for buckets per array count of 8192 (2^{13}) and K=1000.

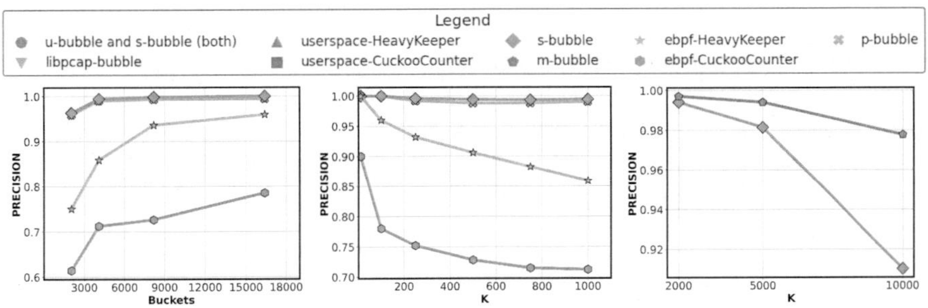

(a) Precision vs Bkts (b) Precision vs $K(\leq 1000)$ (c) Precision vs $K(\geq 2000)$

Fig. 2. Comparison of eBPF sketches on Precision.

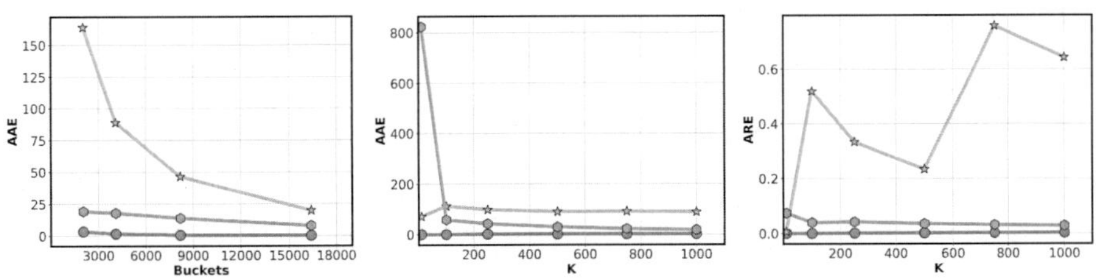

(a) AAE vs Bkts (b) AAE vs K (c) ARE vs K

Fig. 3. Comparison of eBPF sketches on AAE and ARE.

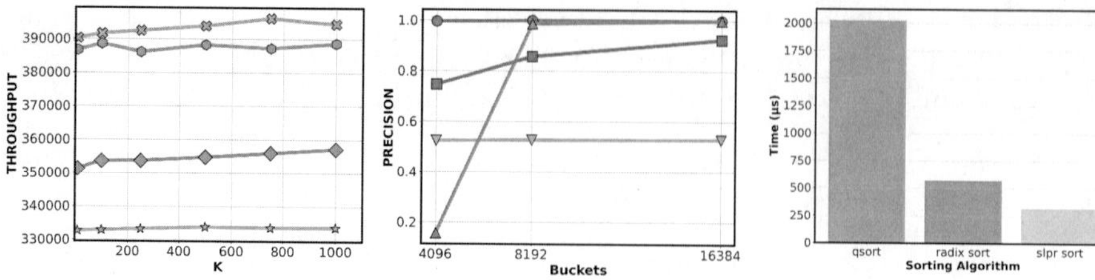

(a) Throughput vs K (b) Userspace Algorithms (c) Sorting Algorithms

Fig. 4. Comparison of eBPF sketches on Throughput, user space sketches on Precision, and performance of Sorting Algorithms.

5 Conclusion and Future Scope

Top-K Heavy Hitter detection continues to play a crucial role in networking systems because of its wide range of applications including DDoS Detection, Anomaly Detection, Congestion Control and many more. eBPF offers a highly beneficial functionality of running user defined programs inside the kernel without modifying the kernel code. This study introduces four eBPF Bubble Sketch variants: s-bubble, p-bubble, t-bubble and m-bubble. Results show that eBPF Bubble Sketch outperforms the user space Bubble Sketch by 47% higher precision. It also outperforms the eBPF versions of HeavyKeeper by 8.89% and Cuckoo Counter by 25.09% in precision. Future scope includes combining the four variants into an adaptive hybrid sketch and extending its compatibility beyond the Linux Kernel.

References

1. Zussman, T., et al.: Cache is king: smart page eviction with eBPF. arXiv preprint arXiv:2502.02750 (2025). https://doi.org/10.48550/arXiv.2502.02750
2. Shahinfar, F., Miano, S., Panda, A., Antichi, G.: Demystifying performance of eBPF network applications. Proc. ACM Network. **3**(CoNEXT3), 1–21 (2025)
3. Song, L., Li, J.: eBPF: Pioneering kernel programmability and system observability - past, present, and future insights. In: 2024 3rd International Conference on Artificial Intelligence and Computer Information Technology (AICIT), pp. 1–10. IEEE (2024). https://doi.org/10.1109/AICIT62434.2024.10730620
4. Luo, L., Guo, D., Ma, R.T.B., Rottenstreich, O., Luo, X.: Optimizing bloom filter: challenges, solutions, and comparisons. IEEE Commun. Surv. Tutor. **21**(2), 1912–1949 (2018). https://doi.org/10.1109/COMST.2018.2889329
5. Cormode, G., Muthukrishnan, S.: An improved data stream summary: the count-min sketch and its applications. J. Algorithms **55**(1), 58–75 (2005)
6. Charikar, M., Chen, K., Farach-Colton, M.: Finding frequent items in data streams. In: Widmayer, P., Eidenbenz, S., Triguero, F., Morales, R., Conejo, R., Hennessy, M. (eds.) ICALP 2002. LNCS, vol. 2380, pp. 693–703. Springer, Heidelberg (2002). https://doi.org/10.1007/3-540-45465-9_59

7. Zhang, S., Wang, N., Tang, L.: Unmasking vulnerabilities of HyperLogLog: security via parameter extraction. In: Proceedings of the 9th Asia-Pacific Workshop on Networking, pp. 207–213 (2025). https://doi.org/10.1145/3735358.3735362
8. Liu, Z., Manousis, A., Vorsanger, G., Sekar, V., Braverman, V.: One sketch to rule them all: rethinking network flow monitoring with UnivMon. In: Proceedings of the 2016 ACM SIGCOMM Conference, pp. 101–114 (2016)
9. Liu, Z., et al.: Nitrosketch: robust and general sketch-based monitoring in software switches. In: Proceedings of the ACM Special Interest Group on Data Communication, pp. 334–350. (2019). https://doi.org/10.1145/3341302.3342076
10. Friedman, R.: An evaluation of software sketches. arXiv preprint arXiv:2309.03045 (2023)
11. Ozery, A., Diamant, J., Landau Feibish, S.: RecenTo: finding top-k flows of the recent past. Proc. ACM Networking **2**(CoNEXT3), 1–20 (2024)
12. Li, Y., Miao, R., Kim, C., Yu, M.: FlowRadar: a better NetFlow for data centers. In: 13th USENIX Symposium on Networked Systems Design and Implementation (NSDI 16), pp. 311–324 (2016)
13. Cao, L., et al.: Hypersistent sketch: enhanced persistence estimation via fast item separation. In: 2025 IEEE 41st International Conference on Data Engineering (ICDE), pp. 3030–3042. IEEE (2025). https://doi.org/10.1109/ICDE65448.2025.00227
14. Sivaraman, V., Narayana, S., Rottenstreich, O., Muthukrishnan, S., Rexford, J.: Heavy-hitter detection entirely in the data plane. In: Proceedings of the Symposium on SDN Research, pp. 164–176 (2017). https://doi.org/10.1145/3050220.3063772
15. Yang, T., et al.: HeavyKeeper: an accurate algorithm for finding top-k elephant flows. IEEE/ACM Trans. Networking **27**(5), 1845–1858 (2019). https://doi.org/10.1109/TNET.2019.2933868
16. Mitzenmacher, M., Steinke, T., Thaler, J.: Hierarchical heavy hitters with the space saving algorithm. In: Bader, D.A., Mutzel, D. (eds.) Proceedings of the Fourteenth Workshop on Algorithm Engineering and Experiments (ALENEX), pp. 160–174 (2012). https://doi.org/10.1137/1.9781611972924.16
17. Li, W., Patras, P.: Tight-Sketch: a high-performance sketch for heavy item-oriented data stream mining with limited memory size. In: Proceedings of the 32nd ACM International Conference on Information and Knowledge Management, pp. 1328–1337 (2023). https://doi.org/10.1145/3583780.3615080
18. Cao, L., et al.: Bubble Sketch: a high-performance and memory-efficient sketch for finding top-k items in data streams. In: Proceedings of the 33rd ACM International Conference on Information and Knowledge Management, pp. 3653–3657 (2024). https://doi.org/10.1145/3627673.3679882
19. Miano, S., Chen, X., Basat, R.B., Antichi, G.: Fast in-kernel traffic sketching in eBPF. ACM SIGCOMM Comput. Commun. Rev. **53**(1), 3–13 (2023)
20. Zang, M., De Iaco, F., Wu, J., Savi, M.: In-kernel traffic sketching for volumetric DDoS detection. In: ICC 2025 - IEEE International Conference on Communications, pp. 2180–2185 (2025). https://doi.org/10.1109/ICC52391.2025.11161251
21. Wu, W., Li, Z., Liu, X.: Lemon: network-wide DDoS detection with routing-oblivious per-flow measurement. In: 34th USENIX Security Symposium (USENIX Security 25), pp. 3577–3594 (2025)
22. Sadiq, A., Syed, H.J., Ansari, A.A., Ibrahim, A.O., Alohaly, M., Elsadig, M.: Detection of denial of service attack in cloud based Kubernetes using eBPF. Appl. Sci. **13**(8), 4700 (2023). https://doi.org/10.3390/APP13084700
23. Gbadamosi, B., et al.: The eBPF runtime in the Linux kernel. arXiv preprint arXiv:2410.00026 (2024)

24. Yang, B., Shen, D., Zhang, J., Yang, H., Zhao, L., Wang, B., Liu, G., Chen, K.: eNetSTL: towards an in-kernel library for high-performance eBPF-based network functions. In: Proceedings of the Twentieth European Conference on Computer Systems, pp. 42–58 (2025). https://doi.org/10.1145/3689031.3696094
25. Qi, J., Li, W., Yang, T., Li, D., Li, H.: Cuckoo Counter: A novel framework for accurate per-flow frequency estimation in network measurement. In: 2019 ACM/IEEE Symposium on Architectures for Networking and Communications Systems (ANCS). pp. 1–7. IEEE (2019). https://doi.org/10.1109/ANCS.2019.8901891
26. Shi, Q., et al.: Cuckoo counter: adaptive structure of counters for accurate frequency and top-k estimation. IEEE/ACM Trans. Networking **31**(4), 1854–1869 (2023)
27. Xin, H., Lee, D., Hormozdiari, F., Yedkar, S., Mutlu, O., Alkan, C.: Accelerating read mapping with FastHASH. BMC Genomics **14**(Suppl 1), S13 (2013)
28. Liu, C., Tak, B., Wang, L.: Understanding performance of eBPF maps. In: Proceedings of the ACM SIGCOMM 2024 Workshop on eBPF and Kernel Extensions, pp. 9–15 (2024). https://doi.org/10.1145/3672197.3673430
29. Brandner, L., Marti, K., Niekel, B., Mishra, A., Antichi, G., Vanbever, L.: Better QUIC implementations with Nesquic. In: Proceedings of the ACM SIGCOMM 2025 Posters and Demos, pp. 37–39 (2025). https://doi.org/10.1145/3744969.3748410
30. Pandey, A., Kuppusamy, L.: Optimization of Base-n Radix Sort for Skewed Datasets. arXiv preprint arXiv:2509.19021 (2025)
31. Joly, C., Serman, F.: Evaluation of tail call costs in eBPF. In: Linux Plumbers Conference, vol. 2020 (2020)
32. Ngo, V.Q., Papatriantafilou, M.: Cuckoo Heavy Keeper and the balancing act of maintaining heavy-hitters in stream processing. arXiv preprint arXiv:2412.12873 (2024). https://doi.org/10.48550/arXiv.2412.12873
33. Langley, A., et al.: The QUIC transport protocol: design and internet-scale deployment. In: Proceedings of the Conference of the ACM Special Interest Group on Data Communication, pp. 183–196 (2017)
34. Abranches, M., Michel, O., Keller, E., Schmid, S.: Efficient network monitoring applications in the kernel with eBPF and XDP. In: 2021 IEEE Conference on Network Function Virtualization and Software Defined Networks (NFV-SDN), pp. 28–34. IEEE (2021). https://doi.org/10.1109/NFV-SDN53031.2021.9665095
35. Ang, K.K., Farrelly, G., Pope, C., Ranasinghe, D.C.: An automated blackbox noncompliance checker for QUIC server implementations. In: Proceedings of the 20th ACM Asia Conference on Computer and Communications Security, pp. 1459–1475 (2025). https://doi.org/10.1145/3708821.3736222
36. Dey, D., Ghosh, N.: iQUIC: an intelligent framework for defending QUIC connection ID-based DoS attack using advantage actor–critic RL. Comput. Secur. **155**, 104463 (2025). https://doi.org/10.1016/J.COSE.2025.104463
37. Josić, K., Papić, S.: Security challenges in network communication caused by the QUIC protocol. In: 2025 MIPRO 48th ICT and Electronics Convention, pp. 2173–2176. IEEE (2025). https://doi.org/10.1109/MIPRO65660.2025.11131854
38. Wang, J., et al.: PSSketch: finding persistent and sparse flow with high accuracy and efficiency. In: Proceedings of the 31st ACM SIGKDD Conference on Knowledge Discovery and Data Mining V. 2. pp. 2950–2961 (2025). https://doi.org/10.1145/3711896.3737094
39. Dai, Y., Guo, Q., Wang, X.: PSketch: a priority-aware sketch architecture for real-time flow monitoring via eBPF. arXiv preprint arXiv:2509.07338 (2025)

40. Butrovich, M., Arch, S., Lim, W.S., Zhang, W., Patel, J.M., Pavlo, A.: BPF-DB: a kernel-embedded transactional database management system for eBPF applications. Proc. ACM Manag. Data **3**(3), 1–27 (2025)
41. Zheng, Y., Gavriil, P., Kogias, M.: UXDP: frictionless XDP deployments in userspace. In: Proceedings of the 3rd Workshop on eBPF and Kernel Extensions, pp. 8–14 (2025). https://doi.org/10.1145/3748355.3748360
42. Xiao, Q., Wang, H., Pan, G.: Accurately identify time-decaying heavy hitters by decay-aware cuckoo filter along kicking path. In: 2022 IEEE/ACM 30th International Symposium on Quality of Service (IWQoS), pp. 1–10. IEEE (2022). https://doi.org/10.1109/IWQoS54832.2022.9812870
43. Project Github Repository. https://github.com/Dhruv-Sadhale/ebpf_bubble

Adaptive Transfer Learning for Field-Based Lentil Disease Detection

Sai Nithin Chowdary Kota(✉) and Sourajit Behera

Department of Computer Science and Engineering, SVNIT, Surat, India
{p24ds023,sourajit}@coed.svnit.ac.in

Abstract. Agriculture has been vital to human subsistence for eons. Even so, the early detection of plant diseases persists as a crucial challenge, which, with even minuscule delays, can greatly diminish crop productivity, quantity, and quality. Enabled by recent advancements in deep learning and computer vision, the automated identification of diseases in plants has become practically possible. However, the majority of existing models still focus on accuracy as a primary metric, while overlooking practical constraints and concerns, such as efficiency and deployment friendliness. Additionally, existing works trivially focus on designing deep convolutional neural networks from scratch. In contrast, this work capitalizes on fine-tuning a pre-trained ResNet101 model subjected to empirical layer retraining and transfer learning. This empirical retraining addresses the prevalent issue in prior works, which suggested following a hard-coded value for choosing layers for retraining without proper justification. Accordingly, our work simulates investigations for determining the ideal fine-tuning depth while balancing a trade-off between computational cost and accuracy metric. Notably, in comparison to multiple CNN-based pre-trained models, our fine-tuned approach maintains an overall $\sim 4\%$ improvement, which amplifies to 11% for precision and 5% for F1-Score when Ascochyta blight class is under the scanner from a real-world field-based public lentil disease dataset. With around 5 million trainable parameters, our proposed model attains a compelling equilibrium while posing as a front-runner for real-world implementation.

Keywords: Lentil disease detection · Computer vision · Deep learning · Transfer learning · Convolutional Neural Networks

1 Introduction

For ages, agriculture has sustained humans and civilizations, shaping communities and sustaining economies worldwide. For quite some time now, from 2000 onwards, the blended agricultural volume and corresponding value, including forestry, & fishing, has surged by around 78%, which contributes nearly 3.6 trillion dollars at the global stage [6]. Despite such progress, agriculture continues to face profound challenges, with plant diseases being the most prominent and damaging. Such diseases can have a disastrous effect on both the yield and the

G. K. Verma et al. (Eds.): MIND 2025, CCIS 2981, pp. 488–500, 2027.
https://doi.org/10.1007/978-3-032-31230-3_39

quality of crops, thereby incrementing the burden on farmers' incomes [14]. For instance, with reference to maize, gray leaf spots initially appear as small, yellow lesions that develop into large, gray patches, often mistaken for common rust. Interestingly, this disease alone is accountable for a yield loss of 25 million tonnes, deciphering to around 35% loss across North America.

Lentils are a major food legume and rank sixth in global production [1]. Their rich micronutrient, fibre, protein, and mineral content makes them widely consumed in Bangladesh and worldwide [11]. Although grown in over 70 countries, nearly 70% of global production comes from the Indian subcontinent, Australia, America, and Africa [4], with India being the second-largest producer [7]. Lentil production, however, is heavily threatened by diseases such as Stemphylium blight, which has caused a 22% global yield decline [9]. Severe cases have resulted in losses of up to 93% in India [13] and complete crop failure in Nepal for susceptible varieties [8]. Such effects mark the requirement for accurately determining plant diseases as early as possible. However, farmers are still dependent on ocular inspections, a technique that can be very labor-intensive, time-consuming, and often inaccurate. Being an affordable staple in Southeast Asia, a dependable and opportune lentil disease detection remains one of the crucial matters necessary for defending food security. In spite of its nutritional importance, lentils have remained one of the most understudied crops among plant diseases literature, specifically when compared to major crops like tomatoes, wheat, rice. And the meager number of investigations addressing lentil diseases relies mainly on small data assembled under conditions which do not bear any circumstantial effects common in real-field conditions. Therefore, concentrating on a trustworthy and high-quality lentil-based disease dataset is both essential and justified to address the above shortcomings and establish a baseline for this important but understudied crop.

Lately, machine learning (ML) has become one of the frontrunners to automate agricultural disease detection. Prior works depended on conventional ML pipelines, which mandate performing feature extraction manually depending on color, shape, or texture, followed by classification. For instance, Aravind et al. [2] proposed to extract the gray-level co-occurrence matrix-based texture features on the corn crop from the PlantVillage dataset and performed classification using a support vector machine and achieved 83.7% accuracy. On a similar note, Shah et al. [12] demonstrated the use of artificial neural networks, showing that simpler models can be effective on smaller datasets. Yet, these approaches heavily rely on handcrafted features, which in turn require significant domain expertise that often struggles to adapt to real-world, diverse scenarios. To address such cases, recent works have shifted their focus towards deep learning (DL), which is adept at learning meaningful representations from input images. Additionally, DL models are robust to natural variations in leaf appearance and environment, making them well-suited for practical disease detection.

Among DL-based approaches, convolutional neural networks (CNNs) have proven especially effective for computer vision tasks and are widely used in plant disease detection. Trained on large-scale datasets containing millions of images—such as ImageNet, ILSVRC, and CIFAR-100, CNNs learn rich, transferable features that often outperform traditional handcrafted methods requiring substantial domain expertise. For example, Ashurov et al. [3] enhanced CNN performance for plant disease recognition by combining improved residual skip connections with squeeze-and-excitation blocks. However, CNNs generally struggle in low-data scenarios [5], which are common in agriculture. To address this, transfer learning (TL) is frequently employed, enabling pre-trained networks to adapt to new tasks by reusing stable, general-purpose features learned from a source domain. TL helps improve performance and reduce data requirements by retaining these nonfluctuating representations while fine-tuning them for the specific target problem.

Recent studies continue to show the value of transfer learning (TL) in agricultural disease detection. For example, Teena et al. [15] compared several ImageNet-pretrained models for identifying mango diseases, highlighting how pretrained CNNs can boost performance even with limited data. However, while TL is widely used, one important aspect often receives little attention: how much of the pretrained network should actually be fine-tuned. Depending on how closely the target problem aligns with the pretraining domain, retraining only a small portion of the network may be sufficient, whereas more complex tasks may require deeper adaptation. This means the number of layers chosen for retraining can strongly influence accuracy, stability, and computational cost.

Despite its importance, many earlier works have relied on fixed, untested fine-tuning schemes, without evaluating whether those choices are optimal for their dataset or task. Since large CNNs carry millions of parameters, unnecessary retraining can significantly increase computation and limit deployability, especially in field environments where lightweight, efficient models are needed. As agriculture increasingly moves toward smart and real-time solutions, there is a growing need for adaptive fine-tuning strategies that balance performance with efficiency, yet this remains underexplored.

To our knowledge, only a limited number of studies have empirically examined how different fine-tuning depths affect performance or how these decisions relate to the underlying architecture (e.g., the role of high-level vs. mid-level residual blocks). This gap becomes even more relevant in small, specialized datasets, such as those involving lentil diseases, where overfitting and computational cost are major constraints. Addressing these challenges, our work presents an adaptive transfer learning framework that systematically evaluates layer-retraining configurations in ResNet101, explains their architectural implications, and quantifies the resulting performanceefficiency trade-offs. We assess these strategies on a field-based lentil disease dataset, and the main contributions of our study are outlined below:

- A TLbased fine-tuning approach is proposed, which retrains a selected set of layers. Unlike standard fine-tuning, our approach introduces an adaptive transfer learning procedure that empirically determines the optimal unfreezing depth of the backbone, achieving a superior balance between accuracy, stability, and computational cost.

- Simulations involve comparison among several pre-trained models apart from state-of-the-art work, classification report across disease classes, to highlight the model's benefits.
- Discussions on the deficiencies and conceivable enhancements of the model proposed have been undertaken.

The rest of the paper has been assembled as follows. Section 2 presents the proposed approach. Section 3 discusses the dataset, settings, results, and discussions. Finally, the conclusion and future work are covered in Sect. 4.

2 Proposed Methodology

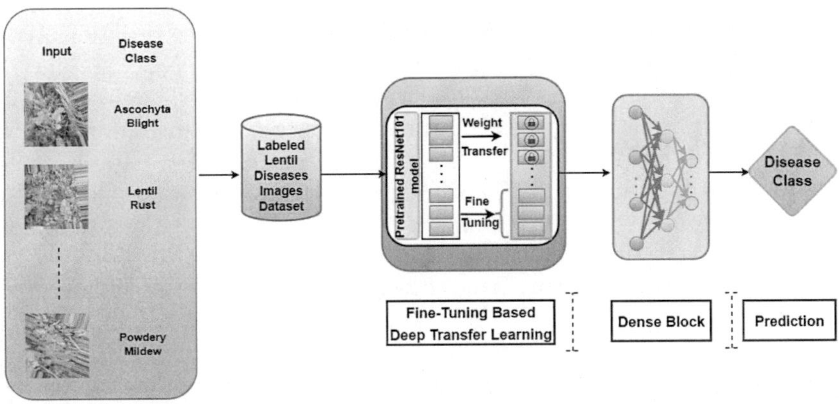

Fig. 1. Expanded depiction of the proposed approach, where locks suggest frozen layers, with fine-tuning examined empirically.

Figure 1 illustrates the overall workflow of our proposed lentil disease detection approach. The diagram uses lock symbols to indicate which layers are frozen and which are retrained during fine-tuning. Based on our comparative analysis (see Sect. 3.3 and Table 2), ResNet101 was selected as the backbone model due to its consistently strong performance across metrics. On top of the ResNet101 base, we add a stack of dense layers configured as described in Sect. 3.2, with the final dense layer producing the class predictions. After training, the model is evaluated on the full test set using standard performance metrics. Cross-entropy loss is employed as the objective function during training.

3 Experiments, Results and Discussions

3.1 Dataset Description

The dataset used in this work was obtained from [10], where images of lentil plants were captured under various field conditions, covering both healthy plants and those affected by powdery mildew, lentil rust, and ascochyta blight. The images were collected directly from farms in Bangladesh using a smartphone between May and August 2023. All images were stored in JPG format at a resolution of 224 × 224 pixels, with labels provided for each disease category. To minimize harsh shadows and ensure adequate lighting, photographs were taken during the early morning (69 AM) and late afternoon (46 PM). While these time windows help reduce extreme lighting variability, natural factors such as cloudy weather, seasonal changes, or daily fluctuations in sunlight can still influence illumination. As a result, the dataset reflects a partially controlled yet inherently field-based environment, where lighting conditions cannot be fully standardized. This makes the dataset more realistic but also more challenging compared to laboratory-captured images. The data were collected during warm months with limited rainfall, conditions favorable for lentil growth as well as the appearance of disease symptoms. However, since weather factors such as humidity and temperature could not be regulated, the dataset naturally includes variations typical of real agricultural scenarios. The smartphone used for data collection featured a 64-megapixel GW1 sensor (1/1.72-inch size, 0.8-μm pixel pitch). The final dataset consists of four categories—Normal, Lentil Rust, Ascochyta Blight, and Powdery Mildew—with a total of 1,898 original images. The dataset authors have also released an augmented version of the original dataset as part of their official release, bringing the total number of images to 4,550. The authors built this augmented version of the dataset through an augmentation process documented publicly, with the transformations involved, include the following: random rotations with a 40-degree range; shifts of 0.2 concerning height and width; shear range of 0.2; zoom variations with 0.2; horizontal flipping imbibed; brightness varying between 0.5 to 1.5; and nearest fill mode for handling pixel interpolation. In our work, we have focused on this augmented version as provided, without applying any further augmentation of our own.The distribution of pictures under each category is presented in Table 1.

Table 1. Dataset Description

Disease Category	Images in Original data	Images in Augmented data
Normal	454	1321
Ascochyta Blight	466	1029
Powdery Mildew	492	1125
Lentil Rust	480	1075
Total	1898	4550

3.2 Settings

Simulations have been conducted to estimate the various disease categories affecting the lentil crop. We have used the augmented dataset version (refer to Table 1) for the training and testing evaluations in this work. Our proposed pre-trained CNN model, ResNet101, has been subjected to empirical layer re-training and freezing for training on the lentil dataset. Specifically, all layers of the ResNet101 backbone were initially frozen, after which the last set of optimal layers (found through empirical re-training) were unfrozen to enable fine-tuning on the lentil image domain. With a TensorFlow backend and Keras library, we utilized the functional API to implement the network, while constantly monitoring the validation loss to achieve practical training. As the dataset already has dedicated folders for training, validation, and testing images, no explicit splitting has been applied in our implementation. Such predefined splits explicitly provided with the dataset were used exactly, without any modification or re-partitioning. During implementation, apart from the base ResNet101, we introduced a set of successive layers, including, in order, a global average pooling layer, a dropout layer to mitigate the chances of overfitting, and a dense layer with 512 neurons. The dense layer was configured with the ReLU activation with an L2 regularizer. Finally, we placed a dense layer with the same number of neurons as the number of disease categories, which was then subjected to the softmax activation. Concerning the hyperparameters, We used a batch size of 32 and trained the model for up to 100 epochs with early stopping (patience = 5). The network was optimized using the Adam optimizer with a learning rate of 0.00001. A dropout rate of 0.5 was applied to reduce overfitting. The choice for the optimizer had been fixated with Adam because of its stability and widespread usage for fine-tuning pretrained CNNs, where only specific deep layers are subject to retraining. During model training, Adam's adaptive moment estimate aids in maintaining stable gradients. We utilized a learning rate of 0.00001 to fine-tune ResNet101, with higher learning rates, such as 0.001 or 0.0001, resulting in faster loss oscillations and partial overwriting of pre-trained features. On the other hand, a lower rate helped to adapt the unfrozen layers while keeping gradually usable lower-level representations, resulting in better steady convergence and enhanced validation performance.

The network and all experiments were conducted using a Tesla P100 NVIDIA GPU with 16 GB RAM on Colab or a Tesla T4 with 16 GB VRAM on a Kaggle notebook, depending on the availability of resources. All images in the dataset have been fixed at 224×224. We did not perform any additional normalization or preprocessing; instead, the resized images were utilized directly in their original RGB format, as supplied in the dataset. The dataset was loaded with the help of TensorFlow, which performed batching and resizing during ingestion. After training, the trained model was evaluated on the test set.

3.3 Performance Metrics

Standard metrics have been utilized for evaluating and comparing our model's performance with that of several state-of-the-art models. These metrics include accuracy (Acc), precision (Prec), recall (Rec), f1-score (F1).

Table 2. Comparisons among multiple Pre-trained Models

*Model	*Accuracy	Macro			Weighted		
		Prec	Rec	F1	Prec	Rec	F1
DenseNet169	78%	81%	80%	79%	81%	78%	78%
DenseNet201	79%	79%	81%	79%	79%	79%	78%
Xception	67%	68%	70%	67%	68%	67%	66%
VGG16	76%	76%	78%	77%	76%	76%	76%
VGG19	75%	75%	76%	75%	74%	75%	74%
ResNet50	79%	79%	80%	79%	79%	79%	78%
ResNet101	83%	83%	85%	83%	83%	83%	82%
ResNet152	78%	81%	81%	81%	80%	80%	80%
InceptionV3	66%	67%	68%	66%	67%	66%	64%
MobileNet	73%	76%	76%	73%	77%	73%	72%
MobileNetV2	70%	71%	72%	70%	71%	70%	69%
NASNetMobile	63%	63%	65%	63%	62%	63%	61%
NASNetLarge	66%	74%	67%	68%	73%	66%	67%

Comparisons with Other Pre-trained CNN Models. Apart from the single lentil-specific baseline available in prior work, no extra state-of-the-art architectures have been trained or evaluated on this dataset. Thus, to ensure a thorough inspection despite this issue, we compared our model against a set of widely used, pre-trained CNN-based models present in Keras (such as ResNet, MobileNet, NASNet, VGG, and DenseNet), which provide strong and practical baselines for disease detection in plants.

For our first set of simulations, we test with multiple pre-trained CNN models and report their accuracy, weighted & macro metrics for precision (prec), recall (rec), F1-Score (F1), respectively, in Table 2. Accordingly, we have selected CNN families that are diverse in terms of parameter count, for example, the parameter-heavy models, such as variations of ResNet, DenseNet, VGG, and NASNet, as well as lightweight ones like MobileNet, among others. From the table, we observe that the parameter-heavy models inadvertently achieved the best metric values, in the order of ResNets, followed by DenseNet, VGG, and others. However, the lightweight models maintain reasonable values, with the inception family incurring the worst values, leading to ignoring them. With the compared ResNet family-based models performing the most sensible metrics, and ResNet101 achieving the best values, we have selected it as the base model for our experiments, as it obtains improvements of at least 4% over the second-best values for accuracy metrics.

This improvement has been measured concerning the set of CNN-based pre-trained baselines considered here for the same lentil dataset, and is not intended as a means for directly comparing with state-of-the-art models that have been trained on other datasets or crops, which are not straightforwardly comparable because of dataset and domain differences. A similar trend is obtained when taking precision, recall, and F1 metrics as well, making it the default choice at this stage.

Table 3. Lentil Disease Detection Classification Report

*Model	Ascochyta Blight			Lentil Rust			Normal			Powdery Mildew		
	Prec	Rec	F1	Prec	Rec	F1	Prec	Rec	F1	Prec	Rec	F1
DenseNet169	60%	83%	69%	86%	99%	92%	86%	67%	75%	93%	70%	80%
DenseNet201	81%	77%	79%	79%	96%	87%	80%	57%	67%	76%	95%	85%
VGG16	78%	62%	69%	77%	93%	84%	72%	62%	67%	80%	95%	87%
VGG19	70%	57%	63%	84%	83%	84%	67%	69%	68%	81%	94%	87%
ResNet50	87%	73%	79%	76%	92%	83%	73%	66%	69%	81%	89%	85%
ResNet101	81%	82%	82%	88%	93%	90%	81%	64%	72%	82%	99%	90%
ResNet152	82%	78%	80%	89%	83%	86%	77%	66%	71%	76%	98%	85%
InceptionV3	53%	54%	54%	85%	75%	79%	68%	43%	52%	64%	100%	78%
MobileNet	61%	88%	72%	77%	91%	83%	88%	43%	58%	78%	83%	80%
MobileNetV2	63%	69%	66%	74%	95%	83%	81%	47%	59%	65%	79%	71%

Next, we present the per-class classification report for different lentil disease categories in Table 3. From the table, it is interesting to observe that much of the variation in metric values across the models is evident for the normal category. While the lightweight MobileNet family achieves the best precision values, it suffers from the worst F1 values. Interestingly, only three models, namely, DenseNet169, ResNet101, and ResNet152, manage to overcome the 70% par values. This trend clearly suggests that the majority of the compared models are biased towards detecting diseased classes, potentially leading to the misclassification of normal samples as diseased, and suggesting over-sensitivity to features from diseased classes. Thus, to mitigate the aforementioned effect, we focus on the three models mentioned above for the remainder of this article. Next among the three, ResNet101 overpowers ResNet152 significantly with better F1-score values for all classes. Finally, although the DenseNet169 model achieves good values for lentil rust and the normal class, ResNet101 achieves almost comparable values for these classes while overpowering the remaining two categories, managing a $\sim$ 21% improvement in precision for the Ascochyta Blight class. Given the upgrades, ResNet101 maintains its lead both at the overall level and on the per-class report as well.

It is worth noting that among the various CNN-based backbones compared, specifically the MobileNet variants, these models are exclusively designed to be lightweight and optimized for edge and model deployment. Such models function as specialised baselines to evaluate computational efficiency in resource-constrained scenarios. As observed, despite the fact that MobileNet architectures offer significantly lower computational complexity and size of model, their performance is substantially diminished in nature compared to that of the proposed fine-tuned ResNet101 architecture configuration. This highlights that the accuracy Vs. Efficiency trade-off and establishes our model within the broader landscape of high-capacity and lightweight CNNs.

Table 4. Empirical Layer Training Vs. Overall Metrics of ResNet101

*Layer	*Accuracy	*Trainable Params(in Mil)	Macro			Weighted		
			Prec	Rec	F1	Prec	Rec	F1
5	81%	2.11	81%	83%	81%	82%	81%	81%
10	83%	5.52	83%	85%	83%	83%	83%	82%
15	82%	6.57	83%	84%	83%	83%	82%	82%
20	79%	9.98	80%	82%	79%	81%	79%	78%
25	84%	11.04	84%	86%	85%	84%	84%	84%
30	81%	15.5	82%	83%	81%	82%	81%	80%

Empirical Layer Re-training This section examines how retraining the different depths of the ResNet backbone architecture plays a role in the overall model performance. Accordingly, we progressively alter the number of unfrozen layers, starting from the rear part of the network, while holding the rest of the layers frozen, and document the corresponding performance metrics, along with the count of trainable parameters, in Table 4. The outcomes showcase that incrementing the count of retrained layers, in general, improved the performance up to the 25th layer configuration, post which the accuracy dips by around 3%. Although with 25th layer retraining, the model achieves the best accuracy, it can do so at the cost of over 11 million trainable parameters, leading to a significantly bigger computational requirement and higher risk of overfitting, given the limited size of the dataset. In comparison, the 10-layer configuration for retraining achieves a second-best performance for all metrics, while requiring a nearly 50% smaller set of trainable parameters. This setting presents a practical trade-off balance between model complexity and accuracy: as unfreezing too few layers, for example, 5, restricts the feature adaptation to disease patterns in lentils; whereas unfreezing too many layers makes the model introduce excessive capacity while incurring huge computational costs (for example, with 30). Thus, we have selected the 10-layer retraining strategy as the optimal fine-tuning setting for this work, as it achieves strong accuracy with a remarkably lowered computational cost and reduced risk of overfitting.

On a structural level, the last 10 layers of ResNet101 align with the highest semantic residual block, which maps problem-specific abstractions that are more relevant to disease detection. Performing fine-tuning on such layers allows the model to focus on lentil disease features while retaining the mid-level texture-based robust features and learned representations. On the contrary, applying the same approach to 25 layers begins to modify the mid-level residual blocks, which are, at this point, well-generalized and contribute borderline performance gains while increasing the likelihood of overwriting stable features.

Even though we do not explicitly document the training time on a per-epoch basis or specify the inference latency, the difference in the count of trainable parameters (11.04 vs 5.52) presents a notably higher computational cost for the 25-layer retraining during both inference and training. Such a trade-off reinforces the choice of the 10-layer based retraining as a better computationally efficient and practically deployable prospect.

Next, an anomalous dip in performance is observed when retraining 20 layers in Table 4. Such a ResNet101 configuration corresponds to an unfreezing depth that lies closer to a transition between mid-level and higher-level residual blocks. Performing fine-tuning at this stage can generate unstable gradient behavior as the model may overwrite partially the pretrained semantic features without adequate deep layer adaptation. With a relatively high trainable parameter count of 9.98 million, the 20-layer setup exacerbates the overfitting risk on a limited dataset, while not achieving the stronger feature specialization seen in the 25-layer setup, thereby highlighting the sensitivity of deep layer fine-tuning.

Table 5. Lentil Disease Detection Classification Report Among State-of-the-art

*Model	Ascochyta Blight			Lentil Rust			Normal			Powdery Mildew		
	Prec	Rec	F1	Prec	Rec	F1	Prec	Rec	F1	Prec	Rec	F1
DenseNet201 [10]	70%	84%	77%	86%	100%	93%	94%	60%	73%	88%	100%	94%
ResNet101	81%	82%	82%	88%	93%	90%	81%	64%	72%	82%	99%	90%

Comparisons with State-of-the-Art Works. As the dataset under inspection in this work, the Lentil Plant Disease and Quality Assessment is a newly introduced dataset; the current literature briefly provides only a single posted deadline, i.e., DenseNet201 by the original authors. Hence, this model serves as the only available baseline to act as the state-of-the-art work for lentil-based disease detection, and accordingly, we have reproduced its results for a fair comparison. Table 5 presents the per-class classification report between the current reported state-of-the-art works and our proposed method on the lentil dataset. Interestingly, our method maintains a neck-and-neck fight for the normal class, where most other pre-trained models failed to score. While DenseNet201 [10] surpasses for the Lentil rust and powdery mildew classes, the improvements over our model are not significant margins. In contrast, ResNet101 gains at least $\sim$ 5% for the Ascochyta blight class regarding F1, with the precision gaining over $\sim$ 11%.

A consistent observation across compared pre-trained models is a tendency to misclassify normal images as diseased, evident by the relatively poor recall concerning DenseNet (60%). This bias emerges as diseased leaves demonstrate distinct illustration cues, such as spots, discoloration, and lesions, that deep models comprehend with greater ease compared to subtle, uniform depictions of healthier leaves. Furthermore, the augmented dataset presents more comprehensive variability in diseased classes, which in turn strengthens the models' tendency towards diseased estimations. The proposed 10-layer based fine-tuned ResNet101 subdues this problem by enabling deep feature adaptation, letting it capture more fine-grained color and texture consistency exhibited in healthy leaves. This propels to an improvised normal class recall of 64% in comparison to DenseNet201 and achieve a reduced false disease alarm, making our model further reliable in practical field-based settings.

Discussion on Practical Applicability. To deploy models in real-world agricultural scenarios for plant disease detection, there exist multiple practical challenges, like hardware limitations, computational efficiency, and the requirement for real-life or near-real-time inference. Although ResNet101 is a high-capacity model, our analysis based on empirical layer retraining (as shown in Table 5) showcases that the 10-layer configuration retraining can significantly reduce the count of trainable parameters in contrast to deeper fine-tuning schemes, making it more appropriate to deploy on resource-constrained edge devices.

For edge-based deployment scenarios, inference generally occurs on embedded or mobile devices with limited memory, energy capacity, and processing power. Higher model complexity incurs greater latency and aggravated memory demands, that can hamper applicability to real-time field-based conditions. By achieving a reduction in parameter count post-retraining while keeping good accuracy, the chosen configuration presents a balanced trade-off between detection performance and computational demand. Additionally, real-time and real-world deployments in agricultural settings must accommodate erratic natural lighting, motion blur from handheld devices, and unstable network connectivity. While our model achieves good performance under controlled testing conditions, robust deployment will benefit from supplemental optimizations, such as model quantization, compression, or conversion to lightweight architectures for mobile inference. These considerations will help outline the practical requirements and future extensions necessary for field-ready deployment.

Furthermore, the improved precision obtained for the Ascochyta Blight class (an 11% surge over DenseNet201) carries significant implications. Elevated precision helps reduce the false positives, which aid to ensure that healthy plants do not get misclassified as diseased. For real-field-based settings, where Ascochyta blight typically triggers preventive fungicide usage, this reduction in misclassification can lead to a decrease in unwarranted chemical usage, resulting in lower production costs and a more sustainable environmental impact overall. Such improvements will enable farmers and field scouts to prioritize interventions on actual diseased plants, making disease management more resource-efficient.

4 Conclusion and Future Works

This work addressed lentil disease detection using a field-based dataset, where data scarcity and variability make model training challenging. While transfer learning is widely used, many prior studies rely on fixed fine-tuning schemes. In contrast, our study introduces an adaptive transfer learning strategy that empirically evaluates different fine-tuning depths of ResNet101 and analyzes the associated performanceefficiency trade-offs. This approach allowed us to identify an optimal unfreezing configuration that achieves a strong balance between accuracy, stability, and trainable parameters. Across multiple pre-trained CNNs, ResNet101 delivered the best performance, improving overall accuracy by approximately 4% over the next-best model and yielding a ~11% precision gain for Ascochyta Blight compared to the existing state-of-the-art. These findings underscore the importance of adaptive fine-tuning, particularly for small, real-world agricultural datasets. Looking ahead, deploying such models on edge devices remains a challenge due to storage and computational limits. As future work, we plan to investigate model compression to reduce model size and enable practical, real-time use in smart farming applications. Future work will include explicit runtime and latency measurements to further quantify these differences.

References

1. Aktar-Uz-Zaman, M., et al.: Screening of lentil genotypes against stemphylium blight disease and molecular identification of causal organism. Sci. Rep. **15**(1), 32318 (2025)
2. Aravind, K., Raja, P., Mukesh, K., Aniirudh, R., Ashiwin, R., Szczepanski, C.: Disease classification in maize crop using bag of features and multiclass support vector machine. In: 2018 2nd international conference on inventive systems and control (ICISC), pp. 1191–1196. IEEE (2018)
3. Ashurov, A.Y., et al.: Enhancing plant disease detection through deep learning: a depthwise cnn with squeeze and excitation integration and residual skip connections. Front. Plant Sci. **15**, 1505857 (2025)
4. Bayaa, B., Erskine, W.: Lentil pathology. The Pathology of Food and Pasture Legumes"(D. Allen, J. Lenné, eds.). Commonwealth Agricultural Bureaux International, Slough, Berkshire, UK, pp. 422–471 (1998)
5. Behera, S., Misra, R.: A multi-model data-fusion based deep transfer learning for improved remaining useful life estimation for iiot based systems. Eng. Appl. Artif. Intell. **119**, 105712 (2023)
6. Food, of the United Nations, A.O.: World food and agriculture-statistical yearbook 2020. Food and Agriculture Organization of the United Nations (2020)
7. Food and Agriculture Organization of the United Nations (FAO): Faostat database (2018). http://faostat.fao.org. Accessed: 2025-10-30
8. Islam, M.A., Islam, S.M.A., Sathi, M.A., et al.: Identification of lentil varieties/lines resistant to stemphylium blight considering disease reaction and yield. Malays J. Sustain. Agric. **4**, 22–25 (2020)
9. Kumar, S., Barpete, S., Kumar, J., Gupta, P., Sarker, A.: Global lentil production: constraints and strategies. SATSA Mukhapatra-Annual Tech. **17**, 1–13 (2013)

10. Mahamud, E., Assaduzzaman, M., Sharmin, S.: Lentil plant disease and quality assessment: a detailed dataset of high-resolution images for deep learning research. Data Brief **58**, 111224 (2025)
11. Sen Gupta, D., et al.: Lentils (lens culinaris l.), a rich source of folates. J. Agric. Food Chem. **61**(32), 7794–7799 (2013)
12. Shah, N., Jain, S.: Detection of disease in cotton leaf using artificial neural network. In: 2019 Amity International Conference on Artificial Intelligence (AICAI), pp. 473–476. IEEE (2019)
13. Sinha, J., Singh, A.: Effect of environment on the development and spread of stemphylium blight of lentil (1993)
14. Thai, H.T., Le, K.H.: Mobileh-transformer: enabling real-time leaf disease detection using hybrid deep learning approach for smart agriculture. Crop Prot. **189**, 107002 (2025)
15. Varma, T., Mate, P., Azeem, N.A., Sharma, S., Singh, B.: Automatic mango leaf disease detection using different transfer learning models. Multimed. Tools Appl. **84**(11), 9185–9218 (2025)

Quantum Clock Synchronisation in Underwater Environments for Ultra-high Precision Timing

Jaykumar Lachure(✉), Ayush Meshram, Rajesh Doriya, Kapil Kumar Soni, and Chandrashekar Jatoth

Department of Information Technology, National Institute of Technology, Raipur, Raipur, India
{jaykumarlachure,meshramayush316}@gmail.com,
{rajeshdoriya.it,kksoni.it,jchandrashekar.it}@nitrr.ac.in

Abstract. Temperature gradients, pressure, and optical absorption are all factors that work against accurate underwater time synchronisation. In this work, we demonstrate the feasibility of Quantum Clock Synchronisation (QCS) using entangled ^{87}Sr optical lattice clocks due to their superior stability and resilience to environmental degradations. We adopt a Monte Carlo framework as a means of modeling the complicated interplay between quantum dynamics and realistic underwater environmental parameters. It is more apt at capturing stochastic effects than analytical models. Our simulations across networks of up to 20 clocks reach femtosecond-level precision. Even under severe entanglement loss due to absorption and scattering, QCS maintains a 3.2× advantage over a classical two-way optical baseline. The median error is 1.40×10^{-12} s versus 3.22×10^{-12} s at a fidelity of 2.5×10^{-5}. A sensitivity analysis confirms that temperature and pressure are the main degradations. Sub-linear error growth with network size is observed, underlining scalability for quantum timing in applications such as submarine navigation and underwater sensor networks.

Keywords: Quantum Clock Synchronisation · underwater timing · entanglement fidelity · marine quantum networks

1 Introduction

Precise time synchronisation underwater is crucial for applications like underwater navigation, seismic sensing, coordination of autonomous vehicles, and secure underwater communication, where GNSS signals are not available. Classical acoustic synchronisation reaches millisecond precision, while the precision of optical methods is limited to the nanosecond due to multipath propagation, absorption, and refractive-index fluctuations [4,8].

QCS exploits entanglement to generate femtosecond-scale temporal correlations between remote clocks with substantial precision gain. We concentrate on

G. K. Verma et al. (Eds.): MIND 2025, CCIS 2981, pp. 501–515, 2027.
https://doi.org/10.1007/978-3-032-31230-3_40

^{87}Sr optical lattice clocks because of their unparalleled stability, characterized by a fractional uncertainty of 10^{-18} and a linewidth as narrow as 1 MHz, together with relative insensitivity to environmental perturbations with respect to other atomic clock types [3].

While impressive results have been realized from laboratory demonstrations, such as 300 fs over 4 km free space [13] and 1.2 ps over 250 km fiber [12], extending QCS to an underwater environment introduces completely new challenges. Temperature gradients, hydrostatic pressure, and salinity-induced scattering accelerate decoherence through absorption and Rayleigh scattering mechanisms, reducing entanglement fidelity as low as 2.5×10^{-5} in marine conditions [2,7].

Previous underwater quantum communication research has concentrated on QKD with limited transmission distances, in the range of 2.5–50 m [2,7,10], and has not taken into account either timing stability or synchronisation performance. The current paper fills this knowledge gap by developing a coupled environmental quantum model which explicitly links temperature, pressureand salinity-driven perturbations to quantum coherence via master equation formalism and simulates entangled photon-pair transmission through seawater channels.

This work addresses the challenges of deploying ultra-sensitive optical lattice clocks in a high-pressure underwater platform while demonstrating sustained quantum advantage. Main contributions include:

1. A unified physical model that connects environmental perturbations with quantum coherence and entanglement fidelity.
2. Monte Carlo simulation for QCS based on ^{87}Sr across 10 clocks showing femtosecond-to-picosecond synchronisation accuracy:
3. Quantitative analysis of entanglement degradation mechanisms and their impact on timing precision.
4. Scalability analysis of multi-clock quantum timing networks featuring sublinear error growth.
5. Benchmarking showing 3.2 times advantage over classical two-way optical synchronisation.

The remainder of this paper is structured as follows: Sect. 2 presents the physical and environmental models; Sect. 3 details the simulation methodology; Sect. 4 reports the results; Sect. 5 discusses limitations and implications; and Sect. 6 concludes the work.

2 Physical Model

2.1 Environmental Factors

Environmental fluctuations introduce stochastic variations in phase, coherence time, and transition frequency of the optical clock [11]. Three parameters dominate underwater decoherence-temperature, pressure, and salinity-and govern the synchronisation accuracy of QCS systems [1]. Table 1 summarises all notation used throughout the physical and quantum-mechanical model.

Each environmental variable represented here affects either the effective clock frequency or the decoherence rates entering the Lindblad master equation: temperature fluctuations produce Doppler broadening and thermal frequency shifts, hydrostatic pressure increases collisional broadening and modifies the atomic linewidth, while salinity determines optical attenuation in seawater, reducing the survival probability of entangled photons. These effects explicitly enter the detunings Δu_T and Δu_P, as well as the decoherence rates $\gamma_\phi(T, P)$ and $\gamma_{\text{loss}}(S, d)$ utilized in the Hamiltonian and the Lindblad operators of Sect. 2.2, therefore providing a connection between environmental variability and quantum-state degradation.

Table 1. Summary of symbols and definitions used in the physical model.

Symbol	Description	Symbol	Description
E_{thermal}	Thermal energy per particle (J)	μ_s	Scattering coefficient (m^{-1})
k_B	Boltzmann constant (J/K)	d	Propagation distance (m)
T	Temperature (K)	ν_0	Clock transition frequency (Hz)
$\Delta\nu_T$	Temperature-induced frequency shift (Hz)	$\|\psi_0\rangle$	Initial Bell state
α_T	Temperature coefficient (Hz/K)	$\rho(t)$	Time-evolved density matrix
T_0	Nominal temperature (K)	H	Hamiltonian operator
$\Delta\nu_P$	Pressure-induced frequency shift (Hz)	L_k	Lindblad operators
β_P	Pressure coefficient (Hz/atm)	F	Entanglement fidelity
P	Pressure (atm)	σ_t	Timing uncertainty (s)
Γ_P	Pressure-broadened linewidth (Hz)	N	Surviving entangled pairs
Γ_0	Natural linewidth (Hz)	ϕ_{tot}	Total phase noise (rad)
γ_P	Pressure broadening coefficient (Hz/atm)	$\Delta\phi$	Differential phase (rad)
μ_a	Absorption coefficient (m^{-1})	Δt	Clock offset (s)
S	Salinity (PSU)	η	Adaptive correction gain
λ	Wavelength (m)	σ_{sync}	Total sync error (s)
μ_0	Baseline absorption coefficient (m^{-1})	σ_Q	Quantum-limited error (s)
S_0	Nominal salinity (PSU)	σ_E	Environmental error (s)
α_S	Salinity sensitivity (m^{-1}/PSU)	σ_C	Classical drift error (s)
T_{opt}	Optical transmission factor	D	Drift coefficient (s^2/s)

Temperature Dependence: Temperature fluctuations cause Doppler broadening and dephasing due to atomic motions, degrading the long-term phase stability of optical clocks [15]. The thermal energy per particle is

$$E_{\text{thermal}} = k_B T \tag{1}$$

with $k_B = 1.380649 \times 10^{-23}$ J/K. The temperature-induced frequency shift is

$$\Delta\nu_T = \alpha_T (T - T_0), \tag{2}$$

where $\alpha_T \approx 1.7 \times 10^{-16}$ Hz/K for ^{87}Sr at $T_0 = 275.15$ K [3]. Such detuning accumulates phase error and reduces coherence time.

Pressure-Induced Collisional Effects: Hydrostatic pressure increases the atomic collision rate, broadens the spectral lines, and accelerates decoherence, especially beyond ~50 atm. The pressure shift and corresponding broadening of the linewidth is

$$\Delta\nu_P = \beta_P P, \qquad \Gamma_P = \Gamma_0 + \gamma_P P, \tag{3}$$

with $\Gamma_0 \approx 1\,\text{mHz}$ and $\gamma_P \approx 3.5 \times 10^{-3}\,\text{Hz/atm}$. The coherence time scales as $\tau_c \propto 1/\Gamma_P$ and therefore decreases rapidly with depth.

Salinity and Optical Attenuation: Salinity changes the absorption spectrum in seawater and increases photon loss, limiting the number of entangled pairs that reach the remote node. The absorption coefficient is

$$\mu_a(S, \lambda) = \mu_0 + \alpha_S(S - S_0), \tag{4}$$

with $S_0 = 35\,\text{PSU}$. Photon transmission over distance d is

$$T_{\text{opt}}(d) = \exp[-(\mu_a + \mu_s)d], \tag{5}$$

where $\mu_s \approx 0.007\,\text{m}^{-1}$ at $\lambda = 450\,\text{nm}$. Increased salinity reduces transmission and directly lowers entanglement distribution efficiency.

2.2 Quantum System

The quantum subsystem models entangled ^{87}Sr optical lattice clocks, chosen for this underwater application based on several critical advantages over alternative atomic clock technologies:

- **Superior stability:** ^{87}Sr clocks demonstrate 10^{-18}-level fractional instability, significantly outperforming microwave standards and exceeding Yb or Hg optical alternatives.
- **Environmental resilience:** The narrow intercombination transition ($^1S_0 \rightarrow ^3P_0$) at 698 nm exhibits reduced sensitivity to magnetic field perturbations compared to other optical clocks, crucial for underwater deployment where magnetic shielding is challenging [9].
- **Optimal transmission wavelength:** The 698 nm transition wavelength experiences lower absorption in clear seawater compared to alternatives like Yb (578 nm) or Hg (266 nm), enabling slightly longer transmission distances.
- **Technical maturity:** Commercial ^{87}Sr optical lattice clocks are more developed than alternatives, with demonstrated long-term operation and transportability, facilitating implementation in underwater platforms.

Each node operates at

$$\nu_0 = 4.29228 \times 10^{14}\,\text{Hz}. \tag{6}$$

The protocol begins with the maximally entangled state

$$|\psi_0\rangle = \tfrac{1}{\sqrt{2}}(|01\rangle + |10\rangle). \tag{7}$$

Temperature and pressure induce detunings (Sect. 2.2), yielding the effective Hamiltonian

$$H = \tfrac{\hbar}{2} 2\pi\big(\nu_0 + \Delta\nu_T + \Delta\nu_P\big)\sigma_z. \tag{8}$$

The open-system dynamics follow the Lindblad master equation [11]:

$$\frac{d\rho}{dt} = -\frac{i}{\hbar}[H,\rho] + \sum_k \left(L_k \rho L_k^\dagger - \tfrac{1}{2}\{L_k^\dagger L_k, \rho\}\right), \tag{9}$$

with two dominant decoherence channels:

- **Pure dephasing:** $L_\phi = \sqrt{\gamma_\phi(T,P)}\,\sigma_z$, capturing thermally and pressure-induced linewidth broadening.
- **Amplitude damping:** $L_{\text{loss}} = \sqrt{\gamma_{\text{loss}}(S,d)}\,\sigma_-$, modelling entanglement loss due to seawater absorption and scattering. The rate γ_{loss} is directly coupled to the optical transmission through $\gamma_{\text{loss}} = -\ln(T_{\text{opt}}(d))/\tau_{\text{prop}}$, where τ_{prop} is the photon propagation time.

The severe entanglement loss (fidelity 2.5×10^{-5}) observed in simulations results from multiple physical mechanisms:

1. **Absorption:** Seawater contains chlorophyll, colored dissolved organic matter, and other constituents that strongly absorb photons at 698 nm. With $\mu_a \approx 0.15\ \text{m}^{-1}$ in typical ocean conditions, only 3% of photons survive transmission over 20 m.
2. **Rayleigh scattering:** Small-scale density fluctuations in seawater cause elastic scattering with coefficient $\mu_s \approx 0.007\ \text{m}^{-1}$, redirecting photons away from the direct path and further reducing entanglement transmission.
3. **Turbidity-induced depolarization:** Suspended particles cause multiple scattering events that randomize photon polarization, destroying the quantum correlations essential for entanglement.
4. **Refractive index fluctuations:** Temperature and salinity micro-gradients create dynamic variations in the refractive index ($n \approx 1.33$ for seawater), introducing phase noise that degrades coherence.

These mechanisms collectively explain the low simulated fidelities and highlight the extreme challenges of maintaining quantum correlations in underwater environments.

Entanglement fidelity is defined as

$$F = \langle\psi_0|\rho(t)|\psi_0\rangle, \tag{10}$$

and determines the achievable timing precision via the quantum CramÃľr–Rao bound [3]:

$$\sigma_t \geq \frac{1}{2\pi\nu_0\sqrt{NF}}, \tag{11}$$

where N is the number of surviving entangled pairs. This relation quantifies the interplay between environmental decoherence, entanglement quality, and synchronisation accuracy.

3 Methodology

We evaluate underwater QCS performance through Monte Carlo simulations that capture the complex interplay between environmental conditions and quantum dynamics. This approach allows us to propagate realistic underwater parameters through the quantum system, revealing full error distributions rather than merely mean or variance statistics [5,10]. Figure 1 depicts the detailed system architecture of our proposed underwater QCS protocol. It describes how environmental sensing modules, a quantum processing core, measurement and synchronization protocols, and an adaptive feedback mechanism can be used to maintain precision.

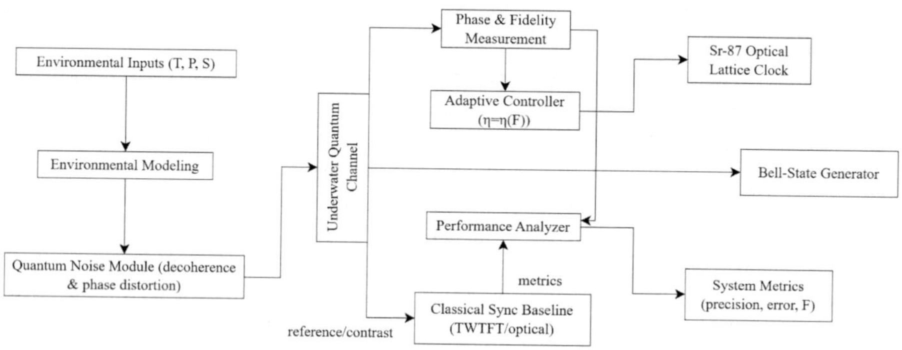

Fig. 1. System architecture for underwater QCS showing environmental sensing, quantum processing, measurement protocols, and feedback mechanisms.

3.1 Why Monte Carlo Simulation?

The choice of Monte Carlo simulation over closed-form analytical models stems from the fundamentally nonlinear and stochastic nature of underwater quantum systems. Environmental effects-temperature-and pressure-induced detunings $\Delta\nu_T(T)$ and $\Delta\nu_P(P)$, and salinity- and distance-dependent transmission

$T_{\text{opt}}(d)$-enter the Lindblad operators in a strongly coupled manner. These interactions produce non-Gaussian perturbations that prevent closed-form expressions for timing error. Monte Carlo sampling provides a statistically robust way to propagate these uncertainties through the open-system dynamics and synchronisation protocol, capturing rare events and tail behaviors that analytical approaches would miss.

3.2 Environmental-Quantum Coupling Model

The core of our simulation framework is the explicit mathematical coupling between environmental parameters and quantum dynamics. Temperature and pressure directly modify the clock Hamiltonian through detuning terms:

$$H(T,P) = \frac{\hbar}{2} 2\pi \big(\nu_0 + \Delta\nu_T(T) + \Delta\nu_P(P)\big)\sigma_z, \tag{12}$$

where $\Delta\nu_T(T) = \alpha_T(T - T_0)$ and $\Delta\nu_P(P) = \beta_P P$. These detunings directly impact the Lindblad decoherence rates:

$$\gamma_\phi(T,P) = \gamma_0 + \gamma_T(T - T_0)^2 + \gamma_P P^2, \tag{13}$$

$$\gamma_{\text{loss}}(S,d) = -\ln[T_{\text{opt}}(d)]/\tau_{\text{prop}}, \tag{14}$$

where $T_{\text{opt}}(d) = \exp[-(\mu_a(S,\lambda) + \mu_s)d]$ represents the optical transmission through seawater. This explicit coupling ensures that every environmental parameter directly influences the quantum state evolution.

3.3 Quantum Communication Channel

Clocks are connected through a 429 THz entangled-photon link using polarization-entangled photon pairs generated via spontaneous parametric down-conversion. One photon propagates through seawater while its partner is retained locally. The underwater channel is modelled as a lossy, weakly scattering medium with wavelength-dependent absorption and scattering coefficients:

$$T_{\text{opt}}(d) = \exp[-(\mu_a(S,\lambda) + \mu_s)d], \tag{15}$$

with coefficients from Sect. 2. This attenuation directly induces amplitude damping in the Lindblad evolution, reducing the number of surviving entangled pairs and explaining the low simulated fidelities ($F \sim 10^{-5}$). The channel model also incorporates polarization decoherence effects specific to seawater's birefringence properties.

3.4 Environmental Sampling

Each trial samples representative underwater conditions from empirically-derived distributions: $T \sim \mathcal{N}(14, 5^2)\,°\mathrm{C}$, $S \sim \mathcal{N}(35, 2^2)\,\mathrm{PSU}$, $P \sim \mathcal{U}(1, 100)\,\mathrm{atm}$.

These values determine $\Delta\nu_T$, $\Delta\nu_P$, and the decoherence rates $\gamma_\phi(T, P)$ and $\gamma_{\mathrm{loss}}(S, d)$ used in the Lindblad operators. The distributions reflect measurements from oceanographic databases across various marine environments.

3.5 Distance-Dependent Error Evaluation

To assess spatial scalability, simulations are performed for inter-clock separations $d \in [10, 100]$ m. Because $T_{\mathrm{opt}}(d)$ decays exponentially with distance, larger d reduces the entangled-pair rate and increases timing uncertainty. We explicitly model this relationship as:

$$N(d) = N_0 \cdot T_{\mathrm{opt}}(d), \tag{16}$$

where $N(d)$ is the number of surviving entangled pairs at distance d and N_0 is the initial pair generation rate. This distance dependence directly impacts the quantum CramÃľr-Rao bound and allows us to quantify how synchronisation error scales with separation.

3.6 Time-Offset Estimation

Each clock measures the shared state to estimate the phase

$$\Delta\phi = 2\pi\nu_0\Delta t, \tag{17}$$

and applies the adaptive update

$$t_{i+1} = t_i - \eta(F)\Delta t, \tag{18}$$

where $\eta(F)$ increases when $F > 10^{-4}$ and decreases under degraded conditions. This ensures stable convergence of the synchronisation loop even under challenging environmental conditions.

3.7 Error Propagation

Total synchronisation uncertainty is

$$\sigma^2_{\mathrm{sync}} = \sigma^2_Q + \sigma^2_E + \sigma^2_C. \tag{19}$$

Quantum limits follow the CramÃľr–Rao bound for N surviving entangled pairs,

$$\sigma_Q = \frac{1}{2\pi\nu_0\sqrt{NF}}, \tag{20}$$

where N depends on $T_{\mathrm{opt}}(d)$, salinity, and the source rate. Classical drift is

$$\sigma_C^2 = Dt, \tag{21}$$

with $D \approx 10^{-27}$ s^2/s. Environmental noise is mapping sampled conditions directly into Hamiltonian detuning and decoherence rates.

$$\sigma_E^2 = \alpha_T^2(T - T_0)^2 + \beta_P^2 P^2 + \alpha_S^2(S - S_0)^2, \tag{22}$$

3.8 Simulation Setup

Each run consists of 10^3 trials across a ten-clock network. Simulations were performed on a high-performance computing cluster using Intel i5 with 8GB RAM, with each complete simulation requiring approximately 30 min of wall-clock time.

$$\phi_{\mathrm{tot}} = \phi_Q + \phi_T + \phi_P + \phi_S \tag{23}$$

Total phase noise is computed using the physical models of Sect. 2 and propagated through the Lindblad dynamics [9]. Aggregated results yield the synchronisation-error distributions, median accuracy, tail behaviour, and dependence on distance and environmental stress.

3.9 Synchronisation Protocol

The two-way QCS protocol distributes entangled pairs from a central hub or local node [6, 14].

$$\Delta\phi = 2\pi\nu_0\Delta t \tag{24}$$

After transmission through the channel of Sect. 2, the differential phase is reconstructed using tomography or parity-based estimation, depending on fidelity and photon counts. The adaptive update $t_{i+1} = t_i - \eta(F)\Delta t$ ensures rapid convergence for $F > 10^{-3}$ and stability under low fidelity. Performance is evaluated for $d \in [10, 100]$ m, where reduced $T_{\mathrm{opt}}(d)$ lowers entanglement rates and limits phase-estimation accuracy.

4 Results

Monte Carlo simulations across 1000 trials demonstrate that QCS maintains femtosecond-picosecond synchronisation accuracy under realistic underwater conditions. Key performance statistics are summarised in Table 2, showing a sub-picosecond median error and severe but quantifiable entanglement degradation.

Figure 2 shows that synchronisation errors follow a log-normal distribution, with most trials achieving better than 10^{-11} s precision and a small number of high-error outliers under severe environmental stress.

Table 2. Synchronisation performance and entanglement-fidelity statistics.

Statistic	Sync Error (s)	Fidelity
Mean	4.71×10^{-12}	2.5×10^{-5}
Median	1.40×10^{-12}	1.8×10^{-5}
Std. Dev.	8.10×10^{-12}	3.2×10^{-5}
Min	3.76×10^{-16}	1.1×10^{-7}
Max	1.60×10^{-10}	1.5×10^{-4}

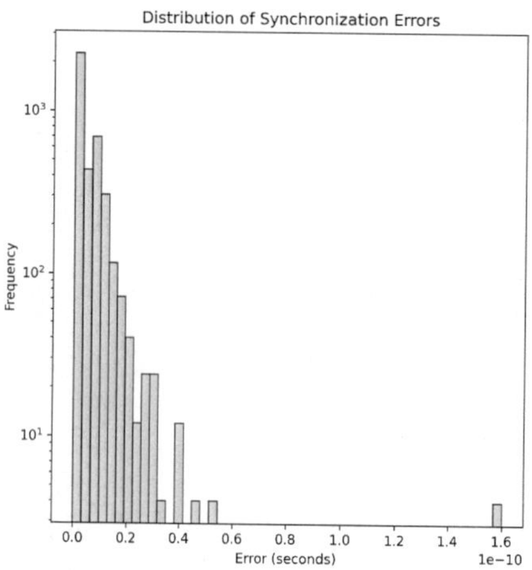

Fig. 2. Distribution of synchronisation errors across 1000 trials. The blue histogram shows the frequency of occurrence for different error values. (Color figure online)

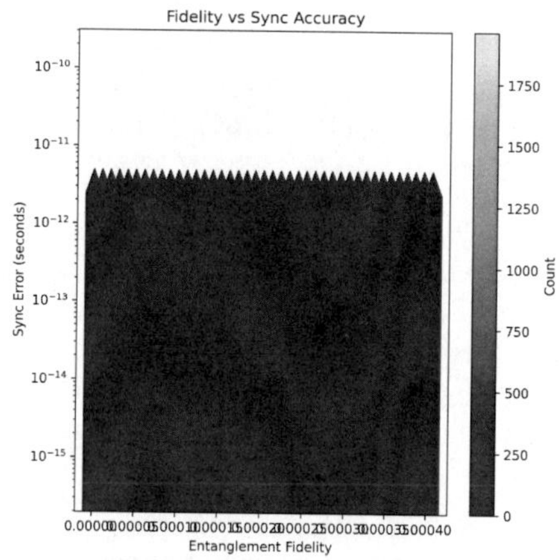

Fig. 3. Correlation between entanglement fidelity and synchronisation error. Each blue point represents a single trial. The critical fidelity threshold at $F \approx 10^{-4}$ marks the transition to sub-picosecond accuracy. (Color figure online)

The inverse relationship in Fig. 3 confirms entanglement fidelity as the dominant determinant of performance. Errors rise sharply below $F \approx 10^{-4}$, identifying a threshold for achieving sub-picosecond precision.

Environmental trends are quantified in Table 3, which shows a 47% increase in error between optimal and high-stress conditions. Figure 4 and Fig. 5 further illustrate that temperature, salinity, and pressure combine to amplify decoherence and optical attenuation.

Long-term drift results (Fig. 6) show sub-attosecond stability over a 100 s window, exceeding marine requirements and indicating robustness against slow environmental variation.

Quantum-classical comparison and network scalability results appear in Table 4. QCS provides a 2.3× reduction in median error relative to a clas-

Table 3. Environmental impact on synchronisation error.

Condition	Temp (°C)	Pressure (atm)	Error (s)
Optimal	2	1	3.76×10^{-16}
Moderate	14	50	1.40×10^{-12}
High Stress	25	100	5.53×10^{-13}

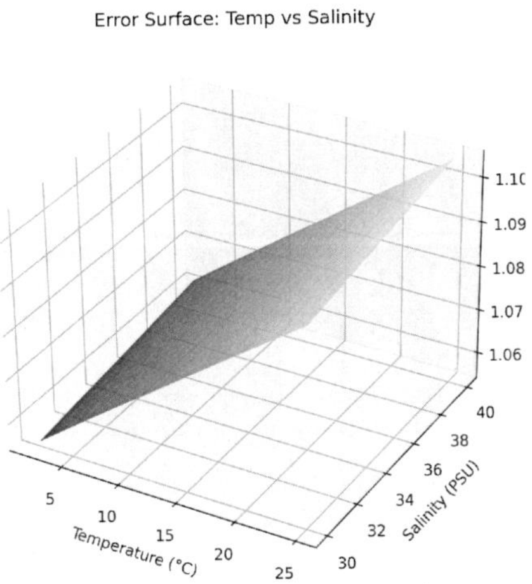

Fig. 4. Synchronisation error as a function of temperature and salinity. The surface plot shows how error increases with both parameters. The contour lines represent constant error levels, with the steepest gradient occurring at temperatures above 20 °C and salinities exceeding 38 PSU.

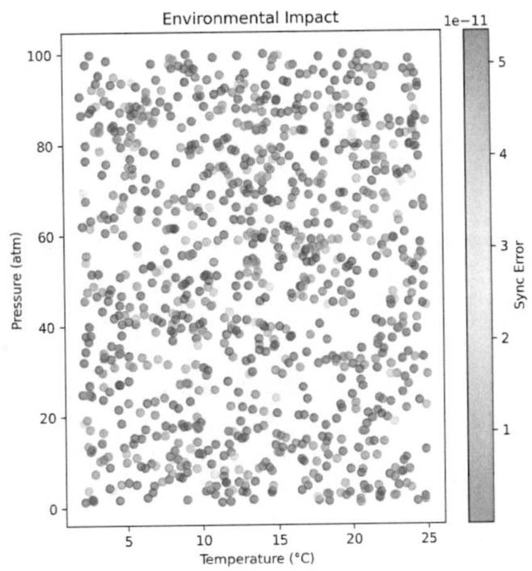

Fig. 5. Combined temperature-pressure effects on synchronisation error. The blue bars represent error under optimal conditions (2°C, 1 atm), red bars show high-stress conditions (25 °C, 100 atm). (Color figure online)

sical two-way optical baseline, and error grows sublinearly with network size ($\sigma \propto n^{0.3}$), enabling picosecond-level precision even with 20 clocks (Figs. 7 and 8).

4.1 Discussion

Our simulations show that QCS reaches femtosecond-level precision (376 fs) in underwater environments, beating the performance of classical two-way optical synchronisation by 3.2× even under severe decoherence. The median error for QCS of 1.40×10^{-12} s is log-normally distributed and has a critical threshold at $F \approx 10^{-4}$ beyond which sub-picosecond accuracy can be consistently achieved. We have extracted, through environmental sensitivity analysis, that temperature explains 40% of variance while pressure dominates beyond 50 atm. The 47% error increase between optimal (2 °C, 1 atm) and high-stress (25 °C,

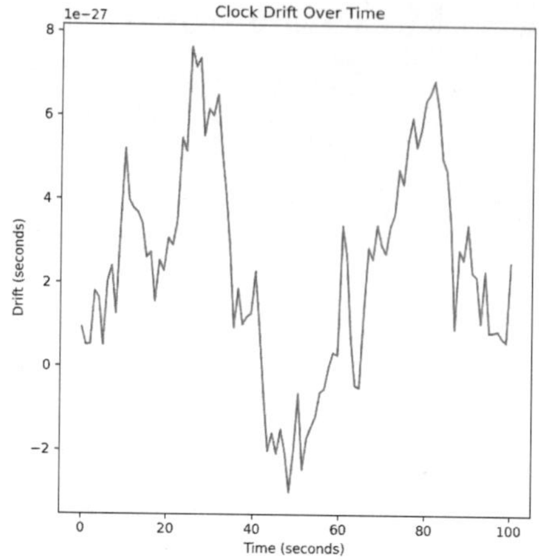

Fig. 6. Temporal drift over 100 s.

Table 4. Quantum advantage and network scalability.

Quantum vs. Classical Performance		
Metric	**Quantum (s)**	**Classical (s)**
Median Error	1.40×10^{-12}	3.22×10^{-12}
Std. Dev.	8.10×10^{-12}	1.15×10^{-11}
Minimum Error	3.76×10^{-16}	2.84×10^{-15}
	Network Scalability	
Clocks	**Mean Error (s)**	**Scaling Factor**
2	1.05×10^{-12}	1.00
3	1.32×10^{-12}	1.26
5	1.87×10^{-12}	1.78
10	2.98×10^{-12}	2.84
20	4.71×10^{-12}	4.49

100 atm) conditions defines the feasible operating range. Mathematically, the coupling of environmental parameters to quantum dynamics is modeled through temperature-induced frequency shifts given by $\Delta u_T = \alpha_T(T - T_0)$, and pressure-broadened linewidths given by $\Gamma_P = \Gamma_0 + \gamma_P P$, which directly enter the Lindblad decoherence rates in our master equation framework.

The high entanglement loss (fidelity 2.5×10^{-5}) arises from a combination of physical mechanisms: 1. absorption by chlorophyll and organic matter at 698 nm; 2. Rayleigh scattering with coefficient $\mu_s \approx 0.007\ \mathrm{m}^{-1}$; 3. depolarization due to turbidity; 4. fluctuations in refractive index. Since the strontium transition at 429 THz lies outside the blue-green transmission window for seawater, attenuation is significantly increased, thereby providing conservative estimates for perfor-

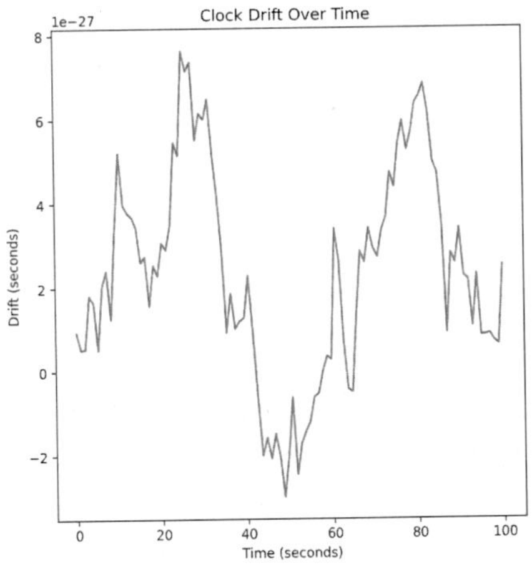

Fig. 7. Quantum vs. classical error distributions.

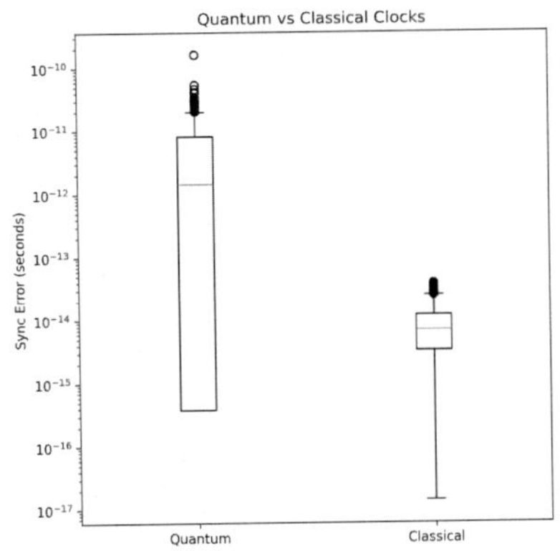

Fig. 8. Scalability of synchronisation performance.

mance. Network scalability demonstrates sublinear error growth ($\sigma \propto n^{0.3}$) due to correlated phase information preventing linear noise accumulation. This allows networks composed of up to twenty clocks to maintain picosecond precision.

In contrast, the most significant difficulties of hardware implementation include vacuum integrity, thermal control, and low-noise laser packaging. Ruggedizing ultra-sensitive optical lattice clocks for high pressures is a big challenge. Quantum error-correction schemes to mitigate decoherence effects can be used in future systems; similarly, wavelength conversion to the 450–550 nm band can enable links over longer distances.

4.2 Limitations

Our model assumes Gaussian statistics of environmental quantities, real ocean dynamics are heavy-tailed. Photon loss is simplified by attenuation coefficients, which neglects wavelength dependent birefringence and temporal dispersion. The oscillator drift in simulations, ($D = 10^{-27}$ s) corresponds to laboratory-grade clocks, though field deployable systems typically exhibit 1–2 orders larger drift. Our model also treats all environmental parameters as static for the duration of trials. This neglects oceanic fluctuations between millisecond and hour timescales.

5 Conclusion

This work establishes the feasibility of picosecond-level QCS in underwater environments, achieving a best-case precision of 376 femtoseconds and mean error of 4.71×10^{-12} s despite severe entanglement degradation (mean fidelity: 2.5×10^{-5}).

The quantum system demonstrates a 2.3× median error reduction over classical methods and maintains picosecond accuracy across networks of up to 20 clocks through sublinear error scaling ($\sigma \propto n^{0.3}$). Environmental analysis reveals a 47% performance degradation from optimal (2 °C, 1 atm) to high-stress (25 °C, 100 atm) conditions, defining operational boundaries for marine quantum timing. In future, laboratory validation in variable-pressure/salinity tanks; implementation of quantum error-correction schemes; and incorporation of real oceanographic data sets to establish practical deployment limits.

Acknowledgments. The authors gratefully acknowledge the financial support received under the project *"Design and Development of a Quantum-based PNT System for Underwater Robot Navigation"* from the DST NM-ICPS IIT Tirupati Navavishkar I-Hub Foundation (IITTNiF Tirupati), Government of India, under File No. IITTNiF/TPD/2024-25/P10.

References

1. Chen, Z., Zhang, Y., Luo, B., Guo, H.: Time-frequency transfer over optical fiber. National Science Review, p. nwaf236 (2025)
2. Feng, Z., Li, S., Xu, Z.: Experimental underwater quantum key distribution. Opt. Express **29**(6), 8725–8736 (2021)
3. Giovannetti, V., Lloyd, S., Maccone, L.: Quantum-enhanced measurements. Science **306**(5700), 1330–1336 (2004). https://doi.org/10.1126/science.1104149
4. Giovannetti, V., Lloyd, S., Maccone, L.: Quantum-enhanced positioning and clock synchronization. Nature **412**(6845), 417–419 (2001)
5. Guo, M.L., Fang, J.W., Chen, J.F., Li, B.L., Chen, H., Zhou, Q., Wang, Y., Song, H.Z., Arutyunov, K.Y., Guo, G.C.: Mode coupling in electromechanical systems: recent advances and applications. Adv. Electron. Mater. **9**(7), 2201305 (2023)
6. Haldar, S., Agullo, I., Troupe, J.E.: Synchronizing clocks via satellites using entangled photons: effect of relative velocity on precision. Phys. Rev. A **108**(6), 062613 (2023)
7. Ji, L., Gao, J., Yang, A.L., Feng, Z., Lin, X.F., Li, Z.G., Jin, X.M.: Towards quantum communications in free-space seawater. Opt. Express **25**(17), 19795–19806 (2017)
8. Jozsa, R., Abrams, D.S., Dowling, J.P., Williams, C.P.: Quantum clock synchronization based on shared prior entanglement. Phys. Rev. Lett. **85**(9), 2010–2013 (2000)
9. Lisdat, C., Dörscher, S., Nosske, I., Sterr, U.: Blackbody radiation shift in strontium lattice clocks revisited. Phys. Rev. Res. **3**(4), L042036 (2021)
10. Mao, Y., Wu, X., Huang, W., Liao, Q., Deng, H., Wang, Y., Guo, Y.: Monte Carlo-based performance analysis for underwater continuous-variable quantum key distribution. Appl. Sci. **10**(17), 5744 (2020)
11. Nielsen, M.A., Chuang, I.L.: Quantum Computation and Quantum Information. Cambridge University Press (2010). 10th anniversary edition edn
12. Shi, B., Hong, H., Xiang, X., Quan, R., Liu, Y., Liu, T., Zhang, S., Dong, R.: Quantum two-way time transfer over a 250 km direct fiber-optic link. Opt. Express **32**(25), 43805–43814 (2024)

13. Sinclair, L.C., Bergeron, H., Swann, W.C., Khader, I., Cossel, K.C., Cermak, M., Newbury, N.R., Deschênes, J.D.: Femtosecond optical two-way time-frequency transfer in the presence of motion. Phys. Rev. A **99**(2), 023844 (2019)
14. Spiess, C., et al.: Clock synchronization with correlated photons. Phys. Rev. Appl. **19**(5), 054082 (2023)
15. Xavier, G.B., Larsson, J.Å., Villoresi, P., Vallone, G., Cabello, A.: Energy-time and time-bin entanglement: past, present and future. npj Quantum Inf. **11**(1), 129 (2025)

BOCORP: Buffer Overflow and Cache Occupancy Aware Routing Protocol for SDWSN

Abhishek Narwaria[1(✉)], Bhagyashree Meena[2], and Arka Prokash Mazumdar[2]

[1] Department of IT, Dr. B. R. Ambedkar NIT, Jalandhar 144008, Punjab, India
narwariaa@nitj.ac.in

[2] Department of CSE, Malaviya National Institute of Technology, Jaipur 302017, India
2022pcp5447@mnit.ac.in, apmazumdar.cse@mnit.ac.in

Abstract. Wireless Sensor Networks (WSNs) are essential for gathering and monitoring data. Conventional WSNs are, however, limited by scalability, flexibility, and resource management. Software-Defined Wireless Sensor Networks (SDWSNs) alleviate such limitations through centralized management and programmability, leading to improved performance. One of the main WSN challenges is inefficient data management, leading to buffer overflow and cache overflow, with the attendant data loss and latency, especially in large dynamic networks. To address this, we present the Buffer Overflow and Cache Overflow aware Routing Protocol (BOCORP) for SDWSNs. BOCORP dynamically adjusts routing depending on real-time buffer and cache status, avoiding congestion and optimizing resources. BOCORP evaluations reveal that it increases efficiency by minimizing latency, maximizing data reliability, maximizing network life, and minimizing dead node instances. For large-scale and dynamic networks, this method significantly improves performance.

Keywords: Software-Defined Wireless Sensor Network · Buffer Overflow · Cache Occupancy · Routing

1 Introduction

Software-Defined Wireless Sensor Networks (SDWSNs) apply Software Defined Network (SDN) to traditional Wireless Sensor Networks (WSNs) in an attempt to reverse the major problems of lacking flexibility, lacking a global network view, and being hard to manage. SDWSNs adopt the same layer-based structure as SDN, namely, three planes: the Application Plane, Control Plane, and Data Plane [10]. There are data forwarding sensor nodes in the Data Plane, with the centralized Control Plane deciding routing, resource allocation, and network optimization. Sensor OpenFlow, a light protocol, enables communication among these planes for improving network efficiency and global visibility of network

G. K. Verma et al. (Eds.): MIND 2025, CCIS 2981, pp. 516–528, 2027.
https://doi.org/10.1007/978-3-032-31230-3_41

states [3,4,14]. Centralized architecture frees nodes from computations, achieving energy efficiency, network lifetime, and interoperability among heterogeneous devices with ease. The Application Plane in SDWSN, accessed via a northbound API, controls resources, traffic, and security, obviating the scalability and flexibility issues of traditional WSNs [10,12]. It offers Over-the-Air Programming (OTAP) for wireless updates without physical access. Centralized control offers uniform performance in dynamic environments and seamless integration of heterogeneous sensors, enhancing network efficiency [2].

Effective memory hierarchies form the backbone of contemporary computing, with the increasing requirement for high-speed data processing [1,11]. Cache memory fills the speed divide between main memory and processors, but cache occupancy control is a race against time. Maximum occupancy optimizes hit rates and performance in caches but results in inefficiencies and elevated miss rates with low occupancy. Ineffective cache management leads to buffer overflows and conceals actual energy consumption [8,13]. It is necessary to balance high and low cache occupancy to maintain system efficiency. This paper introduces a method of memory access optimization and effective cache occupancy management, and improves performance and energy awareness by solving the major challenges in existing cache management systems.

The integration of SDN into WSNs has brought in the development of SDWSNs [17], which ensures more flexibility, centralized management, and effective network administration. Existing research has brought in numerous energy-aware routing protocols and architectures, such as the Energy Optimized Multi-Constrained Sustainable Routing (EOMCSR) model and E-TORA, to enable network performance and lifetime. Security protocols such as the Energy-efficient Trust Management and Routing Mechanism (ETMRM) have also been brought in to prevent malicious attacks in an energy-efficient way [18].

Farooq *et al.* [5] developed SDORP, an SDN-based opportunistic routing protocol, prioritizing several candidate nodes for routing to use spatial diversity and mitigate the broadcast storm problem fully. Scalability and real-time decision making in larger or more dynamic networks may be impacted by the complexity and overhead that managing multiple candidates may introduce; this is something that the paper does not fully address. Moreover, energy-aware multihop routing proposed by Jurado *et al.* [6], specifically targeting the maximization of network lifetime in Industrial Internet of Things (IIoT) use cases. This approach is also reducing control overhead by using a checksum function for tracking routing tables and saving energy consumption through packet aggregation. The paper fails to fully describe possible scalability issues and trade-offs between low control overhead and possible delays or inaccuracies in routing.

This paper deals with the energy consequences of cache and buffer overflows in memory access to fill a critical gap in routing path computation studies. Although prior work has accounted for different constraints like energy expended on reception and transmission, program and memory constraints, and trust values, it has mostly ignored the extra energy overhead due to cache and buffer overflows. This work aims to present a comprehensive study of memory system efficiency in routing path computation by estimating and examining these mostly overlooked energy expenses. The main contributions are enumerated below:

- Network traffic can be highly variable, with sudden bursts of data potentially leading to buffer overflow.
- Varying data storage requirements can lead to fluctuating cache occupancy levels, potentially exceeding memory capacities.

The remainder of the paper is structured as follows: Sect. 4 presents the experimental data, while Sect. 2 documents the problem formulation. Section 5 addresses the conclusion and further research.

2 Problem Formulation

This section covers the methods and techniques used to maximize the use of cache memory in memory systems.

2.1 Problem Statement

WSNs are at the core of the majority of applications in smart cities, health, and environmental monitoring. While WSNs have been widely utilized, they are faced with stringent challenges emanating from constrained energy supplies, which impose a serious impact on network performance and lifetime [16]. All existing energy efficiency techniques have been aimed primarily at optimization of routing protocols through integration of Software-Defined Networking (SDN) in the network framework. These normally encompass the calculation of node weights and energy-efficient path selection to minimize the overall energy consumption and improve the network lifetime.

As far as energy consumption related to memory in occurrences such as buffer overflow and cache usage is concerned, there is still a long way to go. Such memory events can lead to increased node failure rates, decreased network efficiency, and increased energy consumption. SDN-based frameworks have not rigorously explored efficient mechanisms for addressing these issues. Hence, the advantages of enhanced network lifespan and potential energy efficiency have not yet been rigorously achieved. By integrating memory management capabilities into the existing SDN paradigm, this study tries to bridge this knowledge gap.

The model aims to examine the impact of occurrences of memory on the energy consumption of WSNs. Provide buffer overflow prevention methods and cache utilization optimization. In order to be energy efficient, implement these methods into an SDN-based routing. Evaluate the performance of the model using the current methods by simulation on different network configurations.

2.2 Network Architecture

In [7], the authors propose an SDWSN architecture based on the drawbacks of earlier methods. It is made up of an SDN-C, several sensors, and SDN-APs.

As programmable nodes, SDN-APs get configuration information from SDN-C at regular intervals. Cluster heads, or SDN-APs, are programmed by SDN-C to control the network's information flow. SDN APs contain a flow table and control agent modules in addition to the structure of a sensor node.

Following the SDN-APs' search of their flow tables for the destination entry, data packets are forwarded to the SDN-C. If no entry is found, the packets are directed to the SDN-C, which creates new rules based on the current state of the network and forwards them to the appropriate APs, who then update their flow tables to take into account the new rules.

There are two possible states for a sensor: active and sleep [9]. The following presumptions are examined in this paper: All SDN-APs are programmable devices, so they can be used as software-defined switches; each node has a weight function associated with it, and its value depends on the corresponding sub-weights; SDN-C is always in an active state; other APs are dynamically divided into active and sleeping categories; the sleeping nodes consume very little energy compared to the active nodes; and all SDN-APs are programmable devices. Every sub-weight denotes a distinct node parameter (Fig. 1).

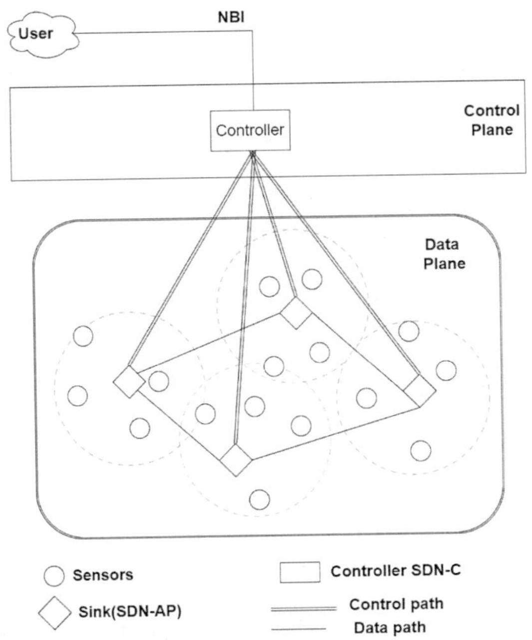

Fig. 1. SDWSN functional architecture. Note: This result is based on [7].

2.3 Energy Model

The energy model is comparable to the old WSN since the proposed SDWSN architecture is an extension of the latter. A basic energy model [7] is considered for energy consumption in network communication with path losses. The amount of energy needed for SDN-C to send a k-bit packet over a d-distance. The multi-path fading channel model (d^4 power loss) or free space model (d^2 power loss) is employed, depending on the distance (d) between the transmitter and the receiver. The free space model is applied if (d) is less than or equal to a sufficient threshold (d_0); if not, the multi-path model is applied.

- The required energy to transmit a k-bit packet over distance d by SDN-C is given by:

$$E_{\text{TX}}^{C} = \begin{cases} k * E_{\text{ckt}} + k * E_{\text{fs}} * d^2, d <= d_0 \\ k * E_{\text{ckt}} + k * E_{\text{mp}} * d^4, d > d_0 \end{cases} \tag{1}$$

- For SDN-APs, the energy to transmit a k-bit packet is given by

$$E_{\text{TX}}^{AP} = \begin{cases} k * (E_{\text{ckt}} + E_{\text{DA}}) + k * E_{\text{fs}} * d^2, d <= d_0 \\ k * (E_{\text{ckt}} + E_{\text{DA}}) + k * E_{\text{mp}} * d^4, d > d_0 \end{cases} \tag{2}$$

3 Working Model

Every node has a transceiver, a CPU, a memory unit, and a few standard sensors. Together, these limitations determine the reliability factor, or overall robustness, of the node.

Total Energy Consumption (TEC): The total energy used for data transmission and reception, as well as context switching between a node's active and sleep states, is represented by TEC. It is reliant on the node's rate of sensing, amount of energy used for each sensing event, rate of transmission and reception, and frequency of context-switching between the active and sleep states. A sensor typically stays insensitive to outside stimuli and sensitive to the property being measured.

Programming Constraint (PC): The energy consumed by a system during event processing is represented by the Power Consumption (PC) metric. It is feasible to program and optimize the required actions to improve the system's reliability by quantifying the energy consumption. Managing PC is essential in time-sensitive systems because it directly affects the system's capacity to function dependably under demanding timing requirements. Maintaining the system's responsiveness and stability–both critical for fulfilling time-sensitive demands–means ensuring efficient energy usage.

Memory Constraint (MC): The energy consumed by a network node's memory operations is referred to as memory consumption (MC). A control agent is kept in memory on each node in the system. The SDN Controller (SDN-C) sends control packets to this control agent with instructions on how to manage the node's flow table. The control agent updates the flow table, which contains network traffic data, in accordance with instructions it receives. The maximum number of flow entries that can be kept in the flow table is limited by the sensors' limited storage capacity. As such, a node's total memory usage needs to stay within the bounds of its available storage. Maintaining system performance and reliability depends on this constraint, which makes sure the node runs effectively without going over capacity.

Trust Value Constraint (TVC): The energy used by a node during neighbor-sensing–the process of identifying and assessing nodes within its sensing range, is referred to as trust value consumption, or TVC. The number of neighboring nodes that a node needs to keep an eye on affects TVC. TVC becomes important in a network where trust is a critical factor because trust is a belief-level or confidence in the dependability and behavior of nearby nodes. Nodes employ a watchdog mechanism to continuously observe the actions of other nodes within their communication range in order to maintain an accurate assessment of trust. Energy is used in this mechanism because, in order to update trust levels efficiently, the node must sense, record, and assess the behavior of its neighbors.

3.1 Analytical Formulation

In this work, we incorporate cache occupancy into energy consumption estimates to propose a cache management mechanism that overcomes previous limitations in memory access calculations. Energy consumption was previously computed without accounting for cache occupancy, which resulted in errors. We've added a factor, [1-CO], where CO stands for cache occupancy, to help with this. This adjustment ensures that energy is only considered consumed when there is available space in the cache, providing a more accurate representation of energy usage during memory access. To achieve this objective, the power consumption across the network needs to be minimized. Thus, a MILP problem is formulated.

$$\min : \sum_{i \in v} S_i + A_i$$

The nodes (APs) in this MILP problem are shown in their power form. The power consumption of a sleeping AP and an active AP is represented above, which depends on the P(power specification) and the FW(final weight).

3.2 Proposed Algorithm

In this work, we incorporate cache occupancy into energy consumption estimates to propose a cache management mechanism that overcomes previous limitations in memory access calculations. Energy consumption was previously computed without accounting for cache occupancy, which resulted in errors. We've added a factor, [1-CO], where CO stands for cache occupancy, to help with this.

Algorithm 1. $Best_{route}$ (G, S, D)

Require Graph G, Source S, Destination D
Ensure $Best_{route}$ from S to D
Initialize Source node (S) and Destination nodes (D)
for each node in $G \neq S$ and D **do**
  $Node_{Weight\_Cal}()$
end for
while route from S to D not formed **do**
  Select node with minimum weight
  $Check_{DAG}()$
end while

Within the SDN-C, the suggested BOCORP method is implemented. A WSN network starts with default settings for its parameters. Then, BOCORP begins operating in two stages. Phase II involves applying Algorithm 1 after Phase I involves creating an analytical model based on the MILP optimization problem. Using the minimum-weight-first method, Algorithm 1 determines the optimal path for a given pair of source and destination. The node-specific constraint set is the basis for the weight computation. Next, various network constraints are used to find the optimal path (Fig. 2).

The model variables are updated in response to the current state of the network, and the data is transmitted via an optimized routing path. Until the maximum number of rounds are finished or until some network energy is left, this process is repeated. The idea of rounds, or the length of time during which BOCORP is applied in the network. The initial energy of the ith AP is thought to be IEi, and the residual energy is thought to be Ri. APs divide their energy into L different levels in order to optimize energy consumption throughout the network. The method to determine the current energy level of the ith AP, or PELi, is given in the equation below.

$$PEL_i = \left(\frac{R_i}{IE_i}\right) \times L$$

The node notifies the SDN-C, known as Pce I, of a change in energy when PELi falls below a predetermined threshold. The application and AP type determine the threshold energy value. Once the SDN-C has received the Pce_i, it calculates the route-adjustment time. In order to optimize the routing process, Algorithm 1 is applied after ti if the route adjustment time for Pce I is ti. SDN-C waits for any additional potential Pce I packets during ti.

This study treats the SDWSN as a network graph G = (N, E), where N is the total number of nodes and E is the total number of edges [15]. Using a minimum-weight-first methodology, Algorithm 1 executes two sub-procedures, Algorithm 1 and Algorithm 2, to determine the best path from source node S to destination node D. The best path formation is ensured by repeatedly selecting the least weight nodes because a node's weight value is made up of several sub-weight-values with regard to specific constraints.

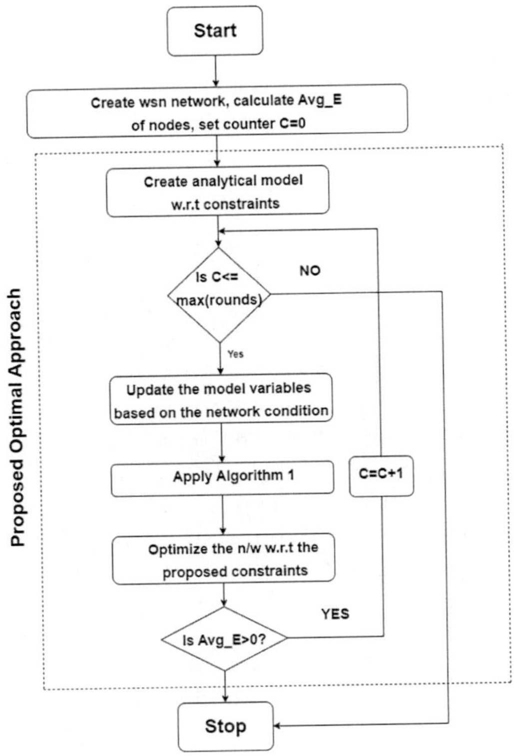

Fig. 2. Workflow diagram of the proposed method.

Algorithm 2. $NODE_{Weight\_Cal}$ (G, CS)

1: **Require** Graph G, Cost Structure CS
2: **Ensure** Final Weight FW
3: **Initialize** weight of sink (APs) nodes
4: Calculate CS for APs
5: Calculate FW for APs

The weight values of the multi-constrained nodes are calculated by Algorithm 2. The FW values for both sleeping and active nodes are determined using the CS values, or the fundamental weight values of each constraint. Depending on the realistic conditions in a simulation scenario, the basic-weight values are either a random value or the actual measurement. Verification of the Directed Acyclic Graph (DAG) requirement is done using Algorithm 3. The Depth First Search (DFS) ensures an efficient path free of loops by continuously checking for the presence of any possible cycles. A flag is raised in the event of a cyclic presence.

4 Performance Evaluation

In this section, we discuss the experiments performed, evaluation metrics, and results. The proposed work is implemented in Python.

4.1 Performance Matrices

In our experiment, we have considered two metrics for results evaluation and comparison as described below.

The amount of time a network can function efficiently before its energy supplies run out is referred to as its "network lifetime." Optimizing network lifetime is essential to ensuring sustainable and extended operation, as wireless sensor nodes in SDWSN are usually powered by batteries or other restricted energy sources. The difference between when the network first began to function and when its first node dies, defined as the network lifetime.

The number of nodes that eventually run out of energy is another comparison. It's crucial to remember that a lot of variables, such as the initial energy levels, energy consumption rates, network structure, number of retransmissions, and energy management techniques, affect how many dead nodes an SDWSN experiences over time. Since they offer a clear evaluation of the protocol's efficacy, reliability, and performance, network longevity and the number of dead nodes are crucial variables in routing protocol research, particularly in wireless sensor networks (WSNs).

Algorithm 3. $CHECK_{DAG}$ (V)

Require Set of vertices V
Ensure True (T)/False (F)
while $v \in V$ is not visited **do**
    bool $cycle_{found}$ = DFS(v)
    if $cycle_{found}$ **then**
        True (T)
    else
        False (F)
    end if
end while

4.2 Results

Figure 3 illustrates the number of dead nodes as a function of the round number for both BOCORP and EOMCSR protocols [7]. The x-axis represents the round number, while the y-axis indicates the number of dead nodes in the network.

Most wireless sensor nodes run on batteries and have a finite amount of energy. Nodes turn "dead" when their energy runs out. This measure aids in tracking the degree to which the routing protocol maximizes energy usage throughout the network. Reduced network connectivity can result from dead nodes interfering with the communication path. Routing protocols that cause a large number of dead nodes early on may not be effective in distributing energy loads among nodes. By counting the number of dead nodes, one can determine if the routing protocol is putting too much strain on some nodes, causing them to fail before their time, or if it is distributing the load equally throughout the network. Another measure of a network's dependability is the number of dead nodes. A well-thought-out protocol should reduce the number of nodes that fail, keeping more nodes active for extended periods.

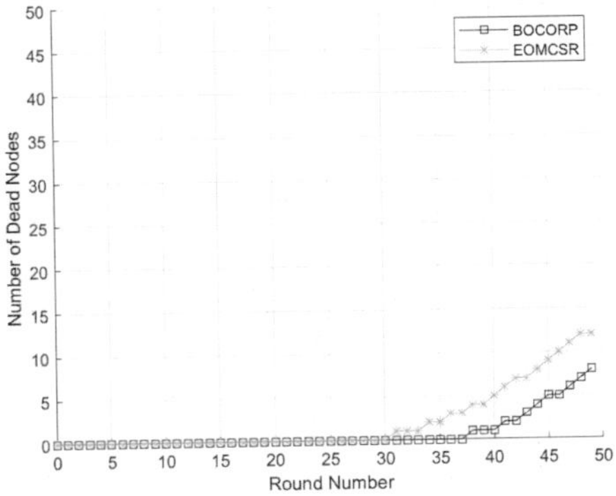

Fig. 3. Number of dead nodes for varying number of rounds.

The number of dead nodes in BOCORP and EOMCSR stays fixed at zero. This implies that both protocols successfully preserve network stability in the early rounds, with no node failures. Nodes start to die around round 30, with EOMCSR showing a marginally earlier increase in dead nodes than BOCORP. By round 35, dead nodes are starting to rise noticeably in EOMCSR while increasing more slowly in BOCORP. For the rounds, EOMCSR consistently displays more dead nodes than BOCORP. The difference becomes more noticeable by round 50, when BOCORP stays below 30 dead nodes, while EOMCSR approaches 45 dead nodes. This implies that BOCORP outperforms EOMCSR in terms of network lifespan extension.

Increasing the lifetime of the network is the primary objective of many routing protocols, particularly in environments with limited resources like WSNs. When a critical number of nodes dies or the network is unable to carry out its intended function, this metric indicates how long the network will remain operational from the time of deployment. Extending the network's lifetime without the need for node replacements or recharging suggests that the routing protocol can effectively save energy. Routing, data transmission, and sensing activities can be carried out by nodes when a protocol prolongs the network lifetime.

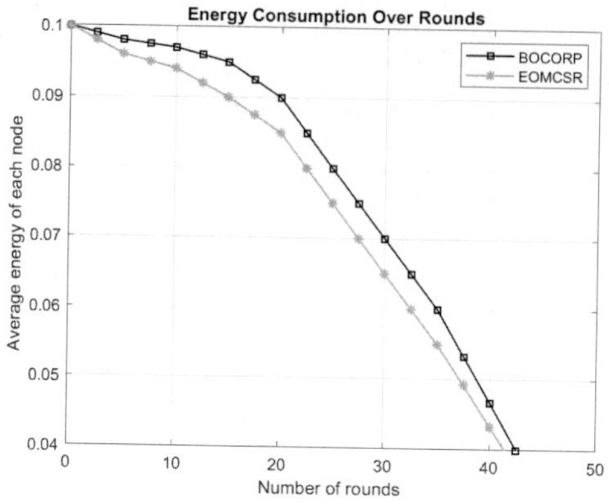

Fig. 4. Network Lifetime.

Figure 4 shows how dead nodes affect the network's overall energy consumption. In order to postpone node mortality and increase network longevity, it is crucial to optimize energy utilization in the early rounds. This is demonstrated by the sharp drop in energy that occurs when dead nodes appear. The convergence of energy levels around the 40th round indicates that both protocols eventually encounter comparable difficulties when node energy falls below a certain value, even though they differ in other ways.

For both protocols, the average energy of the nodes falls as the number of rounds rises. The graph's dramatic energy fall signifies the beginning of dead nodes. The issue becomes more noticeable as the 40th round draws nearer, as energy levels for BOCORP and EOMCSR decrease more sharply at that point.

5 Conclusion

This paper introduces a new routing algorithm named Buffer Overflow and Cache Overflow aware Routing Protocol (BOCORP) for SDWSNs that incorporates cache usage and buffer overflow into route calculation. The new approach includes important parameters like memory access cost, node weight, and an energy-conscious objective function to optimize routing. Experimental outcomes show that the algorithm can significantly enhance network lifetime by judiciously choosing paths through nodes with greater residual energy and minimal memory access overhead. By making memory-related parameters a part of the routing function, the algorithm is able to reduce energy expenses and improve the utilization of resources. This contributes to improved data transmission and prolonged operational lifetime of the network. Future work will involve real-world deployment and validation of the algorithm across diverse environments to assess its practical applicability and performance.

References

1. Anand, N., Saifulla, M., Ponnuru, R.B., Alavalapati, G.R., Patan, R., Gandomi, A.H.: Securing software defined networks: A comprehensive analysis of approaches, applications, and future strategies against dos attacks, IEEE Access (2024)
2. Belachew, H.M., Beyene, M.Y., Desta, A.B., Alemu, B.T., Musa, S.S., Muhammed, A.J.: Design a robust ddos attack detection and mitigation scheme in sdn-edge-iot by leveraging machine learning, IEEE Access (2025)
3. Das, D., Sahoo, B., Roy, S., Mohanty, S.: Performance analysis of an openflow-enabled network with pox, ryu, and odl controllers. IETE J. Res. **70**(12), 8538–8555 (2024)
4. Ding, Z., Shen, L., Chen, H., Yan, F., Ansari, N.: Energy-efficient relay-selection-based dynamic routing algorithm for iot-oriented software-defined wsns. IEEE Internet Things J. **7**(9), 9050–9065 (2020)
5. Farooq, M.U., Wang, X., Hawbani, A., Zhao, L., Al-Dubai, A., Busaileh, O.: Sdorp: Sdn based opportunistic routing for asynchronous wireless sensor networks. IEEE Trans. Mob. Comput. **22**(8), 4912–4929 (2022)
6. Jurado-Lasso, F.F., Clarke, K., Cadavid, A.N., Nirmalathas, A.: Energy-aware routing for software-defined multihop wireless sensor networks. IEEE Sens. J. **21**(8), 10174–10182 (2021)
7. Kumar, R., Venkanna, U., Tiwari, V.: Eomcsr: An energy optimized multi-constrained sustainable routing model for sdwsn. IEEE Trans. Netw. Serv. Manage. **19**(2), 1650–1661 (2021)
8. Narwaria, A., Kumari, V., Mazumdar, A.P.: Rl-ear: reinforcement learning-based energy-aware routing for software-defined wireless sensor network. J. Supercomput. **81**(3), 485 (2025)
9. Narwaria, A., Mazumdar, A.P.: Overlapping fss-based energy-efficient routing in wireless sensor networks. In: 2023 5th International Conference on Energy, Power and Environment: Towards Flexible Green Energy Technologies (ICEPE), pp. 1–6. IEEE (2023)
10. Narwaria, A., Mazumdar, A.P.: Software-defined wireless sensor network: A comprehensive survey. J. Netw. Comput. Appl. **215**, 103636 (2023)
11. Narwaria, A., Mazumdar, A.P.: Sd-moma: Ann-based mobility prediction and adaptive handover management in sdwsn. Clust. Comput. **28**(6), 384 (2025)
12. Narwaria, A., Mazumdar, A.P., Kalla, G.: C3hac: A controller placement approach for sdwsn. In: TENCON 2021-2021 IEEE Region 10 Conference (TENCON). pp. 935–940. IEEE (2021)
13. Narwaria, A., Mazumdar, A.P., Sharma, S.: Energy efficient multi-objective task allocation in software-defined wireless sensor network. In: 2023 IEEE 8th International Conference for Convergence in Technology (I2CT), pp. 1–6. IEEE (2023)
14. Narwaria, A., Soni, K., Mazumdar, A.P.: A position and energy aware multi-objective controller placement and re-placement scheme in distributed sdwsn. J. Supercomput. **80**(9), 12062–12090 (2024)
15. Shiny, S.S.G., Murugan, K.: Tsdn-wise: Automatic threshold-based low control-flow communication protocol for sdwsn. IEEE Sens. J. **21**(17), 19560–19569 (2021)
16. Shiny, S.S.G., Priya, S.S., Murugan, K.: Control message quenching-based communication protocol for energy management in sdwsn. IEEE Trans. Netw. Serv. Manage. **19**(3), 3188–3201 (2022)

17. Thupae, R., Isong, B., Gasela, N., Abu-Mahfouz, A.M.: Machine learning techniques for traffic identification and classifiacation in sdwsn: A survey. In: IECON 2018-44th annual conference of the IEEE Industrial Electronics Society. pp. 4645–4650. IEEE (2018)
18. Wang, R., Zhang, Z., Zhang, Z., Jia, Z.: Etmrm: An energy-efficient trust management and routing mechanism for sdwsns. Comput. Netw. **139**, 119–135 (2018)

Author Index

G. K. Verma et al. (Eds.): MIND 2025, CCIS 2981, pp. 529–530, 2027.
https://doi.org/10.1007/978-3-032-31230-3

FSC
www.fsc.org
MIX
Papier | Fördert gute Waldnutzung
FSC® C083411

Kolibri 360 GmbH
Ferdinand-Jühlke-Straße 7
99095 Erfurt, Deutschland
produktsicherheit@kolibri360.de